Therapist's Guide to Clinical Intervention

The 1–2–3's of Treatment Planning

Second Edition

Therapist's Guide to Clinical Intervention

The 1–2–3's of Treatment Planning

Second Edition

SHARON L. JOHNSON

ACADEMIC PRESS

An Imprint of Elsevier

Amsterdam   Boston   London   New York   Oxford   Paris
San Diego   San Francisco   Singapore   Sydney   Tokyo

Permissions may be sought directly from Elsevier's Science and Technology Rights
Department in Oxford, UK: phone: (+44) 1865 843830, fax: (+44) 1865 853333,
e-mail: permissions@elsevier.com.uk. You may also complete your request on-line
via the Elsevier homepage (http://www.elsevier.com), by selecting
"Customer Support" and then "Obtaining Permissions."

Academic Press
An Imprint of Elsevier
525 B Street, Suite 1900, San Diego, California 92101-4495, USA
http://www.academicpress.com

Academic Press
84 Theobald's Road, London WC1X 8RR, UK
http://www.academicpress.com

Library of Congress Catalog Card Number: 2003109372

ISBN-13: 978-0-12-386588-5
ISBN-10: 0-12-386588-3

PRINTED IN THE UNITED STATES OF AMERICA
09 10 11 12   9 8 7

CONTENTS

Introduction   xvii

Level of Patient Care and Practice Considerations   xix

Decision Tree of Evaluation and Intervention   xxi

Levels of Functioning and Treatment Associated Considerations   xxii

High-Risk Situations in Practice   xxiii

Treatment Plan   xxiv

Solution-Focused Approach to Treatment   xxv

Case Conceptualization   xxvi

Common Axis 1 and Axis 2 Diagnoses   xxviii

Chapter 1
TREATMENT PLANNING: GOALS, OBJECTIVES, AND INTERVENTIONS

Disorders Usually First Evident in Infancy, Childhood, or Adolescence   1
    Mental Retardation (MR)   1   •   Pervasive Developmental Disorders (PPD)   5

Disruptive Behavior Disorders   7
    Attention Deficit Hyperactivity Disorder (ADHD) Oppositional Defiant Disorder,
    Conduct Disorder   7   •   Separation Anxiety   13   •   Avoidant Disorder   14
    Overanxious Disorder   16   •   Eating Disorder (EDO)   18
    Preventing Weight and Body Image Problems in Children   24

Recommendations for Family Members of Anorexic Individuals   25
    Identity Disorder   26

Children   28

Organic Mental Syndromes and Disorders   31

Dementia   32

   Dementia and Organic Mental Disorders   32
   Defining Specific Dementias   34

Psychoactive Substance Abuse Disorders   37

   *Substance Abuse and/or Dependence   38   •   Categories of Pharmacological
   Intervention   41   •   Treatment Settings   41*

List of Symptoms Leading to Relapse   42
Schizophrenia, Delusional, and Related Psychotic Disorders   45

   *Thought Disorders   45   •   Phases of Treatment   49
   Treatment Settings   49   •   Summary of Treatment Recommendations for
   Patients with Perceptual Disturbances   49*

Mood Disorders   51

   *Depression   52   •   Depression Co-occurring with other Illness   56
   Mania   58   •   Children   61*

Bipolar Disorder Hypersexuality   62
Antidepressant Medication and other Treatment   63
Additional Treatment Considerations   64
Anxiety Disorders   65

   Anxiety Disorders   65

Cycle of Anxiety-Provoked Emotional Distress   69

   Trauma Response   70

Somatoform Disorders   72

   *Somatoform Disorders   72   •   Psychosomatic Illness and Personality Disorder   75
   Interpreting Functional Presentations of Symptomology   77*

Dissociative Disorders   78

   Dissociative Disorders   78

Sexual Disorders   80

   Sexual Disorders   80

Adjustment Disorders   81

   Adjustment Disorders   82

Impulse Control Disorders   84

   Impulse Control Disorders   84

Psychological Factors Affecting Physical Condition   86

   Psychological Factor Affecting Physical Condition   86

Personality Disorders   88

   *Avoidant Personality Disorder   89   •   Compulsive Personality Disorder   90
   Dependent Personality Disorder   92   •   Passive-Aggressive Personality Disorder   94
   Paranoid Personality Disorder   95   •   Schizotypal Personality Disorder   97
   Schizoid Personality Disorder   98   •   Histrionic Personality Disorder   99
   Narcissistic Personality Disorder   100
   Borderline Personality Disorder   101*

Physical Factors Affecting Psychological Functioning   104

   Stages of Adjustment   105

Chapter 2
ASSESSING SPECIAL CIRCUMSTANCES

Assessing Special Circumstances   109

*Cognitive-Behavioral Assessment   109   •   Depression And Anxiety Screening   111
Depression   111   •   Anxiety   111*

Structured Interview for Depression   112
Cycle of Depression   113
Suicide   115

*Suicide Assessment Outline   115   •   Adolescent Suicide   116   •   Treatment
Focus and Objectives   117   •   Depression and Suicide Risk Relapse   118*

Dangerousness   119

*Dangerousness Assessment Outline   120   •   Clarifying Risk of Harm   121
Treatment Focus and Objectives   122*

Cycle of Phobic Anxiety   124
Obsessional Disorders: An Overview   125
Assessment of Obsessional Disorders (OD)   125
Gravely Disabled   127

Treatment Focus and Objectives   127

Activities of Daily Living   128

*Living Situation   129   •   Self-Care Skills   129   •   Level of Required
Assistance   129   •   Care of Environment and Chore Responsibilities   129
Meals   129   •   Child Care   129   •   Financial   129   •   Shopping   129
Transportation   130*

Chronic Mental Illness (CMI)   130

General Guidelines for Assessing the Chronic Mentally III   131

Crisis Evaluation   132
Crisis Intervention   133

Critical Incident Stress Debriefing (CISD)   134   •   Screening for Survivors   135

Identifying Traumatic Stress   135

*Recovering from Traumatic Stress   135   •   How Does a Traumatic Event
Affect Someone?   136   •   The Effects of Time   137*

Traumatic Stress and Vehicular Accidents   137
Assessment of Phobic Behavior   139
Postpartum Depression and Anxiety   141

*Definitions   141   •   Postpartum Crisis Psychosis   143   •   How to Break the
Postpartum Cycle   144*

Professional Guidelines for Crisis Intervention   145
Self-Care Behaviors   146
Counseling the Individual in a Medical Crisis   147

*Treatment Framework and Conceptualization   148
The Central Crisis Issue   149*

Dealing with the Challenges of Long Term Illness   151

Working Through the Challenges and Fears Associated with Long-Term Illness   154

Chronic Pain: Assessment and Intervention   157

    Factors Affecting the Experience of Pain   157   •   Clinical Interview   158
    Assessment and Measuring Pain   158

Pain Identification Chart   160

    Location and Type of Pain   160

Pain Management Scale   161

    Interventions for Chronic Pain   162   •   Six Stages of Treatment   162
    Interventions   162

Somatic Problems: A Brief Review   164

The Patient with Psychosomatic Illness Who has an Underlying
   Personality Disorder   165

Eating Disorders Screening Questionnaire   167

The Mood Eating Scale   169

Eating History   169

Eating Disorder Evaluation: Anorexia   170

Eating Disorder Evaluation: Bulimia   172

Adult ADD Screening   174

ADHD Behavioral Review   177

Chemical Dependency Assessment   179

Chemical Dependency Psychological Assessment   182

Withdrawal Symptoms Checklist   185

    Psychological   185   •   Somatic   185

Spousal/Partner Abuse   187

    Assessing Spousal/Partner Abuse   187

The Stage Model of Domestic Violence   191

Assessing for Domestic Violence   192

    Intervention Categories   193

Counseling Victims of Domestic Violence   194

    Objectives   195

Child Abuse and Neglect   195

    Prevention   195   •   Indicators of Abuse   196   •   Treatment   197

Child Custody Evaluation   198

    Guidelines for Psychological Evaluation   198
    Ability of the Child to Bond   199
    Ability of the Parent to Bond and Other Pertinent Information   199
    Child Custody Evaluation Report Outline   200   •   Parental Behavior   201
    Interaction Between Parent-Child(Ren)   201   •   Bonding Study Versus
    Custody Evaluation   201

Parental Alienation Syndrome   202

    Parental Programming   202   •   Subtle and Unconscious Influencing   202
    Child's Own Scenarios   203   •   Family Dynamics and Environment/
    Situtational Issues   203   •   Criteria for Establishing Primary Custody   203
    Behaviors of the Parents   204   •   Children   205   •   Three Categories of
    Parental Alienation   206

Evaluation and Disposition Considerations for Families where Parental
    Alieneation Occurs   207

      Questions to Ask Children   208   •   Questions to Ask the Parents   209

Parental Alienation Syndrome Treatment   209

Visitation Rights Report   211

      Visitation Rights Report   211

Dispositional Review: Foster Placement; Temporary Placement   211

      Dispositional Review Report Outline   212

Psychiatric Work-Related Disability Evaluation   213

      *Identifying Information   213   •   Description of Client at Time
of Interview   213   •   Descriptions of Client's Current Complaints   213
History of Present Illness   213   •   Occupational History   214
Past Psychiatric History and Relevant Medical History   214
Family History   214   •   Developmental History   215   •   Social History
(Distinguish Prior to Disability, Disability Concurrent, After Injury)   215
Mental Status Exam   215   •   Review of Medical Record   215
Findings from Psychological Assessment   215   •   Interviews With
Collateral Sources and Review of Employment or Personnel Records (Compare
Description of Industrial Injury With Clients Description)   216
DSM-IV Diagnosis (Multiaxial, Using DSM Criteria and Terminology)   216
Summary and Conclusions   216*

Psychological Pre-Employment Evaluation   217

      Report Outline   217

Compulsory Psychological Evaluation   218

      Compulsory Psychological Evaluation   218

Forensic Evaluation   219

Report Outline   220

      *Competency   220   •   Competency to Plead and/or Confess   220
Competency to Stand Trial   220   •   Mental Status at Time of Offense   220*

Chapter 3
SKILL-BUILDING RESOURCES FOR INCREASING SOCIAL COMPETENCY

What is Stress?   223

      Stress Review   225

Stress Management   226

      *Early Warning Signs of Stress   228   •   Stress Signals   228
Stress Busting   229*

Effective Management of Stress   229

      *Critical Problem Solving   229   •   Assertiveness   230
Conflict Resolution   230   •   Time Management   230
Self-Care   230*

Tips for Stress Management   230

Tips to Simplify Life   231

    Ten Signs that You Need to Simplify Your Life   232
    How to Improve Planning   233

Pain Management   233
Some Examples of Individualized Time Management Options   234
Self-Care Plan   235
How to Get The Most Out of Your Day   236
Emotional IQ   237
Relaxation Exercises   238

    Deep Breathing   238   •   Mental Relaxation   239
    Tensing the Muscles   239   •   Mental Imagery   239   •   Brief Relaxation   241
    Brief Progressive Relaxation   241   •   Progressive Muscle Relaxation   242
    Preparing for the Provocation   244   •   Confronting the Provocation   245
    It's Time to Talk to Yourself   245   •   A Guide to Meditation   245

Critical Problem Solving   247

    Preparing to Learn Problem-Solving Skills   248
    Managing Interaction During Problem Solving   248
    Developing Good Problem-Solving Skills Equips Individuals To: 248
    *Stages of Problem Solving (As Therapist Facilitates Skill Development
    in Individual):   248   •   Steps for Problem Solving   249*

Problem Solving Diagram   249
Assignment 1   250

    Sample Problems   250

Assignment 2   250
Assignment 3   251
Risks   252
Components of Effective Communication   253

    "I" Statements   253   •   Active Listening   253   •   Reflection   254

Nonverbal Communication Checklist   255
Improving Communication Skills   256

    *How You Present Yourself: Body Language   256   •   How You Say It: Quality
    of Voice   256   •   Effective Listening   257*

Assertive Communication   257
Assertiveness Inventory   258
Nonverbal Communication   260
Developing Assertiveness   261

    Nonverbal Assertive Behavior   261

Personal Bill of Rights   262
Assertiveness   262

    The Steps of Positive Assertiveness   263   •   Practicing Assertive Responses   263

Ten Steps for Giving Feedback   264
Saying "No"   264

    *To Overcome Guilt in Saying "No" 264   •   Review for Yourself the
    Consequences of Saying "Yes"   265*

Accepting "No" for An Answer   265

Ten Ways of Responding to Aggression 265

The Communication of Difficult Feelings 266

     How You Can Deal with Uncomfortable Feelings 266

Writing 267

Areas of Potential Conflict 268

     List of Potential Conflicts 268

List of Feeling Words 269

     Pleasant Feelings 269

     Difficult/Unpleasant Feelings 269

Time Management 270

     Four Central Steps to Effective Time Management 270 • *How to Start Your Time Management Program* 270

Some Examples of Individualized Time Management Options 271

Decision Making 272

     Steps for Decision Making 272

Goal Development 273

     Steps for Developing Goals 273

Setting Priorities 274

     Steps for Setting Priorities 274

Rational Thinking: Self-Talk, Thought Stopping, and Reframing 274

     Self-Talk 274 • *Thought Stopping* 276 • *Reframing* 277

Thinking Distortions 278

Realistic Self-Talk 279

Practice Reframing How You Interpret Situations 281

Defense Mechanisms 282

Defense Mechanism Definitions 283

Anger Management 283

     Seven Steps of Taking Responsibility 284

Understanding Anger 285

Handling Anger 286

     General Principles Regarding Anger 286

     Understanding Your Experience of Anger 286

     Recognizing the Stages of Anger 287 • *Decrease the Intensity of Anger* 287

     Barriers to Expressing Anger 288 • *Inappropriate Expression of Anger: Violence and Rage* 288 • *Penalties for Not Expressing Anger* 288

     Ways to Deal with Anger 289

Ten Steps for Letting Go of Anger 289

Preventing Violence in the Workplace 289

     Negative Work Environment 290 • *The Dangerous Employee* 290

     Bully in the Workplace 291 • *Workplace Violence* 291

How to Handle Angry People 295

What Management Can Do to Minimize Employee Stress 296

Adjusting/Adapting 298

     Life Changes 298 • *Developmental Perspective* 299

Learning History 300

Losses/Opportunities 301

What is Meant by Resolving Grief/Loss? 301 • *Why Are People Not Prepared to Deal with Loss?* 301 • *What Are the Myths of Dealing with Loss?* 302 *How Do You Know You Are Ready?* 302 • *Finding the Solution: The Five Stages of Recovering From Loss* 302 • *How You Deal with Loss* 302 *Other Ways?* 302

Grief Cycle 303

Definition: The Natural Emotional Response to the Loss of a Cherished Idea, Person, or Thing 303

Grief 304

Never Happened 304 • *Bargaining* 305 • *Depression* 305 *Acceptance* 306

History of Loss Graph 307

Example 307

Relationship Graph 307

Example 307

Is Life What You Make It? 308

Journal Writing 308

Steps 1–4 308 • *Steps 5–15* 309

Developing and Utilizing Social Supports 310

Characteristics of a Supportive Relationship 310

How to Build and Keep a Support System 312

Recognizing the Stages of Depression 313

Decreasing the Intensity of Depression 313

Managing Depression 314

The Causes of Depression 314

Depression Symptom Checklist 315

Surviving the Holiday Blues 317

Utilizing Your Support System 318

Examples 318

The Power of Positive Attitude 318

Self-Monitoring Checklist 319

Management Behaviors 319

Daily Activity Schedule 322

Confronting and Understanding Suicide 323

Hopelessness and Despair 323

Depression 324

Phone Numbers 324

Feeling Overwhelmed and Desperate 325

Feeling like Your Life is Out of Control 326

Guilt 327

Loneliness 329

Chemical Imbalance 329

Low Self-Esteem   330
The Self-Esteem Review   332
Ten Self-Esteem Boosters   333
Affirmations for Building Self-Esteem   334
Self-Nurturing: A Component of Self-Esteem   334
Characteristics of Low Self-Esteem   336
Characteristics of High Self-Esteem   338
What Motivates Me?   339
Standing Up to Shyness   339
 Socializing   340

Bad Memories and Fear   341
Seasonal Anniversary of Losses   342
Fatigue or Sleep Deprivation   344
What is Panic Anxiety?   344
 Symptoms   345 • *Treatment   345*

Post-Traumatic Stress Disorder (PTSD)   346
Managing Anxiety   347
 What Do You Do   349

Survey of Stress Symptoms   350
 Psychological Symptoms   350 • *Physical Symptoms   350*
 Estimate Your Stress Level   350

How Your Body Reacts to Stress and Anxiety   351
 Managing Stress   351

25 Ways to Relieve Anxiety   352
Plan of Action for Dealing with Anxiety   353
Relapse—Symptom Reoccurrence   354
 Intervening in the Relapse Cycle   355

Warning Signs of Relapse   356
Systematic Desensitization   357
 The Ten Steps of Systematic Desensitization   357

What is Dementia?   358
 Symptoms   358 • *Conditions Causing Reversible Symptoms   358*
 Conditions Causing Dementia That Are Not Reversible   359 • *Diagonosis   359*

Understanding Schizophrenia   359
 Symptoms and Perceptual Disturbance   360 • *Potential for Violence   360*
 Suicide   360 • *What Causes Schizophrenia   360*

Ten Warning Signs of Alzheimer's Disease   362
Caregiving of Elderly Parents   363
 Common Problems Experienced by Caregivers   365
 Effective Coping Strategies for the Caretaker   365
 Tips for the Caretaker   366 • *Advice for others Close to the Situation   366*

Ten Warning Signs of Caregiver Stress   366
Sleep Disorders   367
 Treatment Focus and Objectives   367

Ten Tips for Better Sleep   368

Health Inventory   370

Assessing Lifestyle and Health   371

Assuming the Patient Role: The Benefits of Being Sick   372

Improving Your Health   373

Heart Disease and Depression   375

    *Facts on Depression and Heart Disease Offered by The National
Institute of Health   375   •   Benefits of Depression Treatment   375
Depression Is Often Undiagnosed and Untreated   375
Effective Treatment for Depression   376*

Eating History   376

How to Stop Using Food as a Coping Mechanism   377

Preventing Body Weight and Body Image Problems in Children   378

    *Obsession with Weight   378   •   Obesity and Self-Esteem   379
What Parents Can Do   379*

Guidelines to Follow if Someone You Know Has An Eating Disorder   379

Dealing with Fear   380

Guidelines for Family Members/Significant Others of Alcoholic/Chemically
Dependent Individuals   381

Detaching with Love Versus Controlling   382

The Enabler—The Companion to the Dysfunctional/Substance-
Abusing Person   383

Substance Abuse/Dependence Personal Evaluation   385

List of Symptoms Leading to Relapse   386

What is Codependency?   387

The Classic Situation   388

Some Characteristics of Codependence   388

Suggested Diagnostic Criteria for Codependence   389

How Does Codependency Work?   390

    *The Rules of Codependency   391   •   How Codependency Affects
One's Life   391   •   Symptom/Effect in Children of Codependents   392
What Can You Do   392   •   Stages of Recovery   392*

Characteristics of Adult Children of Alcoholics   393

Guidelines for Completing Your First Step Toward Emotional Health   394

Relationship Questionnaire   396

Healthy Adult Relationships: Being a Couple   396

    Special Circumstances   397

How to Predict the Potentially Violent Relationship   397

Domestic Violence : Safety Planning   399

    *Most Important to Remember   399   •   Document the Abuse   399
Find A Safe Place to Go   399   •   Create a Safe Room in Your Home   400
Have Money and Keys   400   •   Create a File with Your Important
Documents   400   •   Pack a Suitcase   401
Know When and How to Leave   401*

Why Victims of Domestic Violence Struggle with Leaving   401

Improved Coping Skills for Happier Couples   402

    Evaluate the Problem   402   •   Problem Resolution   403

Couple's Conflict: Rules for Fighting Fair   403

Parenting a Healthy Family   406

> Creating Effective Family Rules   406   •   Effective Coparenting   406
> Maintain the Parent Role   407   •   Be An Active Parent   407
> A Healthy Family Means All of Its Members are Involved   407
> Encourage Communication   407

Guiding Your Child to Appropriately Express Anger   408

The Family Meeting   409

> Guidelines   409   •   Developing Positive Self-Esteem in Children
> and Adolescents   410

Understanding and Dealing with Life Crises of Childhood   411

What Is a Crisis?   411

What Happens During a Crisis   412

Crisis Resolution   413

> What Do You Need to Do to Help a Child   413

Your Child's Mental Health   415

Warning Signs of Teen Mental Health Problems   416

Talking to Children   417

> Rules for Listening   418   •   Rules for Problem Solving and Expressing Your
> Thoughts and Feelings to Children   418   •   Do's   419   •   Don'ts   419

Guidelines for Discipline that Develops Responsibility   419

> Helpful Hints   420   •   Steps in Applying Logical Consequences   420

Surviving Divorce   420

> Physical Stress   421   •   Emotional Stress   421   •   Self-Care   421

Successful Stepfamilies   422

> Honor   422   •   Validation   422   •   Respect   422   •   Responsibility   422
> Communication   423   •   Discipline   423   •   Parent-Centered Structure   423

Helping Children Cope with Scheduling Changes   423

Is Your Behavior in the Best Interest of Your Children?   425

The Rules of Politeness   426

Self-Monitoring   426

> Questions to Ask Yourself   426

Goal Setting   427

Accomplishments   428

Strengths   428

Resources   429

Ten Rules for Emotional Health   429

Chapter 4

PROFESSIONAL PRACTICE FORMS, CLINICAL FORMS,
BUSINESS FORMS

Case Formulation   435

> General Consult Information   435

General Clinical Evaluation   436

Treatment Plan   439

Mental Status Exam   442

    Contents of Examination   442

Mental Status Exam   444

Mental Status Exam   445

Initial Case Assessment   447

Initial Evaluation   449

Brief Mental Health Evaluation Review   451

Life History Questionnaire   454

Adult Psychosocial   463

    Family History   464   •   *Drug and Alcohol Abuse*   465
    Educational History   465   •   *Employment History*   465
    Socialization Skills   465

Summary   466

    Treatment Plans and Recommendations   466

Child/Adolescent Psychosocial   467

    Identifying Information   467

Parent's Questionnaire   475

    Question   475

Self-Assessment   477

Brief Medical History   478

Illnesses and Medical Problems   479

Medical Review Consult Request for Primary Care Physician of an Eating
   Disorder (EDO) Patient   480

Substance Use and Psychosocial Questionnaire   481

    Treatment History   482   •   *Family History*   483
    Social History   483   •   *Medical Problems*   484

Chemical Dependency Psychosocial Assessment   485

Initial Evaluation Consultation Note to Primary Care Physician   488

Brief Consultation Note to Physician   490

Outpatient Treatment Progress Report   491

Progress Note for Individual with Anxiety and/or Depression   494

Clinical Notes   496

Disability/Worker's Compensation   498

Social Security Evaluation, Medical Source Statement, Psychiatric/
   Psychological   499

Worker's Compensation Attending Therapist's Report   500

    Progress   500   •   *Treatment*   500
    Work Status   500   •   *Disability Status*   500

Brief Psychiatric Evaluation for Industrial Injury   502

Brief Level of Functioning Review for Industrial Injury   505

Outline for Diagnostic Summary   509

    Diagnostic Summary   509

Discharge Summary   511

Patient Registration   515

Insured/Responsible Party Information 515 • *Office Billing and Insurance Policy 515*

Contract for Services Without Using Insurance 517
Fee Agreement for Deposition and Court Appearance 517
Limits on Patient Confidentiality 519

Release of Information 519

Treatment Contract 520
Contract for Group Therapy 521
Release for the Evaluation and Treatment of a Minor 522
Authorization for the Release or Exchange of Information 522
Client Messages 523
Affidavit of the Custodian of Mental Health Records to Accompany Copy of Records 524
Referral for Psychological 525

Psychiatric History 525

Release to Return to Work or School 527
Notice of Discharge for Noncompliance of Treatment 528
Duty to Warn 529
Missed Appointment 530
Receipt 531
Receipt 532
Balance Statement 533
Client Satisfaction Survey 534
Form for Checking Out Audiotapes, Videotapes and Books 536
Quality Assurance Review 537

Initial Assessment 537 • *Progress Notes 537*

Bibliography 539
Index 553

INTRODUCTION

THIS second edition, like the first, is intended to serve as a comprehensive resource tool. Because of the positive response to the organization of the original text, the format has remained the same. The *Therapist's Guide to Clinical Intervention* is divided into four sections: Treatment Planning, Special Assessment, Skill-Building Resources, and Clinical/Business Forms. The handbook concept has evolved and expanded, building on the strong foundation of the first edition. Upon review of the current literature, it was unnecessary to alter or delete any of the information contained in the original text. Instead, information viewed as increasing the resourcefulness of the text has been added. In addition to being a time-management tool, helping the therapist to meet the increasing demands of documentation requirements and the expectation of therapeutic effectiveness in identifying and resolving current problems with the brief mental health treatment benefit of managed care, the format supports improved case conceptualization of individualized treatment planning.

Since the publication of the first edition of the *Therapist's Guide to Clinical Intervention*, the prevalence of managed care in the marketplace has increased and the challenge of maximizing effectiveness has increased with it. Managed care companies and consumers alike expect to be informed of the expected number of sessions necessary to resolve the presenting issue(s) and for the therapist to collaterally communicate with the primary care physician and the physician prescribing psychotropic medications. It is a case-management role not sought after by therapists, but bestowed upon them. As a result, additional time and added responsibility are integrated into one's professional practice, again reflecting the importance of adequate documentation. The solution-oriented standard of practice has continued to flourish. The fiscal agenda of the managed care company is clear. What has become more surprising is that many consumers also are seeking brief therapy in association with clearly defined goals. Therefore, in many cases, both the consumer of services and the contractor of services are depending on the therapist to provide refined diagnostic skills, concise treatment planning with defined goals and objectives, crisis intervention, case management with collateral contacts, contracting with the client for various reasons, and discharge planning that is well documented and research supported. The *Therapist's Guide to Clinical Intervention* facilitates the ease of accomplishing these expectations by combining the aforementioned significant aspects of practice. All of this is provided in a single resource, which saves a tremendous amount of time that would be required to review the number of texts necessary to amass a commensurate amount of information.

To review the format for those familiar with the first edition and introduce this format to those who are new to the *Therapist's Guide to Clinical Intervention*, we will provide a brief summary on the four sections of the text. The first part of the book is an outline of cognitive-behavioral treatment planning. This organization of goals and objectives associated with specific, identified problems supports thoroughness in developing an effective intervention formulation that is individualized to each client. Each diagnosis or diagnostic category has a brief summary highlighting the salient diagnostic features. The treatment planning section was designed to be user-friendly and to save time. There is a list of central goals derived from identified diagnostic symptoms and the associated treatment objectives for reaching those goals from a cognitive-behavioral perspective. It goes without saying that not all individuals or diagnoses are amenable to brief therapy interventions. However, cognitive-behavioral interventions can still be very useful in the limited time frame for developing appropriate structure and facilitating stabilization. Often the brief intervention will be used as a time for initiating necessary longer-term treatment or making a referral to an appropriate therapeutic group or psychoeducational group.

The second part of the book offers a framework for assessing special circumstances, such as those involving a danger to self, danger to others, the gravely disabled, spousal abuse/domestic violence, and so forth. Additionally, this section offers numerous report outlines for various assessments with a brief explanation of their intended use. The assessment outlines provide a thorough, well-organized approach resulting in the clinical clarity necessary for immediate intervention, appropriate referrals, and treatment planning.

The third part of the book offers skill-building resources for increasing client competency. The information in this section is to be used as an educational resource and as homework related to various issues and needs presented by clients. This information is designed to support cognitive-behavioral therapeutic interventions, to facilitate the client's increased understanding of problematic issues, and to serve as a conduit for clients to acknowledge and accept their responsibility for further personal growth and self-management. Skill-building resources, whether offered verbally or given in written form, promotes the use of client motivation between sessions, enhancing goal-directed thoughts and behaviors.

The fourth part of the book offers a continuum of clinical/business forms. The development of forms is extremely time consuming. Some of the forms have only minor variations due to their specificity, and in some cases they simply offer the therapist the option of choosing a format that better suits his or her professional needs. Many of the forms can be utilized as is, directly from the text. However, if there is a need for modification to suit specific or special needs associated with one's practice beyond what is presented, having the basic framework of such forms continues to offer a substantial time-saving advantage.

This text is a compilation of the most frequently needed and useful information for the time-conscious therapist in a general clinical practice. To obtain thorough utilization of the resources provided in this text, familiarize yourself with all of its contents. This will expedite the use of the most practical aspects of this resource to suit your general needs and apprise you of the remaining contents, which may be helpful to you under other, more specific circumstances. While the breadth of the information contained in this book is substantial, each user of this text must consider her or his own expertise in providing any services. Professional and ethical guidelines require that any therapist providing clinical services be competent and have appropriate education, training, supervision, and experience. This would include a professional ability to determine which individuals and conditions are amenable to brief therapy and under what circumstances. There also needs to be knowledge of current scientific and professional standards of practice and familiarity with associated legal standards and procedures. Additionally, it is the responsibility of the provider of psychological services to have a thorough appreciation and understanding of the influence of ethnic and cultural differences in one's case conceptualization and treatment, and to see that such sensitivity is always utilized.

Level of Patient Care and Practice Considerations

Decision Tree of Evaluation and Intervention

Assessment

Patient identification
- Presenting problem
- Age
- Gender
- Race/culture
- Prior treatment
- History of substance abuse
- Medical problems
- Medications
- Relationships/family
- Academic/work history and performance

Symptom specification
- Mental status exam
  - Current mood and affect/ stability
  - Memory in tact
  - Orientation
  - Expressive/receptive language
  - Rule out organic mental disorder: age, illness, injury, substance abuse, medication reaction/hallucinations
  - Delusions
  - Suicidal ideation
  - Homicidal ideation
  - Grossly impaired
  - Judgement/insight/impulse control
  - Need for sufficient data

Ambiguous diagnosis

Problem is beyond scope of practice, expertise, or control

Critical issues — Interpretation — Intervention

Abuse
- Child
  - Psychological/emotional
  - Physical
  - Sexual
  - Neglect
- Elder or dependent adult
  - Psychological
  - Physical
  - Fiduciary
- Spousal
  - Psychological/emotional
  - Physical
  - Sexual

Interpretation: Legal/ethical issues

Intervention: Mandated reporting to appropriate agencies / Management of clinical issues related to confidentiality

- Misdiagnosis of pathology
  - *Interpretation:* Delusions/beliefs are culturally acceptable
  - *Intervention:* Educate regarding right to safety and medical treatment / Refer to to shelter/community support group / Explore/investigate cultural issues

- Prior therapists, medications, treatment-programs, hospitalizations
- Substance(s) of choice, recency of ingestion, how much, how often, prior treatment
  - *Interpretation:* Organic basis for diagnosis: overdose, drug interaction, side effects
  - *Intervention:* Communicate with PCP / Make appropriate referrals

- Multiple medications prescribed by...

- Custody issues/visitation/bonding, parental alienation
- Conservatorship
  - *Intervention:* Education, mediation, boundary clarification / Discuss other resources/consultation

Interpretation: Drugs, organicity, psychosis, cultural
- *Intervention:* Record review / Consult with PCP / Medical clearance / Detox

Interpretation: Danger to self / Danger to others
- *Intervention:* Evaluate lethality } Intervene / Evaluate lethality } accordingly

Interpretation: Unable to diagnose with clinical interview/records
- *Intervention:* Psychological testing

Intervention: Refer appropriate resources / Consultation

Referrals:
- Hospital
  - medical clearance, danger to self, danger to others, unable to provide for basic needs
- Substance abuse treatment program
- Child protective services (child abuse)
- Adult protective services (adult abuse)
- Police (tarasoff)
- Conservator(impaired/unable to provide for basic needs)
- Primary care physician (physical exam, rule out thyroid/hypoglycemia, etc.)
- Neurologist (evaluation)
- Psychiatrist (medication, evaluation, and monitoring)
- Neuropschologist (evaluation and treatment recommendations)
- Appropriate community therapy groups
- Women's shelter
- Attorney
- Vocational testing

Levels of Functioning and Associated Treatment Considerations

Level of functioning	Treatment goals[a]	Focus of treatment	Possible treatment modalities

1. Patient demonstrates adaptive functioning with minimal-to-no symptomology	Increase
	  Knowledge
	  Understanding
	  Problem Solving
	  Choices/Alternatives
		Self efficacy
		Education
		Prevention
			Didactic/educational Groups
			Community/church based support groups
			Therapeutic classes/groups focused on developmental Issues
			Recommended reading

2. Patient demonstrates mild-to-moderate symptomology which interferes with adaptive functioning	Cognitive restructing Behavior Modification	Decrease symptomology Self care Improve coping Improve problem solving and management of life stressors	Individual therapy Conjoint therapy Family therapy Group therapy dealing with specific issues and/or long term support
3. Patient demonstrates moderate symptomology warranting higher level of care	Improve daily functioning and self-management	Stabilization Daily activity schedule Productive/pleasurable activities Symptom management Development and utilization of social supports	Urgent care Intensive outpatient (OP) Reinitiate outpatient treatment with possible increased frequency Medication evaluation/monitoring Therapeutic/educational groups Case management
4. Patient demonstrates severe symptomology Danger to self Danger to others Grave disability	Monitor and provide safe environment	Stabilization All aspects of patient's life and environment (family, social, medical, occupational, recreational) Decrease symptomology Psychopharmacology Monitoring Improve judgement, insight, impulse control	Increased OP therapy contact Urgent care Intensive outpatient Partial hospitalization 23-hour unit Inpatient treatment Safely maintained in structural/monitored setting with adequate social support Home health intervention Reinitiate individual treatment when adequately stabilized
5. Patient demonstrating acute symptomology	Provide safe environment and rapid stabilization	Stabilization Decreased symptomology Psychopharmacology Monitoring	Increased OP therapy contact Urgent care Intensive OP 23-hour unit Partial hospitalization Support group Medication monitoring Case management
6. Patient demonstrating acute symptomology with difficulty stabilizing	Provide safe environment Protection of patient Protection of others	Psychopharmacology Monitoring	Inpatient treatment 23-hour unit Urgent care Partial hospitalization Intensive OP Individual therapy Support group Medication monitoring Case management

[a]Treatment goals are cumulative, i.e., a patient at a functioning level of 6 with acute symptomology may include treatment goals of previous, less acute levels, as symptomology decreases and level of functioning increases.

HIGH-RISK SITUATIONS IN PRACTICE

You can substantially reduce or eliminate risk in the following situations by giving heed to the track record of liability insurance companies. To gain perspective in these issues, plan to take a Risk Management Continuing Education course when available in your area.

1. Child Custody Cases
2. Interest Charges
3. Service Charges
4. Patients Who Restrict Your Style of Practice (e.g., Do Not Want You To Take Notes)
5. Release of Information without a Signed Form—To Anyone
6. Collection Agencies
7. Answering Service
8. Interns or Psychological Assistants to Supervise
9. Patient Abandonment
10. Dual Roles
11. High-Risk Patients, Such As Borderline Patients, Narcissistic Patients, or Multiple Personality Patients
12. Repressed Memory Patients or Analysis
13. High Debt for Delayed Payment
14. Appearance of a Group Practice without Group Insurance
15. Sexual Impropriety
16. Evaluations with Significant Consequence
17. Over or Under Diagnoses for Secondary Purposes
18. Failure to Keep Session Notes

Printed by permission from Allan Hedberg, Ph.D.

The Treatment Plan formulation serves as the guide for developing goals and for monitoring progress. It is developed specifically to meet the assessed needs of an individual. The Treatment Plan is composed of goals and objectives, which are the focus of treatment. The following is an example of how to use the treatment planning information to quickly devise a clear Treatment Plan. Listed in the example are five identified treatment goals and the corresponding objectives.

A 12-year-old boy is referred for treatment because of behavioral problems. He is diagnosed as having an Oppositional Defiant Disorder.

TREATMENT PLAN

Goals and
Objectives

Goal 1
Parent Education
Objectives

A. Explore how family is affected, how they respond, contributing factors such as developmental influences, prognosis, and community resource information

B. Parent Effectiveness Training Limit seeting, natural consequences, positive reinforcement, etc.

Goal 2
Develop Appropriate Social Skills
Objectives

A. Role model appropriate behaviors/responses for various situations

B. Identify manipulative and exploitive interaction along with underlying intention. Reinforce how to get needs met appropriately.

C. Identify behaviors which allow one person to feel close and comfortable to another person

Goal 3
Improved Communication Skills
Objectives

A. Teach assertive communication

B. Encourage appropriate expression of thoughts and feelings

C. Role model and practice verbal/nonverbal communication responses for various situations

Goal 4
Improved Self-Respect and Responsibility
Objectives

A. Have person define the terms of self-respect and responsibility, and compare these definitions to their behavior

B. Have person identify how they are affected by the behavior of others and how others are affected negatively by their behavior

C. Work with parents to clarify rules, expectations, choices, and consequences

Goal 5
Improved Insight
Objectives

A. Increase understanding of relationship between behaviors and consequences

B. Increase understanding of the thoughts/feelings underlying choices they make

C. Facilitate problem solving appropriate alternative responses to substitute for negative choice

SOLUTION-FOCUSED APPROACH TO TREATMENT

1. Meet people where they are psychologically and emotionally
   A. Listen
   B. Validate
   C. Reflect

2. Reframe
   A. When necessary/helpful
   B. To facilitate the ability to see alternatives/new possibilities
   C. "Planting seeds"

3. Clarify
   A. Clear descriptions of feelings
   B. Clear descriptions of situations and associated responses
   C. Patterns (relationship between thoughts, feelings, and behaviors)
   D. What are they motivated to work on or change?

4. Develop realistic expectations and limitations
   A. Establish appropriate/obtainable goals
   B. Identify markers of progress

5. Evaluate the response and outcome of prior crises
   A. What/who was helpful?
   B. What does the person think was a turning point?
   C. What did the person learn?

6. Facilitate development of problem solving and decision making
   A. Teach basic skills (Johnson, 1997)

7. Develop a plan of action
   A. Requires specifics which can be broken down
   B. Mutually agreed upon plan/goals
   C. Integrate empirically supported treatments
   D. Self-monitoring

8. Homework
   A. Designed to continue treatment progress
   B. Facilitate personal growth and recovery

9. Follow up
   A. Follow up on homework assignment to clarify
      1. What did or did not work
      2. Motivation
      3. Associated increased awareness and associated choices

10. Reinforce efforts and encourage continued growth
    A. Reinforce efforts throughout the course of treatment

Case Conceptualization
(Given nothing; hypothesize everything)

Part 1: Foundations of
professional practice

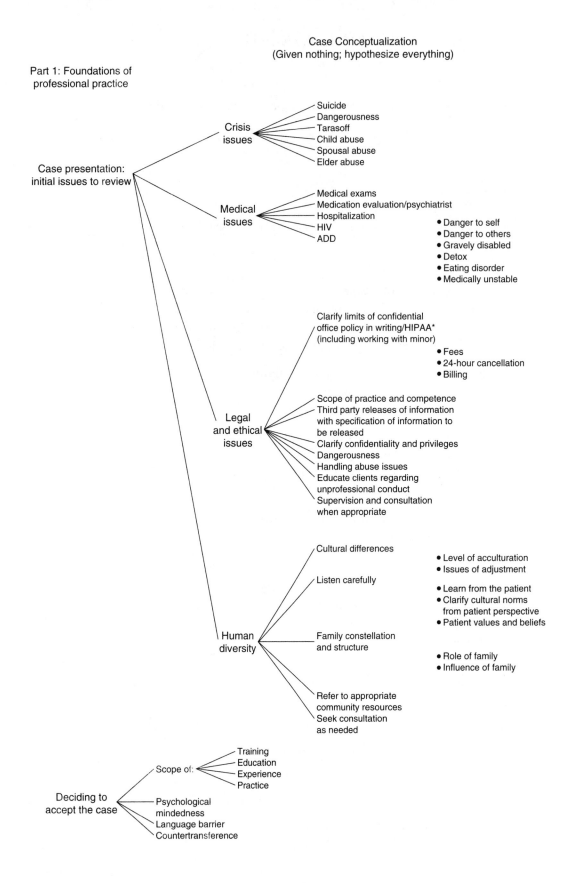

*HIPAA: Health Insurance Portability and Accountability Act. Protecting the privacy of patient's health information.

Part 2:
Treatment planning

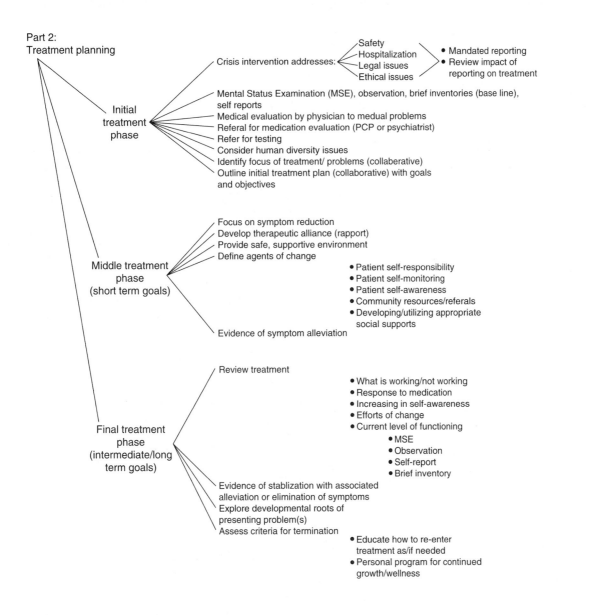

Initial treatment phase

Crisis intervention addresses:
- Safety
- Hospitalization
- Legal issues
- Ethical issues
  - Mandated reporting
  - Review impact of reporting on treatment

- Mental Status Examination (MSE), observation, brief inventories (base line), self reports
- Medical evaluation by physician to medual problems
- Referal for medication evaluation (PCP or psychiatrist)
- Refer for testing
- Consider human diversity issues
- Identify focus of treatment/ problems (collaborative)
- Outline initial treatment plan (collaborative) with goals and objectives

Middle treatment phase (short term goals)

- Focus on symptom reduction
- Develop therapeutic alliance (rapport)
- Provide safe, supportive environment
- Define agents of change
  - Patient self-responsibility
  - Patient self-monitoring
  - Patient self-awareness
  - Community resources/referals
  - Developing/utilizing appropriate social supports
- Evidence of symptom alleviation

Final treatment phase (intermediate/long term goals)

- Review treatment
  - What is working/not working
  - Response to medication
  - Increasing in self-awareness
  - Efforts of change
  - Current level of functioning
    - MSE
    - Observation
    - Self-report
    - Brief inventory
- Evidence of stablization with associated alleviation or elimination of symptoms
- Explore developmental roots of presenting problem(s)
- Assess criteria for termination
  - Educate how to re-enter treatment as/if needed
  - Personal program for continued growth/wellness

COMMON AXIS 1 AND AXIS 2 DIAGNOSES

Depressive Disorders	
Dysthymia	30040
Depression, NOS	31100
Major Depression, Single Episode:	
Mild	29621
Moderate	29622
Severe without psychotic features	29623
In partial remission	29625
Unspecified	29620
Major Depression. Recurrent Episode:	
Mild	29631
Moderate	29632
Severe without psychotic features	29633
In partial remission	29635
Unspecified	29630

Attention-Deficit and Disruptive Behavior Disorders	
Attention-Deficit/Hyperactivity Disorder:	
Combined or hyperactive-implosive types	31401
Predominantly inattentive type	31400
ADHD NOS	31490
Conduct Disorder	31280
Oppositional Defiant Disorder	31381
Disruptive Behavior Disorder NOS	31290

Personality Disorders	
Paranoid	30100
Schizoid	30120
Borderline	30183
Histrionic	30150
Narcissistic	30181
Avoidant	30182
Dependent	30160
Obsessive-Compulsive	30140
NOS	30190

Eating Disorders	
Anorexia Nervosa	30710
Bulimia Nervosa	30751
Eating Disorder NOS	30750

Others	
Psychological Factors Affect on med card	316
Medication Induced Disorder	995.2
Noncompliance with Treatment	v15.81
No Diagnosis on Axis I	v71.09
Diagnosis defined on Axis I	799.9
No Diagnosis on Axis II	v71.09
Diagnosis defined on Axis II	799.9

Adjustment Disorders	
with depressed mood	30900
with anxiety	30924
with mixed anxiety and depressed mood	30928
with disturbance of conduct	30930
with mixed disturbance of emotions and conduct	30940
unspecified	30990

Anxiety Disorders	
Panic, without agoraphobia	30001
Panic, with agoraphobia	30021
Agoraphobia without panic	30022
Specific Phobia	30029
Social Phobia	30023
Obsessive-Compulsive Disorder	30030
PTSD	30981
Acute Stress Disorder	30830
Generalized Anxiety Disorder	30002
Anxiety Disorder NOS	30000

V Codes	
Relational Problem	16190
Parent-Child Relational Problem	16120
Partner Relational Problem, Abuse of Adult	16110
Sibling Relational Problem	16180
Relational Problem NOS	16281
Abuse or Neglect of Child	16121
Noncompliance with Treatment	11581
Malingering	16520
Adult Antisocial Behavior	17101
Child/Adolescent Antisocial Behavior	17102
Religious or Phase of Life Problems	16289
Bereavement	16282
Academic Problem	16230
Occupational Problem	16220
Acculturation Problem	16240

Substance Use	
Alcohol Dependence	30390
Alcohol Abuse	30500
Cocaine Dependence	30420
Cocaine Abuse	30560
Cannabis Dependence	30430
Cannabis Abuse	30520
Opioid Dependence	30400
Opioid Abuse	30550

Impulse Control Disorders	
Impulse Control Disorder NOS	31230
Intermittent Explosive Disorder	31234

Chapter 1

Treatment Planning: Goals, Objectives, and Interventions

DISORDERS USUALLY FIRST EVIDENT IN INFANCY, CHILDHOOD, OR ADOLESCENCE

MENTAL RETARDATION (MR)

Mental retardation is characterized by intellectual functioning being below average (IQ of 70 or below) with concurrent impairments in adaptive functioning, which includes social skills, communication, daily living skills, age-appropriate independent behavior, and social responsibility. There are four degrees of severity in impairment: mild, moderate, severe, and profound.

A medical exam, neurological exam, or evaluation by a neuropsychologist is important to rule out organicity, vision/hearing deficits and to determine the origin of the presenting problems. With the information yielded from such exams, a thorough individualized program can be developed and implemented. An individualized treatment and educational plan addresses the individual needs along with the identification of intelligence level and strengths for the facilitated development of the highest level of functioning for that individual.

Goals

1. Establish developmentally appropriate daily living skills
2. Develop basic problem-solving skills
3. Decrease social isolation and increase personal competence

4. Develop social skills

5. Support and educate parents on management issues

Treatment Focus and Objectives

1. Daily Living Skills (waking by alarm, dressing, hygiene/personal care, finances, taking the bus, etc.)
   A. Realistic expectations and limitations
   B. Repetition of behaviors
   C. Modeling of desired behaviors
   D. Breaking down behaviors into step-wise sequence (shaping)
   E. Positive feedback and reinforcement

2. Impaired Problem Solving
   A. Role-play solutions to various situations
   B. Develop a hierarchy of responses for potential problem/crisis (enlist help of caretaker, parents, neighbor, or other known party who is responsible and inform them as to how to contact the police, EMT, or fire department, etc.)
   C. Practice desired responses
   D. Focus on efforts and accomplishments
   E. Positive feedback and reinforcement

3. Social Isolation
   A. Appropriate educational setting
      1. Most communities have a vocational rehabilitation program and volunteer bureau to offer jobs in the community related to their level of functioning
   B. Special Olympics, or community sporting activities
   C. Programmed social activities
   D. Camps for the MR
   E. Contact local association for mentally retarded persons for community resources
   F. If older, evaluate for vocational training, living arrangement away from family, which includes social agenda (independent living or group home), if low functioning, a day treatment program may be helpful

4. Impaired Social Skills
   A. Realistic expectations and limitations
   B. Teach appropriate social skills (developmental, age appropriate)
      1. Collaboration
      2. Cooperation
      3. Follow rules
      4. Etiquette/manners
   C. Games that practice social skills
   D. Role-play
   E. Practice/repetition
   F. Focus on efforts and accomplishments
   G. Positive feedback and reinforcement

5. Family Intervention/Education
   A. Educate regarding realistic expectations and limitations
   B. Review options and alternatives to various difficulties

C. Identify and work through feelings of loss, guilt, shame, and anger; it is not uncommon for parents/families of severely, handicapped children to feel resentment toward the child, who may be disruptive to the family
D. Facilitate other children in family to deal with their feelings or concerns
E. Encourage acceptance of reality
F. Encourage identification and utilization of community support organizations and other associated resources
G. Teach parents behavior-modification techniques

Additional Considerations

During Assessment

1. If there is adequate verbal skills, utilize open ended questions
2. Clarify with concrete, simple, tightly structured interview questions
3. Be careful to accurately assess for a rich fantasy life versus a diagnosis of psychosis
4. Be sensitive to depression and low self-esteem as clinical issues

Levels of mental retardation by Intelligence Test Range

Mild mental retardation	50–55 to approximately 70
Moderate mental retardation	35–40 to 50–55
Severe mental retardation	20–25 to 35–40
Profound mental retardation	below 20–25

Behavior Competency Expectations Associated with Degree of Mental Retardation (Marsh & Barclay, 1989)

Mild

Preschool (0–5)	Able to develop social and communication skills. The minimal sensory-motor retardation may not be evident until later.
School age (6–18)	Academic proficiency up to 6th grade level. Able to take the lead to social conformity.

Moderate

Preschool	Able to talk/learn to communicate. Poor social awareness. Adequate motor skills. Benefits from self-help skill training with supervision.
School age	Able to benefit from social and occupational skill training. Not likely to advance beyond 2nd grade level. Some independence in familiar setting.

Severe

Preschool	Poor language development. Minimal language skill/little communication. Unlikely to benefit from self-help training.
School age	Able to learn to talk/communicate. Training beneficial for basic self-help skills. Benefits from systematic habit training.

Profound

Preschool	Minimal capacity in sensory-motor functioning. Requires intense care.
School age	Some evidence of motor development. May respond to very limited range of training in self-skill development.

The most common intrauterine causes of mental retardation are the following:

1. Fetal alcohol syndrome (FAS)
2. Asphyxia (from maternal hypertension, toxemia, placenta previa)
3. Intrauterine infections
4. Rubella
5. Toxoplasmosis (often from cats)

The most common prenatal causes of mental retardation are the following:

1. Meningitis
2. Encephalitis
3. Head trauma
4. Anoxia

Dual Diagnosis (developmentally disabled with psychiatric disorder)

Jacobson (1982a, 1982b) surveyed retarded children from infancy to adolescence and found that 9.8% had significant psychiatric impairment, which was categorized into four areas based on features and severity:

1. Cognitive
   A. Major thought disorder
   B. Hallucinations
   C. Delusions

2. Affective
   A. Significant depression
   B. Dysphoric affect

3. Minor behavioral problems (these problems are on a continuum to major problems)
   A. Hyperactivity
   B. Tantrums
   C. Stereotypies
   D. Verbal abusiveness
   E. Substance abuse

4. Major behavioral problems
   A. Physical aggression/assault
   B. Property destruction
   C. Coercive sexual behavior
   D. Self-injurious behavior

Parents and siblings must be evaluated in association with their own risk for significant difficulties (may or may not be related to mentally retarded child in the family system). The family system may lack cohesiveness and harmony.

Parents	Increased risk for depression
	Decreased satisfaction in parenting
	Potential for negative attitude toward retarded child
	Marital stress
	Increased social isolation
Siblings	Behavioral problems
	Feelings of guilt/anger
	Psuedo-adult responsibilities (loss of their childhood)

PERVASIVE DEVELOPMENTAL DISORDERS (PDD)

Pervasive Developmental Disorder is defined by a withdrawal of the child into a separate, self-created fantasy world. The course of this disorder is chronic and often persists into adulthood. It is characterized by such features of impairments as these:

1. Reciprocal Social Interaction: not aware of others' feelings, doesn't imitate, doesn't seek comfort at times of distress, and impairment in ability to make peer relationships.
2. Impaired Communication: abnormal speech productivity, abnormal form or content of speech, and impaired initiating or sustaining conversation despite adequate speech.
3. Restricted Repertoire of Activities and Interests: stereotyped body movements, marked distress over trivial changes, and restricted range of interests.

A medical exam to rule out physical problems such as hearing or vision impairments should be performed prior to the assignment of this diagnosis. PDD show severe qualitative abnormalities that aren't normal for any age in comparison to mental retardation, which demonstrates general delays and the person behaves as if he/she is passing through an earlier stage of normal development. However, MR may coexist with PDD.

Goals

1. Child will not harm self
2. Child will demonstrate trust in his/her caretaker
3. Shaping child's behavior toward improved social interaction
4. Child will demonstrate increased self-awareness
5. Child will develop appropriate means of verbal and nonverbal communication for expressing his/her needs
6. Support and educate parents regarding behavioral management

Treatment Focus and Objectives

1. Risk of Self-Harm
   A. Intervene when child demonstrates self-injurious behaviors
   B. Determine precipitators of self-injurious behaviors (such as increased tension in environment or increased anxiety)
   C. Make efforts to assure, comfort, or give appropriate structure to child during distressful incidents to foster feelings of security and trust
   D. Offer one-to-one interaction to facilitate focus and foster trust
   E. Use safety helmet and mitts if necessary

2. Lack of Trust
   A. Consistency in environment and interactional objects (e.g., toys, etc.) fosters security and familiarity
   B. Consistency in caretaker to develop familiarity and trust
   C. Consistency in caretaker responses to behavior to facilitate development of boundaries and expectations; behavioral reinforcement
   D. Caretaker must be realistic about limitations and expectations. Prepare caretaker to proceed at a slow pace and to not impose his/her own wants and desires of progress on the child who will have to move at his/her own slow pace.

E. Proceed in treatment plan with the lowest level of desired interaction to initiate positive behavioral change. Low-level behaviors could include eye contact, facial expression, or other nonverbal behaviors. Development of these types of behaviors require one-to-one interaction.

F. Keep environmental stimuli at a minimum to reduce feelings of threat or being overwhelmed

3. Dysfunctional Social Interaction
   A. Requires objectives 1 and 2 to be in practice
   B. Support and reinforce child's attempts to interact, with consistent guidance toward goal behaviors
   C. Consistently restate communication attempts to clarify and encourage appropriate and meaningful communication that is understandable (be careful to not alter the intended communication, just clarify it)

4. Identity Disturbance
   A. Utilize activities that facilitate recognition of individuality. Begin with basic daily activities of dressing and mealtime, such as difference in appearance and choices.
   B. Increase self-awareness and self-knowledge. This can be initially facilitated by having the child learn and say the name of the caretaker and then his/her own name and learning the names of his/her own body parts. These types of activities can be done through media such as drawing, pictures, or music.
   C. Reinforce boundaries and individuality

5. Impaired Communication
   A. Consistently make efforts to clarify intent/need associated with communication
   B. Caretaker consistency will facilitate increased understanding of child's communication patterns
   C. When clarifying communication, be eye to eye with child to focus on the communication in connection with the issue of need being presented by the child

6. Parental Intervention/Education
   A. Educate regarding realistic understanding of expectations and limitations
   B. Identify and work through feelings of loss, guilt, shame, and anger
   C. Facilitate other children in the family to deal with their feelings and concerns
   D. Encourage acceptance of reality
   E. Encourage identification and utilization of community support organizations and other associated resources
   F. Identify additional support and respite care
   G. Teach parents specific behavioral management techniques to fit their needs, such as how to solve practical problems (within family, between child/school, family/school, and with other services), how to celebrate progress and how to establish reinforcers
   H. Recognize that parents may be at increased risk for depression or stress-related illnesses

Some conditions produce PDD symptoms, therefore, if a formal diagnosis has not previously been assigned, the following information should be given to the parents and appropriate referral considerations be communicated to the primary care physician.

Medical
Assessment

1. History
2. Examination
3. Rule out associated medical conditions (pica and associated lead intoxication)

4. Visual/audiology exams

5. Neurological assessment important to evaluate for seizures

6. Genetic screening

7. Language/communication assessment, such as articulation/oral motor skills and receptive/expressive skills

Developmental Stage

1. Preschool
   A. Early intervention
   B. Parental education and training
   C. Some eligibility of services

2. School age
   A. Increased eligibility for services (public, social, educational)
   B. Continued education and support of parents, including a focus on problem solving skills and behavior management

3. Adolescence
   A. Expanding eligibility for services by focusing on adaptive skills development, prevocational skills, and vocational programming/education
   B. Clinical clarification of strengths/weaknesses as related to vocational training
   C. When possible include adolescent in treatment planning
   D. Monitor for development of comorbid diagnoses such as depression or seizures

4. Adult
   A. Identification of community resources
   B. Support in planning long-term care, including employment, residential care, social support/activities, and family support

DISRUPTIVE BEHAVIOR DISORDERS

ATTENTION DEFICIT HYPERACTIVITY DISORDER (ADHD) OPPOSITIONAL DEFIANT DISORDER CONDUCT DISORDER

There is somewhat of a continuum and overlap between manifestations of Attention Deficit Hyperactivity Disorder, Oppositional Defiant Disorder, and Conduct Disorder. ADHD may be an underlying issue in both Oppositional Defiant Disorder and Conduct Disorder. A careful assessment taking this into consideration will allow the therapist to rule out the ADHD diagnosis in these instances. Because of the commonality in behavioral symptomology, the treatment focus and objectives will be offered as a single section to draw from based on the needs of the case.

ADHD children are at risk for delinquent behaviors because they do not consistently demonstrate behaviors that will naturally elicit positive reinforcement. Instead they tend to receive negative feedback from their peers and adults. In an effort to fit in with a peer group, they may find acceptance with children/adolescents that have obvious behavioral problems. Generally, there is behavioral evidence of difficulties associated with ADHD in all settings (home, work, school, social), and symptoms are usually worse in situations requiring sustained attention. Although the excessive motor activity characterizing ADHD often subsides prior to adolescence, the attention deficit frequently persists.

In cases where ADHD is suspected, first refer to a physician for a medical exam to rule out endocrine problems or allergies and to address the issue of medication. Rule out mood disorders and abuse. In cases where Oppositional Defiant Disorder or Conduct Disorder is a potential diagnosis, rule out substance abuse, sexual abuse, physical/emotional abuse, and ADHD.

Goals

1. Assess for referral for medication evaluation
2. Enhance parent education regarding familial and clinical aspects of the disorder and behavioral management
3. Collateral cooperation in behavioral management with teaching staff
4. Develop responsible behavior and self-respect
5. Develop appropriate social skills
6. Improve communication
7. Decrease defensiveness
8. Improve self-esteem
9. Improve coping
10. Problem solving
11. Improve insight
12. Impulse control
13. Anger management
14. Eliminate potential for violence

Treatment Focus and Objectives

1. Evaluate for Referral for Medication Evaluation
   A. If parents have a negative or resistant response to medication, direct them to some appropriate reading material and suggest that they meet with a physician specializing in this disorder before they make a decision

2. Parent Education
   A. Overview giving the defining criteria of the specific disorder, explore how the family is affected and how they respond, etiology, developmental influences, prognosis, a selection of reading materials and information on a community support group, if available
   B. Parent effectiveness training. Training to include parenting skills in behavioral modification, contingency planning, positive reinforcement, appropriate limit setting and consequences, encouraging self-esteem, disciplining in a manner that fosters the development of responsibility and respect for others. Consistency is imperative to successful behavioral change and management.
   C. Dysfunctional family dynamics
      1. Explore and identify family roles
      2. Identify modification and changes of person's role in family
      3. Identify the various roles played by family members and the identified patient, and modify or change as needed in accordance with appropriate family dynamics and behavior
      4. Facilitate improved communication
      5. Clarify differences between being a parent and a child in the family system, along with role expectation
      6. Explore the necessity of out of home placement if parents are unable to effectively manage and support behavior change or are actual facilitators of antisocial behaviors. Depending on severity of behaviors, it may require placement for monitoring to prevent risk of harm to self or others

3. Teachers
   A. Define classroom rules and expectation regularly
   B. Break down goals into manageable time frames depending on the task. Time frames could be 15 minutes, 30 minutes, one hour, a day, or a month. Be encouraging by providing frequent feedback. Break tasks into small steps.
   C. Give choices whenever possible
   D. Provide short exercise breaks between work periods
   E. Use a time to encourage staying on task. If these students finish a task before the allotted time, reinforce their behavior
   F. Facilitate the development of social skills
   G. Encourage specific behaviors
   H. Develop contracts when appropriate. It will also help parents reinforce the teacher's program
   I. Develop a secret signal that can be used to remind students to stay on task, which will avoid embarrassment and low self-esteem
   J. Facilitate the development of self-monitoring so that students can pace themselves and stay on task, as well as self-reinforce for progress
   K. Structure the environment to reduce distracting stimuli
   L. Separate these students from peers who may be encouraging inappropriate behavior
   M. Highlight or underline important information
   N. Use a variety of high-interest modes to communicate effectively (auditory, visual, hands-on, etc.)
   O. Position these students close to resources/sources of information
   P. Consistency is imperative
   Q. Work collaterally with all professionals to develop an individualized cognitive behavioral program

4. Lack of Self-Respect and Responsibility
   A. Have person define these terms accurately (may need support or use of external resources) and compare the working definitions to his/her behavior as well as developing appropriate behavioral changes
   B. Facilitate the concept of choices related to consequences, and acceptance of consequences as taking responsibility for one's own actions
   C. Have these children identify how they are affected by the behavior of others and how others are affected negatively by their behaviors. Clarify that they only have control over their own behaviors.
   D. Work with parents to clarify rules, expectations, choices, and consequences

5. Dysfunctional Social Interaction
   A. Role-model appropriate behaviors/responses for a variety of situations and circumstances. Provide situations or vignettes to learn from.
   B. Provide positive feedback and constructive education about their interaction
   C. Identify manipulative or exploitive interaction. Explore intention behind interaction and give information and reinforcement on how to get needs met appropriately.
   D. Focus on the positive demonstrations of interaction over negative ones when reinforcing behavioral change
   E. Have person identify reasons for inability to form close interpersonal relationships to increase awareness and to develop choices for change
   F. Have person identify behaviors that allow one person to feel close or comfortable with another person versus distancing behaviors

6. Impaired Communication Skills
   A. Teach assertive communication skills
   B. Encourage appropriate expression of thoughts and feelings

C. Role-model and practice communication responses (verbal and nonverbal) for various situations and circumstances

D. Positive feedback and reinforcement

7. Defensive Behaviors

   A. Increase awareness for defensive tendencies by defining with examples and encouraging the individual to identify similar behaviors of his/her own

   B. In a nonthreatening way, explore with these individuals any past feedback that they have been given from others about how others perceive them and what contributes to that perception

   C. Focus on positives attributions to encourage positive self-esteem

   D. Encourage acceptance of responsibility for one's own behavior

   E. Have person identify the relationship between feelings of inadequacy and defensiveness

   F. Positive feedback and reinforcement

8. Low Self-Esteem

   A. Through a positive therapeutic relationship, be accepting, respectful, and ask them often what their views are about issues, affirming the importance of what they have to offer

   B. Support and encourage appropriate risk taking toward desired goals

   C. Encourage their participation in problem solving

   D. Reframe mistakes in an effort toward change as an opportunity to learn more and benefit from experiences. Encourage taking responsibility for one's own mistakes.

   E. Encourage self-care behaviors: grooming/hygiene, exercise, no use of substances, good nutrition, engaging in appropriate pleasurable activities

   F. Identify self-improvement activities; behavioral change, education, growth experiences

   G. Identify and develop healthy, appropriate values

   H. Identify strengths and develop a form of daily affirmations for reinforcing positive self-image

   I. Identify desired changes. Be sensitive, realistic, and supportive in development of shaping changes.

   J. Facilitate assertive communication and assertive body language

   K. Educate about the destructiveness of negative self-talk

   L. Create opportunities for person to show his/her abilities

   M. Notice examples of ability and point them out. Build on strengths.

   N. Positively reinforce their efforts and accomplishments

9. Ineffective Coping

   A. Provide appropriate physical activity to decrease body tension and offer a positive choice with a sense of well-being

   B. Set limits on manipulative behavior and give appropriate consequences

   C. Facilitate change in coping by not participating in arguing, debating, excessive explaining, rationalizing, or bargaining with the person

   D. Running away

      1. Identify the nature and extent of running away

      2. Clarify and interpret the dynamics of running away

      3. Work through the identified dynamics

      4. Facilitate the individual to identify the signs of impending runaway behavior

      5. Facilitate identification and implementation of alternative solutions to running away

E. Lying

    1. Identify the nature and extent of lying

    2. Confront lying behavior. Assert the importance of behavior matching what is verbalized

    3. Clarify and interpret the dynamics of lying

    4. Work through the dynamics of lying

    5. Facilitate the development of a behavioral management program for lying. Monitor accurate reporting of information, and encourage the person to make amends to those lied to whenever possible.

F. Focus on positive coping efforts

G. Encourage honest, appropriate, and direct expression of emotions

H. Facilitate the development of being able to delay gratification without resorting to manipulative or acting-out behaviors

I. Have person verbalize alternative, socially acceptable coping skills

10. Ineffective Problem Solving

A. Encourage the identification of causes of problems and influencing factors

B. Encourage the person to identify needs and goals. Facilitate, with the individual's input, the objectives, expected outcomes, and prioritization of issues

C. Encourage the exploration of alternative solutions

D. Provide opportunities for practicing problem-solving behavior

E. Explore goals, and problem-solve how to reach goals

11. Poor Insight

A. Increase understanding of relationship between behaviors and consequences

B. Increase understanding of the thoughts/feelings underlying choices made

C. Facilitate problem solving appropriate alternative responses to substitute for negative choices

12. Poor Impulse Control

A. Increase awareness, and give positive feedback when the person is able to demonstrate control

B. Explore alternative ways to express feelings

C. Facilitate the identification of particular behaviors that are causing problems

D. Facilitate identification of methods to delay response and encourage thinking through of various responses with associated consequences

13. Poor Anger Management

A. Identify antecedents and consequences of angry outbursts

B. Facilitate understanding of anger within the normal range of emotions and appropriate responses to feelings of anger

C. Identify issues of anger from the past and facilitate resolution or letting go

D. Identify the difference between anger and rage

E. Identify affect of anger on close, intimate relationships

F. Identify role of anger as a coping mechanism or manipulation

G. Facilitate the taking of responsibility for feelings and expressions of anger

H. Problem-solve current issues of anger to resolve conflicts

I. Positive feedback and reinforcement for efforts and accomplishments

14. Potential for Violence

A. Assess for signs and symptoms of acting out

B. Maintain a safe distance and talk in a calm voice

C. Provide a safe, nonthreatening environment with a minimum of aversive stimulation

D. Use verbal communication and alternative stress and anger releasers to prevent violent acting out

E. Anger management

    1. Identify the nature, extent, and precipitants of the aggressive behavior (i.e., is the behavior defensive, etc.)

    2. Facilitate identification and increased awareness of the escalators of aggressive behavior

    3. Clarify and interpret the dynamics of aggressive impulses and behavior

    4. Work through the dynamics of aggression

F. Reinforce the use of the skills that the person has developed

G. Have the person discuss alternative ways of expressing their emotion appropriately to avoid negative consequences

H. Encourage the individual to verbalize the wish or need to be aggressive rather than to act on the impulse

I. If the person demonstrates the tolerance of intervention, provide a recreational outlet for aggressive impulses

J. Facilitate the individual to implement alternative actions to aggressive behavior

K. At a later time when the threat of acting out has passed, help the person to benefit from the experience by reviewing the circumstances, choices, and different points of possible intervention and what would have been helpful reinforce the person's problem-solving efforts

Additional Considerations

Regarding culturally diverse and inner-city dwellers, it is imperative to obtain information on the family and neighborhood:

1. Inquire about the possibility of lead intoxication and malnutrition

2. Ask about parental abuse of substances and antisocial behavior/personality disorder (including family members and peer reference group)

3. In the culturally diverse, assess the level of cultural tolerance for certain behaviors

4. Determine if their environment demands physical strength and aggression as survival factors

5. What is the impact of social/economic pressures on lying, truancy, stealing, early substance abuse, sexual behavior, inconsistent/absent parental figures (i.e., single parent who works and is not available), and their values/beliefs

Disorders of behavior are treated with a focus on behavioral interventions. Therefore, therapy is has these features:

1. Highly structured

2. Moderate in supportiveness (some attention to past patterns/difficulties)

3. May include modalities of individual, family, and self-help groups

4. Physical examination with minimal use of medication (not a substitute for modifying inappropriate behavior)

5. Brief duration of treatment

Many children diagnosed with Attention Deficit Disorder (ADD), ADHD, or other behavioral disorders may actually be manic depressive. Bipolar Disorder in children

1. May strike as early as age 7
2. May be prone to rapid cycling
3. May go untreated for years

Similarities between hyperactivity and mania in children are that the children are

1. Excessively active
2. Irritable
3. Easily distracted

However, children with Bipolar Disorder also exhibit

1. Elated mood
2. Inappropriate giggliness
3. Grandiosity
4. Flights of ideas
5. Racing thoughts
6. Decreased need for sleep

SEPARATION ANXIETY

The most prominent feature of this disorder is excessive anxiety concerning separation from those to whom the child is attached. Additional symptoms includes irrational fears, nightmares, emotional conflicts, and refusal to attend school. Explore the presence of domestic issues that are related to or are exacerbating the child's emotional and behavioral problems.

Goals

1. Support and educate parents regarding age-appropriate separation issues
2. Identify and resolve the events precipitating the anxiety
3. Decreased worrying
4. Consistent school attendance
5. Resolution of the emotional conflict
6. Foster cooperative efforts with school personnel to effectively manage behavior

Treatment Focus and Objectives

1. Educating Parents Regarding Age-Appropriate Emotional Separation
2. Exploring Precipitating Events Such as Recent Losses, Stressors, and Changes
   A. Explore the issues of substance abuse in the home or other contributors of instability
   B. Explore parental conflict and spousal abuse issues
   C. Explore possible nightmares or fears associated with separation
   D. Explore the fear of being alone

3. Excessive Worrying
    A. Explore fears related to concerns—rational and irrational
    B. Deal with issues related to rational fears and problem-solve more adaptive coping responses
    C. Confront irrational fears and beliefs

4. Refusal to Attend School
    A. Child needs to attend school
        1. Contact school to prepare the staff for the situation
        2. Parents and teachers to be consistent with a mutual understanding of the plan to manage the child

5. Difficulty Dealing with Emotional Conflict
    A. Play therapy to identify and work through issues
    B. Relaxation training (with reaffirming messages such as "mommy is at work, but will be home at …, Everything is the way it is supposed to be …")
    C. Keeping a journal for venting feelings and for problem solving
    D. Encourage appropriate behavior; do not focus on negative behavior
    E. Explore presence of physical symptoms associated with anticipation of separation. Facilitate development of management skills to decrease symptoms.
    F. Positive feedback and reinforcement

6. Teacher
    A. Inform teacher of difficulties that child is experiencing
    B. Coordinate consistency between efforts of school personnel and parents in being supportive to the child

While separation anxiety is seen as a normal response in young children, when it interferes with age-appropriate tasks (school attendance, peer interaction, daily activities etc.), it needs to be dealt with.

Additional Considerations

For children residing in inner-city settings there may be legitimate issues of safety associated with high crime rates. Parents may be reluctant to let their children go outside and play without adult supervision, feeling anxious and unsafe themselves. Therefore, the parent's level of anxiety and coping must be carefully evaluated. If there is an instance of actual harm or abrupt separation from a caretaking figure, a child's anxiety may increase.

Note that a diagnosis of anxiety disorder is only appropriate when a child's fear, anxiety, worries are persistent and unrealistic.

AVOIDANT DISORDER

The central feature of this disorder is the excessive negative reaction to unfamiliar people. Additional features include heightened anxiety and low self-esteem. These children desire warm and satisfying relationships with familiar people, but their severe reaction to unfamiliar people interferes with social functioning.

Goals

1. Correct irrational thinking
2. Improve self-esteem
3. Facilitate self-management through identification of personal goals and objectives
4. Improve coping

5. Decrease avoidance

6. Decrease anxiety

7. Improve peer relationships

1. Explore Fears and Irrational Beliefs
   A. Challenge irrational thoughts with reality
      - understand fear
      - normalize fear
      - manage fear
   B. Substitute irrational thoughts with rational thoughts
   C. Encourage appropriate risk taking (plugging in some guaranteed successes)

2. Low Self-Esteem
   A. Identify strengths and accomplishments
   B. Create opportunities to demonstrate strengths
   C. Encourage expression of thoughts and feelings on problem-solving issues
   D. Be accepting and respectful
   E. Facilitate development of assertive communication
   F. Positive feedback and reinforcement

3. Lacks Appropriate Goals
   A. Identify strengths and interests
   B. Break down objectives to goal into manageable steps
   C. Focus on efforts and accomplishments
   D. Positive feedback and reinforcement

4. Ineffective Coping
   A. Facilitate identification of feelings
   B. Encourage appropriate venting of feelings
   C. Set limits on avoidant behaviors while encouraging effective coping behaviors
   D. Explore alternatives for dealing with avoidance to specific situations
   E. Practice effective solutions such as homework designed to help individuals face their fears and test cognitions (for example, gradually increasing exposure to feared stimulus)
   F. Focus on efforts and accomplishments
   G. Positive feedback and reinforcement

5. Avoidant Behavior
   A. Teach assertive communication
   B. Teach appropriate social skills
   C. Role-play responses to variety of social situations
   D. Systematic desensitization
      1. Develop hierarchy of increasing anxiety-provoking situations to facilitate feelings of being in control
      2. *In vivo* desensitization may work faster for some individuals then imaginal desensitization
   E. Positive feedback and reinforcement for efforts and accomplishments

6. Increased Anxiety
   A. Identify relationship between anxiety and behavior

B. Teach relaxation techniques
1. Deep breathing
2. Progressive muscle relaxation
3. Visual imagery

7. Improve Peer Relationships
1. Encourage participation in activity where additional benefit is time shared with peers who have the same interest
2. Encourage participation in engaging situations or activities that offer distraction, thereby increasing mastery over anxiety while in the company of peers
3. Parents may have to be more accomodating and lack demonstrations of distress associated with accomodating

Additional Considerations

1. Assess parental response to new people and situations
A. Modeling
B. Level of anxiety

2. Assess
A. Parental encouragement/reassurance of appropriate risk-taking behavior
B. Resolution to distressing situations—learning/increased awareness versus appropriate distrust

3. Work with parents to help them understand their child's behavioral and emotional reactions and the role they can play in modification

OVERANXIOUS DISORDER

This disorder is characterized by irrational anxiety where there is no identifiable situation linked to the fear. Symptoms include worry about the future, low self-esteem (self-confidence), inability to effectively cope, need for reassurance, and somatic complaints. This child is pre-occupied with irrational thoughts.

Goals

1. Correct irrational thinking
2. Improve coping
3. Improve self-esteem
4. Decrease anxiety
5. Family education and intervention
6. Collateral contact with school personnel

Treatment Focus and Objectives

1. Irrational Beliefs
A. Rule out trauma/abuse
B. Explore parental experience of the world (e.g., mother may be over anxious, therefore the world is a dangerous place)
C. Challenge irrational thoughts with reality
D. Encourage appropriate risk taking

2. Ineffective Coping
A. Facilitate identification of feelings
B. Encourage appropriate venting of feelings
C. Identify effective solutions to anxiety-provoking situations

D. Practice positive thinking and effective behaviors in a variety of situations
E. Focus on efforts and accomplishments
F. Positive feedback and reinforcement

3. Elevated Anxiety
   A. Teach relaxation techniques
      1. Progressive muscle relaxation
      2. Deep breathing
      3. Visualization that creates a feeling of calm, reassurance, and safety
   B. Challenge irrational beliefs and behavior
   C. Facilitate development of appropriate substitute self-statements and behaviors for irrational ones
   D. Create mastery experiences. They may need to broken down into successive approximations.

4. Low Self-Esteem
   A. Support and encourage appropriate risk-taking behavior
   B. Encourage participation in problem solving
   C. Reframe mistakes in an effort toward change and an opportunity to learn more
   D. Identify desired areas of change
   E. Identify strengths and develop daily affirmations for reinforcing positive self-image
   F. Facilitate development of assertive communication
   G. Create opportunities for person to demonstrate strengths/desired changes
   H. Feedback and positive reinforcement for efforts and changes

5. Family Intervention/Education
   A. Refer to primary care physician for a physical examination if somatic complaints are present to rule out any organic basis for complaints
   B. Explore what they may be doing to reinforce the beliefs and behaviors
   C. Explore possibility of parental over-concern on child as a deflective response to avoid their own relationship issues, or is this the only method they have for joining?
   D. Strengthen the relationship with siblings, if present
   E. Facilitate appropriate parental focus on the child's behaviors
   F. Educate parents regarding needs for emotional availability, limits/boundaries, encouragement, and positive reinforcement

6. School
   A. Work with school toward mastery behavior versus concern for anxious behavior
   B. Reinforce for efforts and accomplishments

According to Peterson and Brownlee-Duffeck (1989)

1. Fears and anxieties of family members constitute a factor in whether or not to treat the fears and anxieties of a child
2. In the vast majority of cases of child anxiety, there is a positive correlation between parental anxiety and child anxiety
3. This correlation between parental and child anxiety demonstrates stronger lies for younger children than older children
   - Child anxiety is more common among children from lower socioeconomic strata than those from higher economic strata

EATING DISORDER (EDO)

Due to the overlap in symptoms and the blending of features from more than one diagnosis of Eating Disorder, the goals and objectives will be presented as one section instead of separated according to the specific diagnosis.

The central features of Anorexia are refusal to maintain adequate body weight, distorted body image, fear of becoming fat, amenorrhea, eating/food rituals, and excessive exercise. An anorectic may experience feelings of power associated with restricting food.

The central features of Bulimia include recurrent episodes of binge eating and purging, the use of laxatives/diuretics, efforts to diet/fast, and an excess concern with body shape and weight. The binge-purge cycle is initiated by binge eating. This provides relief because the individual ceases to dwell on anything except the food and how to get it down. This behavior replaces all other thoughts, behaviors, and feelings. The purging is initiated to "undo" the consequences of binging. When the binge-purge cycle is over, the bulimic briefly regains control with associated feelings of competence and increased self-esteem. There are no longer any feelings of guilt for having eaten so many calories. The person is on a high or numbed out, feeling relaxed and drained by the behavior.

Due to the relationship of EDO behaviors to physical etiology and consequences, it is important to refer the person to a physician initially (and monitoring if necessary) to rule out the presence of organic problems such as those associated to the endocrine system, gastrointestinal complications, cancer, hypothalamus brain tumor, electrolyte imbalance, assessing the need for hospitalization, etc.

When working with individuals diagnosed with an EDO, be aware of the possibility of a general problem with impulse control. Compulsive behaviors can be oriented around stealing, sex, self-destructive behaviors, and substance abuse. It is not uncommon for individuals diagnosed with an EDO to trade compulsions (even the EDO behaviors) when they are in treatment and are making efforts to alter their behaviors. Be alert to the comorbidity of mood disorder and personality disorder with these individuals, with the associated complications to the clinical picture.

Goals

1. Medical stability
2. Assess for referral for medication evaluation
3. Improve coping
4. Facilitate appropriate autonomy
5. Improve body image
6. Improve rational thinking
7. Improve interpersonal relating
8. Improve communication
9. Improve self-esteem
10. Identify feeling states
11. Differentiate between internal sensations and emotional states
12. Family intervention
13. Self-monitoring
14. Assess psychiatric status and safety

Treatment Focus and Objectives

1. Inadequate Nutrition
   A. Evaluation by physician/dietitian to determine adequate fluid intake and number of calories required for adequate nutrition and realistic weight. These professionals will have to monitor the medical side of the disorder. For the therapist to become involved, serious complications must arise in the therapeutic relationship.

As adequate nutrition and normal eating patterns are established, begin to explore with the person the emotions associated with his/her behavior.

In instances in which intervention has taken place early and the weight loss is not extreme, it may be adequate to do dietary education: the nutritional needs of the body, the effects of starvation, what purpose(s) the illness serves, and contracting for stabilization of weight and normalizing eating patterns. If these limits are transgressed, refer for medical intervention.

If 15% of body weight is lost, refer to physician for monitoring. If the weight loss is 25% or below, hospitalization is necessary. In considering the issues of hospitalization the following factors play a role: (1) how quickly the weight is lost (rapid weight loss is more dangerous), (2) the person's weight prior to weight loss (an obese person has a better tolerance to weight loss), (3) the person's physical condition, as determined by the physician (potassium deficiency, dehydration, hypothermia, low blood pressure, cardiac irregularities, etc.), and (4) the presence of starvation symptoms (cognitive deficits, delayed visual tracking, reduced metabolic rate, fatigue etc.).

 B. Rapid weight fluctuation. This is rarely a problem so extreme to be life-threatening. With severe engagement of the bulimic binge-purge cycle, there can be electrolyte imbalance and dehydration. Additional physical complications are hair loss, pimples, esophageal tears, gastric ruptures, and cardiac arrhythmias.

Ask directly about behaviors of restriction, binging, purging, and laxative/diuretic use.

2. Assess for Referral for Medication Evaluation
 A. Presence of mood disturbance (depression/anxiety)
 B. Potential benefit of psychotropic medication for EDO symptoms

3. Ineffective Coping
 A. Identify person's anger or other feelings associated with loss of control of his/her eating pattern
 B. Explore family dynamics. Facilitate the recognition that maladaptive behaviors are related to emotional problems due to family functioning/structure
 C. Explore fears that interfere with effective coping
 D. Explore history of sexual abuse, physical abuse, emotional abuse, neglect
 E. Identify problem situations and develop alternative responses
 F. Identify manipulative responses
 G. Encourage honest, appropriate expression of emotions
 H. Identify eating rituals and the role they play
 I. Identify the fears associated with stopping the purging behavior
 J. Identify the reasons to choose not to binge and purge
 K. Identify what the bulimics behaviors protect the individual from
 L. Assertive communication
 M. Relaxation training
  1. Progressive muscle relaxation
  2. Visualization
  3. Meditation

4. Difficulty with Autonomy
 A. Teach response options to increase choice and feelings of responsibility
 B. Encourage increased confidence and self-esteem
 C. Encourage self-care and being good to oneself
 D. Explore ways to identify and work through underlying fears
 E. Encourage appropriate risk taking
 F. Reframe mistakes as opportunities for learning and encourage related problem solving

G. Encourage appropriate separation from family

H. Resolve developmental fears

I. Encourage the person's collaboration and input in treatment

J. Identify confusion

1. Separate self-acceptance from performance and the evaluation of others
2. Encourage the validation of the person's own thoughts and feelings
3. Explore the meaning of weight
4. Facilitate accurate perception of self
5. Through positive feedback, help these individuals to accept themselves as they are

5. Distorted Body Image

A. Develop realistic expectations

B. Explore relationships and the belief of needing to be a certain way to maintain the relationship

C. Encourage appropriate grieving for loss of central focus of preoccupation with body and food

D. Increase awareness and expression through guided imagery and art

6. Irrational Thinking (EDO Thinking)

A. Negative self talk, all or nothing thinking, overgeneralizations, and perfectionistic should statement

B. Confronting fear of weight

C. Replacing negative thoughts with realistic and constructive thoughts

7. Impaired Interpersonal Relations

A. Identify trust and honesty issues in relationships

B. Identify fear of "being found out" and of being rejected

C. Encourage appropriate risk-taking behavior in developing relationships

D. Assertive communication

8. Dysfunctional communication

A. Teach assertive communication

B. Encourage appropriate ventilation of thoughts and feelings

C. Model and role-play appropriate responses to various situations

9. Low Self-Esteem

A. Explore ways to change faulty self-perceptions

B. Encourage these person's to develop trust in themselves and their abilities

C. Encourage their participation in problem solving

D. Encourage self-care behaviors and positive self-talk

E. Create opportunities for success

F. Identify strengths and develop daily affirmations for reinforcing a positive self-image

G. Identify personal growth activities

H. Promote feelings of control within the environment through participation and independent decision making

I. Positively reinforce their efforts and successes

10. Identify Feeling States

A. Explore ways for these individuals to separate and maintain their own emotions from the emotions of others

B. Facilitate accurate identification and acknowledgment of feelings

C. Assist person in dealing effectively with feelings

D. Facilitate understanding of feelings such as despair and guilt

E. Encourage daily journal entry related to feelings identification

11. Differentiation between Internal Sensations and Emotional States

A. Explore eating patterns in relationship to denial of feelings, sexuality, fears, concerns, self-comforting, approval, and so on

B. Facilitate development of acknowledging hunger and eating in response to internal hunger cues

C. Identify ritualistic behaviors and substitute appropriate eating patterns

12. Family Therapy

A. Approach family in a nonblaming manner

B. Assume that families have done their best (rule/out)

C. Assume that families want to help (rule/out)

D. Recognize that families are tired and stressed

E. Facilitate age-appropriate separation

F. Identify person's role in the family

G. Identify how family maintains the dysfunctional behavioral/emotional patterns

H. Identify the role of the family in recovery

I. Identify community resources

1. Referral to group therapy and/or self-help groups

Physical Signs of Poor Nutrition and Inadequate Self-Care

Body areas	Nutrient deficiency or other cause of problem	Signs associated with poor nutrition or other cause
Hair	Protein	Lack of natural shine: hair dull and dry; thin and sparse; hair fine; color changes easily plucked
Face	Protein, calories, niacin, zinc, riboflavin, Vit. B6, Essential Fats (A, D, E & K)	Skin color loss; skin dark over cheeks and under eyes; lumpiness or flakiness of skin on nose and mouth; scaling of skin around nostrils
Eyes	Vitamin A	Dryness of eye membranes; night blindness
Lips	Riboflavin, vit. B, folate	Redness and swelling of mouth or lips, especially at corners of mouth
Tongue	Riboflavin, niacin	Swelling; scarlet and raw tongue; magenta color; swollen sores
Teeth	Fluoride, sugar	Missing or erupting abnormally; gray or black spots; cavities
Gums	Vitamin C	"Spongy" and bleed easily; recession of gums
Glands	Iodine, protein	Thyroid enlargement; parotid (cheeks) enlargement
Skin	Protein, niacin, zinc, vit. B6, C, and K, essential fats (A, D, E, and K)	Dryness; sandpaper feel of skin; red swollen pigmentation of exposed areas; excessive lightness or darkness; black and blue marks due to skin bleeding; lack of fat under the skin
Muscles	Protein, calories	Lack of muscles in temporal area, hand between thumb and index finger and calf muscles;
	Thiamin	Pain in calves; weak thighs

13. Self-Monitoring/Relapse Prevention
   A. Identify "red flag" patterns of behavior
   B. Identify resources and support system
   C. Encourage regular review of their program for recovery
   D. Journal Writing
      1. Expressing thoughts and feelings honestly; venting, clarification, and use for problem solving
      2. Record keeping of food consumption, vomiting, purging, and laxative use
      3. Encourage identification of behavioral patterns and related emotional states
      4. Facilitate identification of the kinds of thinking that leads to trouble
      5. To provide a more objective record of changes that do or do not occur
   E. Maintain increased awareness for the role of negative emotional states in relapse
   F. Planning for follow-up with various professionals

14. Assessing Psychiatric Status and Safety
   A. Suicidality
   B. Mood/anxiety disorders
   C. Substance use/dependence
   D. Obsessive Compulsive Disorder/Symptoms
   E. Personality Disorders
   F. Post Traumatic Stress Disorder (PTSD)

Additional Considerations

If an eating disorder is suspected of an individual from a culturally diverse group, it is important to determine the eating behavior and dietary habits that are culturally acceptable, the acculturation issues negatively impacting the individual, and the person's internal struggle with adjustment. The individual's efforts of personal growth and success in a new culture may create significant cognitive dissonance as well as family pressure, disappointment, or alienation.

Possible Signs and Symptoms of Anorexia Nervosa, Bulimia Nervosa, and Compulsive Overeating (Age 13 to Adult)

	Physical symptoms	Psychological symptoms
Anorexia Nervosa	Skin rashes	Perfectionist expectations
	Blueness in extremities	Avoidance of relationships
	Poor circulation	Preoccupation with weight
	Fainting spells	History of sexual abuse/assault
	Anemia	Euphoria
	Chronic low body weight	Sense of omnipotence
	Irregular thyroid	Views self as "fat"
	Postpubertal absence of menses	Overly compliant
	Decreased gastric emptying	Highly motivated
	Water retention	Ritualized behaviors
Bulimia Nervosa	Swollen glands	Impulsive behaviors
	Susceptibility to infections	Intense attachments
	Irregular heart rate	Preoccupation with weight
	Persistent acne	Alcoholic parent(s)
	Menstrual irregularity	Depression
	Frequent diarrhea or constipation	Suicidal thoughts
	Water retention	Poor self-esteem
	Dental erosion	Extreme sense of guilt
	Ipecac poisoning	Mood swings
	Aspiration pneumonia	History of excessive exercise

(Continues)

Possible Signs and Symptoms of Anorexia Nervosa, Bulimia Nervosa, and Compulsive Overeating (Age 13 to Adult) (*Continued*)

	Physical symptoms	Psychological symptoms
Compulsive Overeating	Shortness of breath	Compulsive behavior
	Frequent constipation	Dependent attachments
	Irritable bowel syndrome	Preoccupation with weight
	Elevated blood sugar	Alcoholic parent(s)
	Water retention	Depression
	Nausea	Suicidal thoughts
	Sleep disturbance	Distorted perception of body
	Weight fluctuation	Sense of inadequacy
	Joint inflammation	History of frequent dieting

In addition to forwarding a letter that outlines recommendations for treatment, include this laboratory assessment chart for patients with Eating Disorders when a consultation note is sent to primary care physicians. It will offer them information on assessment in a manner in which they are familiar.

A dental examination should also be performed. In younger patients it is generally useful to assess growth, sexual development, and general physical development. A standard pediatric growth chart is useful for identifying patients who have failed to gain adequate and expected weight or who have experienced growth retardation.

The American Psychiatric Society recommends the following laboratory assessments for patients with eating disorders:

1. Consider the following assessments for all patients with eating disorders;
    A. Basic analyses
        1. Blood chemistry studies
            a. Serum electrolyte levels
            b. Blood urea nitrogen (BUN) levels
            c. Creatinine level
            d. Thyroid function
        2. Complete blood count (CBC)
        3. Urinalysis

2. Consider for malnourished and severely symptomatic patients
    A. Additional analyses
        1. Blood chemistry studies
            a. Calcium level
            b. Magnesium level
            c. Phosphorus level
            d. Liver function
        2. Electrocardiogram

3. Consider for those patients who have been underweight for more than six months
    A. Osteopenia and osteoporosis assessments
        1. Dual-energy X-ray Absorptiometry (DEXA)
        2. Estradiol level
        3. Testosterone level (male)

4. The following are nonroutine assessment procedures
    A. Consider only for specific unusual indications

B. Possible indicator of persistent or recurrent vomiting
   1. Serum amylase level
C. For persistent amenorrhea at normal weight
   1. Luteinizing hormone (LH) and follicle stimulating hormone (FSH) levels
D. For ventricular enlargement correlated with degree of malnutrition
   1. Brain magnetic resonance imaging (MRI)
   2. Computerized tomography (CT)
E. For blood
   1. Stool

PREVENTING WEIGHT AND BODY IMAGE PROBLEMS IN CHILDREN

Increased stress, ever-present media, convenience food and soda, and decreased physical activity have led to an overconcern about physical appearance with decreased tolerance for all the normal variations in body types and an epidemic of obesity in children. Children are becoming more concerned about their weight and body image at an earlier age (as early as 6 to 9 years old). However, children who are obese do not necessarily have lower self-esteem than nonobese children.

Obesity among children has now become a health concern that can make some medical issues worse and lead to others (such as diabetes, joint problems, hypertension, premature onset on periods and irregular periods, etc.). Both genetic and environmental factors affect a child's potential for obesity. Therefore, it may be important to change both you and your child to change some habits. Consult with your family physician or nutritional specialist, attend nutrition classes, and educate yourself by reading about how to eat healthfully. Continuously bringing up exercise and dieting to children and adolescents can create conflicts, resistance, and negative self-esteem. Therefore, problem-solve what changes you will make that sets the tone for nutrition and exercise. Your children will learn from you. Be a more active family. Make activity fun and an important part of your lifestyle.

Obsession with Weight

While being obsess is not necessarily related directly to lower self-esteem there is still warranted concern

1. Peer cruelty
2. Parental focus on weight
   Feelings of inadequacy
   Potential precursor to eating disorders
3. Media continuously portraying cultural perception of thin as attractive

Obesity and Self-Esteem

1. Obesity is not always related to the lowering of self-esteem
2. Self-esteem is more likely to be associated with the following:
   How family members respond to weight issues
   Social experiences
   Development of effective coping skills

What Parents Can Do

1. Set a healthy example
   Physical activity
   Nutrition

Not being negatively judgmental about different body types; children develop adult perceptions of attractiveness as early as age 7

2. Make sure that children know and feel they are loved regardless of their weight
    Do not focus on their weight
    Focus on spending time with them
    Focus on teaching them effective life-management skills

RECOMMENDATIONS FOR FAMILY MEMBERS OF ANOREXIC INDIVIDUALS

1. With child/adolescent anorexics, demand less decision making from the anorexic. Offer fewer choices, less responsibility. For example, they should not decide what the family eats for dinner or where to go for vacation.
2. With child/adolescent anorexics, in conflicts about decisions, parents should not withdraw out of fear that their child/adolescent will become increasingly ill.
3. Seek to maintain a supportive, confident posture that is calming yet assertive. Do not be controlling.
4. Express honest affection, both verbally and physically.
5. Develop communication/discussion on personal issues rather than on food and weight.
6. Do not demand weight gain or put down the individual for having anorexia.
7. Do not blame. Avoid statements like "Your illness is ruining the family." This person is not responsible for family functioning.
8. Do not emotionally abandon or avoid the anorexic family member. Remain emotionally available and supportive. Utilize clear boundaries.
9. Once the individual is involved in treatment, do not become directly involved with the weight issues. If you see a change in the individual's appearance, contact the therapist or other pertinent professional such as the person's physician and dietitian.
10. Do not demand that they eat with you, and do not allow their eating problem to dominate the family's eating schedule or use of the kitchen. Be consistent.
11. For child/adolescent anorexics, do not allow them to shop or to cook for the family. This puts them in a nurturing role and allows them to deny their own needs for food by feeding others.
12. Increase giving and receiving of both caring and support within the family. Develop clear boundaries, and allow each person to be responsible for themselves and setting their own goals.

IDENTITY DISORDER

This disorder is characterized by confusion related to goals, career, friendships, sexual orientation, religion, and morality. The individual experiences distress over his/her inability to clarify and integrate these factors into a self-assured, goal-directed sense of self.

Goals

1. Development of personal goals
2. Responsible behavior
3. Improve communication skills
4. Improve self-esteem
5. Identify and resolve related family issues

Treatment Focus and Objectives

1. Lack of Goals
   A. Identify strengths and areas of interest
   B. Encourage appropriate risk taking
   C. Encourage self-exploration through specific boundaries (individual desires, pleasing self versus pleasing someone else, etc.)
   D. Development of realistic expectations and limitations
   E. Identify fear and anxiety associated with decision making, which interferes with following through on decisions
   F. Refer for vocational counseling

2. Difficulty Taking Responsibility
   A. Discourage parental rescuing
   B. Support appropriate management of anxiety
   C. Encourage appropriate separation and individuation
   D. Encourage appropriate risk taking
   E. Identify strengths
   F. Focus on positives and reinforce trying new things

3. Dysfunctional Communication Skills
   A. Teach assertive communication
   B. Encourage ventilation of thoughts and feelings
   C. Keep a journal for venting thoughts and feelings, clarification of issues, identifying dysfunctional patterns, and problem solving

4. Low Self-Esteem
   A. Be accepting, respectful, and encourage expression of person's beliefs and feelings
   B. Reinforce the trying of new things, and focus on how it felt
   C. Teach assertive communication
   D. Identify strengths and accomplishments
   E. Encourage focusing on strengths and accomplishments
   F. Identify desired areas of change and problem-solve the necessary objectives to meet the defined goals
   G. Encourage and positively reinforce appropriate independent functioning
   H. Facilitate self-monitoring of efforts toward desired goals

5. Dysfunctional Familial Interacting
   A. Identify issues of overcontrol or underinvolvement
      1. Educate and validate regarding impact of such interaction
      2. Encourage person to take responsibility

3. Encourage separation and individuation
4. Educate parents on parenting style and teach effective parenting skills
5. Encourage parents to not rescue or to be aware of detachment and alter
6. Develop realistic expectations and limitations of family for person
7. Identify and encourage appropriate parental interaction

B. Facilitate self-parenting techniques for the person
1. Use affirmative and reassuring self-talk
2. Eliminate irrational, self-critical self-talk
3. Facilitate the experience of learning from mistakes as part of life versus inaction out of fear of making mistakes
4. Encourage thorough review of family experience to facilitate identification of areas of change to increase awareness and to break dysfunctional family patterns in the person's own future family

6. Sexual orientation

Medication and talk therapy do not alter homosexuality or transsexual cross-gender identification. However, talk therapy can be useful in alleviating emotional problems associated with the individual's social experience, relationship with the self, and the experience within their family. Referral for medication evaluation would be based on the same premise of other similar referrals (to eliminate/alleviate/stabilize symptomology).

When working with children and adolescents, a myriad of special issues need to be considered in the assessment, treatment planning, and treatment phases of intervening. A brief and general summary of the biopsychosocial issues to be considered may be quickly reviewed by using the following mnemonic:

CHILDREN

C cultural/gender issues
coping mechanisms
conflicts in marital relationship

H hyperactivity (ADHD)
health issues (chronic/acute)

I information releases for all professionals interacting with child/adolescent
injuries, head trauma (recent fall/physical trauma)
identity issues
intellectual function

L learning disabilities, learning styles (auditory, visual etc.)
low self-esteem
limitations (physical, mental, psychological, parental/family, etc.)

D drug abuse
defiant and oppositional behaviors
deficient mental capacity

R relationship issues (family, peers, educators, other significant people in child's life)
resources and resourcefulness
religious/spiritual beliefs

E emotional disturbances and management (emotional/psychological functioning)
educational issues (academic performance, truancy, compliance with rules)
experimenting sexually/fears or concerns/promiscuity
expectations of life and life goals
empathy and understanding of others
eyes and ears (verify that hearing and vision have been checked)

N nutrition/eating disorders
neglect or other abuse issues

The following three pages offer a summary on the theories of

1. Kohlberg's stages of moral development
2. Erikson's stages of psychosocial development
3. Freud's stages of psychosexual development

Kohlberg's theory of moral development is most often cited. This theory is conceptually founded on the premise that stages of moral development occur in a distinct sequence, in which each stage builds on the previous one and is more cognitively complex.

Kohlberg's Stages of Moral Development

Level 1	Preconventional Morality (Ages 4–10) Stage 1: Punishment-Obedience Orientation Moral judgment based on a desire to avoid punishment. Stage 2: Instrumental-Relativist Orientation Individual is motivated by a desire to satisfy own needs.
Level 2	Conventional Morality (Ages 10–13) Stage 3: "Good Boy/Nice Girl" Orientation Individual motivated by a desire to avoid disapproval or dislike of others. Stage 4: Law and Order Orientation Moral judgments based on a desire to avoid censure by a legitimate authority.
Level 3	Postconventional Morality (Adolescence to adulthood; not reached by most adults) Stage 5: Legalistic Orientation Individual concerned with maintaining the respect of equals and the community, maintaining social order, and obeying democratically determined laws. Stage 6: Universal Ethical Principles Orientation Individual's own conscience is the only criterion of moral conduct.

Erikson's stages of psychosocial development stress social factors in personality development and are characterized by a psychosocial crisis that represents a conflict between the developing individual and society. Erikson viewed development as a process that continues throughout the course of one's life span.

Erikson's Stages of Psychosocial Development

Stage/age	Conflict	Significant relations	Favourable outcome
Oral-Sensory (0–12 mos.)	Trust versus mistrust	Primary caretaker	Trust and optimism
Muscular-anal (12–36 mos.)	Autonomy versus shame	Parents	Self-assertion, self-control, feelings of adequacy
Locomotor-genital (3–6 yrs.)	Initiative versus guilt	Family	Sense of initiative, purpose, and direction
Latency (6–12 yrs.)	Industry versus inferiority	School, neighborhood	Productivity and competence in physical, intellectual, and social skills
Adolescence	Ego identity versus role confusion	Peers, leadership models	Integrated image of oneself as a unique person
Early adulthood	Intimacy versus isolation	Partners in friendship, sex, etc.	Ability to form close personal relationships and make career commitments
Middle adulthood	Generativity versus stagnation	Shared labor and household	Concern for future generations
Maturity	Integrity versus despair	Humankind	Sense of satisfaction with one's life; ability to face death without despair

Freud's constructs of psychosocial development are biological in nature and are based on the inevitable unfolding of different stages in which particular behaviors occur. Abnormal development takes place as a trauma is experienced in early childhood that prevents the flow of libidinal energy through the various stages. If this happens, development is said to be fixated at a particular stage, rendering the individual more vulnerable to crisis later in life. A conflict occurs with each stage. There is a corresponding adult character pattern with each stage.

Freud's Stages of Psychosexual Development

Stage/age	Source of satisfaction	Primary conflict	Personality outcome
Oral (0–12 mos.)	Mouth (sucking, biting, chewing)	Weaning	Fixation produces dependence, passivity, guilibility, sarcasm, or orally focused habits (smoking, nail-biting, eating, etc.).
Anal (1–3 yrs.)	Anal region (expulsion and retention of feces)	Toilet training	Fixation produces anal retentiveness (stinginess, selfishness, obsessive-compulsive behavior) or anal expulsiveness (cruelty, destructiveness, messiness).
Phallic (3–6 yrs.)	Genitals (masturbation)	Oedipus/Electra complex	Successful conflict resolution produces identification with the same-sex parent and development of the superego. Fixation may produce a phallic character (sexual exploitation of others).
Latency (6–12 yrs.)			During this stage, the emphasis is on the development of social skills rather than sexuality.
Genital (12+ yrs.)	Genitals (sexual intercourse)		Sexuality becomes focused in mature, genital love and adult sexual satisfaction.

ORGANIC MENTAL SYNDROMES AND DISORDERS

The various Organic Mental Syndromes and Disorders are manifested in disturbances of cognitive, behavioral, and personality changes. When presented with the symptoms of Dementia and Organic Mental Disorders assessment is crucial in determining the origin of symptom presentation. Just with the symptoms of hallucinations and delusions, the clinician must take into consideration organicity, psychosis, depression with psychotic features, and substance abuse or drug reaction (which can happen easily with the elderly). Substance abuse or drug reaction will be the easiest to clarify because of lab results and history and change in symptom presentation as the person detoxes. Therefore, for the initial refinement in diagnosis the following *general* comparisons are helpful:

Organicity	Depression	Psychosis
History of failing memory	Difficulty concentrating	History of personality disturbance
Disorientation for time	More precise onset	Auditory hallucination/delusions
Perseverations	Low motivation	Disoriented to people and place
Visual/olfactory hallucinations	Self-critical	Perseveration of bizarre thoughts
Neurological signs	Mood congruent hallucinations	Mood inappropriate
Worse at night	Vegetative symptoms (sleep/ appetite)	

Depression can lead to symptoms that may appear to be Dementia. However, depression can also be the response to early signs of Dementia. To clarify whether you are dealing with Dementia or Pseudodementia, the following guidelines may be helpful:

Dementia	Pseudodementia
Age is nonspecific	Elderly ≥ 60
Onset is vague (over months or years)	More precise onset (days or weeks)
Slow course, worse at night	Rapid, uneven course (not worse at night)
Dysphasia, agnosia, apraxia	Sadness, somatic symptoms of depression
Increased cognitive impairment	Increased impairment in personality features in
—Memory	—Confidence
—Disoriented to time/date	—Interests
Mental status—keeps making same mistakes	—Drive
Behavior and affect congruent with degree of impaired though processes and affect	Incongruent mood/affect
Cooperative but frustrated	Self-deprecating
Responses to questions confabulated	Cooperative effects poor
Response to funny/sad situations is normal/exaggerated	Response to questions a pathetic, "I don't know"
	Little or not response to sad or funny situations
Neuroevaluations abnormal (CT, EEG)	Neuroevaluations normal (CT, EEG)

While the diagnostic generalities fit the elderly population, there are differences that warrant clarification because of the impact on treatment plan formulation and care. Those presenting with dementia exhibit a broad range of cognitive impairments, behavioral symptoms and mood changes. Thus, necessitating an individualized and multimodel treatment plan. Since dementia is often progressive, and in conjunction with its evolution is the emergence of new issues to address, the clinician must closely monitor for changes, and whenever possible predict impending change for the individual and/or their family. The following mnemonic provides a useful overview for diagnostic consideration.

DEMENTIA

D drug interaction

E emotional disturbances/current crises or losses

M metabolic/endocrine problems such as diabetes or thyroid dysfunction

E eyes and ears

N nutritional deficiencies

T tumor or trauma

I infection/brain abscess

A arteriosclerosis or other arterisclerotic problems

This mnemonic (Perry et al., 1985) can be utilized while doing a mental status exam and making a thorough diagnostic assessment to rule out reversible dementia such as depression, anemia, hypothyroidism, alcoholic dementia, and so on. Refer for a complete physical which includes a recommendation for a neurological exam, drug screen, endocrine panel, a neuropsychological testing if appropriate.

A family session can be used to educate family members and encourage their consulting with the physician on the case. This will be helpful for increasing their understanding of the medical situation, prognosis, indications, and contraindications of treatment. They need to be educated on how to manage perceptual disturbances and disruptive behaviors, and the importance of medication compliance and signs of toxicity.

DEMENTIA AND ORGANIC MENTAL DISORDERS

Dementia may have various origins. However, the symptomatology does not vary other than for nuances of case individuality and the progression of deterioration. Like Dementia, many of the Organic Mental Disorders (OMD) demonstrate evident symptoms through cognitive, behavioral, and personality changes. There may also be evidence of depression, delirium, or delusions. The dysfunction of OMDs tends to be chronic in that the related physical disorders attributed to these changes are progressive, except in some cases of psychoactive substance-induced OMDs.

The level of functioning must be thoroughly assessed for treatment planning, which includes placement if necessary, and has not been addressed.

Goals

1. Refer for medical evaluation

2. Stabilization and thought processes are intact

3. Note that person will demonstrate improved reality testing or accept explanation/reality testing from others

4. Improve self-care

5. Decrease social isolation

6. Improve self-esteem

7. Person will not experience physical injury

8. Person will not harm self or others

9. Reduce stress of caregiver

1. Refer for immediate medical examination to rule out drug interactions, metabolic or endocrine problems, problems with hearing or vision, presence of tumor, infections, and so on, which could be contributing to the symptom presentation. Additionally medical treatments are available for cognitive symptoms, which offer modest benefit to some. However, the side effects may be difficult to tolerate.

2. Altered Thought Processes
   A. Assist in reality testing. Encourage person to interrupt thoughts which are not reality based.
   B. Instruct caretaker on facilitating person's orientation to time, place, person, and situation
   C. Discourage pattern stabilization of false ideas by talking to the person about real people and situations
   D. Offer simple explanations when necessary, and talk slowly and face to face to increase effective communication
   E. Reinforce accurate reality testing with positive feedback

3. Sensory-Perceptual Changes
   A. Decrease environmental stimuli
   B. Assist in reality testing
   C. Discourage pattern stabilization of false ideas by talking to the person about real people and situations
   D. Provide reassurance for increased feelings of security
   E. Instruct caretaker on facilitating reality testing when person demonstrates inaccurate sensory perception

4. Inadequate Self-Care
   A. Encourage daily independent living skills
      1. Bathing
      2. Cleaning hair, cutting when necessary, and styled appropriately
      3. Brushing teeth
      4. Dressing adequately and appropriately
      5. Cleaning self adequately after using bathroom, and wash their hands

5. Social Isolation
   A. Supportive psychotherapy in early stages of dementia to address issues of loss
   B. Reminiscence therapy
   C. Stimulation oriented treatment
      1. Recreational activity
      2. Art therapy
      3. Pet therapy

6. Low Self-Esteem
   A. Encourage honest expression of feelings loss related to deterioration in functioning
   B. Encourage all levels of communication, and self-care
   C. Problem-solve ways of dealing with cognitive deficits (making labels large and easy to read, signs identifying rooms, etc.)
   D. Focus on abilities and accomplishments
   E. Reinforce accurate reality testing with positive feedback

7. Risk for Injury
   A. Assess
      1. Psychosis
      2. Disorientation
      3. Wanders off
      4. Agitation unmanageable
      5. Excessive hyperactivity
      6. Muscular weakness
      7. Seizures

*Agitation and psychosis are a common presentation in individuals with dementia. If these symptoms are present, a through evaluation to determine what may underlie the disturbance is recommended.

   B. Precautions
      1. Caretaker to remain in close proximity for monitoring, check frequently
      2. Objects/furniture in room should be placed with function and safety in mind
      3. Remove potentially harmful objects
      4. Padding of certain objects may be necessary
      5. Educate caregiver on safety and management issues

8. Risk of Violence
   A. Assess level of agitation, thought processes, and behaviors indicative of possible episode of violent acting outing potentially directed toward self or others
   B. Keep environmental stimuli to a minimum, and remove all dangerous objects
   C. Encourage caregiver to maintain a calm manner
   D. Gently correct distortions of reality
   E. Evaluate need for higher level of care

9. Caregiver Stress
   A. Encourage appropriate expression of feelings such as anger and depression
   B. Identify ways to effectively deal with emotions
   C. Identify feelings of stress and loss in relationship to the person they are taking care of
   D. Identify family conflict related to issues of care
   E. Identify how their own lives have been interrupted/interfered with by caregiver role
   F. Develop rotations of time off to take care of own needs and have time to themselves
   G. Refer to community support group focusing on caregiver situation

DEFINING SPECIFIC DEMENTIAS

1. Alzheimer's Disease: Dimension with an insideous onset, gradual progression, with initial memory deficits. After several years, aphasia, apraxia and agnosia as well as deficits in executive function follows.

*Executive function: High level decision making, performing multiple step tasks, etc. Alzheimer's subtypes: with delirium, with delusions, with depressed mood and uncomplicated

2. Multi-infarct (vascular) Dementia: The consequence of one or more strokes negatively impacting cognitive functioning. Onset is abrupt and pattern of cognitive deficits depends on the region of the brain affected.

3. Dementia associated with Parkinson's Disease: This dementia is demonstrated by a slow progression. Also associated with Parkinson's is a high prevalence of depression and psychosis.

4. Dementia associated with Lewy Body Disease: Clinically similar to Alzheimer's. However, onset is earlier with a faster evolution. There is a prominence of psychotic symptoms and sensitivity to antipsychotic symptoms.

5. Dementia associated with Pick's Disease (and other frontal lobe dementias): Early stages of dementia characterized by changes in personality, executive function, deterioration of social skills, emotional blunting, behavioral disinhibition, and prominent language abnormalities.

6. Others
   a. Dementia associated with Huntington's chorea
   b. Dementia associated with Creutzfeldt-Jakob Disease
   c. Dementia associated with structural lesions (brain tumor, subdural hematoma, head trauma, HIV nutritional deficiencies, endocrine conditions

According to the American Psychiatric Association (2002), the following are underlying conditions commonly associated with delirium:

A. Central nervous system disorder
   1. Head trauma
   2. Seizures
   3. Postictal state
   4. Vascular disease
   5. Degenerative disease

B. Metabolic disorder
   1. Renal failure
   2. Hepatic failure
   3. Anemia
   4. Hypoxia
   5. Hypoglycemia
   6. Thiamine deficiency
   7. Endocrinopathy
   8. Fluid/electrolyte imbalance
   9. Acid-base imbalance

C. Cardiopulmonary disorder
   1. Myocardial infarction
   2. Congestive heart failure
   3. Cardiac arrhythmia
   4. Shock
   5. Respiratory failure

D. Systemic illness
1. Substance intoxication or withdrawal
2. Infection
3. Neoplasm
4. Severe trauma
5. Sensory deprivation
6. Temperature dysregulation
7. Postoperative state

According to the American Psychiatric Association (2000), the following are substances that can cause delirium through intoxication or withdrawal:

A. Drugs of abuse
1. Alcohol
2. Amphetamines
3. Cannabis
4. Cocaine
5. Hallucinogens
6. Inhalants
7. Opioids
8. Phenylcyclidine
9. Sedatives
10. Hypnotics
11. Others

B. Medications
1. Anesthetics
2. Analgesics
3. Antiasthmatic agents
4. Anticonvulsants
5. Antihistamines
6. Antihypertensives
7. Cardiovascular meds
8. Antimicrobials
9. Antiparkinsonians
10. Corticosteroids
11. Gastrointestinal meds
12. Muscle relaxants
13. Immunosuppressive agents
14. Lithium
15. Psychotropic agents with anticholinergic properties

C. Toxins
1. Antocholinesterase
2. Organophosphate insecticides
3. Carbon monoxide
4. Carbon dioxide
5. Volatile organic substances such as fuel or solvents

PSYCHOACTIVE SUBSTANCE ABUSE DISORDERS

This diagnostic section is identified by personality, mood, and behavioral changes associated with the use of substances. These changes are manifested by impairments in the following areas of functioning: social, emotional, psychological, occupational, and physical. Instead of using the terms tolerance and withdrawal to describe substance dependence it may be more helpful to conceptualize "addiction" by the following criteria:

1. Obsessive-compulsive behavior with the substance
2. Loss of control, manifested by the person being unable to reliably predict starting and stopping his/her use of the substance
3. Continued use despite the negative consequences associated with substance use

There are four pathways of use:

1. Oral—absorption in the bloodstream
2. Injection—IV use
3. Snorting—absorbed through the nasal membrane
4. Inhaling—absorbing through the lung

Brown's (1985) developmental model for the stages of recovery offer's a conceptual framework for identifying where an individual is in his/her recovery so that the developmentally appropriate interventions can be made. The stages are as follows:

1. Drinking. The internal and external conflicts of addiction lead the individual to a point of loathing, fear, self-hatred, losses, and other consequences. The individual hits bottom.
2. Transition. The individual makes a shift from using to not using. If the individual does not fully accept and believe that he/she is addicted, the person may slip back and forth between stage 1 and 2. At this stage, work with the resistance as much as possible. Without a constant focus on the substance, the individual is enticed back into the belief that he/she can control use and may initiate the cycle of use once more.
3. Early recovery. The individual begins social integration by interacting with others without the use of a substance. With continued abstinence the person begins to recover some of his/her losses with a return to work, family relationships, and other adjustments. This is a period of new experiences for the individual, which requires the support of others. The individual benefits from participation in a 12 Step group.
4. Late recovery or ongoing recovery. This is the developmental stage of recovery where the more typical psychotherapeutic issues are evident. During this period, there is a move from the self-centered view of the world to a view in which the individual exists in relation to others.

Recovery is not a linear process. It is the up, down, and sideways flow of interaction between all of the experiences. This includes new ideas, new behaviors, new belief system, and the shaping of a new identity integrating the culmination of where the individual has been and where he/she is. This foundation of integrating experience one day at a time is what will take the individual to tomorrow.

SUBSTANCE ABUSE AND/OR DEPENDENCE

Goals

1. Complete assessment with appropriate referrals
2. Encourage abstinence
3. Break through denial
4. Support cognitive restructuring
5. Improve behavioral self-control
6. Develop refusal skills
7. Improve social skills
8. Improve communication skills
9. Improve coping skills
10. Improve problem-solving skills
11. Improve self-esteem
12. Support and educate family

Treatment Focus and Objectives

1. Thorough Assessment for Referral and Treatment
   A. Evaluate substance use (how much, how often, substances of choice, family history, patterns of use, prior treatment, level of impairment in major life areas, inability to control use, etc.)
   B. Refer for general physical examination and consultation with primary care physician. Refer for specific assessment of physiological impairment if warranted by history.
   C. Referrals (assuming detox is not an issue or is completed)
      1. If unable to remain in recovery, refer to residential program
      2. Outpatient chemical dependency program
      3. 12-step meetings or other supportive groups and programs
   D. Evaluate cognitive deficit
      1. Establish baseline assess of fund of knowledge, take into consideration level of education and level of development
      2. Identify strengths and weaknesses
   E. Inadequate nutrition
      1. Facilitate identification of prior eating patterns
      2. Develop and establish eating three balanced meals a day

2. Abstinence
   A. Individual has made a commitment to abstain from substance use
   B. Individual is participating in an outpatient program
   C. Individual has worked with therapist to develop own program for abstinence recovery

3. Denial
   A. Convey an attitude that is not rejecting or judgmental
   B. Confront denial with reality of use and education to correct misconceptions
   C. Identify the relationship between substance use and personal problems
   D. Do not accept or ignore the use of other defense mechanisms to avoid reality

E. Encourage person to take responsibility for choices and associated consequences

F. Provide positive feedback and reinforcement for insight and taking responsibility

4. Negative/Irrational Thinking

    A. Educate regarding positive self-talk to challenge negative self-statements and negative self-fulfilling prophecy

    B. Identify differences in statements prefaced as "can," "can't," "will," and "wont't"

    C. Seek clarification "Does my style of thinking help or hinder me?"

    D. Challenge beliefs with factual information

    E. Accurately reflect reality to individual

5. Lack of Self-Control

    A. Facilitate individual's analysis of substance use patterns and monitoring

        1. Identify situations, people, emotions, and beliefs associated with substance use

        2. Monitor currently or through recollection of past behaviors

        3. Facilitate preparation for anticipated difficult situations and planning strategies either to avoid or cope with these situations (strategies should be both cognitive and behavioral)

        4. Encourage active participation in group affiliation and other self-care behaviors

        5. Build in "reminder" statements or affirmations about the individual's commitment to abstinence

    B. Facilitate development of assertive communication

    C. Offer relaxation training with positive self-statements attached

    D. Increase repertoire of coping skills through modeling, rehearsal, and homework assignments

6. Lack of Refusal Skills

    A. Goal is to develop the skills needed to refuse substances, refuse invitations to participate in activities or be in the company of others associated with substance abuse

    B. Specific tasks to develop to strengthen refusal skills

        1. Asking for help

        2. Honestly expressing thoughts and feelings

        3. Confronting and dealing with fear(s)

        4. Standing up for their rights

        5. How to deal with being left out

        6. How to deal with group pressure and persuasion

7. Ineffective Social Skills

    A. Teach social skills through role modeling, rehearsal, and role playing

    B. Teach effective communication

        1. Nonverbal communication such as positioning, eye contact, and personal space

        2. Verbal communication

            a. Initiating conversation

            b. Reflecting

            c. Giving and accepting compliments

            d. Using "I" statements

            e. Dealing with criticism or teasing

            f. Assertive communication

    C. Develop and utilize social supports

    D. Forming close and intimate relationships

        1. Steps of getting to know someone

        2. Disclosure (how much/what/how soon)

3. Setting limits and boundaries
4. How to be close to someone and not lose focus on your goals
5. Establish trusting relationship reciprocating respect by keeping appointments, being honest, etc.
   a. Facilitate person to clarify the impact that substance abuse/dependence has had on their significant relationships, financial implications, work, physical health, and social supports/interaction or peer reference group
   b. Once these issues are identified, facilitate insight, understanding, and the development of choices in dealing with these various situations

8. Ineffective Communication
   A. Assertive communication. Educate using comparisons of assertive communication to aggressive-passive/aggressive-passive. Use vignettes and role-play.
   B. Facilitate awareness for inappropriate behaviors and verbal expressions as ineffective attempts to communicate
   C. Identify feelings behind inappropriate behavioral and emotional expressions and facilitate problem solving
   D. Use "I" statement to avoid blaming and manipulation
   E. Use vignettes, role modeling, rehearsal, and role play for developing communication skills

9. Ineffective Coping
   A. Facilitate identification of feelings
   B. Encourage appropriate ventilation of feelings
   C. Set limits on manipulative behavior (be consistent)
   D. Facilitate development of appropriate and acceptable social behaviors
   E. Educate person regarding the effects of substance use on social, psychological, and physiological functioning
   F. Explore alternatives for dealing with stressful situations. Problem-solve appropriate responses instead of substance use.
   G. Facilitate the development of a self-care plan that outlines resources, skills to use in various situations, daily structure, red flags to regression, and so on
   H. Encourage person to take responsibility for choices and associated consequences
   I. Positive feedback for independent and effective problem solving

10. Ineffective Problem Solving
    A. Teach problem-solving skills
    B. Develop some sample problems and give homework to practice new skills on
    C. Identify secondary gains which inhibits progress toward change

11. Low Self-Esteem
    A. Be accepting and respectful of person
    B. Identify strengths and accomplishments
    C. Encourage a focus on strengths and accomplishments
    D. Facilitate identification of past failures and reframe with a perspective of how the person can benefit and learn from previous experiences
    E. Identify desired areas of change and facilitate problem solving the necessary objectives to meet the defined goals
    F. Facilitate self-monitoring of efforts toward desired goals
    G. Encourage and positively reinforce appropriate independent functioning
    H. Facilitate development of assertive communication
    I. Facilitate clarification of boundaries and appropriate limit setting in relationships

12. Dysfunctional Family Interaction
    A. Evaluate how family has been affected by behavior of this person (fear, isolation, shame, economic consequences, guilt, feeling responsible for the behavior of others)
    B. Explore how family may help sustain or reinforce this dysfunctional behavior
    C. Teach communication skills
    D. Refer family members to appropriate 12-Step groups, other community resources, or therapy. Decrease isolation.

CATEGORIES OF PHARMACOLOGICAL INTERVENTION

1. Medications to treat intoxication and withdrawal states
2. Medications to decrease the reinforcing effects of abused substances
3. Medications that discourage substance abuse by
    A. Inducing unpleasant consequences through drug-drug interaction
    B. Coupling substance use with an unpleasant drug induced condition
4. Agonist substitution therapy
5. Medications to treat comorbid psychiatric conditions

TREATMENT SETTINGS

As in all cases, individuals should be treated in the least restrictive setting that provides safety and effectiveness. General treatment settings include the following:

1. Hospitalization
    A. Danger to self, others, gravely disabled
    B. There has been an overdose
    C. There is risk of severe/medically complicated withdrawal
    D. Comorbid medical condition(s) prohibits a safe outpatient detox
    E. Psychiatric comorbidity impairs ability to comply and benefit from a lower level of care

2. Residential treatment facility
    A. Does not meet criteria for hospitalization
    B. Lacks adequate social and vocational skills to maintain abstinence
    C. Lacks of social support

3. Partial hospitalization
    A. Requires intensive care but is able to abstain
    B. Requires a transitional level of care following discharge from inpatient care when risk of relapse remains relatively high
    C. Lacks sufficient motivation to continue in treatment
    D. Requires a high level of support (for those returning to high-risk environments). There has not been a positive response to intensive outpatient

4. Outpatient Programs
    A. Clinical conditions/environmental circumstances do not require intensive care

*Duration of treatment is individualized to the specific needs of the person in treatment and may last from several months to several years.

LIST OF SYMPTOMS LEADING TO RELAPSE

1. *Exhaustion*: Allowing yourself to become overly tired. Not following through on self-care behaviors of adequate rest, good nutrition, and regular exercise. Good physical health is a component of emotional health. How you feel will be reflected in your thinking and judgment.

2. *Dishonesty*: It begins with a pattern of small, unnecessary lies with those you interact with in family, social, and at work. This is soon followed by lying to yourself or rationalizing and making excuses for avoiding working your program.

3. *Impatience*: Things are not happening fast enough for you. Or others are not doing what you want them to do or what you think they should do.

4. *Argumentative*: Arguing small insignificant points, which indicates a need to always be right. This is sometimes seen as developing an excuse to drink.

5. *Depression*: Overwhelming and unaccountable despair may occur in cycle. If it does, talk about it and deal with it. You are responsible for taking care of yourself.

6. *Frustration*: With people and because things may not be going your way. Remind yourself intermittently that things are not always going to be the way that you want them.

7. *Self-pity*: Feeling like a victim, refusing to acknowledge that you have choices and are responsible for your own life and the quality of it.

8. *Cockiness*: "Got it made" compulsive behavior is no longer a problem. Start putting self in situations where there are temptations to prove to others that you don't have a problem.

9. *Complacency*: Not working your program with the commitment that you started with. Having a little fear is a good thing. More relapses occur when things are going well than when not.

10. *Expecting too much from others*: "I've changed, why hasn't everyone else changed too?" You can only control yourself. It would be great if other people changed their self-destructive behaviors, but that is their problem. You have your own problems to monitor and deal with. You cannot expect others to change their lifestyle just because you have.

11. *Letting up on discipline*: Daily inventory, positive affirmations, 12-Step meetings, meditation, prayer, therapy. This can come from complacency and boredom. Because you cannot afford to be bored with your program, take responsibility—talk about it and problem solve it. The cost of relapse is too great. Sometimes you must accept that you have to do some things that are the routine for a clean and sober life.

12. *The use of mood-altering chemicals*: You may feel the need or desire to get away from things by drinking, popping a few pills, and soon, and your physician may participate in the thinking that you will be responsible and not abuse the medication. This is the most subtle way to enter relapse. Take responsibility for your life and the choices that you make.

Common Drugs of Abuse

Type of drug	Pharmaceutical or street name	Psychological dependence	Physical dependence	Tolerance	Methods of use	Symptoms of use	Withdrawal syndrome
Stimulant/uppers							
Amphetamines	Benzedrine				Swallowed pill/capsule or injected into veins	Increased activity and alertness euphoria dilated pupils disorientation increased heart rate and *BP insomnia, loss of appetite.	Apathy, long periods of sleep, irritability, depression
Amphetamines	Dexadrine						
Dextroamphetamine	Pep-pills, toot						
Methamphetamine	X-tops, Meth Crystal, Ice						
Cocaine	Bennies, Dexie Uppers, Speed	High	Moderate to High	Yes	snorted injected smoked		
Nicotine					smoke snuff chew	Paranoia, hallucinations anxiety convulsions	
Caffeine					Swallowed pill/ capsule or beverages		
Depressants/downers							
Barbiturates	Phenobarbital, Seconal, Tuinal	High	High		Swallowed in pill or capsule form, or injected into veins	Slurred speech, disorientation, drunken behavior, drowsiness, impaired judgment	Anxiety, insomnia tremors, delirium, convulsions, possible death
Sedative	Quaalude, Soper Barbs, Yellow Jackets, Red Devils, Blue Devils	High	High	Yes			
Hypnotics							
Tranquilizers	Librium, Valium, Equanil, Miltown	Moderate	Moderate				
Alcohol	Beer, Wine, Spirits	High	High		Swallowed in pill or liquid form, injected into veins or smoked	Euphoria, drowsy respiratory depression constricted pupils, nausea chills, sweating cramps, nausea	Watery eyes, runny nose, yawning, loss of appetite, irritibility tremors, panic
Opium	Paregoric (O)	High	High	Yes			
Morphine	(M) Hard Stuff	High	High				
Codeine	School Boy	Moderate	Moderate				
Heroin	H, Horse, Smack	High	High				

(*Continues*)

Common Drugs of Abuse (*Continued*)

Type of drug	Pharmaceutical or street name	Psychological dependence	Physical dependence	Tolerance	Methods of use	Symptoms of use	Withdrawal syndrome
Hallucinogens							
Marijuana (Hashish)	Pot, Grass, Joint Reefer	Possible	Possible		Smoked, inhaled, or eaten	Illusions, hallucinations, poor perception of time and distance	
LSD	Acid, Lucy in the Sky with Diamonds	Possible	No	Yes	Injected or swallowed in tablets sugar cubes	slurred vision	
PCP	Peace Pill, Angel Dust	Possible	No			confusion, dilated pupils, mood swing	
Psilocybin	Magic Mushrooms	Possible	No				
Inhalants/solvents							
Gasoline Taluene Acetone	Trash Drugs Inhalants				Inhaled or sniffed often with use of paper or plastic bag or rag	Disorientation, slurred speech, dizziness, nausea, poor motor control	Restlessness, anxiety irritability
Cleaning fluids Airplane cements		Moderate	No	Yes			
Nitrous Oxide	Laughing Gas	Moderate	No	Yes	Inhaled or sniffed	Light-headed	
Nitrites Amyl Butyl	Poppers, Locker Room Rush, Snappers	Moderate	No	Yes	Inhaled or sniffed from gauze/ampules	Slowed thought, headache	

*BP—Blood pressure.

SCHIZOPHRENIA, DELUSIONAL, AND RELATED PSYCHOTIC DISORDERS

Individuals diagnosed with a thought disorder can exhibit symptoms ranging from mild to bizarre delusions and hallucinations. Symptomatology indicative of psychoticism includes alteration in content of thought, alteration in the organization of thought, and disturbance of sensory input. Additional features include disturbance of mood, affect, sense of identity, volition, psychomotor behavior, and difficulty maintaining satisfactory interpersonal relations. The goal of treatment is usually not to cure the individual but to improve the quality of life.

THOUGHT DISORDERS

Goals

1. Ensure that person will not harm self or others
2. Provide safe environment
3. Refer for medication evaluation
4. Encourage stabilization with decreased/elimination of perceptual disturbances
5. Improve coping skills
6. Improve self-management skills (grooming/hygiene, sleep cycle, etc.)
7. Improve sleep pattern
8. Improve self-esteem
9. Decrease social isolation
10. Improve communication skills
11. Family intervention
12. Medication compliance
13. Educate person and significant others on side effects of medication

Treatment Focus and Objectives

1. Evaluate for risk to self or others (psychotic thinking, rage reactions, pacing, overt aggressive acts, hostile and threatening verbalizations, irritability, agitation, perceives environment as threatening, self-destructive or suicidal acts, etc.)
   A. Keep environmental stimuli low
   B. Monitor closely
   C. Remove dangerous objects from environment
   D. Redirect physical acting out through physical exercise to decrease tension
   E. Medicate as directed/prescribed
   F. Call for crisis team or police of necessary to transport to psychiatric facility

2. Evaluate Environmental Safety
   A. Determine if person demonstrates adequate level of cooperativity
   B. Evaluate adequacy of social support
   C. Adjust level of care if necessary
      1. Day treatment program/partial hospitalization
      2. Inpatient setting-open unit
      3. Inpatient setting-closed unit

3. Refer for Medication Evaluation
   A. If this is an initial evaluation and symptoms of perceptual disturbances are identified, refer for a medication evaluation

B. If this has been an ongoing case and the person is experiencing an exacerbation of symptoms, their functioning has deteriorated, or there are any other signs of decompensation, refer them to their prescribing physician. Additionally, consult with physician yourself to ensure optimal case management.

4. Sensory-Perceptual Disturbance
    A. Identify the nature and etiology of delusions
    B. Rule out the presence of concomitant medical conditions as etiology of delusions
    C. Look for signs of person withdrawing into self
    D. Keep stress and anxiety at a minimum and educate regarding the relationship between stress and anxiety to perceptual disturbance
    E. Increase awareness for patterns of talking or laughing to self
    F. Monitor for disorientation and disordered thought sequencing
    G. Confront distortions and misinterpretations with reality testing, and encourage person to define and test reality
    H. Intervene early to correct reality if person is experiencing perceptual or sensory distortions
    I. Distract the person away from the perceptual disturbance by engaging him/her in another direction of thinking or activity
    J. Skill development for stress and anxiety management
        1. Using progressive muscle relaxation
        2. Listening to soft music
        3. Walking or other appropriate activity
        4. Utilizing support from others

5. Ineffective Coping
    A. Facilitate identification of stressors contributing to increased anxiety and agitation, which result in disorientation of person
    B. Be honest and open about what is or will be taking place so as to decrease suspiciousness and to increase trust
    C. Confront distorted thinking, facilitate reality testing
    D. Encourage consistency in environment
    E. Encourage verbalization of feelings
    F. Facilitate appropriate problem solving
    G. Encourage medication compliance
    H. Educate family to be supportive of appropriate responses, consistency in environment, medication compliance, emotional management, minimal stimuli, necessity for honesty and following through on promises, and so on
    I. Facilitate person's ability to adequately and effective appraise situations and to respond appropriately
    J. Encourage and facilitate appropriate interaction and cooperation

6. Grooming and Hygiene
    A. Encourage daily independent living skills
        1. Bathing
        2. Cleaning hair, cutting when necessary, and styling appropriately
        3. Brushing teeth
        4. Dressing adequately and appropriately
        5. Cleaning self adequately after using the bathroom and washing hands
    B. Encourage appropriate independent efforts
    C. Role-model and encourage the practice of appropriate behavior
    D. Offer positive reinforcement for efforts and accomplishments of independent living skills

7. Sleep Disturbance
   A. Log sleeping pattern to develop treatment plan
   B. Use sedative antipsychotic medications at night (if prescribed)
   C. Clarify if fears or anxiety play a role in difficulty falling to sleep
   D. Develop a pattern for winding down and offer methods to promote sleep
      1. Warm soothing bath or shower
      2. Light snack
      3. Warm milk or herbal tea
   E. Discourage daytime sleeping
   F. Encourage exercise during the day
   G. Use relaxation techniques
   H. Use soft music or nature sounds
   I. Limit caffeine intake

8. Low Self-Esteem
   A. Reinforce accurate reality testing with positive feedback
   B. Encourage assertive communication
   C. Problem-solve through modeling and role-play ways to deal with typical problems encountered by the person in their environment, when interacting in society, and in peer situations
   D. Encourage and positively reinforce self-care behaviors

9. Social Isolation
   A. Educate, role-model, and practice appropriate social skills
   B. Brief, frequent social contacts to facilitate familiarity
   C. Accepting attitude to facilitate trust and feelings of self-worth
   D. Offer patience and support to increase feelings of security
   E. Encourage respect of personal space
   F. Initiate the development and understanding of social cues
   G. Identify feelings or circumstances that contribute to desire or need to withdraw and isolate
   H. Refer person to appropriate social gatherings/groups to practice appropriate social behaviors

10. Ineffective Communication
   A. Encourage person to stay on task with one topic
   B. Encourage appropriate, intermittent eye contact
   C. Clarify communication (I don't understand..., Do you mean...?, etc.)
   D. Help person understand how his/her behavior and verbal expression are interpreted and act to distance or alienate the person from others
   E. Encourage efforts and accomplishments with positive reinforcement
   F. Facilitate person's ability to recognize disorganized thinking
   G. Facilitate person's ability to recognize impaired communication

11. Dysfunctional Family Interaction
   A. Identify how family is affected by person's behavior
   B. Identify behaviors of family members that prevent appropriate progress or behavioral management
   C. Educate family regarding appropriate management of behaviors, the impact of conflict, impact from level of environmental stimuli, importance of medication compliance, reality testing, and how to respond to self-injurious or aggressive behavior. Encourage family to speak with physician and pharmacist regarding the side effects of the medications, the issue of monitoring side effects, and

how to respond to the various side effects. Refer person to med-monitoring group if available.

12. Support Medication Compliance
    A. Educate person regarding role of medication in functioning
    B. Support and reinforce medication compliance as a self-care behavior

13. General Side Effects of Medication
    A. Antipsychotic medication
        1. Nausea
        2. Sedation
        3. Skin Rash
        4. Orthostatic hypotension
        5. Photosensitivity
        6. Anticholinergic Effects
            a. Dry mouth
            b. Constipation
            c. Blurred vision
            d. Urinary retention
        7. Extrapyramidal symptoms (EPS)
            a. Pseudoparkinsonism (shuffling gait, tremor, drooling)
            b. Akinesia (muscle weakness)
            c. Dystonia (involuntary muscular movements of face neck and extremities)
            d. Akathisia (continuous restlessness)
        8. Hormonal Effects
            a. Weight gain
            b. Amenorrhea
            c. Decreased libido
            d. Retrograde ejaculation
            e. Gynecomastia (excessive development of the breasts in males)
        9. Reduced seizure threshold
        10. Agranulocytosis (monitor CBC and symptoms of fever, sore throat, malaise)
        11. Tardive Dyskinesia (bizarre tongue and facial movements)
        12. Neuroleptic Malignant Syndrome (NMS) (monitor fever, severe parkinsonian rigidity, tachycardia, blood pressure fluctuation, and fast deterioration of mental status to stupor and coma)
    B. Antiparkinsonian medication
        1. Nausea
        2. Sedation
        3. Intensifies psychosis
        4. Orthostatic hypotension
        5. Anticholinergic symptoms
            a. Dry mouth
            b. Constipation
            c. Urinary retention
            d. Paralytic ileus (monitor absent bowel sounds, abdominal distention, vomiting, nausea, epigastric pain)
            e. Blurred vision

If the person reports having any side effects from the medication, initiate an immediate consult with the prescribing physician and encourage the person to do so as well.

PHASES OF TREATMENT

1. Acute phase
   A. Goal is to facilitate the alleviation/decrease of acute symptoms in conjunction with improved functioning

2. Stabilization phase
   A. Goal is to minimize stress and provide adequate support in decreasing the possibility of relapse
   B. Adapt/adjust to life in community
   C. Facilitate continued reduction of symptoms while maximizing management and coping

3. Stable phase
   A. Ensure maintaining/improving level of functioning and quality of life
   B. The effective treatment of schizophrenic symptoms
   C. Monitor for adverse treatment effects

TREATMENT SETTINGS

1. Hospitalization
   A. Provide safe, structured, supervised environment and decrease stress on patients as well as their family members
   B. Potential harm to self, others, highly disorganized as a result of delusions/hallucinations or gravely disabled/unable to care for himself/herself
      1. Long-term hospitalization with emphasis on highly structured behavioral techniques
      2. Day hospitalization (crisis unit)
         a. This setting offers less disruption to an individual's life, less restrictive environment, and the avoidance of stigma attached to psychiatric hospitalization
         b. Brief overnight stays in inpatient units should be available when there is evidence of exacerbation of symptoms (decompensation)
      3. Partial hospitalization
         a. This setting benefits the marginally adjusted individual (stabilization to stable range)
         b. The goals are to provide structure, support, prevent relapse, and improve social functioning

2. Supportive Housing
   A. Transitional halfway house
   B. Long-term group residence
   C. Intensive care/crisis community residences
   D. Foster care
   E. Board and care homes
   F. Nursing homes

SUMMARY OF TREATMENT RECOMMENDATIONS FOR PATIENTS WITH PERCEPTUAL DISTURBANCES

For disorders involving loss of contact with reality, the following summary creates a useful overview of areas to consider. Prior to proceeding, be sure to review the specific disorder's diagnostic criteria because of the broad variations in this section.

1. Diagnosis
    A. Schizophrenia
    B. Brief reactive psychosis
    C. Delusional disorder
    D. Schizoaffective disorder
    E. Dissociative disorders
    F. Organic mental syndromes and disorders

*Psuedohallucinations

2. Objectives
    A. Alleviate/eliminate symptoms
    B. Restore contact with reality
    C. Maximize emotional/behavioral adjustment disorders
    D. Improve coping
    E. Prevent relapse
    F. Educate family
    G. Support family
        1. Appropriate referral
            a. Emotional support
            b. Problem solving
            c. Community programs

3. Assessment
    A. Medical: to clarify diagnostic picture, substance use
    B. Neurological: intellectual level, level of functioning
    C. Psychological

4. Treatment team
    A. Medical (PCP, psychiatrist, neurologist)
    B. Psychological (family therapy, individual therapy, group therapy)
    C. Rehabilitation therapist

5. Location
    A. Inpatient
    B. Residential
    C. Outpatient

*Psuedohallucinations:
    fantasized reactions

Person intensely experiences something as real

Intellectually knows it is not real
For example, presence of depersonalization/out-of-body experience

6. Interventions
    A. Medication; monitor closely to limit side effects
    B. Level of care required
        1. Inpatient
        2. Residential
        3. Outpatient

C. Modality
  1. Behavior therapy
    a. Improve coping
    b. Manage stress
    c. Improve socialization/utilization of resources
  2. Family therapy
    a. Education
    b. Support
    c. Adjustment
  3. Psychodynamic therapy
    a. Multiple personality disorder
  4. Group therapy
    a. Rehabilitation counseling
    b. Occupational therapy
    c. Socialization
    d. Respite care

7. Prognosis
  A. Varies based on disorder
    1. Excellent for brief reactive psychosis
    2. Good for psychogenic amnesia
    3. Fair for multiple personality disorder/schizophrenia
    4. Poor for some organic mental disorders

While therapy typically plays a secondary role in the treatment of most organic disorders, it can be an important adjunct to medical treatment. This is particularly true in the early/mind stages of primary degenerative dementia, multi-infarct dementia, an so on. It can serve to do the following:

1. Encourage active/independent living as long as possible
2. Focus on behavioral-cognitive adjustments
3. Facilitate compensation for changes in capacity by building on coping mechanisms
4. Assist in the management of negative affective states and destructive impulses

Adapted from L. Seligman (1990). Selective effective treatment.
San Francisco: Josey-Bass.

MOOD DISORDERS

Mood disorders are divided into Depressive Disorders and Bipolar Disorders. The defining feature of Bipolar Disorder is the experience of one or more manic or hypomanic episodes. This section will deal more simply with the objects and goals related to depressive symptoms and the objectives and goals related to manic symptoms.

According to the *DSM IV* (1994), the central feature of mood disorders is disturbance of mood—manic or depressive. The range of the mood disorders include the following: Major Depression, Dysthymia, Seasonal Affective Disorder, Mania, Hypomania, Bipolar, and Cyclothymia.

DEPRESSION

Goals

1. Assess danger to self and others
2. Provide safe environment
3. Assess need for medication evaluation referral
4. Improve problem-solving skills
5. Improve coping skills
6. Develop and encourage utilization of support system
7. Resolve issues of loss
8. Improve self-esteem
9. Cognitive restructuring
10. Improve eating patterns
11. Improve sleep patterns
12. Develop depression management program
13. Educate regarding medication compliance

Treatment Focus and Objectives

1. Suicide Risk Assessment
   A. Thoughts of killing self, or persistent death wish
   B. Plan
   C. Means to carry out the plan
   D. Feelings of hopelessness
   E. Past history of suicide attempts, or someone close to them that has attempted or committed suicide
   F. Recent losses
   G. Substance abuse
   H. Poor impulse control
   I. Poor judgment

During the interview it may be possible to decrease the level of emotional distress by validating the difficulty that the person is experiencing and encouraging him/her to vent feelings and intentions of suicide. Talking about these issues, which have resulted in such despair and hopelessness, may not only decrease the level of distress, but may create some opportunity for intervention. As the person talks about his/her thoughts of suicide, he/she can be facilitated to begin to understand what a significant impact his/her suicide would have on family, friends, and others. Offering clients validation and reassurance may increase their ambivalence. If there is evidence of adequate social support and cooperation, a short-term verbal contract with a coinciding written contract can offer some structure for dealing with self-destructive impulses.

If the person has resources and does not intend to commit suicide, but is vulnerable, consider increasing the frequency or duration of outpatients contacts for a brief period of time, an intensive outpatient program, or partial hospitalization. If the person is not currently being prescribed antidepressant medication, he/she should be referred for a medication evaluation.

If the person is not able to make any assurances that he/she does not intend to commit suicide, then hospitalization is necessary. Initially, approach the person about voluntary admission to a psychiatric facility. If the person is unwilling to voluntarily admit himself/herself, then an involuntary admission process will ensue. Providing a safe environment with monitoring and support is imperative.

While danger to self is often the critical clinical dilemma requiring immediate attention and intervention, it is also important to assess and rule out any homicidal thoughts and intentions that place others in a position of potential harm. If an assessment reveals the intention to harm another person, the appropriate clinical interventions and legal issue of the duty to warn must be dealt with immediately.

2. Provide Safe Environment
   A. Evaluate whether person is demonstrating adequate cooperation (removal of firearms, medications, etc. that person may have considered for self-harm/suicide)
   B. Evaluate adequacy of social support
   C. Adjust level of care if necessary
      1. Urgent care. Flexible time for meeting, along with extended meeting time to allow the person to ventilate their emotions and initiate problem solving.
      2. Partial hospitalization
      3. Inpatient-open unit
      4. Inpatient-closed unit

3. Referral Assessment for Medication Evaluation
   A. If this is an initial assessment and a history of depression is given that has clearly affected quality of life and functioning, refer for a medication evaluation
   B. If this has been an ongoing case and acute depressive symptoms are present that are interfering with level of functioning, refer for medication evaluation
   C. Assess for mood congruent psychotic features. They can be present and not identified. If positive, convey information to prescribing physician.

4. Ineffective Problem Solving
   A. Define the problem(s)
   B. Brainstorm all plausible solutions
   C. Identify the outcomes in relation to the various solutions
   D. Make a decision that appears to best fit the demands of the problem situation
   E. Prepare the person for the possibility that the solution may not work out as planned; therefore, have a contingency plan

5. Dysfunctional Coping
   A. Help person recognize that he/she can only do one thing at a time
   B. Teach person relaxation skills to use if feeling overwhelmed
   C. Facilitate prioritizing issues that person must deal with
   D. Facilitate clarification of boundaries, especially related to issues of pleasing others versus self-care
   E. Rule out secondary gains
   F. Helplessness
      1. Encourage taking responsibility and making decisions
      2. Include the person when setting goals
      3. Provide positive feedback for decision making
      4. Facilitate development of realistic goals, limitations, and expectations
      5. Identify areas of life and self-care in which the person has control, as well as those areas where the person lacks control
      6. Encourage expression of feelings related to areas of life outside person's control and explore how to let it go

6. Ineffective Development or Utilization of Resources and Social Supports
   A. Resist desire to withdraw and isolate
   B. Identify positive social/emotional supports that the person has have been avoiding
   C. Make commitment to utilize resources and supports in some way every day
   D. Educate regarding role of isolation in maintaining depression

E. Evaluate impaired social interaction
1. Convey acceptance and positive regard in creating a safe, nonjudgmental environment
2. Identify people in the person's life and activities that were previously found pleasurable
3. Encourage utilization of support system
4. Encourage appropriate risk taking
5. Teach assertive communication
6. Give direct, nonjudgmental feedback regarding interaction with others
7. Offer alternative responses for dealing effectively with stress-provoking situations
8. Social skills training in how to approach others and participate in conversation
9. Role-play and practice social skills for reinforcement and to increase insight for how the person is perceived by others
10. Daily structure to include social interaction

7. Dysfunctional Grieving
A. Evaluate stage of grief that person is experiencing
B. Demonstrate care and empathy
C. Determine if the person has numerous unresolved losses
D. Encourage expression of feelings
E. Use the empty chair technique or have the person write a letter to someone he/she has lost, which may provoke the resolution process
F. Educate person on stages of grief and normalize appropriate feelings such as anger and guilt
G. Support person in letting go of his/her idealized perception so that the person can accept the positive and negative aspects of his/her object of loss
H. Positively reinforce adaptive coping with experiences of loss (taking into consideration ethnic and social differences)
I. Refer to a grief group
J. Explore the issue of spirituality and spiritual support

8. Low Self-Esteem
A. Focus on strengths and accomplishments
B. Avoid focus on past failures
C. Reframe failures or negative experiences as normal part of learning process
D. Identify a areas of desired change and objectives to meet those goals
E. Encourage independent effort and accepting responsibility
F. Teach assertive communication and appropriate setting of limits and boundaries
H. Teach effective communication techniques by using "I" statements, not making assumptions, asking for clarification, and so on
I. Offer positive reinforcement for tasks performed independently

9. Distorted Thinking
A. Identify the influence of negativism on depression and educate regarding positive self-talk
B. Seek clarification when the information communicated appears distorted
C. Reinforce reality-based thinking
D. Facilitate development of intervention techniques such as increased awareness with conscious choice of what to focus on (positive thoughts), thought stopping, and compartmentalizing
E. Facilitate person's clarification of rational versus irrational thinking

10. Eating Disturbance
    A. Evaluate eating pattern and fluid intake
    B. Educate regarding importance of good nutrition for energy and clear thinking

11. Sleep Disturbance
    A. Evaluate sleep pattern and overall amount of sleep
    B. Encourage appropriate and adequate sleep cycle
    C. Discourage daytime napping
    D. Avoid caffeine and other stimulants
    E. Perform relaxation exercises or listen to relaxing music before sleep
    F. Daily aerobic exercising such as walking
    G. Administer sedative medications in the evening instead of other times during the day
    H. Suggest activities such as warm bath, massage, herbal tea, light snack, and so on, which promote sleep

12. Difficulty Consistently Managing Depression: This requires a thorough review of lifestyle. Managing depression requires a commitment by the person to take responsibility for improving his/her quality of life. (Refer to skill building section.)
    A. The components of a self-care plan to manage depression include the following:
       1. Structured daily activities
       2. Development and utilization of social supports
       3. Positive attitude and identification of the positive things in one's life
       4. Awareness
       5. Regular aerobic exercise
       6. Eating nutritionally
       7. Living in accordance with one's own value system

13. Educate Person (And Family If Appropriate) on Medication Issues
    A. Emphasize the importance of compliance. Encourage patient to clarify potential side effects including those that require immediate attention.
    B. Recommend that patients familiarize themselves with any restrictions related to medication use
    C. Refer person to clarify medication issues with his/her physician and pharmacist
    D. Educate regarding chemical imbalance related to depression
    E. Educate regarding role of decompensation related to lack of medication compliance
    F. Possible Side Effects of Antidepressant Medication
       1. Sedation
       2. Anticholinergic Effects
          a. Dry mouth
          b. Constipation
          c. Blurred vision
          d. Urinary retention
       3. Orthostatic hypotension
       4. Tachycardia/arrhythmia
       5. Photosensitivity
       6. Decrease in seizure threshold
       7. Hypertensive crisis (monitor for symptoms such as palpitations, nausea, vomiting, sweating, chest pain, severe occipital headache, fever, increased blood pressure, coma)

8. Weight loss or gain
9. Priapism

If the person reports having any side effects from the medication, consult with the prescribing physician immediately and encourage the person to do the same.

If the individual has a diagnosis of seasonal affective disorder, be sensitive to the issue of light treatment to alleviate their depression.

    G. Since a therapist is likely to have significantly more contact with an individual in treatment who is being prescribed psychotropic medication than the prescribing physician, it is imperative to monitor the patient response to medication and communicate salient information to the prescribing physician
      1. At least moderate improvement should be achieved in six to eight weeks
      2. Monitor for presence of side effects (especially those that require immediate attention)
    H. Risk factors for recurrence of major depressive episode
      1. History of multiple episodes of major depression
      2. Evidence of dysthymic symptoms following recovery from an episode of major depression
      3. Comorbid nonaffective psychiatric diagnosis
      4. Presence of chronic medical disorder
    I. Clinical features that influence the treatment plan
      1. Crisis issues
      2. Psychotic features
      3. Substance abuse
      4. Comorbid axis I or axis II disorders
      5. Major depression related to cognitive dysfunction (psuedodementia)
      6. Dysthymia
      7. Severe/complicated grief reaction
      8. Seasonal major depressive disorder
    J. Atypical major depressive disorder features (defined by reversal of vegetative symptoms)
      1. Increased sleep versus decreased sleep
      2. Increased appetite versus decreased appetite
      3. Weight gain versus weight loss
      4. Marked mood reactivity
      5. Sensitivity to emotional rejection
      6. Phobic symptoms
      7. Extreme fatigue with heaviness of extremities
    K. If there is little to no symptomatic response by four to six weeks
      1. Assess compliance
      2. Reassess diagnosis
      3. Reassess adequacy of treatment

DEPRESSION CO-OCCURING WITH OTHER ILLNESS

The co-occurance of depression with other medical, psychiatric, and substance abuse disorders should always be considered. Awareness and treatment can improve overall health and decrease suffering. A thorough assessment and accurate diagnosis are imperative.

1. Depression is a common, serious, and costly illness that affects 1 in 10 adults in the United States
2. It costs the United States $30 to 45 billion per year
3. It causes impairment, suffering, and disruption of all areas of a person's life
4. Two out of three people suffering from depression do not seek treatment
5. Common interventions include therapy, antidepressant medication, or both
6. Most people can be effectively treated for depression
7. Depression can co-occur with medical, psychiatric and substance abuse disorders:
   A. The presence of both illnesses is frequently unrecognized
   B. This may lead to serious and unnecessary consequences for the person/family

Co-occurance with Medical Illness

1. An estimation of 5 to 10% of primary care patients have depression
2. An estimation of 10 to 14% of medical patients have depression
3. Depressed feelings can be a normal response to many medical illnesses
4. Research has shown that major depression (clinical depression) occurs in
   A. 40 to 65% of patients who have had a myocardial infarction (MI). They may also have a shorter life expectancy than nondepressed MI patients
   B. Approximately 25% of cancer patients
   C. 10 to 27% of post-stroke patients

*Failure to recognize and treat co-occurring depression may result in increased impairment and decreased improvement in the medical disorder.

Co-occurance with Psychiatric Disorders

1. There is a 13% co-occurance with panic disorder; in approximately 25% of these patients the panic disorder preceded the depressive disorder
2. 50 to 75% of those with eating disorders have a lifetime history of major depression

*Detection of depression can result in clarifying the primary diagnosis and lead to more effective treatment and improved outcome.

Co-occurance with Substance Abuse Disorders

1. Substance abuse disorders frequently coexist with depression
2. 32% of individuals with depression experience a substance abuse disorder
3. 27% of those with major depression experience substance abuse disorder
4. 56% of those with bipolar disorder experience a substance abuse disorder

*Substance abuse must be discontinued so that a clear diagnosis can be made and the appropriate treatment given. Treatment for depression may be necessary if it continues when the substance abuse problem ends.

MANIA

1. Provide safe environment
2. Eliminate danger to self or others
3. Stabilization and medication compliance
4. Thought processes intact
5. Eliminate perceptual disturbances
6. Improve social interaction/decrease isolation
7. Improve self-esteem
8. Improve self-management
9. Improve sleep pattern
10. Educate regarding medication issues and general side effects

Treatment Focus and Objectives

1. Risk for Injury
   A. Assess
      1. Destructive acting out behavior
      2. Extreme hyperactivity
      3. Extreme agitation
      4. Self-injurious behavior
      5. Loud, and escalating aggressiveness
      6. Threatening behavior
   B. If person lacks control and is a danger to himself/herself or others, hospitalization is necessary. Hospitalization provides a safe environment, monitoring, and an opportunity to stabilize medication. Depending on the level of mania, the person's admission to a psychiatric facility will be voluntary or involuntary (5150)
   C. Keep environmental stimuli at a minimum
   D. Remove hazardous objects
   E. Physical activity such as walking to discharge energy
   F. Medication compliance as prescribed

2. Risk for Violence (Directed Toward Self or Others)
   A. Assess
      1. Extreme hyperactivity
      2. Suspiciousness or paranoid ideation
      3. Hostility, threatening harm to self or others
      4. Rageful
      5. Aggressive body language or aggressive acts of behavior
      6. Provoking behavior (challenging, trying to start fights)
      7. Hallucinations or delusions
      8. Possesses the means to harm (gun, knife, etc.)
      9. Bragging about prior incidence of abuse to self or others
   B. Keep environmental stimuli or a minimum
   C. Monitor closely
   D. Remove all potentially dangerous objects
   E. Physical exercise to decrease tension
   F. Maintain calm attitude with person and do not challenge
   G. Medication compliance as prescribed

As with risk for injury or danger to self or others, hospitalization may be necessary during a manic phase if symptoms are escalating and unmanageable.

3. Medication Noncompliance
   A. As person's functioning improves, educate regarding importance of medication compliance and relationship between decompensation and lack of medication compliance. Medication is clearly the primary mode of treatment for Mania/ Bipolar Disorder. Medication compliance is imperative to symptom management. "If a risk factor for poor outcome is present in 50% of patients (history of nonadherence), it is vital that clinicians are encouraged to ask proactively about problems with adherence and create an atmosphere where such issues can be discussed openly" (Pope, 2002). Research by Rasgon et al. (2002) suggests that women with Bipolar Disorder may be more depressed and experience more frequent mood changes than men.

4. Altered Thought Processes
   A. Do not argue with person or challenge him/her
   B. Communicate acceptance of the person's need for the false belief, but let him/her know that you do not share the delusion
   C. Use clarification techniques of communication (Would you please explain...? Do you mean...? I don't understand....)
   D. Offer positive reinforcement for accurate reality testing
   E. Reinforce and focus on reality by talking about real events
   F. Facilitate development of intervention techniques such as thought stopping, slowing things down, and requesting the support of others in reality testing

5. Sensory-Perceptual Disturbance
   A. Evaluate for hallucination or delusional thinking
   B. Let the person know that you do not share the perception. Point out that although what he/she hears or sees seems real to the individual, you do not hear or see what the person does.
   C. Facilitate understanding between increased anxiety and reality distortions
   D. Distract the person with involvement in an interpersonal activity and do reality testing
   E. Intervene when early signs of perceptual disturbances are evident
   F. Help person recognize perceptual disturbances with repeated patterns and how to intervene
   G. Offer positive reinforcement for efforts and maintenance of accurate reality testing

6. Impaired Social Interaction
   A. Increased awareness for how other people interpret varying forms of behavior and communication
   B. Role-model and practice appropriate responding to social situations
   C. Encourage acceptance of responsibility for own behavior versus projecting responsibility onto others
   D. Encourage recognition of manipulative behaviors
   E. Set limits and boundaries. Be consistent. Do not argue, bargain, or try to reason. Just restate the limit.
   F. Positive reinforcement for recognition and accepting responsibility for own behavior
   G. Positive reinforcement for appropriate behaviors
   H. Facilitate appropriate ways to deal with feelings
   I. Facilitate understanding of consequences for inappropriate behaviors

J. Identify and focus on positive aspects of the person

K. Refer to a support group for bipolar disorder

7. Low Self-Esteem

   A. Validate person's experience. Identify negative impact that disorder has had on the person's life.

      1. Explore what issues he/she controls versus issues involving lack of control

      2. Identify difficulty that person has in accepting the reality of the disorder and as a result not accepting himself/herself

   B. Facilitate identification of strengths

   C. Identify areas of realistic desirable change and break it down into manageable steps

   D. Encourage assertive communication

   E. Offer person simple methods of achievement

   F. Positive feedback and reinforcement for efforts and achievements

8. Improved Self-Management

   A. Increase-awareness of mood changes and how to more effectively manage

   B. Increase understanding of developmental deviations and delays caused by chronic mental illness (CMI)

   C. Confront and deal with the stigmatization associated with mental illness

   D. Challenge fear of recurrent episodes and associated inhibition of normal psychosocial functioning

   E. Problem-solve interpersonal difficulties

   F. Confront and develop appropriate resources to effectively deal with marriage, family, child-bearing, and parenting issues

   G. Improved understanding and development of effective interventions to deal with emotional, social, and legal problems

9. Sleep Disturbance

   A. Monitor sleep patterns

   B. Reduce stimulation, provide a quiet environment

   C. Provide structured schedule of activities, which includes quiet time or time for naps

   D. Monitor activity level

   E. Increase identification and awareness for fatigue

   F. Avoid caffeine or other stimulants

   G. Administer sedative medications, as prescribed, at bedtime

   H. Provide cues and methods to promote sleep such as relaxation, soft music, warm bath, and so on

10. Education on Medication Issues

    A. Person and his/her family should be educated about the disorder and management of the features of the disorder, and they possess a thorough understanding of medication issues

    B. Refer the person and family to the prescribing physician and pharmacist for clarification of medication issues

    C. Educate regarding the chemical imbalance relationship of mania

    D. Educate regarding the issue of decompensation and the lack of medication compliance

    E. General Side Effects of Medication

       1. Dry mouth, thirst

       2. Dizziness, drowsiness

3. Headache
4. Hypotension
5. Pulse irregularities, arrhythmia
6. Nausea, vomiting
7. Fine hand tremors
8. Weight gain

If the person reports having any side effects from the medication, consult the prescribing physician immediately and encourage the person to do the same.

Individual therapy is an extremely beneficial adjunctive treatment to medication for individuals diagnosed with Mania/Bipolar Disorder. It is used to help individuals recover from the symptoms of their disorder, restore normal mood, repair relationship damage, repair career damage, and establish self-monitoring. Therapy is, of course, not attempted during a manic phase, which requires medical/medication stabilization. Family therapy and education are also important to help/support family members in their understanding of the nature of the illness and treatment.

CHILDREN

Bipolar Disorder appears to be more severe in children. Geller et al. (2002) reported that Bipolar Disorder in young children is synonymous with the most severe experiences of bipolar disorder in adults. In adults, the typical Bipolar experience where involves episodes of either mania or depression that lasts a few months with relatively normal episodes of functioning. However, mania in children has been found to be a more severe, chronic course of illness. The report states that many children experience both depression and mania at the same time and may remain ill for years, enduring multiple daily highs and lows without intervening periods of relative normalcy. In a study of 89 subjects with childhood onset of mania, 77 had comorbid ADHD and 67 had comorbid Oppositional Defiant/Conduct Disorder.

Psychiatric management (PM) is an ongoing process with bipolar disorder. PM helps to minimize the negative consequence of unstable mood states by facilitating adaptive responding

1. Interpersonally/socially
2. Professionally
3. Academically
4. Occupationally
5. Financially

Regarding ultra rapid cycling, refer for general medical evaluation

1. With particular focus on thyroid function
2. Comorbid substance abuse
3. Other general medical conditions

Psychosocial variables include the following:

A. Cross-cultural issues
1. Culture may influence experience and communication of symptoms (as with all mental health issues)

2. Culture may influence under diagnosis/misdiagnosis/delayed diagnosis

3. There may be a differential response to antidepressant medications among ethnic groups

B. Environment

1. During manic phase, a calm routine environment is helpful

2. Manic individuals may need room to pace and exercise

3. The individual may benefit from the support of someone in his/her environment who has been educated about realistic expectations and safety associated with mania

C. Stressors

1. Psychosocial stressors may be associated with the precipitation of mania

2. Many episodes of mania have no identifiable psychosocial stressor and as the illness progresses, episodes appear to occur spontaneously

3. May be helpful for individuals with bipolar and their families to work with their therapist to develop an understanding of unique associations to stressful events and the onset of symptoms

BIPOLAR DISORDER HYPERSEXUALITY

For individuals with Bipolar Disorder, the extreme behaviors associated with mania can be devastating. While there is a listing of potential extreme behaviors in the *DSM* indicative of manic episodes, the review of one of those behaviors serves to highlight the damaging results. Hypersexuality is defined as an increased need or compulsion for sexual gratification. A person may be reluctant to expose his/her experience of hypersexuality in treatment because of the associated immense feelings of shame. With the decreased inhibition associated with hypersexuality, individuals find themself engaging in sexual behaviors that they may consider "deviant or forbidden" and that results in feelings of shame. For some, the frequency of their compulsion is at an addictive level. In addition to feelings of shame, hypersexuality can destroy a marriage or a committed relationship and increase the risk of sexually transmitted diseases.

Regarding the issue of the broad patterns of sexual addiction behavior, the Mayo Clinic defines sexual addiction as a loss of control with the focus on compulsion: "compulsive sexual behavior refers to spending inordinate amounts of time in sexual related activity, to the point that one neglects important social, occupational, or recreational activities in favor of sexual behavior." According to the National Council on Sexual Addiction and Compulsivity addiction is characterized as "loss of the ability to choose freely whether to stop or to continue... continuation of the behavior despite adverse consequences, such as loss of health, job, marriage, or freedom... obsession with the activity."

Examples of the specific behaviors that are common to those who struggle with hypersexuality's compulsive and reckless behaviors include the following:

1. Fantasy sex

2. Fetishes

3. Inappropriate sexual touching

4. Sexual abuse and sexual assault

5. Compulsive masturbation

6. Compulsive sex with prostitutes

7. Masochism

8. Patronizing sex-oriented establishments
9. Voyeurism
10. Exhibitionism

The range of consequences associated with hypersexuality include the following:

1. Shame
2. Low self-esteem
3. Fear
4. Financial distress (cost of prostitutes/phone sex and items or activities in sex-oriented establishments)
5. Destruction of relationships
6. Health risk, loss of job (pornography on the computer, inappropriate behavior, etc.)

While evaluating and treating someone with Bipolar Disorder, the aforementioned information should clarify the importance of fully understanding the manic experience of the individual because of the potential deep-seated emotional damage resulting from extreme personally unacceptable behavior. Education and validation are important interventions.

ANTIDEPRESSANT MEDICATION AND OTHER TREATMENT

Everyone views the treatment choices for depression in his or her own individual manner. Some individuals prefer an initial treatment modality for mild Major Depression to be antidepressant medication, while others will prioritize therapy as the initial treatment. There will be some who obtain the desired response in accordance with their treatment choice. Often an individual may be treated most effectively by combining these modalities, especially when there is a history of depression. A referral for antidepressant medication should be provided for those with moderate to severe major depression. If an individual presents with a major depression with psychotic features he/she is likely to be treated with an antidepressant and antipsychotic medication unless Electro-Convulsive Therapy has been planned. For those with difficult-to-treat depression ECT, a stimulant or thyroid supplement is reviewed for potential effectiveness in a given case.

According to the American Psychiatric Association, the following guidelines should be considered in the treatment of major depressive disorder:

1. Should a specific effective psychotherapy be provided?
    A. Mild to moderate depression: preferred as primary treatment or as combination with medication
    B. Moderate to severe depression: in combination with medication or ECT *if* psychosocial issues are prevalent and/or *if* preferred

2. Should medication be provided?
    A. Mild depression: if preferred as primary treatment

B. Moderate to severe depression: with or without a specific effective psychotherapy unless ECT has be planned

C. Psychotic depression: combination of antipsychotic and antidepressant medication unless ECT has been planned

3. Should medication and a specific effective psychotherapy be provided in combination?

A. Mild depression

1. If combination treatment is preferred
2. When there is a history of partial response to a single treatment modality
3. When poor compliance is an issue

B. Moderate to severe depression

1. When there is presence of

a. Prominent psychosocial issues
b. Significant interpersonal problems
c. Personality disorder
d. Poor compliance

4. Should ECT be provided?

A. Chronic, moderate to severe depression

B. With or without specific psychotherapy based on patient preference

C. Severe depression in combination with any of the following:

1. Psychotic features
2. Patient preference
3. Previous preferred response
4. Need of rapid antidepressant response
5. Intolerance of medication

As an individual is receiving any of these treatment modalities in solo or in combination, continue to assess improvement/recovery and review for other treatment considerations.

ADDITIONAL TREATMENT CONSIDERATIONS

1. *Treatment of Depression in the Elderly.* This complex and challenging clinical dilemma is related to the high degree of comorbidity with medical disorders. Some of the complications that confound treatment of depressive disorders in the elderly are as follows:

A. Nonpsychotropic medications may cause depression, alter blood levels of antidepressant medications, and increase the side effects of antidepressant medication.

B. Concurrent psychiatric conditions may result in depression, require the use of different medications, and reduce the response to antidepressant medication.

C. Concurrent medical illnesses may cause biological depression, reduce the effectiveness of antidepressant medication, and change the metabolic rate of antidepressant medications.

D. Complications related to stage-of-life issues include metabolic slowing, which requires lower dosing levels, fixed income with limited resources available to them, issues of loss, dependency and role reversal with children, social isolation, and illness.

2. *Treatment of Depression in Children.* Children and adolescents may not demonstrate the manifestations of depressions as the symptoms readily recognized in adults. Depression in this population is often masked by acting-out or behavioral problems. A careful and thorough diagnostic assessment is extremely important because of the high risk of suicide in troubled adolescents. If depression is diagnosed and psychotropic medication is prescribed it is crucial to monitor medication compliance.

3. *Coexisting Disorders and Conditions.* Diagnostic clarification. Unless the person has a long standing history of depression (Dysthymia), it is the general standard of practice to treat the coexisting disorders and conditions first. If the depression remains then the depressive disorder is clearly diagnosed and treated. Possible associated disorders and conditions include substance abuse, side effects of other medications, the result of medical conditions, other psychiatric conditions such as anxiety disorders, and medical conditions such as menopause.

4. *Coexistence of Depression and Anxiety.* A person may experience a depressive disorder that is accompanied by symptoms of anxiety. However, the symptoms of anxiety may not fully meet the criteria necessary for a diagnosis of an anxiety disorder. The reverse may also be true. A person may have an anxiety disorder accompanied by symptoms of depression. In this situation it is possible that the depressive symptoms are not sufficient to meet the criteria for the diagnosis of a depressive disorder.

ANXIETY DISORDERS

The category of Anxiety Disorders includes diagnoses of Panic Disorder, Agoraphobia, Phobias, Obsessive-Compulsive Disorder, Post-Traumatic Stress Disorder, and Generalized Anxiety.

The central features of these disorders include anxiety, fear, emotional distress, self-defeating cognitive and behavioral rituals, distressing physical symptoms evoked by intense distress and body tension, sleep and appetite disturbance, feeling out of control, and experiencing difficulty effectively coping.

ANXIETY DISORDERS

Goals

1. Assess for need for medication evaluation referral
2. Identify source of anxiety and fears
3. Improve coping skills
4. Improve problem-solving skills
5. Improve self-care skills
6. Improve feelings of control
7. Improve communication skills
8. Cognitive restructuring
9. Improve self-esteem
10. Improve stress-management skills
11. Family education
12. Educate regarding side effects of medication

Treatment Focus and Objectives

1. Assess for Referral for Medication Evaluation. Patients with heightened anxiety, withdrawal, lack of sleep, obsessive thoughts, and compulsive behaviors may benefit from the use of psychotropic medications. If there is comorbidity of depression, convey this information to the referred physician.

2. Feelings of Anxiety and Fear
    A. Validate person's emotional experience
    B. Identify factors contributing to anxiety
    C. Problem-solve factors contributing to anxiety
        1. What is the problem?
        2. Brainstorm various choices for dealing with the problem if it is within the person's control
        3. Make a decision and follow through. Have a contingency plan.
        4. If it is out of the person's control, encourage the person to let go of it
    D. Explore methods of managing anxiety
        1. Relaxation techniques, including deep breathing
        2. Distracting, pleasurable activities
        3. Exercise
        4. Meditation
        5. Positive self-talk
    E. Assess medication for effectiveness and for adverse side effects
    F. Educate regarding signs of escalating anxiety and various techniques for interrupting the progression of these symptoms (refer to section on Managing Anxiety). Also explore possible physical etiology of exacerbation of anxiety.
    G. Fear
        1. Explore the source of the fear
        2. Clarify the reality of the fear base. Encourage venting of feelings of fear. If the fear is irrational, the person must accept the reality of the situation before any changes can occur
        3. Develop alternative coping strategies with the active participation of the person
        4. Encourage the person to make hi/her own choices and to be prepared with a contingency plan
        5. Use systematic desensitization to eliminate fear with gradual exposure to the feared object or situation (exposure can be real or through visual imagery)
        6. Use implosion therapy where exposure to the feared object or situation is not gradual but direct (referred to as "flooding")
        7. Educate person regarding role of internal, self-talk to feelings of fear, and develop appropriate counter statements
    H. Manage obsessive thoughts and compulsive behaviors
        1. Patients with obsessive thoughts should be encouraged to engage in reality testing and to redirect themselves into productive and distracting activity
        2. Patients with compulsive behavior should develop a stepwise reduction in the repetition of ritual behaviors (medication can be very helpful for managing OCD)
    I. Positive feedback and reinforcement for efforts and accomplishments

3. Ineffective Coping
    A. Identify factors that escalate anxiety and contribute to difficulty coping
    B. Identify ritualistic patterns of behaviors
    C. Educate regarding the relationship between emotions and dysfunctional/compulsive behavior
    D. Develop daily structure of activities

E. Gradually decrease time allotted for compulsive ritualistic behaviors, utilizing daily structure of activities that acts to substitute more adaptive behaviors

F. Positive feedback and reinforcement for effort and change to shape behavior

G. Teach techniques that interrupt dysfunctional thoughts and behaviors, such as relaxation techniques, meditation, thought stopping, exercise, positive self-talk, visual imagery, and so on

H. Facilitate shaping of social interaction to decrease avoidant behavior

4. Ineffective Problem Solving

A. Teach problem-solving skills

B. Develop some realistic sample problems and give homework to practice new skills

C. Identify secondary gains that inhibit progress toward change

5. Self-Care Deficiency

A. Support person to independently fulfill daily grooming and hygiene tasks

B. Adequate nutrition

C. Regular exercise

D. Engaging in activities and being with people, all of which contribute to feelings of well-being

E. Use of positive self-talk and affirmations

F. Positive feedback and reinforce efforts and accomplishments

G. Time management

H. Prioritize demands/ tasks

I. Develop and utilize support system

6. Feels Lack of Control over Life

A. Break down simple behaviors and necessary tasks into manageable steps

B. Provide choices that are in their control

C. Support development of realistic goals and objectives

D. Encourage participation in activities in which the person will experience success and achievement

E. Facilitate development of problem-solving skills

F. Facilitate shaping of social interaction to decrease avoidant behavior

7. Ineffective Communication

A. Assertive communication

B. Anger management

C. Role-play, rehearse, and problem-solve appropriate response choices in various situations

D. Positive feedback and reinforcement

E. Learn to say no, avoid manipulation, set limits and boundaries

8. Irrational Thinking/Beliefs

A. Identify negative statements the person makes to themselves

B. Identify the connection between anxiety and self-talk

C. Develop appropriate, reality-based counterstatements and substitute them for the negative ones

D. Keep a daily record of dysfunctional thoughts to increase awareness of frequency and impact on emotional state

E. Disrupt dysfunctional thoughts by increasing awareness for internal self-talk, distracting oneself through relaxation, exercise, or other positive activity, and using thought stopping

F. Irrational Beliefs
1. Identify false beliefs (brought from childhood, integrated parental statements)
2. Challenge mistaken beliefs with rational counterstatements
3. Identify effect that irrational beliefs have on emotions, relationship with self and others, and choices the person makes

G. Self-Defeating Beliefs/Behaviors That Perpetuate Anxiety
1. Identify needs or tendencies that predispose the person to anxiety
   a. Need to control
   b. Perfectionistic
   c. People pleaser with strong need for approval
   d. Ignoring signs of stress
   e. Self-critical
   f. Perpetual victim role
   g. Pessimistic, catastrophizes
   h. Chronic worrier

9. Low Self-Esteem
   A. Self-care
      1. Identifying needs
      2. Setting appropriate limits and boundaries
      3. Seeking a safe, stable environment
   B. Identify realistic goals, expectations, and limitations
   C. Identify external factors that negatively affect self-esteem
   D. Overcome negative attitudes toward self
   E. Address issues of physical well-being (exercise and nutrition) and positive body image
   F. Assertive communication
   G. Identify feelings that have been ignored or denied
   H. Positive self-talk, affirmations
   I. Focus on efforts and accomplishments
   J. Positive feedback and reinforcement

10. Ineffective Stress Management
   A. Facilitate development of stress management techniques
      1. Deep breathing
      2. Progressive muscle relaxation
      3. Visual imagery/meditation
      4. Time management
      5. Self-care

11. Educate Person/Family
   A. Facilitate increased understanding of etiology, course of treatment, and the family role in treatment. Medical exam to rule out any physical etiology.
   B. Encourage person's participation in treatment planning
   C. Educate regarding the nervous system and explain that it is impossible to feel relaxed and anxious at the same time. Therefore, mastery of stress management techniques such as progressive muscle relaxation works to slowly intervene and diminish the symptoms of anxiety.
   D. Educate regarding the use of medication, how it works, the side effects, and the need to make the prescribing physician aware of the person's reaction/responses to the medication for monitoring (the anxious person may need the reassurance from the physician about the medication and how to use it on more than one occasion). Some antianxiety medications exacerbate depressed mood.

12. General Side Effects of Medication
    A. Physical and psychological dependence
    B. May escalate symptoms of depression
    C. Drowsiness
    D. Nausea/vomiting
    E. Orthostatic hypotension
    F. Dry mouth
    G. Blood dyscrasias—if there is easy bruising, sore throat, fever, malaise, or unusual bleeding, report these symptoms immediately to the physician

If the person reports having any side effects to the medication, consult the prescribing physician immediately and encourage the person to do the same. For individuals who suffer from an Anxiety Disorder, internal dialogue, interpretation of their experience, and feeling/belief that something negative is about to happen or will happen significantly affect their ability to effectively cope. Their cognitive distortions act, in part, as a set up for a self-fulfilling prophecy. That is what makes them difficult to treat. They believe that their fears have been validated by their experiences. However, it is actually their negative thinking and distorted beliefs that are keeping them stuck. If they can be supported to adhere to a program of cognitive-behavioral interventions, they are likely to experience a dramatic change in their level of distress. This requires a trusting therapeutic relationship so that the person feels confident of your support and knowledge.

One thing all anxiety disorders share is the behavioral and emotional manifestations of avoidance. These individuals experience thoughts, beliefs, and internal dialogue (self-talk), which perpetuates a cycle of emotional distress. The person wants to participate but experiences fears, cognitive distortions and emotional distress, which escalates and eventually leads to avoidance in order to escape the distress. In other words, their functional performance is compromised by their interpretation, distorted thoughts, and negative self-talk as it pertains to relational and environmental interaction.

CYCLE OF ANXIETY-PROVOKED EMOTIONAL DISTRESS

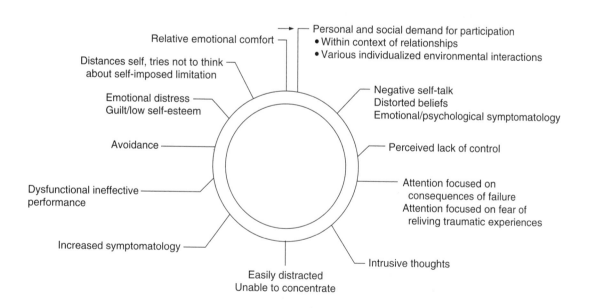

It is evident that unless cognitive-behavioral changes are made, the cycle of anxiety if self-perpetuating.

1. Functional impairment
    A. Sometimes a patient is more focused on the panic attacks themselves than on such issues as avoidance, which significantly impacts his/her daily life (these issues become of secondary importance)
    B. It is important to determine how the individual defines a desired/satisfactory outcome, which influences motivation/compliance
    C. If the defined quality of life is not at an adequate functioning level, the individual should be encouraged to be more realistic

2. Monitoring progress
    A. While there is often an initial positive response in the control of panic attacks, subthreshold panic attacks may continue necessitating further treatment
    B. The feat that attacks may occur in the future often continue when panic attacks cease
    C. It is not uncommon to experience a panic attack after a period of no panic attacks
        1. Predict this possibility for patients
        2. Use as a monitoring tool to rule out the resumption of a poor self-care routine (i.e., increased stress/expanded demands, no exercise, lack of sleep, lack of progressive muscle relaxation)
    D. Be aware of comorbid issues of depression and substance abuse
    E. Be alert to emergent depression

3. Improving treatment compliance
    A. The anxiety associated/produced by treatment may result in noncompliance
        1. Fear side effects of medication (therefore, fear of taking medication)
        2. Sensitive to somatic sensations
    B. Treatment must be sensitive, supportive, honest, reassuring, and, whenever possible, predictive of what to expect (to reinforce choice/control and to validate)

*Anxiety disorders demonstrate a higher than average rate of suicide attempts (Weissman et al., 1989).

TRAUMA RESPONSE

The sequential responses to trauma include the following stage: stressful event, outcry, denial, intrusion, working through, and resolution. Sometimes an individual will bypass the outcry stage and proceed from the traumatic event to denial. Corresponding to the stages of sequential responding are normal reactions or intensification/pathological reactions. Intensifications result when the normal reaction is unusually intense or prolonged.

1. Traumatic/Stressful Event
    A. Normal emotional response: anxiety, fear, sadness, distress

*If normal response is unusually intense or prolonged, the result is a pathological response.

    B. Pathological response: overwhelmed, confused, dazed

2. Outcry
   A. Normal emotional response: anxiety, guilt, anger, rage, shame, protest

*If normal response is unusually intense or prolonged, the result is a pathological response.

   B. Pathological response: panic, exhaustion, dissociative symptoms, psychotic symptoms

3. Denial
   A. Normal emotional response: minimizing, hypersomnia, anhedonia, depression, suppression, repression, obsession, fatigue/lethargy, denial

*If normal response is unusually intense or prolonged, the result is a pathological response.

   B. Pathological response: maladaptive avoidance, withdrawal, substance abuse, suicidality, fugue state, amnesia, rigid thinking, psychic numbing, sleep dysfunction, massive denial of initial trauma or current problems, somatization (headaches, fatigue, bowel problems/cramps, exacerbation of asthma, etc.)

4. Intrusion
   A. Normal emotional response: anxiety, somatosizing, decreased concentration and attention, insomnia, dysphoria
   B. Pathological response: flooded states, hypervigilance, exaggerated startle response, psuedohallucination, illusions, obsession, impaired concentration and attention, sleep/dream disturbance, emotional lability, preoccupation with the event, confusion, fight or flight activation (diarrhea, nausea, sweating, tremors, feelings of being on edge), compulsive reenactments of trauma, impaired functioning

5. Working through
   A. Normal emotional response: find meaning in experience, grieve, personal growth

*If working through is blocked, the result is a pathological response.

   B. Pathological response: frozen states or psychosomatic reaction, anxiety/depression syndromes

6. Resolution
   A. Normal response: return to pre-event level of functioning, psychological/personal growth/integration

*If not achieved the result is a pathological response.

   B. Pathological response: Inability to work/act/feel, personality change, generalized anxiety, dysthymia

Adapted from J.S. Maxmen and N.G. Ward (1995). Modified from M.J. Horowitz (1985).

SOMATOFORM DISORDERS

The central feature of this disorder is the presence of physical symptoms with a lack of demonstrable organic findings as a basis for the symptoms. With this circumstance, there is a strong presumption of a link to psychological factors or conflicts being translated into physical symptoms.

SOMATOFORM DISORDERS

Goals

1. Improve coping skills
2. Rule out cognitive deficits and educate
3. Increase awareness for relationship between emotional functioning and physical symptoms
4. Improve body image
5. Improve self-care
6. Decrease or eliminate perceptual disturbances
7. Improved self-esteem
8. Stress management

Treatment Focus and Objectives

1. Ineffective Coping
   A. Confront irrational beliefs. Consult with physician regarding treatment, lab test, and so on to rule out the possibility of an organic etiology
   B. Identify the extent of somatization
   C. Identify other impairments that may be manifesting as somatizations
   D. Recognize and validate that the symptoms are experienced as real by the person, but confront the associated cognitive distortion that may precipitate, exacerbate, or maintain the symptoms
   E. In the beginning, while developing the therapeutic relationship, gratify the person's dependency needs to develop trust and decrease possibility of symptom escalation
   F. Identify primary and secondary gains of symptomatology experienced by the person
   G. Utilize identified primary and secondary gains to facilitate appropriate problem solving with person
   H. Gradually decrease focus and time spent on physical symptoms to discourage pattern of dysfunctional behaviors. Set limits in a stepwise progression if necessary to decrease focus on symptomatology, and be consistent in not discussing physical symptoms
   I. Encourage venting of anxieties and fears
   J. Facilitate increased awareness and identification for the relationship between stress and symptoms development or symptom exacerbation
   K. Inform patient that development of any new symptoms should be relayed to physician to rule out organic etiology
   L. Identify ways to intervene in dysfunctional pattern of symptomatology in order to avoid resorting to physical symptoms as a coping mechanism
   M. Facilitate identification of how interpersonal relationships are affected by person's behavior
   N. Teach relaxation techniques
      1. Progressive muscle relaxation
      2. Visualization
      3. Meditation

O. Positive feedback and reinforcement for demonstrating effective, adaptive coping

2. Lack of Knowledge or Cognitive Deficits
    A. Evaluate person's knowledge of relationship between psychological functioning and physical functioning
    B. Encourage the person to keep a journal that focuses on psychological functioning (anxiety/stress/fears) to facilitate increased awareness and understanding of mind-body relationship
    C. Assess level of anxiety (which negatively affects learning) and motivation to learn
    D. Consult with physician regarding the results of treatment and tests. Explain to person the reason or purpose of all procedures and the results.
    E. Encourage venting of fears and anxiety
    F. Facilitate identification of primary and secondary gains so that person can understand dysfunctional attempts to get needs met and manipulative behaviors
    G. Identify methods in which the person can get needs met appropriately, such as assertive communication

3. Lack of Awareness for Relationship between Emotional Functioning and Physical Symptoms
    A. Consult with physician regarding treatment, lab test, and so on to rule out possibility of organic etiology
    B. Recognize and validate that the pain is experienced as real by the person
    C. Identify the factors that precipitate the pain
    D. Encourage the involvement in activities that help distract the person from symptoms
    E. Identify unresolved emotional and psychological issues
    F. Facilitate increased awareness and identification for relationship between anxiety and symptoms
    G. Identify alternative means of dealing with stress
    H. Identify ways of intervening to prevent escalation of symptoms, such as the following:
        1. Relaxation
        2. Guided imagery
        3. Breathing exercises
        4. Massage
        5. Physical exercise
    I. Positive feedback and reinforcement for demonstrating effective, adaptive coping

4. Body Image Disturbance
    A. Identify misconceptions and distortions in body image
    B. Decrease focus on distorted perception, as focus is increased on adaptive coping and positive self-care
    C. Facilitate grieving for feelings of loss if person has experienced bodily changes
    D. Facilitate self-care behaviors
    E. Encourage person to strengthen self-esteem
    F. Positive feedback and reinforcement

5. Ineffective Self-Care
    A. Consult with physician regarding disabilities and impairment, and collaborate in developing adequate and effective self-care behaviors

B. Encourage independent fulfillment of daily activities related to hygiene, grooming, and other self-care behaviors (have patient write out a chart of daily behaviors)

C. Be accepting of these individuals—the sympfoms that they experience are real to them. Assure them with information from the physician regarding their *abilities* and what activities they can safely participate in

D. Positive feedback and reinforcement

6. Sensory-Perceptual Disturbance
    A. Consult with physician regarding treatment, lab tests, and so on to rule out possibility of organic etiology. Perform regular mental status exam for ongoing assessment.
    B. Identify primary and secondary gains that symptoms provide for the person
    C. Facilitate the person following through on independent daily activities for self-care
    D. Decrease focus on disturbances, as support and focus is increased on effective, adaptive behaviors
    E. Set limits and be consistent regarding manipulation with disabilities
    F. Reinforce with reality testing
    G. Encourage venting of fears and anxiety
    H. Teach assertive communication to increase appropriate means of getting needs met
    I. Facilitate identification of effective coping tools for dealing with stressful situations
    J. Facilitate development and utilization of support system
    K. Positive feedback and reinforcement for efforts and accomplishments

7. Low Self-Esteem
    A. Facilitate identification of strengths
    B. Focus on efforts and accomplishments
    C. Teach and encourage assertive communication
    D. Replace negative thinking with positive self-talk
    E. Encourage taking responsibility for one's own choices and behaviors
    F. Positive feedback and reinforcement for efforts and accomplishments

8. Ineffective Stress Management
    A. Relaxation techniques
    B. Time management
    C. Self-care behaviors

*Certain medical conditions mimic somatization disorders and need to be ruled out. Examples of such medical disorders include those which present vague, multiple, and confusing symptoms.

1. Multiple sclerosis
2. Systemic lupus erythematusus
3. Porphyria
4. Hyperparathyroidism

Also, women represent the majority of Somatization-Disorder diagnosis. Be careful in assessment. Do not allow this information to serve as a bias leading to an incorrect diagnosis.

PSYCHOSOMATIC ILLNESS AND PERSONALITY DISORDER

The patient with psychosomatic illness that has an underlying personality disorder requires a sophisticated level of clinical expertise. Consider the following issues:

1. Psychosomatic symptoms associated with an underlying personality disorder present a significant challenge to the therapist. In this case, psychosomatic patients may demonstrate impulse-dominated modes of functioning utilizing defenses such as the following:
   A. Denial/splitting
   B. Magical thinking
   C. Feeling omnipotence
   D. Demands of perfection versus worthlessness (extremes)
   E. Displacement/projection/projective identification
   F. Masochistic perfectionism
   G. Fantasized parental relationships (i.e., conflict-free mother-child relationship)

2. Psychosomatic families demonstrate a parental psychosocial profile that can be reviewed for problem solving diagnostically and in the treatment planning approach. The acronym for this system review is PRISES:
   P perfectionism
   R repression of emotion
   I infantilizing decision making
   S organ system choice
   E exhibitionistic parental sexual/toilet activity
   S unconscious selection of the child
   A. Perfectionism-emphasis on the following:
      1. Good behavior
      2. Social conformity
      3. Exemplary childhood/adolescent developmental performance

*Results in indirect communication and separation attempts.

   B. Repression of emotions-caused by the following:
      1. Parental hypermorality (evidenced by)
         a. Strict emotional control in front of children
         b. Aggressive behavior of children not allowed (in general aggression denied)
         c. Downplay/maximizing of successes
         d. Mother deferred to as moral authority

*Rigid internalization of good/bad (without rational review and growth in belief system).

   C. Infantilizing decision-making control
      1. Everything had to represent a noble purpose
         a. Major home activity was intellectual discussion

     b. Scholarly reading

     c. Independent activity/assertiveness led to consequences of humiliation

*Resulting in inability to make decisions with attempts to get others (therapist) to make decisions for them.

  D. Organ-system choice

    1. Development of psychosomatic symptoms

      a. Ulcerative colitis

      b. Anorexia

      c. Asthma

      d. Headaches/migraines

      e. Skin diseases

  E. Exhibitionistic parental sexual/toilet behavior

    1. Significance denied (evidenced by)

      a. Lack of privacy (bathroom/bedroom doors unlocked/left open)

      b. Witnessing f parental intercourse

*Parental exhibitionism coupled with hypermorality and prudishness resulting in inhibition in normal sexual development.

  F. Selection of one child (unconscious selection)

    1. Treated differently than siblings

      a. Used as a confidant

      b. Infantialized (babied)

      c. Total devotion to selected child to the exclusion of spouse/siblings

*Lack of individuality, poor boundaries, and passive-aggressive traits.

Adapted from Wilson and Mintz (1989).

Othmer and DeSouza (1985) developed a brief screening test (mnemonic of Somatization Disorder Besets Ladies and Vexes Physicians) based on their research, which determined that the presence of any two out of seven specific symptoms accurately predicted the correct somatization disorder in 80–90% of screened cases. Their work was adapted by Maxmen and Ward (1995). Each word of the mnemonic is associated with a specific symptoms and organ system.

Somatization	Shortness of breath	Respiratory
Disorder	Dysmenorrhea	Female reproduction
Besets	Burning in sex organs	Psychosexual
Ladies	Jump in throat	Pseudoneurological
And	Amnesia	Pseudoneurological
Vexes	Vomiting	Gastrointestinal
Physicians	Painful extremities	Skeletal muscle

The following questions are used to assess the presence of seven symptoms in the screening test for somatization disorder.

S. Have you ever had trouble breathing?

D. Have you ever had frequent trouble with menstrual cramps?

B. Have you ever had burning sensations in your sexual organs, mouth, or rectum?

L. Have you ever had difficulties swallowing or had an uncomfortable lump in your throat that stayed with you for at least an hour?

A. Have you ever found that you could not remember what you had been doing for hours or for days at a time? (If yes, did this happen even though you had not been using any substances?)

V. Have you ever had trouble with frequent vomiting?

P. Have you ever had frequent pain in your fingers or toes?

If two or more of these seven questions are answered affirmatively, this screening is considered positive. A positive screen simply means that the individual might have a somatization disorder. To confirm the diagnosis, the individual will need to meet the *DSM-IV* criteria for somatization disorder.

INTERPRETING FUNCTIONAL PRESENTATION OF SYMPTOMOLOGY: MALINGERING, FACTITIOUS DISORDER, AND SOMATOFORM DISORDER

1. Malingering
   A. Physical symptoms intentional
   B. False of exaggerated symptoms
   C. Motivated by external incentives
      1. Avoidance driven (legitimate appearance of an excuse)
      2. Benefit driven (some gain associated with symptoms presentation)

*Partial malingering is a combination of definable organic pathology and unconscious psychopathology along with conscious exaggeration of symptoms. Goals include the following:
      a. Relief from work
      b. Relief from family responsibility
      c. Financial gain

2. Factitious disorder
   A. Physical/psychological symptoms intentional
   B. Goal is to assume patient role ("sick role")
      1. To obtain sympathy or be nurtured
      2. External/financial incentives are absent
   C. Does not preclude the coexistence of true physical/psychological symptoms

3. Somatoform disorder
   A. Physical symptoms not intentional
   B. No diagnosable medical condition to account for physical symptoms
      1. Conversion disorder
         a. Symptoms not intentionally produced
         b. Affect, voluntary motor or sensory
         c. Suggests neurological involvement
         d. Undelrying psychological/emotional functioning factors associated, including depression or anxiety manifested as psuedopsychological and symptoms that help resolve a personal conflict
         e. External/financial incentives absent (not financially motivated)

2. Somatization/pain disorder
   a. Chronic pain central focus (more than six months)
   b. Somatic symptoms are out of proportion to objective findings
   c. Psychological factors associated
   d. Characterized by depression, dysfunction, drugs, dependency, diagnostic dilemma, duration, and dramatization of symptoms
   e. Self-sustaining, self-reinforcing, and self-generating
   f. Pain behavior is maladaptive, resulting in despair, alienation from family and society, loss of job, isolation, invalidism, and suicidal ideation
   g. Financial gain rarely present
3. Hypochondriasis
   a. Excessive preoccupation with bodily sensations
   b. Preoccupation/fear of having a serious disease (despite assurances to the contrary)
   c. Misinterpretation of body symptoms

DISSOCIATIVE DISORDERS

The central feature of dissociative disorders is a disturbance in the integration of identity, memory, or consciousness. Selected mental contents are removed or dissociated from conscious experiences; however, they continue to produce motor or sensory effects. The disturbance may have a sudden or gradual onset and may be temporary or chronic in its course. Depending on the mode of disturbance (identity, memory, or consciousness), the individual's life experience is affected in different ways. Conceptually, the course of treatment is to improve coping, maintain reality, and establish normal integrative functions.

DISSOCIATIVE DISORDERS

Goals

1. Thought processes intact
2. Maintain a sense of reality
3. Improve coping skills
4. Stress management
5. Personality integration

Treatment Focus and Objectives

1. Altered Thought Processes
   A. In addition to assessing the person directly, gather information form family and significant others, which acts to broadly define the person (life, experiences, pleasurable activities, likes/dislikes, favorite music, places the person find relaxing, etc.)
   B. Expose person to positive past experiences and pleasurable activities
   C. Slowly elicit personal information from the person to prevent flooding, which could cause regression
   D. As person allows memories to surface, engage the person in activities to stimulate the forthcoming memories such as photographs, talking about a significant person from the past, and the role that various other people have played in the person's life
   E. Encourage the person to talk about situations that have posed significant stress
   F. Facilitate the person to verbalize stressful situations and to explore the feelings associated with those situations
   G. Facilitate increased awareness and understanding of all the factors that have contributed to the dissociative process

H. Facilitate identification of specific conflicts that are unresolved

I. Develop possible solution to the unresolved conflicts

J. Be supportive and offer positive feedback and reinforcement for the courage to work through these issues

2. Sensory/Perceptual Distortion

   A. Identify the nature, extent, and possible precipitants of the dissociative states

   B. Obtain a collaborative history of the nature and extent of the dissociative states from family/friends

   C. Educate the person regarding depersonalization experience, behaviors, and the purpose they generally serve for the person (or did serve originally)

   D. Be supportive and encouraging when the person is experiencing depersonalization

   E. Validate feelings of fear and anxiety related to depersonalization experience

   F. Educate the person regarding the relationship between severe anxiety and stress to the depersonalization experience

   G. Explore past experiences such as trauma and abuse

   H. Encourage the identification and working through of feelings associated with these situations

   I. Identify effective and adaptive responses to severe anxiety and stress

   J. Encourage practice of these new adaptive behaviors. This may be initiated through modeling and role-play.

   K. Facilitate the person's ability to separate past from present to more effectively cope with the traumatic memories and feelings

3. Ineffective Coping

   A. Be supportive and reassuring

   B. Identify situations that precipitate severe anxiety

   C. Facilitate appropriate problem-solving in order to intervene and prevent escalation of anxiety and to develop more adaptive coping in response to anxiety

   D. Explore feelings that the person experiences in response to stressful situations

   E. Consider using environmental manipulation to improve coping

   F. Whenever possible, encourage maintenance of some from of employment as long as possible

   G. Facilitate understanding that the emotion experienced is acceptable and often predictable in times of stress

   H. As the person develops improved coping abilities, encourage him/her to identify the underlying source(s) of chronic anxiety

   I. Encourage identification of past coping strategies and determine if the response was adaptive or maladaptive

   J. Develop a plan of action for effective, adaptive coping to predictable future stressors

   K. Explore with the person the benefits and consequences of alternative adaptive coping strategies

   L. Identify community resources that can be utilized to increase the person's support system as he/she makes efforts to effectively manage

   M. Facilitate identification of how the person's life has been affected by the trauma

   N. Offer positive feedback and reinforcement for efforts and accomplishments

4. Ineffective Stress Management

   A. Relaxation techniques

   B. Time management

   C. Self-care (exercise, nutrition, utilization of resources, etc.)

   D. Educate regarding role of negative self-talk

5. Identity Disturbance
   A. Develop a trusting therapeutic relationship. With a multiple personality, this means a trusting relationship with the original personality as well as the subpersonalities.
   B. Educate person about multiple personality disorder in order to increase his/her understanding of subpersonalities
   C. Facilitate identification of the need of each subpersonality, the role they have played in psychic survival
   D. Facilitate identification of the need that each subpersonality serves in the personal identity of the person
   E. Facilitate identification of the relationship between stress and personality change
   F. Facilitate identification of the stressful situations that precipitate a transition from one personality to another
   G. Decrease fear and defensiveness by facilitating subpersonalities to understand that integration will not lead to their destruction, but to a unified personality within the individual
   H. Facilitate understanding that therapy will be a long-term process, which is often arduous and difficult
   I. Be supportive and reassuring

SEXUAL DISORDERS

For the purpose of this text, the group for Sexual Disorders described as paraphilias are not considered. This discussion does consider the sexual dysfunctions characterized by inhibitions in sexual desire or the psychophysiologic changes associated with the sexual response cycle. Once the diagnosis and underlying factors have been identified, if the issues require more than counseling, problem solving life of relationship issues, or adjustment and resolution that do not alleviate the sexual dysfunction, it is then ethical and appropriate to refer to a certified sex therapist.

SEXUAL DISORDERS

Goals

1. Clarify origin of disorder
2. Make appropriate referrals (physician, certified sex therapist, etc.)
3. Create a baseline for monitoring change
4. Promote education and treatment of emotional and psychological problems

Treatment Focus and Objectives

1. Assess for Predisposing Factors
   A. Review current medications that person is taking. Chronic alcohol and cocaine use have been associated with sexual disorders. Prescription medications that have been implicated include antidepressants, anxiolytics, antipsychotics, anticonvulsants, antihypertensives, cholinergic blockers, and antihistamines.
   B. Assess psychosocial factors. These factors are wide ranging and encompass age of experiences, developmental implications, beliefs systems, interpersonal issues, trauma or pain, and cultural conditioning. These factors may include shame, guilt, fear, anxiety, depression, disgust, resentment, anger toward partner, stress, fatigue, fear of pregnancy, ambivalence, fear of commitment, disease phobia, childhood sexual assault/abuse, moralistic upbringing with negative messages about sexual contact and sexual organs or rigid religiosity, moral prohibition, or inhibition.

C. Consult with physician and refer for medical evaluation. Organic etiologies include the decreased estrogen levels associated with menopause, endometriosis, pelvic infections, tumors, cysts, penile infections, urinary tract infections, prostate problems, damage of irritation or the sexual organs, low levels of testosterone, diabetes, arteriosclerosis, temporal lobe epilepsy, multiple sclerosis, blood pressure, medication reactions, substance abuse, and Parkinson's disease. Pelvic surgery, genitourinary surgery, and spinal cord injuries may also be associated with sexual dysfunction.

2. Assess for Appropriate Referrals
   A. Refer to physician to rule out organic etiology
   B. Refer to other pertinent specialists such as a certified sex therapist if such expertise is needed

3. Establish Baseline Information of Sexual Dysfunction Experience
   A. Time frame associated with onset of dysfunction
   B. Persistent or recurrent (lifelong, acquired, generalized, situational, with or without masturbations, with or without partner, due to psychological or combined factors)
      1. Frequency
      2. Setting
      3. Duration
      4. Level of subjective distress
      5. Effects in other areas of function
   C. Does not occur exclusively during the course of another axis I disorder (major depression, substance abuse, etc.)
   D. Life situation/stress level
   E. Causes marked stress or self-esteem/interpersonal difficulty
   F. Clarify and interpret the dynamics of sexual dysfunction
   G. Work through the dynamics of sexual dysfunction
   H. Relationship issues
   I. Medical issues/medication
   J. Mood and emotion
   K. Misinformation or lack of knowledge
   L. Sexual history
   M. Belief system

4. Lack of Understanding Regarding Dysfunctional Sexual Issues
   A. Educate person regarding the potential for change in satisfaction through various interventions (medical, behavior, psychological)
   B. Identify emotional responses to sex and intimacy
   C. Explore how sensitive and caring the individual's partner is to the person's needs
   D. Determine whether the individual has ever experienced sex as pleasurable or experienced orgasm
   E. Identify the individual's goals, how to incorporate the partner in treatment, and invest the partner as a support and agent of change

ADJUSTMENT DISORDERS

The hallmark of this disorder is a maladaptive reaction to an identifiable stressor(s). The stressor may be single or multiple. The severity of the reaction cannot be extrapolated from the intensity of the stressor. Instead, the reaction is a function of the vulnerability and coping mechanisms of the individual.

ADJUSTMENT DISORDERS

Goals

1. Alleviate emotional, psychological, or behavioral distress
2. Improve coping skills
3. Improve problem-solving skills
4. Improve adjustment
5. Improve stress-management skills
6. Improve self-esteem
7. Improve social interaction
8. Develop social supports

Treatment Focus and Objectives

1. Mood Disturbance
   A. Educate regarding relationship between mood and adjusting
   B. Identify predisposition/history of emotional response to stressors
   C. Review methods of coping in similar situations
   D. Reduce stimuli to decrease agitation/anxiety
   E. Develop appropriate daily structure
   F. Identify precipitating factors that exacerbate mood disturbance
   G. Educate regarding importance of good nutrition
   H. Regular physical exercise to release tension and decrease fatigue
   I. Journal writing to vent thoughts and feelings and to clarify and facilitate problem solving

2. Ineffective Coping
   A. Encourage appropriate venting of thoughts and feelings
   B. Identify physical activities that provide for a healthy outlet for negative feelings
   C. Encourage independent functioning
   D. Facilitate identification of factors that person has some control over and initiate problem solving. Also identify factors that person has no control over and initiate letting go.
   E. Increase awareness for person's response to feelings of powerlessness (victim role, manipulation of others, helplessness, etc.)
   F. Positive feedback and reinforcement toward improved coping

3. Impaired Problem Solving
   A. Facilitate identification of the issues
   B. Facilitate development of alternative ways to manage or resolve issues
   C. Facilitate individual to take action, being aware of the consequences and alternative choices should they be necessary

4. Impaired Adjustment
   A. Have person describe his/her functioning prior to the change
   B. Have the person describe his/her "normal functioning"
   C. Encourage venting of thoughts and feelings associated with change or loss
   D. Encourage independent functioning
   E. Facilitate problem solving about how the person is going to incorporate the change or loss as a life experience

F. Identify problems associated with the change or loss

G. Utilize modeling and role playing to prepare person to follow through on dealing with difficult areas

H. Refer the person to appropriate community resources

5. Ineffective Stress Management

A. Teach relaxation techniques

1. Progressive muscle relaxation

2. Visual imagery/meditation

B. Self-care (exercise, nutrition, utilization of resources)

C. Educate regarding role of negative self-talk

6. Low Self-Esteem

A. Be accepting and nonjudgmental toward person

B. Facilitate identification of realistic expectations (goals) and limitations

C. Facilitate identification of person's assets/strengths

D. Facilitate identification of areas of desired change and develop a problem-solving framework that person can utilize in working toward those goals

E. Encourage and support the person in confronting areas of difficulty

F. Discourage repetition of negative thoughts

G. Encourage taking responsibility for choices and behaviors

H. Facilitate increased self-awareness

1. Journal writing

2. Exploration of thoughts and feelings

I. Facilitate self-acceptance

1. Identify personal beliefs and value system

2. Encourage objectivity and positive regard to the self versus rejecting. Educate the person about the impact of negative self-talk on self-esteem.

J. Focus on the positive; reframe failures as opportunities to learn

K. Positive feedback and reinforcement

7. Impaired Social Interaction

A. Facilitate increased awareness of behavioral responses in relationship and how others experience and interpret the individual's behavior

B. Identify ineffective and inappropriate attempt to get needs met, such as manipulative, angry, or exploitative behavior

C. Identify appropriate verbal and behavioral responses

D. Role-model and practice appropriate verbal and behavioral responses for a variety of anticipated situations

E. Utilize resources

F. Positive feedback and reinforcement for efforts and accomplishments

8. Lacks Social Support

A. Educate and support regarding the development of an appropriate and adequate support system

*The primary goal of treatment is to facilitate the patient in returning to the precrisis level of functioning. The secondary goal is to capitalize on the emotional turmoil of the crisis to change preexisting maladaptive patterns into more useful and self-satisfying ways of responding to the environment. Overall, therapy is supportive in nature, focusing on an individual's strengths in an effort to help individuals adapt and cope effectively with stressors.

Medication might be utilized as a short-term intervention in adjustment reaction when there is a clear target symptom, such as acute anxiety or insomnia, which might impede recovery or impair functioning if not treated.

IMPULSE CONTROL DISORDERS

The central feature of impulse control disorders is the failure to resist an impulse, drive, or temptation that is harmful to the person or to others. Even though there is an increasing sense of tension prior to the act, the act may or may not be premeditated. Additionally, there may or may not be an awareness for resistance to the impulse.

All impulse control disorders have the following pattern in common:

Failure to resist impulse→Increasing sense of tension/arousal
→Gratification/release→Regret/guilt

Goals

IMPULSE CONTROL DISORDERS

1. Eliminate danger to others
2. Eliminate danger to self
3. Improve coping skills
4. Improved stress-management skills
5. Improve self-esteem
6. Relapse prevention

Treatment Focus and Objectives

1. Risk for Violence Toward Others
   A. Reduce environmental stimuli
   B. Clarify positive regard toward the person, but stress that aggressive behaviors are unacceptable
   C. Remove all potentially dangerous objects
   D. Facilitate identification of the underlying source(s) of anger
   E. Remain calm when there is inappropriate behavior to support person in containing impulses
   F. Encourage use of physical exercise to relieve physical tension
   G. Facilitate recognition of warning signs of increasing tension
   I. Facilitate identification of choices
   J. Clarify the connection between behavior and consequences
   K. Positive feedback and reinforcement

2. Risk for Self-Destructive Behavior
   A. Assess
      1. Mental status
      2. History of self-destructive behaviors
      3. Recent crisis, loss
      4. Substance abuse
      5. Plan
      6. Means
      7. Quality of support system

B. Provide safe environment, and intervene to stop self-destructive behaviors (remove dangerous objects, monitor, etc; the person may require hospitalization)

C. Facilitate identification of environmental or emotional triggers associated with self-destructive impulse

D. Facilitate person to identify areas of desired change

E. Develop a plan for behavior modifications to reach goals of desired behavior change

F. Encourage appropriate venting of thoughts and feelings

G. Avoid focus and reinforcement of negative behaviors

H. Focus on efforts and accomplishments

I. Positive feedback and reinforcement

3. Ineffective Coping

A. Increase awareness and insight of their behaviors

B. Facilitate clarification of rules, values—right and wrong

C. Encourage the person to take responsibility

D. Confront denial related to behaviors/choices

E. Facilitate development of understanding the relationship of behaviors to consequences

F. Explore and clarify the person's desire and motivation to become a productive member of society

G. Clarify for person socially acceptable behaviors versus nonsocially acceptable behaviors

H. Facilitate increased sensitivity to others

I. Facilitate increased awareness for how others experience the person and how they interpret the person's behaviors

J. Clarify that it is the person but rather the person's behavior that is unacceptable

K. Facilitate increasing ability to delay gratification

L. Role-model and practice acceptable behaviors with the person over a range of situations

M. Positive feedback and reinforcement for efforts and accomplishments

4. Ineffective Stress Management

A. Teach relaxation techniques
   1. Progressive muscle relaxation
   2. Visual imagery/meditation

B. Self-care (exercise, nutrition, utilization of resources)

5. Low Self-Esteem

A. Focus on strengths and accomplishments

B. Avoid focus on past failures (unless utilized in a positive manner to facilitate hopefulness and the learning of new behaviors)

C. Identify areas of desired change and objectives to meet those goals

D. Encourage independent effort and accepting responsibility

E. Teach assertive communication and appropriate setting of limits and boundaries

F. Positive feedback and reinforcement for efforts and accomplishments

6. Relapse Prevention

A. Self-monitoring

B. Reframe regression issues as an opportunity for taking responsibility to follow the person's program for behavioral change

C. Journal writing to monitor progress and any other changes in behavior

D. Participation in community groups or utilization of other supportive resources

It is necessary to delineate separate characteristics and clarify commonality among the disorders of impulse control in order to determine the course of treatment. These individuals do not often present for treatment of their own volition. As per the *DSM-IV*, the most notable disorders of impulse control include the following:

1. Pathological gambling
   A. Parents tend to show a pattern of alcoholism/gambling
   B. They are unable to resist the impulse to gamble
   C. Gambling disrupts family/vocation/personal endeavors
   D. At least three of the following have occurred:
      1. Arrest for forgery/fraud
      2. Default on debt
      3. Interpersonal difficulties
      4. Borrowing money illegally
      5. Absenteeism
      6. Exploiting others for help

2. Kleptomania
   A. Pattern of being unable to resist the impulse to steal, even with items of no immediate use or monetary value
   B. Increasing sense of tension before acting
   C. No planning or assistance from others

3. Pyromania
   A. Pattern of behavior to resist impulse to set fires
   B. Increasing sense of tension before acting
   C. An experience of intense pleasure/release at time of committing the act
   D. No motivation such as political action/monetary gain involved

4. Intermittent explosive disorder (rare—more often used as an excuse for self-permission to behave badly)
   A. Several discrete episodes of extremely aggressive acts or destruction of property
   B. Act is grossly out of proportion to precipitating social or psychological stressors
   C. No impulsivity or aggressiveness between episodes
   D. No specific organic disorder associated (such as a brain tumor)

PSYCHOLOGICAL FACTORS AFFECTING PHYSICAL CONDITION

When initially assessing an individual, particularly if physical symptoms are present, note if there appears to be a significant relationship between the individual's coping mechanisms and the physical complaint(s). This information will be helpful in treatment planning if the primary care physician clarifies that there is not organic basis for the symptom presentation or that the physical symptoms are exacerbated by the individual's coping mechanisms.

PSYCHOLOGICAL FACTOR AFFECTING PHYSICAL CONDITION

Goals

1. Educate and increase awareness
2. Promote appropriate adjustment to changes

3. Improve coping skills

4. Improve stress-management skills

5. Improve self-esteem

1. Lack of Sufficient Information
   A. Consult with physician regarding tests that have been made and their results
   B. Explore feelings of fear and anxiety related to physical functioning. Unless contraindicated, the person should be given the information related to his/her state of health and treatment issues.
   C. Educate person regarding the mind-body connection. How they think, believe, and interpret things will have an impact on how they experience something.
   D. Encourage venting of thoughts and feelings
   E. Facilitate development of questions that the person can use with the physician to clarify his/her own understanding and to clarify with the physician if there is any symptomatology that would be important for the person to monitor and to report to the physician
   F. Recommend that the person keep a journal to vent thoughts and feelings, to clarify, and problem-solve issues. It may help the person identify dysfunctional patterns.
   G. Recommend that the person keep a daily log of appearance, duration, and density of physical symptoms
   H. Increase awareness and understanding for the relationship between emotional distress and exacerbation of symptomatology
   I. Facilitate identification of primary and secondary gains. The person must identify needs that are being met through sick role to develop more appropriate and effective methods for fulfilling these needs.
   J. Facilitate development of assertive communication so that the person can express self honestly and effectively
   K. Facilitate development of stress-management skills

2. Change in Self-Perception and Role Due to Physical Functioning
   A. Consult with physician to understand the extent of change in physical functioning, if the problem is progressive, or if there is expected progress to be made with return to prior level of functioning
      1. Necessary for appropriate treatment planning
   B. Encourage venting of thoughts and feelings associated with physical functioning
   C. Facilitate identification of stressors that negatively influence functioning
   D. Facilitate increased awareness for the relationship between physical symptoms and emotional functioning
   E. Facilitate identification of maladaptive responses
   F. Facilitate identification of family's response to the situation and its affect on the person
   G. Encourage family participation as necessary in treatment. Educate them regarding prognosis, identify dysfunctional patterns, and in enlisting their support
   H. Facilitate development of appropriate responses to situations
   I. Model and role-play appropriate responses with the person
   J. Facilitate identification of desired changes that the person would like to make
   K. Positive feedback and reinforcement for efforts and accomplishments

3. Ineffective Coping
   A. Consult with physician to obtain thorough picture of what the person has experienced and what the prognosis is

B. Facilitate identification of goals

C. Facilitate development of problem-solving skills

D. Encourage the person to take appropriate risks and challenge irrational thinking

E. Encourage the person to take responsibility by making decisions, following through, and being prepared with a contingency plan

F. Encourage venting of thoughts and feelings (such as powerlessness and lack of control, appearance, etc. associated with physical contion)

G. Facilitate identification of how the person can maintain a feeling of control

H. Facilitate increased awareness for the relationship between physical symptoms and emotional functioning

I. Facilitate increased awareness for learned behavior and secondary gains

J. Facilitate increased awareness for primary or secondary gains that may be present

K. Refer the person to appropriate community resources

L. Journal writing to increase awareness and self-monitor positive efforts

M. Positive feedback and reinforcement for efforts and accomplishments

4. Ineffective Stress Management

A. Teach relaxation techniques

1. Progressive muscle relaxation

2. Visual imagery/meditation

3. Deep breathing

B. Self-care (exercise, nutrition, utilization of resources)

C. Educate regarding the role of negative self-talk

5. Low Self-Esteem

A. Facilitate identification of realistic goals

B. Facilitate identification of strengths

C. Minimize focus on physical symptoms

D. Focus on strengths, positives, efforts, and accomplishments

E. Facilitate development of problem-solving skills

F. Facilitate identification of appropriate responses to variety of situations to increase feelings of ability and capability

G. Break down goals into manageable steps. If the person experiences difficulty, work with him/her to break down steps of change further. Prepare the person that this is an expected experience in behavior modification and that no step is too small.

H. Promote feelings of control by encouraging the person to participate in decision making regarding treatment planning

I. Positive feedback and reinforcement for efforts and accomplishments

PERSONALITY DISORDERS

A person may meet the criteria for more than one personality disorder. Additionally, there is an overlap in the diagnostic criteria of various personality disorders. Because a person suffering as Axis I crisis may demonstrate personality disorder features during the period of that crisis does not warrant the diagnosis of a personality disorder. A diagnosis of personality disorder is only given when enduring personality traits are inflexible and maladaptive and cause significant impairment in how the individual interacts with the environment.

Due to the nature of personality disorders (enduring and pervasive maladaptive behaviors), psychodynamic treatment, in conjunction with results-oriented brief therapy interventions and skills development, offers optimal results toward behavioral change.

AVOIDANT PERSONALITY DISORDER

Goals

1. Decrease resistance to beneficial intervention/change
2. Develop goals
3. Improve social interaction
4. Decrease avoidant behavior
5. Resolve issues of loss
6. Improve coping skills
7. Cognitive restructuring
8. Decrease sensitivity
9. Improve self-esteem

Treatment Focus and Objectives

1. Therapeutic Resistance
   A. Establish a trusting therapeutic relationship
   B. Do not engage the person in clinical issues too quickly
   C. Do not pressure the person with expectations

2. Lack of Goals
   A. Develop appropriate goals for personal growth and behavioral change

3. Impaired Social Interaction
   A. Facilitate identification of fears (rejection, etc.) and feeling that the environment is unsafe
   B. Educate regarding effect of anxiety in avoidant behavior
   C. Facilitate identification of realistic expectations regarding changes in avoidant behavior
   D. Develop a slow-paced stepwise progression of social interaction
   E. Facilitate identification of fear of rejection and hypersensitivity. Increase awareness of alternative ways of viewing the responses of others versus personalizing.
   F. Refer to group therapy to increase awareness for and practice dealing with hypersensitivity
   G. Facilitate small steps toward calculated risks for social/personal gratification
   H. Positive feedback and reinforcement for efforts and accomplishments

4. Avoidance of People and Situations
   A. Systematic desensitization/flooding
   B. Teach assertive communication
      1. Role-play and model effective, honest responses/behaviors
   C. Break down desired behavioral changes into manageable steps
   D. Be supportive, focusing on positives
   E. Positive feedback and reinforcement for efforts and accomplishments

5. Issues of Loss
   A. Facilitate identification of feelings of loneliness, being an outsider, and so forth
   B. Identify behaviors that contribute to isolation and aloneness
   C. Facilitate resolution of losses through venting of feelings, closure on issues where appropriate, problem solving, and behavioral changes

6. Ineffective Coping
   A. Establish a trusting relationship, reciprocating respect by keeping appointments, being honest, genuine, and so on within the therapeutic frame

B. Facilitate identification of feelings

C. Encourage appropriate ventilation of feelings

D. Explore alternatives for dealing with stressful situations instead of avoidance

E. Identify goals for desired changes, and break down each goal into manageable steps for shaping new behaviors

F. Educate regarding role of negative self-talk

G. Teach relaxation techniques
   1. Progressive muscle relaxation
   2. Visual imagery/meditation
   3. Time management

H. Positive feedback and reinforcement for efforts and accomplishments

7. Distorted Beliefs

A. Challenge irrational thoughts, statements, and attributions

B. Reframe beliefs and situations to provide rational, believable alternatives

C. Paradoxical interventions
   1. Prescribing avoidant behaviors. This intervention can sometimes be used to slow down avoidant responding by circumscribing and limiting avoidant patterns of behavior by assigning specific avoidant behaviors.
   2. Prescribing rejections. To fulfill this intervention, seek situations that are predictable and under control.

8. Overly Sensitive

A. Facilitate increased awareness for acute sensitivity
   1. Difficult for the person to benefit from the feedback from others because it is viewed as criticism and disapproval
   2. Interferes with others feeling comfortable with being honest with the person, fearing the person's negative response

B. Role-play social situations to decrease fear/anxiety

C. Initiate person to speak honestly about themselves

D. Explore issues of self-acceptance

E. Refer to group therapy to facilitate increased awareness for acute sensitivity and desensitization

9. Low Self-Esteem

A. Be accepting and respectful to person

B. Identify and focus on strengths and accomplishments

C. Facilitate self-monitoring of efforts toward desired goals

D. Facilitate development of assertive communication

E. Encourage and positively reinforce efforts and accomplishments

These individuals want affection, but not as much as they fear rejection. The slightest disapproval or critique is misconstrued as derogatory. They may ingratiate themself to others in an effort to prevent rejection. A friendly, gentle and reassuring approach is essential in developing a beneficial therapeutic relationship with someone who is hypersensitive to potential rejection and has low self-esteem.

COMPULSIVE PERSONALITY DISORDER

Goals

1. Assess for referrals

2. Develop goals

3. Decrease perfectionism

4. Decrease ritual behaviors

5. Decrease obsessive, ruminative thoughts

6. Increase functional, constructive behavior

7. Improve communication skills

8. Improve self-esteem

Treatment Focus and Objectives

1. Assess Regarding Appropriate Referrals
   A. For medication evaluation
   B. OCD group or other appropriate community resources (for developing increased awareness for maladaptive coping mechanisms and for reinforcing of positive efforts and change)

2. Lack of Goals
   A. Facilitate development of appropriate goals for personal growth and behavioral change
   B. Facilitate understanding and acceptance that therapy can be a long, slow process when dealing with such issues. Avoid power struggles. These individuals can be highly resistant to change and have difficulty dealing with issues of power and authority.

3. Perfectionism
   A. Facilitate identification of feelings and tendency to minimize feelings
   B. Facilitate venting of feelings
   C. Explore issues of control and frustration associated with perfectionism

4. Compulsive Rituals
   A. Identify the nature and extent of compulsions
   B. Identify the internal and external triggers for compulstions
   C. Facilitate the individual in learning to interrupt the compulsions and to substitute with appropriate behavior
   D. Identify the dynamic of the compulsions
   E. Work through the dynamics of the compulsions
   F. Systematic desensitization of increase tolerance for associated anxiety
   G. Explore unacceptable thoughts and intense feelings that are not expressed
   H. Explore fear associated with expression of feelings and thoughts
   I. Facilitate use of behavioral journal
      1. To develop baseline
      2. To develop a reasonable program for decreasing the frequency of ritual behaviors
      3. Reinforce focus on positives and accomplishments

5. Obsessive Ruminations
   A. Identify the nature and extent of obsessions
   B. Identify the internal and external triggers for obsessions
   C. Facilitate the individual in learning to interrupt the obsessions and substitute with rational thinking
   D. Identify the dynamics of the obsessions
   E. Work through dynamics of the obsessions
   F. Encourage decision making
   G. Confront irrational thinking with reality
   H. Facilitate rational, positive self-talk

I. Facilitate the use of rhought stopping

J. Encourage making of choice of distract self from ruminative thoughts by utilizing physical activity or other activities.

K. Explore relationship of the obsessive thoughts and compulsive behaviors

L. Maintain focus of treatment on the person's feelings (because these individuals tend to intellectually defend against threatening feelings)

6. Ineffective Use of Time

A. Facilitate increased awareness for how obsessions and compulsions interfere in normal daily functioning

1. Facilitate identification of losses, activities the person does not have time to participate in or fears that prevent participation in otherwise desirable activities

2. Develop daily structure of activities

3. Person to make support system aware of his/her goals and how the support system can help in efforts toward change

4. Capitalize on positive affect experienced when the person breaks the OCD and pattern such as improved self-esteem, enjoyment of life, and feelings of control over his/her life

7. Ineffective Communication

A. Teach assertive communication

B. Teach anger management

C. Role-play and rehearse, problem-solving appropriate responses to a variety of situations

D. Learn to say no, avoid manipulation, set limits and boundaries

E. Positive feedback and reinforcement for efforts and accomplishments

8. Low Self-Esteem

A. Identify realistic goals, expectations, and limitations

B. Identify factors that negatively affect self-esteem

C. Overcome negative feelings toward the self

D. Assertive communication

E. Positive self-talk and affirmations

F. Identify feelings that have been ignored or denied

C. Focus on efforts and accomplishments

H. Positive feedback and reinforcement for efforts and accomplishments

Compulsives are a difficult population to treat. Their obsessiveness can paralyze attempts of clinical progress. They often want complete explanations of what will happen during the evaluation and course of treatment. Additionally, they often lack insight to initiate change because their thinking is highly concrete. Progress is measured in terms of behavioral change.

DEPENDENT PERSONALITY DISORDER

Goals

1. Increase independent beahvior

2. Develop goals

3. Improve decision-making skills

4. Improve communication skills

5. Improve stress-management skills

6. Promote cognitive restructuring

7. Decrease sensitivity

8. Improve self-esteem

Treatment Focus and Objectives

1. Dependent behavior
   A. Be careful to not push person before the person is ready for change
   B. Identify fears associated with independent behaviors
   C. Identify how dependent behaviors limit the person in getting needs met and/or participating in chosen interests
   D. Identify how dependent behaviors communicate a mixed or incorrect message to others
   E. Facilitate identification of own competence and self-worth
   F. Clarify that seeking autonomy will not be harmful to others

2. Lack of Goals
   A. Facilitate development of appropriate goals for personal growth and behavioral change

3. Difficulty Making Decisions
   A. Teach decision-making skills
   B. Teach problem-solving skills
   C. Facilitate decrease in self-critical behavior/internal dialogue (self-talk)

4. Ineffective Communication
   A. Teach assertive communication
   B. Role-play and model assertive communication
   C. Positive feedback and reinforcement for efforts and accomplishments

5. Ineffective Stress Management
   A. Expose the person to anxiety-provoking situations
   B. Develop situations that program person for success in accomplishing simple tasks that normally elicit stress/anxiety
   C. Educate regarding the influence on negative self-talk on stress
   D. Facilitate development of positive self-talk
   E. Educate the person regarding the stages of relations, which include loss and how to cope with it
   F. Facilitate identification of persons' fear of being alone
      1. Problem-solve constructive time along for brief periods
      2. Positive feedback and reinforcement for efforts and accomplishments
      3. Identify irrational thinking behind fear of being alone
   G. Teach relaxation techniques
      1. Progressive muscle relaxation
      2. Visual imagery/meditation
      3. Time management

6. Distorted Thinking
   A. Challenge irrational beliefs, and offer plausible substitute statement
   B. Facilitate clarification when the information communicated appears distorted
   C. Reframe situations previously viewed as negative as an opportunity for change and growth when appropriate
   D. Facilitate person's clarification of rational versus irrational thinking
   E. Reinforce reality-based thinking

7. Overly Sensitive
    A. Facilitate increased awareness for difficulty that the person has accepting feedback from others and in viewing it as critical or disapproving
    B. Increase understanding for the effect of being overly sensitive in the context of a relationship and how it limits honest communication
    C. Facilitate identification of fear of abandonment and how this fear affects person and how they relate to others

8. Low Self-Esteem
    A. Identify and focus on positives and accomplishments
    B. Identify goals and break them down into manageable steps so that the person can see progress and feel positive about it
    C. Facilitate development of assertive communication
    D. Positive feedback and reinforcement for efforts and accomplishments
    E. Facilitate identification of the person's own competence and self-worth

It is not unusual for individuals with Dependent Personality Disorder to call their therapist constantly clarifying appointments and asking advice or seeking guidance. Clear limits established at the onset of treatment regarding the regularity of appointments and therapist availability are necessary.

PASSIVE-AGGRESSIVE PERSONALITY DISORDER

Goals

1. Decrease procrastination
2. Develop goals
3. Cognitive restructuring
4. Increase positive emotional/behavioral responding
5. Improve social skills
6. Improve self-esteem
7. Effective communication

Treatment Focus and Objectives

1. Procrastination
    A. Facilitate identification of dysfunctional behavioral patterns (e.g., works slow, complains, forgets, pessimistic)
    B. Facilitate improved time management
        1. Increase awareness and productivity. These individuals often do not reach goals because of self-defeating behavior.
    C. Increase awareness for frequent power struggles with authority figures

2. Lack of Goals
    A. Facilitate development of appropriate goals for personal growth and behavioral change

3. Distorted Thinking and Beliefs
    A. Identify thinking/beliefs that interfere with the person taking responsibility for his/her behavior
    B. Identify, clarify, and interpret the dynamics of the passive-aggressive behavior
    C. Work through the dynamics of passive-aggressive behavior
    D. Identify blaming (the problem lies with someone else)

E. Encourage the person to keep a journal
1. To clarify irrational logic and dysfunctional responding
2. To clarify possibility of unrealistic expectations
F. Positive reinforcement and feedback for efforts and accomplishments

4. Negative Emotional and Behavioral Responses
   A. Facilitate increased awareness for negative responding associated with situations that the person does not like (acting out)
   1. Identify efforts of manipulation and avoidance
   2. Facilitate drawing out of covert aggression
   B. Confront veiled threats and efforts of manipulation and direct them back to the person in terms of what he/she has to gain by such actions
   C. Educate regarding how limiting such behavior is
   D. Facilitate problem solving for rational, appropriate responses to various situations that will improve relationships for the person and allow him/her to feel good
   E. Facilitate increased awareness and understanding for how such responding affects self-esteem
   F. Positive feedback and reinforcement for efforts and accomplishments

5. Ineffective Social Skills
   A. Social skills training
   1. Role-play appropriate and cooperative behaviors
   B. Explore the use of manipulative behavior or other means that the person uses to get what he/she wants
   C. Facilitate acknowledgement that behavioral problems negatively affect one's social interaction and the outcome
   D. Teach assertive communication
   E. Facilitate increased awareness for how negative responding has limited developing mature, appropriate responses
   F. Positive feedback and reinforcement for efforts and accomplishments

6. Low Self-Esteem
   A. Be accepting and respectful to the person
   B. Identify strengths and focus on accomplishment
   1. Facilitate recognition of the sense of relief associated with completed tasks, and point out how much more positive things will proceed for the person in his/her environment with increased cooperation
   C. Facilitate self-monitoring toward desired goals with a focus on the positives
   D. Facilitate the development of assertive communication
   E. Positive feedback and reinforcement for efforts and accomplishments

7. Ineffective Communication
   A. Teach assertive communication
   B. Role-play and model appropriate communication
   C. Positive feedback and reinforcement for efforts and accomplishments

PARANOID PERSONALITY DISORDER

Goals

1. Decrease treatment resistance
2. Develop goals
3. Decrease paranoid thinking
4. Improve social skills

5. Manage anger

6. Decrease fear with supportive therapeutic relationship

7. Improve self-esteem

Treatment Focus and Objectives

1. Treatment Resistance
    A. Develop a trusting therapeutic relationship
    B. Explain purpose for a cooperative effort

2. Lack of Goals
    A. Facilitate development of appropriate goals for personal growth and behavioral change

3. Distorted Paranoid Thinking
    A. Identify the nature and extent of paranoia
    B. Facilitate the individual's development of awareness for the presence of paranoia
    C. Explore thoughts and feelings
        1. Identify that person expects to be used or exploited
        2. Identify personal impact/losses for being unable to trust
        3. Identify that the person is always looking for hidden meaning/conspiracy
    D. Be careful to avoid any ambiguity in communication with this person
    E. Medication compliance
        1. Suspiciousness. Encourage the person to ask questions and read literature on medication
        2. Prepare the person for the various side effects that he/she may experience
    F. Facilitate increased awareness for inability to relax. Work with person to develop plausible alternatives for relaxing (and clarify benefit).

4. Ineffective Social Skills
    A. Determine range of paranoid thinking (i.e., within normal limits—paranoid)
    B. Educate and role-play regarding appropriate limits and boundaries within various relationships
    C. Educate regarding appropriate level of disclosure in various relationships
    D. Problem-solve with person about how to deal with paranoid thinking in a social context
    E. Facilitate increased awareness for restricted affect
    F. Positive feedback and reinforcement for efforts and accomplishments

5. Underlying Anger
    A. Encourage venting of underlying anger/jealousy
    B. Validate feelings of anger/jealousy
    C. Increase person's awareness for role he/she plays in situation's and support his/her in taking responsibility for that behavior
    D. Facilitate person recognizing that withholding of anger is not in his/her best interest
        1. Teach anger management
        2. Role-play the appropriate expression of feelings
        3. Teach other constructive methods for dealing with anger and frustration (exercising, finding a trustworthy person to vent to, journal writing with a problem-solving component)
    E. Positive feedback and reinforcement for efforts and accomplishments

6. Fear and Lack of Support
    A. Supportive psychotherapy
    B. Be clear, respectful, hones, open

C. Challenge denial and projection in a supportive manner

D. Empathize with the person's difficult life experience, while encouraging him/her to take responsibility

E. Facilitate increased awareness for relationship ambivalence

F. Facilitate increased awareness for the projection of the person's own unacceptable thoughts

G. Facilitate increased awareness of how the person's distorted perspective interferes in his/her life

H. Facilitate increased awareness for overinvolvement in fantasy and private belief system

I. Through problem solving with person, develop minimally threatening situations for practice and programmed success

J. Positive feedback and reinforcement for efforts and accomplishments

7. Low Self-Esteem

A. Be accepting and respectful to the person

B. Identify and focus on strengths and accomplishments

C. Facilitate self-monitoring efforts toward desired goals

D. Positive feedback and reinforcement for efforts and accomplishments

These individuals rarely present for treatment on their own simply because they do not perceive weakness or faults in themselves. They tend to be guarded in sharing personal information. The central goal of treatment is to minimize the distrust of the therapist and the therapy process. With regard to almost all issues, the paranoid expects the worst but feels assured in being given all the details beforehand. Therefore, it is imperative to give adequately detailed and accurate information.

SCHIZOTYPAL PERSONALITY DISORDER

Goals

1. Decrease treatment resistance

2. Develop goals

3. Improve social skills

4. Decrease isolation

5. Improve communication skills

6. Improve self-esteem

Treatment Focus and Objectives

1. Treatment Resistance

A. Explain purpose of therapy intervention

B. Explain that the person is at risk for premature termination from therapy because of difficulty trusting the therapist and others

C. Assess disordered thinking

2. Lack of Goals

A. Identify what the person wants and needs

B. Develop and utilize resources that support efforts toward identified goals

C. Positive feedback and reinforcement for efforts and accomplishments

3. Ineffective Social Skills

A. Facilitate increased awareness for overinvolvement in fantasy and private belief system

B. Increase awareness for odd and eccentric behavior

C. Increase awareness for how others experience the person

D. Role-play various social situations to demonstrate appropriate and effective responses

E. Positive feedback and reinforcement for efforts and accomplishments

4. Social Isolation

A. Problem-solve ways to decrease isolation with a minimal amount of distress

B. Participation in regular activities to facilitate development of comfort level with familiarity

5. Ineffective Communication

A. Teach assertive communication

B. Role-play and model assertive communication

C. Refer to appropriate group or other social interaction to provide opportunity for practice

D. Positive feedback and reinforcement for efforts and accomplishments

6. Low Self-Esteem

A. Identify and focus on strengths and accomplishments

B. Facilitate development of assertive communication

C. Identify goals and break them down into manageable steps for programmed success

D. Positive feedback and reinforcement for efforts and accomplishments

Schizophrenia should always be considered in those under the age of 35. If there is a clear diagnosis, continue to monitor for decompensation

1. They may become transiently psychotic under stress

2. The condition may evolve into schizophrenia

3. They may develop fanatic beliefs

Medication (antipsychotics) may be beneficial in alleviating some of the intense anxiety and cognitive symptoms (such as odd speech and unusual perceptual experiences). Therefore, consider the referral for a medication evaluation.

SCHIZOID PERSONALITY DISORDER

Goals

1. Decrease treatment resistance
2. Develop goals
3. Improve social interaction
4. Decrease social isolation
5. Improve communication skills
6. Improve self-esteem

Treatment Focus and Objectives

1. Treatment Resistance

A. Explain purpose of therapy

B. Encourage the person to discuss mixed feelings about participating in therapy

2. Lack of Goals

A. Facilitate development of appropriate goals

B. Assess disordered thinking

3. Ineffective Social Interaction
   A. Increase awareness for how others experience the person (cold, detached)
   B. Role-play appropriate and effective responses for various social situations
   C. Facilitate increased awareness for emotional experience in relating to others
   D. Facilitate identification for consequences of cold, aloof responding to others
   E. Positive feedback and reinforcement for efforts and accomplishments

4. Social Isolation
   A. Facilitate identification of the person's experience
   B. Facilitate development of goals. They must be realistic and broken down into manageable steps.
   C. Communicate respect for the person's need for privacy

5. Ineffective Communication
   A. Teach assertive communication
   B. Role-play and model assertive communication
   C. Positive feedback and reinforcement for efforts and accomplishments

6. Low Self-Esteem
   A. Identify and focus on strengths and accomplishments
   B. Facilitate development of assertive communication
   C. Positive feedback and reinforcement for efforts and accomplishments

Because social isolation is such a prominent feature with this disorder, these individuals are not likely to seek treatment. Most schizoids would lack both the bright and the motivation for therapy and likely experience the intioning of therapy as too threatening.

HISTRIONIC PERSONALITY DISORDER

Goals

1. Goal development
2. Appropriate affect and expression of emotion
3. Appropriate social behavior
4. Appropriate emphasis on appearance
5. Improve communication skills
6. Improve self-esteem

Treatment Focus and Objectives

1. Lack of Goals
   A. Facilitate development of appropriate goals
   B. Refer to appropriate group to facilitate clarification of goals as well as efforts toward progress

2. Inappropriate Affect
   A. Facilitate increased awareness for exaggerated emotional display
   B. Facilitate increased awareness for seductive behavior
   C. Explore need for attention and excitement
   D. Facilitate increased awareness for how emotional over-reaction affects his/her relationships
   E. Encourage anger management
   F. Promote clarification of feelings and appropriate, congruent expression
   G. Encourage person to take responsibility for the consequences of his/her actions
   H. Positive feedback and reinforcement for efforts and accomplishments

3. Dramatized Social Interaction
   A. Facilitate increased awareness for inappropriate social responding and the effect that it has on others in the person's relationships
   B. Role-play appropriate responses to various social situations
   C. Facilitate identification of particular areas of difficulty the person experiences in expressing himself/herself (e.g., how does the person respond when he/she feels ignored)
   D. Increase awareness for manipulative behavior
   E. Be supportive and empathic toward person's emotional/social difficulties
   F. Positive feedback and reinforcement for efforts and accomplishments
   G. Increase awareness and improve accuracy in self-image (inflated/distorted)
   H. Address provocative attention-seeking behavior

4. Overemphasis on Appearance
   A. Facilitate identification of distorted beliefs and overinvestment in appearance
   B. Increased awareness and understanding of lack of congruence between looking good on the outside and internal emptiness/lack of fulfillment
   C. Facilitate identification of fears associated with aging, which will affect appearance
   D. Facilitate identification on lack of development of internal resources because the person's energy is consistently used to "look good," whether by physical appearance or by collecting things
   E. Facilitate increased awareness for self-centered actions to gain immediate satisfaction
   F. Positive feedback and reinforcement for efforts and accomplishments

5. Ineffective Communication
   A. Teach assertive communication
   B. Encourage the person to keep a journal to increase awareness for honesty, self-centeredness, and tendency toward shallowness
   C. Role-play and model appropriate, assertive communication
   D. Facilitate increased understanding for shifting emotions, inappropriate exaggerations, and the need to be the center of attention, which are communicated to others. Explore the impact that this has on the person getting needs met and having fulfilling relationships.
   E. Positive feedback and reinforcement for efforts and accomplishments

6. Low Self-Esteem
   A. Identify and focus on strengths and accomplishments
   B. Facilitate the development of goals
   C. Facilitate self-monitoring of efforts toward desired goals
   D. Facilitate the development of assertive communication
   E. Positive feedback and reinforcement for efforts and accomplishments

Since histrionics think in terms of impression not fact, trying to get detailed information during the interview process becomes an arduous task.

NARCISSISTIC PERSONALITY DISORDER

Goals

1. Develop goals
2. Increase sensitivity toward others
3. Improve problem-solving skills
4. Increase self-awareness
5. Improve self-esteem

1. Lack of Goals for Personal Growth and Development
   A. Facilitate development of appropriate goals
   B. Break down goals into reasonable steps
   C. Identify and problem-solve factors that previously inhibited reaching goals
   D. Develop realistic expectations and limitations (these individuals often feel inadequate and helpless when they fail to meet unrealistic goals)
   E. Positive feedback and reinforcement for efforts and accomplishments

2. Lack of Sensitivity Toward Others
   A. Encourage the person to put himself/herself in the place of others to increase understanding
   B. Encourage the person to appropriately express how he/she feels when people are insensitive to the person's needs
   C. Positive feedback and reinforcement for efforts and accomplishments

3. Ineffective Problem Solving
   A. Teach problem-solving skills
   B. Develop sample problems to practice new skills on
   C. Facilitate increased awareness of how feelings of entitlement interfere with appropriate, effective problem solving
   D. Identify secondary gains that inhibit progress toward change
   E. Improve coping by increasing awareness for the power struggle between the person's intense need to be admired by an individual he/she views as important and, at the same time, feeling rage at being disappointed by that person

4. Lacks Self-Awareness
   A. Encourage journal writing to identify thoughts, feelings, and behaviors
   B. Encourage honest self-evaluations
   C. Facilitate increased awareness for how these individuals' constant seeking of love, admiration, and attention from others impedes them taking responsibility for themselves and learning to fill their sense of emptiness on their own
   D. Facilitate insight into feelings of inadequacy and vulnerability

5. Low Self-Esteem
   A. Identify and focus on strengths and accomplishments
   B. Facilitate self-monitoring of efforts toward desired goals
   C. Facilitate development of assertive communication
   D. Facilitate development, and support maintenance of realistic concept of the individual's own self-worth
   E. Positive feedback and reinforcement for efforts and accomplishments

If this individual presents for treatment, it is not likely associated with insight about the need for taking responsibility and making necessary changes. Instead, it is likely due to depression, pressure from a partner, adjustment/loss, or is associated with a medical condition. When a therapist exposes these individuals' issues of grandiosity/self-importance, it should be done in a gentle way with guidance into a proper perspective. Otherwise it will illicit strong resentment. Their self-centeredness is a shield of protection that when fractured exposes insecurity.

BORDERLINE PERSONALITY DISORDER

1. Goal development
2. Appropriate expression of emotions

3. Increase awareness for intensity in relationships
4. Decrease self-destructive behaviors
5. Decrease manipulative behavior
6. Clarify boundaries
7. Improve communication
8. Improve self-esteem

Treatment Focus and Objectives

1. Lack of Goals
   A. Facilitate development of appropriate goals for personal growth and behavioral change
   B. Facilitate development of realistic expectations and limitations

2. Inappropriate Expression of Emotions
   A. Facilitate increased awareness for inappropriate, exaggerated expression of emotions (emotional instability)
   B. Facilitate increased awareness for how inappropriate emotional expression impacts relationships
   C. Facilitate increased awareness for how inappropriate emotional expression impacts person getting their needs met
   D. Facilitate increased awareness for how inappropriate emotional expression impacts self-esteem
   E. Positive feedback and reinforcement for efforts and accomplishments

3. Inappropriate Behavior and Lack of Awareness
   A. Facilitate increased awareness regarding appropriate behavior
   B. Facilitate increased awareness for how inappropriate behavior impacts relationships
   C. Facilitate increased awareness for how inappropriate behavior interferes with getting needs met
   D. Facilitate increased awareness for how inappropriate behavior impacts self-esteem
   E. Role play and model appropriate behavioral responses
   F. Positive feedback and reinforcement for efforts and accomplishments

4. Self-Destructive Behavior
   A. Facilitate increased awareness for pattern of being easily overwhelmed by anger and frustration which often results in impulsive, manipulative and/or self-destructive behavior
      1. Anger management
      2. Encourage appropriate expression of feelings and thoughts
   B. Self-Mutilation
      1. Identify the nature and extent of self-mutilating behavior
      2. Assess the seriousness of the behavior(s) and provide a safe environment when necessary
      3. Clarify and interpret the dynamics of the behavior
      4. Work through the dynamics of self-mutilation
      5. Encourage venting of thoughts and feelings associated with the behavior
      6. Facilitate development of appropriate alternatives for dealing with unpleasant affective states that precipitate self-mutilation behavior
   C. Facilitate development of appropriate communication
   D. Facilitate clarification of wants and needs and how to appropriately get them met
   E. Clarify wants and needs to be met by the individual versus those to be met in a relationship

F. Develop appropriate alternatives of behavioral responses

G. Facilitate recognition of how self-defeating and self-destructive behaviors keep person from getting their needs met

H. Facilitate increased awareness and understanding of the underlying meaning of self-destructive behaviors

I. Positive feedback and reinforcement for efforts and accomplishments

5. Manipulative Behavior

A. Increase awareness of use of manipulative behavior

B. Increase awareness for goal behind manipulative behavior and the positives and negatives associated with it

C. Facilitate awareness of benefits associated with eliminating manipulative behavior

D. Role play and model appropriate and inappropriate behaviors for clarification and to broaden repertoire of appropriate behaviors

E. Positive feedback and reinforcement for efforts and accomplishments

6. Lack of Appropriate Boundaries

A. Facilitate increased awareness for person's lack of boundaries

B. Facilitate increased awareness of relationship difficulties associated with lack of boundaries

C. Facilitate increased awareness for fear of abandonment and role this plays in poor boundaries, as well as other inappropriate behaviors and inappropriate expression of emotion (all issues of appropriate boundaries in interpersonal interaction)

D. Facilitate increased awareness for self-defeating relationship difficulties such as:
   1. Unstable and intense relating
   2. Idealization and devaluation
   3. Manipulation

7. Ineffective Communication

A. Teach assertive communication

B. Facilitate awareness for inappropriate behaviors and verbal expressions as ineffective attempts to communicate

C. Identify feelings behind inappropriate behavioral and emotional expressions and facilitate problem solving with person for appropriate changes to accomplish their goal

D. Role play and model assertive communication

E. Positive feedback and reinforcement for efforts and accomplishments

8. Low Self-Esteem

A. Identify and focus on strengths and accomplishments

B. Facilitate self-monitoring of efforts toward desired goals

C. Facilitate development of appropriate behavior and verbal communication

D. Positive feedback and reinforcement for efforts and accomplishments

This disorder tends to run in families and has a high rate of association to mood disorders. A majority of borderlines have a history of physical, sexual, or emotional abuse by their caregivers who at times were also adequate in their care and were even nurturing. The result is loving and hating the caregiver in a vacillating manner (all good or all bad).

While splitting may be a normal and healthy defense in 18- to 36-month-old toddlers, when the mind is able to handle greater complexity, developmental adjustment facilitates the good, bad dichotomy diversity and is recognized and managed in the ambiguous shades of gray in which good and bad exist. Borderlines do not accomplish this developmental adjustment.

PHYSICAL FACTORS AFFECTING PSYCHOLOGICAL FUNCTIONING

The following is an example of how a person's emotional and psychological functioning are affected by a health issue.

1. Vignette

   An individual is referred for therapy by the person's primary care physician. While the person has been experiencing various symptoms for some time, the individual has recently been diagnosed with multiple sclerosis (MS). For some, a diagnosis of MS being presented months or even years after the onset of symptoms is a relief from the standpoint that the person now knows what is wrong. For others, this diagnosis is a terrible shock.

2. Symptoms of MS possibly experienced prior to diagnosis
   A. Weakness
   B. Fatigue
   C. Low self-worth (associated with the decreased productivity from fatigue)
   D. Depression
   E. Impaired memory
   F. Difficulty concentrating

3. Common reactions to being given the diagnosis of a chronic illness
   A. Disbelief
   B. Fear
   C. Anger
   D. Depression
   E. Guilt
   F. Fear of losing control over one's life
   G. Grieving (Grieving losses in functioning as part of adjustment)
   H. Denial

4. Central emotional crisis issues associated with a medical crisis
   A. Control
   B. Self-image
   C. Dependency
   D. Stigma
   E. Abandonment/rejection
   F. Anger
   G. Isolation/withdrawal
   H. Death

*Refer to information on crisis counseling.

Additionally, some fears associated with a long-term illness where there is decompensation over time include fear of pain, imposed changes in lifestyle, alteration of social patterns, and fear of the future. The impact of such a significant crisis is stressful to clarify, speak about, and, initially, to problem-solve how to deal with imposed changes in the level of physical and cognitive functioning as the illness progresses.

STAGES OF ADJUSTMENT

Adjusting to MS is an ongoing process that evolves over a period of time (which varies among individuals). Some people proceed through cycles of progression and remission, others decompensate with little remission, and yet others may remain in remitted states for a very long period of time. Initially, if there is little evidence of disability, the individual may not experience denial because he or she is not currently confronted with changes in functioning. Evidence of psychological stress and efforts to cope may be evidenced as follows:

1. Denial is a normal defense reaction in not wanting to accept and acknowledge such stressful information. Denial is easily validated with a remission of symptoms ("I don't really have MS").

2. Resistance to letting "this illness" control one's life is an action based response against the illness. While this may be a positive demonstration of will, it may also be an unrealistic expectation of personal control, which could lead to significant depression if the individual is confronted with the reality that he/she cannot conquer the illness (i.e., symptom presentation and decompensation).

3. Affirmation is the acknowledgement that the diagnosis is real.
   This allows the individual to open up, process, and develop resources. It also facilitates a reevaluation of life priorities.

4. Acceptance is the realistic recognition of what the diagnosis means and coming to terms with it.

5. Personal growth is the silver lining in the cloud—responding to a difficult crisis with the attitude that with every experience in life there is the opportunity to grow and continue to evolve in new ways. There may be more appreciation for life in general and genuine gratitude for the things that are "right" in one's life.

There is an unfortunate history of nonintegrated treatment between practioners of physical health and mental health. As a result, there is often negligence in acknowledging and educating patients regarding the emotional and psychological impact associated with various medical disorders and disease states. The following table presents a brief review used to highlight this significant relationship. Such information, when shared with a patient, acts to validate one's experience and leads to appropriate problem solving and interventions.

Medical Causes of Psychiatric Illness

Medical Problem	Depression mood disorders	Anxiety disorders	Personality change	Psychosis	Dementia
Adrenal insufficiency	✓	✓		✓	
Aids	✓	✓		✓	✓
Altitude sickness		✓			✓
Amyotrophic lateral sclerosis	✓				✓ rare
Antidiuretic hormone Inappropriate secretion					✓

(Continues)

Medical Problem	Depression mood disorders	Anxiety disorders	Personality change	Psychosis	Dementia
Brain abscess		Range of cognitive symptoms			
Brain tumor	✓		✓		✓
Cancer	✓	✓			
Cardiac arrhythmias		✓			
Cerebrovascular accident	✓		✓	✓	
COPD (Chronic obstructive pulmonary disease)	✓	✓			
Congestive heart failure	✓	✓			
Cryptococcosis				✓	✓
Cushing's syndrome	✓	✓		✓	
Deafness		Paranoid ideation			
Diabetes mellitus	✓	✓			
Epilepsy	✓			✓	
Fibromyaglia	✓	✓			
Head trauma	Mood swings		✓	✓	✓
Herpes encephalitis		✓		✓	
Homocystinuria					✓
Huntington's disease	✓		✓	✓	✓
Hyperparathyroidism	✓	✓	✓	✓	
Hypoparathyroidism	✓	✓	Paranoid ideation		✓
Hypothyroidism	✓	✓		✓	
Kidney failure	✓				
Klinefelter's syndrome	✓			✓	
Liver failure	✓				
Lyme disease	✓	✓		✓	
Meniere's disease	✓	✓		✓	
Menopause	✓	✓			
Migraine	✓	✓			
Mitral valve prolapse		✓			
Multiple sclerosis	✓		Cognitive impairment		✓
Myasthenia gravis		✓			

(*Continues*)

Medical Causes of Psychiatric Illness (*Continued*)

Medical Problem	Depression mood disorders	Anxiety disorders	Personality change	Psychosis	Dementia
Neurocultaneous disorders	✓	✓			✓
Parkinson disease	✓	✓			✓
Phemochromocytoma		✓			
Pneumonia		✓			
Pernicious anemia					
Porphyria	✓	✓		✓	
Postoperative states	✓	✓		✓	
Premenstrual syndrome	✓	✓			
Prion disease		✓			✓
Progressive supranuclear palsy	Labile mood				✓
Protein energy malnutrition			Cognitive change	✓ Occasional	
Pulmonary throembolism		✓			
Rheumatoid arthritis	✓			✓ Rate	
Sickel-cell disease	✓		Substance dependence		
Sleep apnea	✓				
Syphilis	✓				
Systematic infection					
Systematic lupus erythematosus					
Thiamine deficiency			Amnesia		
Wilson's disease			Cognitive disorder		

Chapter 2

Assessing Special Circumstances

ASSESSING SPECIAL CIRCUMSTANCES

This section begins with the special assessment circumstances of risk of suicide (danger to self), dangerousness (danger to others), and gravely disabled. These constitute three of the most difficult and challenging situations with which the therapist will be presented. They require careful assessment, treatment considerations regarding level of care and providing a safe environment, legal issues, and often a family intervention. Additionally, this section addresses many other important situations in which the therapist may be engaged clinically to assess, provide evaluative reports, and/or to make appropriate interventions, referrals, and recommendations.

Guidelines for assessment provide the framework from which the therapist can establish a reasonable evaluation from a perspective of standard of care. For example, while there is no fail safe method of establishing the issue of risk of violence, using standard assessment criteria in combination with clinical judgment and issues of immediate management offers numerous points of intervening, thereby decreasing risk and increasing safety.

When providing any of the aforementioned services there are guidelines of education, training, supervision, and experience which are necessary.

COGNITIVE-BEHAVIORAL ASSESSMENT

It may not be possible to assess all of the following during the initial assessment. The assessment process continues throughout the course of treatment. The cognitive-behavioral assessment has a general educational element and helps to focus the individual on internal and external variables that may not have appeared relevant to the problem.

Outline of the

Interview

1. Succinct description of the presenting problem
2. Development of the problem
   A. Behavior(s)
   B. Cognition(s)
   C. Affective response(s)
   D. Physiological reaction(s)
   E. To each of these, answer
      1. What
      2. When
      3. Where
      4. How often
      5. With whom
      6. Degree of distress
      7. Degree of disruption
3. Contextual variables or modulating variables
   A. Situation(s)
   B. Behavior(s)
   C. Cognition(s)
   D. Affective response(s)
   E. Interpersonal response(s)
   F. Physiological response(s)
4. Maintaining factors
   A. Situation(s)
   B. Behavior(s)
   C. Cognition(s)
   D. Affective response(s)
   E. Interpersonal(s)
   F. Physiological response(s)
5. Coping
   A. History of responses to difficulty situations
   B. Current resources
      1. Interpersonal
      2. Community
6. Psychiatric history
7. Medical history
8. Previous treatment
   A. General course of treatment
   B. How responded
   C. What was helpful
9. Beliefs and interpretations associated with presenting issue
10. Mental status
11. Psychosocial factors
    A. Family/social relationships
    B. Psychosexual development
    C. Occupation

D. Personal interests/leisure activities

E. Adjustment/accommodation

DEPRESSION AND ANXIETY SCREENING

While a complete clinical evaluation is necessary to establish a diagnosis of depression or anxiety, a simple screening instrument serves a useful purpose to do the following:

1. Clarify symptom presentation
2. Explore the history of symptoms
3. Explore treatment history
4. Educate the patient regarding treatment choices
5. Make appropriate referrals

DEPRESSION

Criteria for Major Depressive Episode

Five or more of the following symptoms have been present during the same two-week period and represent a change from previous functioning. At least one of the symptoms is depressed mood or loss of interest/pleasure.

1. Fatigue or loss of energy
2. Feelings of worthlessness
3. Diminished interest/pleasure in all/almost all activities
4. Recurrent thoughts of death or suicide or suicide attempts
5. Significant weight loss or weight gain
6. Insomnia or increased need for sleep
7. Inability to concentrate
8. Depressed mood most of the day
9. Agitation or lethargy

ANXIETY

Many individuals with persistent anxiety present with somatic symptoms as well. For these individuals, consider a diagnosis of generalized anxiety disorder.

Generalized anxiety disorder is described as excessive anxiety and worry that occurs more days than not for a period of at least six months. The individual experiences difficulty controlling the excessive worry. Anxiety and worry are associated with three or more of the following symptoms.

1. Feelings of restlessness/on-edge/keyed-up
2. Easily fatigued
3. Difficulty concentrating/maintaining attention
4. Irritability/low frustration tolerance
5. Muscle tension
6. Sleep disturbance

STRUCTURED INTERVIEW FOR DEPRESSION

When depression has been identified as the presenting or underlying issue, the next task is to clarify the nature of the depression and its severity so that appropriate treatment (including referrals for medication evaluation/hospitalization) can ensue.

1. Current level of functioning
   A. Symptoms
   B. Relationship
   C. Work/school
   D. Home
   E. Negative/self-defeating thoughts
   F. Onset of depression
   G. Development of depression
   H. Context of depression

*Collaborate with individual to develop a problem list from their perspective.

    I. Mental status
   1. Mood
   2. Affect
   3. Memory
   4. Processes
   5. Perceptual disturbances
   6. Judgment
   7. Insight
   8. Impulse control

2. Define treatment goals
   A. Collaborative
   B. Willingness

3. Educate
   A. Regarding cycle of negative thinking and depression cycle
   B. Possibilities of change, offering hope
   C. Importance of self-care

4. Homework/feedback
   A. Do reinforce movement toward treatment goals
   B. Awareness
   C. Self-responsibility
   D. Preventative strategies developed

5. Prepare for self-monitoring
   A. What to look for
   B. What process to use (journals, self-respect, survey, pre and post test instrument, etc.)

CYCLE OF DEPRESSION

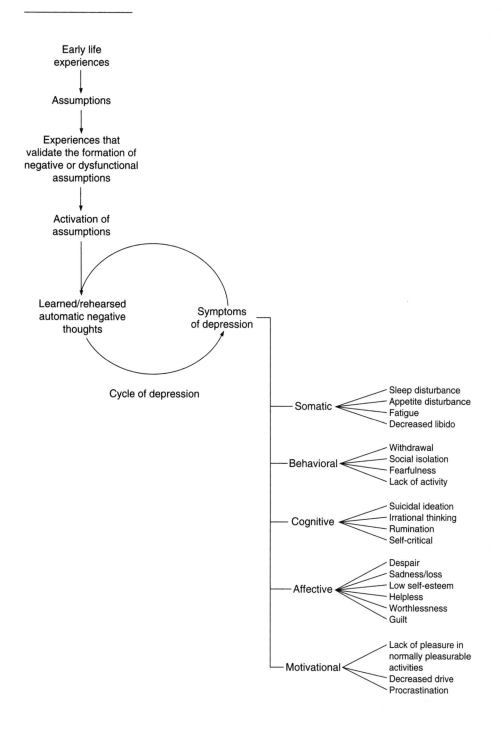

Early life
experiences

↓

Assumptions

↓

Experiences that
validate the formation of
negative or dysfunctional
assumptions

↓

Activation of
assumptions

↓

Learned/rehearsed
automatic negative
thoughts

Symptoms
of depression

Cycle of depression

Somatic
- Sleep disturbance
- Appetite disturbance
- Fatigue
- Decreased libido

Behavioral
- Withdrawal
- Social isolation
- Fearfulness
- Lack of activity

Cognitive
- Suicidal ideation
- Irrational thinking
- Rumination
- Self-critical

Affective
- Despair
- Sadness/loss
- Low self-esteem
- Helpless
- Worthlessness
- Guilt

Motivational
- Lack of pleasure in
  normally pleasurable
  activities
- Decreased drive
- Procrastination

Adapted from A. Beck, Model of Depression (1967, 1976)

Subjective Patient Review of Self Awareness and Presenting Problems

Name: _____ Date: _____

Please fill out the following by checking the correct space that applies.

	None or a little of the time	Some of the time	A good part of the time	Most or all of the time
I feel downhearted and blue.				
I enjoy my time alone.				
I have crying spells or feel like having them.				
I have trouble sleeping at night.				
I eat as much as I used to.				
I enjoy sex.				
I notice that I am losing weight.				
I have trouble with constipation.				
My heart beats faster than usual.				
I get tired for no reason.				
My mind is as clear as it used to be.				
I find it easy to do the things I used to do.				
I am restless and cannot keep still.				
I feel hopeful about the future.				
I am more irritable than usual.				
I find it easy to make decisions.				
I feel that I am useful and needed.				
My life is pretty full.				
I feel that others would be better off if I were dead.				
I still enjoy the things I used to do.				
I spend time with friends.				
Describe your personality.				
What problem are you seeking help for?				

SUICIDE

Assessing self-destructive threats, gestures, and suicide potential refers to the degree of probability that a person may harm or attempt to kill themselves in the immediate or near future.

Suicidal impulse and suicidal behaviors constitute a response by a person whose coping mechanisms have failed. They are often desperate and feel ashamed. If the person has attempted suicide a medical evaluation and issues of medical stability supersede a clinical interview. Be calm and caring in your approach, establishing a setting conductive to eliciting the necessary information. Be reassuring in letting the person know how you plan to proceed regarding referral for medical evaluation if needed, and that you want to talk to them in order to understand what has been happening in their life which brought them to the point of suicidal intent and suicidal behavior.

SUICIDE ASSESSMENT OUTLINE

1. Assessing suicidal ideation
   A. Ask directly if they have thoughts of suicide
   B. Are the thoughts pervasive or intermittent with a definite relationship to a given situation
   C. Do they have a plan; if so, how extensive is their plan
   D. Lethality of the means/method defined
   E. Is there access to the identified means

2. Suicide attempt
   A. Immediate referral for a medical evaluation for medical stability if method of attempt warrants it
      1. Means, location, collaborator, rescuer, number of attempts
      2. Thoroughness of plan and its implementation
      3. Note signs of impairment and physical harm
      4. Level of treatment required

*Intention, plan, method, means, lethality, and prior attempts

3. Risk factors
   A. Intention and history
      1. recent/prior attempts or gestures
      2. direct or indirect communication of intent
      3. extensiveness of plan
      4. lethality of means
      5. access to means
      6. family history of suicidal behaviors
   B. Demographics
      1. age (teens, middle age, and elderly are at highest risk)
      2. gender (males more often succeed at suicide attempts because of the lethality of means, but females make more attempts)
      3. homosexuals (additional stressors/lack of social supports)
      4. race (white)
      5. marital status (separated, widowed, divorced)

6. social support (lack of support system, living alone)
7. employment status (unemployed, change in status or performance)
C. Emotional functioning
   1. diagnosis (major depression, recovery from recent depression, schizophrenia, alcoholism, bipolar disorder, borderline personality disorder)
   2. auditory hallucination commanding death (bizarre methods may also indicate psychosis)
   3. recent loss or anniversary of a loss
   4. fantasy to reunite with a dead loved one
   5. stresses (chronic or associated with recent changes)
   6. poor coping ability
   7. degree of hopelessness or despair
D. Behavioral patterns
   1. isolation
   2. impulsivity
   3. rigid
E. Physical condition
   1. chronic insomnia
   2. chronic pain
   3. progressive illness
   4. recent childbirth

While many of these factors appear to be of a general nature it is the clustering of these factors which contribute to the person's mood, belief system, and coping ability that may lead to the risk of suicide.

ADOLESCENT SUICIDE

Behavioral and Social Clues
1. Heavy drug use
2. Change in academic performance
3. Recent loss of a love object, or impending loss
4. Pregnancy
5. Homosexuality (additional stressors/lack of social support)
6. Running away
7. Prior suicide attempts or family history of suicide
8. Intense anger
9. Preoccupation with the violent death of another person
10. Impulsivity
11. Learning disability
12. Ineffective coping
13. Lack of resources and feelings of alienation
14. Hopelessness, depression
15. Risk-taking behaviors (playing in traffic, intentional reckless driving, etc.)
16. Loss of support system
17. Recent move, change in school

18. Loss of family status (family member leaves or is removed from the home, change in economic level of family)
19. Feeling anonymous and unimportant
20. Peer group activity associated with issue of death

In assessing adolescents, the symptoms of depression may not be indicated as directly as when assessing an adult. This is referred to as masked depression. Masked depression can be described in two ways:

1. Classic: Somatic complaints take the place of the general criteria of depression. There are chronic complaints of headaches, backaches, and stomach ache.
2. Behavioral: Evidenced by acting out behaviors such as substance abuse, promiscuity, shoplifting. These are all representations of ways of converting affective state interpreted as boredom into something exciting. Young people are sometimes ineffective in expression depression. Therefore, they translate it into something else and project it outward, finding boredom in school, peers, and family. The use of substances may be an attempt to cope with emotional distress, lack of identity, or boredom. They may see the world as boring and unfulfilling. Males tend to act out more aggressively in their environments.

TREATMENT FOCUS AND OBJECTIVES

The type of intervention is based on efforts to problem solve and provide a safe environment for the suicidal person.

1. Outpatient Therapy and Management: Utilized when the risk of suicide is low, the precipitating crisis is no longer present, there is an adequate support system, and the person contracts that they will contact the therapist if they are unable to cope. Least restrictive and appropriate means of intervention are always utilized.
2. Hospitalization: Utilized if the person is at high risk for suicide, lacks adequate social supports, lacks adequate impulse control, is intoxicated or psychotic. For the benefit of the person, initially pursue the least restricitive course of a voluntary admission. If they are unwilling and the criteria are present an involuntary admission is warranted which will necessitate an evaluation by the appropriately designated persons/facility in your area.
3. Techniques
   A. Alleviate the person's isolation by recommending that they stay with family or friends
   B. Facilitate the removal of weapons or other means of a suicide attempt from their environment. Deal with issues of substances (abuse) if necessary
   C. Support the development and utilization of a support system, or the reestablishment of their support system
   D. Facilitate the appropriate expression of anger or other feelings which are contributing to self-destructive impulses
   E. Validate the person's experience of the crisis, but also identify their ambivalence and the fact that suicide is a permanent solution to a temporary problem

F. Refer for medication evaluation making sure that the physician is aware of the person's suicidal ideation/impulses

G. Educate the person regarding the impact that a lack of sleep has on effectively coping, and reassure them that the depression can be managed or eliminated

H. Identify irrational, negative beliefs. Help the person recognize that the associated negative self-talk contributes to keeping them in a state of hopelessness. Facilitate the identification of alternatives to the difficulties that they are currently experiencing

I. Do not verbally or nonverbally express shock or horror

J. Do not emphasize how much they have upset other people

K. Do not offer psychological or moral edicts of suicide

L. Explore with person what they hoped to accomplish by suicide

M. Identify life issues which have contributed to person's emotional state

N. Discuss the fact that suicide is a permanent solution

O. Review resources and relationships (family, friends, family physician, clergy, employer, police, emergency response team, therapist, community support groups, 12-step groups, emergency room, psychiatric hospital)

P. Be reassuring and supportive

Q. Facilitate improved problem solving and coping

R. Facilitate development of a self-care program
   1. Daily structure
   2. Inclusion of pleasurable activities
   3. Resources/support system (including therapy and medication compliance)
   4. Identify crisis/potential crisis situations and plausible choices for coping
   5. Identify warning signs (self-monitoring) that indicate that the person is not utilizing their self-care plan, medication difficulties, etc.
   6. Regular aerobic exercise and good nutrition

DEPRESSION AND SUICIDE RISK RELAPSE

Suicide does not begin with the self-destructive gesture. It begins with feelings of isolation, hopelessness, sleep disturbance, inability to cope, and other symptoms related to change, loss, or impulse control. Warning signs that serve as a potential red flag that there is an impending crisis include:

1. A general feeling that things are not going well. A pervasive negative outlook. They feel that life is not worth living and they cannot manage day-to-day activities.

2. Denial. A belief that they lack control over their life. Tendency to blame other people or situations for how they feel. As a result of not dealing with what they are experiencing, there is a tendency toward decompensation.

3. Attempts to help others while disregarding the priority of self-care. They become involved in other people's issues and avoid dealing with their own.

4. Defensiveness. Taking the position that they are doing fine and do not need the help of other people, resources, or medication.

5. Old behavior that the person has changed because of its negative role emotionally begins to surface. This could be looking at pictures or listening to songs that make them sad, reading old love letters, etc.

6. Focus on negatives. The person focuses on the view rather than the positive view of things, which increases feelings of helplessness.

7. Impulsive behaviors. The person begins to make rash decisions and participates in risk-taking behavior. Decisions are often made under stress and without thinking through choices and consequences.

8. Isolation and withdrawl continues. The person makes up excuses and avoids socializing and utilizing other resources.

9. Physical symptoms begin to appear such as appetite disturbance, sleep disturbance, fatigue, headaches, etc.

10. The person does not maintain their daily schedule, finding it difficult to get everything done as they previously had been able to do.

11. Hopelessness. The person feels that nothing will ever improve, that everything is a mess, and that life is not worth living.

12. The person is often confused and irritated. This low frustration tolerance affects all areas of life.

13. Breaking relations and associations. The person disengages from their support system. They may not feel the energy to participate or may believe that anything will make a difference.

14. Energy level is diminished. The person does little or nothing, spends their time daydreaming, and does not follow through on tasks.

15. Lack of sleep or poor sleep patterns begin to negatively impact their ability to effectively cope.

16. Depression becomes more severe in intensity and chronic. As a result, quality of life and relationships are significantly affected.

17. The person begins to miss therapy appointments. Self-care and treatment are a low priority.

18. The person expresses a dissatisfaction with life, immersed in a negative perspective of everything going on around them.

19. The person takes on the victim role which fosters helplessness and hopelessness.

20. Having thoughts of death or a "death wish." They do not want to kill themselves, but they want to escape their pain and see death as a state of not feeling the pain.

21. The person gets their life in order by making a will, giving things away, or saying goodbye as they emotionally detach.

22. The person appears to be doing much better following a depressive episode, which gives them enough energy to attempt suicide.

23. Feeling overwhelmed and unable to cope. Not able to adequately problem solve situations that normally would not present any difficulty.

24. Thoughts of suicide begin, and the person starts thinking about methods of suicide.

25. The person begins to demonstrate self-destructive patterns of behavior.

DANGEROUSNESS

The role of the mental health professional in assessing the potential for violence is to prevent injury and to provide the necessary care to people who are acting out violently or on the verge of losing control. The imminent concern of violent behavior is the potential harm of one person by another.

Violence itself is not a diagnosable mental disorder or illness, but rather the symptom of an underlying disorder and problems with impulse control. It is important to not discount or disregard the signs of potential violence. Instead, it provides a crisis situation which requires effective control before further interventions can be made.

The central priority of dealing with the potentially violent person is to insure the safety of the person, other individuals within close proximity, and your own safety. If the person assumes an aggressive and hostile position, steps must immediately be taken to maintain a safe environment. Often these people are fearful of losing control over their violent impulses, and as a result, are defending against feelings of helplessness, or have learned intimidation serves as a method of perceived control when in emotional distress. The immediate goal in intervening is to help the person regain control over their aggressive impulses.

DANGEROUSNESS ASSESSMENT OUTLINE

1. Assess thoughts of violence
   A. Ask directly if they have thoughts of harming another person
   B. Are the thoughts pervasive or transient (venting without intent) in relationship to a response to a given situation
   C. Do they have a plan, if so, how extensive is their plan
   D. What are the means to be used in harming someone
   E. Do they have access to the planned means/method

2. Do they have a history of violent behavior (have they ever seriously harmed another person)

3. Does the person wish to be helped to manage the aggressive impulses

4. If you are in the process of interviewing someone with a history of violent behavior be alert to signs of agitation and losing control:

   If it is determined that the person is at risk to harm another person, immediate steps need to be taken. If they demonstrate some semblance of being reasonable aside from their aggressive impulse toward another person focus on their ambivalence and talk with them about voluntary admission to a hospital to gain control over the impulses and to learn appropriate means of dealing with their feelings. If there is concern that such a discussion would only escalate a person who is already demonstrating significant agitation then contact the police for transport to a hospital.

   Remember: Having thoughts of wanting to harm someone and having the intention of acting on them are two different issues. If threats with intent to harm are present there is a duty to contact the police and the intended victim so that precautions can be taken.

5. Risk Factors
   A. Intention and History
      1. specific plan for injuring or killing someone
      2. access or possession of the intended weapon of use
      3. history of previous acts of violence
      4. history of homicidal threats
      5. recent incident of provocation
      6. conduct disorder behavior in childhood/antisocial adult behavior
      7. victim of child abuse

B. Demographics
   1. gender (males are at higher risk to act out aggressive impulses)
   2. low socioeconomic status (increased frustrations, general feelings of lack of control in life, aggressive environment or survival issues)
   3. social support (lack of support system)
   4. overt stressors (marital conflict, unemployment)
C. Emotional Functioning
   1. diagnosis (depression with agitation, drug/alcohol intoxication or withdrawal, delirium, mania, paranoid or catatonic schizophrenia, temporal lobe epilepsy, antisocial personality disorder, paranoid personality disorder)
D. Behavioral Patterns
   1. poor impulse control
   2. extreme lability of affect
   3. excessive aggressiveness
   4. easily agitated and signs of tension
   5. loud or abusive speech
   6. bizarre behavior or verbalization

CLARIFYING RISK OF HARM

Current Risk Factors

Suicidality _____ None _____ Ideation _____ Plan _____ Intent w/o means _____ Intent w/means

Homicidality _____ None _____ Ideation _____ Plan _____ Intent w/o means _____ Intent w/means

If risk of suicidality or homicidality exists, client is able to contract to not harm:
_____ Self _____ Others

Impulse control _____ Sufficient _____ Moderate _____ Minimal _____ Inconsistent _____ Explosive

Medical risks _____ None _____ Present If present, explain: _____

Substance abuse _____ None _____ Abuse _____ Dependence _____ Unstable remission _____ Stable remission

If substance abuse exists, specify substance, quantity, date of last use, ability to abstain, and prior CD treatment: _____

_____

Does significant substance abuse or dependence exist in client's living situation? _____ Yes _____ No

Current physical abuse, sexual abuse, and/or child/elder neglect? _____ Yes _____ No

If yes, client is: _____ Victim _____ Perpetrator _____ Both _____ Neither, but abuse exists in family

Does abuse involve a child and/or elder? _____ Yes _____ No Legally reported? _____ Yes _____ No

Specifies _____

_____

Risk History

Explain any *significant history* of suicidal and/or homicidal behavior, problems with impulse control, substance abuse, and/or medical risks that may affect client's *current* level of risk or may impair client's functioning.

_____

_____

Functional Impairments (*As applicable, explain how the symptoms affect daily functioning or place the client at risk.*)

Please rate severity of impairment. 1 = Mild   2 = Moderate   3 = Severe

Area	Severity	Description
Job/school	_____	_____
Relationships	_____	_____
Other	_____	_____

Disability? _____ None _____ Medical _____ Mental health

*Claiming workers' comp? _____ Yes _____ No

Currrent Medications _____ None _____ Psychiatric _____ Medical _____ No information

Specify dosage, frequency, and compliance: _____

Prescribed by: _____ _____ Psychiartist _____ Other physician

TREATMENT FOCUS AND OBJECTIVES

1. Outpatient Setting
   A. Have a prior plan worked out with office staff for intervening with reinforcement of security guards or police if escalation is a concern
   B. Establish a nonthreatening setting for the interview. Do not turn your back to the person, be aware of personal space, and position yourself close to the door in case an exit for safety is necessary
   C. Provide supportive feedback, reflecting to them that you recognize that they are upset. Encourage them to talk about what is wrong
   D. Set firm and consistent limits on violent behavior, and encourage the person to verbally express what they are feeling instead of acting on the aggressive impulses
   E. Establish a collaborative environment, being respectful to the person
   F. Be reassuring, calm, and if necessary assist in reality testing
   G. Refer for medication evaluation
   H. Identify personal and community resources
   I. Encourage them to take responsibility and emphasize appropriate choices
   J. Clarify the connection between actions and consequences
   K. Initiate counseling on anger management or refer to a community group focusing on anger management
   L. Teach assertive communication
   M. Encourage appropriate physical exercise to discharge body tension

N. Positive reinforcement for efforts and accomplishments

O. Maintain keen awareness for your own reaction to the person

P. End the interview if there are signs of increasing agitation. Inform the person that you sense the difficulty that they are experiencing in maintaining self-control

2. Inpatient setting

If the person is hospitalized the appropriate intervention selection will be based on the person's level of agitation and their ability to self-monitor and to respond appropriately. The basic goal is to provide a safe environment.

A. Give supportive feedback, and encourage appropriate ventilation and expression of feelings

B. Maintain personal safety behaviors at all times (don't turn your back on the person, position yourself close to the door, leave the door open, maintain adequate distance)

C. Set clear and consistent limits. Educate the person about what is expected of them and how they will benefit by cooperation and collaboration

D. Provide them with appropriate structure to discharge body tension

E. Set physical limits on violent behaviors when verbal limits are not sufficient. Call for help immediately if there are signs of escalation with impending violent behavior. As attending you must assume a role of leadership to assure the staff and the person that you are prepared to take charge and direct the necessary step to insure safety of the person, unit peers, and staff. If possible, offer the person choices of self-restraint for regaining control. If necessary seclude the person, and if warranted use restraints. At the very least the person should spend some time in the quiet room which is free of objects and easy to monitor, until they have time to regain composure and take responsibility for their behavior and be able to offer plausible alternatives for dealing with feelings of agitation or hostility. Consult with the treatment team psychiatrist regarding medication if person is unable to calm down and remains in an agitated state

F. Provide education on assertive communication

G. Provide education on anger management

H. Provide education regarding the relationship between behavior and consequences

I. Encourage the person to take responsibility for their behaviors

J. Positive reinforcement for efforts and accomplishments

CYCLE OF PHOBIC ANXIETY

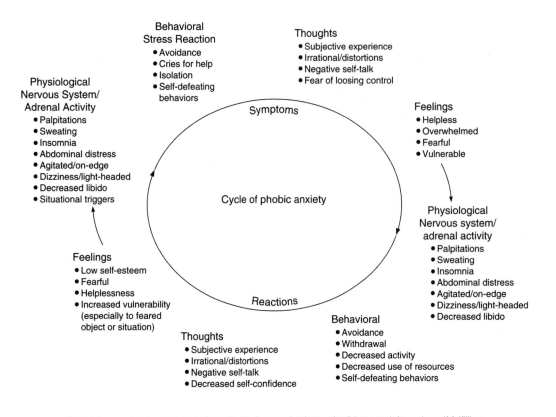

Behavioral Stress Reaction
- Avoidance
- Cries for help
- Isolation
- Self-defeating behaviors

Thoughts
- Subjective experience
- Irrational/distortions
- Negative self-talk
- Fear of loosing control

Physiological Nervous System/Adrenal Activity
- Palpitations
- Sweating
- Insomnia
- Abdominal distress
- Agitated/on-edge
- Dizziness/light-headed
- Decreased libido
- Situational triggers

Symptoms

Cycle of phobic anxiety

Feelings
- Helpless
- Overwhelmed
- Fearful
- Vulnerable

Physiological Nervous system/adrenal activity
- Palpitations
- Sweating
- Insomnia
- Abdominal distress
- Agitated/on-edge
- Dizziness/light-headed
- Decreased libido

Feelings
- Low self-esteem
- Fearful
- Helplessness
- Increased vulnerability (especially to feared object or situation)

Reactions

Thoughts
- Subjective experience
- Irrational/distortions
- Negative self-talk
- Decreased self-confidence

Behavioral
- Avoidance
- Withdrawal
- Decreased activity
- Decreased use of resources
- Self-defeating behaviors

This vicious cycle of symptoms and reactions mirror each other and validate or reinforce the self-fulfilling prophecy of expectations of the phobic individual. This cycle maintains and perpetuates fear-based symptoms and reactions (symptom-reaction list is not exhaustive—It is a sample list which can/should be individualized).

OBSESSIONAL DISORDERS: AN OVERVIEW

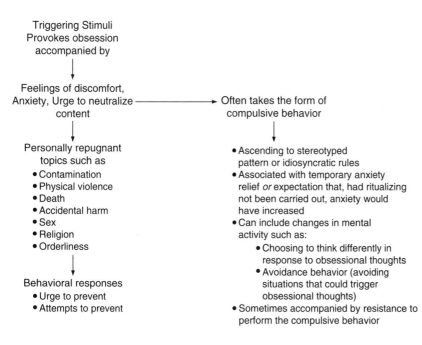

Defined as unwanted and intrusive thoughts/images and impulses associated with attempts to neutralize the emotional discomfort

Triggering Stimuli
Provokes obsession
accompanied by

↓

Feelings of discomfort,
Anxiety, Urge to neutralize ——————→ Often takes the form of
content   compulsive behavior

↓   ↓

Personally repugnant
topics such as
- Contamination
- Physical violence
- Death
- Accidental harm
- Sex
- Religion
- Orderliness

- Ascending to stereotyped
  pattern or idiosyncratic rules
- Associated with temporary anxiety
  relief *or* expectation that, had ritualizing
  not been carried out, anxiety would
  have increased
- Can include changes in mental
  activity such as:
  - Choosing to think differently in
    response to obsessional thoughts
  - Avoidance behavior (avoiding
    situations that could trigger
    obsessional thoughts)
- Sometimes accompanied by resistance to
  perform the compulsive behavior

↓

Behavioral responses
- Urge to prevent
- Attempts to prevent

When calm, the individual usually can objectively regard his/her obsessional thought and compulsive behaviors as senseless or excessive (at least to some degree).

ASSESSMENT OF OBSESSIONAL DISORDERS (OD)

1. Presenting problem
   A. General description
      1. Recent and specific examples
      2. Description of situational trigger (nighttime, leaving the house, etc.)

2. Detailed cognitive, behavioral, physiological analysis
   A. Cognitive
      1. Form of obsession(s): thoughts/images/impulses
      2. Content of obsessions
      3. Cognitions that trigger obsessions
      4. Neutralizing
      5. Avoidance
      6. Perceived resistance to obsessions
      7. Senseless/excessive ruminations
   B. Emotional
      1. Mood changes associated with obsessions
         a. Anxiety
         b. Depression

     c. Other forms of distress_____

     d. Mood change before/after obsession

  C. Behavioral

    1. Triggers for obsessional thinking

    2. Avoidance

     a. Of situations in which obsessional thoughts might occur

     b. As an effort to control occurrence of obsessive thoughts

    3. Rituals

    4. Requesting reassurance

    5. Requesting others carry out tasks associated with their obsessions

  D. Physiological

    1. Triggers

    2. Changes associated with obsessions/compulsions

3. History of obsessional disorder

  A. Development of problem

    1. Obsessions

    2. Neutralizing

    3. Avoidance

  B. Negative impact on

    1. Intimacy/sex

    2. Personal growth and goals

    3. Work

    4. Social interactions/functioning

    5. Domestic role and functioning

    6. Significant relationships

     A. Patterns

     B. Dynamics

     C. Negative impact

    7. Benefits/costs associated with change

4. Monitoring

  A. For additional information

  B. For change

  C. Self-monitoring/reporting

  D. Questionnaire/survey/tests

    1. Maudsley Obsessive-Compulsive Inventory

    2. Compulsive Activity Checklist

    3. Beck Depression Inventory

    4. Beck Anxiety Inventory

    5. Others_____

5. Observation by others

  A. Significant other

  B. Relatives

  C. Friends

  D. *In-vivo* home visits

GRAVELY DISABLED

The gravely disabled individual is unable to provide for their basic necessities of food, clothing, and shelter. The gravely disabled state may be due to:

1. confusion
2. hallucinations
3. delusional thinking
4. impaired reality testing
5. psychomotor agitation
6. lack of motivation
7. memory impairment
8. impaired judgment
9. undersocialization

Some behavioral indicators of being gravely disabled include:

1. unable to dress self
2. incontinent (without responsibly dealing with it)
3. not eating/drinking
4. deterioration of hygiene
5. inability to maintain medical regime
6. unable to provide residence for self

TREATMENT FOCUS AND OBJECTIVES

1. Inadequate Hygiene (Teach basic hygiene and activities of daily living [ADL])
   A. Person to seek assistance with bowel/bladder function
   B. Person will bathe/shower on their own
   C. Person will brush teeth, comb hair, shave, and dress appropriately daily

2. Uncooperative
   A. Person will be able to verbalize/demonstrate acceptance of daily assistance
   B. Person will comply with medication/medical regimen
   C. Person will accept assistance with living arrangement
   D. Person will accept long-term assistance

3. Inadequate Nutrition/Fluids
   A. Person will drink an adequate intake of fluids to maintain hydration
   B. Person will eat a balanced diet

4. Family Nonsupportive or Lacks Understanding Intervention
   A. Family education regarding person's prognosis and necessary support/structure
   B. Community support group

5. Inadequate Coping
   A. Consequences of noncompliance with medication
   B. Self-care management
   C. Facilitate problem solving and conflict resolution for practical situations that the person is likely to encounter
   D. Facilitate development of adequate social skills
      1. provide opportunities for social interaction
      2. model and role play appropriate social behaviors
   E. Facilitate development of management of anger and frustration
   F. Teach relaxation training
   G. Identify leisure skills

6. Improve Inability to Manage and Improve Judgment
   A. Evaluate for conservatorship

7. Inadequate/Inappropriate Living Arrangement
   A. Consider placement
      1. Board and care facility
      2. Planned senior citizen community with therapeutic and medical care
         a. must ask permission of spouse for participation in appropriate adult activities
         b. social isolation
         c. reluctance of a spouse (offender) to allow spouse to be seen alone
         d. history of child abuse
         e. behavior problems in children

ACTIVITIES OF DAILY LIVING

In evaluating competency as it pertains to self-care and self-sufficiency there are standard behavioral issues to be assessed. This is a general review of Activities of Daily Living (ADLs) which need to be adapted to age-appropriate criteria when making an assessment.

LIVING SITUATION

Assessing the living situation encompasses the level of support needed in any given living situation/environment.

1. Does the individual live independently in their own home or apartment.
2. Do they reside with family members or other individuals, Board and Care Facility, Custodial Care Facility, Residential Drug Treatment Facility, Nursing Home, Skilled Care Facility, etc.
   A. Do they live there independently or require the care/support/monitoring of those with whom they reside.
3. Do they utilize community support services such as "meals on wheels," home health services, someone hired to care for them, etc.
4. Do they attend school, Sheltered Workshop, Day Treatment, Day Activities Center, Social Club, Rehabilitation/Training Program

SELF-CARE SKILLS

Assessing the level of knowledge of basic needs such as food, clothing, hygiene, grooming, compliance with treatment issues.

1. Feeds self appropriately, adequately
2. Bathes regularly, shaving if necessary, deodorant, hair cut/combed
3. Dresses self appropriately, buys clothes, does laundry
4. Medication and treatment compliance

LEVEL OF REQUIRED ASSISTANCE

Assessing the level of ability of assistance required.

1. Incapable or unable to provide sufficiently for some of own self-care needs
2. Limited by physical or mental condition
3. Can only carry out simple tasks
4. Can only carry out simple tasks under the supervision or direction of others
5. Can initiate and complete tasks without being reminded, assisted, or prompted by others

State if ADLs are done by another individual for this person and to what degree assistance is required.

CARE OF ENVIRONMENT AND CHORE RESPONSIBILITIES

1. Individual takes care of all basic housecleaning tasks and yard tasks.
2. The quality of care in these tasks are: functional, neat, clean, (un)cluttered, (dis)organized, completion, done in an orderly manner.

MEALS

Eats fast food, carry-out, junk foods, snacks, prepared foods, sandwiches, simple cooking, boils/fries, full menu, able to use all kitchen appliances, coordinates all aspects of a meal.

CHILD CARE

Assess for neglect, abuse, people living in household and their contact to the child, leaves child alone, issues related to entertainment, teaches age-appropriate information/tasks, appropriately advocates for child.

FINANCIAL

Assess ability to count, make change, recognition of coins and paper currency. Is able to write checks, deposit checks/currency, able to do routine banking procedures, demonstrates ability to spend and save appropriately, effectively manages financial resources.

SHOPPING

Assess ability to shop for personal toiletries, clothing, food, etc.

TRANSPORTATION

Assess ability to effectively available modes of transportation and to plan for necessary scheduling.

CHRONIC MENTAL ILLNESS (CMI)

This population can be described as individuals with disabling chronic conditions who are unable to sustain an adequate range of functional independent skills. Historically, most of the clinical focus has been on those diagnosed as schizophrenic. There is no question of the value of behavioral treatment in conjunction with the sensitive use of maintenance medication for many individuals. There is additional benefit in including the significant people in their life for reinforcement of targeted behavior change or management. This population is observed as socially deteriorating, demonstrating poor hygiene and lack of self-care, slow speech and motor response, high rate of shouting, living in various residential settings (family home, board and care, various institutional environments, etc.), and they are often homeless, delusional, and periodically violent in some cases. Many have an inability to participate in and maintain normal social interaction.

Clinically, their symptoms are classified as "positive" (for example, auditory hallucinations) or "negative" (for example, poverty of affect and apathetic). These behavioral deficits and excesses do not demonstrate correlation between individuals. Additional clinical descriptors associated with causation of symptomology include the following:

1. *Premorbid deficits* are the symptoms or difficulties experienced before the psychiatric illness existed, such as social stability and academic/vocational stability. The significant importance of this history is that it often has a predictive function in the final outcome or level of functioning of the individual with CMI.
2. *Primary deficits* are those that directly emerge as the fundamental nature of the disorder. It is these deficits that result in a diagnosis.
3. *Secondary deficits* are those experienced as a consequence of the illness or the adverse personal reactions that continue even when primary deficits are managed or eliminated—for example, property damage that results in lost opportunities for the individuals and possibly others as well (such as a wrecked car).
4. *Institutional deficits* are those that can be identified as the consequence of being institutionalized.
5. *Iatrogenic deficits* are the side effects of long-term medication use.
6. *Pain deficit* is experienced as an increased threshold for pain, or the individual may not present symptoms or illnesses to be treated medically, which is related to CMI individuals having a higher level of morbidity than the general population.

Therapists working with CMI recognize the importance of stimulation level in the individual's environment. Too much stimulation is agitating and can contribute to decompensation, while too little stimulation produces higher levels of social withdrawal and general apathy. When there is motivation and effort, appropriately include those with CMI in treatment planning outlining goals and objectives which relate to perceived needs. Offer direct inquiry into personal desires of improvement and offer or work with them to develop appropriate and helpful means of achievement. Encourage and facilitate as much social responsibility and opportunity as possible. As with all treatment, the lowest level of clinical intrusiveness should be applied along with adequate support. When the treatment plan has been established, there is the added clinical responsibility to educate and teach those involved in the direct care as to their role and skill development for interaction with the identified individual.

GENERAL GUIDELINES FOR ASSESSING THE CHRONIC MENTALLY III

1. General interview and demographic information
2. Current behavior
   A. Remaining skills/assets
   B. Deficits/losses
   C. Deviation/oddities/excesses

3. Past behavior
   A. Identified in prior treatment (hospital/outpatient)
   B. Self-reports
   C. Collateral reports
   D. Antecedents of episodes of decompensation (people, place, situation, timing)

4. Potential target problems (those identified for treatment)
   A. Substance abuse
   B. Sexually exploited (poor judgment, etc.)
   C. Medical treatment

5. The use of rating scales
   A. Standard measures (for general behavior/psychiatric rating)

6. Time sampling
   A. Observation at predetermined intervals
   B. Observation in specific environments/situations

7. Identifying community resources
   A. Applicable for unique needs of individuals
   B. Specific groups which encourage positive maintenance and desired changes

8. Changing sensitive treatment goals
   A. Checklist for specific steps of change
   B. Update goals as needed

9. Developing brief treatment planning
   A. When working with a motivated individual (avoid overwhelming them)
   B. When working with collateral contacts such as family members or other care givers

10. Treatment team
    A. Consult as needed

In general, the results would be the development of the following:

1. A cognitive-behavioral program
2. Individualized treatment planning
3. Treatment in the context of larger groups
4. Treatment in the context of smaller groups (individuals with their families)

CRISIS EVALUATION

The crisis evaluation is utilized when urgent care is required or there is the presentation of acute symptomology during the course of an initial interview. The areas of evaluation includes the following:

1. Tentative diagnosis
   A. Multiaxial
   B. Underlying the current acute symptomolgy

2. Identification of other potential diagnoses to be ruled out (R/O)
   A. Multiaxial
   B. Influencing/contributing factors to acute symptomology
   C. Short-term treatment
   D. Implications for long-term treatment
   E. What diagnostic issues are longer term regarding being confirmed/disconfirmed during the course of treatment?

3. Biopsychosocial factors that play a role in the current and long-term symptom presentation, including ethnic and cultural issues.

4. Patient's participation in current and future treatment. Consider the following:
   A. Abilities/limitations (current/long term)
   B. Willingness
   C. Motivation
   D. Cooperativity

5. Crisis issues presenting risk (voluntary/involuntary inpatient admission)
   A. Danger to self
      1. Precautions to take (safety, legal, ethical)
      2. Hospital admission
      3. Short-term/long-term interventions/treatment
   B. Danger to others
      1. Precautions to take (safety, legal, ethical)
      2. Hospital admission
      3. Short-term/long-term interventions/treatment
   C. Gravely disabled (safety, legal, ethical)
      1. Precautions to take
      2. Hospitalization
      3. Short-term/long-term interventions/treatment
   D. Violence/abuse (child, spousal/partner/elder/dependent adult)
      1. Precautions to take (safety, legal, ethical)
      2. Hospitalization
      3. Shot-term/long-term interventions/treatment

6. Disposition
   Immediate placement and treatment for necessary level of care and expected level of transition during course of treatment

7. Consideration and recommendation associated with discharge planning

8. Follow up

CRISIS INTERVENTION

When a person experiences an unexpected traumatic experience, an intervention is most beneficial when it follows the event as closely as possible. A discussion about what happened and the associated response facilitates working through and resolving the crisis experience. The personal response to a traumatic crisis includes emotional, psychological, physical, and behavioral factors, and the response pattern varies among individuals.

The individual response pattern is a function of the following:

1. Past experiences and how the person has coped
2. Access and utilization of a support system
3. Emotional health at the time of the crisis
4. Physical health at the time of the crisis
5. Beliefs
6. Attitudes
7. Values
8. How others/society respond to the individual and the event that the person experienced.

Here are some of the more common responses:

Emotional	Mental	Physical	Behavioral
anxiety	confusion	fatigue	angry outbursts
fear	forgetfulness	exhaustion	increased substance use
agitation	difficulty	gastrointestinal	isolation
irritability	concentrating	problems	withdrawal
anger	distractibility	respiratory	restless
guilt	intrusive thoughts	problems	interpersonal problems
grief/loss	flashbacks	headaches	appetite disturbance
vulnerability	nightmares	twitching	sleep disturbance
fragility	obsessing	sweating	change in libido
disbelief	hypervigilance	dizziness	easily agitated

In an effort to decrease the intensity of the emotional and psychological response, decrease physiological arousal, and facilitate resolution of the crisis with a return to previous level of functioning, discussion of the traumatic experience should be initiated as soon as possible following the crisis. Early intervention will prevent the development of PTSD for some individuals. Be careful to not overstimulate the individual and add to the experience of trauma.

1. Listen carefully and pay close attention to the responses of these individuals (detachment, agitation, emotional reactiveness, flashbacks, etc.)
2. Decrease physiological arousal
3. Facilitate appropriate support(s)
4. Normalize their responses to crises

5. Educate them about the range of responses to crises, with care to avoid the following:
   A. Compounding social stigmatization of those with more symptoms
   B. Creating feelings of guilt for experiencing fewer symptoms than others
   C. Using confusing jargon/language not used by the general public
   D. Overpathologizing and focusing on disability
6. Assure them that their response is temporary
7. Let them know that there is not a specific time frame in which to recover from a crisis. However, if they engage in self-care behaviors, healing is likely to be expedited.
8. Foster resilience and recovery
9. Assess for substance abuse
10. Follow up

When providing psychological interventions to those recently traumatized and experiencing acute stress or individuals with PTSD validated treatment elements include direct therapeutic exposure and cognitive restructuring. Early cognitive-behavioral interventions include the following techniques:

1. Deep breathing
2. Progressive muscle relaxation
3. Imaginal and *in-vivo* exposure therapy
4. Regular physical activity
5. Positive daily structure with reinforcers
6. Utilization of resources
7. Journaling
8. Self-monitoring

CRITICAL INCIDENT STRESS DEBRIEFING (CISD)

Mitchell and Everly (2000) have suggested a seven-phase structured group discussion, which is provided within 10 days of a crisis (1–10 days). The purpose is to alleviate acute symptoms, assess for need of resources and follow-up, and provide a sense of closure to the crisis experience. The phases are as follows:

1. Introduction and guidelines for participation
2. Discussion of relevant facts
3. Discussion of thoughts
4. Discussion of reactions/emotions
5. Discussion of developing symptoms
6. Education about responses and coping strategies
7. Reentry
   A. Summarize
   B. Discuss additional available resources

SCREENING FOR SURVIVORS

The Institute of Medicine (IOM) offers screening program guidelines. Visit these two websites to access such information:

http://books.nap.edu/books/0309068371/html/index.html
http://www.quic.gov/report/toc.htm

IDENTIFYING TRAUMATIC STRESS

Be aware of the following warning signs for traumatic stress:

1. Recurring thoughts about the event (intrusive thoughts)
2. Recurring nightmares about the event
3. Sleep disturbance/appetite disturbance
4. Acting or feeling as if traumatic event is recurring, changes in appetite
5. Experience of anxiety and fear, especially when exposed to event reminiscent of trauma
6. Being on edge
7. Hypervigilant
8. Feeling depressed/sad
9. Low energy/fatigue
10. Memory difficulty, including difficulty in remembering aspects of the trauma
11. Difficulty with attention and concentration, unable to focus on work tasks or daily activities
12. Difficulty making decisions
13. Low frustration tolerance, easily agitated, angry or resentful
14. Feeling numb and withdrawn
15. Feeling disconnected or different from others
16. Mood swings, crying without provocation, feeling a sense of despair and hopelessness
17. Restricted range of affect
18. Sense of foreshortened future
19. Feeling overly fearful and protective of the safety of loved ones
20. Avoidant behavior (avoiding people, places or activities that provoke thought of the event)
21. Flashbacks of the event

RECOVERING FROM TRAUMATIC STRESS

Traumatic stress results from a crisis that tends to be both sudden and overwhelming. The psychological and emotional consequences range from a brief episode, which is acute but adequately coped with, to sustaining interference in ability to adequately cope with normal daily stressors accompanied by significant intrusion of thought, emotional reactivity, and physiological reactivity. Understanding the individualized experience of trauma is the first step to recovery.

HOW DOES A TRAUMATIC EVENT AFFECT SOMEONE?

It is common for an individual to experience shock and denial not long after a traumatic event has occurred. This is an almost automatic self-protective response. During this reactive stage, an individual may feel dazed, confused, or stunned. Another way to describe this emotional experience is that the individual feels numb and disconnected from life in general. Thought, emotion, and behavior are affected by the experience of trauma. There may also be stress associated physiological responses.

1. Changes in thought/mental Images
   A. Intrusive thoughts
   B. Racing thoughts
   C. Difficulty with concentration/attention
   D. Low frustration tolerance
   E. Feelings of being on edge
   F. Flashbacks
   G. Rumination
   H. Cognitive distortions
   I. Dissociation

2. Changes in emotion
   A. Moodiness
   B. Depression
   C. Acute anxiety
   D. Fear
   E. Easily overwhelmed

3. Changes in behavior
   A. Unable to remain on task
   B. Avoidance
   C. Restless/unable to sit still
   D. Difficulty maintaining a normal daily routine
   E. Detached/withdrawn
   F. Easily agitated/argumentative (low frustration tolerance)

4. Physical responses (commonly experienced with acute stress)
   A. Rapid heart rate
   B. Chest pain
   C. Abdominal distress
   D. Nausea
   E. Headaches

5. Additional Issues
   A. Self-medication
      1. Alcohol/drug abuse
      2. Prescription medication abuse
   B. Anniversary of events (may trigger)
      1. Intrusive thoughts
      2. Distressing memories

3. Nightmares
4. Feelings of helplessness
5. Feelings of being overwhelmed
6. Difficult emotions

C. Contact with stimuli similar in some way to the event acts as a trigger and could be experienced by any of the five senses
1. Visual
2. Auditory
3. Tactile
4. Olfactory
5. Taste

THE EFFECTS OF TIME

There is no way to predict the amount of time it will take to recover or if events of trauma will continue to linger in some evident manner throughout the course of an individual's lifetime. It is expected that all significant life experiences carry with them some impact of change. Numerous factors affect the recovery process. Therefore, outcome of such experiences is based on the following factors:

1. Prior experiences and how they were resolved
2. How others (society/victim blaming) respond to the individual in association with the crisis
3. Repetition or number of trauma events
4. General coping ability
5. How the individual views herself or himself
6. How the individual views his/her environment
7. Self-care
8. Resources
   A. Social support
   B. Professional intervention
9. Learning
10. Whether the response to the trauma was immediate or delayed
11. Integration
12. Resolution

TRAUMATIC STRESS AND VEHICULAR ACCIDENTS

This information also applies to other experiences of trauma where there has been significant physical harm to an individual's physical integrity.

1. Physical review: What happened to the person physically.
   A. Physical trauma and near death/disfigurement
   B. Multiple injuries

C. Chronic/acute pain

D. Physical limitations

E. Continued medical treatment with associated physical recovery

    1. Invasive procedure(s)

    2. Experimental procedure(s)

    3. Rehabilitation

F. Time that it takes to achieve stability where further procedures are not anticipated and the person is in a state of true adjustment in the recovery process

G. Time that it takes to heal (often someone who is released from medical treatment is in the initial stages of healing; healing can take a long time)

H. Effects/risks of medications

    1. Dependence

    2. Used as the only intervention for pain and acute anxiety management

2. Physical status affecting emotional and psychological functioning

A. Depression/anxiety/stress may be associated with the following:

    1. Losses

    2. Changes

    3. Adjustment

    4. Chronic pain

    5. Continuing medical treatment

    6. Medical instability

    7. Rehabilitation

    8. Decompensation (feared or predicted)

B. The *body* may be depressed just because of what it is going through and continuing to endure resulting in

    1. Fatigue

    2. Low tolerance

    3. Stress/difficulty/pain associated with normal movement

    4. Decreased stamina

C. Ongoing medical treatment may present the following issues:

    1. How functional will the person be?

    2. Will the physical integrity of the person's body be maintained?

    3. Identity issues: "How have I been changed"

       a. Self-awareness

       b. Other's reflecting a change in personality/mood

3. Role of depression and PTSD

A. Depression

    1. Decreased energy/fatigue

    2. Sleep disturbance

    3. Mood vulnerability

    4. Increased potential for illness (people who are depressed are ill more often)

*Recovery is a lot of work. Depression slows the process, but it is also a normal part of adjustment.

4. PTSD (near death trauma/disfigurement with sustaining influence)
   A. Ongoing medical treatment/continuing stress or trauma
   B. Chronic pain
   C. Physical limitations
   D. Emotional vulnerability
   E. Unpredictable good and bad days (may be emotion or pain related)
   F. Health implications
      1. Musculoskeletal disorders
      2. Neurochemical changes resulting in an increased susceptibility to infection and immunological disorders
      3. Association of physical trauma and fibromyalgia

5. Physiology of stress
   A. Stress negatively affects physiology
   B. Stress suppresses the immune system
   C. Stress impairs resistance to
      1. Infection
      2. Illness
      3. Complications of surgery
   D. Stress accelerates metabolic activity
      1. Insomnia
      2. Nervousness (muscle tension)
      3. Fatigue/exhaustion

*Stress is four times as likely to precede infection.
*Stress compromises the immune system enough for infection to take hold.

ASSESSMENT OF PHOBIC BEHAVIOR

This is a special assessment associated with the fear(s) experienced by the individual and the identification of the practices, thoughts, or situations that reinforce and sustain phobic anxiety. Situational triggers alone influence physiology, thoughts, behavior, and feelings that perpetuate the cycle. When an individual is able to clarify the chain of experience, thought, physiology, behavior, or emotion that is specific to their phobic response, he/she will be able to problem solve reaction management and behavior modification/change.

Once the presenting problem phobia has been clearly identified, use the following information to develop an accurate clinical picture and treatment plan.

1. List symptoms in the following areas:
   A. Physiology (nervous system/adrenal activity)
      1. Palpitations
      2. Sweating/chills
      3. Insomnia
      4. Abdominal distress
      5. Dizziness/light-headedness
      6. Decreased libido
      7. Others _____

B. Behavior
   1. Stress reaction
      a. Avoidance (identify full range for developing hierarchy)
      b. Cries for help (decreased functionality)
      c. Isolation
      d. Self-defeating behaviors
C. Thoughts
   1. Subjective experience
   2. Irrational thinking
   3. Distortions of reality
   4. Negative self-talk
   5. Fear of losing control
D. Feelings
   1. Helpless
   2. Overwhelmed
   3. Fearful
   4. Vulnerable

2. Maintaining factors (interfere with progress)
  A. Avoidance
  B. Cognitive factors, thoughts of dangerousness of phobic stimulus
    1. Doubting the value of treatment
    2. Doubting one's ability to follow through on treatment decisions
  C. Presence of generalized (heightened) anxiety
    1. Associated depression (dysthymia)
  D. Possible underlying fear associated with overcoming the phobia
    1. Secondary gain
    2. Security associated with what is known eliminated, thereby increasing distress
    3. Would other problems develop?

3. Existing coping skills
  A. Methods of coping previously employed (may be helpful in treatment)
  B. Use of substances (alcohol/tranquilizers)
  C. What has been tried in an effort to overcome phobia?

4. Resources
  A. Hobbies
  B. Sources of pleasure
  C. Sources of success
  D. Helpful and caring family and friends
  E. Community resources
  F. Personal characteristics (persistent, sense of humor, intelligence, etc.)

5. Suitability for treatment
  A. Most cases improve with treatment
  B. Potential for noncompliant factors
    1. Severe depression
    2. Substance dependence   > Requires prior treatment intervention
    3. Personality disturbance

4. Other difficulties
   a. Fluctuating motivation
   b. Excessive emotional dependence
   c. Excessive hostility

6. Measures
   A. Baseline
   B. Information on progress
   C. Treatment plan and associated time frame
   D. Standardized rating scales
   E. Self-reports/self-monitoring

POSTPARTUM DEPRESSION AND ANXIETY

Baby Blues
Postpartum Depression Syndrome
Postpartum Stress Syndrome
Postpartum Anxiety Syndrome
   Postpartum Panic Disorder
   Postpartum Obsessive Compulsive Disorder

This syndrome refers to an illness that has a typical pattern of symptoms clustered together but does not have an identified specific single cause. This is the underlying reason why postpartum depression, postpartum stress, and postpartum anxiety syndromes often go undiagnosed and untreated. Also, it is imperative that prior to treatment of postpartum emotional syndromes there be a thorough medical examination to rule out other illnesses that may present similar symptoms but require very different treatment (such as thyroid dysfunction).

It is estimated that in the United States approximately 400,000 women experience postpartum depression each year. The experience of postpartum depression most commonly takes place six to eight weeks following childbirth. One in four first-time mothers will experience postpartum depression syndrome or postpartum stress syndrome. When postpartum anxiety syndromes are added, the number of women affected by postpartum emotional difficulties is one in three. The most severe postpartum disorder is postpartum psychosis, and approximately two women per 1,000 will experience it. Generally, there are no early warning signs or identified predispositions for postpartum disorders. Many women do not even present with a history of depression or anxiety. Also, postpartum syndromes can happen following any pregnancy (first, second, third, etc.). Therefore, it is not an exclusive experience for a first pregnancy; nor is there an assurance that a woman who experiences a postpartum disorder with one pregnancy will not experience this disorder after another pregnancy as well.

While postpartum syndromes are common, only a small number of women who experience some form of postpartum emotional distress will get help. Often it is not identified by the woman or her physician. However, this has began to change in recent years. Women have increased awareness and are seeking help.

DEFINITIONS

1. Baby blues

   The "baby blues" is not postpartum depression. However, someone with postpartum depression may have the baby blues. The baby blues is the most common experience of depression following childbirth. The baby blues is not an illness and resolves on its own. Approximately 60 to 80% of women experience brief and temporary moodiness (crying or feeling sad, irritable, frustrated) following childbirth. It generally takes place three to four days following childbirth and lasts for only a few hours or several days. If severe, the baby blues may last for about two weeks. It is brought on by the following:

A. Hormone changes

B. Breast engorgement

C. Transition from hospital to home

2. Postpartum Depression Syndrome

Following childbirth, a woman experiences emotional and physical symptoms of the syndrome of clinical depression. During the course of postpartum depression, a woman may also experience the baby blues. The following list presents physical and emotional symptoms associated with postpartum depression.

Postpartum Depression Symptom Checklist

———— 1. I can't shake feeling depressed no matter what I do.

———— 2. I cry at least once a day.

———— 3. I feel sad most or all of the time.

———— 4. I can't concentrate.

———— 5. I don't enjoy the things that I used to enjoy.

———— 6. I have no interest in making love at all, even though my doctor says I'm now physically able to resume sexual relations.

———— 7. I can't sleep, even when my baby sleeps.

———— 8. I feel like a failure all of the time.

———— 9. I have no energy; I am tired all the time.

———— 10. I have no appetite and no enjoyment of food (or I am having sugar and carbohydrate cravings and compulsively eating all the time).

———— 11. I can't remember the last time I laughed.

———— 12. Every little thing gets on my nerves lately. Sometimes, I am even furious at may baby. Often, I am angry with my husband.

———— 13. I feel that the future is hopeless.

———— 14. It seems like I will feel this way forever.

———— 15. There are times when I feel that it would be better to be dead than to feel this way for one more minute.

3. Postpartum Stress Syndrome

This condition is also known as Adjustment Disorder. The level of emotional distress falls between minor baby blues and severe postpartum depression. Approximately one in five women experience postpartum stress syndrome. Since symptoms are generally not as striking as postpartum depression, no one may notice how awful the new mother feels.

4. Postpartum Anxiety Syndromes

A. Review the Postpartum Panic Disorder Symptom List to see if you identify with the symptoms. Panic disorder symptoms occur without warning and generally last for about 10 to 30 minutes. Talk to your physician if you have these symptoms.

Postpartum Panic Disorder Symptom Checklist

———————— 1. I can't catch my breath.
———————— 2. My heart pounds, races, or skips a beat.
———————— 3. My hands shake or tremble.
———————— 4. I have stomach pains, nausea, or diarrhea.
———————— 5. I get hot flashes or chills.
———————— 6. I feel that something terrible is about to happen.
———————— 7. I get dizzy or light-headed.
———————— 8. Things appear "funny" or "unreal."
———————— 9. I feel like I'm choking.
———————— 10. I feel like I'm dying or about to have a heart attack.
———————— 11. I am afraid to leave my house or be alone because I might have an anxiety attack and not be able to get help.
———————— 12. I feel numb or tingly in my hands or around my mouth.

B. Obsessive Compulsive Disorder

While there may be many different symptoms, they all involve recurrent intrusive ideas or compulsive behaviors that cause significant distress or consume a great deal of time. There is the experience of certain repeated thoughts, urges, or images that are irrational and cannot be ignored, which result in discomfort and distress. Common examples include the following:

1. Horrifying violent images (including thoughts of harming a child)
2. Extreme doubts
3. Severe fear of becoming contaminated by germs
4. Compulsive housekeeping
5. Checking and rechecking things
6. Unnecessary repeated handwashing, counting, or touching certain items

POSTPARTUM CRISIS PSYCHOSIS

The rare and severe postpartum experience of postpartum psychosis is when a woman experiences hallucinations or delusions with other symptoms. This is an overwhelming and terrifying experience. The outcome of a postpartum crisis is potentially tragic. If a woman is concerned that she may be experiencing symptoms of postpartum psychosis, she should contact her physician immediately so that she can receive appropriate treatment and support as quickly as possible.

Suicide is a consequence of postpartum psychosis more often than harm to a child. There may not be adequate concern for a woman harming herself because the media sensationalizes the circumstances when a child is harmed by a mother. As a result, equal weight may not be applied to potential risks of harm to a mother and child (children) associated with postpartum psychosis. Below is a symptom checklist. If any of the symptoms are being experienced or the woman is concerned about her safety or the safety of the child, she should get medical and psychological intervention immediately.

Postpartum Crisis Symptom Checklist

———————— 1. I am afraid that I might harm myself in order to escape this pain.
———————— 2. I am afraid that I might actually do something to hurt my baby.
———————— 3. I hear sounds or voices when no one is around.
———————— 4. I do not feel that my thoughts are my own or that they are totally in my control.
———————— 5. I am hearing voices telling me to hurt my baby.
———————— 6. I have not slept at all in 48 hours or more.
———————— 7. I do not feel loving toward my baby and can't even go through the motions of taking care of him/her.

———— 8. I am rapidly losing weight without trying to.

———— 9. I am being controlled by forces beyond myself.

———— 10. I am thinking about hurting myself.

When a woman experiences difficulty coping effectively, hospitalization should be considered:

1. When medication requires very close monitoring
2. When necessary support of family and friends is not available
3. When outpatient treatment is not effective and a higher level of care is necessary
4. When symptoms are severe and unmanageable

Hospitalization is necessary when the individual is not able to adequately function and there is a lack of support in the home environment to ensure appropriate care and supervision (not functioning adequately):

1. A woman is suicidal
2. A child is at risk of harm
3. There are psychotic symptoms (heating voices, feeling paranoid, delusional beliefs)
4. A woman is not able to care for basic daily needs herself or her child
5. A woman cannot tolerate being left alone/or is on able to cope adequately with normal stressors

HOW TO BREAK THE POSTPARTUM CYCLE

1. Seek professional help
   A. Physician for medication and appropriate referrals
   B. Group therapy
   C. Individual therapy

2. Seek support from caring family and friends

3. Accept that you are experiencing a postpartum syndrome so that you can deal with it
   A. "It is not my fault" (affirmation)
   B. "I will not always feel this way."
   C. "I will choose to participate in my treatment and help myself improve." (follow treatment recommendations)

4. Identify patterns of negative response, deal with "what is" not "what if"

5. Increase awareness for situations, mood changes, tasks, and so forth that trigger negative responses or escalate symptoms

6. Stop it with increased awareness of negative response patterns, problem-solve helpful and appropriate ways to respond
   A. Thought stopping
   B. Thought substitution
   C. Behavior change

7. Distract yourself
   A. Find something to replace negative response patterns like going for a walk, calling a friend, meditating

8. Create options
   A. Give yourself permission to do what would be helpful and have a backup plan where a husband or someone else can take care of tasks while you
      1. Take a bath
      2. Exercise
      3. Engage in specific relaxation techniques
      4. Meditate
      5. Listen to music
      6. Pray

9. Be reasonable
   A. Remind yourself that it won't last forever
   B. Only do what needs to be done
   C. Get help

10. Set limits on telephone time
11. Limit visits from family and friends
12. Assert yourself to conserve energy, say no
13. Talk about your experience with someone you trust
14. Deal with difficult feelings
    A. Feelings of loss for the perfect pregnancy
    B. Feelings of loss for the perfect mother-baby experience
    C. Correct romanticizing childbirth and new motherhood
    D. Feelings of guilt
    E. Feelings of failure
    F. Low self-esteem
    G. Fear

Adapted from Kleiman & Raskin (1984). *This Isn't What I Expected.* Bantam Books.

PROFESSIONAL GUIDELINES FOR CRISIS INTERVENTION

If this is a crisis group instead of an individual session, address group rules, identify group goals, and establish an outline for the series of group sessions.

1. Explain the professional process. Therapist's role, client's role, issues of confidentiality, expectations, and goals.
2. Elicit the client's description of what occurred. Encourage a thorough description of visual, auditory, and olfactory experience. Does the client play a role in what happened. If not, what do they know about it, and how did they learn about it.
3. Review their previous level of functioning and rule out a cumulative effect from prior crisis experiences which have not been resolved.

4. What was the person feeling and thinking before, during, or immediately after the event? What have been their feelings and thoughts about the situation since then?

5. Clarify the person's reaction. Identify what had the most impact on them—the worst aspect of it for them—what part of the experience has made it the most difficult for them to deal with the situation.

6. What has been their emotional, mental, physical, and behavioral response to the crisis. Use the aforementioned symptoms to help them identify their response by breaking it down. Seeing that there are parts to what they are experiencing makes it more manageable and creates choices for them. They may feel more capable of dealing with one issue than another, and being in a position to make a choice gives a feeling of control which also contributes to progress toward working through and resolving of the crisis.

7. Interventions
   A. Educate the person regarding the range of experience accompanying a crisis.
   B. Identify strengths. Provide support for strengths and facilitate understanding how these can be utilized in the current situation.
   C. Identify vulnerabilities. Facilitate problem solving to avoid, strengthen, or reframe these issues.
   D. How have they coped with difficult situations and crises in the past?
   E. How do they view their own ability to cope, and why?
   F. Educate them on how prior crisis experiences that are unresolved may act in concert with the current crisis to create a cumulative effect. In other words, not all of what they are currently experiencing may be due to the recent crisis.
   G. Educate regarding the working through stages for resolution of a crisis. Also, educate regarding the importance of developing a self-care program to improve coping while dealing with and resolving crisis issues.

8. Resolution

As a client reaches the end stages of crisis resolution summarize what they have experienced, what they have learned and resolved. Review their self-care plan, including resources and "red flags" that might be a signal to regression. Give feedback regarding their recovery within the context of a normal response and focus on the positives and internal resources as they prepare to terminate.

SELF-CARE BEHAVIORS

Develop a personalized self-care plan for optimal results. This does require a commitment to health and follow through. It is recommended that there be a medical exam for medical clearance, as well as providing the opportunity for a medication evaluation which may be useful in dealing with unmanageable symptoms following a crisis.

1. Utilize relaxation techniques to decrease body tension and stress level.
2. Process the experience by:
   A. Utilizing your support system. Talking about the experience and how you have been affected. Don't isolate and withdraw. Instead spend time with people who offer a feeling of comfort and care.

B. Initiate a journal. Instead of keeping thoughts and feelings inside where they build up, get them down on paper. Some individuals have difficulty expressing themselves to others, or are afraid of being judged. In order to benefit a similar degree of relief as talking, journal writing can be useful.

C. Enter therapy for a safe, nonjudgmental environment where you can speak freely about your thoughts and feelings without feeling how others will respond, or feeling the need to protect those close to you. Therapy can be extremely beneficial for resolving a crisis.

3. Regular, moderate exercise. Aerobic exercise such as walking, appears to be most helpful in alleviating and maintaining decreased body tension.

4. Approach each day with a purpose. Be productive by outlining daily structure which includes adequate sleep, good nutrition, exercise, relaxation, utilization of resources, task accomplishment commensurate with level of functioning (no task is too small to feel good about).

5. Avoid anxiety-provoking talks or making significant life decisions during this time. You are still vulnerable and do not want to experience a relapse.

6. Avoid being self-critical. Be as kind and understanding to yourself as you would be to another. Use positive self-talk to reassure yourself that the symptoms that you are currently experiencing will subside with time.

What are some additional things that you could add to a self-care plan to meet your specific needs?

COUNSELING THE INDIVIDUAL IN A MEDICAL CRISIS

The goal for working with individuals presenting with medical crisis is not to affect a cure, but to optimize quality of life by facilitating individuals and their families to cope with the emotional and psychological trauma which often accompany the medical crisis. As they learn to cope with the crisis and associated life changes they will begin to integrate the illness as part of their life experience, to adjust to what has happened and/or will happen to them, and to live their life as fully as possible. For a therapist to intervene effectively requires that they be prepared to be:

1. Holistic in their approach of uniting mind and body
2. Aware and recognize the context of the ecosystem in which the individual is a part of
3. Able to provide a perspective which is able to assume that this is an individual with a healthy ego and defenses whose emotional equilibrium has been disrupted or affected by the intrusive force of a medical crisis versus an underlying psychopathology

Medical crises can be acute or chronic. In either case, appropriate interventions can help an individual avoid psychiatric complications and in some cases reduce the intensity or the onset of physical symptoms. While many of the issues being addressed would benefit an individual experiencing an acute medical crisis, the focus is on intervening with the individual experiencing a chronic medical crisis. The three heightened points of distress associated with a medical crisis where intervention is most effective are when a diagnosis has been made, an individual is released from the hospital, and an exacerbation in symptomatology. The initial focus of intervention is to reduce stress, address fears, and activate coping mechanisms.

Adaptive coping mechanisms are facilitated by:

1. Developing a clear picture of the situation. In order to process their medical condition they must have accurate information about its progression and the prognosis. Other factors which need clarification include an understanding of financial issues, medical treatment and resources, and family resources

2. Increasing emotional awareness. Asking questions of the self. How they feel and how they show their emotions

3. Effectively managing emotions. Using clear communication to express themselves and to get their needs met. Making an effort to remain as flexible as possible regarding the possible changes of all conditions

4. Ventilation of feelings and thoughts, verbally, with writing, drawing, or other expressive media

5. Utilizing resources and support—both personal and professional. Creating a list of all personal and professional resources, their availability, specifically what context of resources or support is offered, and if possible put the list in order according to the associated difficulty for which the individual seeks an intervention. This will help alleviate frustration and other negative feelings unnecessarily initiated by dead ends and other limitations.

The fears associated with long-term illness include fear of pain, body mutilation, imposed changes in lifestyle, alteration of social patterns, low self-esteem, fear of the future, and fear of death. The individual may experience many losses. Loss of body parts, physical functioning, sexual functioning, job, home, relationships, self-image, feelings of control, and death itself. The fear of living with losses and limitations can be as overwhelming as the fear of death.

Intervening with an individual in a medical crisis requires that these biopsychosocial issues be applied to the practical problems of daily living which confront an individual with a chronic illness such as: medical management, treatment compliance, symptom control/management, dealing with social isolation and developing new resources and supports, adjusting to physical changes and loss of functioning, establishing some level of comfort in a new lifestyle, dealing with financial consequences, and how those close to the individual respond. An entirely different issue not covered here, but of significant importance is the needs and issues of family members, specifically those who may be the central caregivers. Similar to the individual they care for, these people are also confronted with isolation, fear, uncertainty, and changes in their role.

TREATMENT FRAMEWORK AND CONCEPTUALIZATION

1. The focus of treatment are the medical crisis and condition (disease progression and prognosis)

2. Medical crises are often temporary, but if they appear to be of more a chronic nature (cycles of flareups or exacerbation), they still provide an opportunity for growth and learning

3. The issues of adjustment facing people with chronic illness are often predictable (physical, emotional, financial, lifestyle, relationships, identity, etc.)

4. The focus is on an individual's capacity and ability to facilitate maximal coping

The interventions for medical crisis are short term. However, there may be some individuals who will require more than one treatment of intervention due to underlying personality issues which interfere with their adjustment, the issue of secondary gains, or in response to a new crisis.

As previously stated, there are predictable issues which an individual experiencing a medical crisis associated with a chronic illness will experience. Support in confronting these issues will alleviate the fear and make the issue less overwhelming. It is important to validate the reality basis for the identity of issues and the fear or other emotion associated with it.

These issues are not experienced as a sequence of stages, but rather are assumed to be present all of the time. However, one issue may be dominant over another because of certain circumstances in a given time frame. Clinically, the therapist simply meets the person where they are emotionally at any given time. Take the cue from the individual as to what seems to be a prominent issue at the time, do as much resolution around the issue, do not diffuse it by focusing on other issues at the same time.

THE CENTRAL CRISIS ISSUES

1. Control
   A. How did they feel when a diagnosis was given? What did it mean to them? People do not know what the future will bring and often catastrophize, assuming the worst possible progression of the illness.
   B. Daily experiences of pain.
   C. What is the expected course of treatment, and treatment regimens?
   D. Facilitate venting of fears, and uncertainty of outcome.
   E. Facilitate expressed feelings of loss.

2. Self-Image
   A. Acknowledge the impact on an individual living in our society where there is a high social regard for good health and physical appearance.
   B. Validate feelings of loss and having to cope and adjust to the reality that they will never be the same again. "Who am I?"
   C. What are their personal strengths and resources which can help them cope?
   D. What was their life like before the diagnosis? Medical treatments? Doing an inventory of what the individual perceives as valued qualities and abilities can facilitate the grieving process. This can in turn facilitate a modified version of the individual's original self-image so that other problem solving can transpire.
   E. Explore the individual's general feelings/belief system about impairments and disabilities prior to the illness. This clarification will help them correct how they assume the attitudes of others.

3. Dependency
   A. Threats to independence: emotional, physical, financial. This can contribute or lead to depression and suicidal ideation.
   B. Negative feelings associated with the need for support or additional resources in making the necessary adjustments and accommodations of change.
   C. Facilitate the cultivation of self-reliance within the limits of their capabilities. Validate their fear of loss of personal independence and to effectively deal with the fear of being a burden on their family. Encourage optimal independence.
   D. In evaluating issues related to fears of dependency take into consideration the following factors: gender, age, psychosocial development, etc.
   E. Spousal and/or Family Related Issues
      1. What was the type/degree of independence of each individual in the family system/couple prior to the illness?
      2. How troubling is the dependency to each (all) involved?

3. How easy/difficult is it for the ill person to ask for help?

4. How freely is support given by others?

5. How difficult has it been to accept help/support from others?

6. What are the practical demands of the situation (routines, needs, wants, financial stressors, time demands, time for self, etc.)?

7. What are the helpful/useful community based resources such as home health, etc.?

8. Role play scenarios with individual and family members/partner.

9. Facilitate reality checks for objective evaluations.

10. Talk to physician regarding limitations/prognosis.

4. Stigma

A. Issues of self-acceptance.

B. Facilitate development of social skills and belief system to deal with the attitudes of others.

C. Be aware of the different social impact on the evaluation of men versus women. Males are more likely to be viewed as being more damaged and heroic, whereas, there is a tendency to view females as weak, ineffective, and being self-absorbed or feeling sorry for themselves.

5. Abandonment/Rejection

A. This issue may be more emotionally distressing than the fear associated with dying. There is a double bind for the individual: (a) There is a fear of abandonment, but they also feel bad about being a burden. (b) They want the care, but are aware of the difficulty that it poses on others. This is also a bind for caregivers who want to give the necessary care and offer comfort and feelings of security, but also wish that they did not have to deal with the problem.

B. It is extremely important to facilitate clear communication and joint decision making as soon as possible.

C. An awareness for the issue of caregiver burnout may prevent it from happening. With interventions such as acknowledging the caregiver's sacrifices and building in respite breaks into the regular routine caregiver burnout can be circumvented. For this to be successful, the individual must be sensitized to the caregiver's need for time away/breaks.

D. Reframe breaks as part of a functional pattern of long-term management to alleviate the interpretation of abandonment/rejection.

E. Facilitate utmost self-reliance.

6. Anger

A. Identify, validate, and constructively redirect the anger.

B. Be aware of the possible lack of awareness or denial for feelings of anger.

C. Reframe anger as a normal response to frustration when an individual is unable to control their life or illness.

D. Facilitate appropriate expression of anger. Possible modes of expressing anger include, appropriate ventilation, humor, talking, activity, meditation, etc.

E. Facilitate identification of the positive aspects of life: strengths, opportunities, and life pleasures.

7. Isolation/Withdrawal

A. Physically unable to continue in previous life activities such as work, social life, and other normal activities. Promote development of abilities.

B. Be aware that the consequences of social, physical, and emotional isolation can include increased depression, hopelessness, and despair.

C. Being cutoff from friends and family significantly increases the risk of sickness and death.

D. Feelings of low self-esteem and unworthiness can lead to withdrawal and refusal of invitations to be with other people and being involved socially.

This issue is just as important for the caregiver as the chronically ill individual. Their world has been radically decreased. Therefore facilitate development and utilization of a support system. Also, facilitate identification of options and the setting of realistic goals. Lastly, recognize that isolation and withdrawal may be a consequence of depression, fear, or rejection (real or perceived).

8. Death
    A. Facilitate acceptance.
    B. Recognize that the individual may vacillate between grief stages.
    C. Emphasize being in the here and now to maximize quality of life.
    D. Facilitate the individual to concentrate on living the life they have. Initiate conversations/discussions about life to promote living life to its fullest.
    E. Support the individual in accomplishing important and necessary tasks and to talk to family members/partner and other significant people in their life.
    F. Facilitate problem solving and resolution of practical issues which can contribute to their investment in living and decreasing a preoccupation with death.
    G. Facilitate clarification of priorities and values:
        1. Identifying the most meaningful aspects of life
        2. How does the individual want to be remembered.
        3. What is important for them to take care of.
        4. What are they able to let go of.
        5. Facilitate exploration of beliefs about death and life.
        6. Clarify philosophical and spiritual beliefs and resources.
        7. Facilitate clarification of what gives them both strength and comfort.
        8. Facilitate and support grieving.

This has been adapted and summarized from I. Pollin & S.B. Kannan (1995). *Medical Crisis Counseling*, New York: Norton.

DEALING WITH THE CHALLENGES OF LONG-TERM ILLNESS

1. Confronting your medical crisis: Recognize that you are not alone
    A. Learn skills to help you effectively cope. Instead of the goal to be cured, how do you learn to live with it and improve your quality of life.
    B. By confronting the illness and associated fears, you acknowledge what is happening and how it affects you. This is the path necessary for problem-solving how you will live with the illness. Every experience you have becomes a part of you.
        1. Acknowledge it
        2. Accept it
        3. Learn how to cope with how it changes your life.
        4. Learn to cope with how it has changed and is still changing you

C. To accomplish this, review the 8 central crisis issues associated with chronic illness and consider the following general points for improved coping and management:

1. Identify and accept adjustment as a normal part of life
2. Identify your general style of coping with difficult circumstances
3. Clarify
   a. Your view of your illness
   b. The stress it creates
   c. Your emotional reaction
4. Identify your strengths and weaknesses
5. Maximize resources
   a. Personal (psychological and emotional endurance; physical strength)
   b. Social (support network such as family, friends, community participation, support groups, professional help)
6. Decrease negative emotion
   a. Stress
   b. Anxiety
   c. Depression
7. Find ways to improve relaxation and being in the moment
   a. Prayer
   b. Visualization
   c. Meditation
   d. Stretching/yoga
   e. Formal relaxation techniques
8. Improve positive daily structure and daily functioning
9. Be a positive and cooperative member of your treatment team
   a. Ask questions
   b. Make decisions
   c. Be compliant with treatment
10. Decrease isolation/social withdrawal
11. Foster a sense of control (do what you can do)
12. Continue to strive for quality of life and satisfaction in life

2. Impact of chronic illness on relationships

Once the diagnosis is made or onset of chronic illness is evident, relationships may change. Not only may it be a time of stress and adjustment, but it may also be a time when you require an increased level of attention and care from those closest to you. As a result, everyone experiences a greater degree of stress. This may be a time of extreme anxiety for you and your family. Because of the range of intense emotions for all involved, people sometimes try to avoid friction and pull away with "silencing" being a possible consequence.

A. Keep communication open
B. It is appropriate to experience anxiety, depression, anger, fear, frustration, resentment, shame, guilt, and fatigue. Talking about it is the only way to find creative methods of dealing with such changes in yourself and significant relationships.
C. While you work at identifying how you are emotionally/psychologically responding, it is also important to understand how your loved ones feel. Don't wall yourself off. This medical crisis is shared by all those close to you.
D. Take charge
   1. Put problems in perspective
   2. Identify what is exacerbated or changed by the diagnosis/illness
   3. Do not personalize the illness

E. Facilitate a family discussion to address
1. Feelings
2. Responses
3. Fears
4. Impact on the life of each person
5. Problem-solving for managing changes as a family
6. Validating all feelings and thoughts
7. Separating difficult behaviors from the person
8. Expressing care and love

F. Develop realistic expectations and limitations for all family members (including yourself)

G. Clarify what you need from significant others
1. Tell them how you feel
2. Tell them what you miss (deal with it too)
3. Reassure their feelings about the medical crisis
4. Give them guidance in how to help you
5. Do not manipulate with your illness
6. Share appreciation for help and support

H. Help significant others to
1. Adjust to changes in responsibilities (some will feel a higher level of demand and others may feel displaced, so be aware and ready to talk about it)
2. Maintain as much responsibility and involvement in medical decisions as is possible
3. Keep awareness for overprotectiveness from family

I. Don't use family guilt as an avenue to gain desired attention

J. Make sure scheduling is structured so everyone gets respite care if necessary

K. Develop an effective partnership with your physicians by getting as much information about your illness as possible. Create a personal list of questions for you physicians aimed at increasing knowledge and understanding:
1. Are you sure of the diagnosis?
2. How did I get the disease?
3. What factors make it worse or better?
4. How long must I stay in the hospital?
5. What should I expect as far as disabilities?
6. Will the disease get worse?
7. Can the symptoms be controlled?
8. What treatments are available?
9. Is the treatment you are recommending the latest?
10. What is its success rate?
11. What are the risks of this treatment?
12. Do the benefits outweigh the risks?
13. Are there any experimental treatments I should know about?
14. If I take this medication for many years, what are the potential side effects?
15. If I have surgery, will it stop the disease or will the process continue?
16. What should I be doing to take care of myself?
17. What would make me feel better?
18. What would make me feel worse?

L. Clarify what you expect from your physician and what your physician expects from you

M. Feel confident if you choice to do the following:
  1. Seek a second opinion if you're dissatisfied with the specialist or feel uncertain about the diagnosis
  2. Get as much information about your disease as possible, but only as much as you are comfortable with. It should help with your treatment.
  3. If you are anxious in your doctor's office, bring in prepared questions and take notes. Have someone accompany you.
  4. Share your feelings and concerns with your doctor and his/her staff, especially if you feel you are being mistreated
  5. If you're going into surgery, put your surgeon's name on the release form. This will ensure that this particular surgeon will be performing the operation—not another member of the medical staff.
  6. Get copies of your medical records if it helps you to keep track of your treatment
  7. Speak up clearly if you are dissatisfied with a nurse's treatment of you. Start by speaking with your nurse directly. If that doesn't work, speak to the head nurse and then with your doctor.

WORKING THROUGH THE CHALLENGES AND FEARS ASSOCIATED WITH LONG-TERM ILLNESS

1. Loss of control
  A. Acknowledge you may not be able to control what is medically happening to you, but that you have a choice in how you deal with it. Your emotional state can affect your physical state and your physical state can affect your emotional and psychological functioning. So when you are confronted with some limitations and forced life changes, you still have power of choice over your psychological and emotional life.
  B. Find a way to come to terms with the loss of control and life changes
  C. Evaluate what you do and do not have control over
  D. Find ways to regain maximum control
    1. Clarify and separate long-term from short-term issues
    2. Make your own decisions whenever possible
    3. Review your life before and after the diagnosis
      a. What was a priority?
      b. How have you changed?
      c. What part of your life remains intact?
      d. What changes do you need to make?
    4. Identify areas of stress
    5. Develop realistic expectations and limitations
    6. Continue using coping mechanisms that are or can be effective
    7. Explore new ways of decreasing stress
    8. Identify/develop your support system (determine who you can depend on and under what circumstances)
    9. Consider joining a support group that focuses on your specific health issue
    10. Be creative
    11. Be flexible
    12. Plan ahead to maximize choices and control in situations
    13. Never underestimate the power of how you think
    14. Live an attitude that strives for quality of life

2. Changes in self-image
   A. Identify what was familiar that is now changed or lost in appearance or in physical, emotional, or psychological functioning
   B. Determine if these changes are permanent, temporary, or progressive
   C. Grieve your losses, let go, and validate normal responses
   D. Identify what losses are ahead of you as a result of the illness
   E. Develop a self-image that currently fits your strengths
   F. Remind yourself that change is a normal part of life
   G. Encourage family and friends as partners in your efforts of change
   H. Do things that make you feel good about yourself
   I. Seek professional support

3. Dependency concerns
   A. Identify what you can do for yourself versus relying on others
      1. Physically
      2. Financially
      3. Medically
      4. Daily life (shopping, house chores, child care, etc.)
   B. Find a balance between autonomy and reliance on others
   C. Identify how you are emotionally affected by dependency issues
   D. Develop realistic expectations and limitations
   E. Develop new goals
   F. Give to others and participate in their lives
   G. Resolve financial issues
   H. Participate in your own medical decisions
   I. Maintain as much independence as possible

4. Stigma—real and perceived
   A. Have a realistic view of the world
   B. Examine how you have dealt with the disabilities of others (insight into you own perceptions, which may result in your own distress with changes in you)
   C. Confront and resolve your own distortions of disabilities
   D. Participate in a support group
   E. Do not personalize the words or behaviors of others
   F. Talk with your family and friends
   G. Find ways to laugh at difficult situations and yourself
   H. Respond to others in an educative way—"I do things this way because..."
   I. Take control of how you present yourself

5. Abandonment
   A. Be aware of your sensitivity
   B. Avoid misinterpretations in family communication
   C. Confront your fear(s)
   D. Discuss your fears and concerns with family members and friends
   E. Identify negative thinking that is not reality based or shades of reality
   F. Be realistic and don't let your fear control you
   G. Be sensitive to the needs of your family
      1. Be empathic
      2. Be appreciative
   H. Stay emotionally involved with those you care about

I. Continue to participate as much as possible in the lives of family and friends (there are lots of ways to do the same thing or to be supportive)

J. Do not withdraw and then distort it as a validation of abandonment by others

6. Anger
   A. Begin with self-evaluation
   B. Assess your feelings of anger and how you have learned to deal with anger throughout the course of your life
   C. Do not personalize normal responses of anger from those close to you
   D. Determine where feelings of rage are being focused
   E. Do not burden yourself with being "angry at you"
   F. Take responsibility for the future without blaming yourself for the past
   G. Talk rationally and appropriately about your anger
   H. Find appropriate and helpful ways to vent your anger
      1. Be creative
      2. Be forgiving
      3. Take action
      4. Find positive ways to use your energy
   I. Acknowledge and accept realty

7. Isolation
   A. Identify the different forms of isolation
      1. Physical limitations (difficulty walking, wheelchair, bed-ridden)
      2. Social isolation (fewer contacts)
      3. Emotional isolation
   B. Be empathic; family members may also experience isolation
   C. Prepare yourself to deal with issues of isolation (let people know you want to be included)
   D. Participate in a support group for encouragements validation, and problem solving
   E. Identify how much support you need and want
   F. Have realistic expectations about family and friends
   G. Problem-solve how to reintegrate yourself socially and develop new interests

8. Death
   A. Decrease your fear of death
      1. Talk about it with family and friends
      2. Be helpful to others to decrease self-focus
      3. Write about your thoughts and feelings
      4. Read
      5. Talk with clergy
      6. Plan for it—take control
   B. Ask the hard questions
   C. Plan for the future
   D. Face death as you have faced life
   E. Comfort your fear of death in your own way
   F. Identify what is important to you and accomplish it on your own or with help
   G. Continue to make your own decisions
   H. Stay close to loved ones and invest yourself in important relationships
   I. Remain hopeful and believe in miracles—they do happen

J. Live life to its fullest

K. Be in the moment and enjoy the moment

Adapted from I. Pollin and S. Golant (1994). *"Taking charge": Overcoming the challenge of long term Illness*. New York: Times Books

CHRONIC PAIN: ASSESSMENT AND INTERVENTION

Everyone suffers from acute pain when injured, but acute pain abates quickly. Chronic pain is defined as pain that has not gone away or reoccurs often even after 6 months have passed. The management of chronic pain is so difficult because traditional methods of pain management frequently fail to bring relief.

The most common types of chronic pain are back pain, headaches, and pain associated with arthritis. However, there are many other origins of chronic pain. Unfortunately, in many of these cases, the underlying cause of the pain is not identified.

The most common pain syndrome is *myofascial pain*, which refers to pain in the muscles or connective tissue. This pain tends to be diffuse and described as "achy," and is often associated with the muscles of the head, neck, shoulders, and lower back. The onset can be rapid or gradual and generally will diminish on its own. There can be a cycle with myofascial pain which: (1) originates with muscle tension which produces pain; (2) focuses attention on the pain; (3) increased muscle tension; and (4) resulting in more pain. When an individual is not focusing on the pain, but instead doing other things and thinking about other things the distraction acts to minimize the experience and a normal alleviation or subsiding of the pain occurs.

Another pain syndrome, *neuralgia*, is similar to myofascial pain in that there appears to be a lack of tissue damage. The primary sign of neuralgia experienced by people is a severe sharp pain along a nerve pathway. This pain can occur suddenly with or without stimulation. It is transient and brief, but can reoccur and at times be intense enough to be incapacitating.

FACTORS AFFECTING THE EXPERIENCE OF PAIN

1. Cultural. Varying cultures offer different explanations of origin or meaning and expectation. However, there are few differences in sensation thresholds cross culturally.

2. Cognitive Response. The thoughts and beliefs that an individual has are one of the strongest influences on the perception of pain. Cognitive distortions such as excessive worrying, catastrophizing, negative self-fulfilling prophecy, overgeneralization, and personalization are common to individuals who suffer chronic pain. This type of thinking can play a role in the exacerbation of depression, requiring a thorough assessment of mood disturbance issues. The interpretation of pain will determine the overall experience of it, as well as feelings of control and self-efficacy in pain management.

3. Affect and Stress. As stress increases there is also an increase in the perception of pain. Psychogenic pain is chronic pain which lacks any physical etiology, and is believed to be a response to psychological need or disturbance. Often, people with depression or other emotional distress will manifest their distress in pain.

4. Prior Experiences of Pain. Even though the reaction to pain is autonomic, earlier experiences influence pain perception. There is no cure for pain; it is a survival mechanism to prevent harm and death.

CLINICAL INTERVIEW

Individuals with pain often present with additional coping difficulties. Chronic pain is exhausting, physically limiting, and challenges an individual's identity and sense of control. Be sensitive to not minimize or invalidate their experience of pain.

1. Identifying information
2. Relationship history
3. Work/academic history
4. Relevant background information and developmental history
5. History of pain (intensity, frequency, quality)
6. Medical history (injuries, hospitalization/surgery, medication, etc.)
7. Psychiatric history (therapy, biofeedback, hospitalization, medication)
8. Mental status
9. Coping mechanisms and problem-solving ability
10. Strength and weakness
11. Diagnosis
12. Tentative treatment plan listing planned collateral contacts for further information and case management

Use of the MMPI. MMPI scales can be very helpful when used as predictors of pain-coping strategies likely to be preferred by individuals with chronic pain.

ASSESSMENT AND MEASURING PAIN

1. Behavioral Observation. Observed outward manifestations of pain may be offered by any significant person in the individual's life and by the therapist. These observations may include distorted posture, distorted ambulation, negative affect (irritable, fatigue, etc.), avoidance of activity, verbal complaints, and distressful facial expressions.
2. Subjective Reports. The accuracy of subjective reports of pain are highly variable. It can be helpful to offer a conceptual range of pain from no experience of pain to pain that is intolerable (can't be any worse). This information can be clarified by using:
   A. A basic anatomical chart for identifying location/points of pain and type of pain.
   B. Facilitate the initiation of a journal for a brief period of time if clarification is necessary. **Concern is creating increased focus on the pain. However, information which can be gathered includes location, frequency, intensity, time of day which is worse, pain management techniques (what is helpful), etc.

Using the pain chart on the next page show where you experience pain. There are different symbols for making the location of pain on the diagram which are descriptors of the type of pain that can be experienced.

Every area that you mark as a location where pain is experienced should also be numbered between 0 and 10 to indicate the intensity of the pain experienced. For example if a location had the symbols and numbers such as:

/ / / / 4
/ / / /

It would mean that at the location marked there is an experience of stabbing pain with a low-moderate intensity.

About how often do you get the pain?
__ more than once every day
__ once a day
__ at least once per week
__ at least once per month
__ less than once per month
__ only during specific activities (if yes, please explain)

_____

_____

_____

_____

_____

How do other people try to help you when you have pain?_____

_____

_____

_____

How does the pain interfere in your life? What activities does it prevent you from doing?

_____

_____

_____

_____

_____

_____

PAIN IDENTIFICATION CHART

Name _____   Date _____

Mark the areas on your body where you feel the described sensations. Use the appropriate symbol. Mark areas of radiation. Include all affected areas.

LOCATION AND TYPE OF PAIN

Numbness = = = =   Pain and Needles + + + +

         = = = =   + + + +

Burning   0 0 0 0   Stabbing   / / / /

         0 0 0 0   / / / /

Please rate the average pain intensity for each location on a 10 point scale.

0 = no pain;   10 = very intense pain

FRONT

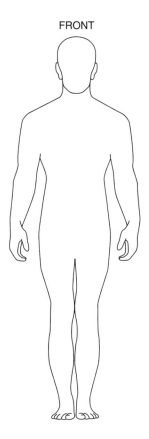

BACK

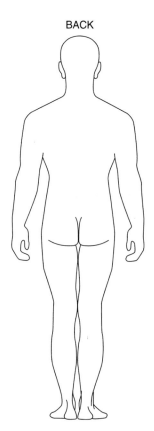

COMMENTS

_____

_____

_____

PAIN MANAGEMENT SCALE

Medical understanding of pain management continues to improve. In conjunction with the body chart, which shows where pain is experienced along with the type of pain, the use of a pain scale would be beneficial in communicating the degree of pain distress an individual is experiencing. Below is an example of the type of pain scales being utilized by hospitals and pain management specialists. As a therapist working with individuals recovering from various physical injuries and surgical procedures, this information may be valuable in your consultation with the individual's primary care physician, who is generally the case manager.

Directions
On a scale of 0 to 10 (with "0" meaning no pain and "10" meaning the worst pain) circle where your experience of pain is on the number line.

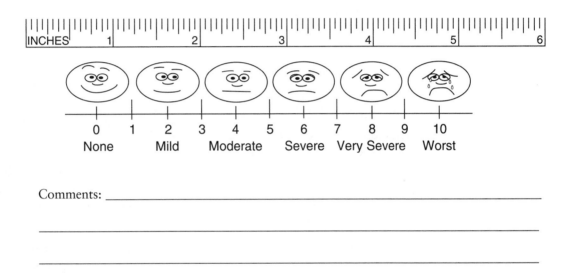

Comments: _____

_____

_____

If the individual is unable to use the 0 to 10 pain intensity scale, assess the following behavioral changes he/she experienced:

1. No behavioral/physiological changes indicating pain
2. Facial expressions (frowning, grimacing, fearful look)
3. Vocalizations (crying, moaning, grunting). Under what circumstances?
4. Sleep disturbance
5. Withdrawal or decreased social interaction
6. Guarding, rigidity, tension
7. Irritability, fidgeting
8. Physiological measures
   A. Increased heart rate/pulse
   B. Increased blood pressure

INTERVENTIONS FOR CHRONIC PAIN

There are two perspective of intervention which must be addressed:

1. Understanding the physiological processes of the body
2. Taking into consideration the individuals' belief system and perspective and response to pain

Case Management requires a multidisciplinary, multimodal, and multilevel approach which offers individual flexibility and stepwise progression where possible (emotional and physical rehabilitation).

SIX STAGES OF TREATMENT

1. Assessment
2. Reconceptualization which offers an understanding of the multidimensional nature of the pain (psychological, emotional, cultural, social, and physical associations).
3. Skills development (cognitive and behavioral)
4. Rehearsal and application of skills developed
5. Generalization of new skills and effective management skills
6. Planned follow-up treatment sessions to maintain progress

INTERVENTIONS

1. Collateral contact(s) with treating physician(s) for clarification of etiology, lab results, and pharmacologic treatment.
   A. Assess individual's knowledge regarding their pain, its etiology, and its impact on their life and relationship. Have the individual verbalize in their own words their understanding of what is happening to them to cause the pain that they are experiencing and why it is happening.

2. During the initial phase of treatment prepare an individual for their role in treatment planning and being the most significant person on the treatment team. Their compliance on recommendations and defined treatment interventions is imperative to the effective management of the case. Predict for them that, long term, there is a tendency for regression due to their decrease in compliance and activity. Therefore, it is beneficial to schedule intermittent follow-up sessions for maintenance.

3. Refer for psychopharmacological evaluation if there is evidence of underlying emotional factors such as depression and anxiety.

4. Cognitive Behavioral Interventions
   A. Cognitive restructuring
      1. Educate regarding the impact of negative thinking and negative self-talk. Develop calming self-talk and cognitive reappraisal.
      2. Facilitate development of compartmentalizing, or being able to "put things away." In other words, not having to deal with something all of the time. It creates some experience of control.
      3. Facilitate a focus on "what is" versus "what if"
      4. Facilitate a focus on capabilities versus disabilities
      5. Prayer helps some individuals alter their thinking patterns
      6. Selective attention.

7. Identify thoughts and feelings of helplessness and in a supportive manner confront with realistic information.

B. Relaxation training
   1. Progressive muscle relaxation
   2. Visualization
   3. Hypnosis
   4. Meditation
   5. Systematic desensitization

C. Correcting maladaptive pain behavior patterns
   1. Time contingent versus pain contingent programs (e.g., taking pain medication every 6 hr. as prescribed instead of "as needed").
   2. Functional rehabilitation through the use of physical therapy and occupational therapy to reclaim loss of functioning through a progressive hierarchy of task mastering.
   3. Decrease avoidant behavior and being self-absorbed/self focused through increased interests and utilizing resources.
   4. Assess for abuse of pain management medication or other substances.

D. Biofeedback (review the literature for efficacy of treatment for specific etiology of pain). One example is use of the EMG.

E. Stress management
   1. Relaxation training
   2. Stress inoculation training utilizing breathing techniques, imagery/visualization, progressive muscle relaxation, self-hypnosis or other focusing strategies, and cognitive restructuring
   3. Development and use of a self-care program
   4. Participation in pleasurable activities
   5. Regular, appropriate exercise
   6. Adequate nutrition
   7. Time management/prioritizing

F. Identify any precipitating stressors

G. Encourage venting of feelings and explore the meaning that pain holds for the individual. This will help the individual connect symptoms of pain to emotional states.

H. To redirect the individual to other areas of their life offer them attention when they are not focusing on the pain. This serves as a reinforcer to encourage their adaptive behaviors. It may also act to facilitate as a transition to invest individual in behaviors that distract them from the pain.

I. Explore with individual various methods of intervention to utilize when symptoms intensify. Emphasize consistency in treatment compliance issues.

J. Facilitate effective coping
   1. Validate individual's experience of pain. Acknowledgment and acceptance of their pain creates a foundation improved coping.
   2. Identify any evident or presumed secondary gains related to pain experience such as attention, increased dependency, decreased responsibility, etc.
   3. Following initial fulfillment of dependency needs, begin to gradually withdraw attention from pain. Eventually any complaints of pain will be referred to the physician, therefore, reinforcing compartmentalization by the individual.
   4. Encourage venting of anxiety and fears. Confront and problem solve with reality-based information.
   5. Facilitate individual's insight into the relationship between psychosocial stressors and experience of pain.
   6. Explore and problem solve the impact that chronic pain has had on relationships. Educate in a caring manner how the fears and frustration of others regarding this individual's experience of pain creates emotional distancing.

7. Positive feedback and reinforcement for efforts and accomplishments.
  K. Issues of control
    1. Facilitate identification of choices.
    2. Facilitate identification of how person (can) manages issues which appear out of their control or are out of their control.
  L. Body image issues
    1. Encourage grieving for any issues of loss related to changes in functioning. This also affects personal identity and requires adjustment.
    2. Facilitate identification of distortion individual has regarding body image.
    3. Encourage self-acceptance.
    4. Encourage development and utilization of self-care program.
    5. Positive feedback and reinforcement for individual's acknowledgment of realistic body/physical perceptions.
    6. The development and utilization of a self-care program can serve to reorient the person's perspective of the self and begin to heal damaged self-image.

SOMATIC PROBLEMS: A BRIEF REVIEW

Somatic presentation is characterized by the following:

1. Observable and identifiable disturbances of bodily functions,
2. Disturbances of bodily functions, which are perceived rather than observed, *or*
3. Mixed (some combined presentation of items 1 and 2).

Somatic problems commonly seen in the mental health setting include these:

1. Headache
2. Insomnia
3. Abdominal distress
4. Irritable bowel syndrome (IBS)
5. "Often ill" (as seen with some depressive individuals)
6. Hypochondriasis

Both the causation and maintenance of somatic conditions require exploration and treatment. Sometimes treatment is complicated by the presence of an actual physical condition. Such situations need a sophisticated direct psychological approach that does not focus on ruling out a physical condition, but instead frames in a positive psychological manner the problems experienced by the individual. A consultation with the treating physician is necessary to appropriately consider the following:

1. A realistic description of the individual's physical state
2. The course of the physical condition
3. Any physical limitations that affect psychological treatment

Individuals presenting with somatic problems believe that their problems have a physical cause, which may be accurate or inaccurate. When this perception is distorted and exaggerated, it becomes a source of difficulty and anxiety. They look for evidence to support their perceptions and as a result misinterpret symptoms. Sometimes this may be an issue of miscommunication between the individual and a medical professional whereby the individual's physical functioning may be slightly different from the norm but is considered as relative to the individual and not an impairment as the individual may believe. Regardless, when the therapist initially assesses the individual, he/she is likely to feel

1. Fearful of the possibility of further decompensation
2. Fearful emotional distress of dependency
3. Dealing with issues of loss
4. Overwhelmed by the process of making associated adjustments
5. Angry
6. Depressed/anxious

Therefore, one's reaction to physical impairment, real or perceived, can be changes in thoughts, behavior, mood, and physiological functioning.

THE PATIENT WITH PSYCHOSOMATIC ILLNESS WHO HAS AN UNDERLYING PERSONALITY DISORDER

Such a case requires a sophisticated level of clinical expertise. Consider the following issues:

1. Psychosomatic symptoms associated with an underlying personality disorder presents a significant challenge to the therapist. In this case, psychosomatic patients may demonstrate impulse- dominated modes of functioning utilizing the following defenses:
   A. Denial/splitting
   B. Magical thinking
   C. Feelings of omnipotence
   D. Demands of perfection versus worthlessness (extremes)
   E. Displacement/projection/projective identification
   F. Masochistic perfectionism
   G. Fantasized parental relationships (i.e., conflict-free mother-child relationship)

2. Psychosomatic families demonstrate a parental psychosocial profile that can be reviewed for problem solving diagnostically and in the treatment planning approach. The acronym for this system review is PRISES:
   Perfectionism—emphasis on
   a. Good behavior
   b. Social conformity
   c. Exemplary childhood/adolescent developmental performance

*Results in indirect communication and separation attempts.

Repression of emotions-caused by

A. Parental hypermorality (evidenced by)
1. Strict emotional control in front of children
2. Aggressive behavior of children not allowed (in general aggression denied)
3. Downplay/maximizing of successes
4. Mother deferred to as moral authority

*Rigid internalization of good/bad (w/o rational review and growth in belief system.

Infantilizing decision-making control

A. Everything had to be a noble purpose
1. Major home activity was intellectual discussion
2. Scholarly reading
3. Independent activity/assertiveness led to consequences of humiliation

*Resulting in inability to make decisions with attempts to get others (therapist) to make decisions for them.

Organ-System choice

A. Development of psychosomatic symptoms
1. Ulcerative colitis
2. Anorexia
3. Asthma

Exhibitionism by parent(s)

A. Doors to bathrooms or bedroom left unlocked or open
1. Facilitating child curiosity
2. Over-exposure paired with parental hypermorality
3. Resulting inhibition in normal psychosexual development

Selection of one child (unconscious selection)

A. Treated differently than siblings
1. Used as a confidant
2. Infantialized (babied)
3. Total devotion to selected child to exclusion of spouse/siblings

*Lack of individuality, poor boundaries, passive-aggressive.

Adapted from C. P. Wilson, I. L., Mintz (1989). Psychosomatic Symptoms: Psychodynamic Treatment of the Underlying Pennality Disorder

EATING DISORDERS SCREENING QUESTIONNAIRE

1. Have you ever been diagnosed and treated for an eating disorder?

    _____ Yes _____ No

    If so, please explain _____

    _____

2. Height: _____
3. Weight: _____
4. Highest weight in the past six months: _____
5. Lowest weight at your current height: _____ How recently? _____
6. Have you missed two or moree menstrual periods in the past six months?

    _____ Yes _____ No

For the following questions answer never (N), sometime (S), often (O), or always (A).

__Do you worry about gaining weight?

__Do you avoid certain foods because of calories, carbohydrate, sugar, or fat content?

__How often do you think about wanting to be thinner?

__Are you distressed about having fat on your body?

__Do you feel guilty after eating?

__Do you feel that food controls your life?

__During the past six months, have you exercised to control your weight, even when you were not feeling well or against the recommendation of your physician?

__During the past six months, has exercising to control your weight interfered with other activities?

__Do your concerns or eating behaviors interfere with your relationships?

__Do your concerns or eating behaviors interfere with academic/work performance?

__Do your concerns, eating behaviors, or weight gain cause you a lot of distress?

During the past six months, have you had periods where you ate unusually large amounts of food within two hours (binging), and have you felt unable to control how much you were eating at these times?

    __Never

    __Less than one time per month

    __About one time per month

    __About one time per week

    __Two or more times per week

If you have experienced binge eating episodes (as described in the previous question), would you describe the experience as any of the following:

___ Yes ___No Eating faster than usual?

___ Yes ___No Eating until you felt uncomfortable?

___ Yes ___No Eating a lot of food when you didn't feel hungry?

___ Yes ___No Eating alone because you were embarrassed about the amount of food you were eating?

___ Yes ___No Feeling depressed, guilty, or disgusted with yourself for overeating?

For the following statements, answer never (N), less than once a month (LM), about once a month (AM), about once a week (AW), or two or more times a week (MW).

___I have self-induced vomiting in an attempt to avoid gaining weight or to lose weight.

___I have taken laxatives in an attempt to avoid gaining weight or to lose weight.

___I have restricted my eating in an attempt to avoid gaining weight or to lose weight. (eating less than 500 calories a day or skipping two or more meals a day).

___I have taken diuretics (water pills) in an attempt to avoid gaining weight or to lose weight.
___I have exercised in an attempt to avoid gaining weight or to lose weight.

How did these behaviors start? _____

_____

_____

_____

_____

_____

_____

_____

_____

_____

How do you feel when you engage in these behaviors? _____

_____

_____

_____

_____

_____

_____

_____

_____

_____

_____

_____

THE MOOD EATING SCALE

If you agree with a statement, check it off.

__When I feel overwhelmed, eating can help me to feel relieved.

—Eating helps to calm me down when I feel nervous.

__If someone treats me badly, I find myself eating after it happens.

__If I am feeling frustrated, eating may not make me feel better.

__When I am feeling really happy, eating makes me feel even better.

__When I eat certain foods I feel guilty, but I find myself eating more of those foods than others (those foods are_____)

__When I am feeling stressed, I eat more food than usual
   (for example, when I have relationship problems, exams, or significant changes such as job, moving, school).

__If I had conflict with someone that I care about, eating would help to make me feel better.

__I generally do not eat when I am bored.

__If I feel inadequate, I find myself wanting to eat.

__If things feel out of control, I seem to eat more than usual.

__If I am angry with someone, eating doesn't make me feel better.

__If I am disgusted with myself, I feel like eating.

__I snack a lot while studying for tests.

__At times when everything seems to go wrong, I don't eat any more than usual.

__If someone makes fun of how I look, I find myself wanting to eat.

__When I feel like I am about to explode from stuffing my feelings, I feel better if I eat.

__If I fail at something I don't eat any more than usual.

__If someone has taken advantage of me, it will make me feel better if I eat.

__When I feel stressed and under pressure, I find myself eating more often.

__When I am lonely, I eat more.

Use this information for increasing your awareness for the connection between thoughts, feelings, and behaviors. Such information can be explored in journal writing and in therapy.

Adapted from L. L. Jackson and R. C. Hawkins II (1980).

EATING HISTORY

Please use the following form to record your eating history. Write about your loss of control associated with food use, rituals and practices regarding the food you choose. When you have completed your eating history, share it with another person to break the cycle of secrecy and loneliness.

Consider the following:

1. Kinds, amounts, and frequency of food use
   Put this information in a time line (at what age, what were/are the triggers)

2. Foggy memories or difficulty concentrating after eating too much
   Not able to think clearly

3. Feeling high after vomiting or starving
4. Feeling powerful and in control after vomiting or starving
5. Behavior changes
    A. Mood swings with eating/not eating
    B. Withdrawal from others to eat or starve
    C. Compulsive patterns, such as purchasing food to binge or changing to another compulsion when eating behavior becomes more healthy

6. Rituals surrounding food use
    A. Overeating or binge eating on certain foods
    B. Frequent eating out
    C. Sneak eating
    D. Weighing self daily or more often
    E. Selecting specific foods and why
    F. Exercise

7. Preoccupation
    A. Thinking about eating/not eating
    B. Eating for relief from problems, boredom, frustration, etc. (using food as a coping mechanism)
    C. Protecting your food supply; hiding food/hoarding
    D. Preoccupation with body size
    E. Carefully choosing clothes that mask starvation
    F. Preoccupation with secrecy and control

8. Beliefs
    A. What life changes are expected with weight loss/control of eating?
    B. How would the relationship with yourself change with weight loss/control of eating?

9. Attempts to control eating and/or weight
    A. Doctor's diets
    B. Fad diets
    C. Diet pills and/or shots
    D. Starving, vomiting, laxative use, or manual extraction of stool
    E. Diet clubs or fat farms
    F. Hypnosis, acupuncture, stomach stapling, or gastric bypass surgery
    G. Spending money to control eating or weight
    H. Cosmetic surgery

EATING DISORDER EVALUATION: ANOREXIA

1. Psychological evaluation
    A. Eating behaviors
    B. Weight
    C. Emotional symptoms
    D. Stressful life events
    E. Stressful life circumstances

F. Parental verbal abuse

G. History of mental/emotional illness

H. Mental status

I. Strengths/weaknesses

J. Motivation for treatment

K. Prior treatment experiences and outcome

L. Collateral contact with family members/other treating professionals

2. Review diagnostic criteria

A. Significant weight loss (less than 85% of ideal weight)

B. Significant failure to gain weight normally

C. Denial of the seriousness of the weight loss or low body weight

D. Excessive influence of body and weight on self-perception and self-evaluation

E. Intense fear of gaining weight

F. Loss of menstruation or delayed onset of menses

G. Exploring other compulsive behaviors such as substance abuse

H. Coexisting disorders (depression, anxiety disorders, Post Traumatic Stress Disorder (PTSD), Obsessive Compulsive Disorder (OCD) substance abuse)

3. Physical symptoms and signs

A. Dry skin

B. Sallow skin/complexion

C. Appearance/increase in fine hair on the body

4. Medical complications (physician review). Note: This is not an exhaustive list.

A. Cardiac abnormalities (arrythmias, slow heart rate)

B. Low blood pressure

C. Low body temperature

D. Low white blood cell count

E. Chronic constipation

F. Osteoporosis

G. Infertility

H. Hair loss

I. Nail destruction

5. Referrals

A. Physician-medical evaluation

B. Registered dietician

C. Family therapy

D. Group therapy

E. Specific eating disorder program

F. Inpatient treatment

6. Treatment recommendations

A. Psychotherapy (Cognitive-Behavioral, interpersonal, psychodynamic)

1. Individual, family, conjoint, group

B. Antidepressant medication

C. Medical evaluation and possible monitoring

D. Nutritional counseling

E. Self-help groups

EATING DISORDER EVALUATION: BULIMIA

1. Psychological evaluation
   A. Eating behaviors
   B. Weight
   C. Emotional symptoms
   D. Stressful life events
   E. Stressful life circumstances
   F. Parental verbal abuse
   G. History of mental/emotional illness
   H. Mental status
   I. Strengths/weaknesses
   J. Motivation for treatment
   K. Prior treatment experiences and outcome
   L. Collateral contacts with family members/other treating professionals

2. Review diagnostic criteria
   A. Episodic binge eating (eating an extremely large amount of food within a specified period of time while feeling out of control)
   B. Episodic purging behavior, which includes vomiting, laxative use, diuretic use, enema use, fasting, or excessive exercise to prevent weight gain
   C. Overconcern with body weight and shape
   D. History of other compulsive behaviors such as shoplifting or substance abuse
   E. Coexisting disorders (depression, anxiety disorders, PTSD, OCD, substance abuse)

   *Binge eating disorder lacks purging behaviors

3. Physical symptoms and signs
   A. Dental enamel erosion and cavities
   B. Swelling of cheeks, hands, and feet
   C. Abdominal fullness, constipation, diarrhea
   D. Abrasions on nuckles
   E. Headaches
   F. Fatigue
   G. Hair loss

4. Medical complications (physician review). Note: This is not an exhaustive list.
   A. Electrolyte and fluid abnormalities (low serum potassium values)
   B. Dehydration
   C. Enlarged parotid glands (glands in the cheeks associated with salivation)
   D. Dental enamel erosian and cavities
   E. Bowel abnormalities

5. Referral
   A. Physician-medical evaluation
   B. Registered dietician
   C. Family therapy

D. Group therapy

E. Specific eating disorder program

F. Dentist

6. Treatment recommendations

   A. Psychotherapy (Cognitive Behavioral, interperson, psychodynamic)

   B. Individual, family, conjoint, group

   C. Antidepressant medication

   D. Medical evaluation and possibly monitoring

   E. Nutritional counselling

   F. Self-help groups

ADULT ADD SCREENING

A symptom checklist is a quick way to screen this specific diagnostic area and identify a constellation of symptoms that may warrant referral to an ADD specialist. The following areas of review will only take a few minutes. Check off areas identified as a problem and with each one checked "yes," explore the frequency of experience (never, rarely sometimes, almost always).

History
__Experienced ADD symptoms in childhood, such as difficulty maintaining attention, tendency to be easily distracted, impulsive, restless (it is a disorder that initiates in childhood not adulthood)
__Has not performed up to level of potential in school or work
__History of behavioral problems
__Experienced bed wetting beyond age 5
__Family history: ADD
        Learning disabilities
        Mood disorders
        Substance abuse problems
        Impulse control problems

Attention Span/Distractibility
__Short attention span, unless very interested and engaged
__Easily distracted
__Fails to pay adequate attention to detail
__Difficulty listening carefully to directions
__Often misplaces things
__Difficulty learning new games or tasks
__Easily distracted during intimacy
__Poor listening skills
__Tendency to space out
__Tendency to get bored

Problems Initiating and Following through on Tasks
__General procrastination
__Does not complete tasks once started
__Motivated beginning, poor ending
__Tasks take longer due to inefficiency
__Inconsistent school/work performance

Poor Organizational Skills
__Poor organization and planning skills
__Difficulty maintaining organization in work/living environment
__Common to have piles of stuff
__Easily overwhelmed by daily tasks
__Poor financial management
__Able to be effective only with the organizational support of others

Restlessness
__Constant motion, fidgeting
__Needs to be moving to think about things
__Difficulty sitting still for too long (work, home, leisure)
__Feels anxious, nervous, on edge

Impulsivity
__Impulsive (spending, speaks before thinking)
__Difficulty following protocol/proper procedure
__Impatient

___Difficulty living beyond the moment
___Embarrasses others
___Lies or steals
___Frequent traffic violations
___Does not consider consequences associated with actions
___Tendency toward addictions (food, alcohol, substances, work)

Internal Feelings/Self-Esteem
___Negative self-esteem
___Chronic bad feelings about self, which are associated with underachievement
___Unhappy with self for not having accomplished more at this stage of life
___Feelings that "the other shoe is about to drop"
___Negative thinking
___Mood swings
___Often feels demoralized
___Often feels that things will not work out well
___Tendency to worry needlessly and endlessly

Relationship Issues
___Difficulty maintaining relationships (friendships, significant relationships)
___Promiscuity
___Difficulty with intimacy
___Immature behavior
___Immature interests
___Difficulty empathizing with or understanding the needs of others
___Difficulty communicating within a relationship
___Self-focused
___Difficulty with authority
___Avoids group activities
___Verbally abusive

Anger Management
___Short fuse to real or imagined negative personal remarks
___Rageful outburst
___Damages property

Need for Stimulation
___May be argumentative
___May create conflicts
___Gravitates toward a high degree of stimulation (gambling, high-stress job)

Dyslexic Responses
___Switches numbers, letters, words
___Switches words in conversation

Coordination
___Poor writing skills (difficulty translating thoughts to written form)
___Often prints versus cursive handwriting
___General coordination difficulties

Pressure and Performance
___Performance deteriorates under pressure
___Tendency to go blank during tests (test anxiety)
___Tendency to shut down during social pressure/social situations
___Difficulty remaining focused during reading (may feel tired and fall asleep)
___No matter how hard one tries, it just gets worse
___Easily overwhelmed with pressure

Sensitivity
___Easily startled by unsuspecting noises
___Sensitive to noise

__Sensitive to touch
__Sensitive to the feeling of clothing
__Sensitive to light

Sleep/Wake Cycle
__Difficulty resting mind and falling asleep (continues to think about things)
__Does not awaken feeling alert
__Needs morning ritual of coffee or activity to get going

Energy Level
__Episodes of fatigue
__Energy low in morning and afternoon
__Often feels tired

A history of ADD symptoms in childhood, short attention span, and a high level of distractibility are necessary to consider a diagnosis of ADD.

ADHD BEHAVIORAL REVIEW

Below are a list of behaviors one can review in establishing difficulties experienced by a child with a potential diagnosis of ADHD. When a therapist is consulting with teachers or parents, this information can be used to indicate the importance of an ADHD evaluation and referral for medical treatment.

Child's name: _____

Gender: M   F

Age: _____   Grade: _____

1. Does not give close attention to details.
2. Makes careless mistakes in schoolwork.
3. Squirms in seat and fidgets hands/feet.
4. Demonstrates difficulty maintaining attention on tasks/play activities.
5. Does not stay in seat or room as directed.
6. Does not appear to listen when being directly spoken to.
7. Exhibits behavior that is inappropriate to situations (climbing on things/getting into things when it is appropriate to be relatively quiet).
8. Does not follow instructions.
9. Fails to complete work.
10. Demonstrates difficulty playing quietly.
11. Demonstrates difficulty organizing tasks/activities.
12. Seems to be constantly on the go.
13. Avoids tasks that require consistent/sustained mental effort.
14. Talks constantly.
15. Constantly losing things that are needed for tasks/activities.
16. Is not able to wait his/her turn to talk or blurts out answers.
17. Is not able to wait for questions to be fully stated before answering.
18. Demonstrates difficulty waiting his/her turn.
19. Is easily distracted.
20. Demonstrates forgetfulness in daily tasks/activities.
21. Interrupts others.
22. Is intrusive in behavior/talking.

Adapted from G. J. Di Paul et al. (1998). ADHD Rating, Scale-IV, School Version.

Diagnosing ADHD:
Decision tree for clarifying ADHD diagnosis.

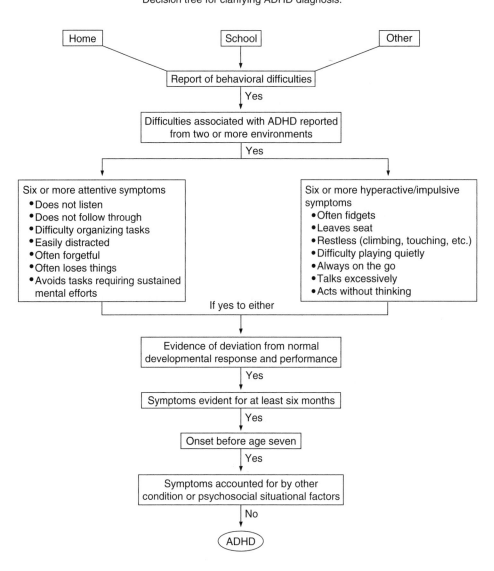

Adapted from A. D. Anastopolous and T. L. Shelton. (2001). *Assessing Attention Deficit/Hyperactivity Disorder.*

CHEMICAL DEPENDENCY ASSESSMENT

Date: _____

Name: _____

1. Description of Patient (identifying information):

   _____

   _____

   _____

   _____

2. Reason for Referral:

   _____

   _____

   _____

   _____

3. Patient's Perception of Chemical Use:

   _____

   _____

   _____

   _____

4. Patient's Treatment Expectations and Goals:

   _____

   _____

   _____

   _____

5. Effects of Lifestyle/Symptomatology:
   A. Family (History of family problems in origin and/or present family including chemical dependency);

   _____

   _____

   _____

B. Social (Description of peer association, isolation/hypersocialization):

_____

_____

C. Occupational/Scholastic (Absenteeism because of chemical use, decreased performance, dismissal):

_____

_____

D. Physical (Emesis, blackouts/passouts, hallucinations, tremors, convulsions, serious injury/illness, surgery, handicaps):

_____

_____

E. Psychological/Emotional (Cognitive functioning, emotionality, paranoia, history of treatment, behavioral problems):

_____

_____

F. Spiritual (Change or conflict within belief system):

_____

_____

G. Financial:

_____

_____

H. Legal Implications (Underage consumption, driving while under the influence, dealing; include disposition if any):

_____

_____

6. Diagnostic Impression (Multiaxial):

   I. _____

   II. _____

   III. _____

   IV. _____

   V. _____

7. Impressions and Recommendations:

Client's response to therapist: ☐ cooperative ☐ fearful ☐ suspicious
☐ hostile ☐ negative ☐ other _____

Mental Status:

Mood	__normal __depressed __elevated __euphoric __angry __irritable __anxious
Affect	__normal __broad __restricted __blunted __flat __inappropriate __liable
Memory	__intact __short-term problems __long-term problems
Processes	__normal __blocking __loose associations__confabulations __flight of ideas __ideas of reference __grandiosity __paranoia __obsession __preseverations __depersonalization __suicidal ideation __homicidal ideation
Hallucinations	__none __auditory __visual __olfactory __gustatory __somatic __tactile
Judgment	__good __fair __poor
Insight	__good __fair __poor
Impulse Control	__good __fair __poor

Client's Attitude Toward Treatment: ☐ accepting ☐ neutral ☐ resistant

Communications: ☐ talkative ☐ satisfactory ☐ open ☐ guarded
☐ answers questions only ☐ other _____

_____   _____
Therapist   Date

CHEMICAL DEPENDENCY
PSYCHOLOGICAL ASSESSMENT

Date: _____   Age: _____

Name: _____

S.O. Name _____   Phone: _____

Religious/ethnic/cultural background: _____

_____

Marital Status: _____   Children: _____

Living with Whom: _____

Present Support System (family/friends): _____

Chemical History:

Chemical Use	Route	Age started	Amt.	Freq.	Last Dose/ Last Used	Length of Use

Description of Presenting CD Problems (pt's view): _____

_____

Previous Counseling:

When	Where	Therapist/Title	Response To
_____	_____	_____	_____
_____	_____	_____	_____
_____	_____	_____	_____
_____	_____	_____	_____

Family/S.O. relationships/History of Chemical Use: _____

_____

_____

_____

S.O. Relationships and History of Chemical Use: _____

_____

_____

_____

Effects of CD on Family/Support System: _____

_____

_____

_____

Daily Activities that: A. Support Abstinence: _____

                       B. Encourage Usage: _____

History of Sexual/Physical Abuse (victim/abuser): _____

_____

Sexual Orientation: _____

Education: _____

Vocational History: _____

Leisure/Social Interests: _____

_____

Current Occupation: _____

Current Employer: _____

Impact of CD use on Job Performance: _____

_____

EAP? Yes _____ No _____ Name: _____ Phone: _____

Socioeconomic/Financial Problems: _____

_____

_____

Legal: _____ DWI: Yes _____ No _____   Court Ordered: Yes _____ No _____

Patient's Perceptions of Strengths and Weaknesses: _____

_____

_____

Preliminary Treatment Plan: List presenting problems based on initial assessment of the
client's physical, emotional, cognitive, and behavioral status

Detox: Yes _____ No _____ Explain: _____

Rehab: Yes _____ No _____ Explain: _____

Problem #1: _____

Problem #2: _____

Problem #3: _____

_____

Immediate treatment recommendations to address identifying problems: _____

_____

_____

_____

_____

_____   _____
Therapist   Date

WITHDRAWAL SYMPTOMS CHECKLIST

Ratings: 0 = none   1 = mild   2 = moderate   3 = severe

PSYCHOLOGICAL

__ Drowsiness
__ Excitability (jumpiness, restlessness)
__ Unreality
__ Poor memory/concentration
__ Confusion
__ Perceptual distortion
__ Hallucinations
__ Obsessions
__ Agoraphobia/phobias
__ Panic attacks
__ Agitation
__ Depression
__ Fear
__ Paranoid thoughts
__ Rage/aggression/irritability
__ Craving

SOMATIC

__ Headache
__ Pain (limbs, back, neck)
__ Pain (teeth, jaw)
__ Tingling/numbness altered sensation (limbs, face, trunk)
__ Stiffness (limbs, back, jaw)
__ Weakness ("jelly legs")
__ Tremor
__ Muscle twitches
__ Ataxia (lack of muscle coordination)
__ Dizziness/lightheadedness
__ Blurred/double vision
__ Ringing in the ears
__ Speech difficulty
__ Hypersensitivity (light, sound, taste, smell)
__ Insomnia/nightmares
__ Tantrums
__ Nausea/vomiting

__ Abdominal pain
__ Diarrhea/constipation
__ Appetite/weight change
__ Dry mouth
__ Metallic taste
__ Difficulty swallowing
__ Skin rash/itching
__ Stuffy nose/sinusitis
__ Influenza-like symptoms
__ Sore eyes
__ Flushing/sweating
__ Palpitations
__ Overbreathing
__ Thirst
__ Frequency/polyuria, pain on micturition
__ Incontinence
__ Abnormal heavy periods
__ Mammary pain/swelling
__ Other symptoms (specify)_____

Chemical Use History

| Check if used | Chemical classification | Description of substance | Past history | | | | Current use (last 6 months) | | | |
			First use (onset)	Age of regular use	Frequency and amount	Range of frequency (include date of last use)	Range of amount	Route of administration	Comments (cost, chemical of choice)
	Alcohol								
	Amphetamines								
	Cannabis								
	Cocaine								
	Hallucinogens								
	Inhalants								
	Opiates								
	Phencyclidine (PCP)								
	Sedatives/Hypnotics/ Anxiolytics								

SPOUSAL/PARTNER ABUSE

The victim of spousal abuse is often reluctant to acknowledge and admit that abuse has occurred. They have been beaten down emotionally, suffer from low self-esteem, feelings of worthlessness or unworthiness, and convinced that they are incapable of managing their own lives. Therefore, the clinician needs to be astute in recognizing the signs of abuse.

The cycle of abuse can be recognized by three stages. Stage 1 is indicative of stress and mounting tension. There may be what are described as minor incidents of battering such as pushing. The individual facing abuse tries to cope by staying out of the way of the abuser and by making sure that they are not doing anything to upset the abuser. This stage can endure for a long time. The major coping mechanism for this stage is denial. Stage 2 is where the explosion occurs. There is a lack of control and predictability by the abuser. Acute battering occurs, and can lead to the police being called or the abused individual seeking out a shelter/safe environment. Attempts to cope with these circumstances often include shock and denial. Stage 3 is the honeymoon. This is where the abuser is apologetic, loving, and promises to change. This leads to a denial of the violence and the cycle repeats itself.

ASSESSING SPOUSAL/PARTNER ABUSE

1. Indicators of Spousal Abuse
    A. Obvious injuries at various stages of healing
    B. Obvious erroneous explanation for their injuries
    C. Repeated bruises and other injuries
    D. Chronic depression, insomnia, nightmares, and anxiety
    E. Fear and hypervigilance
    F. Reluctance to offer more than general, superficial information
    G. Vague somatic complaints
    H. Overdependence on spouse
    I. Complaints of marital problems
    J. History of alcohol/substance abuse of the offender
    K. Spouse makes decisions of what they wear, who they see, and what they do

2. Immediate Interventions

    The primary goal is to protest the individual and their children.
    A. Obtain medical treatment for the victim.
    B. Provide the victim with the information for a shelter, and encourage them to call from your office.
    C. Educate the victim regarding their right to safety and legal intervention.
        1. File a police report and press charges so that an intervention can be made with the abusive partner.
        2. Obtain a restraining order so that law enforcement can offer protection and enforce the law with the offender.
    D. Offer support and understanding for what effects the experience has had on them and reinforce that they deserve better.
    E. Educate the victim about the cycle of violence in their own life, and how continuing to live in that environment perpetuates the roles of victim and abuser for the children.
    F. If the victim has a safe place to go to other than a shelter strongly encourage them to participate in groups offered by the shelter for battered women.
    G. Positive reinforcement for efforts and accomplishments of self-care:
        1. Decrease feelings of responsibility for the abusive behavior
        2. Develop safety plans for the protection of self and children

3. Develop and utilize support system
4. Decrease isolation
5. Decrease fear and feelings of helplessness
6. Decrease dependency on relationship
7. Increase constructive expression of anger and other feelings

3. Issues for the Abused Individual
   A. Financial and emotional dependency
   B. Control of life is lacking
   C. Fear
   D. Isolation
   E. Distressing emotions, ambivalence
   F. Low self-esteem, shame, embarrassment
   G. Frustration
   H. Competency
   I. Minimizing
   J. Self –blame or low self-worth
   K. Harassment
   L. Learned acceptance, passivity, and submission

Because of the emotional distance, fear, and defenses of the abused individual, the therapist needs to be direct, honest, and genuinely caring. Use joining techniques and unconditional positive regard to reduce the resistance that will be innately present of this type of client.

Identify if the client has someone or something of value that he/she wants to protect (children, friends, job), and refer to this during treatment to empower the client. Clients may not feel motivated toward protecting themselves until sometime after this initial work is accomplished.

Identify faulty belief systems that keep clients in the victim role and instruct in cognitive reframing, thereby offering a healthy alternative to adopt and to utilize constructively as an agent of change.

Refer to other community resources that will assist clients in their independent functioning and separate from them the abusers, such as job training, child care services, legal aid, AFDC, self-help groups, and so on.

There are two central features for assessing the perpetrator of violence:

1. Assessing Lethality
   A. Homicide risk (weapons, threats, degree of violence)
   B. Suicide risk (history and current status of risk factors)
   C. Frequency of violence (complete inventory of when violent behavior started, last episode of violence, typical degree of violence, most violent behavior, range of violent behavior, i.e., physical, sexual, property, emotional/psychological, cycle of violence, and current stage of violence)
   D. History of violence (own experiences of being abused, witnessing a parent being abused, violence in previous relationships)
   E. Substance use/abuse
   F. Assaults on other family members or other individuals
   G. Criminal history, criminal behaviors
   H. Isolation
   I. Proximity of abuser and victim
   J. Attitudes and beliefs related to violence
   K. Ownership of partner, feelings of being entitled to partner's service, obediance, and loyality

    L. Centrality of partner

    M. Depression

    N. Prior involvement of law enforcement

    O. Evaluation of life stressors

    P. Psychiatric history and mental status

    Q. Hostage taking

2. Assessment of the Offender's Motivation for Change

    A. Listen and carefully observe degree of interest in change.

    B. Is the motivation for change internally or externally driven?

    C. Do the person acknowledge having a problem with anger?

    D. Do the person acknowledge having a problem with violence?

    E. Is the person willing to discuss his/her violent behavior?

    F. Does the person minimize and deny violence?

    G. Are there any signs of remorse?

    H. Does the person feel his/her violent behavior is justified?

    I. Does the person acknowledge in any way a belief of being able to benefit from treatment, with any expression of wanting a violence-free relationship?

    J. Does the person have any insight into why he/she uses violence?

    K. Does the person see violence as a functional or integral part of the relationship?

    L. Is the person cooperative with treatment?

    M. What is the degree of externalization?

    N. Does the person keep appointments and arrive on time?

Issues related to motivation must be observed over time. The reasons for entering treatment are varied. Clients may not be presenting for treatment out of their own personal desire for change, but rather as a response to an external demand.

It is recommended that the individual participate in individual therapy, group therapy, and anger management class as modalities of intervention prior to the possibility of conjoint therapy, if that is an option. It is also important to assess for substance abuse. The modality or modalities used will be based on the needs of the client.

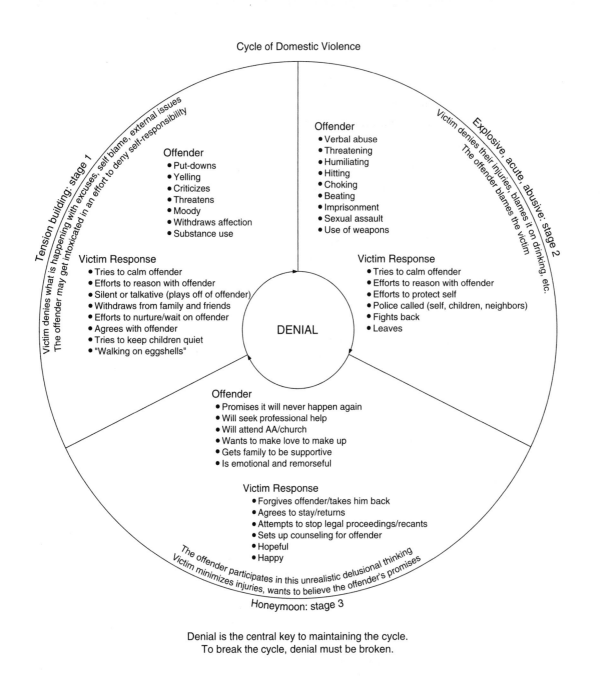

Cycle of Domestic Violence

Tension building: stage 1
Victim denies what is happening with excuses, self blame, external issues
The offender may get intoxicated in an effort to deny self-responsibility

Offender
- Put-downs
- Yelling
- Criticizes
- Threatens
- Moody
- Withdraws affection
- Substance use

Victim Response
- Tries to calm offender
- Efforts to reason with offender
- Silent or talkative (plays off of offender)
- Withdraws from family and friends
- Efforts to nurture/wait on offender
- Agrees with offender
- Tries to keep children quiet
- "Walking on eggshells"

Explosive, acute, abusive: stage 2
Victim denies their injuries, blames it on drinking, etc.
The offender blames the victim

Offender
- Verbal abuse
- Threatening
- Humiliating
- Hitting
- Choking
- Beating
- Imprisonment
- Sexual assault
- Use of weapons

Victim Response
- Tries to calm offender
- Efforts to reason with offender
- Efforts to protect self
- Police called (self, children, neighbors)
- Fights back
- Leaves

DENIAL

Offender
- Promises it will never happen again
- Will seek professional help
- Will attend AA/church
- Wants to make love to make up
- Gets family to be supportive
- Is emotional and remorseful

Victim Response
- Forgives offender/takes him back
- Agrees to stay/returns
- Attempts to stop legal proceedings/recants
- Sets up counseling for offender
- Hopeful
- Happy

The offender participates in this unrealistic delusional thinking
Victim minimizes injuries, wants to believe the offender's promises

Honeymoon: stage 3

Denial is the central key to maintaining the cycle.
To break the cycle, denial must be broken.

Adapted from the Domestic Abuse Intervention Program, Deluth Minnesota.

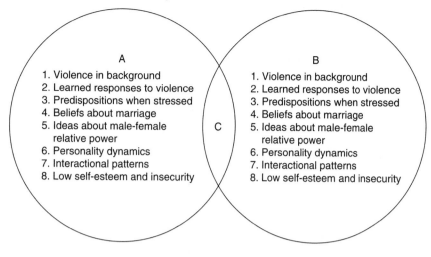

A General Systems Model of Domestic Violence

A
1. Violence in background
2. Learned responses to violence
3. Predispositions when stressed
4. Beliefs about marriage
5. Ideas about male-female relative power
6. Personality dynamics
7. Interactional patterns
8. Low self-esteem and insecurity

C

B
1. Violence in background
2. Learned responses to violence
3. Predispositions when stressed
4. Beliefs about marriage
5. Ideas about male-female relative power
6. Personality dynamics
7. Interactional patterns
8. Low self-esteem and insecurity

THE STAGE MODEL OF DOMESTIC VIOLENCE

The conceptual framework of systems theory is utilized to demonstrate the stepwise progression of the physically abusive relationship. Both the pattern of violence and the response to violence are learned early and can affect how a person deals with stress within a relationship. This is a process of adaptive change. The proposed stages of domestic violence (DV) include the following:

1. The establishment of the family system
   A. How did earlier life history affect the new family system?
   B. How did family boundaries evolve?
   C. What are the rules of dominance and power?

2. The first violent event
   A. How did the interaction between the couple during the first episode of violence affect the potential for future violence?

3. Stabilization of violence
   A. What functions within the system allow violence to escalate?
   B. What role does internal goals between the couple play in the evolution of DV?

4. Pivotal crisis point
   A. At what point do patterns of violence become intolerable?
   B. What are the criteria for intolerance aside from the amount of violence?

5. Reorientation
   A. How do the boundaries that previously defined the system shift?
   B. How does leaving the system cause a shift in thinking and personal dynamics?
   C. How does the offender respond to the victim's attempts to change the boundaries of the system?

6. Reorientation and conversion or status quo
   A. Does the victim leave the relationship?
   B. Is the victim successful in developing new interactional patterns in a new system?

C. If the victim remains in the relationship, will reorientation of system functioning and boundaries be successful, or will they remain the same?

Adapted from J. Giles-Sims (1983). *Wife battering: A systems theory approach.*

ASSESSING FOR DOMESTIC VIOLENCE

According to O'Leary et al. (1992), less than 5% of couples seeking conjoint therapy report any incident of domestic violence (DV) during intake. However, as many as 66% of those screened report some form of relationship violence experienced when given written self-report measures. Therefore, if specific questions are not asked during the interview, DV will not likely be identified and treated.

1. Reasons for not reporting DV
   A. Fear
   B. Shame
   C. Guilt/responsibility
   D. Belief that DV is not the problem

2. Complications of same-sex relationships
   1. Less likely to report DV than heterosexual couples
   2. May be more difficult to identify victim versus offender

*Advocates for Abused and Battered Lesbians has developed an assessment model to distinguish victim from offender (Veinot, T.,)

3. Complications for ethnic minority groups
   A. Language difficulties and associated limitations
   B. Isolated from their communities
   C. Obtaining services may result in increased community isolation

4. Children who are exposed to DV may present with the following concerns:
   A. Academic problems
   B. Social problems
   C. Low self-esteem
   D. Externalization demonstrated by behavioral problems
   E. Internalization of emotional effects
   F. Anger
   G. Aggressiveness
   H. Depression
   I. PTSD

5. Considerations to rule out in screening children (family history important):
   A. Other forms of trauma
   B. Depression
   C. ADD
   D. Conduct disorder

6. Victim symptom presentation
   A. Depression
   B. Anxiety
   C. Sleep disorder
   D. Eating disorder
   E. Substance abuse disorder
   F. Somatization disorder
   G. Panic attacks
   H. Hypervigilance
   I. Intrusive thoughts
   J. Suicidality

Housekamp and Foy (1991) stated that most symptoms are PTSD related. As a result, one or more of the preceding symptoms/disorders would be a common presentation. Additionally, be aware of a misdiagnosis of borderline or histrionic personality disorder. According to Root (1992), the development of personality disorder symptoms are a normal reaction to abnormal situations, and the condition may have developed as a coping mechanism.

Once DV has been identified, then assessment regarding the level of risk can be made. Assessment instruments include (but are not limited to) the following:

1. Dangerousness Assessment (Campbell, 1995)
2. Dominance Scale (Hamby, 1995)
3. Propensity for Abusiveness Scale (Dutton, 1995)
4. Psychological Maltreatment of Women Inventory (Tolman, 1989)
5. Relationship Conflict Inventory (Bodin, 1996)
6. Risk checklist/Psychological Violence Inventory (Sonkin, 2000)
7. Spousal Assault Risk Assessment (SARA) (Kropp & Hart, 1997)
8. Women's Experience with Battering (Smith, Earp, & DeVillis, 1995)

*Assessment for children: See Trauma Symptom Checklist for Children (TSCC) (Briere, 1996).

INTERVENTION CATEGORIES

1. Crisis intervention
   A. Resolution of immediate threats
   B. Resolution of other issues that may impair safety
   C. Identification of resources (medical, legal, community, social)
   D. Facilitation of access to resources
   E. Minimizing or eliminating dangerousness
   F. Development and implementation of a safety plan

2. Intervention for victims
   A. Immediate or short-term objectives
      1. Identify impact of violence and abuse
      2. Promote personal sense of empowerment
   B. Emphasis on long-term adjustment
      1. Resolution of emotional/psychological difficulties

C. Modalities
    1. Support group
    2. Psychoeducational programs
    3. Psychotherapy
    4. Shelter

3. Intervention for children exposed to DV
    A. Resolution of psychological and emotional consequences
       1. Distorted views of couple/family relationships
       2. Secondary trauma
       3. Assumption of age-inappropriate roles
    B. Modalities
       1. Support group
       2. Psychoeducational programs
       3. Psychotherapy
       4. Shelter (or some other safe placement)

4. Intervention for offenders
    A. Social control
    B. Psychoeducational programs
    C. Psychotherapy (accepting responsibility/commitment to refrain from acts of DV)

5. Intervention for couples or families of DV
    A. Requirements for conjoint therapy to proceed
       1. Maintenance of no violence
       2. Successful completion of individual goals in prior treatment interventions
       3. Both parties equally invested in safety for all parties involved as a priority over conjoint therapy and resolution of couple's issues

The literature is controversial regarding conjoint therapy. Some believe that conjoint therapy is prone to perpetuating further abuse, others believe that it is an essential intervention. Geffner and Mantooth (2000) have identified the following factors as being contraindicative for conjoint therapy:

1. Offender does not refrain from violence
2. Failure to accept responsibility for his/her actions
3. Failure to accept the discontinuance of abuse as the primary treatment objective
4. Inability to promote and preserve safety of all parties
5. High degree of fear and intimidation
6. Stalking or other obsessive behaviors
7. Use of alcohol or other substances
8. High degree of dangerousness and lethality
9. Disinterest or discomfort by either party to participate in conjoint therapy

COUNSELING VICTIMS OF DOMESTIC VIOLENCE

Primary goal: To protect self and children.

OBJECTIVES

1. Enhance experience of self-empowerment
2. Decrease/eliminate responsibility for the behavior of others
3. Develop social support
4. Increase utilization of resources (medical, legal, welfare, social support)
5. Decrease isolation
6. Increase protections skills (for self and children)
7. Improve self-care skills
   A. Stress management
   B. Self-presentation
   C. Nutrition
   D. Self-affirmation
   E. Health care
8. Increase utilization of self-care skills
9. Decrease fear, immobilization, and helplessness
10. Decrease dependency on relationship with offender
11. Educate regarding family and social facilitators of domestic violence
12. Improve assertive communication
13. Begin vocational training/education
14. Increase awareness of behavioral patterns and vulnerability

CHILD ABUSE AND NEGLECT

Child abuse encompasses physical abuse, emotional/psychological abuse, neglect, and sexual abuse. The report of suspected child abuse is a written narrative describing the suspected abuse, a summary of statements made by the victim or person(s) accompanying the child, and an explanation of known history of similar incident(s) for the minor victim on a form which can be obtained from child protective services or other agency whose jurisdiction oversees and investigates suspected child abuse. The foundation of the report is based on the verbalized statements of alleged abuse as well as the physical and emotional indicators of child abuse.

A therapist may participate at various levels of prevention, intervention, and treatment. As mandated reporters of child abuse, all therapists should be familiar with identifying families at risk for abuse as well as the interdisciplinary and community resources available to victims of child abuse and their families.

PREVENTION

Primary Prevention

is community education aimed at improving the general well-being of families and their children. The focus is to facilitate the development of skills which improve family functioning and to prevent or alleviate stress or problems which could lead to child abuse.

Secondary Prevention

is the available or specifically designed services which identify high-risk families and help them prevent abuse.

| *Tertiary Prevention* | is defined as the intervention or treatment services which assist a family in which child abuse or neglect has already occurred and acts to prevent further abuse or neglect. |

INDICATORS OF ABUSE

Indicators of Physical Abuse

1. Bruises
2. Burns
3. Bite marks
4. Abrasions, lacerations
5. Head injuries
6. Whiplash (shaken baby syndrome)
7. Internal injuries
8. Fractures

Indicators of Emotional/ Psychological Abuse

1. The child is depressed and apathetic
2. The child is withdrawn
3. The child is overly conforming to authority figures
4. Demonstrates behavioral problems or "acting out"
5. Demonstrates repetitive, rhythmic movements
6. Overly concerned with detail
7. Unreasonable demands or expectations are placed on the child
8. The child is triangulated into marital conflicts
9. The child is viewed as property of the parent (referred to as "it" instead of by name)
10. The child is used to gratify parental needs
11. The child demonstrates exaggerated fears or antisocial behaviors
12. The child is unable to perform normal, age-appropriate behaviors/skills
13. Constantly seeking the attention and affection of adults

Indicators of Child Neglect

1. Lack of adequate medical/dental care
2. The child demonstrates poor personal hygiene
3. The child is always dirty
4. The child is inadequately dressed
5. Poor supervision/left home alone
6. Unsanitary environmental conditions
7. Lack of heating and plumbing
8. Fire hazards and other unsafe home conditions
9. Inadequate sleeping arrangements (cold, dirty, etc.)
10. Inadequate nutrition/children fend for their own nutritional needs

These conditions existing as chronic and extreme constitute the definition of an unfit home and neglect.

1. Enuresis or fecal soiling
2. Eating disturbances
3. Fears/phobias/compulsive behaviors
4. Age-inappropriate behaviors (pseudomaturity or regressive behaviors)
5. Problems with school performance and attitudes
6. Difficulty concentrating
7. Sleep disturbance
8. Depression, low self-worth, and withdrawal
9. Overly compliant
10. Poor social skills
11. Acting out/runaway/antisocial behaviors
12. Substance abuse
13. Age-inappropriate excessive self-consciousness of body
14. Sudden possession of money, new clothes, or other gifts
15. Self-destructive behavior, self-defeating behavior
16. Suicidal thoughts, plans, attempts
17. Crying without apparent reason
18. Fire setting
19. Sexually transmitted diseases, genital infection
20. Physical trauma or irritation to the anal or genital area
21. Difficulty walking or sitting due to genital/anal pain
22. Pain on voiding/elimination
23. Psychosomatic symptoms
24. Age-inappropriate knowledge of sexual behavior
25. Inappropriate sexual behavior with siblings, peers, or objects
26. Compulsive masturbation
27. Excessive curiosity about sexual issues and/or genitalia
28. Promiscuity or prostitution

TREATMENT

When dealing with issues of neglect or psychological abuse, appropriate education and support are often sufficient to alter the identified circumstances of neglect. There are, of course, instances in which the psychological/emotional functioning of the parent(s) is not adequate to consistently provide the child's necessities for health and wellness without an increased level of intervention and treatment, possibly removing the child from a home.

With issues of physical abuse, child safety is the central focus. The court relies on expert witness testimony, collateral observations and information, interview of the victim and the parent(s) or other offender if not a parent to make the determination of setting appropriate goals. Treatment goals could range from removal of the child to insure safety with a tentative plan for early reunification to long-term placement of a child who cannot be safety returned to their home.

While a child experiencing any level of abuse may benefit from therapy, a child who has been sexually abused should be referred for therapy as soon as possible. Even if the family is participating in a treatment program, the child should be referred for individual therapy so that the impact of abuse can be evaluated without the family dynamics overshadowing the child's intrapersonal-interpersonal experience resulting from the abuse.

Likewise parent(s) or caretaker(s) need assistance in understanding what the assessed abusive behaviors are, why they are abusive, how to effectively manage their own lives, and how to effectively parent. These families need to have resources identified for them that can be helpful for ongoing support, education, and crisis intervention.

CHILD CUSTODY EVALUATION

When mediation has not been successful, a qualified psychologist is often called on to conduct a child custody evaluation. Requirements of standard of care following ethical and professional guidelines act to protect and preserve the rights of all with the best interest of the children being the central focus of outcome.

GUIDELINES FOR PSYCHOLOGICAL EVALUATION

A. Examination of Child
   1. Mental status with behavioral observations noted.
   2. Developmental milestones.
   3. Coping methods, especially with regard to issues of change in lifestyle, family constellation in their daily environment, use of transitional objects in lieu of absence of a parent, and dealing with loss.
   4. Degree of attachment to parents.
   5. Stage of development and what type of parenting indicative of each parent.
   6. Presence of psychosocial impairment, severity, interventions recommended.
   7. Use of psychological testing instruments as deemed necessary.

B. Individual Examination of Parents
   1. Mental status with behavioral observations noted.
   2. Personality functioning and parenting skills. Are there issues/concerns related to parental functioning which could compromise and/or damage the child's well-being?
      a. Psychopathological states which are indicative or have demonstrated the fostering of delinquent/antisocial behavior.
      b. Pathology which impairs the ability to parent consistently and safely such as psychosis, substance abuse issues, character disturbances.
      c. An unhealthy focus or unconscious concerns related to dependency, power, sexuality, anger, and using the child(ren) to meet their own needs.
   3. Personal history with reference to their own childhood experiences, i.e., how did their family deal with anger, discipline, emotional needs met, parental relationship, etc.
   4. Demonstration of flexibility in accepting feedback related to their parenting responsibilities, skills, and recommendations for change.
   5. Likely method of restoring missing partner—cooperative or noncooperative.
   6. Ability and willingness to form treatment alliance serving the best interest of their child(ren).
   7. Use of psychological testing instruments as deemed necessary.

C. Conjoint Examination of Parents
   1. How do they complement each other in appropriate parenting ability?
   2. How do personality dynamics affect minimal cooperative efforts in managing the needs of child(ren)?
   3. How will they likely respond to their ex-partner's choices such as remarriage?

The purpose of the Bonding Study is to develop an understanding of the degree to which the child demonstrates an attachment with their perspective family.

ABILITY OF THE CHILD TO BOND

1. Is the child bonded to the parent(s)?
2. What is the quality of attachment?
3. Does the child have the capacity to bond to anyone?
4. If the child were removed from this home would it result in psychological damage?
5. Are the visitations between child and parent(s) meeting developmental/psychological needs of the child?
6. Compare/contrast the relationship of the child to both parents and both parents to the child.
7. Observe leave-taking behavior and affect.
8. Be aware of any impediments to child bonding such as child or parent deafness.

Some children identified as "at risk" and requiring special care may need specific parental qualities of nurturance and positive regard. The potential parents must be thoroughly evaluated for their ability and desire to care for a special-needs child. In observing the child and interactions with the potential parents it is necessary to have a clear picture of the level of child development and maturity.

Additional issues include:

1. History and current status of the child's health.
2. Any changes in the child's behavior observed by the custodial/foster parent on the way to a visit, on the way home from a visit, or for the reset of the day following the visit.
3. Be prepared by being familiar with the history of the child and the relationship being observed.

ABILITY OF THE PARENT TO BOND AND OTHER PERTINENT INFORMATION

1. Thorough review of background and court-related history.
2. Observation of parent's mental status.
3. Clinical interview.
4. Psychological testing if necessary for clarification on issues of functioning.
5. Observe nature of family relationships.
6. Collateral contacts for information related to history of child (number of caretakers, quality of care, history of abuse, previous psychological treatment, etc.) history of perspective parent(s) (similar issues).
7. Stage of development versus behavioral manifestations in various settings.
8. Additional considerations if present related to cultural or familial factors, substance abuse, support system, reunification, etc.

The unique information required in a Bonding Evaluation can be applied to the report outline of a Child Custody Evaluation.

CHILD CUSTODY EVALUATION REPORT OUTLINE

A. Identification of Case
   1. Parties and minor children
   2. Legal issues and standards
   3. Referral source(s)
   4. Referral question(s)
   5. List collateral contacts and cite the form of contact such as phone, record review, etc.

B. Schedule of Appointments
   1. Individual(s) seen
   2. Date(s) of service
   3. Amount of time devoted to evaluation of each individual and the methods of evaluation utilized.

C. Assessment
   1. Document the stated objectives of each party related to custody and visitation.
   2. What does each party view as the primary issues such as conflicts, and allegations.
   3. Parent statements, from their perspective, of their own strengths, weaknesses, and limitations as a parent and their view of the child(ren) in terms of needs and impairments—and their view on the same issue as it pertains to the other parent.
   4. Information gathered from prior findings (records, summary analyses, etc.) which establish a foundation of relevant background and context for the current evaluation.

D. Results of Evaluation
   1. Statement of evaluation findings which includes:
      a. mental status exam
      b. interview information as it pertains to child custody
      c. observations
      d. relevant psychological testing information

E. Interpretation of Findings
   1. Parental abilities, strengths/concerns/impairments that either enhance or detract from competent parenting.
   2. Mental health of child(ren) clarifying developmental needs, special considerations, vulnerabilities, etc.
   3. Quality of parent–child interaction, parent–parent interaction with issues of consistency and congruence.
   4. Issues of credibility related to these findings.

F. Discussion of Findings

This section utilizes specific references to detail each parent's competencies as it pertains to the best interest of the child(ren). Address issues of health, safety, and welfare of the child(ren). Include relevant issues such as child abuse, neglect, etc. Use this section to integrate all relevant findings presented in the evaluation.

G. Opinions

If requested regarding specific referral questions and legal issues in reference to legal and physical custody, visitation, activities, contact with other significant people in the support system of the child(ren), etc.

H. Parent–Child Interaction
  1. How does the child(ren) spontaneously respond to the parent—valued, devalued, close, distant—and the reason behind it.
  2. Is the parent appropriately engaged with the child(ren), listens and communicates with them, facilitates appropriate self-management by the child(ren), provides them choices, etc.?
  3. Is the parent nurturing and resourceful to the child(ren)?

During the assessment of the parent–child(ren) interaction, the interaction is broken down or defined by the following factors:

PARENTAL BEHAVIOR

1. Eye contact
2. Age-appropriate structure/limit setting/discipline
3. Type of objects brought by parents for the child(ren): food, toys, clothing, etc.
4. Amount and emotional quality of physical contact
5. Initiative toward interaction
6. Age-appropriate expectations
7. Appropriateness of verbal interaction, questions, etc.
8. Attitude and behavior, before, during, and after interview

INTERACTION BETWEEN PARENT–CHILD(REN)

1. Child(ren) behavior toward parent, and parent's response to it
2. Eye contact or avoidance on the behalf of parent or child(ren)
3. Affectionate, positive, nurturing body language
4. Quality and type of physical contact between parent and child(ren), i.e., sit together in chair, together on floor, playful, engaged in any way
5. Verbal exchanges
6. Parent limit setting/structure and child(ren) response

BONDING STUDY VERSUS CUSTODY EVALUATION

The reference of bonding is related to the issue of adoption. A bonding study minimally requires:

1. An observation of the minor
2. Interviews with the bonding parent(s)
3. Observations in combinations of parent, parents–child, parent–child, whole family
4. Some of the observations are to be made in the home environment
5. Psychological testing will be utilized if the perspective parents have not been previously evaluated
6. Interviews with anyone significant to the child's life: prospective siblings, teachers, etc.
7. Thorough review of available documents
8. Recommendations

Specify treatment recommendations, individual (parent or child), conjoint remediation between parent or between parent–child(ren), need of special programs, etc. Be sure that all issues and questions raised by the court have been addressed.

PARENTAL ALIENATION SYNDROME

Parental alienation syndrome (PAS) occurs when parental influence or programming is combined with a child's own disparaging views of a parent. Overall, there are four contributing factors to PAS:

PARENTAL PROGRAMMING

1. Most often overt and obvious
2. Often there is an infrequency of visits or lack of contact with the alienated parent (which decreases opportunity to correct the alienating parent's distortions. Without actual experience, the child may completely accept the alienating parents criticisms)
3. Common complaints of the preferred parent
   A. He/she has to pay for everything
   B. He/she cannot depend on the alienated parent
      He/she "abandoned us"
      He/she destroyed the family
      He/she is mean, abusive, or sick
   C. The preferred parent exaggerates the psychological problems of the alienated parent
      1. Uses sarcasm to highlight how undesirable the alienated parent is
      2. Interferes with phone calls from alienated parent
      3. Mentors child in being deceitful to alienated parent, making the child an accomplice in warfare (message is that alienated parent is not worthy of honesty and respect)
      4. Labels attempts of hated parents to contact child or be involved in their lives as harassment

SUBTLE AND UNCONSCIOUS INFLUENCING

1. Preferred parent may state that he/she never criticizes the other parent to the child, however, says things like "I could tell you some things (about the other parent), but I'm not the kind of parent who speaks badly about the other parent"
2. Respects the child's wishes to spend time with the alienated parent, but the child generally knows that the preferred parent doesn't want him or her to or uses subtle sabotage: "If you don't visit, he/she will take us to court"
3. Provokes feelings of guilt for abandoning the preferred parent when the child spends time with the alienated parent
4. Finds neutral ways to convey the inadequacies of the alienated parent
5. Undoing (i.e., criticizes the other parent and then says, "I didn't mean it" or "I was just kidding")

CHILD'S OWN SCENARIOS

These are experiences or perceptions of the child, which play a role in the alienation process by feelings of validation, juvenile punishment of the alienated parent, protectiveness of the preferred parent, experience of viewing emotional/physical abuse perpetrated by alienated parent toward the preferred parent, and so forth

1. Lack of nurturance from alienated parent
2. Lack of bonding
3. Anger or disappointments
4. Seeing preferred prerent as a victim or fragile
5. Experiencing parent as nongratifying
6. Seeing alienated parent as mean and rigid (difficult to get the child's needs met)

*It is important to not lose sight of the child's contribution in parental alienation.

FAMILY DYNAMICS AND ENVIRONMENT/ SITUATIONAL ISSUES

1. System structure parents create (nurturer, disciplinarian, understanding, rigid rules, encouragement, controlling, etc.)
2. Closed versus open family system
3. History of colluding behavior
4. Poor health in a parent
5. Prioritizing (work, couple's time, individual time, family time, etc.)
6. Values/morality

For the alienated parent, PAS only applies when this parent has not engaged in any degree of abusive behavior that would warrant such a response from the child. Generally, these parents have provided relatively normal nurturing parenting. Sometimes there is evidence of minor weakness/deficiencies, which are exaggerated and become the benchmark of focus in the development of PAS. Children are preoccupied in an unjust and exaggerated manner on these deficiencies in the parent.

As instruments to be used, these children become an ally with the preferred parent in an effort to preserve what they identify to be the most desirable living arrangement. This happens without awareness that in some situations primary custody by the alienated parent might actually be in the child's best interest. Here the child becomes a weapon, thereby enabling the preferred/loved parent to gratify his/her hostility toward the alienated/hated parent through the child. The loved parent is also preoccupied with the hated parent's defects, thus creating and reinforcing a distorted image.

CRITERIA FOR ESTABLISHING PRIMARY CUSTODY

1. Preference is given to the parent with the stronger and healthier bond
2. The primary caretaker during the early formative years of a child's life is likely to exhibit the stronger/healthier bond
3. The more extensive time between these formative years and the time of the custody decision, the greater the likelihood that other factors may influence custody in either direction.

BEHAVIORS OF THE PARENTS

1. The preferred parent
   A. Denies positives in relationship between the child and the alienated parent
   B. Describes behaviors in absolutes of "always" or "never"
   C. Emotional boundary disintegration
      1. Merges his/her own feelings/views with the child ("We won't let them take us to court and hurt us anymore")
   D. Makes direct/indirect attempts to interfere with the relationship between the child and the alienated parent
   E. When the child is with the alienated parent, creates intrusive interference by numerous phone calls
   F. Involves the child in spying and information gathering
   G. Uses child as confidant, sharing adult issues about divorce, blaming, and so on
   H. Uses child as a messenger between parents
   I. Creates family splitting and feuding

*The evaluator will need to take into consideration if the behaviors of the preferred parent are associated with real or perceived deficiencies of the alienated parent. Depending on what is found, there needs to be recommendations that address these issues. If the issues are addressed in the recommendations in the form of intervention, to whom they are directed depends on whether they are genuine or not (i.e., does the alienated parent need to modify or cease certain behaviors, or does the alienating parent need to alter perceptions and acknowledge the ways in which a child is negatively affected by the situation?).

2. The alienated parent
   A. Healthy relationship with child prior to separation
      1. Being shut out of the child's life
      2. Insightful, willing to accept responsibility and examine a range of possibilities associated with a child's behavior
      3. History of actively participating in his/her child's life
      4. Nurturing qualities with possible tendency toward passivity
      5. May experience some difficulty dealing with overwhelming emotion

*These factors provide an environment for alienation to take hold. In such family systems, the preferred or alienating parent is typically emotionally over-reactive and extreme, whereas the alienated parent is empathic, sensitive, nurturing, and passive or avoidant of conflict (peacemaker). Therefore, when the alienation is put in motion the alienated parent may initially respond in a more passive manner, feel overwhelmed and not knowing what to do. Unfortunately, there may be a tendency to detach to avoid conflicts, and this reinforces the behavior of the alienating parent. Additionally, if the court system reinforces or rewards the alienating parent's behavior, it creates a momentum to the alienation that seems impossible to stop. In this situation, when the alienated parent has finally had enough and responds with repeated efforts to participate more in the child's life, he/she is easily labeled with harassment, and when he/she sets firm limits with the alienating parent, he/she is labeled vengeful and often reprimanded and told he/she is fueling the situation.

   B. The parent claims alienation is the source of estrangement, however, he/she is defensive, avoidant, externalizes blame, and has difficulty with self-responsibility, which are really the original souces of estrangement

1. Had little to do with the child prior to separation (workaholics/self-centered)
2. Quickly involved in a new relationship with an insensitivity to child's feelings and issues of adjustment and relationship building
3. Controlling, powerful, dominating (blame/externalizing is common)
4. Expectation of child exceeds their investment in the relationship (demanding without nurturing, but expects the child to be a certain way following separation)
5. Less child centered and less empathic
6. Parent-child relationship has a superficial quality due to years of neglect
7. Has a keen sense for showing up at the right moments for credit as being supportive—"Kodak moments"
8. May report being active in the child's life via encouragement in activities or coaching sports, but the child actually feels pushed into these activities
9. May alleged alienation as a means to continue to control and blame

*Identification of these parents is initially challenging, but clarity can be achieved by exploring the history of their investment in family and the parent-child relationship coupled with defensiveness, control, self-focus, blaming/externalization, and overall superficial quality to the parent-child relationship.

CHILDREN

The relationship between parents and children can be fragile and tenuous, even if it were a positive one prior to separation. Children don't have the ability, let alone the power, to maintain the necessary boundaries for normal and healthy relationships with their parents. They are dependent on parents setting and maintaining the guidelines for healthy relationships. As a result, when parents lack respect and responsibility in guiding their own behaviors and making decisions that are truly in the best interest of their children, the children are eclipsed and caught in the middle. It is these dynamics in which parental alienation is initiated and encouraged. The child become a pawn in vengeance and in meeting the needs of the parent. The needs of the child are secondary.

As the war ensues, causation and reason for the conflicts are often not clearly discernible. What is clear is that anyone or anything that is not supportive of the preferred parent's perception is viewed as negative and rejected. The child may already have his/her own slightly tainted image of the alienated parent, but this is accelerated under the influence of the preferred parent. If a child is somewhat passive, dependent, and feels a need to care/protect/nurture the alienating parent, he/she is even more susceptible to alienating programming. This boundariless fusion of feelings enmeshes the child and the alienating parent. Some of the psychological/emotional problems that these children are at risk for developing include the following:

1. Depression
2. Dependency
3. Psychological vulnerability
4. Abandonment issues
5. Splitting
6. Inability to tolerate anger/hostility
7. Anger and rage
8. Difficulty developing intimate relationships
9. Conflicts with authority figures
10. Psychosomatic symptoms

11. Eating disorders

12. Entitlement

Often when these children are evaluated, there is little evidence of them being placed in the middle. Many have experienced one parent being controlling or dictatorial, severe hostility, and spousal abuse. There is a quality of sadness in them and either ambivalence associated with a desire for a healthy relationship with the alienated parent or just the lack of a relationship with this parent. This would indicate being aligned to the preferred parent, but not total alienation for the other parent.

As the clarity of systems dynamics develops, several other issues may become apparent regarding the quality of the relationship the child shares with each parent. There may be an alignment with one parent, but it is not due to alienation. Time is spent with a specific parent because of shared interest (sports, arts/music, outdoors). The child also spends a modified amount of time with the other parent. Second, alignment with one parent may be an adaptive maneuver that removes the child from the middle as conflict escalates in an effort to decrease anxiety and vulnerability. In this case, the child is demonstrating a desire to not be a part of parental conflicts, not as an instrument in parental alienation, and it may not even matter which parent it is. Therefore, it is the conflict (anxiety and vulnerability) that drives the parental alignment and splitting.

THREE CATEGORIES OF PARENTAL ALIENATION

1. Mild (as evidenced by)
   A. Subtle attempts to alienate a child against the other parent may take place
   B. The child is influenced to take on the preferred parent's point of view with unconscious or conscious efforts and a lack of insight of how it makes a child feel
   C. The alienating parent maintains the importance of a relationship with both parents
   D. Generally, both parents recognize that alienation from either parent is not in the best interest of the child
   E. Communication between parents exists and there is a more conciliatory approach to requests by the alienated parent to be involved in the child's life
   F. Even though the preferred parent wants sole custody and believes that it would be best for the child, he/she recognizes that protracted legal proceedings may cause more suffering for the child
   G. Children develop their own views, with slight prodding from the preferred parent
   H. Children though ambivalent regarding visitation, are free to express their feelings

*For most children the consequences are minimal and include minor loyalty conflicts and anxiety, there is no fundamental change in the child's own view of the alienated parent

2. Moderate (as evidenced by)
   A. Preferred parent often feels hurt, angry, and vengeful
   B. Preferred parent expects the child to take sides and be loyal to him/her
   C. Preferred parent actively interferes with visitation arrangements and relationship with the alienated parent
   D. Preferred parent supports the notion of a relationship with the other parent, yet consciously/unconsciously perpetrates sabotage
   E. Preferred parent may ignore court orders (if he/she can get away with it)
   F. Paranoid projections are not as extreme as in severe PAS
   G. There is some ability to differentiate between allegations that are dishonest/outlandish versus genuine complaints

H. Significant desire to withhold child from the alienated parent as vengeful maneuvering

I. Though unreceptive, the preferred parent complies with court orders under pressure, threat of sanctions, transfer of custody, and so on

J. Psychological bond may be healthy but is compromised by anger/rage

K. The preferred parent likely demonstrated good parenting prior to divorce

*Common consequences for children

1. Insecurity
2. Distortions (viewing the alienating parent as the good parent and the alienated parent as the bad parent with some integration of positives about the alienated parent)
3. Anxiety
4. Splitting/manipulating
5. Limited relationship with the alienated parent

3. Severe (as evidenced by)

A. Preferred parent is angry, bitter, and possibly feels abandoned and betrayed by the alienated parent

B. Conscious, consistence disparaging programming of the alienated parent by the preferred parent and the child (initiated by parent and adapted by child)

C. In most cases, the child and alienated parent had a relatively positive and healthy relationship previously

D. The preferred parent will utilize every mechanism and opportunity to prevent visitation

E. These parents are not logical, reality based, or appeal to reason

F. Paranoid projections

G. Impaired child rearing capacity prior to separation/divorce

H. The alienated parent is outraged by the influence and changes in the child and blames the other parent

EVALUATION AND DISPOSITION CONSIDERATIONS FOR FAMILIES WHERE PARENTAL ALIENATION OCCURS

The degree of parental alienation syndrome may be viewed as reflective or directly related to the degree of motivation demonstrated by parents who present or are court-ordered for psychological evaluations and treatment from family court. As a result, these are inherently difficult cases, which pose an issue for risk management on behalf of the therapist involved in such a case. Document your case well. The following information presents the mother as the loved or preferred parent and the father as the hated or alienated parent. However, this scenario works in the reverse direction as well. Consider the following points and questions in your evaluation and recommendations.

1. Proper placement of the child is imperative. Without proper placement, treatment will be futile.

2. Though the parental alienation syndrome is actually a continuum with discrete markers defining the severity, it is necessary that the therapist evaluating a case

specifically differentiate between moderate and severe cases because of the implication on placement.

3. A guardian ad litem for the children at the center of a custody litigation may be useful. However, if the guardian ad litem is not familiar with the dynamics of PAS, his/her involvement could prove to be a detriment to the outcome of the disposition in the case.

4. If the situation does not render reasonable certainty as to what would be the best decision, offer a "tentative" recommendation subject to review and reevaluation. However, when possible, every attempt to make a permanent recommendation is preferred.

5. Create a balance sheet overview of assets and liabilities, including stepparents if they are in the current clinical picture being evaluated.

6. The parent who is going to discourage the child from visitation is most likely to deprive the child from important information from the other parent. The healthier parent, even with his/her own personal issues associated with the divorce, recognizes the importance of continuing as positive a relationship as possible with both parents. This is a very important issue in determining primary custody. The decision of custody is extremely difficult, and there is no completely satisfactory solution to this issue.

QUESTIONS TO ASK CHILDREN

1. Ask the children to describe one parent and then the other. If PAS is present, the children will describe one parent with a number of criticisms and the other with a clear delineation of positive responses.

2. Ask the child to describe each parent's family. If PAS is present, the responses will reflect a distinct similarity to the answers in the prior question—thus, preferring the family of the preferred parent and alienation toward the family of the alienated parent.

3. If PAS has been established by the information gathered and, for example, the mother is the preferred parent and the father has been alienated, ask the child if his/her mother interferes with visitation of the father. It is very likely that the child will describe his/her mother as being neutral and not interfering, stating that the decision of visitation is entirely the child's own.

4. Again, assuming that the father is the hated/alienated parent, ask the child why he/she does not want to visit the father. The response initially may be vague. When pressed for specifics, horrible abuses may be conjured, which are exaggerations not warranting concern. Sometimes there will be a proclamation that the child's desire is to have absolutely no contact with the hated/alienated parent.

5. If the mother is the loved/preferred parent, ask the child if the mother harasses his/her. Normally, it would be expected that a child would offer several situations where he/she is not gratified. When PAS is present, the mother is likely to be described more in terms of being a perfect parent. The alienated parent's attempts to have contact and be involved with the child is what would be viewed as harassment.

6. Ask the child if the hated/alienated parent harasses him/her. The response would generally validate the harassment with any attempt (phone calls, letters, legal intervention, etc.) identified as harassment.

QUESTIONS TO ASK THE PARENTS

1. What is their opinion of parent-child relationships?
   A. What is the history of each relationship?
      1. What has changed?
      2. How has the child been affected?
   B. How does each parent demonstrate support of the child's relationship to the other parent?
   C. What do the parents think the child should know about what has happened in the marriage?
2. What are their ideas of how to improve the circumstances?
3. How do they believe that their behavior has affected their child?
4. What are they willing to do differently?
5. If they make the change recommended, what would be the evidence of that change in three months, six months, or one year.

PARENTAL ALIENATION SYNDROME TREATMENT

1. Mild PAS
   A. Most cases do not require intervention
   B. Generally, a final court order will confirm the custody arrangement, often with the preferred parent due to history of being the primary caretaker and demonstrating a stronger bond with the child

2. Moderate PAS
   A. It is recommended that there be one therapist for the family system
      1. Reduce fractionization of communication
      2. Decrease antagonistic subsystems
      3. Beneficial if therapist is court ordered (with the court being willing to impose sanctions)
   B. Some parents in this category may involve themselves meaningfully in the treatment process. They may even pursue individual therapy in an effort to take responsibility for and work through unresolved issues.
   C. Because they are good child rearers, the child is often to remain in custody of the preferred parent
   D. Combined effort of therapist and court realigns children to resume normal visitation

3. Severe PAS
   A. One therapist for the family system
   B. The alienating parent is not receptive to therapy
      1. Will consider a therapist who believes his/her position or is at least passively supportive by not implementing necessary change or confrontive of the PAS he/she is instigating
   C. The literature's view of how to proceed on the disposition of custody varies
      1. Gardner (1989) has stated that the child should be removed from the custody of the alienating parent with custody being transferred to the alienated parent. He has recommended a period of decompression/debriefing where there is no contact from the alienating parent to allow for the reestablishment of a

relationship with the alienated parent. If there is visitation, it is minimal and in the presence of a designated third party contracted with the court to formally monitor the interaction. Once there has been stabilization with parent-child realignment, the contact with the alienating parent is proceeded with slowly to prevent a reoccurrence of the previous level of dysfunction. The belief is that if no intervention has been made, the risk of lifelong alienation between the child and the alienated parent will result.

Both parents are to be educated about the PAS and what is expected of them regarding their interaction the child and with issues associated with the other parent. Addressing the importance of a strong bond with both parents

    a. Child's exaggerated hatred is generally a façade (not allowed to be honest, fear of displeasing, protective, etc.)
    b. The need to develop a thick skin to deal with negative outbursts from the child
    c. The importance of neither parent withdrawing from participation in the child's life
2. Stahl (1999) stated that any abrupt custody change may have significant negative consequences on the child. Therefore, any proposed changes should be thoroughly problem-solved so as to not cause more problems for the child. He has advocated a more balanced custody arrangement of equal time sharing in larger chunks (two weeks or more at a time). The belief is that in some families there may never be a viable relationship between the child and the alienated parent, even with structural changes in custody, therapy, and monitoring. In such cases, with guidance from the therapist, there may be the recommendation that the alienated parent temporarily withdraw from the child's life in order to prevent the child from experiencing any pain due to being in the middle. The decision to withdraw is only to help their child. It is also made clear that the parent loves the child, highly desires a relationship with the child, and will make contact every several months. The parents further states that the child will always know where the parent is and how to contact him/her.

Research has not been conclusive or consistent on what the right intervention is in severe PAS cases. Instead, it appears that there should be a thorough review about how to proceed on a case-by-case basis. One intervention that may be helpful in every case for monitoring of change and information that the court could concretely reinforce for outcome-oriented specified results would be to explain to each parent the effects of PAS on the child:

1. Have the information reiterated in written form
2. Have both parents sign a form acknowledging their understanding
3. Develop a written treatment plan that breaks down the expected changes and outlines the associated consequences if there is not compliance have parents sign the form.
4. Referral for individual therapy for resolution of personal issues is made and a consultation is made with the individual therapist so that he/she understands the situation and what is expected
5. Meet intermittently to review progress or lack of progress

The information on PAS was adapted from R. A. Gardner (1989) and P. Stahl (1999).

VISITATION RIGHTS REPORT

When there has been a marital separation, divorce, or out-of-the-home placement it is sometimes necessary to evaluate the parents and child for the purpose of visitation rights. The goal is to serve the best interest of the child by assuring adequate contact with each parent in a safe environment under which the visitation occurs. If there is concern related to safety or a history of difficulties associated with the contact of either parent with the child then appropriate steps must be taken to provide for the safety of the child.

VISITATION RIGHTS REPORT

1. Dates of gathering information for the report
2. Names of father, mother, and child
3. Referral source
4. Identifying information for each party
5. Relevant background information
6. Site of visitation (and reason for that selected site)
7. History of visitation
8. Child's relationship with mother/evaluation of mother
9. Child's relationship with father/evaluation of father
10. Conclusions
    A. Temporary arrangement pending further information, supervision, completion of recommended classes (anger management/parenting/first aid/etc.), or other identified issues to be resolved
    B. Trial visitation arrangements
    C. Permanent arrangement
    D. Other parameters/considerations
11. Recommendations

DISPOSITIONAL REVIEW: FOSTER PLACEMENT; TEMPORARY PLACEMENT

A primary responsibility of mental health professionals (MHP) working with mistreated children and their families is to remedy difficult situations and prevent placement if possible. Placement of a child outside of the family home is indicated only as the last option or when a child is in danger of harm. The task of the MHP may be as a consultant to a child protective service agency in directing the appropriate disposition of the child and family, what necessary placement would be appropriate, and the monitoring of all parties participating in a place (Disposition Review).

In evoking the placement process it is important to minimize traumatic disruption and replacement of caretakers and environments. Placements should be thoroughly screened to ensure that potential caretakers are prepared to cope effectively with the behaviors of troubled children. The last thing an abused or neglected child needs is the validation of rejection. Therefore, there should be continuity of care where the caretakers are consistent, dependable, and the basic needs of physical comfort, nurturance, affection, encouragement, gratification, intellectual development, and social development are offered and facilitated.

Because the court monitors such placements and because there can be planned or warranted charges in placement there may be a request by the court for a Dispositional Review. The Dispositional Review is a thorough evaluation of all parties and the environment of the placement. Historically, it addresses the background leading to placement and the placement goals. The conclusion must address issues of adjustment, and status of goals and objectives. The last segment of the report is the area of recommendations. This report serves as a baseline for review and must lend itself to updated addendums to supply to the court with necessary information during the course of the placement.

DISPOSITIONAL REVIEW REPORT OUTLINE

1. Identifying information of minor/family court-appointed caretakers
2. Reason for referral
3. Relevant background information
4. Sources of data
5. Evaluation of
   A. Minor
   B. Mother
   C. Father
   D. Court-assigned caretakers
   E. Interaction/relationship functioning between minor and parents and minor and court-assigned caretakers
   F. Environment of placement
6. Conclusions
7. Recommendations

PSYCHIATRIC WORK-RELATED DISABILITY EVALUATION

This is a formal report format for the evaluation of an individual who is believed to be unable to work due to psychiatric disability.

Name _____

Date of Report _____

Date of Birth _____

Date of Last Day Worked _____

Case Number _____

IDENTIFYING INFORMATION

A. Date, place, and duration of examination
B. Reason for referral and referral question(s)
C. Names of all individuals participating in the examination. Include the use of interpreter or any other party present and why they are present.
D. Sources of Information
   1. Collateral contacts
   2. Prior reports/progress notes/medical records
   3. Clinical interview
   4. Mental status exam
   5. Psychological tests

DESCRIPTION OF CLIENT AT TIME OF INTERVIEW

A. Appearance (include any physical variance)
B. General behavior, demeanor, presentation
C. The observed effective state
D. Stream of speech

DESCRIPTIONS OF CLIENT'S CURRENT COMPLAINTS

A. Subjective complaints, described in their own words
B. The client's view of the impairment created/resulting from the described complaint

HISTORY OF PRESENT ILLNESS

A. Client's description of work-related/industrial stressors, onset of the complaints, and the alleged injuries/illness associated with the onset
B. Psychological/emotional response to the alleged injury situation

C. History of mental health problems since the alleged injury

D. History of treatment since the alleged injury

E. Current treatment
1. Medication (including medication taken on the day of the interview)
2. Psychotherapy
3. Group therapy
4. Alternative approaches used for management of complaints

OCCUPATIONAL HISTORY

This section includes work events prior to injury, concurrent with injury, and after injury.

A. Educational level and profession, technical, and/or vocational training

B. Sequence of work experience/occupations pursued including military and internship trainings
1. Training and skills required
2. Management/supervisory responsibilities
3. Career mobility (vertical or lateral moves)

C. Accomplishments and/or difficulties in each position and occupational setting

D. Previous occupational injuries, time lost, leaves of absence, and outcome to all situations addressed

PAST PSYCHIATRIC HISTORY AND RELEVANT MEDICAL HISTORY

A. Prior experiences in therapy

B. Hospitalizations

C. Psychotropic medication history/prescribed by whom

D. Medical history resulting from occupational setting or exacerbated by it

FAMILY HISTORY

A. Family of Origin
1. Parent's age, education, and occupational history
2. Sibling's age, education, and occupational history
3. Composition of family during client's childhood and adolescence
4. Mental health history and relevant medical history of family members
5. Family response to illness
6. Relevant social history of family members
7. Quality of family relations

B. Family of Procreation
1. Present marital status/history of previous marital relationships
2. Spouse's age, education, occupational history
3. Number of offspring (if offspring are of adult age obtain same data as for spouse)

4. Mental health history and relevant medical history of family members
5. Relevant social history of family members
6. Quality of family relations

DEVELOPMENTAL HISTORY

A. Developmental milestones (met at appropriate ages/delays/difficulties)

SOCIAL HISTORY (DISTINGUISH PRIOR TO DISABILITY, DISABILITY CONCURRENT, AFTER INJURY)

A. Interpersonal relationships
B. Previous life changes/crises/losses and how responded to
C. Educational history
D. Relevant legal history (prior workers' compensation and personal injury claims with circumstances and outcome)
E. Relevant criminal history
F. Substance use and abuse
G. Client's description of a typical day

MENTAL STATUS EXAM

A. Hygiene, grooming, anything remarkable about appearance
B. Mood (normal, depressed, elevated, euphoric, angry, irritable, anxious)
C. Affect (normal, broad, restricted, blunted, flat, inappropriate, labile)
D. Memory (intact, short-term/remote memory)
E. Orientation (time, place, person, situation)
F. Speech (descriptors, expressive language, receptive language)
G. Processes (normal, blocking, loose associations, confabulations, flight of ideas, ideas of reference, grandiosity, paranoia, obsession, perseverations, depersonalization, suicidal ideation, homicidal ideation)
H. Hallucinations
I. Evidence of deficit (learning, problem solving, and judgment)
J. Impulse control
K. Behavioral observations/evidence of physiologic disturbance (somatoform or conversion symptoms, autonomic, skeletal muscle system)
L. Client's response to the examiner/appropriateness during course of interview

REVIEW OF MEDICAL RECORD

FINDINGS FROM PSYCHOLOGICAL ASSESSMENT

(attach complete psychological report which has been completed as per workers' compensation guidelines)

INTERVIEWS WITH COLLATERAL SOURCES AND REVIEW OF EMPLOYMENT OR PERSONNEL RECORDS (COMPARE DESCRIPTION OF INDUSTRIAL INJURY WITH CLIENTS DESCRIPTION)

DSM-IV DIAGNOSIS (MULTIAXIAL, USING DSM CRITERIA AND TERMINOLOGY)

SUMMARY AND CONCLUSIONS

A. Brief summary of relevant history and finding

B. Present and justify an opinion concerning the current cause(s) of disability if present
   1. The relationship of the work environment to the disability
   2. Nonindustrial causes of disability and preexisting causal factors
   3. Aggravating or accelerating factor (industrial and nonindustrial)
   4. Natural progression of preexisting disorder
   5. Active or passive contribution of the workplace to the disability
   6. Client's subjective reaction to stress at work

C. Indicate any diagnostic entities which were work disabling prior to the alleged industrial injury and provide evidence.

D. State whether the disability is temporary or has reached permanent stationary status and cite evidence. If the condition is permanent and stationary, state on what date it became so and cite evidence. Consider the history of the disorder, and the response to treatment. If the condition is not yet considered to be permanent and stationary, state when you expect it will be so. If the opinion is that reasonable medical treatment will improve the condition, then describe the treatment and the expected benefits.

E. If the disability is permanent and stationary, offer an opinion regarding the nature and severity of the disability. Describe the disabling symptoms (subjective and objective), citing symptoms, mental status findings, psychological test data, and history to support opinion.

F. Make an advisory apportionment of disability. Do this by describing the disability that would exist at this time in the absence of the workplace injury. Cite the evidence on which the estimated preinjury level is based on.

G. Recommend treatment and/or rehabilitation if indicated and define using the following:
   1. The effects of the injury, combined or not with any previous injury
   2. Whether the individual is permanently precluded or likely to be precluded from engaging in their usual and customary occupation, or the occupation in which they were engaged in at the time of the injury (if different).

H. Be sure that all referral questions have been addressed and address any questions and/or issues raised in the referral reports.

Indicate whether or not actual events of employment were responsible for a substantial degree of the total causation from all sources contributing to the psychiatric injury (clarify if the state that you practice in stipulates a percentage of total causation related to employment for valid work-related disability claim).

PSYCHOLOGICAL PRE-EMPLOYMENT EVALUATION

The purpose of a pre-employment evaluation is to determine whether the individual being considered for a certain position has the psychological suitability (emotional nature and psychological character) necessary to effectively perform the job requirements and the ability to cope with the emotional factors to which they are likely to be exposed to.

REPORT OUTLINE

Name of Candidate _____

Date of Birth _____

Date Tested _____

Date Interviewed _____

Referral Source _____

1. Identifying Information
    A. Age, ethnicity, marital status, the position being sought by the candidate, and any other pertinent information designated to identification.

2. Procedures
    A. Clinical interview
    B. Adult History Questionnaire (thorough exploration of life experience)
    C. Minnesota Multiphasic Personality Inventory
    D. California Psychological Inventory
    E. Rotter Incomplete Sentence Blank
    F. Bender-Gestalt Sentence Blank

3. Relevant History
4. Behavioral Observations and Mental Status
5. Assessment Results
6. Interpretation of Results
7. Summary and Conclusions
    A. Designating reasoning for conclusion of supporting or not supporting candidate for selection for employment position.

The areas of psychological suitability being assessed include attitude, impression formation, moral and ethical behavior, dominance, emotional control, anxiety, social adjustment, mood, somatic concerns, intelligence, maturity, sensitivity/guardedness, independence, and conformity.

COMPULSORY PSYCHOLOGICAL EVALUATION

A compulsory evaluation is used for a variety of circumstances. A common reason for referral is to establish the following:

1. Work-related problems
   A. Job performance
   B. Inappropriate behavior in the workplace

2. Determining remediation of difficulties and/or criteria for returning to work

3. A thorough assessment of psychiatric difficulties in order to clarify psychopathology and to offer treatment planning

COMPULSORY PSYCHOLOGICAL EVALUATION

1. Client Name
2. Date of Birth
3. Dates Tested
4. Dates Interviewed
5. Tests Administered
6. Referral Source
7. Reason For Referral
8. Identifying Information
9. Relevant Background Information (historical and of current problem)
10. Behavioral Observations and Mental Status
11. Significant Test Results
12. Summary
13. Recommendations

FORENSIC EVALUATION

The legal issue of competency in a criminal proceeding are related to stages of the legal process, and may demonstrate some overlap in their definitions. Every state has its own definition of competency which includes with deficiencies described in the context of mental disorders, disease, or defect. However, this does not mean that all defendants in a criminal proceeding who present with a documented or currently evaluated mental disorder are incompetent. It is also important to note that a defined incompetency in a civil situation does not automatically translate to incompetency in any level of a criminal proceeding.

A competency evaluation is not a quest for clarification of treatment issues, but rather a format in which to present relevant information to the court when making legal decisions related to the defendant. Therefore, competency evaluations deal with issues of legal concern. According to Grisso (1988), the five objectives of competency evaluations are:

1. *A functional description of specific abilities* which defines the defendant's strengths and deficits by the legal standard or criteria for competency. This aspect of the evaluation is the assessment of understanding and reasoning about trials and the defense process.

2. *Information indicative of the cause of deficits in competency abilities.* This aspect of the evaluation offers information derived from clinical observation and other data to determine:
   A. Symptoms or criteria of a mental disorder
   B. The identification of any other plausible explanations
   C. The logical relation between a mental disorder or other plausible explanation(s) and functional deficit(s)

3. *The interactive importance of deficits in any competency ability.* This aspect of the evaluation demonstrates the degree or level of practical significance to the identified deficits in relationship to the demand of the legal process confronting the defendant.

4. *Conclusory opinions about legal competency and incompetency.* This is the examiner's opinion about the defendant's ability to stand trial given their strengths, deficits, and the demands of the process. This aspect of the evaluation is not necessary unless requested to make comment. Generally, this is not a component of the evaluation.

5. *Advised remedy for the deficits identified in competency abilities.* This aspect of the evaluation offers the court methods or recommendations to remedy deficits or other options for dealing with the current disposition. As previously noted, it is not the court's quest to determine necessary treatment but rather what treatment or time frame would be required to restore the defendant to a level of functioning appropriate for resocialization in the community.

REPORT OUTLINE

COMPETENCY

1. Interview Date
2. Patient/Admonishment (optional if civil versus criminal proceeding)
3. Sources of Data
4. Reason for Referral and by Whom
5. Relevant Background Information (including family if information is available)
6. Determination of Competency
   A. Behavioral observations
   B. Assessment of intellectual functioning
   C. Assessment of adaptive functioning
7. Conclusions
8. Recommendations

COMPETENCY TO PLEAD AND/OR CONFESS

1. Interview Date
2. Patient/Defendant Identifier/Admonishment
3. Sources of Data
4. Reason for Referral and by Whom
5. Relevant Background Information
6. Personal History
7. Mental Status
8. Observations Concerning Competency to Confess
9. Observations Concerning Competency to Plead Guilty

COMPETENCY TO STAND TRIAL

1. Interview Date
2. Patient/Defendant Identifier/Admonishment
3. Sources of Data
4. Referral Source
5. Relevant Background Information
6. Mental Status
7. Defendant's Understanding of the Legal Situation
8. Conclusions Concerning Competency to Stand Trial
9. Recommendations for Treatment (optional)

MENTAL STATUS AT TIME OF OFFENSE

1. Interview Date
2. Patient/Defendant Identifier/Admonishment
3. Sources of Data

4. Referral Source
5. Relevant Background Information
6. Circumstances of the Offense
7. Present Mental Status/Pre-defense Mental Status
8. Mental Status At Time of Offense

Chapter 3

Skill-Building Resources for Increasing Social Competency

In an effort to be efficient and timely, therapists need to develop their own resources for facilitating cognitive and behavioral changes with the individuals that they work with. This section offers resources in a form that can be used as homework, education, and increasing awareness as agents of change.

WHAT IS STRESS?

Stress is the body's physical, emotional, and psychological response to any demand. It is generally perceived mentally as pressure or urgency to respond, which is experienced as mental strain. Stress is associated with the more primitive survival "fight" or "flight" response. When confronted with danger, the body responds physiologically with the release of adrenalin and hydrocortisone (cortisol). Short term, these chemicals shut down some biological mechanisms in order to conserve energy, which may be needed for fight or flight. After the challenge has been met and resolved, the body returns to normal. Normal body functioning is demonstrated by muscles relaxing, hands becoming dry, stomach unwinding, and gastrointestinal relaxation heart rate and blood pressure returning to normal. Long term adrenalin and hydrocortisone can result in numerous negative influences physiologically, psychologically, and emotionally. One of these negative consequences is suppression of the immune system. If managed effectively, stress is not necessarily bad for you. It can provide momentum to get things going and increase productivity. Review some differences between positive stress and negative stress:

1. Positive stress
   A. Is short term
   B. Motivates
   C. May feel exciting
   D. Improves productivity
   E. Improves performance
   F. Is pleasant
   G. Is beneficial
   H. Is important to physical and mental fitness
   I. Focuses energy
   J. Sharpens the mind

2. Negative stress (referred to as distress)
   A. Can be harmful, especially if experienced for a long period of time
   B. Drains energy reserves
   C. Causes emotional depression
   D. Suppresses immune system
   E. Builds over time instead of diminishing
   F. Can lead to mental and physical problems
   G. Can change the way a person thinks

Stress has no boundaries, everyone experiences it. It is a part of daily life. Most individuals live a lifestyle and life circumstances at a medium level of stress. This level is enough to keep one's attention sharp and motivation high in order to remain task oriented with the goal of alleviating stress. It is when stress escalates beyond this moderate level that it can become harmful. No one is immune from the negative effects of stress, and it may be cumulative in how individuals are able to respond over time (burnout).

Since everyone evaluates their experiences differently, no particular factors are identified as the causes of stress. Stress can come from pressures at home or work, from relationships from school, or as the result of other personal situations. Oftentimes, stress is associated with the "too much" phenomenon:

1. Too many changes
2. Too high of expectations
3. Too much responsibility
4. Too much information (overload)

The more stressors you have in a short period of time, the more severe their effects. In all likelihood, if one were able to experience these stressors over time allowing one to process and resolve each situation, then the stressors would be manageable. When there is not enough time between stressful events, however, the experience is overloading and debilitating.

There are generally two ways to define the source of stress: internal factors or external factors. Additionally, how each individual responds to stressful events can either increase or decrease the overall experience of stress. Failure to effectively cope with a stressful situation contributes to a feeling of things being more difficult, adding to the level of stress already felt from external sources. Self-care, use of resources, and self-talk form the foundation of effective stress management.

The difference between being stressed and not being stressed is associated with three factors:

1. Individual perception of stress
   A. People often view the same situation very differently, depending on their life experiences, personality, and health. A visit to a personal physician for the same purpose may be stressful to one individual and not stressful to another.

*An individual's perception of stress will determine its effects on him/her.

2. Personal and family resources
   A. Time, skill, financial resources, and family resources all affect one's ability to handle stress. For example, money is double-edged: it can either be a stressor or a resource for resolving it. Personal management styles such as patience and perseverance also affect the way an individual or family system deals with stress.

3. Social support
   A. Your relationships with family, friends, and your community as well as access to professional resources can all be avenues for relieving stress

Aside from stress being derived from internal or external factors, there is another way to define the kinds of stress experienced:

1. Ordinary daily life stressors
   A. Regular daily schedule (getting up, going to work/school, etc). These stressors can be dealt with by setting priorities, following a schedule, having resonable expectations, and delegating when possible.

2. Developmental Stresses
   A. Stage of life issues
   B. Learning new things/changing old habits

These stressors can be dealt with by looking forward to known developmental changes, looking forward to the challenge. Being proactive in thinking through choices and how one wants to deal with things versus being forced to deal with the event when it happens can also minimize stress.

STRESS REVIEW
1. Keep a journal. Write what you think and feel to improve self-understanding
2. Identify the issues or situations that cause stress
3. Brainstorm a list of all possible ideas for dealing with these issues and situations
4. Clarify ideas
5. Evaluate all possible outcomes
6. Choose the best solution
7. Plan who does what (individual, family, outside resource); delegate, but be realistic
8. Create a trial period (day, week, month, etc.) for putting a plan into action

9. Evaluate the plan: What worked? what didn't work?
10. Integrate the new information you have in order to improve effectiveness of stress management

STRESS MANAGEMENT

Often, when a person enters therapy they are feeling overwhelmed by the stressors in their life. This crisis presents an opportunity for cognitive-behavioral changes which are beneficial to the person's overall ability to cope effectively. During a period of crisis a person's normal defenses are down and emotional distress is high. The person feels an urgency to decrease the level of emotional distress. Because they are motivated toward alleviating emotional distress they are open to new ways of thinking and behaving.

Some people have little awareness of the role that negative stress or too much stress plays in the complaints and physical ailments that they are reporting which are reactions to the pressures and circumstances in their lives. The body generally offers several opportunities for the person to intervene via some method to decrease distress. If ignored these signals often lead to emotional problems and physical ailments.

Change is stressful, even when it is beneficial. Change requires effort and conscious awareness. In preparing to engage someone in the process of change, it is important to understand how they normally interact with their environment. A life stress assessment includes a review of life events occurring in the last year, personality characteristics, and a review of significant historical life stressors which have not been resolved and/or have contributed to how the person currently copes.

The responses to stress are numerous, and so are the approaches for dealing with it. What works for one person may not work for another. Therefore, it is necessary to be prepared with a number of strategies for handling stress.

The mind plays a powerful role in illness and in health. Because cognitions or mental processes have a strong influence, negative or positive, on the physical and emotional reactions to stress cognitive restructuring is an important intervention.

The five aspects of mental processing that play a significant role in stress include:

1. *Expectations/Self-Fulfilling Prophecy.* What a person believes will happen or expects to happen sometimes influences their behavior in a way that makes that outcome more likely to happen. Negative expectations increase anxiety and stress. Identifying goals for change and facing such challenges with optimism and a positive attitude will facilitate optimal coping and management.

2. *Mental Imagery/Visual Imagery.* Along with expectations for a given situation a person will develop an accompanying mental picture and internal dialogue. This mental imagery can itself elicit emotional and physiologic responses. Negative mental imagery increases anxiety and stress reactions; whereas positive mental imagery minimizes the effects of life stressors and increases effective coping.

3. *Self-Talk.* This is the internal dialogue that the person carries on with themself all day long. Most people do not have a conscious awareness for self-talk or the influence it has on anxiety, stress, and self-esteem. Self-talk has a similar influence to that of mental imagery. Negative mental images and negative self-talk can result in anxiety and psychosomatic symptoms, whereas positive mental images and positive self-talk encourages self-confidence, effective coping, and a general feeling of well being. Initially, an awareness for negative self-talk

must be facilitated, followed by the development of rational substitute statements to replace the negative thoughts for cognitive restructuring.

4. *Controlling and Perfectionistic Behavior.* Perfectionism and unrealistic expectations often go together. Responses of controlling and perfectionistic behaviors are frequently an effort to avoid abuse, conflict, the unknown, or a feeling of uneasiness and inadequacy associated with perfectionism. Placing unrealistic expectations on others is a form of controlling behavior. It takes enough energy to manage yourself. Efforts to control the behavior of others leads to stress, anxiety, frustration, and anger. The goal is for the person to develop realistic expectations for themself and accept that they have no control over the behavior of another.

5. *Anger.* Anger is a normal, healthy emotion when expressed appropriately. It can be damaging to the self and others when not expressed appropriately because of the internal stress and tension it causes as well as predisposing the person to "blow-ups" with others. This behavior results in low self-esteem and poor interpersonal relating. Chronic anger and hostility are related to the development or exacerbation of a number of physical symptoms, illnesses, and diseases. A person has a choice in how they evaluate a situation. Appropriate management of anger will decrease stress.

For a person to effectively manage stress they must understand what they need and want emotionally, take responsibility for their own thoughts and behaviors, release themself from the self-imposed responsibility of and efforts to control others, develop realistic expectations and limitations, have appropriate boundaries in relationships, express themself honestly, and take care of themself (by getting adequate sleep, eating nutritionally, exercising regularly, and utilizing relaxation techniques).

The central strategies for effective stress management focus on living healthy. This includes exercise, eating habits, how stress is dealt with, belief system, and attitude. Effective living requires goals, appropriate prioritization, and time management.

Given the pace of daily living and the demands placed on people it is not difficult to understand the level of stress experienced by the average person. Because it is physiologically impossible to be stressed and relaxed at the same time developing techniques for alleviating distress (negative stress) is an important step in coping effectively with life stressors.

Excellent results have been found in the treatment of numerous physiological symptoms and emotional or psychological problems through the regular use of relaxation techniques. Regular use of relaxation techniques prevents the development of cumulative stress. Cumulative stress is generally associated with high levels of anxiety which have become unmanageable. The effective discharge of stress and tension associated with relaxation techniques creates the opportunity for the body to recover from the consequences of stress and places an individual in an optimal position for managing normal stressors, especially if they are engaging in regular exercise, getting adequate sleep, and eating nutritionally.

Difficulties leading to stress are often related to a person's style of managing or interacting with their environment. An approach which results in unnecessary stress includes:

1. Attempting to do too much at one time.
2. Setting unrealistic time estimates, or poor time management.
3. Procrastinating on the unpleasant.
4. Disorganization.
5. Poor listening skills.
6. Doing it all yourself.

7. Unable to say "no."

8. Trouble letting other people do their job.

9. Impulsive, snap decisions.

10. Not taking responsibility for the quality of your own life. Blaming others.

EARLY WARNING SIGNS OF STRESS

Emotional Signs

1. Apathy, feelings of sadness, no longer find activities pleasurable

2. Anxiety, easily agitated, restless, sense of unworthiness

3. Irritability, defensive, angry, argumentative

4. Mentally tired, preoccupied, lack of flexibility, difficulty concentrating

5. Overcompensating, avoiding dealing with problems, denial that you have problems

Behavioral Signs

1. Avoidance behavior, difficulty accepting/neglecting responsibility

2. Compulsive behaviors in areas such as spending, gambling, sex, substances

3. Poor self-care behavior (hygiene, appearance, etc.), late to work, poor follow through on tasks

4. Legal problems, difficulty controlling aggressive impulses, indebtedness

A Life Events Survey can be administered to determine the specific stressors as well as a rough estimate of stress experienced by an individual. This can clarify acute crises and chronic problems which therapeutic interventions can seek to alleviate and resolve.

STRESS SIGNALS

The following messages from your body may indicate that you have a health problem or are on the road to developing a health problem. Also explore family history for any predisposition to a particular disease.

1. *Insomnia.* If you go to bed thinking about things or worrying, the physiological response is adrenaline, which is activating and interferes with getting to sleep or achieving restful sleep. Create a routine for winding down and putting your mind to rest. Before bed, swim, walk, meditate, drink warm milk or herbal tea (no caffeine), take a hot bath, or choose to think of peaceful, pleasant thoughts.

2. *Headaches and sore muscles.* When you body is in high gear, you are continuously on alert to respond and body tension accumulates. If tension is chronic, the result can be muscle soreness and rigidity. A tight neck, upper back, and shoulders can lead to a headache. Stretching and light exercise every couple of hours throughout the day may help to relieve these symptoms.

3. *Stomach problems.* When you are stressed, acid is secreted in the stomach, which can cause heartburn, stomach cramps, or other digestive problems. Over-the-counter antacids may alleviate the symptoms, but don't ignore the real culprits of irritation: stress, caffeine, smoking, alcohol, poor nutrition, inadequate sleep and relaxation, or spicy foods. Use physical activity, deep breathing, and self-soothing activities for calming your digestive track. Be sure to consult you physician. Don't ignore these symptoms.

4. *Addictive behavior.* Efforts to escape chronic stress by drinking too much, increased smoking, overeating, overspending, gambling, or other negative patterns lead to increased stress. Find helpful and healthful ways to deal with stress. Talk with your physician and seek professional help.

5. *Low sex drive.* While this can be a signal of stress and fatigue, a variety of other issues need to be explored with your physician:
   A. High blood pressure
   B. Sedentary lifestyle
   C. Decreased testosterone
   D. Excessive salt consumption
   E. Excessive alcohol use
   F. Certain drugs and diseases that may cause high blood pressure in some people

STRESS BUSTING

1. Deal with stress when it strikes. Breath slowly and deeply. Exercise to diminish adrenalin.

2. Think positively. What causes stress is not the situation but how you think about it.

3. Practice improved management of stress by visualizing stressful situations and how you will manage them effectively. That way, when the stressful event occurs it feels like you have already successfully dealt with it numerous times before.

4. Set limits. Create a work frame of time and when the time is up, shift gears and stop thinking about work. Consider how unfair it is to the people you care for if you are always thinking about work when you are with them, rather than being emotionally available and listening.

5. Be honest about what you have control over and what you don't control. If you have control, take action and plan for a resolution. If it belongs to someone else, let go of it.

EFFECTIVE MANAGEMENT OF STRESS

There are two approaches for coping with excessive stress:

1. Self-control, which requires taking responsibility for reactions to a situation.
2. Situation control, which includes problem solving, assertiveness, conflict resolution, and time management.

CRITICAL PROBLEM SOLVING

1. Acknowledge and clarify the problem or issue.
2. Analyze the problem, and identify the needs of those who will be affected.
3. Employ brainstorming to generate all possible solutions.
4. Evaluate each option, considering the needs of those affected.
5. Select the best option and implement the plan.
6. Evaluate the outcome or problem-solving efforts.

ASSERTIVENESS

To assert oneself positive includes:

1. Acting in your own best interest.
2. Standing up for yourself, expressing yourself honestly and appropriately.
3. Exercising your own rights without diminishing the rights of others.

CONFLICT RESOLUTION

Conflict resolution can be achieved cooperatively through a combination of problem-solving skills, assertiveness, good listening skills, and mutual respect until differing viewpoints are understood. This is followed by a course of action that satisfies the parties involved.

TIME MANAGEMENT

1. Clarify a plan(s) of action, or tasks to be completed
2. Clarify priorities
3. Divide the plan of action into manageable goals and tasks
4. Allot a reasonable amount of time to complete all tasks

For optimal time management eliminate procrastination, combine tasks when possible, do things one time, and delegate when possible.

SELF-CARE

1. Adequate sleep and good nutrition
2. Good hygiene and grooming
3. Regular exercise
4. Relaxation techniques or other strategies for decreasing tension
5. Development and utilization of a support system
6. Use of community resources
7. Personal, spiritual, and professional growth
8. Self-monitoring for staying on task self-care behaviors to develop a routine

TIPS FOR STRESS MANAGEMENT

1. Learn to meditate and use other relaxation techniques (yoga, progressive muscle relaxation, visualization, etc.)
2. Practice good nutrition and be physically active
3. Review how you choose to think about things. How you think influences your stress level:
   A. Is your cup half empty or half full?
   B. Are you a chronic worrier?
   C. Do you catastrophize?
   D. Are you always thinking about "what if" instead of dealing with "what is?"

    E. Are you a perfectionist?

    F. Are you overly critical?

4. Take short breaks

    A. Reenergize with a short, refreshing time out

5. Manage your time

    A. Set priorities

    B. Be realistic about the amount of time it takes to do tasks

6. Talk about it

    A. Talk out your problems with a friend or family member to relieve stress and put problem into perspective

7. Live a balanced life

    A. Balance work with play

    B. Develop interests or hobbies

    C. Participate socially

*Make sure you have laughter in your life.

8. Develop goals

    A. Set realistic goals

    B. Make sure you have what is required to successfully meet your goals

    C. When necessary, break tasks into small, manageable steps

    D. Reevaluate goals from time to time

9. Anticipate stress

    A. Use your awareness of situations coming up and plan ways to respond

    B. Review what you have control over and what you don't control

    C. Identify anything that can be done ahead of time to reduce the stress that will be a part of expectations associated with a given situation

10. Get help

    A. When you feel overwhelmed by stress, get professional help

    B. Identify supportive resources in the community

TIPS TO SIMPLIFY LIFE

Are you exhausted? Do you feel overwhelmed and overworked? If you answered yes to these questions, take the time to step back, look at the choices you are making, and make simple changes. Small changes can often lead to an improved quality of life. Consider the following recommendations in reviewing life changes:

1. Reduce the "to do" list. Separate the following items:

    A. What needs to be done

    B. What does not need to be done

    C. What you want to do

2. Stop procrastinating
   A. Be honest with yourself about what you are willing to do
   B. Acknowledge what needs to be done and just do it
   C. Accept that motivation is not something you have, it is something you do

3. Take some time to yourself every day
   A. Keep your lunchtime personal
   B. Do what you want to do during your brief "personal" time
   C. Try to increase personal time gradually

4. Set a stop time
   A. Set a time to stop working a task, and stick to it
   B. Move on to a restful enjoyable task to balance things
   C. Make others aware of your "stop time" so that it will be respected

5. Financial responsibility
   A. Consider how many hours you have to work pay for a purchase and then ask yourself, "Is it worth it?"
   B. Disengage from "retail therapy" (buying to feel good for a while)
   C. Get a handle on debt and create a special fund for desired purchases

6. Streamline
   A. Do not reinvent the wheel
   B. Do not do more than is necessary to complete a task (get over perfectionism)
   C. Consider the purpose of a task its importance

7. Organize
   A. Create manageable order to belongings
   B. Utilize time management
   C. Create a central information center for family demands

8. Identify quality-of-life issues
   A. Identify what matters most
   B. Enjoy the moment
   C. Spend time with people you enjoy or doing activities you enjoy
   D. Calm your soul—find peace

TEN SIGNS THAT YOU NEED TO SIMPLIFY YOUR LIFE

1. You feel that people are always expecting you to do things and are always making demands on you
2. Your storage spaces (cabinets/closets) are a disaster
3. You don't keep up on small daily tasks (making bed, spiffing the kitchen)
4. You are easily upset or overwhelmed when something goes wrong
5. You find it difficult, if not impossible, to complete all the tasks on your to-do list
6. You take on another task before finishing the one you are working on
7. Tasks seem too complicated or take too long to complete
8. You have little or no patience and snap at people around you
9. You often misplace things
10. You find it difficult to concentrate and to keep things straight

HOW TO IMPROVE PLANNING

1. Keep a list of tasks and errands posted on the refrigerator (all family members can be helpful)
2. Keep a phone book in you car in case you need to find a new resource
3. Carefully think out the rout of running errands in order to save time
4. Choose one day a week for appointments and errands
5. Make a master list of home chores done monthly, quarterly, and yearly, and note these chores on the calendar so you don't have to try to remember them
6. Coordinate with your partner to save time and energy—two work faster than one
7. Ask you partner for input on planning
8. Identify individual strengths when you explore your resources
9. Always weave in desired activities
10. Reevaluate effectiveness and identify necessary changes

PAIN MANAGEMENT

Over time, deep relaxation may be as helpful for relieving pain as medication. Even if medication is used, relaxation and physician-recommended exercise should be used daily as part of a pain-management program, Deep relaxation relates specifically to relieving muscle tension and focusing on breathing. One relaxation technique is meditation. The foundation of meditation is to focus on a specific word, sound, thought, or rhythm of breathing. Meditation, as with other forms of relaxation, is most beneficial when practiced routinely on a daily basis. Many individuals with chronic pain become more debilitated over time, being less physical than they could have been and participating less in life. When this happens, a person's entire life may focus on the pain and its effects.

Deep relaxation can short-circuit pain, improve mood, increase energy, diminish feelings of helplessness, and result in an overall sense of well-being. Developing a sense of control in pain management can decrease feelings of stress and the degree of discomfort associated with chronic pain.

Be patient. When you first begin to practice relaxation, it may be difficult to remain focused. It is not uncommon for those preoccupied by acute distress of any kind to report that they experience difficulty not thinking about other things while trying to engage in deep relaxation. However, with continued practice they find that part of deep relaxation is reconditioning the mind and body and teaching it to relax. Therefore, it may be easiest to start out learning the technique of deep breathing.

Follow these steps to enhance deep breathing:

1. Be comfortably seated with feet on the floor or elevated
2. Dim the lighting or turn off the lights
3. Breath in deeply so that you are ware of your stomach expanding before your chest
4. Once you have taken air deeply into your lungs, hold for a count of five
5. As you exhale, imagine the tension leaving your body and mind

To master meditation, one must practice deep breathing and other relaxation techniques repetitively. Some people find it helpful to start with an audiotape that guides them. After a period of regular use, they find that they do not need the tape any longer. This is such an easy way to improve the quality of life. Get started immediately!

Talk with your therapist about the different types of relaxation training. He/she may have specific recommendations for what would be most helpful for you. The therapist may also be able to give you a printed dialogue of a relaxation technique that you could use to make a tape in your own voice. There are many choices, so begin to get to work on improving your pain-management program with the addition of relaxation.

SOME EXAMPLES OF INDIVIDUALIZED TIME MANAGEMENT OPTIONS

Effective time management contributes to a balanced lifestyle. Review the following list and choose some time management tips that you can incorporate into your life to accomplish more and to feel less stress.

1. Be realistic with yourself regarding how much you can actually accomplish in a given span of time.

2. Say "NO" to additional responsibilities that infringe on personal/leisure or work time.

3. Prioritize your tasks because they are not equally important. Set priorities on a daily, weekly, and monthly basis for maximizing accomplishments.

4. Develop an awareness for your peak energy periods and plan to do the activities with the highest energy demand at that time.

5. On a regular basis, review what the best use of your time is currently.

6. Striving for perfection is generally not necessary and can burn up time better spent in another way. Complete tasks well enough to get the results that you really need.

7. Delegate tasks and responsibilities to others whenever appropriate. Just be sure to communicate your expectations clearly.

8. Don't waste time thinking and rethinking the decisions for basic issues. Make those decisions quickly and move on.

9. If you have a difficult task to do that you are not looking forward to, do yourself a favor and approach it with a positive attitude. You will be surprised about how much stress that can relieve from you.

10. Break big overwhelming tasks into small manageable ones, that way it is easier to keep track of your progress and achievements.

11. Be prepared to make good use of "waiting" time by having small tasks or activities to do. Another way to deal with it is to always be prepared to take advantage of potential relaxation time when there are no demands on you.

12. When you need time to focus on your goals without interruption then request it. Take responsibility for creating a conductive work environment at home and at work.

13. Set goals and reward yourself when have accomplished them. If it is a big goal you may want to build in rewards at certain milestone of effort and accomplishment as a reinforcer.

14. From time to time remind yourself how good it feels to accomplish tasks, what the benefits of accomplishment are, and the relief of having that weight off your shoulders.

15. Good use of time means more than completing "necessary" tasks. It means building in time for self-care like leisure activities and exercise. You being the best that you can be is a priority.

SELF-CARE PLAN

Develop a personalized self-care plan for optimal emotional health and a positive sense of well-being. This does require a commitment to health and follow through. It is recommended that there be a medical exam for clearance to participate in desired physical activity. Components of a self-care plan include:

1. Utilization of relaxation techniques to decrease body tension and to manage stress.

2. Review the social supports available to you. If necessary, work at developing and adequate and appropriate support system. Utilizing your social supports can offer relief, distraction, and pleasure. Make a list of your supports.

3. Initiate a journal. Instead of keeping thoughts and feelings inside, where they can build up and cause confusion and emotional/physical distress, get them down on paper. A journal is useful for venting thoughts and feelings, clarifying issues, and problem solving. It can also be helpful in determining patterns, relationships, health, and emotional functioning. Keeping a journal will help you monitor progress in life goals.

4. Get adequate sleep and rest.

5. Smile and have laughter in your life. Be spontaneous at times and playful.

6. Feed your body, mind, and spirit. Eat meals regularly and nutritionally. Practice good hygiene and grooming. Participate in life for personal, spiritual, and professional growth.

7. Approach each day with a purpose. Be productive by outlining daily structure. No task is too small to feel good about. Each step can be important to reach goals that you develop.

8. Avoid being self-critical. Be as kind and understanding of yourself as you would be to another person. Use positive self-talk to reassure yourself, to cope effectively, and to allow yourself to see that there are always choices.

9. Be sure to build in to your schedule time for relationships and pleasurable activities.

10. Take responsibility for your own life. Life is about choices. Understand yourself, your behaviors, your thoughts/beliefs, and your motivations.

HOW TO GET THE MOST OUT OF YOUR DAY

Whether you are simply considering a project or wanting to change something about your current lifestyle, the following tips will be useful.

1. *Start your day right.* Eat a light breakfast followed by some quiet time meditating or reading inspirational material.
2. *Choose to greet the day with a positive attitude.* You have the choice of setting the right tone for a positive outlook or a negative outlook every day. You get back what you give out. What do you choose to create?
3. *Organize your daily tasks on a list.* You will feel great every time you put a line through an accomplished task. Be realistic about what is reasonable for you to accomplish and how much time a task really requires to complete.
4. *Inspire yourself by seeing yourself in a positive light.* Overall, success is the adding up of all the little successes along the way. Each day, make a positive contribution.
5. *Remind yourself of past successes.* Tell yourself, "I am a capable person." Do not overwhelm yourself by thinking about all you had to do. Just do it. Life is genuinely difficult. However, it does not seem so bad when you just do what you need to do.
6. *Work on your gratitude.* Do you take the time to appreciate your blessings? Genuine gratitude offers a great attitude adjustment.
7. *Be prepared.* Break a task down into manageable steps if necessary and establish a routine for accomplishing it.
8. *Practice self-improvement.* From time to time, do a personal inventory. Work toward positive changes and personal growth while you actively make changes that you know will benefit you in all areas of your life.
9. *Increase motivation.* Enhance your actions by remembering this statement: "Motivation is not something you wait to get, motivation is something that you do."
10. *Incorporate creativity into your life.* Being creative leads to personal growth and is a great way to relax.
11. *Bring out the child in you and play.* Playing is a great way to rejuvenate and reenergize.
12. *Be active.* Use your body-walk or do some other activity. Walking is great for decreasing stress, increasing energy, improving sleep, and improving libido.
13. *Have faith in yourself and your ability.* The power of positive thinking works.
14. *Practice self-discipline.* Set goals. Decide what it is you need to do to accomplish the goals, and remind yourself on a daily basis of the importance of the goals that you set.
15. *Convince yourself about the importance of your goals.* Write a list about why it is important to you and why you believe you will accomplish it.
16. *Make your vision a reality.* Imagine yourself successful. Take that mental picture with you wherever you go.

17. *Stay with it.* Persevere. Never quit. Eventually you will accomplish what is important to you.

18. *Be committed to being your best.* If you stick with it, it will come true.

19. *Reward yourself for your efforts.* Sometimes the accomplishment is the reward itself. Other times, create a reward that is waiting for you at the finish line.

20. *Always have things to look forward to.* Anticipate things that are going to be. How exciting!

Each day carries with it its own significance in our lives. It is not what happens to us that necessarily creates problems; it is the manner in which we choose to deal with the event.

EMOTIONAL IQ

Emotional IQ plays an important role in our personal and professional success. Some of the central qualities that make up emotional intelligence are the following:

1. Self-awareness
   A. The ability to recognize a feeling as it happens
   B. Increased awareness and understanding of "gut feeling"
   C. Being able to answer the following two questions objectively. They address taking responsibility for your own choices and an understanding of the motivation behind the choice of response.
      1. "What am I doing?"
      2. "Why am I doing it?"

2. Mood management
   A. We generally have little control over experiences that provoke or result in negative emotional experiences (anger, frustration, hurt feelings). However, we do have the choice/self-control over how we feel, how long, and how we demonstrate the feelings we have. For example, the more you think about how angry you are, the angrier you get.
   B. Reframe. When situations are emotionally difficult, choose to reinterpret the situation in a realistic or more positive light.
   C. Take time to yourself to calm yourself down and think clearly
   D. Don't waste time on negatives. If you have control over something, deal with it in a productive manner and then move on. If you do not have control over it, let the other person own it.
   E. Distract yourself from negatives with positives
   F. Engage in self-care
      1. Meditation
      2. Prayer
      3. Formal relaxation techniques
      4. Regular exercise
      5. Adequate rest and good nutrition
      6. Positive use of resources
   G. Be aware of your mood and thoughts about your mood

3. Self-motivation

Motivation is not something that you have, it is something that you do.

A. Requires clear goals, with an optimistic "I can do this" attitude

B. Catch negative, self-defeating thoughts as they occur and reframe them in less negative terms. For example, when optimistic people experience failure, they blame the situation, not themself. They think in terms of what they learned, what they can do, how to improve something, or break it down so that it is manageable. Regardless, they have rational and realistic belief in themselves. They say, "I can do it."

4. Impulse control or delay of gratification

A. This is emotional self-regulation—the ability to delay a desired impulse in order to reach a goal. This is a very important trait associated with success. It is also associated with social competence, self-awareness, and the ability to cope with frustration. The ability to resist impulses can be developed through increased awareness and practice. Remind yourself the long-term goal. It will be worth it.

B. Delaying gratification helps to regulate your mood. You don't allow yourself to get focused on the disappointment of not getting what you want now; instead you look at the big picture of ultimately achieving your goals and doing what is necessary—even waiting. This perspective facilitates positive problem solving, which motivates a person to continue to try in the face of setbacks by finding more ways to perform effectively.

5. Social skills

A. Empathy is the capacity to understand how another person feels, whether you are at work, with friends or family, or in romance. Go back to self-awareness. Do you leave people feeling dismissed, unimportant or patronized versus genuinely appreciated and cared for? Remember, It is not all about you.

B. The better we are at paying attention to signals that other people put off, the better we are at choosing effective signals that we send to people because we have improved understanding of how others experience us.

The interrelationship among all of the factors associated with emotional IQ results in knowing yourself and knowing how others experience you.

RELAXATION EXERCISES

DEEP BREATHING (5 MIN)

1. Select a comfortable sitting position.

2. Close your eyes, and direct your attention to your own breathing process.

3. Think about nothing but your breathing, let it flow in and out of your body.

4. Say to yourself: "I am relaxing, breathing smoothly and rhythmically. Fresh oxygen is flowing in and out of my body. I feel calm, renewed, and refreshed."

5. Continue to focus on your breathing as it flows in and out, in and out, thinking about nothing but the smooth rhythmical process of your own breathing.

6. After 5 minutes, stand up, stretch, smile, and continue with your daily activities.

MENTAL RELAXATION (5 TO 10 MIN)

1. Select a comfortable sitting or reclining position.

2. Close your eyes, and think about a place that you have been before that you found to be a perfect place for mental and physical relaxation. This should be a quiet environment, such as the ocean, the mountains, a forest, a panoramic view, etc. If you can't think of a real place, then create one.

3. Now imagine that you are actually in your ideal relaxation place. Imagine that you are seeing all of the colors, hearing all of the sounds, smelling all of the different scents. Just lie back and enjoy your soothing, rejuvenating environment.

4. Feel the peacefulness, the calmness, and imagine your whole body and mind being renewed and refreshed.

5. After 5 to 10 minutes, slowly open your eyes and stretch. You have the realization that you may instantly return to your relaxation place whenever you desire, and experience a peacefulness and calmness in body and mind.

TENSING THE MUSCLES (5 TO 10 MIN)

1. Select a comfortable sitting or reclining position.

2. Loosen any tight clothing.

3. Now tense your toes and feet. Hold the tension, study the tension, then relax.

4. Now tense your lower legs, knees, and thighs. Hold the tension. Study the tension, then relax.

5. Now tense your buttocks. Hold and study the tension. Relax.

6. Tense your fingers and hands. Hold and study the tension, then relax.

7. Tense your lower arms, elbows, and upper arms. Hold it, study it, relax.

8. Tense your stomach, hold the tension, feel the tension, and relax.

9. Now tense your chest. Hold and study the tension. Relax. Take a deep breath and exhale slowly.

10. Tense the lower back. Hold and study the tension and relax.

11. Tense the upper back. Hold the tension, feel the tension, then relax.

12. Now tense the neck, back, and front of your neck. Hold the tension, study the tension, then relax.

13. Now tense the shoulders. Hold and study the tension. Then relax.

14. Now tense your entire head. Make a grimace on your face so that you feel the tension in your facial muscles. Study the tension and then relax.

15. Now try to tense every muscle in your body. Hold it, study it, then relax.

16. Continue sitting or reclining for a few minutes, feeling the relaxation flowing through your body. Know the difference between muscles which are tense and muscles which are relaxed.

17. Now stretch, feeling renewed and refreshed, and continue with your daily activities.

MENTAL IMAGERY (10 TO 15 MIN)

Mental imagery can deepen relaxation when used with other techniques, or may be used by itself. The purpose is to calm your body, thoughts, and emotions. It gives you the opportunity to take a break from tension and stress. Mental imagery uses all of your senses to create and recreate a relaxing place, perhaps a meadow, a walk through the woods, along the beach, or perhaps a special place from your memory.

Prepare your environment so that you can complete this relaxation exercise without interruption. Spend some time getting comfortable. Close your eyes, as you scan your body for any tension. If you find tension, release it. Let it go and relax.

Relax your head and your face.
Relax your shoulders.
Relax your arms and hands.
Relax your chest and lungs.
Relax your back.
Relax your stomach.
Relax your hips, legs, and feet.

Experience a peaceful, pleasant, and comfortable feelings of being relaxed as you prepare to make an imaginary trip to a beautiful place.

Take a deep breath, and breathe out slowly and easily. Take a second deep breath, and slowly breathe out. Allow your breathing to become smooth and rhythmic.

Picture yourself on a mountaintop. It has just rained and a warm wind is carrying the clouds away. The sky is clear and blue, and the sun is shining down.

Below you are beautiful green trees. You enjoy the fragrance of the forest after the rain. In the distance you can see a beautiful white, sandy beach. Beyond that, as a far as you can see, is a crystal clear, brilliant blue water. A fluffy cloud drifts in the gentle breeze until it is right over you. Slowly, this little cloud begins to sink down on you. You experience a very pleasant, delightful feeling. As the fluffy cloud moves down across your face, you feel the cool, moist touch of it on your face. As it moves down your body, all of the tension slips away, and you find yourself completely relaxed and happy.

As the soft cloud moves across your body, it gently brings a feeling of total comfort and peace. As it sinks down around you it brings a feeling of deep relaxation. The little cloud sinks underneath you, and you are now floating on it. The cloud holds you up perfectly and safely. You feel secure. The little cloud begins to move slowly downward and from your secure position on it, you can see the beautiful forest leading down to the beach. There is a gentle rocking motion as you drift along. You feel no cares or concerns in the world, but are focused completely on the relaxed feeling you experience. The cloud can take you any place you want to go, and you choose to go to the beach. As you move to the beach, the cloud gently comes to the ground and stops. You get off the soft cloud onto the beach, and you are at peace. You take some time to look around at the white sandy beach, and the beautiful blue water. You can hear sea gulls and the roar of the waves. As you feel the sun shining on you, you can smell the ocean air. It smells good. As you walk slowly on the beach, you enjoy the feeling of the warm clean sand on your feet. Just ahead on the beach is a soft blanket and pillow. You lie down and enjoy the feeling of the soft material on the back of your legs and arms. As you listen to the waves and the sea gulls and feel the warmth of the sun through the cool breeze, you realize that you are comfortable, relaxed, and at peace. You feel especially happy because you realize that you can return to this special and beautiful place any time you want to. Feeling very relaxed, you choose to go back to the place where you started, knowing that you will take these peaceful and relaxed feelings with you. There is a stairway close by that leads you back to the room where you started. As you climb the five steps, you will become more aware of your surroundings, but you will feel relaxed and refreshed. You are at the bottom of the stairs now, and begin climbing.

Step 1 to Step 2:   moving upward
Step 2 to Step 3:   feeling relaxed and more aware
Step 3 to Step 4:   you are aware of what is around you, and your body is relaxed
Step 4 to Step 5:   your mind is alert and refreshed, open your eyes and stretch gently

BRIEF RELAXATION (5 TO 10 MIN)

Get comfortable.

You are going to count backwards from ten to zero.

Silently say each number as you exhale.

As you count, you will relax more deeply and go deeper and deeper into a state of relaxation. When you reach zero, you will be completely relaxed.

You feel more and more relaxed, you can feel the tension leave your body.

You are becoming as limp as a rag doll, the tension is going away.

You are very relaxed.

Now drift deeper with each breath, deeper and deeper.

Feel the deep relaxation all over and continue relaxing.

Now, relaxing deeper you should feel an emotional calm.

Tranquil and serene feelings, feeling of safety and security, and a calm peace.

Try to get a quiet inner confidence.

A good feeling about yourself and relaxation.

Study once more the feelings that come with relaxation.

Let your muscles switch off, feel good about everything.

Calm and serene surroundings make you feel more and more tranquil and peaceful.

You will continue to relax for several minutes.

When I tell you to start, count from one to three, silently say each number as you take a deep breath.

Open your eyes when you get to three. You will be relaxed and alert.

When you open your eyes you will find yourself back in the place where you started your relaxation.

The environment will seem slower and more calm.

You will be more relaxed and peaceful.

Now count from one to three.

BRIEF PROGRESSIVE RELAXATION

Clench both fists, feel the tension. Relax slowly ... feel the tension leave. Feel the difference now that the muscles are relaxed.

Tighten the muscles in both arms. Contract the biceps ... now relax the arms slowly.

Curl the toes downward until the muscles are tight up through the thigh ... now slowly relax. Feel the tension ease.

Curl the toes upward until the muscles in the back of the legs are tight ... now relax slowly. Feel the tension ease.

Curl the toes upward until the muscles in the back of the legs are tight ... now relax slowly. Feel the tension ease.

Push the stomach muscles out and make it tight. Now slowly ... relax. Your arms are relaxed, your legs are relaxed, and your even breathing gives you a feeling of calmness and releases stress.

Pull your stomach in up until your diaphragm feels the pressure. Now ... slowly relax ... slowly. Feel the tension ease.

Pull your shoulders up to your ears. Feel the tension in your back and chest. Now ... slowly relax. Let your arms relax. You are feeling good. Your beating is easy and restful.

Tilt your head backward as far as you can. Stretch the muscles. Feel the tenseness. Now ... slowly ... relax. Feel the tension go.

Wrinkle your forehead. Hold it. Feel the tension. Now, relax. Feel the tension go.

Squint your eyes as tight as you can. Hold it. Now ... relax.

Make a face using all of your face muscles. Hold it. Now relax ... slowly ... let it go. Your arms are relaxed ... your breathing is easy and you feel good all over.

In a perfect state of relaxation you are unwilling to move a single muscle in your body. All you feel is peaceful, quiet and relaxed. Continue to relax. When you want to get up count backward from four to one. You will feel relaxed and refreshed, wide awake and calm.

PROGRESSIVE MUSCLE RELAXATION (20 TO 25 MIN)

Prepare your environment so that you can complete this relaxation exercise without interruption. Spend a little time getting as comfortable as you can. Prepare yourself for a pleasant and comfortable experience. Lie down or recline in a comfortable chair. Uncross your legs, loosen any tight clothing, and remove your shoes and glasses. Your arms should be placed comfortably at your sides. Slowly open your mouth and move your jaw gently from side to side. Now let your mouth close, keeping your teeth slightly apart. As you do this, take a breath, and slowly let the air slip out.

As you tighten one part of your body, try to leave every other part limp and relaxed. Keep the tensed part of your body tight for a few seconds and then let the tension go and relax. Then take a deep breath, hold it for a moment, and as you breath out, think the words, "Let go and relax." You don't have to tense a muscle so hard that you experience discomfort or cramping. The goal of this technique is to recognize the difference between tension and relaxation. It's time to begin progressive muscle relaxation.

First, tense all the muscles in your body. Tense your jaw, eyes, shoulders, arms, hands, chest, back, legs, stomach, hips, and feet. Feel the tension all over your body. Hold the tension briefly, then think the words, "Let go and relax." Let your whole body relax. Feel a wave of relief come over you as you stop tensing. Experience feeling calm.

Take another deep breath, and study the tension as you hold your breath. Slowly breath out and think the words, "Let go and relax." Feel the deepening relaxation. Allow yourself to drift more and more with this relaxation. We will continue with different parts of your body. Become aware of the differences between tension and relaxation in your body.

Keeping the rest of your body relaxed, wrinkle up your forehead. Feel the tension. Your forehead is very tight. Be aware of the tense feeling. Now let the tension go, and relax. Feel the tension slipping away. Smooth out your forehead and take a deep breath. Hold it for a moment, and as you breathe out, think the words, "Let go and relax."

Squint your eyes as if you are in bright sunlight. Keep the rest of your body relaxed. Feel the tension around your eyes. Now, let the tension go, and relax. Take a deep breath and think the words, "Let go and relax," as you breathe out.

Open your mouth as wide as you can. Feel the tension in your jaw and chin. Experience the tension. Now, let your mouth gently close. As you do, think the words, "Let go and relax." Take a deep breath, and as you breathe out, think the words, "Let go and relax."

Close your mouth. Push your tongue against the roof of your mouth. Feel the tension in your mouth and chin. Hold the tension for a moment, then let it go and relax. Take a deep breath. Now think the words, "Let go and relax" as you breathe out. When you breathe out, let your tongue rest comfortably in your mouth, and let your lips be slightly apart.

Keeping the rest of your body relaxed, clench your jaw. Feel the tension in your jaw muscles. Hold the tension for a moment. Now let it go and relax. Take a deep breath out, think the words, "Let go and relax."

Focus now on your forehead, eyes, jaw, and cheeks. Are these muscles relaxed? Have you let go of all the tension? Continue to let the tension slip away and feel the relaxation replace the tension. Your face will feel very smooth and soft as all the tension slips away. Your eyes are relaxed. Your tongue is relaxed. Your jaw is loose and limp. All of your neck muscles are also very relaxed.

The muscles of your face and head are becoming more and more relaxed. Your head feels as though it could roll gently from side to side. Your face feels soft and smooth. Allow your face, head, and neck to continue becoming more and more relaxed as you now move to other areas of your body.

Become aware of your shoulders. Lift your shoulders up and try to touch your ears with each of your shoulders. Become aware of the tension in your shoulders and neck. Hold on to that tension, now let the tension go and relax. As you do, feel your shoulders joining the relaxed parts of your body. Take a deep breath. Hold it, and think the words, "Let go and relax" as you slowly breathe out.

Notice the difference between tension and relaxation in your shoulders. Lift your right shoulder up and try to touch your right ear. Become aware of the tension in your right shoulder and along with the right side of your neck. Hold on to that tension, and now, let it go and relax. Take a deep breath and think the words, "Let go and relax" as you slowly breathe out.

Now lift your left shoulder up and try to touch your left ear. Notice the tension in your left shoulder and along the left side of your neck. Hold on to that tension. Now, let the tension go, and relax. Take a deep breath, and think the words, "Let go and relax" as you slowly breathe out. Feel the relaxation spread throughout your shoulders. Feel yourself become loose, limp, and relaxed.

Stretch out your arms in front of you and make a fist with your hands. Feel the tension in your hands and forearms. Hold that tension. Now, let the tension go and relax. Take a deep breath and think the words, "Let go and relax" as you slowly breathe out.

Press your right hand down into the surface it is resting on. Be aware of the tension in your arm and shoulder. Hold the tension. Now, let the tension go and relax. Take deep breath and as you slowly breathe out, think the words, "Let go and relax."

Now push your left hand down into whatever it is resting on. Experience the tension in your arm and shoulder. Hold on to that tension. Now let go and relax. Take a deep breath and think to yourself, "Let go and relax" as you slowly breathe out.

Bend your arms toward your shoulders and double them up as if you were showing off your muscles. Feel the tension, and hold on to it. Now let it go. Take a deep breath and think the words, "Let go and relax" as you slowly breathe out.

Move your attention to your chest. Take a deep breath that completely fills your lungs. Feel the tension around your ribs. Think the words, "Let go and relax" as you slowly breathe out. Feel the relaxation deepen as you continue breathing easily, freely, gently.

Take another deep breath. Hold it and again experience the difference between relaxation and tension. As you do, tighten your chest muscles. Hold on to that tension and as you slowly breathe out, think the words, "Let go and relax." Feel the relief as you breathe out and continue to breathe gently, naturally, and rhythmically. With each breath, you are becoming more and more relaxed.

Keeping your face, neck, arms, and chest relaxed, arch your back up (or forward if you are sitting). Feel the tension along both sides of your back. Hold that position for a moment. Now, let the tension go, and relax. Take a deep breath and think the words, "Let go and relax" as you breathe out. Feel the relaxation spreading up into your shoulders and down into your back muscles.

Feel the relaxation developing and spreading all over your body. Feel it going deeper and deeper. Allow your entire body to relax. Your face and head are relaxed. Your neck is relaxed. Your shoulders are relaxed. Your arms are relaxed. Your chest is relaxed. Your back is relaxed. All of these areas are continuing to relax more and more, as you are becoming more deeply relaxed and comfortable.

Move your attention to your stomach area. Tighten your stomach muscles, and briefly hold that tension. Let the tension go, and relax. Feel the relaxation moving into your stomach area. All the tension is being replaced with relaxation, and you feel the general well-being and peacefulness that comes with relaxation. Take deep breath and think the words, "Let go and relax" as you breathe out.

Now push your stomach out as far as you can. Briefly hold that tension. Now let it go and relax. Take deep breath. Hold it, and think the words, "Let go and relax" as you breathe out.

Now pull your stomach in. Try to pull your stomach into your backbone. Hold it. Now, relax and let it go. Take a deep breath and think the words, "Let go and relax" as you breathe out.

You are becoming more and more relaxed. Each time you breathe out, feel the gentle relaxation replace the tension in your body. As you continue to do these exercises, your body will relax more and more. Check the muscles of your face, neck, shoulders, arms, chest, and stomach. Make sure they are still relaxed. If they are not as relaxed as they can be, just tense and release them again. You are experiencing control over your body. Whatever part is still less than fully relaxed is starting to relax more and more. You are learning to recognize when you have tension in any part of your body. You are learning that you can become relaxed and let go of the tension you may find in any part of your body.

Now, focus your attention on your hips and legs. Tighten your hips and legs by pressing your heels down into the floor or couch. While you are tightening these muscles, keep the rest of your body as relaxed as you can. Hold on to the tension. Now, let the tension go and relax. Feel your legs float up. Take a deep breath and think the words, "Let go and relax" while breathing out. Feel the relaxation pouring in. Be aware of the differences between the tension and relaxation. Let the relaxation become deeper and deeper. Enjoy the comfortable feeling.

Keeping your feet flexed toward your knees, tighten your lower leg muscles. Feel the tension, hold on to that feeling. Now, let it go and relax. Take a deep breath and think the words, "Let go and relax" as you breathe out.

Now, very gently, curl your toes downward toward the bottom of your feet. Be careful that you don't use so much tension that you experience cramping. Feel the tension. Now, let go of the tension. Feel the relaxation taking the place of the tension. Take a deep breath and think the words, "Let go and relax" as you breathe out.

Keeping your lower legs relaxed. Bend your toes back the other way, toward your knees. Feel the tension. Hold on to the tension. Now let it go and relax. Feel the tension slip away. Take a deep breath, and think the words, "Let go and relax" as you slowly breathe out. Feel the tension leaving your body and the relaxation coming in.

You have progressed through all of the major muscles in your body. Now, let them become more and more relaxed. Continue to feel yourself becoming more and more relaxed each time you breathe out. Each time you breathe out, think about a muscle and think the words, "Let go and relax." Your hands are relaxed. Your chest is relaxed. Your back is relaxed. Your legs are relaxed. Your hips are relaxed. Your stomach is relaxed. Your whole body is becoming more and more relaxed with each breath.

Focus on the peaceful, comfortable, and pleasant experience you are having. Realize that this feeling becomes more readily available to you as you practice becoming aware of your body.

In a moment, I will start counting from five to one. At the count of three, I will ask you to open your eyes. On the count of two, just stretch your body as if you were going to yawn. And at the count of one, you have completed this relaxation exercise and can feel well rested and refreshed. 5 … 4 … 3 … open your eyes … 2 … stretch your muscles gently … 1 … you have completed the progressive muscle relaxation exercise.

When a relaxation technique has been completed, visual imagery can be utilized while the person is still in the relaxed state. The visual imagery can range in emotional intensity from neutral to overwhelming anxiety. Its utility can be in the form of a hierarchy or in the repetition of a single troubling scene for the person that they are striving to master and resolve. In this form of imagined rehearsal, the person gains more practice in coping with anxiety-provoking situations. This acts to build behavioral repertoire and confidence.

The following example (from Navaco as cited in Meichenbaum and Turk, 1976, pp. 6–9) is a demonstration of the type of statements that can be used in conjunction with stress management and relaxation training to enhance or facilitate behavioral change. This particular example counters the negative self-statements indicative of an anger reaction. Because the individual is in a relaxed state with their defenses down they are psychologically less resistant to changing their schemata. This is a beneficial way to increase coping in a variety of anxiety-provoking situations.

What can you tell yourself to control your feelings?

PREPARING FOR THE PROVOCATION

What is it that you have to do to?
You can work out a plan to handle it.
You can manage the situation.
You know how to regulate your anger.
There won't be any need for argument.

Take time for a few deep breaths of relaxation. Feel comfortable, relaxed, and at ease.

CONFRONTING THE PROVOCATION

Stay calm. Just continue to relax.
As long as you keep cool, you're in control.
Don't take it personally.
Don't get all bent out of shape, just think of what to do here.
You don't need to prove yourself.
There is no point in yelling.
You're not going to let them get to you.
Don't assume the worst or jump to conclusions.
Look for the positives.
It's really a shame this person is acting the way they are.
For a person to be that irritable, they must be really unhappy.
There is no need to doubt yourself, what they say doesn't matter.

Your muscles are getting so tight, it's time to slow things down and relax.
Getting upset won't help.
It's just not worth getting so angry.
You'll let them make a fool of themselves.
It's reasonable to get annoyed, but let's keep a lid on it.
Time to take a deep breath.
Your anger is a signal of what you need to do.

IT'S TIME TO TALK TO YOURSELF*

You're not going to get pushed around, but you're not going to be aggressive and out of control either.
Try a cooperative approach, maybe you're both right.
They'd probably like for you to get angry. Well, you're going to disappoint them.
You can't get people to act the way you want them to.

It worked!
That wasn't as hard as you thought it would be.
You could have gotten more upset than it was worth.
You're doing better at this all of the time.
You actually got through that without getting angry.
Guess you've been getting upset for too long when it wasn't even necessary.

The components of the last paragraph can progressively change in accordance with behavioral and cognitive modification and change.

A GUIDE TO MEDITATION (THE TIME FOR MEDITATION IS DECIDED BY THE INDIVIDUAL)

Meditation is a silent, internal process in which an individual attempts to focus their attention on only one thing at a time. It doesn't matter what the focus of attention is, only that all other stimuli are screened out. There are a variety of ways in which to practice meditation. Different meditation techniques are suited for specific purposes. Therefore, it is necessary to determine the needs or desired goal prior to determining the meditation technique to be utilized. The following meditation technique is general in nature and may be altered accordingly. Meditation does not eliminate the problems in a person's life. However, the resulting decrease in stress and tension would be an obvious contribution to an improved ability to cope.

Five steps of instruction on meditation will be presented. It is suggested that an individual experiment with the various techniques to determine which step they elicit the most comfort, ease, and benefit from. During periods of experimentation make an effort to increase the awareness for changes in both internal and external experiences.

STEP 1:

Preparation and Determining Your Posture

Find a quiet place. Practice daily, at the same time each day, for at least 5 minutes. Choose a comfortable sitting position. Sit with your back straight and remain alert. Be sure that you are comfortable, that clothing fits loosely, and that the environment lacks distractions.

STEP 2:

Breathing

Close your eyes and focus on the sensations you are experiencing. With your eyes closed take several deep, cleansing breaths. Notice the quality of your breathing. Notice where your breath resides in your body, and how it feels. Try to move your breath from one area to another. Breathe deeply into the stomach (i.e., the lower area of the lung) and continue up until you reach the chest (i.e., the upper lung region). Likewise, when you exhale, start at the bottom, gently contracting the abdomen and pushing the air out of the lower lung. During this process be focusing on how you feel and how the breathing feels. This technique takes the shortest amount of time.

STEP 3:

Centering

There are focal points, or centers in the body which enhance certain abilities when focused on. The middle of the chest is the heart center, the center of the forehead is the wisdom center, and the navel is the power center. There are other focal points, but these are most commonly used. Concentrating on the heart center increases and intensifies a person's compassion and offers the experience of being one with the universe. Focusing on the wisdom center expands wisdom and intuition. Focusing on the power center enhances the experience of personal power. The collective focus on all three centers represents compassion, wisdom, and power.

STEP 4:

Visualization and Imagery

Visualization creates mental imagery impressions that can consciously train your body to relax and ignore stress. The use of visualization is wide ranging. It has been used to improve athletic performance, and can be a powerful contributor toward the goals of self-development and self-exploration. To fully experience the varying sensations associated with different images meditate on the following topics, adding others to expand your experience if you choose:

1. A mountain lake
2. A forest
3. A happy time in your life or pleasing experience
4. Having as much money and success as you want
5. Radiating physical health
6. White light
7. Nirvana
8. A spiritual icon (Jesus, Buddha, Mohammed)

Choose a visualization that symbolizes what you want or are looking for in your life and mediate on that symbol daily.

STEP 5:

The Word

Words are powerful and focusing your meditation on certain words or phrases can be enlightening. The word or phrase is similar to what was described for visualization and imagery except, instead of a mental picture, the power of words are used instead. Most people are familiar with associating the power of words with positive affirmations.

Meditating words is generally done by repeating the word or phrase that have meaning to you. Some examples are:

1. Love, God, Peace, or Creator
2. I am prosperous or my life is spiritually filled
3. Relax and feel the peacefulness

CRITICAL PROBLEM SOLVING

An intervention strategy that has special potential for enhancing your ability to cope is problem solving. Mastering these principles prepares you to cope more effectively with the diverse problems of life. Much of your negative life experience is likely related to ineffective behavior that fails to solve life's challenging problems and leads to undesired effects such as psychosomatic illness, depression, anxiety, and various other difficulties.

It is generally found that individuals lacking adequate problem-solving skills:

1. Generate fewer possible solutions.
2. Suggested solutions that often don't include social supports.
3. Have inaccurate expectations about probable consequences of alternate solutions.

By mastering a systematic approach to making decisions and solving problems, individuals gain the following benefits:

1. Learn a process that promotes collaboration, cohesiveness, and mutual respect among family and group members.
2. Prevent interpersonal conflicts produced by dysfunctional modes of reaching decisions or solving problems (such as authoritarian patterns or competitive power struggles).
3. Reduce tension, anxiety, and depression by solving stress-producing problems effectively.
4. Generate a wider range of options for coping with problematic situations, thereby enhancing chances of selecting maximally effective decisions or solutions.
5. Enhance the likelihood that family and group members will commit themselves to implementing options that are selected.
6. Increase confidence, self-efficacy, and self-esteem by acquiring a mode of problem solving that can be employed in future problematic situations.

PREPARING TO LEARN PROBLEM-SOLVING SKILLS

Preparing yourself to learn this skill is critical and requires motivation and commitment along with practicing the components of problem solving. This challenge is not simple because marital partners and family members typically view themselves as victims of unreasonable and offensive behavior on the part of other significant members of their system. Failing to see how they contribute to their difficulties, they perceive the solution as consisting of favorable changes by the "offending" person. Therefore, they see no need for collaborative problem solving. Often having assumed an adversarial quality, their interactions tend to be characterized by arguments, mutual recriminations, put-downs, and power struggles.

Begin by clarifying what the problem-solving process is all about. Basically, it is a systematic approach that will help you collaborate in solving problems or in reaching decisions effectively. It involves a number of steps that will assist you to define problems accurately and to generate several possible solutions so that you can select the best possible option. The best option is the one that best meets your needs, so another step involves helping you to identify and understand each other's needs. The process also involves guidelines that will assist you to work together as a team and avoid needless and unproductive hassles.

The process is effective and you can succeed in applying it, but only if you commit to following the steps and guidelines.

MANAGING INTERACTION DURING PROBLEM SOLVING

As individuals prepare to begin practicing problem-solving steps they need to observe the following guidelines:

1. Be specific in relating problems.
2. Focus on the present problem rather than on past difficulties.
3. Focus on only one problem at a time.
4. Listen attentively to the concerns and feelings of others who are sharing problems.
5. Share problems in a positive and constructive manner.

DEVELOPING GOOD PROBLEM-SOLVING SKILLS EQUIPS INDIVIDUALS TO:

1. Identify the causes of emotional difficulties.
2. Recognize the resources they have to deal with their difficulties.
3. Give them a systematic way to overcome their current problems.
4. Enhance their sense of control.
5. Prepare them to deal more effectively with future problems.

STAGES OF PROBLEM SOLVING (AS THERAPIST FACILITATES SKILL DEVELOPMENT IN INDIVIDUAL):

1. To acknowledge and define the problem.
2. Identify their resources—assets and supports.
3. Obtain information from other sources if helpful.
4. Decide on practical arrangements—who will be involved.
5. Establish a therapeutic contract which clarifies the individual's and therapist's responsibilities in problem solving.

Implementing the process does not ensure that resultant decisions and solutions will always produce desired results. However, using the process does avoid discord and substantially enhances the chances of achieving favorable outcomes.

STEPS FOR PROBLEM SOLVING

1. Acknowledge/identify the problem.
2. Analyze the problem, and identify needs of those who will be affected.
3. Employ brainstorming to generate possible solutions.
4. Evaluate each option, considering the needs of those affected.
5. Implement the option selected.
6. Evaluate the outcome of problem-solving efforts.

PROBLEM-SOLVING DIAGRAM

Take a few minutes to focus on yourself. Are you (1) a person who generally copes well but is having current difficulties associated with a specific situation or (2) a person who experiencing difficulty coping? If you identified yourself as generally experiencing difficulty coping, be prepared to be patient as you learn to improve your problem-solving skills, and use the necessary resources for reaching this important goal.

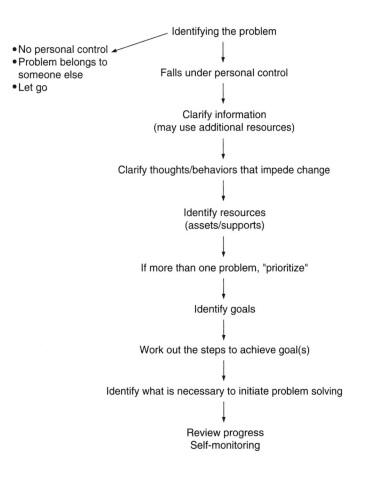

ASSIGNMENT 1

SAMPLE PROBLEMS:

1. "I wish you would ask me in advance about taking the car. When you wait until the last minute, it really annoys me and puts me in a bind because sometimes I need the car. I would like to be considered when you think about taking the car."

_____

_____

_____

_____

2. "I don't like you going to the bar with your buddies several nights in a row. I feel unimportant to you when you spend so little time with me. I would like to share more evenings with you."

_____

_____

_____

_____

3. "It humiliates me when you get on my case in front of my friends. I would like to feel I can bring my friends home without fear of being embarrassed."

_____

_____

_____

_____

Make a list of your own problems and how you plan to resolve them.

ASSIGNMENT 2

1. Discuss a situation that you have experienced that was easy to get into, but difficult to get out of.
   a. Why was the situation so difficult to get out of?
   b. What have you learned from your experience, has it changed you, and what would you do differently next time or in a similar situation?

ASSIGNMENT 3

Taking Risks

1. What is the meaning of risk?

2. Discuss a "risk" you need to take in your life.

3. What keeps you from taking the risk?

4. Why do you feel this risk should or should not be taken?

5. What is possible positive outcome(s) if the risk is taken?

RISKS

Nothing ventured, nothing gained.

A venture is a risk. It is trying something new, or approaching the same problem in a different way.

There are many times when we must take certain risks to bring about desired change, growth, and learning. By avoiding risk you *may* avoid suffering and sorrow. However, you will also avoid learning, feeling, change, growth, love—living. To avoid risk is to remain a prisoner of fear and doubt.

1. What does the statement, "nothing ventured, nothing gained" mean?

   _____

   _____

2. Do you live your life taking well thought out risks or do you fear risk and remain stuck? Explain.

   _____

   _____

3. Does the way you approach problems offer you few choices or more choices with alternatives in case something doesn't work out the way you planned?

   _____

   _____

4. Explain how you currently live your life, and what you want to try to do differently.

   _____

   _____

COMPONENTS OF EFFECTIVE COMMUNICATION

"I" Statements, Active Listening, Reflection, and Nonverbal Communication

"I" STATEMENTS

Rationale: To improve communication by being able to rephrase statements into more assertive statements.

Goal: To be able to identify assertive statements.

Objective: To be able to see the difference between hostile blaming and manipulative statements versus assertive statements. It is also important to take responsibility for your own emotions. Taking responsibility for how you feel instead of blaming someone for how you feel allows you to express yourself honestly and appropriately.

Material Needed: Pencil and paper.

Activity: Rephrase each statement by starting with "I."

Example; You don't care about anyone.
versus
I feel sad when I'm left out.

1. You are wrong.
2. You make me mad.
3. Go away.
4. Give it back.
5. You embarrass me.
6. It's your fault.
7. This is mine.
8. That is bad.

Notes:

_____

_____

ACTIVE LISTENING

Rationale: To demonstrate that attention is being paid to what is being communicated to you.

Goal: To define and be able to demonstrate active listening.

Objective: To be able to pick up the emotional message and be able to restate it in your own words, without analyzing, criticizing, or giving advice.

Activity: Use one of the following sentences for an idea to practice. Have one person give and one person receive.

Example: #1 says: "My purse was just stolen by a man as I walked to my car when I left the store."
#2 responds; "Are you alright? That must have been frightening."

1. Describe your feelings prior to your first date.
2. Describe your feelings prior to an important exam.
3. Describe your feelings prior to tryout for a team.
4. Describe your feelings prior to a confrontation.
5. Describe your feelings when you were intimidated by someone.

Remember: Active listening demonstrates interest with appropriate concern and questions for clarification.

Notes:

_____

_____

_____

_____

_____

REFLECTION

Rationale: To demonstrate interest and understanding of what is being communicated to you.

Goal: To be able to give feedback or reflect emotional messages using "I" statements.

Objective: To clarify message offered by another person.

Activity: Using the same format as with Active Listening and the same sentences.

Example: "I feel you ..."
"It sounds like ..."

Notes:

_____

_____

_____

_____

_____

NONVERBAL COMMUNICATION CHECKLIST

Behavior observed (check all observed)	Yes	No
A. Eye Contact		
1. Spontaneous eye contact and eye movements	_____	_____
2. Breaking eye contact	_____	_____
3. Staring too intensely	_____	_____
4. Looking down	_____	_____
5. Looking directly at helper when speaking	_____	_____
6. Looking directly at helper when listening	_____	_____
7. Looking away	_____	_____
8. Staring blankly	_____	_____
B. Body Posture		
1. Slight forward lean	_____	_____
2. Body facing helper	_____	_____
3. Relaxed posture	_____	_____
4. Relaxed hand position	_____	_____
5. Spontaneous hand and arm movements	_____	_____
6. Gestures for emphasis	_____	_____
7. Touching helper	_____	_____
8. Relaxed leg position	_____	_____
9. Slouching	_____	_____
10. Fixed, rigid position	_____	_____
11. Physically distant from helper	_____	_____
12. Physically too close to helper	_____	_____
13. Arms across chest	_____	_____
14. Body turned sideways	_____	_____
C. Head and Facial Movements		
1. Affirmative head nods	_____	_____
2. Calm, expressive facial movements	_____	_____
3. Appropriate smiling	_____	_____
4. Expressions matching helper mood	_____	_____
5. Face rigid	_____	_____
6. Continual nodding	_____	_____
7. Extraneous facial movements	_____	_____
8. Continual smiling	_____	_____
9. Little smiling	_____	_____
10. Cold, distant expression	_____	_____
11. Frowning	_____	_____
12. Overly emotional expression	_____	_____
D. Vocal Quality		
1. Pleasant intonation	_____	_____
2. Appropriate loudness	_____	_____
3. Moderate rate of speech	_____	_____
4. Simple, precise language	_____	_____
5. Fluid speech	_____	_____
6. Monotone	_____	_____
7. Too much affect	_____	_____
8. Too loud	_____	_____
9. Too soft	_____	_____
10. Use of jargon	_____	_____
11. Use of slang	_____	_____
12. Too fast	_____	_____
13. Too slow	_____	_____
14. Use of "you know"	_____	_____
15. Use of "um," "ah"	_____	_____
16. Voice quiver	_____	_____
E. Distracting Personal Habits		
1. Playing with hair	_____	_____
2. Fiddling with pen or pencil	_____	_____
3. Chewing gum	_____	_____
4. Smoking	_____	_____
5. Drinking	_____	_____
6. Tapping fingers or feet	_____	_____
Other		

IMPROVING COMMUNICATION SKILLS

Less than 10% of what you communicate to someone will be interpreted based on what you say. Over 40% of interpretation is derived from how it is said, and over 40% is interpreted by how you present yourself physically. An additional problem in communication, which contributes to its ineffectiveness, has to do with nonverbal behaviors or habits that are distracting to the person you are communicating with (such as smoking, drinking, fidgeting, tapping fingers/feet, tapping a pin/pencil, chewing gum, playing with one's hair, mustache or beard, etc.).

HOW YOU PRESENT YOURSELF: BODY LANGUAGE

1. Eye contact
   A. Look directly at the person you are speaking to
   B. Remain relaxed, spontaneous/normal, serious but not overly intense

2. Body posture
   A. Face the person you are speaking to
   B. Slightly lean forward toward the person
   C. Maintain a relaxed, attentive posture
   D. Keep your hands loosely clasped or on your lap
   E. The occasional fluid movement of arms and hands is okay
   F. Keep legs parallel or comfortably crossed
   G. Avoid being, rigid, tense, or threatening

3. Head/facial movements
   A. Occasionally nod your head affirmatively
   B. Use appropriate facial responses
   C. Mirror the person you are talking to

HOW YOU SAY IT: QUALITY OF VOICE

1. Tone of voice
   A. Effective tone of voice
      1. Pleasant
      2. Interested intonation
      3. Appropriate loudness
      4. Moderate rate of speech
      5. Natural and relaxed conversation
      6. Simple and precise language
      7. Fluid speech
      8. No to minimal use of slang

Work at increasing your awareness for how you are experienced by others. Do they clearly understand what you want them to? Do you leave them with the thoughts and feelings about you that you intended as a result of your communication efforts? Identify what communication skills you effectively demonstrate and what you need to work on. Observe others you feel are skilled communicators, and try to learn from their modeling of effective communication.

Use the checklist of items describing the quality of your communication to improve your effectiveness and to maintain good communication skills.

EFFECTIVE LISTENING

1. Focus on what is being said
2. Acknowledge *what* has been said (not your interpretation of it)
3. Ask questions for clarification
4. Pay attention to body language
5. Resist the usage to interrupt or give advice
6. Know your "hot buttons"

ASSERTIVE COMMUNICATION

Assertiveness means to communicate your thoughts and feelings honestly and appropriately. Assertive communication can be verbal and nonverbal. To express yourself assertively requires self-awareness and knowing what you want and need. It means showing yourself the same respect that you demonstrate toward others.

If you do not assert yourself, by letting other people know what your thoughts, feelings, wants, and needs are then they are forced to make assumptions about you in those areas. Assumptions have about a 50% chance of being correct. That means that you only have half a chance of people understanding you and responding to you in a way that you desire.

Once you begin to assert yourself you will find that you will feel better about yourself, have more self-confidence, that you get more of what you want out of life, and that others will respect you more.

Be prepared that not everyone will be supportive of your changes in thinking and behavior. Some people that you interact with, such as family members or a significant other, may even demonstrate some negativity toward these changes. This could be because change is difficult for them to accept, they are comfortable with what is familiar to them, they benefited from your passive, people-pleasing behavior, or they fear losing you through change. However, you can't give up who you are to please other people, or to keep certain people in your life. Take one day at a time, focus on the positive, and be the best that you can be.

To clarify the variations of responses and styles of communication/behavior review the following descriptions.

1. *Passive:* Always giving into what others want. Don't want to make waves. Don't express your thoughts or feelings. Afraid to say no. Discounting your own wants and needs.

2. *Aggressive:* Being demanding, hostile, or rude. Insensitive to the rights of others. Intimidates others into doing what they want. Is disrespectful.

3. *Passive-aggressive:* You tell people what they want to hear which avoids conflict. However, you really feel angry inside and you don't follow through on the expectations or requests which results in the other person feeling frustrated, angry, confused, or resentful.

4. *Manipulative:* Attempt to get what you want by making others feel guilty. Tend to play the role of the victim or the martyr in order to get other people to take responsibility for taking care of your needs.

5. *Assertive:* Directly, honestly, and appropriately stating what your thoughts, feelings, needs, or wants are. You take responsibility for yourself and are respectful to others. You are an effective listener and problem solver.

ASSERTIVENESS INVENTORY

The following questions will help determine how passive, assertive, or aggressive you are. Answer the questions honestly and write out how you would handle each situation.

1. Do you say something when you think someone is unfair?
2. Do you find it difficult to make decisions?
3. Do you openly criticize the ideas, opinions, and behavior of others?
4. If someone takes your place in line do you speak up?
5. Do you avoid people or events for fear of embarrassment?
6. Do you have confidence in your own ability to make decisions?
7. Do you insist that the people you live with share chores?
8. Do you have a tendency to "fly off the handle?"
9. Are you able to say "no" when someone is pressuring you to buy or to do something?
10. When someone comes in after you at a restaurant and is waited on first do you say something?
11. Are you reluctant to express your thoughts or feelings during a discussion or debate?
12. If a person is overdue in returning something that they have borrowed from you do you bring it up?
13. Do you continue to argue with someone after they have had enough?
14. Do you generally express what you think and feel?
15. Does it bother you to be observed doing your job?
16. If someone's behavior is bothering you in a theater or lecture, do you say something?
17. Is it difficult for you to maintain eye contact while talking with someone?
18. If you are not pleased with your meal at a restaurant, do you talk to the waitress about correcting the situation?
19. When you purchase something that is flawed or broken do you return it?
20. When you are angry do you yell, name-call, or use obscene language?
21. Do you step in and make decisions for others?
22. Are you able to ask for small favors?
23. Do you shout or use bullying tactics to get your way?
24. Are you able to openly express love and concern?
25. Do you respond respectfully when there is a difference of opinion?

You can tell by your pattern of responses if you generally fall within the descriptor of being passive, assertive, or aggressive. Use this exercise to better understand yourself and to help you set a goal for change if necessary.

Share the results with your therapist.

(Adapted from R. Alberti & M. Emmons, Stand Up, Speak Out, Talk Back, 1975.)

To further clarify what style of communication and behavior that you use, explore how you would handle the following situations.

1. You are standing in line and someone cuts in front of you, or it is your turn and the clerk waits on someone else.
2. Your doctor keeps you waiting for half an hour for your appointment.
3. You are not served something that you ordered at a restaurant.
4. Your neighbors are keeping you awake with loud music.
5. Your teenager is playing the stereo too loud.
6. Your friend borrowed some money from you. It is past the date that they promised to pay you back.
7. You receive a bill and it looks like there is an error on it.
8. You purchased something and decide that you want to return it to the store for a refund.
9. The people behind you at the theater are talking during the movie.
10. You realize that the person that you are talking to is not listening to you.
11. You are displeased by your partner's behavior.
12. The dry cleaners did a poor job on several articles of clothing.

This exercise will help you better understand yourself, and help you determine appropriate and effective responses to normal, everyday experiences.

Passive: Failing to stand up for yourself or standing up for yourself ineffectively which can lead to a violation of your rights.

Assertive: Standing up for yourself in a way that does not violate the rights of other. It is a direct, appropriate expression of thoughts and feelings.

Aggressive: Standing up for yourself in a way that violates the rights of another person. They may feel humiliated or put down by your response.

NONVERBAL COMMUNICATION

Rationale: To explore ways of communicating.

Goal: To show that we always communicate even when we try not to.

Objective: To become more aware of your own nonverbal communication. To make sure your non-verbal communication accurately projects what you are thinking and feeling

Materials Needed: 3×5 cards with words describing a feeling/emotion.

Example:
happy	depressed	nervous
sad	surprise	tired
angry	fear	embarrassed
bored	mischievous	curious

Activities:

A.

1. Get your partner.
2. Sit facing your partner.
3. For one minute, try and "not communicate" anything to your partner.
4. Discuss how "we" always communicate.
5. Did you laugh, look away, make faces, etc?
6. How did you feel?

B.

1. Select a card and try to act out the word using only facial expressions (no hands).

Notes:

_____

_____

_____

_____

_____

_____

_____

DEVELOPING ASSERTIVENESS

1. What do you want (negotiable)?
2. What do you need (non-negotiable)?
3. What are you thinking and feeling that you are not expressing that prevents you from getting what you want and need?

Learning assertive communication and behavior and using it effectively requires the development of all aspects of what it means to be assertive. Effective, assertive communication is like a circle—to be complete all aspects of it must be continuous.

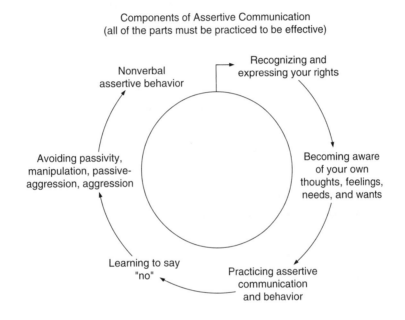

Components of Assertive Communication
(all of the parts must be practiced to be effective)

Recognizing and expressing your rights

Becoming aware of your own thoughts, feelings, needs, and wants

Practicing assertive communication and behavior

Learning to say "no"

Avoiding passivity, manipulation, passive-aggression, aggression

Nonverbal assertive behavior

NONVERBAL ASSERTIVE BEHAVIOR

1. With square shoulders and good posture, look directly at a person when talking to them.
2. Maintain personal space and openness (don't cross arms or legs).
3. To express yourself in an effective assertive manner, don't back up or move from side to side while speaking. Maintain eye contact and be respectful.
4. Remain calm. Do not become emotional. Express yourself appropriately.

PERSONAL BILL OF RIGHTS

1. I have a right to ask for what I want.
2. I have a right to say no to requests or demands that I cannot meet.
3. I have a right to express all of my feelings—positive and negative.
4. I have a right to change my mind.
5. I have a right to make mistakes and do not have to be perfect.
6. I have a right to follow my own values and beliefs.
7. I have the right to say no to anything if I feel that I am not ready, if it is unsafe, or if it conflicts with my values.
8. I have the right to determine my own priorities.
9. I have the right not to be responsible for the actions, feelings, or behavior of others.
10. I have the right to expect honesty from others.
11. I have the right to be angry at someone I love.
12. I have the right to be myself. To be unique.
13. I have the right to express fear.
14. I have the right to say, "I don't know."
15. I have the right not to give excuses or reasons for my behavior.
16. I have the right to make decisions based on my feelings.
17. I have the right to my own personal space and time.
18. I have the right to be playful.
19. I have the right to be healthier than those around me.
20. I have the right to feel safe, and be in a nonabusive environment.
21. I have the right to make friends and be comfortable around people.
22. I have the right to change and grow.
23. I have the right to have my wants and needs respected by others.
24. I have the right to be treated with dignity and respect.
25. I have the right to be happy.

If you are not familiar with your personal rights then take the time to read this daily until you are aware of your rights and begin to assert them. It may be helpful to post a copy of this where you have the opportunity to see it intermittently for reinforcement.

ASSERTIVENESS

1. Enables a person to act in their own best interest.
2. Supports a person to stand up for themselves without mounting anxiety, to express their feelings honestly, and assertively.
3. Facilitates a person to exercise their own personal rights without denying the rights of others.

THE STEPS OF POSITIVE ASSERTIVENESS

1. Prepare for a neutral conversation by first diffusing your emotions and by waiting until the other person is likely to be least reactive and most receptive.
2. Deliver your message as briefly and directly as possible, without being sarcastic, condescending, or judgmental. Contribute to the interaction being a positive one.
3. Be respectful. Allow enough time for the other person to respond without pressure.
4. Reflectively listen. If the person becomes defensive reflect to them what you hear them saying and validate their feelings.
5. Reassert your message. Stay focused on the original issue, do not be derailed.
6. Reuse this process, using a lot of reflective listening to decrease emotionality, debating, or arguing. It takes two people to escalate things. Don't participate.
7. Focus on the solution, without demanding that the person respond as you do. Because you brought it up, you have probably been thinking about it and resolved some aspects of the situation. Therefore, it is important that you facilitate their participation in problem solving the issue so that they don't feel like they have been railroaded.

Nonverbal behaviors are as important as verbalizing your assertiveness. The signals that a person sends, as well as receives, are crucial to the success of assertive communication. Nonverbal cues include eye contact, body posture, personal space, gestures, facial expressions, tone of voice, inflection of voice, vocal volume, and timing. Other variables include smile, head nodding, and appropriate animation.

Entering an ongoing conversation requires the observation of those already involved. As you observe the body language of others, make eye contact, and become part of the group. Join in with appropriate statements and comments.

Ending a conversation can take place by stating a form of closure. "I've really enjoyed this discussion," or "I see someone I must say hi to that I haven't seen for some time." Other solutions could include a change in content, less self-disclosure, and fewer open-ended statements which encourage ongoing conversation. For body language, there is less eye contact, less head nodding, and increasing physical distance.

PRACTICING ASSERTIVE RESPONSES

1. Describe several problem situations. Arrange them in order of increasing discomfort or emotional distress that they cause you. In describing a problem situation include who is involved, when it happens, what bothers you about this particular situation, how you normally deal with it, and what fears you have about being assertive in this situation.

Once you have fully describe a problem situation then determine your goal. How would you like to deal with it, and what is the outcome you want.

2. Developing an Assertive Response
   A. Determine what your personal rights are in the situation.
   B. Speak directly with the person involved, clearly stating how the situation is affecting you. Use "I" statements so that your communication is not blaming or provokes defensiveness (e.g., I feel this way … when … happens).
   C. Express your thoughts and feelings honestly and appropriately. Respect demonstrates that you are taking responsibility for yourself and that you are motivated to cooperatively resolve issues.

D. Clarify what it is that you want by requesting it directly. Stay focused on the issue and don't be side-tracked.

E. Seek to make them aware of the consequences of having or not having their cooperation. Initiate it from a positive perspective of win-win, helping them to see that you will both benefit, e.g., "If you help me clean up the kitchen after dinner we can leave early for the game like you want to do."

TEN STEPS FOR GIVING FEEDBACK

1. Describe what you see or observe instead of making an evaluation or giving your judgment.

2. Be specific instead of general. Specifics are helpful.

3. Feedback should provide information about that which can be controlled and changed, otherwise it only adds to frustration.

4. Timing is important; always consider it, but do not use it as an excuse.

5. Check out what the person you were giving feedback interpreted you as saying. Assumptions cause problems and can lead to hard feelings.

6. Check out the validity of your feedback with others.

7. Encourage feedback, but do not pressure others or impose yourself on them if it is not wanted.

8. Do not overwhelm others with a lot of information. Offer your feedback in small pieces.

9. Own your own feedback, and feelings by using "I" statements. After all, it is only your opinion.

10. Share your feedback with others in a way that makes it easy for them to listen to what it is you want to express.

SAYING "NO"

Many individuals find it difficult to say "no" or to accept someone saying "no" to them, without experiencing negative emotions. Saying "no" can be thought of as a way of taking care of oneself, not to make another individual feel rejected, or to experience feelings of guilt if you are the individual saying "no."

TO OVERCOME GUILT IN SAYING "NO"

Ask yourself the following questions:

1. Is the request reasonable?

2. Ask for more information to clarify what all the facts are.

3. Practice saying "no."

4. Quit apologizing, if it is something that you do not want to do or cannot do. Therefore, quit saying, "I'm sorry, but…"

REVIEW FOR YOURSELF THE CONSEQUENCES OF SAYING "YES"

1. End up angry with yourself for doing something you don't want to.

2. Gets in the way or distracts from things you want to do.

3. Resentment begins to develop and build up.

4. Because you are doing something that you don't want to do, but aren't being honest, it leads to a lack of communication and dishonest communication.

ACCEPTING "NO" FOR AN ANSWER

Each time you hear someone saying "no" to a request that you have made, think to yourself, "I am not being rejected as an individual, it is my request that is being rejected."

Rejection comes up emotionally because your need for approval is strong. You view accepting your requests as an acceptance and approval of you. It is not.

Remember, assertive communication does not mean getting what you want. Assertiveness means honest communication which contributes to respectful relationships.

TEN WAYS OF RESPONDING TO AGGRESSION

1. Reflection: Reflect back to demonstrate that the message has been received. If you like, add information, self-disclosure, or limit setting.

2. Repeated assertion: Instead of justifying personal feelings, opinions, or desires, repeat the original point. This requires ignoring issues that are not relevant or are meant to push buttons.

3. Pointing out assumptions of the aggressor's opinion or position: Do this and then wait for a response. Then state your own opinion or position.

4. Use "I" statement: "I think," "I feel," etc.

5. Ask questions: Questions are especially effective against nonverbal aggression. Questions help the individual become more aware of nonwarranted reactions and behaviors.

6. Paradoxical statements: Making a statement that will make others realize that their aggressive statement could backfire on them.

7. Time out: Stop, and pause. You can do this by excusing yourself in some way, such as ending a phone conversation. This is helpful when you need time to think about how you want to respond, such as refusing a request or demand.

8. Repeat back: When you do not think that another individual is listening to you, ask the a question such as, "What do you think I am asking for?", or "What is your understanding of what I just said?"

9. Feedback reversal: Clarify what you think is being said to you by restating what has been said, in your own words. For example, "Are you saying yes?".

10. Clipping: If you feel like you are under attack, do not want the discussion to be prolonged, and do not feel like you want to defend your position then answer directly: "yes" or "no."

THE COMMUNICATION OF DIFFICULT FEELINGS

HOW YOU CAN DEAL WITH UNCOMFORTABLE FEELINGS

1. Talk to someone
   A. Report the fact of the situation. Do not use the word "you." When you use the word "you," the person that you are speaking to generally becomes defensive, because they are responding like they are being blamed for something.
   B. Use "I" statements. I feel... (angry, happy, scared, upset, etc.) when this happens or when this is said. An "I" statement identifies that you are taking responsibility for your feelings and are speaking assertively with the person to deal with the outcome of any given experience.
   C. Compromise. Ask: "what can we do about this?" This demonstrates respect for the other person's point of view as well as facilitates desired changes, which can benefit both parties.

2. Take action
   A. Call a friend and get together.
   B. Go for a drive.
   C. Write in a journal your feelings and thoughts.
   D. Write an uncensored letter that you do not intend to send.
   E. Go to a movie.
   F. Do something creative (paint, draw, needlework, etc.)
   G. Help someone else.
   H. Read a book that helps to relax and distract you.
   I. DO SOMETHING!

3. Physical activity

Physical exercise is an excellent way to decrease stress and clear your mind so that you can think more rationally. Often, when people are upset they say and do things which complicate an already difficult situation. Emotional distress of any kind creates muscle/body tension. When you feel less distressed you are in a better position to participate in constructive problem solving—alone or with someone else.

Problems occur or get worse when you ignore or neglect to deal with your emotions, or deal with them in a nonproductive pattern.

Three common errors:

1. Fight. If you know how to argue things through to resolution it can be helpful. However, most people lack this skill. Therefore, they end up causing more problems.
2. Flight. Walking out on others and on your own emotions can have negative effects for your emotional and physical well-being.
3. Withdrawal. When you don't deal with things they pile up. Things that pile up over time show up as headaches, fatigue, depression, anxiety, panic attacks, etc.

Sometimes people are no longer able to talk constructively to their partner because either a person lacks the skills of good communication, or they are in an emotionally difficult situation that has been dragging on because they are unable to resolve it. The poor communication may be isolated to specific subjects or it can be a general problem that now crosses many boundaries. If this is the case try writing about your feelings.

Writing about your feelings allows you to describe them more accurately and more honestly. An additional benefit to writing about your feelings is that it allows you to understand yourself and your feelings more deeply. You can put away your defenses, fears, and anxiety. This may not feel safe with others, but when it is only you that you explore the depth of your emotions with the honesty can be a relief and can create opportunities for change never before considered.

Feelings are a spontaneous inner reaction connected to your interpretation of life experiences. Over time you may begin to recognize that how you choose to view or interpret things has a significant impact on how you feel emotionally. It is your responsibility to identify accurate and inaccurate interpretations. For example, sometimes you may take personally someone's behavior or what they said. We cannot take responsibility for others. However, we are responsible for our own thoughts, feelings, and behavior. Once this issue is clarified you will find that you conserve your energy in a constructive way, especially if, in the past, you often interpreted things negatively and tended to personalize them as well.

Feelings are constantly changing. You can have many feelings at once. If you are honest emotionally and accurate in your interpretation of situations *then* you are ready to begin to speak openly about many of the issues you have only felt safe writing about. Do not speak for others, only yourself. Communicating your own feelings accurately, responsibly, and with care eliminates an atmosphere of judgment and blame.

When you express your feelings with care it is an act of giving. No one can describe your feelings as clearly and accurately as you. Communication on a feeling level is an important aspect of a couple's relationship. It is the giving and receiving of each other. This is true of all feelings, even unpleasant and difficult feelings.

To make an assumption or judgment about another opens the door to criticism, blame, defensiveness, accusations, and argument. All of these things lead to the distancing of two people who care about one another. Sometimes the way in which information is given makes it difficult to hear. Therefore, ask yourself, "Am I saying this in a way that the other person can hear what I want them to hear?"

Begin your self-exploration with writing. As soon as you feel comfortable, begin sharing some of the things that you have learned about yourself, and about yourself in your relationship. A lot can be learned, understood, and resolved when two people write. Consider the possibility of each person doing what has been stated as a couple's project in personal and relationship growth.

WRITING

Remember: Keeping a personal journal can be useful for clarification and deeper self understanding, but in this particular writing project you are writing to your partner and your partner is writing to you. Therefore, you will be writing in the same manner that you would like to verbally express yourself. This means writing in a caring and tender manner with honesty and sincerity.

This requires that you clarify the difference between thoughts and opinions and your feelings. Make an effort to describe your feelings as thoroughly as possible and in terms that your partner will be able to relate to and understand. To begin, use the next sheet (List of Potential Conflicts) which defines some potential topics of relationship conflicts. Together you will choose one area to write about using the directions given.

This writing project is not to be a means to vent and get things off your chest. Nor is it the means to make your partner feel bad or to put them in their place. Its purpose is to improve the understanding and communication between the two of you in order to build a stronger and more satisfying, sharing relationship.

In your writing be sure that you do not blame your partner for how you feel or try to change them. The purpose of your writing is to reveal the real you with an invitation for them to symbolically take your hand and grow toward a stronger bond of genuine respect and positive regard and love for one another.

The outcome of improving your communication will be to come to mutually agreeable solutions and problem solving.

Once the two of you have completed your writing it is time to exchange your notebooks. This exchange is done in a gentle, caring manner without any discussion. To share yourself with one another so openly and honestly is a gift. Each person is to read what their partner has written two times without saying anything. Try to understand the words that they have written to you about their feelings.

The next step is to talk about what you have shared with one another through your writing. Listen to one another carefully so that there can be full understanding between the two of you. Remind yourself that this is a time of growth. A time to grow closer through understanding and validation.

AREAS OF POTENTIAL CONFLICT

1. Read through the list. Put a check by any area that you identify as an area of difficulty, where you believe that others do not understand how you feel, or where you may lack understanding in how other people feel.

2. If you have marked more than one area, choose the one that elicits the strongest feelings for you.

3. Write a letter to your partner as described on the handout. As you describe how you feel in detail be sure that the manner of your expression is respectful as you attempt to grow in awareness and understanding of one another.

LIST OF POTENTIAL CONFLICTS

__ Money/finances
__ Time management
__ Work
__ Leisure time
__ Couple's time
__ Sexual relationship
__ Intimacy/touching/hugs
__ Children/parenting issues
__ In-laws or other family members
__ Atmosphere of the home
__ Maintenance of home
__ Decision making
__ Friends
__ Differences in religious or spiritual beliefs
__ Use of alcohol/drugs
__ Other

LIST OF FEELING WORDS

PLEASANT FEELINGS

OPEN	HAPPY	ALIVE	GOOD
understanding	great	playful	calm
confident	gay	courageous	peaceful
reliable	joyous	energetic	at ease
easy	lucky	liberated	comfortable
amazed	fortunate	optimistic	pleased
free	delighted	provocative	encouraged
sympathetic	overjoyed	impulsive	clever
interested	gleeful	free	surprised
satisfied	thankful	frisky	content
receptive	important	animated	quiet
accepting	festive	spirited	certain
kind	ecstatic	thrilled	relaxed
	satisfied	wonderful	serene
	glad		free and easy
	cheerful		bright
	sunny		blessed
	merry		reassured
	elated		
	jubilant		

LOVE	INTERESTED	POSITIVE	STRONG
loving	concerned	eager	impulsive
considerate	affected	keen	free
affectionate	fascinated	earnest	sure
sensitive	intrigued	intent	certain
tender	absorbed	anxious	rebellious
devoted	inquisitive	inspired	unique
attracted	nosy	determined	dynamic
passionate	snoopy	excited	tenacious
admiration	engrossed	enthusiastic	hardy
warm	curious	bold	secure
touched		brave	
sympathy		daring	
close		challenged	
loved		optimistic	
comforted		re-enforced	
drawn toward		confident	
		hopeful	

DIFICULT/UNPLEASANT FEELINGS

ANGRY	DEPRESSED	CONFUSED	HELPLESS
irritated	lousy	upset	incapable
enraged	disappointed	doubtful	alone
hostile	discouraged	uncertain	paralyzed
insulting	ashamed	indecisive	fatigued
sore	powerless	perplexed	useless
annoyed	diminished	embarrassed	inferior
upset	guilty	hesitant	vulnerable
hateful	dissatisfied	shy	empty
unpleasant	miserable	stupefied	forced
offensive	detestable	disillusioned	hesitant
bitter	repugnant	unbelieving	despair
aggressive	despicable	skeptical	frustrated
resentful	disgusting	distrustful	distressed
inflamed	abominable	misgiving	woeful
provoked	terrible	lost	pathetic
incensed	in despair	unsure	tragic

infuriated	sulky	uneasy	in a stew
cross	bad	pessimistic	dominated
worked up	a sense of loss	tense	
boiling			
fuming			
indignant			

INDIFFERENT	AFRAID	HURT	SAD
insensitive	fearful	crushed	tearful
dull	terrified	tormented	sorrowful
nonchalant	suspicious	deprived	pained
neutral	anxious	pained	grief
reserved	alarmed	tortured	anguish
weary	panic	dejected	desolate
bored	nervous	rejected	desperate
preoccupied	scared	injured	pessimistic
cold	worried	offended	unhappy
disinterested	frightened	afflicted	lonely
lifeless	timid	aching	grieved
	shaky	victimized	mournful
	restless	heartbroken	dismayed
	doubtful	agonized	
	threatened	appalled	
	cowardly	humiliated	
	quaking	wronged	
	menaced	alienated	
	wary		

TIME MANAGEMENT

Time is defined by how we use it. If you feel like you are constantly rushing, don't have enough time, are constantly missing deadlines, have many nonproductive hours, lack sufficient time for rest or personal relationships, feel fatigues, and feel overwhelmed by demands, it is likely that you suffer from poor time management.

FOUR CENTRAL STEPS TO EFFECTIVE TIME MANAGEMENT

1. *Establish priorities.* This will allow you to base your decisions on what is important and what is not, instead of wasting your time.
2. *Create time by realistic scheduling.* People tend to misjudge how much time tasks will really take to accomplish. Therefore, give yourself adequate time to accomplish a given task and eliminate low-priority tasks.
3. *Develop the skill of decision making.*
4. *Delegate tasks to others.* If you tend to control everything or believe that only you can do whatever it is, then realistically evaluate all the tasks that you do and you will be surprised to find that many people in your life are capable of doing some of the things that you do.

HOW TO START YOUR TIME MANAGEMENT PROGRAM

1. Making an initial assessment of how you spend your time takes approximately 3 days of observation. Keeping a journal specifically to log how you spend your

time will clarify your time management or lack thereof. This will be easy to manage if you break up the day into three parts:

   A. From waking through lunch.

   B. From the end of lunch through dinner.

   C. From the end of dinner until you go to sleep.

2. It will take one day to define and prioritize your goals and activities.

3. To adequately develop a habit of effective time management will take between 3 and 6 months.

Once you begin your time management program continue to do a weekly review to monitor your consistency and progress. Maintain an awareness of what you are doing and why. You will find that effective time management will significantly reduce your stress.

SOME EXAMPLES OF INDIVIDUALIZED TIME MANAGEMENT OPTIONS

Effective time management contributes to a balanced lifestyle. Review the following list and choose some time management tips that you can incorporate into your life to accomplish more and to feel less stress.

1. Be realistic with yourself regarding how much you can actually accomplish in a given span of time.

2. Say "NO" to additional responsibilities that infringe on personal/leisure or work time.

3. Prioritize your tasks, because they are not equally important. Set priorities on a daily, weekly, and monthly basis for maximizing accomplishments.

4. Develop an awareness for your peak energy periods and plan to do the activities with the highest energy demand at that time.

5. On a regular basis, review what the best use of your time is currently.

6. Striving for perfection is generally not necessary and can burn up time better spent in another way. Complete tasks well enough to get the results that you really need.

7. Delegate tasks and responsibilities to others whenever appropriate. Just be sure to communicate your expectations clearly.

8. Don't waste time thinking and rethinking the decisions for basic issues. Make those decisions quickly and move on.

9. If you have a difficult task to do that you are not looking forward to, do yourself a favor and approach it with a positive attitude. You will be surprised about how much stress that can relieve.

10. Break big overwhelming tasks into small manageable ones so that way it is easier to keep track of your progress and achievements—which is reinforcing.

11. Be prepared to make good use of "waiting" time by having small tasks or activities to do. Another way to deal with it is to always be prepared to take advantage of potential relaxation time when there are no demands on you.

12. When you need time to focus on your goals without interruption then request it. Take responsibility for creating a conducive work environment at home and at work.

13. Set goals and reward yourself when you have accomplished them. If it is a big goal you may want to build in rewards at certain milestones of effort and accomplishment as a reinforcer.

14. From time to time, remind yourself how good it feels to accomplish tasks, what the benefits of accomplishment are, and the relief of having that weight off your shoulders.

15. Good use of time means more than completing "necessary" tasks. It means building in time for self-care like leisure activities and exercise. You being the best that you can be is a priority.

DECISION MAKING

Life is about choices. Decision making is a skill that can help you to make choices that are necessary and right for you. It is an active process that requires you to take responsibility for yourself, your life, and your own happiness. People who are good at making decisions have the self-confidence that comes from knowing how to make good choices in their life.

STEPS FOR DECISION MAKING

1. *Isolate the problem.* Sometimes things are not what they seem.
   Be careful in not just looking at the surface issues and making a decision based on that. Instead, try to understand any underlying issues that may actually be the source of the problem. If you allow yourself to examine the problem from a number of different perspectives or angles, you may find yourself defining the problem in a number of different ways. The more options you have the better your chance of making the best choice.

2. *Decide to take action.* Once you have identified and isolated the problem, the next step is deciding whether or not you need to take action now. Sometimes the best decision is to do nothing. However, there is a difference between making a choice to do nothing versus procrastination, and avoidance of dealing with an uncomfortable situation.

3. *Gather resources.* Ideally it is best to gather as much information as possible about the situation. Sometimes this may even mean consulting with a professional or expert could be beneficial. Gather as much information as you can, but use common sense. Gathering information could be a way to delay taking any action based on the premise that you don't have all the information that you know its out there.

4. *Make a plan.* In other words, "make a decision." You have analyzed the problem, looked at it from all the different angles. Now it is time to decide how you will carry out your decision.

5. *Visualize your plan of action.* It is not possible to anticipate the outcome of any decision you make, because making a decision involves some degree of risk. However, you can do a test run on your plan by visualizing the potential outcome of your decision. Use your gut feeling or intuition. If it doesn't feel right, don't ignore it, try to understand the source of your discomfort with the decision.

6. *Take action.* You have successfully completed all the steps required for good decision making. Now it is time to take action, and put your decision to work. At this point you should feel confident about the work you have done in making this decision, and you will be able to maintain that feeling of self-confidence as you take action.

GOAL DEVELOPMENT

Before a person can reach goals they must set goals. Often, people have a lot of different things on their mind that they would like to see happen. However, they have not taken the time to sit down and thoroughly think through all that is required to see those things happen. Strategizing for success is an easy process, doesn't take much time to do, and when you are completed you will have a much clearer idea of what you want and how you are going to go about making it happen.

STEPS FOR DEVELOPING GOALS

1. *Keep it simple.* Define the goal as clearly as possible. If you are not sure of exactly what you want, the course to get there will be bumpy, and it will take more time and energy than necessary.

2. *Break it into small steps.* Once you have clearly defined the goal, break it down into small steps that you take to reach your goal. Small steps are helpful because they are manageable, require the least amount of stress, and allow you to see the progress that you are making toward your goal.

3. *Choose a starting point.* Once you have broken your goal down into steps, the next thing to do is to choose a starting point. When will you begin working on your goal? This is a question which clarifies how much of a priority it is to you. Life is about choices, and everyone is responsible for the quality of their own life.

4. *Redefine the goal.* Sometimes it becomes necessary to redefine a goal that you have set. Maybe it was an unrealistic goal because you lacked the resources to reach it, it is not as important to you as it once was, or maybe as time has gone on you have learned some new information which changes the way that you are looking at things. In redefining the goal you go through the same steps as setting the original goal. Redefining goals is often related to personal growth.

5. *Act on your plan.* By the time you actually initiate a formal starting point of your goal you will already have completed several of the steps toward it. You will have thought it through, and actually planned it out. Accomplishing steps toward your goal will reinforce positive self-esteem, and following through on other important changes in your life if that is your choice.

SETTING PRIORITIES

Once you have set major goals and decided on your plan of action, you need to determine how important it is for you to reach your goal. This is what is meant by "setting priorities." Sometimes people get frustrated with themself because they start things that they never finish. It is important to explore the reason behind the lack of accomplishment. It could be that motivation is low, avoidance is at work, or that it is simply not a priority for you.

STEPS FOR SETTING PRIORITIES

1. *Develop a strategy.* This relates back to the steps of clearly defining your goals. Once the goal is decided, you then break it down into steps that will ensure that you are able to reach it. Because you remain focused your goal the steps to getting there are each a priority set in sequence.

2. *Know what is important.* To be satisfied with the outcome of your goal it is important to be aware of all of the issues related to it. In some ways your goal may open the door for other opportunities, or it may present some limitations. Understand where you are going and how things may change for you over time, which may alter priorities.

3. *Investigate alternatives.* Use your resources, take the time to educate yourself, and ask as many questions as possible. Because goals can include investments of time, money, and effort, thoroughly investigate the different paths for getting to the same goal. Then, when it comes time to put your plan into action, you will know if there is more information that you need to update yourself or if you feel assured that you are ready to proceed.

4. *Reaching your goal.* By having a clearly defined goal and a plan which is broken down into manageable steps, you will be able to reach your goal. You will have put your priorities into place and will be on your way to accomplishing your goal.

RATIONAL THINKING: SELF-TALK, THOUGHT STOPPING, AND REFRAMING

SELF-TALK

Much of what a person feels is caused by what they say to themselves. People talk to themselves all day long with little awareness for it. This is because self-talk is automatic and carried out repeatedly. However, people generally have some idea for the type of self-talk they use once exploring the subject of self-talk begins.

When people are not sure why something is the way it is they often start looking outside themselves for the source of unhappiness or other form of emotional distress. They have the impression that what is happening around them is what "makes" them feel the way they do. While there is likely to be some contribution from their environment, it is really their thoughts and interpretation about the situation that causes the associated feelings.

Situation or _____ Distorted-Negative _____ Emotional Response
Experience   Self-Talk

Therefore, what a person thinks about a situation is likely the greatest factor influencing how they feel and respond. The most positive aspect about this is that a person has choices. Choices with effort leads to change in the way they interpret events and think about them.

It is likely that if they do engage in negative self-talk that they have been doing it for a long time. It may have even started when you were very young.

It starts by a person telling themselves negative things about themselves and their life situation. Not surprisingly, these types of internal messages could start when a person is young because they are unhappy, a negative thing may be repeatedly said to them which becomes part of their identity, they didn't feel like they had control over their life, and/or they have not been taught good coping skills. All of this makes it easier for a person to externalize or blame the way that they feel and their responses to some entity outside of themselves and their control instead of taking responsibility for their own feelings and actions.

As an adult all of this negative self-talk is seen as perfectionism, chronic worrying, always being a victim, self-critical, low self-esteem, phobias, panic attacks, generalized anxiety, depression, and hopelessness. It is also possible that when people feel so bad emotionally that it affects them physically.

For example: headaches, abdominal distress, intestinal disorders, seems to be sick all the time.

If you experience physical symptoms, you should consult your physician. Examples:

Distorted

Thinking—

Negative

Self-Talk

_____

1. What if I don't pass the employment exam (worrier).
2. I am a weak person (critic).
3. I will never get over this (victim).
4. I will be devastated if I don't get acceptance/approval (perfectionist).

List some negative self-statements that you are aware of:

1. _____

    _____

2. _____

    _____

3. _____

    _____

4. _____

    _____

5. _____

    _____

6. _____

_____

7. _____

_____

8. _____

_____

9. _____

_____

10. _____

_____

The realization that you are mostly responsible for how you feel is empowering. When you take responsibility for your reactions you begin to take charge and have mastery over your life. Once you become aware of the distortions in your thinking you will be able to change negative thoughts to positive ones.

Accomplishing this is one of the most important steps to living a happier, more effective and emotionally distressing free life.

THOUGHT STOPPING

Now that you are aware of negative self-talk and how it affects how you think, feel, and respond you are ready to learn some additional strategies to facilitate new ways of thinking.

Thought stopping is a technique that has been used for years to treat obsessive and pho-bic thoughts. It involves concentrating on the unwanted thoughts, and after a short time, suddenly stopping and emptying the thoughts from your mind. The command "stop" or a loud noise is generally used to interrupt the unwanted and unpleasant thoughts.

As previously discussed regarding negative self-talk, it has been well documented that negative and frightening thoughts invariably precede negative and frightening emotions. If the thoughts can be controlled, overall levels of stress and other negative emotions can be significantly decreased.

Thought stopping is recommended when the problem is primarily cognitive, rather than acted out. It is indicated when specific thoughts or images are repeatedly experienced as painful or leading to unpleasant emotional states. Assess which recurrent thoughts are the most painful and intrusive. Make an effort to understand the role that these thoughts have had on emotional functioning and how you experience your environment in general, based on the following statements.

Explore Your List of Stressful Thoughts (from self-talk section)

1. No Interference. This thought does not interfere with other activities.
2. Interferes a Little. This thought interferes a little with other activities, or wastes a little of my time.
3. Interferes Moderately. This thought interferes with other activities, or wastes some of my time.
4. Interferes a Great Deal. This thought stops me from doing a lot of things, and wastes a lot of time every day.

1. Close your eyes and imagine a situation where the stressful thought is likely to occur. Include the neutral as well as distressing thought related to this situation.

2. Interrupt the thought

   A. Set a timer or alarm of some sort to go off in 3 min. Close your eyes and imagine the stressful thought as stated in #1. When the alarm goes off, shout "stop." Let your mind empty of the stressful thoughts, leaving only neutral and nonstressful thoughts. Set a goal of about 30 sec after the stop, with your mind remaining blank. If the stressful thoughts return during that brief period, shout "stop" again.

   B. Using a tape recorder, record yourself shouting "stop" at the varying intervals of 3 min, 2 min, 3 min, 1 min. Repeat the taped "stop" messages several times at 5-sec intervals. Proceed the same way with your timer or alarm. The tape recording is beneficial to strengthen and shape your thought control.

   C. The next step is to control the thought-stopping cue without an alarm or tape recorder. When you are thinking about the stressful thoughts shout "stop." When you succeed in eliminating the thought(s) on several occasions by interrupting the thought with "stop" said in a normal voice, then start interrupting the thought by whispering the "stop" cue. When you are able to interrupt the thought with the whispered cue begin to use a subvocal cue of "stop" (moving your tongue as if you were saying it out loud). When you have success at this level then you will be able to stop the thoughts alone or in public without making a sound and not calling attention to yourself.

   D. The final step of thought stopping involves thought substitution. In place of the distressing thought, use a positive, affirming, and assertive statement. For example, if you were afraid to go out on a lake in a boat you might say to yourself, "This is beautiful and relaxing out here." Develop several alternative statements to combat the negative one, since the same response may lose its power through repetition.

Special Considerations

1. Failure with your first attempt at thought stopping means that you have selected a thought that is very difficult to eliminate. In this situation choose a stressful thought that is either less stressful or intrusive than your first choice. Repeat the technique.

2. If the subvocalized "stop" is not successful, and saying "stop" out loud embarrasses you, then keep a rubberband around your wrist so that no one can see it and when the thought occurs snap it. Or pinch yourself, or press your fingernails into your palms.

3. You should be aware that thought stopping takes time. The thought will return and you will have to eliminate it again. The main idea is to stop the thought when it returns again, and to concentrate on something else. The thoughts will return less and less in most cases and eventually cease.

REFRAMING

You have learned about how negative self-talk affects how you think, feel, and respond. Now you are going to learn additional strategies for changing how you think and what you do related to how you will interpret situations and how you feel.

Often the way you interpret things is linked to irrational beliefs or negative self-statements. Reframing, or relabeling is a technique you can use to modify or change your view of a problem or a behavior. You will also find it helpful in decreasing defensiveness and to mobilize your resources.

Therefore, reframing provides alternative ways to view a problem behavior or perception. Look for overgeneralizations like never and always.

For example:

if labeled   stubborn   independent or persistent
                   greediness   ambitious
                   anger   loving concern

When a behavior is labeled negatively ask the following questions:

1. Identify a situation which typically produces uncomfortable or distressing feelings.
2. Try to become aware of what you automatically focus on during the situation.
3. What are you feeling and thinking?

To challenge the long-term negative labeling ask the following questions:

1. Is there a larger or different context in which this behavior has positive value?
2. What else could this behavior mean?
3. How else could this situation be described?

Steps to Successful Reframing

1. To understand and accept an individual's belief that perceptions about a problem situation can cause emotional distress.
2. To become aware of what is automatically attended to or focused on in problem situations. You can use imagery or role paying to reenact situations to become more aware of what thoughts and feelings are present. When you identify your perceptions and feelings you will be able to be prepared for the next step.
3. Identification of alternative perceptions. Generally this means to attend to other features of the situation that have a positive or neutral connotation. The reframe must fit, be acceptable to the individual, and at least as valid as the perception they are reframing.
4. Modifying the perceptions in a problem situation are designed to break the old patterns by creating new and more effective reframes. This requires commitment and practice.
5. Homework using real-life situations and recording it in your journal will reinforce desired change(s). The experience, perception with associated thoughts, feelings, and responses, and the chosen reframe (it may be helpful to list several possible alternative reframes).

THINKING DISTORTIONS

1. All-or-Nothing Thinking. You see things in black and white categories. If your performance falls short of perfect, you see yourself as a total failure.

2. Overgeneralization. You see a single negative event as a never-ending pattern of defeat.

3. Mental Filter. You pick a single negative detail and dwell on it exclusively so that your vision of all reality becomes darkened, like the drop of ink that discolors the entire beaker of water.

4. Disqualifying the Positive. You reject positive experiences by insisting that they don't count for some reason or other. In this way you can maintain a negative belief that is contradicted by your everyday experiences.

5. Jumping to Conclusions. You make a negative interpretation even though there are no definite facts that convincingly support your conclusion.
    A. Mind Reading. You arbitrarily conclude that someone is reacting negatively to you, and you don't bother to check it out.
    B. The Fortune Telling Error. You anticipate that things will turn out badly, and you will feel convinced that your prediction is an already established fact.

6. Magnification, Catastrophizing, or Minimization. You exaggerate the importance of things (such as failure, falling short of the mark, or someone else's achievement), or you inappropriately shrink things until they appear tiny (your good and desirable qualities or someone else's limitations).

7. Emotional Reasoning. You assume that your negative emotions necessarily reflect the way things really are, "I feel it, so it must be true."

8. Should Statements. You try to motivate yourself with shoulds and shouldn'ts, as if you had to be whipped and punished before you could accomplish anything. "Musts" and "oughts" also fall into this faulty-thinking category. The emotional consequence is guilt. When you direct should statements toward others, you feel anger, frustration, and resentment.

9. Labeling and Mislabeling. This is an extreme form of overgeneralization. Instead of describing your error, you attach a negative label to yourself, "I'm a loser." When someone else's behavior rubs you the wrong way you attach a negative label to him, "He's a jerk." Mislabeling involves describing an event with language that is highly colored and emotionally loaded.

10. Personalization. You see yourself as the cause of some problem, or take on someone's opinion as having more value than it does.

REALISTIC SELF-TALK

1. This too shall pass and my life will be better.
2. I am a worthy and good person.
3. I am doing the best I can, given my history and level of current awareness.
4. Like everyone else, I am a fallible person and at times will make mistakes and learn from them.
5. What is, is.
6. Look at how much I have accomplished, and I am still progressing.
7. There are no failures only different degrees of success.

8. Be honest and true to myself.

9. It is okay to let myself be distressed for awhile.

10. I am not helpless. I can and will take the steps needed to get through this crisis.

11. I will remain engaged and involved instead of isolating and withdrawing during this situation.

12. This is an opportunity, instead of a threat. I will use this experience to learn something new, to change my direction, or to try a new approach.

13. One step at a time.

14. I can stay calm when talking to difficult people.

15. I know I will be okay no matter what happens.

16. He/She is responsible for their reaction to me.

17. This difficult/painful situation will soon be over.

18. I can stand anything for a while.

19. In the long run who will remember, or care?

20. Is this really important enough to become upset about?

21. I don't really need to prove myself in this situation.

22. Other people's opinions are just their opinions.

23. Others are not perfect, and I won't put pressure on myself by expecting them to be.

24. I cannot control the behaviors of others, I can only control my own behaviors.

25. I am not responsible to make other people okay.

26. I will respond appropriately, and not be reactive.

27. I feel better when I don't make assumptions about the thoughts or behaviors of others.

28. I will enjoy myself, even when life is hard.

29. I will enjoy myself while catching up on all I want to accomplish.

30. Don't sweat the small stuff—it's all small stuff.

31. My past does not control my future.

32. I choose to be a happy person.

33. I am respectful to others and deserve to be respected in return.

34. There is less stress in being optimistic and choosing to be in control.

35. I am willing to do whatever is necessary to make tomorrow better.

PRACTICE REFRAMING HOW YOU INTERPRET SITUATIONS

You have a choice in how you view or interpret situations. If you tend to overgeneralize or focus on the negatives you make it difficult to cope effectively, you decrease your opportunity for happiness, and you remain stuck instead of adjusting and adapting.

1. Identify several situations which typically produce uncomfortable or distressing feelings.

_____

_____

_____

_____

_____

2. What is your automatic focus, thoughts, and feelings in each situation?

_____

_____

_____

_____

_____

3. What is a more useful way to view each situation which offers you choices and the potential for growth?

_____

_____

_____

_____

DEFENSE MECHANISMS

Defense mechanisms are a way of coping with anxiety, reducing tension, and restoring a sense of balance to a person's emotional experience. Defense mechanisms happen on an unconscious level and tend to distort reality to make it easier for the person to deal with. Everyone uses defense mechanisms as a way to cope with the everyday garden variety mild to moderate anxiety. When defense mechanisms are used to an extreme, they interfere with a person's ability to tell the difference between what is real and what is not.

Defense mechanisms are used independently or in combination with one another. They are used to various degrees, depending on how well they meet our needs.

Choose three defense mechanisms and describe how you use each. Additionally, describe how it prevents your personal growth. Identify constructive alternatives for coping that you could use instead of the defense mechanisms.

1. Defense Mechanism: _____

_____

_____

_____

_____

_____

_____

2. Defense Mechanism: _____

_____

_____

_____

_____

_____

_____

3. Defense Mechanism: _____

_____

_____

_____

_____

_____

_____

DEFENSE MECHANISM DEFINITIONS

1.	Denial	Protecting oneself from unpleasant aspects of life by refusing to perceive, acknowledge, or face them.
2.	Rationalization	Trying to prove one's actions "made sense" or were justified; making excuses.
3.	Intellectualization	Hiding one's feelings about something painful behind thoughts; keeping opposing attitudes apart by using logic-tight comparisons.
4.	Displacement	Misdirecting pent-up feelings toward something or someone that is less threatening than that which actually triggered the feeling response.
5.	Projection	Blaming. Assuming that someone has a particular quality or qualities that one finds distasteful.
6.	Reaction Formation	Adopting actions and beliefs, to an exaggerated degree that are directly opposite to those previously accepted.
7.	Undoing	Trying to superficially repair or make up for an action without dealing with the complex effects of that deed, "magical thinking."
8.	Withdrawal	Becoming emotionally uninvolved by pulling back and being passive.
9.	Introjection	Adopting someone else's values and standards without exploring whether or not they actually fit oneself; "shoulds" or "ought to's."
10.	Fantasy	Trying to handle problems or frustrations through daydreaming or imaginary solutions.
11.	Repression	Unconsciously blocking out painful thoughts.
12.	Identification	Trying to feel more important by associating oneself with someone or something that is highly valued.
13.	Acting Out	Repeatedly doing actions to keep from being uptight without weighing the possible results of those actions.
14.	Compensation	Hiding a weakness by stressing too strongly the desirable strength. Overindulging in one area to make up for frustration in another.
15.	Regression	Under stress, re-adopting actions done at a less mature stage of development.

ANGER MANAGEMENT

Anger is a normal, healthy emotion. When it is expressed appropriately you are letting go of the stress and frustration that you are experiencing, and those around you understand and accept that you are upset. When anger is expressed inappropriately with blame and aggression it can be a destructive force—both to the person experiencing it and for those subjected to it.

As with other things that are negative, there is a tendency to hold something or someone else responsible. When you hold someone else responsible for your stress, anxiety, or frustration you feel that you have the right to express it in an aggressive manner.

1. You are responsible for your own life, the choices you make, and the quality of your life experience.
2. Clarify your thoughts, feelings, needs and wants. You are the only one who knows what goes on inside of you.
3. Compromise with others when wants or needs are in conflict, or an issue of some contention. It is unreasonable to always or rarely get what you want. Therefore, with mutual respect, compromise, and negotiation people can seek an equitable solution.
4. Develop effective skills for managing your life. Examine the difficulties that you experience, assess how you contribute to the difficulties, and decide what you are willing to do differently.

SEVEN STEPS OF TAKING RESPONSIBILITY

1. Make a commitment to change in order to improve the quality of your life.
2. Be aware of how the behavior of others affect you. Seek activities which are pleasurable and beneficial to you. People who feel good about their lives are less negative and angry. They are happy, accepting of responsibility and take good care of themselves.
3. Self-care is the core of taking responsibility for yourself. Balance your life; Nutrition, adequate rest, regular exercise, people and activities that you enjoy, personal growth, things to look forward to, etc.
4. Broadening your resources and support system is a life-long endeavor. Don't limit yourself with minimal resources. Create as many choices for yourself as possible.
5. Clear boundaries and setting limits reinforces everyone being responsible for themselves. Don't do things just to please others. Give yourself permission to say "no." If you ignore this step you are likely to feel used, abused, and resentful.
6. Define your goals. Break each goal down into manageable steps. Regularly check on the progress you had made toward your goals. You create your own destiny.
7. Let go. If something is unresolved then take care of it and move on. If there is something that you don't have any control over then make peace with it, accept it, and let go. Letting go is also important if you choose to remain in situations or relationships which are frustrating to you. You only have control over yourself. You are responsible for your own happiness.

UNDERSTANDING ANGER

1. What are the stressors, fears, and frustrations that are at the bottom of your anger?

   _____

   _____

2. Triggers: What do you think or say to yourself that increases anger?

   _____

   _____

3. Is anger effective in getting others to do what you want them to do? Explain.

   _____

   _____

4. What are more effective techniques you can use to get what you want and need?

   _____

   _____

5. What are resources or sources of support you utilize when you are feeling angry?

   _____

   _____

6. What are you going to do differently to manage anger? How can you decrease or eliminate feelings of anger?

   _____

   _____

7. Are there things that you need to limit or eliminate from your life (obligations, relationships, saying yes to everyone, etc.)?

   _____

   _____

8. How can you get what you want and need through compromise and problem solving?

   _____

   _____

9. What are your goals of anger management and how are you going to go about the changes needed to reach your goals?
   (e.g., Goal: I choose to no longer feel angry all about my husband's behavior. Object: Recognize and accept that he is responsible for his own behavior)

   _____

   _____

10. If you feel that you have tried everything and are unable to resolve issues with a person or situation the only thing left for you to do is to LET GO. How will you be able to make peace with such a situation?

   _____

   _____

How do you feel about having wasted so much of your energy, time, and life on anger?

   _____

   _____

   _____

   _____

HANDLING ANGER

GENERAL PRINCIPLES REGARDING ANGER

1. Anger is a common emotion.
2. Anger needs to be expressed for healthy adjustment.

UNDERSTANDING YOUR EXPERIENCE OF ANGER

1. Socialized to believe that anger is wrong.
2. Anger is associated with anxiety.
3. Anger is used to control and intimidate others.
4. Fear of anger.
   A. Fear of your own anger.
   B. Fear of the anger of others.
5. Anger is a normal reaction to a stimulus.
6. A belief that you are unable to control anger.
7. Physiological response with anger (survival emotion).
8. Pretending that you don't get angry can make you sick.
9. Blocked and unexpressed anger does not go away.
10. When not expressed assertively and appropriately, anger tends to pop up in destructive ways, such as resentment and hostility.

RECOGNIZING THE STAGES OF ANGER

It is not uncommon for people to deny that they have any feelings of anger or to simply be unaware that they are angry until it escalates to a rageful explosion. Once anger begins to intensify, this feeling may be carried over into your communication with others. Unfortunately, when this happens people do not listen to what you are trying to tell them; instead they either discount your message or become defensive to the display of anger. This could simply mean that your anger has built to a level that is overwhelming to you, and when it is expressed to someone else it overwhelms that person as well.

Start paying more attention to what you are thinking, feeling, and the physical changes you experience when you are angry. It would be expected that the more intense the feeling of anger, the more intense the emotion and physical response associated with it. It is important to increase your awareness for anger so that it can be expressed at an earlier stage with less intensity and to decrease the impact on you physically.

The following list identifies feelings that lead to a progressively intense level of anger. Read through the list and identify your feelings. Use this awareness to monitor these feelings and to take responsibility for effectively dealing with them. If you do this, you will find that you are increasingly expressing your feelings appropriately at an earlier stage of anger, which is less distressful to you emotionally and physically.

1. Uneasy
2. Uncomfortable
3. Withdrawn
4. Irritated
5. Agitated
6. Annoyed
7. Upset
8. Mad
9. Angry
10. Furious
11. Rageful

The following is a brief list of physical responses to anger:

1. Headache
2. Muscle tension
3. Clenched fists
4. Changes in breathing
5. Upset stomach
6. Tight stomach
7. Sleep disturbance (ruminating)
8. Yelling/screaming
9. Hitting/breaking things

DECREASE THE INTENSITY OF ANGER:

1. Clarify your needs, thoughts, and feelings
   A. Express them
   B. If other are not supportive or caring, problem-solve appropriate ways to get your needs met

2. Take time out

3. Exercise or do relaxation techniques to decrease body tension

4. Write about your feelings

5. Decide how you are going to take responsibility for you, and take positive action.

BARRIERS TO EXPRESSING ANGER

1. Fear of disapproval.

2. Fear of the power of your anger.

3. Denial of the fact of your anger.
   A. Stressed out
   B. Tired
   C. Sick

4. Allow others to deny your right to be angry.

5. Avoidance of all feelings.
   A. Out of touch with emotional experience. Not aware of when angry, sad, happy.

INAPPROPRIATE EXPRESSION OF ANGER: VIOLENCE AND RAGE

1. Take responsibility for your emotional experience.

2. Acknowledge that inappropriate expression of anger is not acceptable.

3. Learn anger management.

4. Identify how your behavior has affected and harmed others.

PENALTIES FOR NOT EXPRESSING ANGER

1. Depression—experienced as feeling incompetent.

2. Anxiety—often experienced with fear.

3. Guilt—socialized to believe that it is wrong to feel angry.

4. Self-destructive activities.
   A. Drinking/drugs
   B. Eating to mask feelings
   C. Psychosomatic Illnesses
      1. Headache
      2. Gastrointestinal problems
      3. Hypertension

5. Aggression/violence.

6. Disguised anger.
   A. Hostile humor (sarcasm)
   B. Nagging
   C. Silence and withdrawal
   D. Withholding sex
   E. Displacement

WAYS TO DEAL WITH ANGER

1. Recognize anger when you are experiencing it.
2. Express it appropriately when it occurs.
    A. Express how you feel with an "I" statement and in a courteous, respectful, assertive manner.
3. What if you are intensely angry?
    A. Acknowledge and take responsibility for dealing with it in an appropriate and constructive manner.
        A. Activities
        B. Exercise
        C. Talk—express your emotions with someone who can empathize
        D. Journal writing

THE STEPS FOR LETTING GO OF ANGER

1. Awareness of your feelings and behaviors.
2. Taking responsibility for your emotions and responses.
3. Attitude—will greatly influence your success or failure. If you have a negative attitude don't expect good things to happen.
4. Self-talk. What you say to yourself will determine how you think and feel. It is a choice.
5. Don't take responsibility for people and other things that you don't have control over.
6. Develop resources and a support system that encourages the positive changes in you and in your life.
7. Self-care behaviors. People who take care of themselves feel better about who they are, have more energy, and are more likely to be happy.
8. Develop positive self-esteem.
9. Develop positive alternative responses to counter the older anger responses.
10. Practice rehearsing the new responses. Keep a journal to track and reinforce change. A journal will also clarify issues which require further problem solving, or dysfunctional patterns which are keeping you from the progress and change that you desire.

PREVENTING VIOLENCE IN THE WORKPLACE

The Northwest National Insurance Co. (1995) presented the results of a study of 600 workers, which demonstrated that one in four workers was harassed, threatened, or attacked in the period 1992–1993. The results additionally stated that the rate of work-related homicide had tripled in 15 years. Therefore, when a therapist interfaces with workplace issues, it is important to be prepared to discuss the following:

1. The negative work environment
2. The bully in the workplace
3. Workplace violence
4. Prevention

NEGATIVE WORK ENVIRONMENT

A negative work environment contributes to stress and violence. Some specific contributing factors include the following:

1. Feeling disrespected and unappreciated
2. A lack of appropriate/earned advancement
3. Authoritarian and unpredictable management
4. Invasion of privacy
5. A high degree of secrecy
6. A high level of demand with inadequate support
7. The influence of substances (drug and alcohol use is correlated to acts of violence)
8. Media influences, which offer a disgruntled employee the attentive forum he/she is seeking

THE DANGEROUS EMPLOYEE

The following characteristics are not to be used to profile an employee, but instead are to be used to increase awareness for potential factors often seen in dangerous employees. These include the following characteristics:

1. Male
2. 35 years old age or older
3. Has a history of violence toward women, children, or animals
4. Owns a firearm
5. Is invested in the job for self-esteem and identity
6. Has few interests or hobbies
7. Is a loner/socially withdrawn
8. Externalizes
9. Has a history of substance abuse
10. Has a history of emotional/mental illness
11. Is extreme in opinions/attitudes
12. Has a history of making unwelcome sexual comments
13. Has difficulty with authority
14. Frequently engages in conflicts
15. Makes threatening statements

BULLY IN THE WORKPLACE

A bully in any environment creates difficulties. A bully can be a coworker or a manager. Bullying can be described as follows:

1. An intense method of threat used to exert pressure on others.
2. Harassment with a purpose.

WORKPLACE VIOLENCE

Causes of Workplace Violence

There is no way to determine a specific cause. There are different categories of violence and a number of contributory factors. The general categories are the following:

1. Work-related causes
   A. Robbery is the number one cause of violence in the workplace, and the offenders come from outside the workplace
   B. Terrorism or hate crimes

2. Personal Causes
   A. Fear of losing a job
   B. Loss of a job
   C. Warning/reprimand from a supervisor
   D. Not receiving an expected promotion or raise
   E. Acts or words viewed as unfair, threatening, or hostile
   F. Unresolved hostility or conflicts with coworkers
   G. Personal problems
      1. An abusive partner may follow an employee to work where a physical attack is triggered by rage, fear, or jealousy
      2. A romantic fantasy or grudge becomes an obsession leading to stalking, threats, harassment, or attack
      3. An individual is unable to cope with stressors and lashes out at others
      4. The use of substances contributes to decreased inhibition for normative expected social behavior or influences violent acting out (use of crack, PCP)

3. Behavioral patterns indicative of potential violent acts
   1. Evidence of substance abuse
   2. Emotional outbursts or threatening statements/belligerent
   3. Attendance problems
   4. Decreased productivity/evidenced deterioration in performance
   5. Inconsistent work patterns (extremes)
   6. Poor workplace relationships
   7. Difficulty with concentration and attention
   8. Safety issues/accident prone
   9. Fascination with weapons (guns/knives)
   10. Evidence of unmanageable stress (death of loved one, bill collectors, emotionality)
   11. Poor hygiene and grooming
   12. Continual excuses, blaming others for problems
   13. Chronic depression, suicidality
   14. Destruction of property/theft
   15. Abusive language and general uncooperativity
   16. Disregard for policies and procedures

17. Acts of violence
18. Sees self as victimized by coworkers or management

4. Early warning signs of potential workplace violence
   A. Direct or veiled threats of harm
   B. Intimidation of others. This can be physical or verbal intimidation. Harassing phone calls and stalking are examples
   C. Carrying a concealed weapon or flashing a weapon to test reactions
   D. Paranoid behavior. Perceiving that the whole world is against one.
   E. Moral righteousness and believing the organization is not following its rules and procedures
   F. Inability to take criticism of job performance. Holding a grudge, especially against a supervisor. Oftentimes verbalizing hope for something to happen to the person against whom the employee has the grudge
   G. Expression of extreme desperation over recent family, financial, or personal problems
   H. History of violent behavior
   I. Extreme interest in semiautomatic or automatic weapons and their destructive power to people
   J. Fascination with incidents of workplace violence and approval of the use of violence under similar circumstances
   K. Disregard for the safety of co-employees
   L. Obsessive involvement with the job, often with uneven job performance and no apparent outside interests
   M. Being a loner and having a romantic obsession with a coworker who does not share this interest

5. Level of violence
   A. Level 1
      1. Refuses to cooperate with immediate supervisor
      2. Spreads rumors and gossip to harm others
      3. Consistently argues with coworkers
      4. Is belligerent toward customers/clients
      5. Constantly swears at others
      6. Makes unwanted sexual comments
   B. Level 2
      1. Argues increasingly with customers, vendors, coworkers, and management
      2. Refuses to obey company policies and procedures
      3. Sabotages equipment and steals property for revenge
      4. Verbalizes wishes to hurt coworkers or management
      5. Sends sexual or violent notes to coworkers or management
      6. Sees self as victimized by management (me against them)
   C. Level 3—Frequent displays of anger resulting in the following:
      1. Recurrent suicidal threats
      2. Recurrent physical fights
      3. Destruction of property
      4. Utilization of weapons to harm others
      5. Commission of murder, rape, or arson

Prevention
Not all angry people become violent. However, most violent people are angry. The moment in which a situation is unfolding and what takes place are the most important factors in

determining if acts of violence will occur. Therefore, the most basic information may be how to be in control of one's own anger: don't take anger personally, do not counterattack, do not respond with verbal abuse (escalate), and do not invalidate the other person's experience of anger.

1. Dealing with the bully
   A. Train employees to avoid being the victims of bullies
      1. Report to a supervisor, union representative, or human relations personnel immediately
      2. Educate employees regarding the harassment policy and procedure in the workplace

2. Employee safety
   A. Increase security
   B. Restrict entry to the workplace via specialized identification, sign-in sheets, and so on
   C. Improve lighting where needed in workplace interiors like stairwells and parking areas
   D. Screen potential employees for a history of violent or threatening behavior
   E. Instill a no-tolerance policy for threats
   F. Instill a no-tolerance policy for weapons in the workplace
   G. Do not allow former employees on the premises without management permission
   H. Establish an employee hot line to report harassment, threats, bullying, or bizarre behavior
   I. Promote rapid firm responses to workplace threats, harassment, aggressive behavior
   J. Educate and train employees on conflict resolution
   K. Offer counseling to employees in distress

3. Learning to reduce tension
   A. Remain calm and courteous
   B. Be respectful to others, even when you do not agree
   C. Focus on the problem/behavior, not the person
   D. If a situation feels like it is possibly escalating, talk with appropriate management immediately
   E. Do not argue, raise one's voice, or respond to threats

4. Appropriate responses to criminals who enter the workplace
   A. Do not try to be a hero, give robbers what they demand
   B. Report all suspicious or criminal behavior to the authorities
   C. If an assault takes place (especially sexual assault), do not change clothing or bath before a physical examination can take place
   D. Acknowledge emotional responses
      1. Pain, fear, stress
      2. Do not blame yourself; the offender is responsible for acts of violence
      3. Counseling should be offered for validation, improved coping, and resolution

5. Investigation of threats

It is important to consider the various roles available for dealing with threats of violence in the workplace. The investigation is often best handled by a professional, independent third party trained to deal with such situations. The common investigative and intervention roles and where their alliance exists include the following:

    A. Management consultant-allied with management exclusively

    B. Mediator-neutral party to problem-solve and resolve conflicts

    C. Counselor-allied with suspected perpetrator

    D. Counselor-allied with alleged victim

    E. Professional evaluator of suspected perpetrator, though neutral investigator, they are referred to by management and will likely be viewed as biased by suspected perpetrator

    F. Risk assessment evaluator—allied with management

    G. Risk prediction specialist—allied with management

6. Guidelines for reporting threats
    A. Obtain identifying information
    B. Collect information from direct sources
    C. Separate fact from embellishment
    D. Remain neutral

7. Assessing level of risk
    A. Has anyone been physically/emotionally harmed?
    B. Is anyone in imminent danger (as evidenced by what?)?
    C. Have there been threats (details)?
    D. Are weapons involved? Are there any weapons on workplace premises (or part of the threat)?
    E. Do involved parties appear out of control (as evidenced by what?)?
    F. Where are the involved parties at this time?
    G. Have authorities been notified (management, human resources, security, police)?
    H. Who has been interviewed about the situation and given details (indirect sources)?

8. Professional crisis response
    A. Identify and proceed with crisis response options
    B. Develop an threat management team (TMT) whose purpose is to provide ongoing monitoring and assessment
    C. Notify identified management of the incident
    D. If warranted, notify security, law enforcement, and emergency response services
    E. Be prepared with the development of a central processing center for dealing with such issues (know how to process intake information and disseminate information, what actions are to be taken and under what circumstances)

*If someone is dealing with an angry person, the following recommendations may be helpful in preventing an escalation of aggression:

1. Stay calm, composed, and confident that you can manage the situation. This is easier to say than do, but portraying a lack of confidence and fear may be an unexpected escalator in a difficult situation.

2. If possible, arrange for the two of you to sit down

3. Use the person's name. Being personally addressed can get someone's attention and have a calming effect.

4. Lowering one's tone of voice or toning down speech and body movements may have a calming effect
5. Be careful to not hurry the person off. If an angry person feels that he/she being invalidated and brushed off, it may escalate anger.
6. Be receptive to what is being said
7. Adopt open posture
8. Maintain positive eye contact (pay attention)
9. Demonstrate good listening skills
    A. Listen attentively
    B. Be open minded
    C. Reflect on what has been heard
    D. Reman focuses
    E. Show care for the problem being presented
    F. Answer questions
    G. Talk; don't argue as arguing escalates anger
    H. Avoid attempts at humor, which demonstrates discounting and invalidation
    I. Facilitate resolution by clarifying questions
    J. Demonstrate a sharing of mutual interests/goals
    K. When appropriate offer, "I don't know" or " I apologize"
    L. Explore potential solutions
    M. Remain respectful

HOW TO HANDLE ANGRY PEOPLE

Backlund and Scott (*Assertiveness: Get What You Want Without Being Pushy*) offer the acronym "BULLETS" to consider when dealing with people who are angry:

<u>Be seated</u>. Place yourself in a relaxed position sitting down and ask the other person to also sit down. This could slow behavioral reactiveness as well as maintain a measure of distance for personal space.

<u>Use the person's name</u>. Speak directly to someone who is angry in a calm and low tone of voice addressing them by name.

<u>Lower your voice</u>. With awareness for the tension that is present, systematically lower your voice and do not verbally react.

<u>Listen</u>. Listen and be validating about what the person has to say. Remember, validation does not mean agreement; it is only acknowledgment for the other person's thoughts or feelings. Listen thoroughly to what the person has to say and do not try to rush him/her out the door and minimize the anger that the person is experiencing.

<u>Eliminate humor</u>. Do not try to make light of the situation when someone is upset. Such a response feels disrespectful and minimizing. It immediately conveys that the person is not being taken seriously, which would escalate anger.

<u>Talk, don't argue</u>. Arguing increases tension and escalates feels of anger. When things have calmed down, then share your ideas if you have points to share that you feel are important. Discussing things rationally requires people to be relatively calm and prepared to validate and problem-solve.

<u>Slow down</u>. Slowing the rate of speech is a way to initiate calm and role-model to the other person the manner in which to speak without addressing it directly.

For problem solving and negotiation to take place, both parties must remain calm, rational, and mutually respectful.

WHAT MANAGEMENT CAN DO TO MINIMIZE EMPLOYEE STRESS

1. Be familiar with community resources and company resources available to employees
2. Be sensitive to work demand and adequate support to get tasks done
3. Make sure that employees are given advance notice of upcoming deadlines
4. Keep employees informed of changes taking place in the organization or changes in philosophy so that they feel included in change
5. Be respectful of general ongoing work demand when considering adding demands unless it is absolutely necessary, and be realistic, validating, and supportive
   A. Acknowledge the extra stress and inconvenience
   B. Demonstrate appreciation
   C. When possible, reward for extra efforts
6. Make sure that adequate training is offered
7. Whenever possible, offer continuing education
8. Maintain regular evluations so that people are aware of how they are doing the job
9. When employees request support or are in obvious need of support, offer it
10. Reinforce positive efforts, contributions, and accomplishments
11. Whenever possible, challenge employees with interesting work
12. Promote employees who have earned advancement
13. Clearly define employee roles, expectations, areas of responsibility, and limits of authority
14. Encourage employees to take breaks and mealtime breaks
15. Encourage good health behaviors in employees. Offer smoking cessation information, nutrition and exercise education, stress management, and so forth whenever possible. If your company is not large enough, then have available a list of community resources

16. Recognize that work stress and personal stress mutually affect all areas of a person's life

17. Educate management about the signs and symptoms of stress in employees

18. Consult with a professional who specializes in workplace environments and employee issues to maintain an optimally positive work environment

19. As management, be aware of your own level of stress, and be a role model in practicing stress management techniques yourself

20. Recognize your own limits of responsibility and power in the workplace

ADJUSTING/ADAPTING

A. LIFE CHANGES

Factors involved in personality and social development include heredity, family factors, peer factors, and age. It can be helpful to understand what experiences have contributed to how you respond to your environment because if there are difficulties such information offer indications of necessary change and growth. Looking at your past for information and understanding can be emotionally painful, but it can also help you take responsibility for making the change that will help you reach your goals.

Because a significant review of your life experience will be related to parental interaction it is important to maintain awareness for what you are trying to accomplish. Don't get stuck blaming your parents or other people for what is wrong. As an adult, only you can take responsibility for your choices and behavior.

There are common stages of development that everyone experiences. There are also experiences that individuals have that for various reasons have a significant impact on their life, how they define themselves, and how they deal with things.

Some Common Life Changes Which Require Adjusting and Adapting

1. Selecting a mate.
2. Learning to live with a partner.
3. Starting a family.
4. Rearing children.
5. Getting started in an occupation, and then changing and growing professionally.
6. Developing a support system/peer group affiliation.
7. Developing adult leisure time activities.
8. Relating oneself to one's partner as a person.
9. Accepting and adjusting to physiological changes.
10. Altering one's role in family as appropriate and necessary.

What are all the life changes that you have experienced?

Understanding Your Skill of Adjusting and Adapting

1. Write about a difficult or challenging experience you had in which you were able to adjust.
2. What did you do, and how were you able to accomplish it?

_____

_____

_____

_____

3. What is something that you have experienced that you have had difficulty adjusting to or have not been able to adjust to?

4. What has prevented the necessary adjustment?

_____

_____

_____

B. DEVELOPMENTAL PERSPECTIVE

The basic view of development begins with a look at your family experience. There are five specific aspects of family functioning to consider.

1. Leadership. The parents serve as models. The parental modeling is determined by each parent's personality, the relationship between the parents, the presence or absence of mutual support and esteem, the effectiveness of their communication, absence of mutual support and esteem, the effectiveness of their communication, their way of relating to relatives and others in the community, power, and discipline.

2. Boundaries. Family boundaries include the individual's self boundaries, the boundaries between generations, and the boundaries between the family and the community. Boundaries need to be semipermeable. Boundaries serve as a guideline to appropriate interaction between individuals and between generations. The family–community boundary needs to become increasingly permeable. As children grow they need to cross it more freely to participate in community. Boundaries that are inadequate, overly rigid, or overly loose present a risk because they interfere with optimal family functioning as an open system (versus closed system).

3. Emotional climate. Emotional forces are the glue that holds the family together. No family can function well unless its family members care for and support each other. The family needs to be a place where intimacy and anger can be tolerated (to a greater extent than in the community and where people can relax more freely than they can outside the home). Discipline and how parents exercise their power are related to and often determine the emotional climate of the family. *There are also wide cultural variations in emotionality and its expression.

4. Communication. Language, the basis for social interaction, is learned in the family. Language develops best when children are talked to, read to, sung to, and encouraged to respond to others and to express feelings and experiences verbally. Communication consonant with the thinking and values of the community and culture underlies an important aspect of sociocultural development. Any communication handicap is a potential risk factor, and communication difficulties and deviance are significant risk indicators in children's development.

5. Family goals and tasks. The understanding of family goals and tasks throughout the life cycle is the most important component of family functioning to decrease risk. Society expects families to nurture and socialize the young to become productive members of society with appropriate value systems. The family life cycle begins with marriage and family formation and passes through many stages.

LEARNING HISTORY

1. What did you learn from your family that you have carried on in how you interact with other people, the community (POSITIVE AND NEGATIVE)?

   _____

   _____

2. How do you deal with your emotions?

   _____

   _____

3. How do you deal with anger?

   _____

   _____

4. How would you rate your self-esteem?

   _____

   _____

5. How do you take care of yourself?

   _____

   _____

6. What are the consequences of your behaviors?

   _____

   _____

7. What are your choices?

   _____

   _____

8. What changes do you need to continue working on in order to reach your goals?

   _____

   _____

LOSSES/OPPORTUNITIES

Sometimes changes in life, even positive changes, result in losses. When you experience a loss it is important to work through the associated thought and feelings. This working through is called grieving. Grief is a normal and natural response to loss. People grieve over the death of someone they love and sometimes over life changes including changes in family patterns or behavior. Grieving is related to adjusting and adapting.

Examples of situations which may facilitate grieving include:

1. Children starting school
2. Children going away to school
3. Marriage
4. Divorce
5. Addictions
6. Retirement

The negatives or losses in each of these situations seems pretty easy to pick out. Can you pick out the potential positive. Quite often with losses also comes opportunity, and you need to be prepared to look for it. There are stages to the grieving process:

1. Denial
2. Anger
3. Bargaining
4. Despair
5. Acceptance

These stages do not occur in the same order for everyone.

WHAT IS MEANT BY RESOLVING GRIEF/LOSS?

1. Claiming your circumstances instead of them claiming you (discuss what this means).
2. Being able to enjoy fond memories without having the precipitation of painful feelings of loss, guilt, regret or remorse.
3. Finding new meaning in living, and living without the fear of future abandonment.
4. Acknowledging that it is okay to feel bad from time to time, and to talk about those feelings.
5. Being able to forgive others when they say or do things that you know are based on a lack of knowledge and understanding.

WHY ARE PEOPLE NOT PREPARED TO DEAL WITH LOSS?

1. They have been taught to acquire things not to lose them.
2. They have been taught that acquiring things will help them feel complete or whole.

3. They have been taught that if they lose something replacing the loss will make it easier (i.e., bury their feelings).

WHAT ARE THE MYTHS OF DEALING WITH LOSS?

1. Put off until later to do things that are frightening or painful.
2. Regret the past (get stuck wanting it different, better, or more).
3. Just give it time.
4. Grieve alone (don't need to talk about thoughts or feelings).

Two major issues bury your feelings and forget the loss.

HOW DO YOU KNOW YOU ARE READY?

1. You have acknowledged that a problem exists.
2. You have acknowledged that the problem is associated with the loss.
3. You acknowledge that you are now willing to deal with your loss.

FINDING THE SOLUTION: THE FIVE STAGES OF RECOVERING FROM LOSS

1. Growing Awareness—that issues are unresolved
2. Accepting Responsibility—for resolving the loss
3. Identifying—what you need to do to resolve the loss
4. Taking Action—to resolve the loss
5. Moving Beyond Loss—through sharing with others and taking action which facilitates resolution and growth

HOW DO YOU DEAL WITH LOSS

People deal with loss in various ways. Do you identify with any of the following examples?

1. Intellectualize—don't deal with feelings, don't talk or write about how they feel
2. Be fine and put on a happy face for those around you "Academy Award Winning Recovery."
3. Want the approval of others; want others to be accepting of your feelings.
4. Acting out ("don't expect anything of me because I hurt so bad").

OTHER WAYS?

Write about how you have dealt with the loss(es) you have experienced, and be prepared to discuss it.

GRIEF CYCLE (WHERE ARE YOU STUCK?)

DEFINITION: THE NATURAL EMOTIONAL RESPONSE TO THE LOSS OF A CHERISHED IDEA, PERSON, OR THING

1. DENIAL (Isolation)
   A. Powerlessness
   B. Psychological Buffer (defense)—protects knowledge or awareness of thoughts or feelings that you are not ready to deal with mentally, emotionally, or spirituality
   C. Denial of Reality
      1. The more you have depended on the last object, the stronger your denial

2. ANGER (Self-Disappointment, Self-Hatred)
   A. Anger over loss and not being able to find it
      1. Regrets
   B. Can become destructive if not expressed in healthy ways
      1. Out of control anger = rage, violence
      2. Held in, stuffed anger = out of control physical illness
         a. anger turned inward toward self = Depression
         b. Despair, suicide

3. BARGAINING (Postponing the inevitable. Attempt to control the uncontrollable)
   A. "What If's" and "If Only"
   B. Desperate attempt to regain control
   C. Keeps you from facing reality
   D. Destructive if one gets stuck here

4. DEPRESSION (Sorrow, Despair)
   A. Anger channeled back into self, turned inward against self
   B. Response typically associated with grief but actually only one part of the whole process
      1. Tears, funerals, wakes allow you to be sad
      2. Trapped (stuck) sorrow = self-pity leads to destructive behavior
      3. Can be immobilizing = total helplessness
      4. Crying is a good way to express sorrow. It washes away sadness. Heals. Is a sign of strength when used as part of the grieving process, but if stuck crying can become a chronic behavior which does not effectively promote grieving

5. ACCEPTANCE
   A. Final goal with achieving resolution of grief
   B. Belief that it is possible to heal and recover
   C. Surrender to reality
   D. Recognition of responsibility = ACTION

GRIEF

Grief is intense emotional suffering caused by a loss. When unresolved, it can lead to acute anxiety and depression. Usually when we think of loss and the grief process, we think of someone very close to us dying or leaving. When this happens, we experience intense emotional pain (hurt, sadness). So we can say that grief is the natural, normal, inevitable process that all human beings experience when they lose something that is important to them. The stages of grief are denial, anger, bargaining, depression, and acceptance.

The varying things that a person can experience during the course of their life that can result in feelings grief and loss include:

1. Death of a loved one.
2. The ending of an important relationship (boyfriend-girlfriend).
3. Loss of relationship with a parent through divorce.
4. Feelings of loss for a friend that moved away (or you moved away).
5. Feelings of loss associated with school, neighbors, house, etc. because you moved away.
6. Loss of job due to restructuring, lack of transportation, drinking, etc.
7. Loss of your special place in the family because another child was born.
8. Damaged reputation due to someone who doesn't like you, your own poor judgment, mistakes, etc.
9. Physical impairment—accident illness.
10. Loss of a pet.
11. Not being able to return to school, friends, family, or spouse for some reason.
12. Recognizing that life dreams will not be realized.
13. Others _____

What are the things that you may have wanted to happen that never occurred and you feel hopeless about.

NEVER HAPPENED

1. Happy childhood.
2. Normal or happy home perhaps like a friend has or you saw on TV or a movie.
3. To belong to a certain group.
4. Get a particular person to care about you.
5. Parents you didn't have.
6. A beautiful or great body (according to the narrow and damaging social perspective that slim is okay and any variation from that is not as good as....).
7. A smooth and clear complexion (this can be a painful experience).
8. Color of hair or eyes (not accepting of self).
9. Parents that were home or spent time with you or didn't get drunk and abusive.
10. Grandparents.

From this place of pain, hurt, and disappointment comes a wall of protection called *denial*:

1. I don't care.
2. It's not really that.
3. Who wants it anyway.
4. Everyone does it.
5. There's no problem.
6. Drugs aren't my problem.

When we quit denying our loss, we move into the next stage: *ANGER*. Your anger may be reasonable or unreasonable and it may be felt in varying degrees.

Hate	Rage	Anger	Frustrated
Hurt	Upset	Irritated	

This is a stage where blaming occurs. Perhaps distrust, revenge, or get even. Externalization takes place—"It's all his fault."

Make a list of all the people, places, and things that you are angry about to some degree.

BARGAINING

When anger begins to calm down there is an attempt to bargain with:

1. Life
2. Ourselves
3. Another person
4. God
   A. I'll try harder to please...
   B. Maybe if I had...
   C. Bargaining in an attempt to postpone the inevitable; in an attempt to prevent it.

DEPRESSION

It begins when there is realization that bargaining has not worked, the struggle to ward off reality, and the belief that the experience has been unfair an overwhelming depression can take over. This is when the full force of the loss is experienced and is accompanied by crying, and intense emotional pain. Feelings associated with this stage include:

1. Helpless
2. Powerless
3. Self-pity—Why me?
4. Sadness
5. Guilt
6. Suicidal thoughts
7. Self-destructive or self-defeating behaviors

ACCEPTANCE

This is the last stage of the grieving process. Acceptance is not necessarily a happy stage. It is almost void of feeling. It is as if the pain is gone and the struggle is over. There is peace, but it does not mean that healing is complete or the feelings of emptiness are gone.

1. At peace
2. Learn coping skills
3. Accept our past
4. Accept life as it is
5. Accept our present circumstances
6. Accept our loss
7. Free to go on with your life
8. Begin to feel comfortable with your life again
9. Adjusting
10. Set new goals
11. May strive for some understanding of the loss
12. Stop avoiding issues associated with the loss or rumination about the loss

Are you or someone in your life going through this grief process for a major loss? What stage do you think you are in?

Review your life and consider the major losses and changes you have gone through. Recall your experiences with the grief process. Write about your feelings as you remember them.

HISTORY OF LOSS GRAPH

On your graph write:

1. What happened
2. When did it happen

Below your graph write about:

1. How did it affect your life
2. What issues do you now have to resolve

EXAMPLE:

year	1977	1980	1981	1987
loss	lost job	Father died	son went off to college	spouse had an affair
year				
loss				

RELATIONSHIP GRAPH

Above the time line write down the happy experiences, and below the line write the unhappy experiences. Start with your first conscious memory or recollection of a loved one. Include on your graph relationships with people, things, or changes.

1. How many positive experiences were never acknowledged or talked about?
2. How many negative events were never acknowledged or talked about?
3. Did you become aware of other unspoken communications, either things you wish you had heard or things you wish you had said?

EXAMPLE:

Happy	1st memory	family vacation		time
Unhappy	1969 bad argument w/dad	1972 separation from spouse	1975 death of mother	
Happy				time
Unhappy				

IS LIFE WHAT YOU MAKE IT?

1. Write about what the following statements mean.
2. Do you apply this type of attitude/perspective to your life?
   If yes—how do you apply it to your life.
   If no—how do you go about changing it.

SOMETHING LOST—SOMETHING GAINED

IS YOUR CUP HALF EMPTY OR HALF FULL

JOURNAL WRITING

Sometime changes can occur just by recognizing the source of the problem. However, most changes come from an accumulation of changes in beliefs, priorities, and behaviors over a period of time. Consistency and an investment in yourself is necessary. Journal writing can be useful for keeping track of a wide variety of things that can help you achieve your goals. Use your journal to record your thoughts and feelings. "Just doing it" can make a difference. Acknowledging underlying thoughts and feelings and writing about them can help increase self understanding, and self-awareness which can make it easier to change old patterns of behavior and to start new ones. Consistently keeping a journal is a strong message to yourself that you want to change and that you are committed to make it happen.

People often experience greater successes when they have established goals. Unpredictable situations do occur which can cause setbacks, but they can also allow for a reevaluation of your problems and can offer an opportunity. However, when goals are defined and the unexpected happens, you are more likely to reach them even if you are initially thrown off course. Most people don't clearly establish their goals, let alone write them down and think about what it will take to accomplish them.

STEP 1

Write down the goals you want to accomplish in the next 12 months. Make them as specific as possible. They should be realistic, but also challenging.

STEP 2

Write down ten goals you want to accomplish this month. These should help you move toward some of your goals for the year. The monthly goals should be smaller and more detailed then the yearly goals.

STEP 3

Write down three goals you want to accomplish today. Goals need to be accompanied by plans to make them happen. If your goals are too large, you are likely to stop before you start. Better to start small and build upward. Small successes build big successes.

STEP 4

Self-monitoring: Keep track of where you are now. Create realistic plans that can get you to your goals.

STEP 5

Begin observing which self-talk has been maintaining the old patterns you want to change. List at least five to ten negative self-statements that feed into your old patterns.

STEP 6

List five to ten positive statements that are likely to help create the new patterns you want to create.

STEP 7

Create challenges that will replace the negative self-talk you listed in Step 5.

STEP 8

Programming new healthy self-talk. Each day, say at least ten positive self-statements to your-self.

STEP 9

Imagination and visualization: Five times each day, take one minute to visualize a positive image.

STEP 10

Building self-esteem: Use your journal to list good things about yourself. Be supportive to yourself.

STEP 11

Each day record three of the days successes—big or small. Praise yourself. Plan small rewards for some accomplishment each week.

STEP 12

In your journal, frequently ask what parts of yourself you are involved with. The various issues you face (e.g., the needy child, the rebellious adolescent, etc.).

STEP 13

Each day, forgive yourself for something you have done. Like self-esteem, forgiveness is one of the keys to successful change. Forgiving yourself for past actions allows you to take responsibility for what happens in the future.

STEP 14

List the fears of success that the different parts of you may have. Work on making success safe.

STEP 15

Be willing to do things differently. If you don't, nothing is going to change.

DEVELOPING AND UTILIZING SOCIAL SUPPORTS

When someone lacks emotional health they tend to withdraw from pleasurable activities and socially isolate. One important way to regain emotional health is to develop and utilize social supports.

We all need several good friends to talk to, spend time with, and to be supported by with their care and understanding. For someone to be a part of your support system requires that you care for them and trust them. A partner or family member is a likely candidate for your support system. You may develop relationships with people through activities or interests that you share. These relationships could become strong enough to become part of your support system. Other resources could be clubs or other social group affiliations that you feel a part of and feel important to. Whoever the person or group is, it is necessary that there be mutual care, positive regard, and trust.

CHARACTERISTICS OF A SUPPORTIVE RELATIONSHIP

1. Objectivity and open-mindedness. They let you describe who you are and how you feel. They validate you.
2. They support and affirm your individuality and recognize your strengths. They validate and encourage your goals.
3. They empathize with you. They understand your life circumstances and how you are affected by your life experiences.
4. They accept you as you are without being judgmental. You can ask one another for help and support.
5. You can laugh with them and be playful. You will both enjoy it.
6. They are at your side, supporting you to do whatever is important to you.

List the People that Make Up Your Support System:

1. _____

2. _____

3. _____

4. _____

5. _____

If you didn't have anyone to list as your support system or only one to two people don't feel bad about yourself and give up. What you have done is to accomplish the first step in understanding what you need to do: change your situation. The good news is that there is a lot you can do to change your situation.

What Stands in Your Way of Developing Your Support System (check the items that apply to you):

__you have a hard time reaching out
__you have a hard time making and keeping friends

__low self-esteem
__you tend to very needy and draining to others
__you become overly dependent and wear people out
__you lack the social skills necessary to develop relationships
__you have inappropriate behaviors which embarrass others
__you are unreliable

What Is It That You Need and Want From Your Support System (check the items that apply to you):

__someone to talk to
__understanding
__someone to stand up for you
__companionship
__caring
__sharing
__someone to watch or monitor you
__someone who will listen to you
__someone to do things with
__someone who writes to you or phones you
__mutual support and positive regard

Are there other things that you would want or expect from a friend?

_____

_____

_____

People that help you get started in making the changes necessary to develop a strong support system include your therapist, minister, and various support groups. There are also many helpful books that have been written that you can find in the psychology or self-help sections of a bookstore. The main thing to is make a commitment to yourself to develop a support system and to not give up.

HOW TO BUILD AND KEEP A SUPPORT SYSTEM

1. To be emotionally well and keep my moods stable.
   What do you do to maintain stable moods? _____
   _____

2. To take care of myself.
   List your self-care behaviors: _____
   _____

3. To recognize and accept that others can help, but that I am responsible for making myself okay.
   Define what you must do for yourself versus what is reasonable for others to do for you: _____
   _____

4. Develop appropriate social skills.
   This can be done by working with your therapist, reading and practicing the techniques you read about, participating in activities in the community or special groups, taking a class at adult education programs if available, watching what other people do and what responses they get. Be involved.
   What resources are available to you? _____
   _____

5. Do volunteer work and be supportive of others.
   Whether it is doing volunteer work or being supportive to people you know, it is good practice.
   Where could you volunteer? _____
   Who supports you and how can you be supportive back to them? _____
   _____

6. Make it a point to keep in touch with friends and acquaintances.
   When was the last time you invited someone to do something or made an effort to get together? If it didn't work out was it the timing, the activity, or someone who really isn't capable of being a social support for you? What are you going to do to become more successful with this point? _____
   _____

7. How will you know if you are making progress in developing a support system?
   _____

RECOGNIZING THE STAGES OF DEPRESSION

There is a wide range in the experience of depression. Sometimes we feel sad about something happening, we experience depression with grief when we have experienced a serious loss, or we have a building depression, which does not go away when something serious has happened and it is not resolved or lots of difficult things happen over time without our having the opportunity to resolve them. Also consider the following issues as related to the experience of depression:

1. You do not express your needs, thoughts, or feelings in order to keep the peace
2. You have lost your sense of identity
3. Have you lost hope with what you need and feel
4. Do you feel empty and confused
5. Have you stopped expressing your hopes and goals
6. Have you given up on your hopes and goals

Is it possible that your experience of depression is the result of you not being true to yourself? If so, think about the following statement: If you are not true to yourself and are denying yourself, you lose yourself, and when you lose yourself you become depressed.

The following is a list of feelings that progressively lead to depression. Read through the list and identify your feelings. With this awareness you will then begin to monitor these feelings and take responsibility for the appropriate self-care to decrease or eliminate these feelings and therefore decrease or eliminate your experience of depression.

1. Withdrawn and quiet
2. Sad
3. Decreased enthusiasm
4. Lonely
4. Melancholy
5. Sense of helplessness and hopelessness
6. Feeling overwhelmed
7. Despair

DECREASING THE INTENSITY OF DEPRESSION

1. Clarify your needs, thoughts, and feelings
   A. Express them
   B. If others are not supportive or caring, problem-solve appropriate ways to get your needs met
2. Be assertive; say "no" to certain activities and people
3. Identify and change negative self talk. It takes you down and keeps you there.
4. Get regular exercise; walk, it relieves stress, increases energy, and changes brain chemistry to decrease depression
5. Prioritize tasks and do not overload yourself
6. Engage in creative projects that are fun and distracting from other stressors
7. Practice good nutrition
8. Get adequate rest (not too much or too little)

9. Ask for help and delegate when possible

10. Develop a supportive social network

11. Develop goals and get focused

12. Pamper yourself with a pedicure or manicure, get a massage, buy yourself a small gift, and so on.

MANAGING DEPRESSION

Depression is a common human experience. Most people will at some time in their life experience depression. The most dramatic sign is a lack of pleasure in normally pleasing life activities and feeling fatigued. Most experiences of depression do not interfere in daily activity. People go on doing the things they have to do, but they must push themselves.

When the level of depression becomes severe and does interfere in a person's ability to follow through on their daily activities it is called major depression. The difference between normal depression and major depression is that symptoms are more severe, last longer, and impair a person's ability to function. What used to be satisfying is frustrating or tedious. You may withdraw from people and isolate, you may avoid people and situations, experience negative thinking, experience hopelessness, feel overwhelmed, experience disturbance of appetite and sleep. You may feel that you are a prisoner of this state of emotion and fear/believe that it will never end. Some people with major depression experience suicidal ideation or death wish (where they wish something would happen to them so they didn't have to live with the struggle any longer, but do not actively think about taking their own life).

THE CAUSES OF DEPRESSION

1. Environmental or Situational Factors. This depression is triggered by the stress of changes or losses such as losing a job, divorce, or death of a family member or friend.

2. Biological Factors. There are chemicals in the brain called neurotransmitters which communicate messages between the nerve cells of the brain. If there is an imbalance in these brain chemicals the result can be changes in thought, behavior, and emotion.

   Other biological relationships to depression could be hypothyroidism, medications, chronic pain or other medical illness, and the long-term experience of stress with a component of hopelessness.

3. Genetic Factors. There appears to be a relationship between family history of mood disturbances. This suggests that if there are family members who have chronic depression there may be a predisposition to having depression. Approximately 25% of people who experience depression have a relative with some form of depressive illness.

If you experience depression there a number of interventions that you can use which can improve the quality of your life experience.

Therapy is a key factor in understanding the source of your depression and making the appropriate interventions. Also, discuss the possibility of antidepressant medications with your physician.

DEPRESSION SYMPTOM CHECKLIST

The symptoms of depression vary widely from person to person. Which of the following feelings and symptoms do you experience?

__ feeling low	__ tense	__ fatigue
__ feeling sad	__ agitated	__ heaviness
__ difficulty with sleep	__ quiet	__ fear
__ compulsive eating	__ withdrawn	__ disorganized
__ no appetite	__ guilty	__ cries easily
__ low self-esteem	__ hateful	__ empty, void
__ hopelessness	__ angry	__ like a failure
__ obsessed with the past	__ hoping to die	__ unbearable
__ hating my life	__ plan to kill self	__ dead inside
__ helplessness	__ self-critical	__ body aches
__ anxious	__ no motivation	__ miserable
__ apathetic	__ worthless	__ alone
__ difficulty concentrating	__ excessive worrying	__ feelings of loss

If there are other symptoms that you experience please list them.

_____

_____

It is important to identify the symptoms that you are experiencing so that a course of intervention can be determined. Often, when someone is depressed they have numerous physical symptoms. These symptoms or sensations can be purely related to stress and depression or may have a physical basis. Therefore, if you have not been recently examined by your physician it is a good idea to make an appointment to rule out any physical complications that are contributing to your experience of depression.

Possible medical causes could be:

__ endocrine system problems (such as a malfunctioning thyroid)
__ medication interactions
__ acute or chronic stress reactions
__ allergies
__ PMS
__ chronic health problems
__ drug/alcohol abuse or dependence
__ recently stopped smoking
__ recent surgery
__ seasonal affective disorder

Managing depression requires that you gain some sense of control over the depression. Because everyone's experience is unique to them it is necessary that you take the time to increase your awareness, take the risk of trying some interventions, and make the commitment to follow through. Managing depression requires that you take responsibility for improving the quality of your life. If your depression has been chronic and severe discuss antidepressant medication with your physician. There may be a biological or genetic factor influencing your mood which requires a medical intervention. Once this is determined then you must decide what you are going to do. This is accomplished by developing a Self-Care Plan. The significant components of a Self-Care Plan include:

1. *Structure.* How you will structure your day to include the factors or interventions of taking care of yourself. This can be easily established by using a daily activity chart until you are able to consistently engage in self-care without constant reminders.
2. *Support.* Developing and utilizing resources to eliminate social isolation and withdrawal.
3. *Positive Attitude.* Choosing positive thoughts instead of negative ones, reminding yourself that depression is a temporary emotional state, and focusing on taking one day at a time.
4. *Awareness.* To maintain and continue the progress that you make in managing your depression requires that there be an increased awareness for what works and is beneficial and what does not help you. Keeping a journal can be useful for self-monitoring. You will want to identify the "red flags" of potential regression and any patterns of behavior which affect you negatively.
5. *Exercise.* Before you initiate any exercise program check with your physician. Walking aerobically (quick paced 35–40 min.) at least every other day is helpful in reducing body tension, improving sleep, creating a sense of well-being, increasing energy, and decreasing stress.
6. *Nutrition.* Eating daily well-balanced meals. If you are unsure of what it means to eat healthy consult your physician, dietitian, or go to a bookstore where you will find many resources. People who are depressed often experience some disturbance in a normal healthy eating pattern, and as a result, there can be weight loss or weight gain.
7. *Value System.* Clarify what your values are and do an inventory. If you are not living in accordance with your value system this could be contributing to your experience of depression.

As you can see managing depression means total self-care. If you neglect to take care of yourself once you begin to feel better you will likely begin to reexperience some symptoms of depression. Emotional health, as well as physical health, is about lifestyle.

SURVIVING THE HOLIDAY BLUES

For some, the holidays are an emotionally difficult time because of negative and hurtful childhood and adolescent experiences. For others, holidays emphasize the fact that the structure of our lives change over time. These changes can be associated with children growing up, leaving home, and creating new rituals with a life partner, the modification of traditions as in-laws are incorporated into available holiday time, changes in health, death, or other crises. It is highly uncomfortable to face the holidays when they are anticipated with dread or distress. If, for any reason you feel out of sync with the holidays, consider the following:

1. *Develop new holiday traditions.* If you do this, start out with realistic expectations. Whatever you do, it is not going to feel the same way to you as the way it was. It may take repeating the new tradition several times before it begins to feel like something that you are really looking forward to. However, because many people do not have the resources of a large family or the money to travel far to see family, developing new traditions is something you have control over, so make the effort to create a special time.

2. *Choose to participate.* Do not withdraw from everything during the holidays. Do not isolate yourself. While it may be difficult to feel much enthusiasm for social gatherings, choose to do it. Chances are once you are in the midst of participating you will be distracted and find yourself feeling better. Participate at a level that feels comfortable to you—but participate. Also, even participating a little may lift your spirits.

3. *Take care of you.* The commercialization of the holidays can be overwhelming. Do not let that influence how you choose to participate in the holiday season. This is also a time to reflect and give yourself a little tender loving care. Don't park yourself in front of the television and be in a trance. Instead, choose a movie you have wanted to see, read a good book, listen to pleasing music, send cards, or write letters. You may be surprised to find that taking a little time for yourself can help you feel better.

4. *Volunteer.* Sometimes we get so focused on our on losses or distress that we forget all we have to be grateful for. A lot of social service programs really try to reach out to those who have no resources and are destitute, as well as other holiday-oriented extras like special programs at museums. These organizations would be pleased to have the gift of some of your time. Sometimes helping others who are in a more difficult place than ourselves can fire up appreciation for the good things in our own lives. There are numerous ways to give some of your time: call the volunteer bureau, look in the paper, and ask others.

5. *Talk about it.* The holidays blues are more common than you may realize. Do not suffer in silence. There is the risk that the blues could get worse and become depression. Take some time to think about why the holidays are distressful for you. Again, get informed about what is happening in your community. Churches and community centers often offer special programs for people who are alone or experiencing difficulty during the holidays. Also, if it seems to be getting worse, talk to your physician and seek advice from other professional resources. Talking about it is an important step to increased self-understanding, validation, and problem solving.

UTILIZING YOUR SUPPORT SYSTEM

EXAMPLES:

1. Talking about your feelings or thoughts with an understanding person
2. Talking to a therapist or counselor
3. Talking to staff at a clinic, hospital, or hot line
4. Arranging not to be alone
5. Going to a support group
6. Spending time with people you like
7. Spending time with a pet
8. Planned activities with a caring and supportive person

Make a list of the things that you plan to do or have done in the past that have been helpful in decreasing your depression.

_____

_____

_____

_____

_____

_____

Make sure that some of the information you have listed is put into the structure of daily scheduled activities that you developed. This will reinforce a lifestyle of self-care.

THE POWER OF POSITIVE ATTITUDE

Your attitude will have a significant influence on how you feel and how you evaluate your life experiences. If you are an optimistic person it is likely that you tend to expect a positive outcome even from difficult situations. If you are pessimistic you are likely to expect the worst and probably even look for it. This tendency to expect or look for the negative is sometimes referred to as a self-fulfilling prophecy.

If you have a habit of negative thinking there are things that you can do to improve your attitude.

1. *Change your negative thinking to positive thinking.* This is not as hard as it sounds. Taking the following steps will help you change your negative thinking patterns.
   A. Awareness. Work to increase your awareness for negative thoughts. Keep a journal and write down your negative thoughts. You cannot change the way you

think unless you clearly understand how you think and talk to yourself about situations.

    B. Correcting negative thoughts and statements. Once you have identified your negative thoughts and negative patterns of thinking then you can develop positive statements to substitute for the negative ones. It generally is not too difficult to find a different and positive way of viewing things, but it does take a consistent effort to change.

    C. Monitoring your efforts and progress. Again, this is where the journal can be helpful. However, an even better way of assessing your success is by how you feel. If you are changing to a positive pattern of thinking you will find that you worry and catastrophize less, which also contributes to a sense of well-being.

2. *Be Active.* Exercise and other pleasurable activities. Exercise promotes a sense of well-being, decreasing body tension, and decreasing stress. All of which contribute to decreasing depression and feeling good. Spending time with people you like and participating in activities you enjoy are also positive ways of managing depression.

3. *Live one day at a time.* People often waste a lot of energy worrying about "what if." That means that they are worrying and suffering about something that might not even happen. Then, because they are expecting the worst they do not take care of themselves or other things that need to be taken care of today. Deal with "what is" not "what if."

4. *Remind yourself that depression ends.* States of emotional distress are generally temporary. If you have felt chronically depressed for a long time talk to your physician about medication that may help. However, it is also important that you take responsibility for yourself and your emotions. Review what you are doing in the way of self-care behaviors to promote emotional and physical well-being.

5. *Refuse to feel guilty.* If there is something that you need to take responsibility for then do it. Apologize or make amends. Then make peace with whatever it is and let go. Feelings of guilt consume emotional energy and prevent a person from moving forward.

6. *Life is about choices.* Some choices have positive consequences and some have negative consequences. Do the best you can and learn from your errors. Accept that throughout your life you will continue to learn, sometimes from mistakes.

SELF-MONITORING CHECKLIST

MANAGEMENT BEHAVIORS

__ getting up in the morning
__ getting dressed and ready for the day
__ practicing good hygiene
__ start the day off with a positive affirmation
__ thinking positive through the day
__ maintaining good awareness for my thoughts and behaviors
__ problem-solving issues instead of avoiding
__ attending work or school daily

__ participating in pleasurable activities
__ spending time with people I enjoy
__ getting my needs met appropriately
__ getting adequate sleep and rest
__ exercise
__ eating nutritionally
__ meditation or relaxation techniques
__ getting in touch with your spirituality
__ not engaging in self-defeating behaviors
__ not engaging in self-destructive behaviors
__ spending time outside
__ keeping busy
__ consistently taking medication as prescribed
__ maintaining a balance of rest and pleasurable activities
__ using my resources
__ attending support groups or meetings
__ attending therapy
__ Find Something Positive In Every Day

What strategies have you found for decreasing or eliminating your depression?

_____

_____

_____

_____

_____

Using a schedule of Daily Activities can alleviate the pressure of trying to get through a day in a positive and useful manner because it outlines expected activity.

A person who is feeling depressed may spend an entire day or many days doing nothing but existing. This inactivity and lack of accomplishment can maintain or contribute to your depression. Because self-esteem is an active process, when a person is lacking activity and accomplishments in their life they develop low self-esteem. When they have low self-esteem they tend to devalue their efforts, viewing whatever they do as unimportant. To feel worthwhile will take a commitment to develop a self-care program which includes a positive attitude, adequate nutrition, exercise, relaxation, participation in pleasurable activities, and a daily structure for facilitating the development of a healthy and fulfilling lifestyle.

In everyone's life there are responsibilities which must be taken care of ranging from professional duties to housekeeping chores. Some of these tasks may be enjoyable while others are not. When you develop your Daily Activity Schedule be sure to create a balance of pleasure and accomplishment. This will contribute to a sense of wellness. Some things may be both a pleasure and an accomplishment. Some examples are given so that you will have an idea of the types of things to include in your Daily Activity Schedule.

__ get out of bed
__ get dressed
__ good hygiene
__ go to work
__ read the paper
__ have coffee/tea

___ balance the checkbook
___ go for a walk
___ paint/draw
___ talk with a friend
___ lunch with a friend/someone special
___ go to a support group
___ make dinner
___ wash the dishes
___ do the laundry
___ gardening
___ watch a movie
___ write a letter
___ journal writing
___ relaxation/meditation/affirmations
___ helping others
___ listening to music

DAILY ACTIVITY SCHEDULE

DATE: _____

MOOD(S): _____

Time	Planned Activity and Expectations	Actual Activity	How It Felt
7–8 a.m.			
8–9 a.m.			
9–10 a.m.			
10–11 a.m.			
11–12 noon			
12–1 p.m.			
1–2 p.m.			
2–3 p.m.			
3–4 p.m.			
4–5 p.m.			
5–6 p.m.			
6–7 p.m.			
7–8 p.m.			
8–9 p.m.			
9–10 p.m.			

Keep a Daily Activity Schedule until your depression is manageable and you feel that you do not need the support of this strategy to remain stable.

CONFRONTING AND UNDERSTANDING SUICIDE

Everyone is unique in the life crisis that they experience which can contribute or result in suicidal thoughts and behavior. However, there are 12 factors which often trigger suicidal thoughts:

__ hopelessness/despair
__ depression
__ feeling overwhelmed or desperate
__ life is out of control
__ guilt
__ loneliness
__ chemical imbalance
__ low self-esteem
__ bad memories/fears
__ recent loss
__ seasonal anniversary such as a loss
__ fatigue/sleep deprivation

HOPELESSNESS AND DESPAIR

__ no hope that things will ever change and be better
__ no hope for the future
__ no hope that there will ever be stability and wellness
__ no hope that life goals will ever be met
__ no hope that there will ever be a feeling of happiness or enthusiasm
__ no hope that there will ever be a successful career
__ no hope that there will ever be a successful relationship
__ a feeling and belief that life is a miserable existence
__ no point in being alive

When a person is severely depressed they are unable to see things clearly and objectively. As a result, everything is perceived and experienced from a position of hopelessness and despair. However, there is hope.

If you have ever experienced hopelessness and despair describe how you felt and what your beliefs were or are: _____

_____

_____

_____

What are the positive things in your life that you may take for granted, such as a good partner, a pet, home, friends, job, etc.?: _____

_____

_____

_____

DEPRESSION

When a person experiences the hopelessness and despair of profound depression they may feel that the only way to end their painful existence is suicide. The black, slippery hole of depression seems impossible to escape from and suicide is seen as a relief. The person may become obsessed with thoughts of death to stop the endless and overwhelming pain of hopelessness and despair.

As previously stated, a person experiencing severe depression is likely to not be thinking clearly or objectively. Therefore, it is difficult for them to acknowledge or reason that there is an end to the depression.

If you have had prior episodes of depression do you remember that hopeless feeling that it would never end? Write a little bit about your experience and how that episode of depression ended: _____

_____

_____

_____

_____

_____

_____

Use this information, which demonstrates to you that your depression did go away or became manageable, to confront the irrational thinking that the depression is a miserable, permanent state of existence. By changing circumstances, beliefs, using self-care behaviors, and taking medication if prescribed by a physician, depression can be alleviated or even disappear.

If you feel unable to cope, and find that it is hard for you to distract yourself from thoughts or suicide or destructive impulses then you must reach out to others for support. Develop a list of resources that you can contact so that if you are in crisis you can just look at your list and call someone to help you get through and take care of yourself.

PHONE NUMBERS

Family Member _____

Friend(s) _____

Therapist _____

Crisis Hotline _____

Hospital _____

Other_____

FEELING OVERWHELMED AND DESPERATE

When a person is depressed they often lack the energy to resolve problems as they arise. As a result, all of the new problems pile up on top of the difficulties which originally contributed to the state of depression. When this happens a person becomes overwhelmed. Being overwhelmed feels like there is just too much to deal with. They feel desperate because it seems like no matter what they do they will be unable to accomplish all that they have to. It may feel like there are no choices which can really help them. When this happens it may appear that suicide is the only way to escape from the awful, trapped feeling that they are experiencing.

Unfortunately, they are considering a permanent solution to temporary problems. There is always another way no matter how difficult the problems may be. If a person is at the point where they feel desperate and unable to cope the thing to do is to ask for help. If they are feeling that bad then they know that they are not emotionally well and it may require that others who care (family members, friends, therapists, ministers, physicians) are needed to break this downward spiral. Reach out to the people in your support system. If you don't have a support system tell your physician or call a hospital emergency room for help. Get whatever help is necessary to problem solve the solutions that will create the support and structure to stabilize and manage the potentially destructive behavior. Sometimes someone else can offer a solution that a person in a state of being overwhelmed would not even be able to see because they are focusing only on how to escape these awful feelings.

If you have ever felt overwhelmed and desperate describe how you felt. _____

_____

_____

_____

How did you resolve the situation? _____

_____

_____

What did you learn that could help you now? _____

_____

_____

FEELING LIKE YOUR LIFE IS OUT OF CONTROL

When a person feels like their life is out of control their negative thinking increases, they feel overwhelmed and desperate, their self-esteem plummets, and there does not seem to be anything that they can do to get back in control. It is like having a lot of conversations in your head with yourself and you cannot turn it off. It is such a frightening feeling that suicide may appear like the only way to get away from it all. Most people experience this feeling a little bit when they have a lot of different things going on at one time and the demand is greater than what they can give to take care of everything.

It may not be what would be expected, but when a person is feeling like this they tend to engage in behaviors which contribute to feeling and being more and more out of control. It can be like a vicious cycle. The thing to do is to get help from someone who is trusted and can be objective. There are choices, but to effectively make good choices a person will have to slow things down, evaluate and define what the problems are, and then prioritize the identified issues so that they can be systematically resolved one by one. You can only do one thing at a time. When this process is followed it becomes possible to take one step at a time toward any goal that has been set. It helps to deal with "What Is" instead of "What If."

If you are feeling like your life is out of control describe it. _____

_____

_____

What are all of the things that you are feeling pressure from? _____

_____

_____

What resources can you use to help you slow things down to get a handle on your situation?

_____

_____

*Remember: Take one day at a time.
   You can only do one thing at a time.
   Give yourself credit for your efforts and accomplishments because every step
   You take contributes to regaining control over your life.

GUILT

A person who is experiencing feelings of guilt is focusing on something that they have done that is embarrassing, harmful to another person, or some other behavior which has contribute to negative consequences for themselves or someone else. Sometimes this feeling of guilt becomes so big that they feel an intense need to escape, and the only way out appears to be suicide.

Feelings of guilt and shame are very hard to deal with, mainly because it requires that you forgive yourself for whatever has happened. Forgiving yourself requires honesty and self-acceptance. When you own your behavior and confront it with appropriate problem solving it will feel like a huge weight has been taken off of your shoulders.

If you regret your actions, do you attempt to learn from them so that your future behavior does not repeat the same mistakes. Or do you choose to suffer over the past and remain passively stuck in the patterns of behavior you know are not helpful or appropriate?

Self-forgiveness requires an understanding for the possibility of special circumstances, assuming the responsibility for the damage or consequences of your behavior, to make amends for your actions, and to make a firm commitment to do things differently in the future. If you do not make this commitment to change and follow through on it you will not be free from guilt. In fact, you will very likely repeat the same dysfunctional behavior patterns.

Change can be difficult because there is some comfort in what is familiar to you. Who knows what life may confront you with if you did not have your depression, hopelessness, and self-loathing. Misery can provide its own kind of insulation from the rest of the world, whereas happiness, in its own way, is more demanding. Happiness requires energy, consciousness, commitment, and discipline. So it takes time, energy, and work to liberate yourself from guilt.

What have I done or said which makes me feel guilty? _____

_____

_____

How can I take responsibility for what I have done? _____

_____

_____

How can I make peace with what has happened, accept and forgive myself, and move on?

_____

_____

How does what has happened help me understand what my values are? _____

_____

_____

When I feel defensive about positives _____

_____

_____

If I hide myself through fear, envy, or resentment _____

_____

_____

_____

_____

_____

When I act against what I understand and know to be right_____

_____

_____

_____

_____

_____

I will imagine how I would feel if I did things differently in the future _____

_____

_____

_____

_____

_____

LONELINESS

When a person feels that one cares or they really do not have anyone that they feel close enough to talk to and to get help this can contribute to thoughts of suicide. The factor of loneliness can work in two directions with severe depression. When a person feels depressed they may isolate and withdraw from their resources which leads to feelings of loneliness. Or, when someone lacks resources they may experience an increasing sense of isolation and loneliness. Both increase depression and the likelihood of suicide.

When trying to understand and deal with the issue of loneliness consider, on the most basic level, that behavior has only two purposes: To bring people closer together or to push them apart. People who experience depression may find it difficult to maintain close relationships for several reasons.

1. They may not follow through on friendship behaviors because of their negative thinking and expectations of rejection and abandonment.
2. Because of their depressed mood people may feel helpless themselves and not know what to do.
3. People may get frustrated with the depressed person who talks about how bad they feel or who obviously looks like they are having a difficult time, but do not appear to follow through on behaviors to help themselves.

Even though you may think that no one cares about you, you probably do have friends and family who care and are genuinely concerned about you. Do you take advantage of community resources which can help you to establish or reestablish a feeling of belonging and connectedness?—A feeling that you are a part of life and the world.

Make a list of the people who care about you and the resources in your community that you could participate in to decrease your feelings of loneliness and isolation.

1. _____
2. _____
3. _____
4. _____
5. _____
6. _____

CHEMICAL IMBALANCE

There are a variety of things that can contribute to a chemical imbalance. To identify and appropriately treat a chemical imbalance requires that you make an appointment with your physician and explore some simple possibilities and test for others.

Some examples of health or other treatment factors which could cause a chemical imbalance are:

__ thyroid dysfunction
__ diabetes with poor nutrition

__ some medications can contribute to depression
__ medication interactions
__ alcohol and drug abuse

Do not avoid taking care of yourself. You are responsible for your mental health and physical well-being. Utilize your resources and comply with treatment interventions that can help you to feel better and to more effectively manage your emotional state and life.

If you experience chronic health issues explore how your life has been affected, and if there are different resources available to help you manage and cope with your specific situation. Health issues have a significant impact on how people feel emotionally.

LOW SELF-ESTEEM

Self-esteem is composed of such factors as self-worth, self-competence, and self-acceptance. When a person is severely or chronically depressed their self-esteem is diminished. The cloak of depression perceives everything from the dark or negative side and offers little hope of change. This, most importantly, affects how the person views themselves. If their self-esteem has been lost they view themselves as worthless and cannot imagine what others could see in them. This feeling of unworthiness and failure as a person can play a large role in a person considering suicide to be the answer to their worthless existence.

If this is how you are feeling it is time to take an honest, objective look at your accomplishments. Your accomplishments will include the things you have done in efforts to obtain goals as well as things you have done to help other people. Self-esteem is an active process so it is related to behaviors and thoughts that are promoting growth and change. Another way of stating this is that a person with good self-esteem is a person who does not just talk about it—they do it. This activity affirms a sense of worthiness through accomplishment. It does not matter how small the step is as long as it is a step forward.

People who take responsibility for their own existence tend to generate healthy self-esteem. They live an active orientation to life instead of a passive one without hope of change. They make change happen. They understand that accepting full responsibility for their life means growth and change. They recognize that they must make the decisions and use the resources presented to them. They also recognize that it is smart to ask for help when they need it, and for that help to benefit them they must use it. As a result, they have healthy self-esteem.

Avoiding self-responsibility victimizes people. It leaves them helpless and hopeless. They give their personal power to everyone except themselves. Sometimes when this occurs people feel frustrated and blame others for the losses in their life. When a person takes responsibility for their feelings they quit being passive and start taking the necessary action to reclaim their life. They recognize that nothing is going to get better until they change the way they look at things, the way they choose to feel about things, and the way they respond to things.

As you objectively evaluate the different areas of your life you may find that you are more responsible in some areas and less responsible in other areas. It is likely that the areas where you practice greater responsibility are the same areas that you like most about yourself. To accept responsibility for your existence is to recognize the need to live productively. It is not the degree of productivity that is an issue here, but rather the choice to exercise whatever ability that you do have. Living responsibly is closely associated with living actively which translates into healthy self-esteem.

If you wish to raise your self-esteem you need to think in terms of behaviors. If you want to live more responsibly you need to think in terms of turning your thoughts into behaviors. For example, if you say that you will have a better attitude describe how that will be seen in behaviors.

Describe the behaviors associated with having a positive attitude. _____

_____

_____

List the resources you can use for the support of developing healthy self-esteem. _____

_____

_____

Making the changes to improve self-esteem requires increased awareness and understanding of myself. Complete the following sentences to initiate this process:

1. As I learn to accept myself _____

_____

_____

2. If no one can give me good self-esteem except myself _____

_____

_____

3. What follows is an honest and objective evaluation about the positive and negative things in my life.
   A. Negatives _____
   B. Positives _____

4. The things that I can do to raise my self-esteem include _____

_____

_____

THE SELF-ESTEEM REVIEW

Directions: Review the following statements. Rate how much you believe each statement, from 1 to 5. The highest rating, 5, means that you think the statement is completely true, 0 means that you completely *do not* believe the statement.

<u>Rating</u>

1. I am a good and worthwhile person. _____

2. I am as valuable a person as anyone else. _____

3. I have good values that guide me in my life. _____

4. When I look at my eyes in the mirror, I feel good about myself. _____

5. I feel like I have done well in my life. _____

6. I can laugh at myself. _____

7. I like being me. _____

8. I like myself, even when others reject me. _____

9. Overall, I am pleased with how I am developing as a person. _____

10. I love and support myself, regardless of what happens. _____

11. I would rather be me than someone else. _____

12. I respect myself. _____

13. I continue to grow personally. _____

14. I feel confident about my abilities. _____

15. I have pride in who I am and what I do. _____

16. I am comfortable in expressing my thoughts and feelings. _____

17. I like my body. _____

18. I handle difficult situations well. _____

19. Overall, I make good decisions. _____

20. I am a good friend and people like to be with me. _____

0   100

Total lack of self-esteem   High self-esteem

Your score

TEN SELF-ESTEEM BOOSTERS

1. Be realistic
   A. Do not compare yourself to others
   B. Be Satisfied with doing your best

2. Focus on your accomplishments
   A. Each day review what you *have* done
   B. Give yourself credit for what you do

3. Use positive mental imagery
   A. Imagine success
   B. Mentally rehearse confidence

4. Look inside not outside
   A. Avoid being materialistic or identifying yourself by what you have
   B. Identify your sense of purpose

5. Actively live your life
   A. Set goals
   B. Think strategically

6. Be positive
   A. Substitute negative thoughts with realistic positive thoughts
   B. Acknowledge that how you think affects how you feel

7. Have genuine gratitude
   A. Be grateful for all that you have
   B. Appreciate your life as a gift

8. Meditate
   A. Think of peaceful, pleasant things
   B. Learn to relax and let go of stress
   C. Use positive affirmations

9. Develop positive self-care as a lifestyle
   A. Believe you are worthy of taking care of yourself
   B. Take care of your health

10. Appropriately get your needs met
    A. Identify what you need
    B. Identify your choices for getting those needs met

Positive self-esteem is an active process. Daily efforts will make a difference in your life experience.

AFFIRMATIONS FOR BUILDING SELF-ESTEEM

1. I am a valuable and important person, and I'm worthy of the respect of others.
2. I'm optimistic about life; I look forward to and enjoy new challenges.
3. I am my own expert and I am not affected by negative opinions or attitudes of others.
4. I express my ideas easily, and I know others respect my point of view.
5. I am aware of my value system and confident of the decisions I make based on my current awareness.
6. I have a positive expectancy of reaching my goals, and I bounce back quickly from temporary setbacks.
7. I have pride in my past performance and a positive expectancy of the future.
8. I accept compliments easily and give them freely to others.
9. I feel warm and loving toward myself, for I am a unique and precious being, ever doing the best I can, and growing in wisdom and love.
10. I am actively in charge of my life and direct it in constructive channels. My primary responsibility is for my own growth and well-being (the better I feel about myself, the more willing and able I am to help others).
11. I am my own authority, and I am not affected by the negative opinions or attitudes of others.
12. It is not what happens to me but how I handle it that determines my emotional well-being.
13. I am a success to the degree that I feel warm and loving toward myself.
14. No one in the entire world is more or less worthy, more or less important, than me.
15. I count my blessings and rejoice in my growing awareness.
16. I am an action person; I do first things first and one thing at a time.
17. I am kind, compassionate, and gentle with myself and everyone.
18. I am a genuine person who lives consciously.

SELF-NURTURING: A COMPONENT OF SELF-ESTEEM

You will know that you are developing self-care and self-love when you feel worthy, confident, and secure about who you are. The following are demonstrations of progress in self-nurturing:

1. You spend a day alone and are able to enjoy your own company and peacefulness.
2. You are able to make choices and do things to make yourself feel better.

3. You are able to be objective and loyal to yourself. You are able to hear the opinions of others while maintaining your own point of view.

4. While you strive to avoid becoming materialistic, you also feel worthy of giving yourself things that are important to you.

5. You take care of your health and well-being.

6. You do not engage in self-destructive behaviors or choices.

7. When you laugh, you laugh deeply and you laugh often.

8. You feel good about all of your successes large and small. You feel good about all that you achieve. You always strive to be the best you can be.

9. If someone is rejecting or hurtful, you do not take it personally. You are objective and honest with yourself. You realize that the problem may belong to the other person. Likewise, you are honest with yourself about you, take responsibility, and make changes as needed.

10. You are assertive in asking for what you need and want in your relationships with others. You set appropriate boundaries in relationships.

Adapted from a handout by J. Hays, author of *Smart Love*.

CHARACTERISTICS OF LOW SELF-ESTEEM

1. Fearful of exploring his/her real self
2. Believes that others are responsible for how he/she feels
3. Fearful of taking responsibility for his/her own emotions and actions
4. Fearful of assertively communicating wants and needs to others
5. Feels and acts like a victim
6. Judgmental of self and others
7. Does not live according to your his/her values (chameleon)
8. Covert, phony, "social personality"
9. Exaggerates, pretends, lies
10. Puts self down, shameful, blaming, self-critical, condemning
11. Nice person, approval seeking, people pleaser, puts the needs of others first
12. Negative attitude
13. Triangulates by talking badly about one person to another
14. Rationalizes
15. Jealous/envious of others, has trouble being genuinely happy for the successes of others
16. Perfectionistic
17. Dependencies/addiction, compulsive, self-defeating thinking and behavior
18. Complacent, stagnates, procrastinates
19. Does not like the work one does
20. Focuses on what doesn't get done instead of what does
21. Leaves tasks and relationships unfinished and walks away without resolving issues
22. Judges self-worth by comparing to others, feels inferior
23. Does not accept or give compliments
24. Excessive worry or catatrophizing
25. Is not comfortable with self, hard to be alone with self
26. Avoids new endeavors, fears mistakes or failure
27. Irrational responses, ruled by emotions
28. Lack of purpose in life
29. Lack of defined goals
30. Feels inadequate to handle new situation, easily stressed
31. Feels resentful when doesn't win
32. Vulnerable to the opinions, comments, and attitudes of others
33. Feel like one's life is in the shadow of another
34. Gossips to elevate self
35. Continues to blame past experiences (or family) instead of dealing with the current self (the past is an explanation, not an excuse)

Identify your characteristic of low self-esteem. What have you learned from this self-review?

_____

_____

_____

_____

_____

_____

_____

_____

_____

_____

_____

_____

_____

CHARACTERISTICS OF HIGH SELF-ESTEEM

1. Lives authentically
2. Demonstrates self-responsibility—does not blame others
3. Takes responsibility for life and consequences of actions
4. Sets goals and is committed
5. Has purpose in life
6. Is emotionally and intellectually honest with self and others
7. Confronts and deals with fears
8. Is aware of both strengths and weaknesses (self-objective)
9. Is self-respectful and sets appropriate limits and boundaries
10. Does not lie about the choices he/she makes
11. Self-accepting and self-soothing (does not seek external sources to "make it okay")
12. Self-sufficient (thinks and makes decisions independently)
13. Does not hold grudges
14. Is persistent in all efforts
15. Is genuinely grateful
16. Positive attitude (cup is half full not half empty)
17. Accepts others
18. Genuinely pleased for the success of others
19. Does not compare oneself to others
20. Directs efforts toward being the best he/she can be (recognizes that life is about continual personal growth with an aim for excellence not perfection)
21. Lives according to one's own internal values, principles, and standards
22. Chooses to see opportunity and challenges instead of problems
23. Is spontaneous and enthusiastic about life
24. Is able to praise oneself and others for efforts and accomplishments
25. Is able to see the big picture versus being trapped by stumbling blocks (mistakes have value)
26. Appropriately asks for help and utilizes resources
27. Is an active participant in life
28. Is comfortable with self and can enjoy alone time
29. Is true to oneself
30. Has quiet self-confidence

Identify your characteristics of high self-esteem. What have you learned from this self review?

_____

_____

_____

WHAT MOTIVATES ME?

1. First, identify the life goals for which you are striving. If you do not identify your goals on the list below, write them down.

wealth   security   love   self-acceptance   power

status   achievement   success   peace   fulfillment

truth   contribution   social change   personal growth

excellence   lasting relationships   comfort   challenge

2. What values guide you in the pursuit of your goals?

commitment   marriage   experience   excitement

self-discipline   integrity   honor   self-respect

pain avoidance   leisure   cooperation   decency

kindness   meaning   sexual gratification   serving others

happiness   education   friendship   affection

instant gratification   actualization   honesty   health

control   anger   independence   non-commitment   anger

revenge   adventure   travel   children   family

position   superiority   self-importance   laziness   freedom

self-sacrifice   substance use   isolation   job satisfaction   intimacy

assertiveness   accountability   pain seeking   advantage

dishonesty   selfishness   irresponsibility   pleasure   justice

self-serving   resentment   insecurity   vulnerability

play   shyness   equality   hatred   compulsiveness   conflict

curiosity   self-confidence   illness   affluence   resisting change

STANDING UP TO SHYNESS

Shyness is very common. Most people who are shy can share experiences of being embarrassed which resulted in making them feel more self-conscious and shy. It is also common for people who are shy to have unrealistically high expectations of themselves. They overestimate the amount of attention they receive from others, especially when they are feeling intensely self-conscious.

Those who are shy often believe that others are observing them and judging them. What they do not realize that most people are focusing more on themselves than on the presentation or performance of others.

If you want to overcome your shyness, it will require a commitment to change. This means practicing change several times a week to desensitize your level of anxiety. This weekly practice could take place specifically in a group for overcoming shyness, or use the following tips in social settings:

SOCIALIZING

Meet people and talk with them. Everyone's social skills get rusty when they are not used. Practice, practice, practice.

1. Break experiences down into small, manageable steps. Be consistent.
    A. Set a goal to make eye contact
    B. Say hello
    C. Inquire into how someone is doing
    D. Ask another's opinion on a community event

2. Learn to ask questions
    A. Ask open-ended questions
    B. Listen to responses, which may bring up more questions

3. Choose to be in control
    A. Structure social situations
        1. Have dinner with a friend
        2. Have lunch with one or two coworkers
        3. Attend a structured class like photography, dancing, painting where
        4. Conversation is minimal and optional

4. Learn to accept yourself and your imperfections. Be honest and objective with yourself about your struggles in conversation and use this information to come up with several ways of dealing with your discomfort. This will contribute to feeling in control.

5. Let it go. Do not put yourself down if you think you have made a mistake or done something you think is embarrassing. How you think about yourself and how others perceive you are often very different. Take the "oh, well" attitude, and try again.

6. Help someone else. Since you know how uncomfortable you can feel at a large social gathering, help yourself and someone else. It won't be hard for you to identify someone else who is withdrawn and looks uncomfortable. Take that person under your wing and provide support.

BAD MEMORIES AND FEAR

Feeling depressed in combination with feeling overwhelmed by disturbing memories can lead to thoughts of suicide or to self-destructive behavior.

People overwhelmed by bad memories from painful experiences often find it difficult to adequately cope. It could be that they were in some way abused as a child. Such abuse can be physically, emotionally, and psychologically traumatizing and damaging. One of the most upsetting things about a situation such as this is that while they were being hurt by someone else in the past, now they may be engaging in behaviors that continue to harm them.

In addition to haunting memories the fears which make it very difficult to trust others. If this is the case, then it is likely that it has been hard to utilize resources even if you are aware of them. However, because you have decided that you no longer want to feel this way any longer there are some things that you can do to initiate a program of hope and recovery.

1. Therapy. Individual and/or group therapy will be very helpful in facilitating the release of the memories which have held you hostage. Make sure that the therapist is familiar with these issues. Whether or not you participate in short- or long-term therapy will depend on your needs and goals.

2. Venting Your Feelings and Thoughts. Talking with a friend, family member, or therapist that you trust will help you to get out your feelings instead of carrying them around inside, and will help you begin to identify what you need to do to take care of yourself and to heal.

3. Journal Writing. This is a very helpful strategy. Instead of using emotional energy to hold everything inside, write your feelings and thoughts in a journal. Writing is a constructive way to vent thoughts and feelings, to clarify issues, and to problem solve what you need to do to take care of yourself. A journal is always there when you need it.

4. Creative Expression. You do not have to be a trained artist to express yourself in a variety of creative or artistic ways. This can be helpful for distracting yourself so that you can have a break from painful memories or it can give form and texture to your feelings, emotions, and mood.

5. Self-Help Resources. There are so many things available to help such as self-help groups, books, tapes, and community presentations. Check out a local bookstore, see if the local newspaper offers a listing of available support groups and also inquire with your physician or local mental health associations for information on resources.

Painful or fearful memories that I need to let go of are _____

_____

_____

Things that I have done that have been helpful to me in the past are _____

_____

_____

Resources that I am aware of that would be helpful are _____

_____

_____

Helpful resources that I am willing to use are_____

_____

_____

Formulate a plan for letting go of painful and fearful memories so that they no longer interfere with the quality of your life _____

_____

_____

_____

_____

_____

_____

_____

SEASONAL ANNIVERSARY OF LOSSES

The anniversary of a death or other major loss can trigger thoughts of suicide or self-destructive behaviors. Additionally, another time of year that is difficult for a number of people is the holiday season. There are expectations of a loving and caring family coupled with the excitement and enthusiasm of being with others and sharing the holiday spirit. For people who grew up experiencing tension and emotional distress or other issues associated with the holidays this can be a very difficult time. Yet, other people suffer from Seasonal Affective Disorder (SAD). When the days are shorter, the number of hours of daylight are reduced which makes some people experience depression.

Identify which of these issues presents a difficulty for you. _____

_____

What has made it so difficult to deal with this issue(s)? _____

_____

What are things that you have done in the past that was helpful in managing this distressing situation? _____

_____

_____

What is your plan for managing this issue in the future or resolving it? _____

_____

_____

_____

_____

_____

_____

FATIGUE OR SLEEP DEPRIVATION

There is a noted relationship between fatigue and sleep deprivation to severe difficulty coping. Sometimes the inability to cope results in suicidal thoughts. If you experience either or both of these issues get help immediately. Tell your physician, therapist, family members, and/or friends so that you can receive the appropriate support in intervening in this difficult situation. If you are suicidal, let someone in your support system know and allow them to be there with you so that thoughts do not escalate into actions.

If you are not in treatment then talk to your physician about the options for treating depression. There are a range of interventions encompassed by medication, therapy, and the development of your own self-care program. At the very least components of self-care include good nutrition, adequate sleep and rest, exercise, relaxation, being involved in pleasurable activities, and spending time with people that you enjoy.

If I am not getting adequate rest and sleep I will _____

_____

_____

If I am feeling fatigued I will _____

_____

_____

_____

If you experienced these difficulties before what did you do that was helpful _____

_____

_____

_____

My plan for managing the problem with sleep, fatigue, and depression is _____

_____

_____

_____

WHAT IS PANIC ANXIETY?

There is not a single answer to the question "What causes panic attacks?" However, biological, environmental, and genetic factors play a role.

1. It is possible that separation anxiety during childhood may be a predisposing factor for the development of panic anxiety later in life

2. Imbalance in brain chemistry may be responsible
3. Genetic predisposition may be evident when looking at family history of anxiety disorders
4. Learned behaviors play a role—for example, continuously taking care of the needs of others while neglecting your own needs, build up of stress over time, or the chronic feeling of being overwhelmed and not having enough time to get to everything that demands your attention
5. The experience of losing someone close to you such as a family member can result in panic anxiety. A death can result in feelings of being helpless and out of control.
6. Physical trauma past or present may trigger panic anxiety.
7. Sexual trauma past or present may trigger panic anxiety.
8. Positive life events (marriage, job promotion, etc.) may also contribute to panic anxiety. This may be because there are feelings or concerns of some loss associated with the change. It could be that a person does not feel worthy or believes he/she does not deserve to be happy, which may result in negative ruminating and anxiety associated with the change.

SYMPTOMS

Panic attacks are diagnosed when an individual experiences at least 4 of the following 13 symptoms. Additionally, the symptoms develop and peak in a short period of time, which results in feelings of significant distress.

1. Palpitations/pounding heat/accelerated heart rate
2. Chest pain/tightness
3. Sweating
4. Chills/hot flashes
5. Trembling/shaking
6. Feeling short of breath/smothering
7. Feeling of choking
8. Nausea/abdominal distress
9. Feeling dizzy/lightheaded/faint
10. Numbness/tingling in hands or feet
11. Derealization (feelings of unreality)
12. Depersonalization (being detached from oneself)
13. Fear of losing control/going crazy
14. Fear of dying

TREATMENT

1. Cognitive-behavioral therapy
2. Medication
3. Health behaviors (exercise, decrease or eliminate caffeine and alcohol, develop a self-care plan)

POST-TRAUMATIC STRESS DISORDER (PTSD)

When a person is given specific information that is traumatic and overwhelming, witnesses, or has an experience of a traumatic event, the person may experience anxiety, fear, distress, or relive of the traumatic event for months and sometimes years after. Often the experience may have been life threatening or physically harming.

Post-traumatic stress disorder affects twice as many women as men. Half of all adults will experience a significant trauma, and 20% of them will develop post-traumatic stress disorder. Immediately following a traumatic experience, a person may develop acute stress, which if treated may prevent the onset of the more enduring post-traumatic stress disorder. Additionally, some individuals do not have an apparent acute stress reaction, but at a later date the trauma is triggered by some event or significant level of emotional distress and the person then experiences a delayed onset of post-traumatic stress disorder.

Individuals most at risk for PTSD are

1. Victims of sexual assault
2. Victims of child sexual abuse
3. Victims of child neglect, emotional abuse, and physical abuse
4. Victims of spousal abuse
5. Victims of random acts of violence
6. Survivors or witnesses of
    A. Car accidents
    B. Plane crashes
    C. Fires
    D. Natural disasters
7. Veterans and victims of war
8. Family or friends of someone who has died suddenly
9. Individuals who experience a life-changing medical condition

Three major categories of symptoms are present when a person is diagnosed with a post-traumatic stress disorder:

1. Intrusive memories
    A. Bad dreams
    B. Sudden thoughts
    C. Images/flashbacks

*These symptoms can result in physical reactions such as feelings of panic, shortness of breath, sweating, tightness in the chest or palpitations.

2. Avoidance behavior or loss of joy
    A. As thoughts of the trauma are pushed out of conscious awareness or to some corner in one's mind the person may avoid anything that could trigger thoughts of the trauma. As a result, these individuals quit participating as they normally would and no longer find joy in previously enjoyed activities.

3. Hypervigilance (being on guard)
   A. Feeling on-edge
   B. Easily startled
   C. On high alert

*These symptoms can result in difficulty sleeping, difficulty concentrating, irritability, emotional reactivity, or anger.

Treatment includes therapy and the consideration of medication. Other sources of information include the PTSD Alliance at 877-507-PTSD and the Moving Past Trauma hotline at 800-455-8300.

MANAGING ANXIETY

Anxiety is a part of everyday life. It is a normal emotional experience. Something that is different from the anxiety which is a normal response to environmental stressors are anxiety disorders. In an anxiety disorder the anxiety is much more intense, it lasts longer, and it may be specific to people, places, or situations.

The goals in managing anxiety are to understand what your personal reaction to anxiety-provoking situations are, identify what your related concerns are, and to learn to "let go" of anxiety. You may need the help of a therapist to learn the skills useful for managing and eliminating anxiety disorder symptoms. You may also benefit from the use of antianxiety medications in conjunction with therapy to accomplish these goals. The hope is that, by reading that there are a number of strategies, you can learn to deal with anxiety you feel.

As with almost everything, if you want things to be different then you need to be willing to do things differently. It takes a commitment to change and consistency in following through in the use of the strategies that you will develop to manage the distress of anxiety disorders. Some people experience anxiety in specific situations whereas others experience a certain level of anxiety all the time. To develop a treatment plan that will help you manage anxiety effectively requires that you clearly identify your symptoms, the circumstances related to the onset of the symptoms if there are any, and what efforts you have used to cope with the distress of anxiety.

In identifying the possible issues related to anxiety you may have to pay better attention to the thoughts in your mind. People talk to themselves continually throughout the day. When you talk to yourself about the emotion or fear that you attach to it, you can have a significant impact on the development and maintenance of anxiety disorders. Increasing your awareness for what these self-talk statements are will allow you to begin to change and correct thinking that has contributed to your unmanageable anxiety.

It is recommended that you keep a journal. A journal is useful for venting your feelings, clarifying what the problem is, and then problem solving the situation by taking the appropriate action. To problem solve the situations that you write about ask yourself if this is something that you have control over. If the answer is yes then consider the options for dealing with it, and make a decision after considering the various consequences or outcomes. Be prepared to try an alternative if the first attempt does not work effectively. If it is something that you do not have any control over then "let go." Learning to accept what you cannot change will relieve anxiety. It takes time to learn how to let go, but the increased energy, freedom, and relief that you will experience are well worth it.

During the course of your journal writing, as you become more aware of the internal selftalk, you may begin to become aware of the relationship between your thoughts and feelings. Thoughts affect feelings, feelings affect actions. When you choose to think more positively about a situation you will feel better. Likewise, when you worry excessively, expect the worst to happen, and when you are self-critical you can expect to feel bad.

Now that you know that beliefs affect emotion and behavior you will want to pay more attention to your own beliefs.

1. Do you feel an intense need for approval from others? People pleasing behavior means that you put the needs of others before your own needs. This leads to frustration and, over time, resentment. Frustration and resentment are intense feelings that can contribute to chronic anxiety and tension.

2. Do you have an intense need for control? Do you worry about how you appear, do you feel uncomfortable in letting other people be in charge of a situation? Do you believe that if you are not in control, that you are weak and a failure?

3. Do you tend to be perfectionistic and self-critical? Do you often feel that what you do is never enough or not good enough? Do you often criticize your own efforts and feel a constant pressure to achieve?

These patterns of beliefs and behavior are irrational. If this is your approach to life expect to experience chronic stress, anxiety, and low self-esteem. Who could feel calm and relaxed with this approach to life. Chances are that if you engage in any of these behaviors and beliefs that you also have a tendency to discount what you are experiencing physically. The mind and body function as one. When there is emotional distress you know it. Generally, there are physical symptoms as well, especially with chronic stress. Often when people ignore all of the ways that their body tries to tell them to slow down and take care of themselves the result is an escalation in symptoms. When this happens it is called a panic attack. Symptoms of panic attacks include:

1. anxiety
2. palpitations, accelerated heart rate, or pounding heart
3. chest pain or discomfort
4. shaking or trembling
5. muscle tension
6. shortness of breath
7. nausea or abdominal distress
8. feeling dizzy or lightheaded
9. numbness or tingling
10. feelings of unreality
11. feelings of being detached from oneself
12. fear of losing control or going crazy
13. chills or hot flashes
14. feeling of impending doom/fear of dying

If you have not had a panic attack, you can recognize by looking at the symptoms that it is a terrifying experience. Yet, the person who has experienced a panic attack has likely been building up to it for a long time, ignoring their own high level of chronic emotional, psychological, and physical distress.

WHAT DO YOU DO

Ineffective and dysfunctional approaches to relationships with others and with yourself need to be changed. To be the best that you can be in a relationship requires that you be the best you can be as an individual.

1. Develop good boundaries. This means having a realistic view of other people's approval, and that you don't depend on it to feel worthy or accepted. It also means learning to deal with criticism in an objective manner. Everyone is entitled to their opinion. If they offer information that is beneficial to you then use it. If not, then let go. If you have a tendency to put the importance of their needs above your own then recognize your codependency and take responsibility for changing it. This can be a big contributor to states of chronic anxiety and stress.

2. Develop realistic expectations and limitations. Change your belief that your worth is based upon what you accomplish and achieve. Focus on what is right. You can drive yourself to the point of exhaustion with self-criticism. Once you develop realistic goals you will have the time you need for other personal necessities such as spending time doing things that you find pleasurable and being with people that you enjoy.

3. Recognize that not everything can be neat and predictable. Learning acceptance and patience will help you be more comfortable with the things that are not predictable. The next step is learning to trust that most problems eventually work out. One of two things will happen; either you will find a solution to the problem or you will see that it cannot be changed. If it cannot be changed then you find a way to accept it or make some decision based on its influence in your life and do something else. Overall, things become clearer and coping is easier.

As previously discussed, people with chronic anxiety and stress tend to ignore their body's response to stress. This means that you may be ignoring physical symptoms. If this is the case, you will keep pushing yourself without slowing down to take care of yourself. One consequence of pushing yourself with controlling, codependent, perfectionist standards is a chronic high level of stress that turns into panic attacks. A panic attack is also a warning sign. This warning sign is not as easy to ignore as others. If you have a panic attack, chances are that you have ignored taking good care of yourself for some time and that irrational thinking is playing a large role.

In order to learn to manage stress requires that you be able to identify your own symptoms of stress. Once you have this awareness then you can do things to relieve your stress and anxiety. You are responsible for your own physical and emotional health.

It is important to note that it is not uncommon for someone with an anxiety disorder to also be experiencing some level of depression.

SURVEY OF STRESS SYMPTOMS

Check each symptom that you have experienced in the last month, and then count the number of items that you have checked. The symptoms must be experienced to the level that you identify it as a problem

PSYCHOLOGICAL SYMPTOMS

__ anxiety
__ depression
__ difficulty concentrating
__ forgetful
__ agitation, hyper
__ feeling overwhelmed
__ irrational thoughts/fears
__ compulsive behavior
__ confusion
__ feelings of unreality
__ feeling of being detached from oneself
__ restless/on edge
__ mood swings

__ loneliness
__ intrusive thoughts
__ relationship problems
__ family problems
__ work problems
__ irritability
__ excessive worry/obsessing
__ feelings of guilt
__ tearful
__ nightmares
__ social isolation/withdrawal
__ apathy/indifference
__ sexual dysfunction

PHYSICAL SYMPTOMS

__ headaches
__ muscle tension
__ low back pain
__ upper back, neck, or shoulder pain
__ clenching teeth
__ abdominal distress
__ nausea
__ shaking or trembling
__ numbness or tingling

__ feeling of choking
__ chills or hot flashes
__ sweating
__ sleep disturbance

__ fatigue
__ high blood pressure
__ sleep disturbance
__ appetite disturbance
__ diarrhea
__ digestive problems
__ constipation
__ rash/hives/shingles
__ use of alcohol/cigarettes or other drugs to deal with stress
__ bowel problems
__ thyroid dysfunction
__ other stress-related health problems

ESTIMATE YOUR STRESS LEVEL

Number of items checked	estimated level of stress
0–7	low (within the normal range)
8–14	moderate (experiencing some distress)
15–21	high (experiencing difficulty coping)
22+	very high (unable to cope)

As you review your symptom list think of ways that you can take care of yourself, make changes, delegate tasks to others, etc. that can alleviate the physical and emotional distress that you experience.

HOW YOUR BODY REACTS TO STRESS AND ANXIETY

Stress is a part of everyday life. Even "good" stress can affect you by leaving negative consequences such as fatigue and body tension. The body's response to stress is its conditioned habit for coping with difficult situations.

The physiological changes associated with stress and anxiety are initiated with the brain's interpretation of the experience. The brain then sends a message to a gland in the brain (hypothalamus), which then sends the message to another gland in the brain (pituitary—known as the master gland). From there, hormones are released that relay messages to other glands in the body, which also release hormones (like adrenalin). If the stress reaction is brief no significant damage is done. However, if the stress reaction lasts a long time, other stress hormones are released, which begin to negatively affect the immune system and the body becomes more susceptible to infection and disease. The weakest part of the body will be the first to show signs of dysfunction as the ravages of chronic stress takes their toll.

Remember, the body's initial response to stress is the same whether the stress is positive or negative. It is the experience of prolonged stress that is damaging.

MANAGING STRESS

It is physically and psychologically impossible to be stressed and relaxed at the same time. Therefore, the goal is to create a state of relaxation. When the body has been exposed to acute stress for too long or stress has been chronic (one difficult situation after the other), the body forgets what it feels like to be relaxed.

To retrain or recondition to your body to the experience of being relaxed, seek the following:

1. Adequate sleep
2. Good nutrition
3. Laughter and recreation
4. Aerobic physical activity (walking is great)
5. Deep breathing techniques
6. Relaxation techniques (aside from deep breathing, which is a first step in the process)

The mind needs to rest and be distracted so that there can be relief from body tension. Meditation, deep relaxation, and the other reconditioning factors listed earlier help to alleviate tension in the muscles/body and the mind. The result is as follows:

1. An increase in energy
2. A sense of well being
3. Balance in lifestyle

For emotional, psychological, and physical health, learn to relax physically, emotionally, and psychologically. Don't worry about things you can't control, let go of issues that belong to someone else, be effective in your life by accomplishing tasks and then moving on, and practice good self-care behaviors.

1. Positive thinking. Look for the opportunity instead of the negative.
2. Task oriented. Feel good about your efforts and accomplishments.
3. Accept yourself. Don't be self-critical. If there is something you want to change then change it.
4. Be flexible. Not everything is black and white. Be open to the gray area of things.
5. Develop realistic goals. Evaluate what it will take to reach a goal.
6. Develop a positive view of life.
7. Nurture your spirituality.
8. Distract yourself from stressors. Sometimes you have to put everything aside to relax and have fun.
9. Deep breathing, relaxation, meditation, or visualization.
10. Finding humor in things.
11. Spending time with people you enjoy.
12. Keeping a journal for venting, and at the end of every entry closing with something positive.
13. Take time regularly to do activities that you enjoy.
14. Utilize your support system. This could be friends, family, individual therapy, group therapy, or community support groups.
15. Practice being assertive. You will feel better for taking care of yourself.
16. Good communication.
17. Take short breaks throughout the day. Take 5 to 10 minute breaks throughout the day to relax and remove yourself from stressors or demands.
18. Regular exercise. Walking is excellent for decreasing body tension and alleviating stress.
19. Get adequate rest and sleep. If you don't get enough sleep you can't cope well.
20. Practice good nutrition.
21. Massage. A good way to relieve muscle tension and relax.
22. Choose to be in environments that feel good to you.
23. Work on your financial security.
24. Practice good time management.
25. Do things that demonstrate respect, care, and nurturing of the self. That means take good care of you.

Develop a self-care plan. Incorporate these strategies and others to develop a plan of selfcare behaviors, beliefs, and attitudes that can become a new and healthy lifestyle. That is preventive medicine.

PLAN OF ACTION FOR DEALING WITH ANXIETY

1. Recognize and identify anxiety symptoms, and situations related to it.

2. Develop relaxation skills. Most people will be able to feel relaxed by using progressive muscle relaxation. If you have made a good effort to use it and do not find that it is relaxing for you then it is your responsibility to try other techniques until you find one that is effective for you. Other techniques include deep breathing, visualization, meditation, body scanning, and brief forms of progressive muscle relaxation. This is a very important part of managing anxiety. Because of the way the nervous system works it is physically impossible to be stressed and relaxed at the same time. Learn a relaxation technique.

3. Confront anxiety. Make a commitment to understand and deal with the issues underlying your experience of anxiety.

4. Problem solve. Once you have identified the underlying issues contributing to the anxiety you experience deal with the issues that you can do something about and let go of the issues that you cannot do anything about.

5. Develop positive self-esteem. If you do not accept and like who you are, how can you effectively manage the things that are causing your anxiety. The managing of anxiety is about lifestyle changes. This requires a commitment to yourself. To make this commitment and follow through will depend on how important your well-being is to you.

6. Exercise. Aerobic exercise, especially walking is a good stress reliever. It decreases muscle tension, increases energy, and can improve sleep. You will experience the benefits of walking after several weeks of commitment to this anxiety relieving strategy. It feels good to take care of yourself.

7. Using positive self-talk. How you talk to yourself will make a big difference in how you interpret things around you, how you choose to feel, and how you choose to respond. In other words, how you talk to yourself affects your entire life experience. Practice positive, rational self-talk and incorporate daily use of positive affirmations.

8. Keeping a journal. A journal is a great tool for venting your feelings and thoughts. It takes emotional energy to keep all of this "stuff" inside. Get it out. Writing your thoughts and feelings can also clarify issues. Problem solve these issues to alleviate distress and to unclutter your mind. A journal is also a great way to monitor your consistency and actual commitment to the changes necessary for managing your anxiety.

9. Confront and change self-defeating behavioral patterns and personality traits. This means changing perfectionistic, controlling, codependent behaviors. These behaviors do not help you get your needs met and they do not make you feel better. Contrary, they generally leave you feeling stressed, frustrated, anxious, angry and over time resentful.

10. Desensitize phobias. If there are specific situations that elicit extreme anxiety for you then work with your therapist using a technique called systematic desensitization.

11. Utilize your support system. If you do not have a support system then develop one. Start by putting in place the supports that you need for confronting and dealing with your anxiety. A support system can include your therapist (individual or group), your physician, family members, friends, people at your church, etc. Generally the reason why a person lacks a support system is because they have made the choice to not allow others to help them. Instead, they have this distorted belief that it is only themselves that can be there to support other people.

12. Energize yourself with pleasure and humor. This means spending time with people you enjoy and doing activities that you like. Laughter is a great stress reliever. Have laughter in your life everyday.

13. Practice good nutrition and get adequate sleep. You must take care of yourself to live life fully which includes work, relaxation, and pleasure.

14. Develop assertive communication. Being able to say "no" and to otherwise effectively express yourself is a skill. If you do not have it learn it. To get your needs appropriately met requires that you speak honestly and appropriately about what you want and need.

15. Develop self-nurturing behaviors. You are so good at taking care of the needs of others. Practice doing things that feel good to you.

If you have developed a program for managing anxiety and are consistently practicing it you are probably feeling much better. Because change is difficult, people need to feel motivated to do things differently. Originally, it was the extreme distress and physical symptoms that facilitated your change. Sometimes when people start feeling better they quit following through on the changes in their thinking and their behaviors. This can lead to a relapse of symptoms. If a relapse happens to you view it as an opportunity to understand the importance of the components of your management program and the validation that if you do not make a commitment to take care of yourself your body will keep sending you the message that it needs to be taken better care of.

Some people experience relapse as a normal part of their recovery from extreme stress and anxiety. It could be that they are consistently practicing all of the parts of their program but reexperience some symptoms. This has likely happened because there was so much body tension that you may go through one or more stages of a readjustment. So if you are consistently doing what is prescribed in the way of changes continue even if some symptoms reoccur. They will subside. Remember, it took a long time to get to this state, and it may take a while to alleviate all of the emotional and physical distress. Therefore, think of relapse as a normal, predictable part of recovery.

Be prepared to deal with the possibility of a relapse. If it does occur, it is likely that the symptoms will not be as intense or last as long as they did before. This is because you have developed skills to manage your anxiety.

RELAPSE—SYMPTOM REOCCURRENCE

When you have a relapse you fall back into old behaviors and old ways of thinking. When you started feeling better you probably thought that you had conquered the anxiety and would not be bothered by those symptoms again. What happens in relapse is just a recycling of the old patterns. Relapse is a predictable and expected part of recovering.

In preparing yourself for the management of a relapse remind yourself of the self-perpetuating cycle of extreme anxiety.

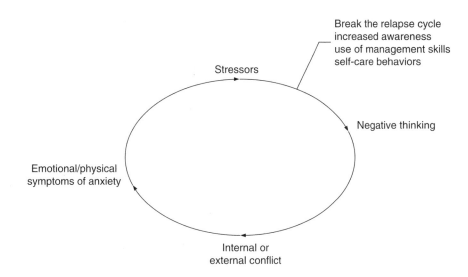

When you experience any relapse, take the time to assess your reactions so that you can evaluate your feelings and behaviors. This will help you to appropriately intervene in the relapse cycle earlier and earlier. The result will be decreased setbacks and stronger progress and stabilization.

INTERVENING IN THE RELAPSE CYCLE

1. Managing Stress
   A. use strategies such as relaxation, meditation, exercise, utilization of support system, delegating tasks to others, etc.

2. Challenging Negative/Irrational Thinking
   A. use positive self-talk, remind yourself that the anxiety will not last forever, use positive affirmations, use your journal so that you can identify patterns of negative self-talk being initiated by specific situations and deal with it.

3. Resolving Internal/External Conflicts
   A. the conflicts were initiated by the stressors at the beginning of the cycle and then again through negative self-talk. Take the opportunity to understand the conflict and problem solve it. This is an opportunity to resolve and let go of past issues and dysfunctional thinking patterns.

You will break the relapse cycle with your increased awareness, use of management skills (assertiveness, relaxation, spending time with people you enjoy, participating in activities that are pleasurable, improving your self-esteem, positive self-talk, etc.), and self-care behaviors (adequate rest/sleep, good nutrition, exercise, etc.)

Your consistency and repeated efforts to cope effectively with stressors using the strategies that you develop will pay off. Remember to use your journal or other source to monitor your efforts and consistency in changing your lifestyle to one in which you take care of yourself and avoid exhaustion.

You know that the progress that you have made is becoming more stable when you have learned to experience normal anxiety without panicking. Therefore, continue to be consistent in your efforts to overcome anxiety. You are responsible for your health.

WARNING SIGNS OF RELAPSE

1. negative thinking
2. controlling behavior
3. excessive worrying/catastrophizing
4. perfectionistic behavior
5. codependent behavior
6. change in appetite
7. difficulty with sleep
8. difficulty getting up in the morning
9. fatigue/lethargy
10. feeling bad about yourself
11. feeling less hopeful about the future
12. decreased exercise
13. unwilling to ask for what you want or need
14. procrastination
15. social isolation
16. withdrawal from activities
17. use of alcohol or other drugs
18. irritable/agitated
19. impatient
20. negative attitude
21. lacking confidence
22. feeling insecure
23. poor judgment
24. misperceptions
25. self-defeating behaviors
26. destructive risk-taking behaviors
27. distrustful of others
28. obsessive thoughts
29. difficulty concentrating
30. not experiencing pleasure in anything you do
31. suicidal thoughts
32. others

In the early stages of your recovery from anxiety you can use this item survey to regularly review for the presence of symptoms that indicate that currently there is a relapse, or that a relapse is inevitable if immediate intervention with management strategies is not made. As your progress begins to stabilize, intermittently review this list to maintain awareness and to reinforce efforts and accomplishments.

SYSTEMATIC DESENSITIZATION

Systematic desensitization is a technique which couples progressive relaxation training and visual imagery for the extinction of maladaptive anxiety reactions.

To ensure that anxiety is inhibited by the counter response to anxiety of muscle relaxation, the anxious individual is instructed to imagine anxiety-provoking scenes arranged in a hierarchy. Hierarchies of anxiety-provoking situations are formulated as a range from mildly stressful or nonthreatening to very threatening. This imaging of these events occurs while the individual is deeply relaxed. Should any imaginary event in the hierarchy elicit much anxiety the individual is instructed to cease visualization and regain their feelings of relaxation. Depending on the situation, the hierarchy is adjusted accordingly (broken down into smaller steps or reorganized) or the imaginal representation of the event is repeated until the individual does not experience anxiety in response to the event image.

THE TEN STEPS OF SYSTEMATIC DESENSITIZATION

1. Identify the event which provokes the extreme anxiety.

2. Develop a hierarchy of ten steps leading to the anxiety-provoking event. Begin with the least stressful aspect in the chain of events leading to the anxiety-provoking event which is avoided because of the associated distress.

3. Make sure that there will not be any disruptions or distractions as the process is initiated. Begin with 15 to 20 minutes of progressive muscle relaxation.

4. Once deep relaxation is achieved, present the first scene from the hierarchy. Talk the person through this scene with realistic detail, utilizing all senses if appropriate. Instruct the individual to picture fully this scene in their mind. Draw their attention to their emotional experience while visualizing this scene. Pause for 15 to 20 sec while they visualize this scene.

5. Instruct the individual that if they experience any anxiety they are to signal by raising their right index finger. If there is an experience of intense anxiety or early symptoms of a panic attack instruct the individual to raise two fingers. If this occurs, instruct the individual to let go of distressful scene and to imagine a safe serene place (discussed and developed prior to the initiation of the systematic desensitization process). Instruct the individual to stay in that safe serene place until they feel relaxed again. When relaxation is achieved, proceed again. If this happens in a later stage and the individual experiences difficulty regaining the relaxed state, back up to the previous imagined event and consolidate the mastery at that step or break down the event further if necessary before proceeding.

6. If there is a signal from the individual that they are experiencing anxiety, have them stay in the scene briefly. While they are still visualizing the scene instruct them to, "take a deep breath and exhale the anxiety, to imagine the tension and anxiety leaving their body. Let go of the anxiety and relax." Allow the person to remain in the relaxed state with the visualized image for one minute.

7. Once relaxation has been achieved with that step of the hierarchy, instruct the individual to turn off that image and again enter a state of relaxation without a visualized event from the hierarchy. This relaxation period can be done with further relaxation statements or a guided imagery to a safe and relaxing place. Allow them to remain in the relaxed state for a one minute.

8. Have the individual signal with raising the right index finger when total relaxation has been achieved. Check in at intervals of one minute monitoring the state of relaxation versus anxiety. When there is no anxiety present proceed to the next step.

9. Repeat the initial scene, going through the entire desensitization process. Continue to repeat this scene with desensitization until there is visualization of the scene without provoking anxiety. This can take two to four repetitions per scene.

10. Once anxiety has been eliminated at one step/event proceed onto the next imagined event, repeating the process as previously stated.

WHAT IS DEMENTIA?

Dementia is a medical term that describes when a person's intellectual capacity is impaired. Dementia is not a normal part of growing old. Older and younger people can develop dementia. A variety of diseases and disorders cause dementia. There are numerous kinds of dementia:

1. Presenile
2. Senile
3. Chronic
4. Organic brain syndrome
5. Arteriosclerosis
6. Cerebral atrophy

SYMPTOMS

1. Short-term memory loss
2. Inability to think problems through
3. Inability to complete simple tasks without supervision and stepwise instruction
4. Difficulty concentrating
5. Paranoia/distrust
6. Inappropriate/bizarre behavior

The National Institute on Aging states that there are more than 100 conditions that mimic serious disorders that are often treatable and reversible. These are referred to as psuedodementias.

CONDITIONS CAUSING REVERSIBLE SYMPTOMS

1. Reaction to medication
2. Emotional distress
3. Metabolic disturbances
4. Vision and hearing deficits
5. Nutritional deficiencies

6. Endocrine abnormalities
7. Infections
8. Subdural hematomas
9. Normal pressure hydrocephalus
10. Brain tumors
11. Atherosclerosis

CONDITIONS CAUSING DEMENTIA THAT ARE NOT REVERSIBLE

1. Head trauma
    A. Fall or accident (can cause personality, thinking, and behavior changes)
    B. If brain injury is mild, the previous level of functioning may be restored

2. Cerebral degenerative disease
    A. Progressive cognitive deterioration
        1. Alzheimer's Disease
        2. Parkinson's Disease
        3. Huntington's Chorea
        4. Pick's Disease
        5. Cereborvascular accident (stroke)
        6. Anoxia (loss of oxygen to the brain)
        7. Creutzfeld-Jakob's Disease
        8. Binswanger Disease
        9. AIDS
        10. Multiple Sclerosis

DIAGNOSIS

1. Complete physical and neuropsychological evaluation is recommended

*Much of the diagnostic testing is done to rule out any possible treatable causes of dementia.

UNDERSTANDING SCHIZOPHRENIA

Schizophrenia appears equally in men and women. However, if often appears earlier in men. The age of onset for women is in their twenties or thirties, whereas the age of onset for men is in their late teens or twenties. It is also possible for children to develop the disease, but it is uncommon for children to experience hallucinations or delusions prior to adolescence.

The experience of schizophrenia can be terrifying

1. Hearing internal voices
2. Belief that others are reading one's mind
3. Belief that others are controlling one's thoughts
4. Belief that others are plotting to cause one harm

SYMPTOMS OF PERCEPTUAL DISTURBANCE

1. Hallucinations and delusions
    A. Hallucinations can be auditory (sound), visual (sight), tactile (touch), olfactory (smell), and gustatory (taste)

*The most common type of hallucination is hearing voices that others do not hear. Auditory hallucinations can be of different associations:

    1. Describing the person's activities
    2. Carrying on a conversation
    3. Warning of impending danger
    4. Issuing orders to other individuals
    B. Delusions
    1. False beliefs with evidence to the contrary and numerous possible themes
    2. One-third of schizophrenics are of the "paranoid type" with delusions of persecution, which are false and irrational beliefs
    3. Other delusions include being cheated, harassed, poisoned, conspired against, being a victim of mind control by magnetic waves or television transmitting special messages, or granduer
    C. Disordered thinking
    1. Thoughts come and go rapidly
    2. Unable to concentrate on one thought for very long
    3. Easily distracted and unable to focus
    4. Unable to sort out what is and is not relevant
    5. Unable to connect thoughts in a logical sequence or continuity of thought
    D. Emotional expression
    1. Blunted or flat affect (severe decrease in emotional expression)
    2. May not show signs of normal expression
    3. May speak in monotone voice
    4. Diminished facial expression
    5. Appears extremely apathetic

POTENTIAL FOR VIOLENCE

Most individuals with schizophrenia are not prone to violent behavior. Instead, they are generally withdrawn. The use and abuse of substances increase the risk of violent behavior for those with schizophrenia just as it does in the general population. Individuals who discontinue medication that was prescribed to treat paranoia and psychotic symptoms are at increased risk for violent behavior. If violent behavior does transpire, it is generally focused on family members or friends and usually takes place in the home.

SUICIDE

Those with schizophrenia are at increased risk for suicide. It is a difficult illness to live with, and numerous losses are experienced.

WHAT CAUSES SCHIZOPHRENIA

1. Genetic relationship
    A. The illness does run in families
    B. Identical twins have the highest risk (40 to 50% if one's twin has the illness)

C. Children of a parent with schizophrenia have approximately a 10% risk

D. It appears that multiple genes are involved in creating a predisposition

E. There is evidence that prenatal trauma may be involved (intrauterine starvation, viral infections, perinatal complications, etc.)

F. It cannot yet be predicted who may develop the illness

G. To learn more about current research, visit the website at www-grb.nimh.nih.gov/gi.html

2. What is happening in the brain

A. There is continuing research regarding neurotransmitters (brain chemicals)

B. Studies show subtle abnormalities in the structure of the brain of some individuals

C. It may be a developmental disorder originating during fetal development

Source: Adapted from NIH Publication No. 00-3517.

TEN WARNING SIGNS OF ALZHEIMER'S DISEASE

According to the Alzheimer's Disease and Related Disorders Association, we should familiarize ourselves with the following ten warning signs of Alzheimer's disease:

1. *Memory loss.* This is specifically most identifiable when it affects job skills. Everyone forgets a name or an assignment once in a while, but frequent forgetfulness with confusion in the home or workplace is definitely a sign that something is wrong.
2. *Difficulty performing normal and familiar tasks.* For example, preparing a meal and then forgetting to serve it. This is not an issue of getting distracted or forgetting one course of a meal. You could apply this type of situation to many different tasks and see the disconnection.
3. *Difficulty with language.* Everyone from time to time has the experience of not being able to find a certain word when speaking or thinking about something. However, people with Alzheimer's forget simple words and substitute inappropriate words making it difficult to understand what they are saying.
4. *Disoriented to time and place.* This issue creates great concern for the family members of someone who has Alzheimer's disease. These individuals become lost in environments that have been familiar to them for years. They don't know where they are, how they got there, or how to get back home (like their own street and neighborhood).
5. *Poor judgment or a decrease in effective judgment.* They seem to lack the common sense of even self-care such as getting a sweater or coat on a cold day or wearing layers on a hot day. They do not dressing appropriately to go out on errands (such as wearing a bathrobe over clothes to the store).
6. *Difficulty with abstract thinking.* Recognizing numbers or performing elementary math operations may be impossible.
7. *Misplacing things.* Unlike the situation where someone misplaces their keys, the Alzheimer's patient may file away all kinds of items in totally inappropriate places and then not remember how they got there.
8. *Changes in mood or behavior.* A broad range of emotional expression is normal. Those with Alzheimer's disease may display quick inappropriate changes in emotion for no known reason. There may be an expression of being blank, vacant, or flat.
9. *Changes in personality.* While its not uncommon for our personalities to change as we age, the Alzheimer's patient's personality can change dramatically over a dramatic short period of time or over a longer period of time.
10. *Loss of initiative.* Everyone loses interest and wants to shirk responsibilities every now and then. However, when the individual with Alzheimer's disease has this experience, he/she may not reexperience or regain that interest and may remain uninvolved.

CAREGIVING OF ELDERLY PARENTS

It may be helpful to first clarify exactly what is taking place between you and your parents. Caregiving is a supportive role in which you are helping someone who is actively taking care of himself/herself. Caretaking involves doing for others what they are capable of doing for themselves and what they should do for themselves.

If you currently find yourself in a caretaking codependent relationship with your parents, you are likely rescuing and helping them to be less capable. These behaviors may result from efforts to please or elicit some other response from your parents. Old family patterns that may have had a negative influence on early emotional development can resurface and intensify as you become more codependently involved in your parent's lives. There are many issues that require attention and management:

1. The degree of help necessary
2. Transportation
3. Living arrangements
4. Health care
5. Financial issues
6. Emotional support
7. Issues of loss

The potential for blurred boundaries is significant. To avoid unnecessarily becoming a caretaker requires awareness and appropriate boundaries. Consider using the following information to create a healthy caregiving relationship while you continue to effectively live your own life:

1. Set appropriate boundaries
   A. Set limits
   B. Decide what you will, won't, and can't do
      1. Problem-solve alternatives
      2. Effectively utilize community resources

2. Live in the here and now
   A. Don't worry about what cannot be changed
   B. Don't worry about "what if"—deal with "what is"
   C. Live the feelings of today, stop anticipating what you may feel later
   D. Do what is right for you to do (for your heart and your conscience)
   E. Accept that parents may not follow medical recommendations (you can't control others)

3. Avoid excessive unnecessary worry
   A. This coincides with living in the here and now
   B. Don't second-guess decisions, acknowledge you are doing the best you can
   C. Stay focused on self-care and self-responsibility

*If you are feeling anger and resentment, you may not be taking care of your own needs. This is your first responsibility. If you are not the best you can be it will eventually take a toll on your supportive care of others.

4. Cope with what needs to be done
   A. No "What ifs"—the circumstances are what they are
   B. When you do what needs to be done without over thinking it doesn't feel so bad.
   C. Deal with it—even if that means the decision is to delegate, use other resources and assert your own limits

5. Avoid emotional blackmail
   A. Do not give into intimidation, tantrums, anger, silence, or being guilted into sympathy
   B. If you give in to negative efforts to get you to respond, you are likely to feel resentful and that is not fair. Take responsibility for the choices you make.
   C. Give adequate, appropriate care

6. Avoid the useless feeling of guilt
   A. Be clear about what you are doing and why you are doing it
   B. Recognize your own limitations
   C. Feel at peace by doing the best you can
   D. Don't self-criticize with "shoulds"

7. Exercise conservation of energy
   A. Avoid the stance of "I can do it all"
   B. Identify and utilize appropriate resources
   C. If you find yourself complaining a lot, use this awareness as an opportunity to make necessary changes
   D. If you find yourself experiencing physical fatigue or depression, you need to review your own needs and commitment to self-care and self-responsibility

8. Take care of yourself first
   A. If you are going to take care of some of the needs of another, it is imperative that you take care of yourself so that you have the physical and emotional energy to do what you feel is necessary
   B. Utilize resources
      1. Family
      2. Friends
      3. Professionals
      4. Community resources
   C. Get adequate rest, eat well, do things that you enjoy, spend time with people that are fun and who can distract you from your daily obligations. You need to laugh and to have fun.

9. Acceptance of current circumstances
   A. Don't waste your energy trying to think your way out—it won't change the situation
   B. Look realistically at the situation and make sensible choices
   C. Participate in a support group if one is available in your community
   D. If there are not any support groups for caregivers in your community, read on the subject to reinforce your positive efforts

10. Self-review
    A. From time to time, take an inventory of your
       1. Emotions
       2. Use of time
       3. Self-care
       4. Personal goals

B. Make amends when necessary

C. Evoke self-responsibility

D. Be honest with your parents about realistic limits

11. Obtain help for yourself

    A. It is painful to see those you love in pain and decompensating physically or psychologically

    B. Find resources in your community that are helpful and healing to you

    C. Review personal losses

        1. Health

        2. Relationships

        3. Enjoyed activities

        4. Finances

    D. Problem-solve what must be done

12. Grieve

    A. Grieving is a necessary part of letting go

    B. Share your thoughts and feelings of grief with those who care about you

    C. This is often a time of painful losses and the acknowledgment of powerlessness

    D. Don't get stuck with immobilizing grief over difficult changes. Some losses simply leave a hole in your heart that doesn't go away or heal over. That does not mean that you do not continue to move on normally in your life. It means you will always miss that person and, if you choose, you can get in touch with those feelings

COMMON PROBLEMS EXPERIENCED BY CAREGIVERS

1. Concerns about medical advice and expense

2. Learning how to maintain positive social supports

3. The resulting strain on a marriage and other important relationships

4. Less time and energy for other important people in the person's life and for himself/herself

5. Balancing the pressures of additional obligations such as work, child care, school, managing home/yard, and so on

EFFECTIVE COPING STRATEGIES FOR THE CARETAKER

1. Find a support group of others facing similar issues

2. Self-care

    A. Time for yourself

    B. Exercise

    C. Adequate sleep/nutrition

    D. Recreation

    E. Time with people you enjoy (laughter/distraction)

    F. Relaxation techniques

3. Ask for help from others when you need it

4. Be honest with your parents about

    A. Realistic limitations

    B. The need to feel appreciated

TIPS FOR THE CARETAKEE

1. Obtain the best possible medical care and always get a second opinion for serious diagnoses
2. Stay involved with friends and activities
3. Stay active mentally and physically
4. Take as much responsibility for yourself as possible

ADVICE FOR OTHERS CLOSE TO THE SITUATION

1. Communicate
   A. Talk honestly about the situation
   B. Be realistic about limits

2. Problem-solve how to be supportive
3. Use available community resources
4. Maintain the mutual giving and sharing in realtionships

*Remember, at some point in our lives we are likely to experience both roles. This thought may help to guide you in the decisions you make.

TEN WARNING SIGNS OF CAREGIVER STRESS

1. *Anger and frustration.* The person feels angry about the lack of effective medical treatment and diminishing feelings of hope. Frustration develops due to the lack of support available and insight with the experience.
2. *Denial.* The caregiver is in denial about the issues of loss, how things have changed, and how an illness has affected the person being cared for.
3. *Fatigue and exhaustion.* Fatigue is evident by never feeling like one adequately catches up with rest and sleep. Exhaustion makes even the smallest daily task seem impossible to complete. This chronic tiredness and feeling of ineffectiveness in one's own life takes a serious toll.
4. *Sleep disturbance.* Sleep is interfered with by continuous thoughts of what needs to be done and ongoing concerns.
5. *Social withdrawal.* Withdrawal from one's own support system occurs. What used to feel pleasurable no longer seems to matter.
6. *Feeling irritable.* Low frustration tolerance develops. These individuals become moody and restless. As a result, they seem to respond to others in a negative way more and more often. They make it clear by their tone of voice, what they say, and their body language that they would rather be left alone.
7. *Difficulty with concentration and attention.* Good concentration and attention requires adequate rest and energy. If you cannot keep you mind on what you are doing, it becomes increasingly difficult to get even simple tasks completed.

8. *Anxiety and stress.* Anxiety begins to develop as stress is experienced just by thinking about facing the responsibilities of another day. It is difficult to have positive feelings and hopefulness for the future.

9. *Depression.* Depression affects a person's ability to cope and effectively manage the demands of life.

10. *Health deterioration.* With depression, anxiety, and exhaustion, the immune system is suppressed and a person becomes more vulnerable to health problems.

If you are currently a caregiver to another, review these warning signs and consider the following recommendations:

1. Maintain a strong support system
2. Maintain your own daily schedule apart from the person who is cared for
3. Join a support group for caregivers
4. Utilize therapy as a resource
5. Make an appointment with your primary care physician and get a thorough examination

SLEEP DISORDERS

Sleep Disorders can be present due to factors such as physiological changes, changes in environment, distressing experiences, emotional difficulties, stress, or changes in daily routine. In dealing with Sleep Disorders there is a single goal: Improved sleep accompanied by increased feelings of restfulness.

TREATMENT FOCUS AND OBJECTIVES

1. Identify the nature and extent of the sleep disturbance
   A. Have the individual keep a sleep journal to more accurately determine the number of hours of sleep per night
   B. Assess the need to refer to specific support resources or for further evaluation

2. Rule out presence of concomitant impairment in physiological/psychological/emotional state which is contributing or responsible for the sleep disturbance

3. Evaluate and refer for psychopharmacological treatment

4. Devise and implement a behavioral management program for treating the sleep disturbance

Individuals who experience sleep disturbance may develop a "phobic"-type reaction which exacerbates their sleep difficulties and further negatively impacts their coping with lack of sleep because of self-defeating internal dialogue. Rule out substance abuse, medication reactions, menopause, pain, and excessive caffeine use.

TEN TIPS FOR BETTER SLEEP

People suffer from insomnia for different reasons. Sleep disturbance can be related to physiological changes such as menopause, medical problems such as hyperthyroidism, emotional distress such as depression or anxiety, changes in lifestyle such as having a baby or any other changes which may influence daily patterns, and general life stressors. Take a few minutes to review what may possibly be related to the difficulty that you are experiencing with sleep. If it has been some time since your last physical examination or you think that there may be a relationship between the sleep disturbance and physiological changes or a medical problem make an appointment with your physician to identify or rule out health-related issues. If health-related issues are definitely not a factor then consider the following ways to improve your sleep.

If you are not able to identify the exact symptoms of your insomnia keep a sleep journal for 2 weeks and write down your sleep-wake cycle, how many hours you sleep, and all the other details related to your sleep disturbance.

1. *Establish a regular time for going to bed, and be consistent.* This helps to cue you that it is time for sleep. Going to sleep at the same time and awakening at the same time daily helps stabilize your internal clock. Having a different sleep-wake schedule on the weekends can throw you off. For the best results be consistent.

2. *Do not go to bed too early.* Do not be tempted to try to go bed earlier than you would normally need to. If you have started doing this then identify the reason why (depression, stress, boredom, pressure from your partner). When people go to bed too early it contributes to the problem of fragmented sleep. Your body normally lets you sleep only the number of hours it need. If you go to bed too early you will also be waking too early.

3. *Determine how many hours of sleep you need for optimal functioning and feeling rested.* Consider the following to determine the natural length of your sleep cycle.
   A. How many hours did you sleep on the average as a child?
   B. Before you began to experience sleep difficulty how many hours of sleep per night did you sleep on the average?
   C. How many hours of sleep do you need to awaken naturally, without an alarm?
   D. How many hours of sleep do you need in order to not feel sleepy or tired during the day?

4. *Develop rituals which signal the end of the day.* Rituals that signal closure for the day could be tucking the kids in, putting the dog out, and closing up the house for the night ... then ... it's time for you to wind down by watching the news, reading a book (not an exciting mystery), having a cup of calming herbal tea, evening prayers, or doing something like meditation, deep breathing exercises, or progressive muscle relaxation. All of these behaviors are targeted for shifting your thinking from the daily stressors to closure that the day is over and it is time for rest so that you can start a new day tomorrow.

5. *Keep the bedroom for sleeping and sex only.* If you use your bedroom as an office or for other activities your mind will associate the bedroom with those activities which is not conducive to sleep.

6. *A normal pattern of sex can be helpful.* However, it is only helpful if you are engaging sex because you are interested in being close to your partner. Sexual stimulation releases endorphins that give you a mellow, relaxed feeling. Be careful to avoid trying to use sex to fall asleep. It can backfire because you are taking a pleasurable, ultimately relaxing behavior and putting expectations on it that can lead to pressure and feeling upset.

7. *Avoid physical and mental stimulation just before sleep time.* Exercising, working on projects, or house cleaning, watching something exciting on television, or reading something that has an exciting plot just prior to going to bed can energize you instead of helping you to have closure at the end of the day.

8. *Be careful of naps.* Some people are able to take naps and feel rejuvenated by them without interfering with their sleep-wake cycle. Other people may be overtired for various reasons and benefit from an hour nap early in the afternoon. However, for others it can be sabotaging. If you take naps skip them for a week. If you find that you are sleeping better without the naps then stop napping.

9. *Get regular exercise.* Regular aerobic exercise like walking can decrease body tension, alleviate stress, alleviate depressive symptoms, and contribute to an overall feeling of wellbeing. Less stress better sleep.

10. *Take a warm bath one to two hours before bedtime.* Experiment with the time to determine what works best for you. A good 20 minute soaking in a warm bath (100–102°F) is a great relaxer. It raises your core body temperature by several degrees which naturally induces drowsiness and sleep.

Be careful not to obsess about sleep. When someone is experiencing sleep disturbance they can become so focused on the issue of sleep that they nearly develop a phobia about not getting it, which creates a lot of stress and tension for them at the end of the day instead of relaxation which is necessary for the natural sleep rhythms to be initiated. Instead, try to relax and think about something pleasant. If, after 20 minutes, that does not work get up and go to another room to meditate, or engage in some other ritual that you find helpful to inducing feelings of drowsiness so you can sleep.

HEALTH INVENTORY

Use the following list to identify basic health-related habits:

1. Exercise regularly
2. Maintain good nutrition
3. Do not smoke
4. Avoid excessive snacking
5. Get seven to eight hours of sleep per night
6. Maintain normal weight
7. Avoid having more than three drinks in at a given time to prevent substance abuse
8. Maintain regular health checkups
9. Avoid overeating or weight gain
10. Be aware of chronic stress or anger

Other health concerns: _____

Take some time to consider the impact of your self-care/health behaviors.

1. What are your assets, and what is the current and potential benefit?

2. What are your problem areas, and what is the current and potential liabilities?

3. What areas of change are necessary?

4. What are you willing to change?

Plan: _____

_____

_____

_____

ASSESSING LIFESTYLE AND HEALTH

A. Current Risk Factors
    __hypertension   __elevated triglycerides   __elevated cholesterol
    __overeating   __excess salt, sugar, fat   __lack of exercise
    __chronic stress   __smoking   __overweight
    __alcohol abuse   __sleep disturbance   __prescription medication abuse

B. Nutrition
When you review your diet and compare it to one year ago and five years ago, is it the same, less healthy, or more healthy?

    1. The positive changes made are _____

    _____

    _____

    2. Changes that need to be made are _____

    _____

    _____

C. Stress Management
    1. Current level of stress is   __low   __moderate   __high
       To the following, respond never (N), sometimes (S), often (O), or always (A):
    2. In an effort to deal with stress;
       a. Exercise is used to decrease tension __
       b. Relaxation techniques are help for for releasing tension __

    3. Characteristics I have in common with those who manage stress well:
       a. Daily moments of peace and solitude __
       b. Playfulness and humor to improve mood __
       c. Positive relationships with family and friends __
       d. Distracting activities __
       e. Good level of frustration tolerance __
       f. Good ability to manage criticism __
       g. An ability to avoid overloaded scheduling __
       h. A good balance of work and pleasure __

D. Answer each of the following questions regarding your negative lifestyle habits:
    1. How is it a problem?

    2. How did it begin and develop?

    3. What could be some appropriate substitutes?

    4. What do you want to change?

E. Plan of change:

ASSUMING THE PATIENT ROLE: THE BENEFITS OF BEING SICK

_____

With real or perceived symptoms of chronic illness, an individual may experience benefits. To better understand yourself and your potential motivation to change, thoroughly think through the following issues.

Accidents, illnesses, symptoms (please list)

_____   _____

_____   _____

_____   _____

_____   _____

_____   _____

Choose an accident, illness, or symptom from your list to complete the following statements:

1. It happens when _____

2. It feels like _____

3. It prevents _____

4. It results in _____

5. I encourages _____

6. It demonstrates that I have a deep need for _____

7. It benefits me with _____

8. An appropriate way to get this need met would be to _____

_____

My plan for dealing with this issue:

_____

_____

_____

_____

_____

IMPROVING YOUR HEALTH

Ready to turn your life around? It may require that you make some changes in basic health behaviors, but the results are worth it. It's simple.

1. Eat right
2. Quit smoking
3. Decrease or eliminate alcohol consumption
4. Exercise and get fit
5. Learn to relax
6. Get adequate sleep
7. Live authentically (be honest, learn from life, and be true to yourself)

Even small changes can lead to significant health improvements. According to an article in *Time* (February 2001), 50 million Americans still smoke and 60% of the American population is obese or overweight:

1. Eating Right
   Educate yourself about the types of fat and their health consequences (for example, omega-3 from cold water fish is good and certain nuts are good; sparingly consume saturated fats, watch out for trans-fatty acids, which are found in crackers and cookies)
   A. Emphasize fruits and vegetables
   B. Promote low-fat dairy
   C. Promote high-fiber grains
   D. Promote modest portions of lean meat
   E. Reduce sodium intake
   F. Reduce alcohol intake (some studies demonstrate a health benefit for small portions of red wine; again, take responsibility and educated yourself)

2. Smoking
   A. The day you quit smoking, carbon monoxide levels in your blood drops significantly
   B. Within one week, blood becomes less sticky and death by heart attack declines
   C. After four to five years of not smoking, risk of heart attack is decreased to nearly the same as someone who has never smoked

3. Alcohol Consumption
   First of all, clarify why you are drinking. Is a glass of wine part of enjoying a good meal, or do you drink to relax, sleep, get high, or numb out? Be honest with yourself, and if you are not able to substitute positive health behaviors for self-medication, or if you cannot decrease drinking or stop drinking on your own, then seek professional help. Remember, some people can drink alcohol and experience some health benefits, others, not necessarily alcoholics, cannot tolerate alcohol use. Be honest and smart.

4. Exercise

A 40-year-old sedentary individual who starts walking briskly for half an hour a day, four days a week, has almost the same low risk of heart attack as the person who has always exercised.

5. Learning to Relax

Adequate rest includes getting enough hours of rejuvenating sleep and reconditioning your body to know what it feels like to be relaxed. With the fast pace of life and daily demands, people sometimes forget what it feels like to not be making lists in your head, stressing about deadlines today, and worrying about the tasks of tomorrow. Exercise, soothing music, doing art, hobbies, pleasure reading, formal relaxation, and meditation are all choices for relaxing. Make sure to throw in a healthy dose of laughter every day. Genuine laughter, smiling, and happy/pleasing thoughts are healing. Likewise, attitude influences health, emotional functioning, and how you share your life with others. Are you honest, friendly kind, and optimistic, or sour, angry, hostile, and negative? Guess what is good for health and happiness and which isn't?

6. Sleep

Research continues to confirm the importance of sleep in optimal physical, emotional, and psychological functioning. If you are experiencing difficulty sleeping, talk with your physician to make sure that there are not any physical reasons contributing to sleep disturbance (such as sleep apnea). Also, it is important to have a regular schedule, which conditions your body to wind down and prepare for sleep.

7. Living Authentically

Be true to yourself. Take responsibility for your own thoughts and feelings. Don't live in the past or hold grudges. If there are issues that you need to resolve do so, learn, heal, and move forward integrating whatever you learn into your life experience—it is a part of who you are and cannot be erased. Consciously choose how you think about things, and respond in the way that is best for you. Self-responsibility is the only way to successfully bring sustaining positive changes to your life.

As you review your life and health, use a journal to record the following:

1. Identify what is good (be grateful)
2. Identify what needs to be changed
   A. Why?
   B. What is the goal?
   C. What steps need to be taken?
   D. How can changed be reinforced and maintained?
   E. What will you need to self-monitor?
3. Clarify and understand why you have chosen negative health behaviors or emotional responses
   A. Self-medication
   B. Lack of insight and awareness
   C. Lack of motivation/self-responsibility
   D. What motivates the decision to change now?

4. What resources may be helpful in reaching you goals?
   A. Gym, walking, jogging, cycling, exercise videos, organized sports
   B. Yoga or other classes
   C. People who are supportive of positive health behaviors
   D. Maintaining a journal

5. Educate yourself on the role of emotions on healthful or harmful thinking or feeling:
   A. Anger
   B. Hostility
   C. Anxiety

HEART DISEASE AND DEPRESSION

FACTS ON DEPRESSION AND HEART DISEASE OFFERED BY THE NATIONAL INSTITUTE OF HEALTH

1. Depression is common and treatable. Nearly 10% of the adult population experiences depression. Unfortunately, it is often not identified.

2. Depression affects those with heart disease at a much higher rate and can have devastating consequences

3. Among individuals with heart disease, depression occurs in 18 to 20% of those who have not had a heart attack

4. Among those who have a history of having a heart attack, the rate of depression is 40 to 65%

5. Major depression appears to increase disability in heart patients
   A. It may contribute to a worsening of symptoms
   B. It may contribute to poor adherence to cardiac treatment regimens

6. Heart attack survivors with major depression have a three to four times greater risk of dying within six months than those who do not suffer from depression

7. Treating depression when it occurs in heart patients can minimize or help patients to avoid some of the serious health consequences

BENEFITS OF DEPRESSION TREATMENT

1. Treatment of depression can benefit the heart patient through
   A. Improved medical status
   B. Enhanced quality of life
   C. Reduced pain and disability
   D. Improved cooperation with treatment

2. Early treatment of depression can reduce the risk of relapse or recurrence of depression

DEPRESSION IS OFTEN UNDIAGNOSED AND UNTREATED

1. There are several reasons why depression in cardiac patients goes untreated
   A. Depressive symptoms are dismissed as temporary low mood, which is often associated with serious illness

B. It may be overlooked

C. It may be viewed as the side-effects of cardiac treatment

D. If the person is older, if may be viewed simply as a part of aging

2. Major depression presents with symptoms that are more severe, last longer, and are more disabling than the expected reaction

EFFECTIVE TREATMENT FOR DEPRESSION

1. With treatment, up to 80% of depressed individuals can improve

2. Treatment usually includes medication and psychotherapy

3. The severity of depression, the other conditions present, and the medical treatment being used must be considered to determine appropriate treatment

Depression can be overcome through appropriate diagnosis and treatment. Persons with a heart disorder, their loved ones, and their physician should be alert to symptoms of depression so that early treatment can be initiated.

EATING HISTORY

To increase your awareness for eating patterns and bahavioral patterns associated with eating, please use the following to write your eating history. Use this as an opportunity to better understand and be honest about your loss of control in regard to food use or rituals and practices surrounding your food use. Share your eating history with another person or with your therapist.

Consider the following:

1. Kinds, amounts, and frequency of food use

2. Foggy memories or difficulty concentrating after eating too much

3. Feeling high after vomiting or starving.
    a. Feeling powerful when "choosing to withhold food or correcting food mistakes" by throwing up (fully of power in demonstrating this self-control to self others.)

4. Behavior changes
    a. Mood swings with eating/not eating
    b. Withdrawal from others to eat or starve
    c. How relationships change and why

5. Rituals surrounding food use
    a. Overeating or binge eating on certain foods
    b. Frequent eating out
    c. Sneak eating/eating in secret
    d. Weighing self daily or more often
    e. Eating/not eating certain food(s)

6. Preoccupation
    a. Thinking about eating/not eating
    b. Eating for relief from problems, boredom, frustration, and so on

  c. Protecting your food supply; hiding food

  d. Preoccupation with body size

7. Attempts to control eating or weight

  a. Doctor's diets

  b. Fad diets

  c. Diet pills or shots

  d. Starving, vomiting, laxative use, diuretics, or manual extraction of stool

  e. Diet clubs or fat farms

  f. Hypnosis, acupuncture, stomach stapling, or gastric bypass surgery

  g. Spending money to control eating or weight

8. Family/friend response

  a. To your eating patterns

  b. To changes in your appearance

HOW TO STOP USING FOOD AS A COPING MECHANISM

Some people experience difficulty expressing their emotions and resolving associated issues. Over time, they may identify food as the source of comfort hey are looking for. By this time it is quite possible that they are experiencing depression. Therefore, their use of food as a mechanism to cope has (1) created a cycle of conditioned behavior that maintains depression and (2) become a demonstration of self-medication.

| Emotional distress | → | Internalizes distress | → | Thinks about food/eating | → | Engages in compulsion | → | Numbs out | → | Feels guilty/bad |

The irony of this cycle is that these individuals often do not even notice the taste or how much they are eating. The distress and emptiness cannot alleviated with food. The foods often eating under these condition are sugars and starches. These foods increase serotonin in the brain and temporarily alleviate emotional distress. Therefore, these two issues must be confronted: (1) reconditioning, which involves learning new ways to cope and take care of yourself and (2) understanding the role of your specific brain chemistry. Consider the following information as resources for developing new coping mechanisms:

1. Increase self-understanding and self-awareness. Keep a self-awareness journal that records what are you doing and why are you doing it. Keep a food journal. Write down exactly what you eat, when, and how you felt.

2. Create a habit of asking yourself why you feel like eating. If you are not hungry, take responsibility for making a better choice. Create a list of behaviors you can do in an effort to get redirected.

3. Identify what you are feeling. Identify what the feeling is associated with (thoughts and experiences), and identify your choices for "dealing" with the feeling.

4. Acknowledge that life is never without issues to deal with. Don't ruminate about it, don't worry about it, don't procrastinate. Whatever it is, deal with it (without food) and move on.

5. Be assertive about how you feel instead of using food as a coping mechanism. Compulsive eating is a negative way of expressing feelings that are being stuffed.

6. Develop realistic expectations about working through emotional distress that has built up over a period of time. Just because you have identified the problem and are practicing positive health behaviors and improved coping does not mean that everything is immediately resolved. Continue to journal for increased clarity and problem solving, and practice appropriately and honestly expressing your thoughts and feelings.

7. Focus on what is working in your life, use positive self-talk, and develop genuine gratitude. Find the silver lining in clouds. What positive things have you learned through difficult experiences? You often do not have any control over things that happen, but you do have control in how you choose to deal with them.

8. Identify triggers. What thoughts, feelings, and situations serve as setups for relapse. This would be a good topic for putting your journal to good use. Be prepared and be self-responsible. Life is about choices, so use choices that help you.

9. Consider joining a support group that reinforces positive health behaviors and self-care.

10. Talk with your doctor about health changes and medications that increase serotonin.

PREVENTING WEIGHT AND BODY IMAGE PROBLEMS IN CHILDREN

Increased stress, ever-present media, convenience food and soda, and decreased physical activity have led to an overconcern about physical appearance with decreased tolerance for all the normal variations in body types, and an epidemic of obesity in children. Children have become more concerned about their weight and body image at an earlier age (as early as 6 to 9 years old). However, children who are obese do not necessarily have lower self-esteem than nonobese children.

Obesity among children has now become a health concern that can make some medical issues worse and lead to others (such as diabetes, joint problems, hypertension, premature onset on periods and irregular periods, etc.). Both genetic and environmental factors affect a child's potential for obesity. Therefore, it may be important for both you and your child to change some habits. Consult with your family physician or nutritional specialist, attend nutrition classes, and educate yourself by reading about how to eat healthfully. Continuously bringing up exercise and dieting to children and adolescents can create conflicts, resistance, and negatively affect self-esteem. Therefore, problem-solve what changes you will make that sets the tone for nutrition and exercise. Your children will learn from you. Be a more active family. Make activity fun an important part of your lifestyle.

OBSESSION WITH WEIGHT

While being obsess is not necessarily related directly to lower self-esteem, there is still warranted concern:

1. Peer cruelty
2. Parental focus on weight

A. May cause a child to develop feelings of inadequacy
B. A develop potential precursor to eating disorders

3. Media continuously portraying the cultural perception of thin as attractive

OBESITY AND SELF-ESTEEM

1. Obesity is not always related to the lowering of self-esteem
2. Self-esteem is more likely to be associated with how
   A. Family members respond to weight issues
   B. Social experiences
   C. Development of effective coping skills

WHAT PARENTS CAN DO

1. Set a healthy example
   A. Physical activity
   B. Nutrition
   C. Not being negatively judgmental about different body types

*Children develop adult perceptions of attractiveness as early as age 7

2. Make sure that children know and feel they are loved regardless of their weight
   1. Do not focus on their weight
   2. Focus on spending time with them
   3. Focus on teaching them effective life-management skills

GUIDELINES TO FOLLOW IF SOMEONE YOU KNOW HAS AN EATING DISORDER

1. Don't pretend that everything is okay when it is not. Anorexia and bulimia are serious illnesses. These eating disorders are self-destructive behaviors (starving, binging, purging). They are scream for help with underlying problems like depression, and they can become life threatening. So don't be silent-be honest and address your concerns.
2. Approach you family member or friend in a gentle, caring manner, but be persistent. Listen without interrupting. However, let your family member know how concerned you are. Do not expect an admission of a problem or changes just because you address your concern.
3. Pay attention to what you witness or experience in the way of changes in your family member or friend, such as anorexia, which is indicated by significant weight loss, obsessive dieting, hyperactivity, distorted body image (seeing oneself as fat when the person is thin) or Bulimia, indicated when someone eats a lot of food and then rushes to the bathroom, or uses laxatives.

4. Do not focus on the eating habits of those you are concerned about. Instead, try to encourage an understanding of why they are engaging in eating disorder behaviors.

5. Encourage them to get help because of their unhappiness. If you have noticed increased fatigue, irritability, depression, anxiety, or compulsiveness, be supportive in their getting help.

6. Being supportive is the best that you can offer. It is important to show you believe in them. Be emotionally available, and do not judge.

7. If possible, offer a written list of resources in your community, online, and in books. Again, do not expect an admission of a problem, just share the resources.

8. Do not keep this to yourself and deal with alone. Colluding with secrecy is not helpful—things are likely to get worse. Confide in someone that you trust. Be honest about not keeping it a secret, and say that you are speaking out because you care.

9. Deal with your own emotions. How have you been affected by this experience? Talk to someone about your own feelings.

10. Be clear that you are not responsible for your family member or friend. You can only encourage these loved ones to help themselves.

Adapted from *Glamour* Magazine (1985, March). Conde Nast Publications.

DEALING WITH FEAR

Fear is not a character flaw. It is a survival mechanism designed to protect you. It is meant to be a warning. However, it does more than just warn you, it makes the heart beat faster as your body prepares itself for fight or flight. However useful fear may be at times, when it becomes irrational and prevents you from doing normal things, it then becomes a problem. Use the following information to appropriately manage and recover from problem fear.

1. *Stop looking for the answer—it doesn't matter why you are afraid.* When you think about something that scared you as a kid (and still does), does thinking about it take away the fear? The memory may not even be accurate. You don't need to know exactly how or when you developed your fear to put your fear to rest. Instead, work on ways to overcome the fear you experience.

2. *End fear by knowledge.* Since fear is a protective mechanism, find out what you are afraid of. A powerful part of the experience of fear is unpredictability or uncertainty. Therefore, when the situation becomes predictable, fear decreases. The more accurate and realistic your information, the more prepared you will feel in dealing with it.

3. *Practice doing it.* The more you know how to do something or are clear about how you want to respond, the more fear seems to evaporate. If there is something you want to do but are afraid, train for it so that you develop a sense of "can do" or self-confidence.

4. *Find positive role models who you can learn from.* They are rational and accurate in what they do. Their courage is calming and contagious.

5. *Talking helps.* Opening up about your fears can decrease distress even when you can't change the situation. Likewise, trying to keep your feelings of fear a secret isn't going to get you the help you need.

6. *Use your imagination.* Remind yourself that fear isn't the end of the world. For example, fear of public speaking is the number one phobia. There are numerous "mind tricks" for dealing with this fear, such as imagining you are speaking to children or that something is funny about everyone in the audience, which decreases the fear of being judged by them. Get creative in problem-solving. How you think about a situation may be helpful.

7. *Focus on the little things.* Little things are always manageable. Figure out what you have to do and do it one step at a time.

8. *Give yourself permission to get help.* If the symptoms are severe, you may have an anxiety disorder that could be treated by medication and therapy. However, even if the symptoms are not severe, it may be useful to seek professional help.

9. *Find ways to decrease the physical and emotional stress associated with fear.* These may include exercise, positive self-talk, and progressive muscle relaxation or meditation.

10. *Develop a hierarchy of experiences that range from not causing fear or/minimal fear leading up to the most feared experience which is the goal to overcome.* This is called systematic desensitization and a therapist can do this technique with you. Another technique is called "flooding," whereby you are continually exposed directly to the feared object or situation until the fear response is diminished.

GUIDELINES FOR FAMILY MEMBERS/SIGNIFICANT OTHERS OF ALCOHOLIC/CHEMICALLY DEPENDENT INDIVIDUALS

1. Do not view Alcoholism/Chemical Dependency as a family or social disgrace. Recovery can and does happen.

2. Do not nag, lecture, or preach. Chances are that they have already told themselves everything that you might say. People tune out to what they do not want to hear. Being nagged or lectured may lead to lying and may put them in a position of making promises they cannot keep.

3. Be careful that you do not come off sounding and acting like a martyr. Be aware, because you can give this impression without saying a word. Look at your own attitudes and behavior.

4. Do not try to control their behavior with "if you loved me." Because the individual using substances is compulsive in their behavior such pleas only cause more distress. They have to decide to stop because it is their choice.

5. Be careful to guard against feelings or jealousy or feeling left out because of the method of recovery that they choose. Love, home, and family is not enough to support abstinence from substance abuse. Gaining self-respect is often more important in the early stages of recovery than other personal relationship responsibilities.

6. Support responsible behavior in the chemically dependent individual. Do not do for them what they can do for themself or do what they must do for themself. No one can do this for them, they must do it for themselves. Instead of removing the problem, allow them to see it, solve it, and deal with the consequences of it.

7. Begin to accept, understand, and to live One Day At A Time.

8. Begin to learn about the use of substances and what role it plays in an individual's life and what role you have played in the life of a substance abuser. Be willing to assume responsibility for your own life and totally give up any attempt to control the behavior and to change the substance abuser—even for their own good.

9. Participating in your own support group, like a 12-Step meeting such as Alanon can help you in your own recovery from the dysfunctional behaviors in this relationship and possibly similar behaviors in other relationships as well.

10. Recognize and accept that whatever you have been doing does not work. Understand what your own behavior is about. Acknowledge that your life has become as unmanageable as the substance abuser so that you can learn to be free to make better choices instead of reacting to what is the responsibility of someone else. Know where you end and they begin.

DETACHING WITH LOVE VERSUS CONTROLLING

One of the hardest, but most important goals for people close to an individual in recovery to learn, is to detach from the behaviors/substance abuse process and continue to love the person.

What does detachment mean? It can sound frightening, given that everyone's life (especially family members) has revolved around the chemically dependent person—always trying to anticipate what will happen next, covering up for them, etc. Detaching with love is an attitude which is associated with behaviors that are not controlling.

What does controlling mean? Controlling behavior is the need to have people, places, and things, be "my way." Expecting the world to be what you want it to be for you. Living your life with "shoulds" and "ought to be." Not expressing your feelings honestly, but with self-centeredness and manipulation of the environment around you. Feeling okay if things are the way you want them to be regardless of the needs or desires of others. It is a behavior that comes from fear—fear of the unknown, of "falling apart" if people and situations are not the way you want them to be. It is a symptom of a family or systems dysfunction. It is a reaction to the substance abuse that evolves out of feeling increasing responsibility for the substance-abusing person.

As the illness within the substance-abusing individual progresses so do the projections: "If it were not for you I would not drink to drink/use other substances." Statements like this contribute to a deterioration of self-worth with the result being that you believe that you are the key to change this awful mess by controlling your world, and the people in it. You become exhausted, frustrated, and resentful. Resentment comes from people not doing what you want them to do—and resentment kills love.

You must accept that:

1. Chemical dependency is an illness.
2. You did not cause it.
3. You cannot control it.
4. You cannot cure it.

Detaching from the illness and the substance-abusing individual's behaviors allows them to take responsibility for themselves—and allows you to be free to feel the love for the individual.

When you begin taking care of yourself and doing and being responsible for yourself, you have the key to peace, serenity, sanity, and really feeling good about who you are.

THE ENABLER—THE COMPANION TO THE DYSFUNCTIONAL/SUBSTANCE-ABUSING PERSON

Substance abuse and substance dependency can have devastating consequences for the individual using the substances as well as for those closely associated with them. Of most concern is the individual who may reside with the substance-abusing individual or who spends a significant amount of time with them. Typically, they begin to react to the symptoms of the individual, which results in the "concerned person" unsuspectingly conspiring with the dysfunctional behavior/illness and actually enabling it to progress and get worse. This "enabling" behavior surrounds and feeds the dependency.

How does the dysfunctional behaviors/illness affect the dependent individual? For the substance-dependent individual they completely lose their ability to predict accurately when they will start and stop their substance use. Because of this they become engaged repeatedly and unexpectedly in such behaviors as:

1. Breaking commitments that they intended to keep.
2. Spending more money than they planned.
3. Driving under the influence (DUI) violations.
4. Making inappropriate statements to friends, family, and co-workers.
5. Engaging in arguing, fighting, and other antisocial behaviors.
6. Using more of the substance(s) than they had planned.

These types of behaviors violate their internal value system resulting in feelings of guilt, remorse, and self-loathing. However, these feelings get blocked by rationalizations and projections. The rationalization is that "last night wasn't that bad." The projection causes the individual to believe that "anyone would be doing what I am doing if they had to put up with what I do." The effects of such use of defenses is to progressively lead the individual to be out of touch with reality. This distortion becomes so solid that the individual using substances or engaging in other dysfunctional behaviors is the last to recognize that their behavior represents any type of personal problem.

What is an enabler? It is the person who reacts to the above symptom of illness/dysfunctional behavior in such a way as to shield and protect them from experiencing the consequences of their problem. Thus, they lose the opportunity to gain insight regarding the severity of their behavior. Without this insight they remain a victim of the defenses and are incapable of recognizing the need to seek appropriate and necessary help. Tragically, the enabler's well-intentioned behavior plays an increasingly destructive role in the progression of the illness/dysfunctional behaviors.

The enabler continues their behavior because they see all that they have done as a sincere effort to help. While they see the negative behavior as isolated attempts to cope with difficult situations or something that just got a little out of hand, their behavior serves to reinforce the issues of rationalization, denial, and projections related to the substance abuse/dysfunctional behaviors.

The enabler may be in denial themselves about the significance or severity of the problem. Their thinking may be that the problem does not really exist or that it will disappear as soon as the real problem disappears. This makes the enabler highly vulnerable to developing beliefs and attitudes which victimize the individual engaging in substance abusing/dysfunctional behaviors. The rationalizations of both persons are now supporting each other's misunderstanding of the true nature of the problem. The result is that they are both engaged in a successful self-deception which allows the disease to remain hidden and to progress to a more serious stage.

The substance abuse/dysfunctional behaviors continue to have an increasingly adverse effect on both individuals. To understand the progression of the type of thinking that the individual engaged in substance abuse/dysfunctional behavior has it is important to understand what a successful defense system projection serves:

1. They take the unconscious and growing negative feelings about the self and put them onto other people and situations. This relieves some of stress that they feel inside and allows them to continue to live in an increasingly painful situation. The individual does not have any insight, and as a result they continue to experience more pain which leads to further projections or putting it off on other—What a vicious circle.

2. As the individual with the substance abuse/dysfunctional behavior problem continues to verbalize their projections on the other person, there is no realization from either party that this is being said out of hatred. Both believe that the individual hates the enabler and for good reason (because of the view that they are the source of the problem). The consequence is that they now both focus on the enabler's behavior and this allows the problem behavior to continue to go unseen as the central issue.

It is easy to see how this defense can have a significant emotional affect on the enabler. This becomes a pivotal point in the process of enabling. As the pain from the projections becomes more painful and uncomfortable, the enabler reacts by feeling hurt, injured, and guilty. The result is avoidance behavior. Less and less is expected of the individual with the substance abuse/dysfunctional behaviors because of the distress that it causes. These avoidant reactions only allow the progression of the problem. The individual with substance abuse/dysfunctional behaviors remains out of touch with reality, does not receive honest feedback of the behaviors causing the difficulties at home, work, school, etc. What develops is a "no talk" rule. By the enabler not directly expressing the issues, the individual with substance abuse/dysfunctional behaviors becomes more removed from any insight into their behaviors and its harmful consequences.

The enabler is not always able to avoid the individual with substance abuse/dysfunctional behaviors. Where relationships are very close, then the increasing projections create in the enabler a growing feeling of guilt and blame. They begin to feel responsible for the individual's self-defeating and self-destructive behavior. These feelings of self-doubt, inadequacy, and guilt continue to increase with the progression of the severity of the problem.

Unfortunately, the tendency is for the enabler's controlling behavior to escalate. The only way for them to feel positive to "try to make sure that the behavior does not get out of control." "If there are things that I did to cause this, then I can make it go away." Most of their efforts are manipulative. They do things indirectly in an effort to get the behavior they want. These manipulations are destined to fail. Nothing is being confronted and dealt with. As the enabler's feelings of low self-worth increase, it triggers even more desperate attempts of control. The cycle continues and escalates as both parties become increasingly alienated and dysfunctional.

The way to break the cycle is through knowledge and understanding:

1. Learn about the dynamic of chemical dependency and other dysfunctional behaviors.
2. Learn about the dynamics of being an enabler and the importance of self-care.
3. Become aware of the personal identification with the compulsive behavior of enabling.

With the development of this knowledge and insight the enabler can begin to respond to an individual with substance abuse/dysfunctional behavior in a meaningful and honest way versus control and manipulation. This will help the enabler let go of the responsibility for the behavior of others. The result is that the enabler become a person who lives life consciously and takes responsibility for themselves, thus becoming an agent of change who no longer reinforces dysfunctional behaviors through control and manipulation. This allows them to intervene directly in functional ways which promotes change not maintains the status quo.

SUBSTANCE ABUSE/DEPENDENCE PERSONAL EVALUATION

1. Age of first drug use?
2. What drug did you use?
3. Who introduced you to drugs?
4. What drug(s) did you go on to use after that?
5. What was your reason for using drugs?
6. Did you ever try to stop?
7. If so, what is it like when you aren't using?
8. Do your friends use?
9. Are you easily influenced by others?
10. Family history of substance abuse?
11. Do you and your significant other use together?
12. How has drug abuse affected your life?
13. What do you see as your options?
14. What do you have to do to abstain from drug abuse?
15. Have you been to a treatment program before or attended 12-Step meetings?
16. What do you feel like when you are using?
17. How do you think you benefit from using/or what do you get out of it?
18. How do you view drug screening in the workplace/school?

LIST OF SYMPTOMS LEADING TO RELAPSE

1. *Exhaustion.* Allowing yourself to become overly tired. Not following through on self-care behaviors of adequate rest, good nutrition, and regular exercise. Good physical health is a component of emotional health. How you feel will be reflected in your thinking and judgment.

2. *Dishonesty.* It begins with a pattern of small, unnecessary lies with those you interact with in family, socially, and at work. This is soon followed by lying to yourself or rationalizing and making excuses for avoiding working your program.

3. *Impatience.* Things are not happening fast enough for you. Or, others are not doing what you want them to do or think they should do.

4. *Argumentative.* Arguing small insignificant points which indicates a need to always be right. This is sometimes seen as developing an excuse to drink.

5. *Depression.* Overwhelming and unaccountable despair may occur in cycle. If it does, talk about it and deal with it. You are responsible for taking care of yourself.

6. *Frustration.* With people and because things may not being going your way. Remind yourself intermittently that things are not always going to be the way that you want them.

7. *Self-Pity.* Feeling like a victim, refusing to acknowledge that you have choices and are responsible for your own life and the quality of it.

8. *Cockiness.* "Got it Made." Compulsive behavior is no longer a problem. Start putting self in situations where there are temptations to prove to others that you don't have a problem.

9. *Complacency.* Not working your program with the commitment that you started with. Having a little fear is a good thing. More relapses occur when things are going well than when not.

10. *Expecting Too Much From Others.* "I've changed, why hasn't everyone else changed too?". All that you control is yourself. It would be great if other people changed their self-destructive behaviors, but that is their problem. You have your own problems to monitor and deal with. You cannot expect others to change their lifestyle just because you have.

11. *Letting Up On Discipline.* Daily inventory, positive affirmations, 12-Step meetings, therapy, meditation, prayer. This can come from complacency and boredom. Because you cannot afford to be bored with your program, take responsibility to talk about it and problem solve it. The cost of relapse is too great. Sometimes you must accept that you have to do some things that are the routine for a clean and sober life.

12. *The Use Of Mood-Altering Chemicals.* You may feel the need or desire to get away from things by drinking, popping a few pills, etc., and your physician may participate in thinking that you will be responsible and not abuse the medication. This is about the most subtle way to enter relapse. Take responsibility for your life and the choices that you make.

WHAT IS CODEPENDENCY?

Codependency is defined as when someone becomes so preoccupied with someone else that they neglect themself. In a way it is believing that something outside of themselves can give them happiness and fulfillment. They payoff in focusing on someone else is a decrease in painful feelings and anxiety.

Some people are in an emotional state of fear, anxiety, pain, or feeling like they are going crazy, and they feel these emotions strongly almost all the time. These people tend to think they can make those around them happy, and when they can't, they feel somehow less than others, they feel like they have failed.

These are people who tend to hold things in and then at inappropriate times they overreact, or they just have a tendency to overreact (e.g., something frightening happens and instead of experiencing normal fear they panic or experience anxiety attacks).

Codependency is when people operate as if they are okay only if they please the people around them.

They live with the false belief that the bad feelings they have can be gotten rid of if they can just "do it better" or if they can win the approval of certain important people in their life. By doing this they make those people and their approval responsible for their own happiness.

Often codependent people appear gentle and helpful. However, in this situation, two different things may be going on:

1. They may be struggling with a strong need to control and manipulate those around them into giving them the approval they believe they need to feel okay.
2. They minimize their emotions until they hardly experience any emotion at all. No fear, pain, anger, shame, joy, or pleasure. They just exist from one day to the next—numb.

It was actually the families of alcoholics and other chemically dependent people who brought these two clusters of symptoms to the attention of professionals.

THE CLASSIC SITUATION

The codependents' efforts were apparently to get the alcoholic or chemically dependent person sober and free from drugs. If they could help the alcoholic the family members would be free of pain, shame, fear, and anger.

But they found that that doesn't really work because even when the alcoholic got sober the family stayed sick and sometimes even appeared to resent the sobriety. Sometimes they sabotaged it.

It was as if the family needed the addict to stay sick and dependent on them so that they could maintain their dependence on the addict as a way of explaining their own experience and how they felt.

In other words, the addict and the codependent are trying to solve similar basic symptoms of the same disease: the addict with alcohol or drugs and the codependent with the addictive relationship.

Codependency may be difficult to see from the outside because people who suffer from codependency generally appear adequate and successful. This is because they are involved in things to win them the all important approval they need.

It's a vicious cycle of addiction because it is common for the codependent to at some point turn to drugs to numb their discomfort. Codependents are set up to be alcoholics or other kinds of addicts.

As you read these examples what do you identify with?

_____

_____

_____

_____

_____

_____

SOME CHARACTERISTICS OF CODEPENDENCE

1. My good feelings about who I am stem from being liked by you and receiving approval from you.
2. Your struggles affect my serenity. I focus my mental attention on solving your problems or relieving your pain.
3. I focus my mental attention on pleasing you, protecting you, or manipulating you to "do it my way."
4. I bolster my self-esteem by solving your problems and relieving your pain.
5. I put aside my own hobbies and interests. I spend my time sharing your interests and hobbies.
6. Because I feel you are a reflection of me, my desires dictate your clothing and personal appearance.
7. My desires dictate your behavior.

8. I am not aware of how I feel. I am aware of how you feel.

9. I am not aware of what I want. I ask you what you want.

10. If I am not aware of something, I assume (I don't ask or verify in some other way).

11. My fear of your anger and rejection determines what I say or do.

12. In our relationship I use giving as a way of feeling safe.

13. As I involve myself with you, my social circle diminishes.

14. To connect with you, I put my values aside.

15. I value your opinion and way of doing things more than my own.

16. The quality of my life depends on the quality of yours.

17. I am always trying to fix or take care of others while neglecting myself.

18. I find it easier to give in and comply with others than to express my own wants and needs.

19. I sometimes feel sorry for myself, feeling no one understands. I think about getting help, but rarely commit or follow through.

SUGGESTED DIAGNOSTIC CRITERIA FOR CODEPENDENCE

1. Continued investment of self-esteem in the ability to control both oneself and others in the face of adverse consequences.

2. Assumption of responsibility for meeting other's needs to the exclusion of acknowledging one's own needs.

3. Anxiety and boundary distortions around intimacy and separation.

4. Enmeshment in relationships with personality-disordered, chemically dependent and impulse-disordered individuals.

5. Exhibits at least three of the following.
   A. excessive reliance on denial
   B. constriction of emotions (with or without outbursts)
   C. depression
   D. hypervigilance
   E. compulsions
   F. anxiety
   G. alcohol or other drug abuse
   H. recurrent victim of sexual abuse
   I. stress-related medical illnesses
   J. has remained in a primary relationship with an actively mistreating or abusing person for at least 2 years without seeking outside support.

Adapted from Cermak (1986). Cermak believes that approximately 95% of the population grew up in a dysfunctional home, and that 5% of those individuals fit this diagnostic criteria.

Another model describing codependence is called the "iceberg model." Again this model depicts the codependent as growing up in a dysfunctional family of origin as well as living in an unhealthy society with two major criteria at the foundation: abandonment and shame.

As children they feel many things; there is a dominance of emptiness. In many ways their life journey is an effort to fill the emptiness. This may result in experiencing painful consequences which include: depression, anxiety, chemical dependence, eating disorders, other compulsions, relationship addiction, and stress-related disorders.

Codependency can be thought of as the growth stopping behaviors that occur between two people. Such behavior is on a continuum from infrequent and not particularly significant to frequent and destructive.

Examples that might exist on a continuum are:

1. A father who is contacted by the school about his teenage son being absent. The father covers for the teenager so that he won't get in trouble. This prevents the son from experiencing the consequences of making bad choices. The result is that it creates an opportunity to reinforce poor decision-making skills.

2. The house always needs to be picked up, but instead of making everyone responsible to pick up after themselves the oldest daughter always does it "to avoid an argument."

3. The alcoholic who has a hangover and can't make it to work every other Monday never is confronted with the consequences of his substance dependence because his wife always calls in the office that he is sick. This is just one of the ways she protects him. However, there are also enumerable fights about her wanting him to quit drinking.

In each situation you have somone trying to control what another person's experience will be. As a result the person is denied being put in a situation in which they have no choice but to deal with the consequences of their behavior are. Additionally, each person has the risk or tendency to become more embedded in their role.

Others_____

_____

_____

_____

_____

_____

HOW DOES CODEPENDENCY WORK

Codependency creates a set of rules for communicating and interacting in relationships.

1. It's not okay to talk about problems.
   "Don't air your dirty laundry in public."
   Never hear mom and dad arguing but there is often a lot of tension.
   This results in learning to avoid problems

2. Feelings are not expressed openly.
   Taking pride in being strong and not showing emotion.
   "Big boys don't cry."
   The result is coming to believe it is better (safer) not to feel, eventually we get so cut off from self that we are unsure what we feel.

3. Communication is often indirect, with one person acting as a messenger between two others.
   Dad tells son "I wish your mom was more understanding" (he talks to mom) Using someone else to communicate for you results in confusion, misdirected feelings, and an inability to directly confront personal problems.

4. Unrealistic expectations: be strong, good, right, perfect, makes us proud.
   Doing well and achieving is the most important thing.
   Enough is never enough.
   Results in creating an ideal in our head about what is good or right or best that is far removed from what is realistic and possible. This leads to us punishing others because they don't meet our expectations. We may even blame ourselves for not pushing someone enough to meet our expectations.

5. Don't be selfish.
   Views self as wrong for placing their own needs before the needs of others.
   End up trying to feel good by taking care of others.

6. Do as I say ... not as I do.
   This rule teaches us not to trust.

7. It's not okay to play.
   Begin to believe that the world is a serious place where life is always difficult and painful.

8. Don't rock the boat.
   The system seeks to maintain itself. If you grow and change you'll be alone.

THE RULES OF CODEPENDENCY

1. It's not okay to talk about problems.
2. Feelings are not expressed openly.
3. Communication is often not direct, having a person act as a messenger between two other people.
4. Unrealistic expectations: be strong, good, right, perfect. Make us proud.
5. Don't be selfish.
6. Do as I say, not as I do.
7. It's not okay to play.
8. Don't rock the boat.

HOW CODEPENDENCY AFFECTS ONE'S LIFE

1. When I am having problems feeling good about myself and you have an opinion about me that I don't want you to have, I try to control what you feel about me so that I can feel good about myself.

2. I can't tell where my reality ends and someone else's reality begins. Leads to making assumptions, belief that you can read the thoughts of others, and as a result choosing your behavior based on your perception of what the other person's opinion of you is.

3. Have trouble getting my own needs and wants met.

4. Resenting others for the pain or losses they have caused you. This can lead to obsessively thinking about them and how to get back or punish them.

5. Avoid dealing with reality to avoid unpleasant feelings.

6. Difficulty in close or intimate relationships. Relationship implies sharing—one person giving and the other receiving (without trying to change each other). Also affects how we parent our own children.

SYMPTOM/EFFECT IN CHILDREN OF CODEPENDENTS

Difficulty with self-esteem/inability to appropriately esteem our children.

Difficulty setting boundaries/inability to avoid transgressing our children's boundaries.

Difficulty owning and expressing our own reality and imperfections/inability to allow our children to have their reality and be imperfect.

Difficulty taking care of adult needs and wants/inability to appropriately nurture our children and teach them to meet their needs and wants.

Difficulty experiencing and expressing our reality/inability to provide a stable environment for our children.

WHAT CAN YOU DO

First of all, it is necessary to examine objectively your life to see if you have codependent behaviors. If you do, but generally not that often (like a parent who occasionally covers for their teenager) then just understanding the impact of the behaviors may be enough to cause change. However, more chronic use of codependent behaviors warrants more intervention to understand what is happening, how it got started, and what the choices are. This can be accomplished in various ways which include:

1. Education. There are many self-help books written on the subject.

2. Self-help groups such as Codependents Anonymous.

3. Male/Female Support Groups (facilitated by a licensed therapist).

4. Individual therapy.

STAGES OF RECOVERY

1. The process actually begins by seeing yourself where you are right now. Before you start recovery you are in the mode of "survival and denial." This is existing, not living. There is a denial of having any problems or that behaviors are self-defeating.

2. Acceptance for the realization that you cannot change others and learning to deal with it.

3. Identifying and working through personal issues. This is where you see and understand more about yourself.

   Awareness is increasing. There is an understanding of the past, but living in the present.

4. Reintegration. Learning to be okay with yourself—not identifying yourself by what you do for others. This prepares you for taking responsibility of self-care and getting your own needs met.

5. A new beginning. Living a new, emotionally healthy way of life.

CHARACTERISTICS OF ADULT CHILDREN OF ALCOHOLICS

Adult children of alcoholics appear to have characteristics in common as a result of being raised in an alcoholic home. Review the characteristics listed. If you identify with these characteristics then seek appropriate sources of support to understand and resolve them. You will find many books at the bookstore on this subject. Additionally, there is Adult Children of Alcoholics 12-Step self-help community meeting, individual therapy, and group therapy facilitated by a therapist.

1. Isolation, fear of people, and fear of authority figures.

2. Difficulty with identity issues related to seeking constantly the approval of others.

3. Frightened by angry people and personal criticism.

4. Have become an alcoholic yourself, married one, or both. A variation would be the attraction to another compulsive personality such as a workaholic. The similarity is that neither is emotionally available to deal with overwhelming and unhealthy dependency needs.

5. Perpetually being the victim and seeing the world from the perspective of a victim.

6. An overdeveloped sense of responsibility. Concerned about the needs of others to the degree of neglecting your own wants and needs. This is a protective behavior for avoiding a good look at yourself and taking responsibility to identify and resolve your own personal difficulties.

7. Feelings of guilt associated with standing up for your rights. It is easier to give into the demands of others.

8. An addiction to excitement. Feeling a need to be on the edge, and risk-taking behaviors.

9. A tendency to confuse feelings of love and pity. Attracted to people that you can rescue and take care of.

10. Avoidance of feelings related to traumatic childhood experiences. Unable to feel or express feelings because it is frightening and/or painful and overwhelming. Denial of feelings.

11. Low self-esteem. A tendency to judge yourself harshly and be perfectionistic and self-critical.

12. Strong dependency needs and terrified of abandonment. Will do almost anything to hold onto a relationship in order to avoid the fear and pain of abandonment.

13. Alcoholism is a family disease which often results in a family member taking on the characteristics of the disease even if they are not alcoholics (para-alcoholics). Dysfunctional relationships, denial, fearful, avoidance of feelings,

poor coping, poor problem solving, afraid that others will find out what you are really like, etc.

14. Tendency to react to things that happen versus taking control and not being victim to the behavior of others or situations created by others.

15. A chameleon. A tendency to be what others want you to be instead of being yourself. A lack of honesty with yourself and others.

GUIDELINES FOR COMPLETING YOUR FIRST STEP TOWARD EMOTIONAL HEALTH

The first step is simply an honest look at how your life experiences have affected you. This includes how you perceive things, how you react and respond to various situations and other people, your coping ability, problem-solving skills, conflict resolution skills, what motivates you, and the ability to form healthy relationships.

Answer all of the questions that follow as thoroughly as possible, citing specific incidents, the approximate date, how you felt, what you thought, and how you responded. It may be an emotional experience for you to review your life experiences in detail, but remind yourself that there is nothing that you will write about that you haven't already experienced and survived. This writing will help you understand yourself better, clarify what the problems are, and find what you need to do to solve these problems.

1. Describe in detail your childhood home life. Include descriptions of relationships with family members, and extended family members that you view as significant.

2. What is your earliest memory? What emotion(s) does this memory evoke?

3. Share two of your happiest/pleasant and two of the most painful life experiences that you have had. Be specific in describing the experiences.

4. How did these experiences affect you?

5. What did you learn from your family about:
   A. What it means to be a family member.
   B. How to be a partner to someone.
   C. How to resolve conflicts and problem solve issues.
   D. How to deal with anger and other emotions.

6. How do you function in social relationships?
   A. Are you friendly, reserved, distrustful, easily hurt?
   B. How do you respond to the ideas or opinions of others?
   C. Do you easily form acquaintances/friendships?
   D. Are you able to maintain relationships?
   E. Do you have any behaviors or attitudes which create difficulties for you?

7. How did your early life experience affect self-esteem and self-confidence?

8. When did you become aware that you have emotional and behavioral difficulties that contribute to negative life experiences?

9. Explain how your difficulties have prevented you from reaching desired goals and having fulfilling relationships.

10. What are your fears, and how do they affect your life?

11. Do your difficulties increase during times of stress or discomfort resulting from job, family, or personal problems? Give examples of each.

12. Discuss how your emotional and behavioral difficulties have had negative impact on significant relationships, intimacy, trust, caused you social problems, such as loss of friends, inability to perform sexually, unreasonable demands on others, allowing yourself to be taken advantage of, etc. Tell how they interfered with your relationships. How do you feel about that now?

13. How have your emotional and/or behavioral difficulties affected your health?

14. List the emotional and behavioral problems that you have attempted to resolve. How successful have you been?

15. Review all that you have written. Use this information to take responsibility for your life. No matter what has happened to you or what others have done it is up to you to make yourself and your life what you want them to be. This requires that you live consciously maintaining a good awareness for what you are doing and why you are doing it. Marketing things right is an active process not just a thinking exercise.

RELATIONSHIP QUESTIONNAIRE

This questionnaire is intended to estimate the current satisfaction with your relationship. Circle the number between 1 (completely satisfied) to 10 (completely unsatisfied) beside each issue. Try to focus on the present and not the past.

1. List the things that your partner does that please you:
2. What would you like your partner to do more often?
3. What would your partner like you to do more often?
4. How do you contribute to difficulties in the relationship?
5. What are you prepared to do differently in the relationship?
6. Is there a problem of alcohol/substance abuse?
7. Do you often try to anticipate your partners wishes so that you can please them?
8. What are your goals or what do you hope to accomplish?

	completely satisfied									completely unsatisfied
General Relationship	1	2	3	4	5	6	7	8	9	10
Personal Independence	1	2	3	4	5	6	7	8	9	10
Spouse Independence	1	2	3	4	5	6	7	8	9	10
Couples Time Alone	1	2	3	4	5	6	7	8	9	10
Social Activities	1	2	3	4	5	6	7	8	9	10
Occupational or Academic Progress	1	2	3	4	5	6	7	8	9	10
Sexual Interactions	1	2	3	4	5	6	7	8	9	10
Communication	1	2	3	4	5	6	7	8	9	10
Financial Issues	1	2	3	4	5	6	7	8	9	10
Household/Yard Responsibility	1	2	3	4	5	6	7	8	9	10
Parenting	1	2	3	4	5	6	7	8	9	10
Daily Social Interaction	1	2	3	4	5	6	7	8	9	10
Trust in Each Other	1	2	3	4	5	6	7	8	9	10
Decision Making	1	2	3	4	5	6	7	8	9	10
Resolving Conflicts	1	2	3	4	5	6	7	8	9	10
Problem Solving	1	2	3	4	5	6	7	8	9	10
Support of One Another	1	2	3	4	5	6	7	8	9	10

HEALTHY ADULT RELATIONSHIPS: BEING A COUPLE

Because people change over time so do their relationships. When two people initially get together there is the excitement and passion of a new relationship. Then they make a commitment to one another. During this time of commitment each person has an expectation that things will feel wonderful forever. This period of relationship development lasts for 1 to 2 years. During this time they begin to notice that there are differences in beliefs and how each would like to handle various situations. However, they continue to put their best foot forward, feeling close and enjoying one another.

As this period of discovery continues there are disagreements and differences of opinion, but they don't talk about it. They tend to hold back fearing an increase in disagreements. They are struggling to find a way to go beyond being two people in a relationship to being two people who are sharing their lives together and building a future.

Unfortunately, avoiding conflicts make them go away. In fact, if issues are being talked about a lot but it is not accompanied by problem solving there can be increased frustration and distancing from one another. The two people struggling to be a couple earlier may be doing things separately now. With this drifting there are questions which arise regarding the stability of the relationship. This leads to a fork in the road for them. They can choose one of two courses of action: (1) being disillusioned and pulling away from one another more and ending it in a separation, or (2) recognize that they have not been making the necessary efforts to strengthen their relationships and make a commitment to invest themselves in creating a successful partnership.

With a recommitment to each other a couple feel as if they have found that excitement that they originally experienced. They have found out some very important things:

1. To feel good about your partner you must have positive thoughts about them in your heart and in your head.

2. For a successful relationship there must be an enduring commitment to get through the good and the bad together.

3. There must be an effort to share your lives cooperatively.

4. As you leave your family of origin to begin your own new family:
   A. Recognize that now it is your partner who comes before others.
   B. From the positive perspective your parents have gained your partner not lost you. Make sure they include your partner as they would you.

5. Since life is very hectic make sure that you are spending adequate time together, focusing on one another and your relationship.

6. Validate your partner. Listen without interrupting when your partner is talking to you. Reflect to them your understanding of what they have shared. Accept and acknowledge how they feel.

SPECIAL CIRCUMSTANCES

1. If you are a single parent you need to have a strong support system. This includes supportive family and one or more very good friends to talk to and have fun with. Strive to keep some balance in your life.

2. If partners get together where there have been children from a previous relationship there are different difficulties that they must deal with. Couples in a blended family have to work harder to maintain their life together.

HOW TO PREDICT THE POTENTIALLY VIOLENT RELATIONSHIP

At the core of any violent relationship is the use of power and control. Women often express interest in how they might be able to predict if a potential partner may be someone who is emotionally, sexually, or physically abusive. Consider the following points in increasing awareness for concern.

1. *Controlling behavior.* Where they are allowed to go, who they are allowed to see or talk to, how they dresses, and how they do their hair and make-up.

This behavior tends to escalate under the guise of trying to be protective or to prevent someone from being harmed by their poor judgment—therefore, they need to be told what to do and how to do it.

2. *Jealousy.* Expresses jealousy as a sign of love and concern. There may be accusations of flirting or questioned for talking to someone. They are often isolated from family and friends. As jealousy intensifies, they will be monitored by frequent phone calling and will not be allowed to make personal decisions. Ultimately, they may not be allowed to do anything without the permission of their partner.

3. *Neediness.* Insecurity is expressed as " I have never felt like this about anyone or "I have never been able to talk to someone or trust someone like you." There is pressure to commit quickly to an exclusive relationship. There may be pressure to have sex or to move in together.

4. *Isolation.* There is an attempt to isolate the abused person from family and friends. There will likely be efforts to sabotage close relationships and accuse others of causing difficulties in the relationship. There may also be efforts to limit phone contact, use of a car, or even from going to school or work.

5. *Projecting blame onto others.* Almost anything that goes wrong will be blamed on the woman or other people.

6. *Unrealistic expectations.* Expectations of the perfect wife, who has nothing out of place and will be his everything. He will have the expectation that *all* needs will be met in this relationship.

7. *Blaming others for the abuser's feelings.* Does not take responsibility for their own emotions. Blames the woman or others for how they feel and may use it as a means to manipulate. Makes light of abuse through minimizing, denying, and blaming.

8. *Verbal and emotional abuse.* Saying things to be hurtful and cruel—minimizing ability, accomplishments, and overall degradation. There may be awakening during the night out of sleep to be verbally assaulted, questioned, and called names. There may be added manipulation such as threats to end the relationship, harm themselves, abandonment, or kick the person out of their home. There is game playing, resulting in the abused experiencing low self-esteem and feeling crazy.

9. *Rigidly traditional roles.* Expectation of the woman being in the home, being the central caretaker, being submissive, being unable to make decisions independently and seen as inferior. This can be a part of economic abuse. The abused may become totally financially dependent on the abuser. This is also where children can be used to make the abused feel guilty for won strivings or using children to relay messages. Using male privilege, treating her like a servant, creating the rules for men and women.

10. *Coercion and threats.* Cruelty to children or pets. Having unrealistic expectations about children's abilities. Pets may be harmed or even killed.

11. *Using force sexually.* Desires to act out fantasies during sex in which the woman is forced, bound, or hurt. There is little concern about what the woman wants or needs. They may use manipulative behavior such as withdrawal, anger, or guilt to get the woman to comply. There may be no empathy for illness, and they may make demands for sex or initiate sex while the woman is sleeping.

12. *Using force during conflicts.* The use of force such as being prevented from leaving a room, held down or restrained. Being held against one's will.

13. *History of violence in a relationship.* History of physically hurting a past partner but blames them for what happened.

14. *Threats of violence.* Making or carrying out threats of harm, threatening to leave, or harm self. Coercing someone into illegal behavior. This is meant to control. There may be excuses later, such as "I was just upset because of what you did. I wouldn't do that."

15. *Throwing or breaking things.* This behavior is threatening and is often used as a punishment and to terrorize another person into submission.

16. *Mood swings.* This is the confusing behavior where one minute the person is nice and the next minute the person is upset, angry, or out of control.

DOMESTIC VIOLENCE: SAFETY PLANNING

MOST IMPORTANT TO REMEMBER

1. Help is available
2. You are not alone
3. You are not to blame

*No one deserves to be hit!

Even if you do not believe that there will be a "next time," decide now what you will do and where you will go.

DOCUMENT THE ABUSE

1. Keep a journal. Make sure that it is hidden in a secret place
2. Take photos of any physical harm to yourself or to property
3. If you are physically harmed, show bruises or injuries to a friend, neighbor or family member
4. Make the following copies and keep them in your secret place
   A. Hospital bills
   B. Property damage bills

FIND A SAFE PLACE TO GO

1. A shelter
   A. Know how to get there
   B. Memorize the phone number

2. Make arrangements to stay with family or a friend
   A. Make friends with a neighbor
   B. Ask neighbors to call the police if they hear suspicious noises from your home

3. Decide ahead of time if you plan to take the children with you. Always try to take the children in order to get yourself and them out of an unsafe environment. An abusive environment may teach your children things about behavior and relationships that you don't want them to learn.

4. Develop a code word with your children, neighbor, friends, or supportive family that lets them know that you need to get out or you need them to call the police

*If there have been serious threats to your safety and you are fearful, contact local law enforcement.

CREATE A SAFE ROOM IN YOUR HOME

1. Choose a room with a window
2. Get a cordless phone for that room
3. If possible, arrange a signal system for help with a neighbor
4. Plan a barricade
5. Install interior locks on the door (ask about locks at the local hardware store)
6. Make sure that there are not any weapons in the room
7. Call the police immediately should you need to use the safe room

*If things are building up, try to leave immediately to prevent the situation from getting out of control. If you can't get out, don't get backed into a corner. Try to keep your back toward an opening such as a door or window.

HAVE MONEY AND KEYS

1. Make duplicate keys for your vehicles, house, safety deposit box, post office box, and so on
2. Start hiding money in amounts that will not be missed
3. Open your own bank account
4. Save paystubs and other important receipts

CREATE A FILE WITH YOUR IMPORTANT DOCUMENTS (IF YOU ARE TAKING YOUR CHILDREN, ALSO PUT THEIR DOCUMENTS)

1. Temporary restraining order
2. Driver's license
3. Car title and registration
4. Social security card(s)
5. Birth certificate(s)
6. Immigration paper(s)
7. Social services documents
8. Prescriptions
9. Tax records/receipts for property purchases
10. Bank statements
11. Address book

PACK A SUITCASE

1. Pack basic clothing
   A. Shoes
   B. Socks
   C. Underwear
   D. Nightclothes
   E. Change of clothes
   F. Toiletries
   G. Special children's needs such as diapers

2. Pack keepsakes that cannot be replaced
   A. Photos
   B. Documents

3. Hide it in a safe place
   A. At a neighbor's house
   B. Under the bed
   C. At church
   D. In the garage
   E. In a public locker
   F. At a family member's home

KNOW WHEN AND HOW TO LEAVE

1. Leave while the offender is away
2. Ask the police to help you
3. If your children are in danger, contact child protective services or the police
4. Consult an attorney or legal resource at a shelter about your parental rights if you are leaving your children while you seek safety

*Safety is the priority.

WHY VICTIMS OF DOMESTIC VIOLENCE STRUGGLE WITH LEAVING

1. *Fear in general.* Often they have been cut off from all of their resources and have lived under threat and control, not being able to rely on their own decision making.
2. *Low self-esteem.* People who have been emotionally beaten down over a period of begin to see themselves as failures at everything they do. Offenders reinforce this belief to maintain their control.
3. *Self-blame/responsibility.* Victimized people blame themselves for the abuse. This is constantly reinforced by the offenders who blame them for the abuser's violent behavior.
4. *Holding the family together.* Women are raised and socialized to see themselves as the center of family cohesiveness—for keeping their families

safe and together. Women often believe they must do this at any cost to themselves, while at the same time questioning their parenting abilities.

5. *Fear of being crazy.* When you are told you are crazy often enough you begin to believe it. As a result, these victims question their ability to cope with all of the responsibilities of the outside world.

6. *Dependence.* Victim of domestic violence have likely had their worlds made very small so that they could be controlled. As a result, they lack experience in making their own decisions and acting independently.

7. *Isolation.* One of the most common things done to victims of domestic violence is to isolate them from family and friends, physically and emotionally. The more isolated they are , the less likely they will seek help or be aware of the help available in their community.

8. *Traditional values.* Traditional male-female roles are in conflict with separation and divorce and support the notion of "keeping the family together at all costs." There may also be a strong religious influences and unsupportive family members that reinforce a victim's belief that she must stay in an abusive relationship.

9. *Learned behavior.* When you live in an isolated and abusive environment, over time the experience takes on a normalcy because there is nothing else to compare it to. When combined with a lack of belief in oneself, the victim may come to believe that the situation is impossible to change. This may be further embedded if the victim grew up in an abusive home.

10. *The honeymoon stage and promises of change.* Victims often love their partners and want a good marriage and a stable family life for their children. With the promise of change is the hope that all of these things are possible. In the hopes that the promise of change will be kept, the victims will forgive and give the relationship another chance for a new beginning.

Deal with what is, not what if. If things were going to change on their own they would have. If there is to be any chance of hope for change, for the victim and the victim's family, it is necessary to take action.

IMPROVED COPING SKILLS FOR HAPPIER COUPLES

There is no way to eliminate all conflicts between two people. However, by improving your coping skills, you can go a long way to alleviate the distress of seeing things differently. By evaluating your problems, learning effective ways to resolve them, and knowing when to seek professional help you, and your partner can ensure the lifelong loving relationship you want. Keep in mind, both people must be prepared to take responsibility, work at becoming aware of their contribution to positive and negative outcomes, and be prepared to make changes when needed. This is a demonstration of mutual respect and responsibility.

EVALUATE THE PROBLEM
Just bringing two lives together quickly highlights basic differences:

1. Style
2. Beliefs

3. Process of how to accomplish tasks
4. Parenting
5. Family expectations
6. Traditions
7. Priorities
8. Goals (short/long term, personal development, and family achievements)

Differences may initially result in mutual attraction, but over time become sources of frustration. Therefore, while differences or complimentarity may bring you together, it is the sharing of common goals that keeps you together.

PROBLEM RESOLUTION

Every couple has differences in opinion. However, people who feel respected, loved, and appreciated experience less conflict. Make it a point every day to say positive and supportive things to your partner. Simply saying, "I love you" is reassuring and feels good. Give compliments about how the other looks or what he/she has done. Compliments are a nice way to say, "I noticed," "I am aware of all that you do."

Talk to each other about fears, concerns, plans, goals, ideas, and financial management. Explore different solutions to the issues that confront you. That will give you more information into the discussion of what the two of you can do to reach your desired outcome. Use the basic problem-solving outline for approaching issues:

1. Identify the problem (agree on what the problem is)
2. Generate all the different ways that are available for resolving the problem
3. Make a mutually agreed on method for resolving the problem
4. Do it!
5. Be supportive and prepared to go to plan B with out blaming if it is necessary

If you have baggage from the past that you (as an individual) have seen interferes with positive outcomes, take responsibility for working through it. If there are couple's issues that you don't seem to be able to resolve to your satisfaction or feel that there is increasing distance in what was a loving and sharing relationship, seek professional help. Also check into community presentations or activities that may improve your functioning as a couple. Many churches also offer helpful groups or programs to the community. Do whatever you need to in order to give your relationship the opportunity to get back on track.

COUPLE'S CONFLICT: RULES FOR FIGHTING FAIR

1. Do not use threats during the argument. Stay focused on the issue(s).
2. Do not use blanket or labeling judgments such as "You never..." or "You are thoughtless." Doing and saying hurtful things is not helpful. Be respectful and treat others as you wish to be treated.
3. Stay on the topic. Save other topics for a later discussion. Focus on specific problem, behaviors or situations that you are striving to resolve.

4. It is not fair to interrupt. Stay at the same eye level. Take responsibility for being a good listener and being sure that you understand what the message is before you respond with your own thoughts and feelings. How you act will be a demonstration of your own agenda or goal. Do you want to work through a problem and resolve it or keep the conflict going?

5. Do not use "always" or "never." Be realistic and honest. Exaggerating prolongs and intensifies a conflict.

6. Stay in the present tense. Bringing up past issues is usually utilized to "win" or prove a point. Just because someone acted in a certain or behaved in a certain way in the past does not mean that person will always do the same thing. What is in the past cannot be changed. Also, if you are held hostage by the past, your partner may start to think that no matter what he/she does, it will not make a difference. This does not mean, however, that one should not take responsibility for past actions and make amends.

7. Do not argue in the dark or in bed.

8. It is not fair to walk away or leave the house while you are in the midst of a conflict. Be respectful and responsible for your own behavior. If tempers are escalating, then make a mutual decision to cool off and come back to resolve the conflict.

9. Avoid finger pointing, which will seem like lecturing. Pay attention to your body language. People pay more attention to how a message is delivered than the words said. What do you want to communicate?

10. Take responsibility for change. Always do your part. Take the high road. Be true to yourself.

11. Take responsibility for your own feelings. Rather than saying, "You make me mad," take responsibility for your emotions by saying, " I am mad." You are responsible for your own thoughts, feelings, and behaviors.

12. If you suspect that a conflict is brewing, write down the issue or problem before it evolves into an emotional volcano. This helps a couple to stay in control and more effectively problem-solve the issues at hand. Also, taking the time to write it down can slow the building of tension and clarify the problem.

13. Drama and exaggeration is not helpful. Being dramatic is likely to escalate the situation. Take responsibility to do your part honestly and in a straight-forward manner.

14. Both partners have the right to take time to calm themselves and to think about their thoughts and feelings so that they can express them appropriately.

15. Be sure that you know what you are having conflict about. What is the real issue? Choose your battles carefully. Don't sweat the small stuff. What is worth fighting about?

16. Approach conflict with a problem-solving attitude. Be honest about your own agenda and take responsibility for how you choose to deal with it.

17. Don't say things that are critical, hurtful, or attacking that offers your partner no recourse but to avoid or retaliate. You can't erase hurtfulness.

18. Don't store up feeling and then erupt like a volcano with your accumulated resentments. This is overwhelming and confuses the current issue. Deal with important issues as they come up.

19. Be honest even when it hurts. Avoid making assumptions. When you make assumptions, you run the risk of totally being off base 50% of the time. It is always easier to see what is wrong with the other person than it is to see what is wrong with yourself. Be honest about your own shortcomings and contributions to relationship difficulties. People grow and change. Also, just because someone loves you does not mean that the person knows what you want or need. It is your responsibility to express your wants and needs directly, clearly, and respectfully.

20. Does it matter who is right? Is it about winning? If you answered yes to either of these questions, you are not investing yourself in a conflict resolution process that is best for your partnership. You are investing yourself in what you think is best for you. When you approach conflict resolution, it must be from a position that both partners just win, both must benefit, and neither will be harmed. When issues are resolved, it is a win-win situation. You are going to have to decide if you are two teams or one. With two teams, each has its own agenda. A single team works together toward a common goal.

Be Clear About What You Want	1. Everyone should occasionally take the time to review where they are with consideration to goals, interests, and friendships.
	2. Consider goals, interests, and friendships as an individual.
	3. Consider goals, interests, and friendships as a couple.

Be Clear in Communicating What You Want	1. A successful couple is one that works hard at making decisions that are acceptable to both parties.
	2. Establish a good time to talk over issues.
	3. Remain on one topic until it has been resolved. Then move on to the next topic of discussion.
	4. Avoid criticizing, judging, or coercing your partner into what you want and they don't. It may feel like you get what you want in the short run, but you will both pay for it later because your partner will feel hurt and cheated.
	5. Avoid stating things from a position of what you don't want. Instead, state what your goals are.
	6. Stay focused, respectful, and concentrate on the discussion topic.
	7. Avoid bringing up negative experiences from the past. Remain focused on the here and now.

How Can Both of You Get What You Want	1. If there is a difference in what you both want be prepared to negotiate.
	2. If there is something you need or want from your partner, request it, don't make a demand for it.
	3. When negotiating be prepared to offer something that your partner wants if you want them to give you what you want. There must be balance. Both partners must feel that they get out what they put into the relationship.

4. Don't hold back waiting to see how your partner is going to help you. Instead, show them how you can assist in completing any task. Remember, balance. Each must feel like they get out what they put in.

5. Self-monitor. Make short-term agreements with a built-in time for reviewing what has been accomplished.

6. Always reinforce the efforts and accomplishments of your partner in assuring that your needs are met. Therefore, when you get what you want make sure you let them know in a loving and appreciative manner.

PARENTING A HEALTHY FAMILY

CREATING EFFECTIVE FAMILY RULES

1. Rules hold the family together. They create a foundation for learning responsibility, developing mutual respect, and encouraging age-appropriate independence.

2. Create rules from a positive perspective. Make rules which facilitate what you want.

3. Have as few rules as possible, be clear, and be specific.

4. Choose consequences that are logical, and that you are willing to enforce.

5. Take the time to educate the child of each rule and the associated consequences. Life is about choices, and early on this is how a child learns responsibility.

6. Have the child reflect to you in their own words and understanding of the rules and consequences.

7. Whenever possible and appropriate include children in making rules as well as other decision-making situations.

8. Be consistent in adhering to rules.

9. Be aware when it is appropriate to change a rule because of developmental changes and increased maturity, in order to facilitate responsible behavior.

EFFECTIVE COPARENTING

1. Make rules together. Agreement on the rules is important so that children receive consistent information from both parents.

2. If you don't agree on certain rules negotiate until there is agreement.

3. Be supportive of each other. Remember, this was a joint decision and children will be confused if there is conflict between parents over rules. Not being consistent and supportive can lead to manipulation and power struggles.

4. If one parent intervenes in a situation and the other disagrees with the intervention do not voice the disagreement and undermine the intervening parent. Instead, discuss and resolve later.

MAINTAIN THE PARENT ROLE

1. Be specific in telling a child exactly what actions are expected.
2. Be flexible in how a child accomplishes a task. If you aware of different ways of doing something show them to the child. It is important for the child to work effectively, to have accomplishments, and to master their environments.
3. Don't lecture. Talk less, act more.
4. Give positive feedback, rewards, and reinforcement for efforts and accomplishment of the behaviors you want.
5. Be consistent, and don't argue.
6. Follow through with rewards and consequences to shape the behaviors you want.

BE AN ACTIVE PARENT

1. Help your child learn by teaching how to do things "their way." Don't expect them to have the same level of expertise as someone older.
2. Be aware that you are always a role model to a child. They learn by watching and copying what they see.
3. Demonstrate your love through actions. Words lack meaning and value if a child does feel the love from a parent through attention and affectionate and caring behaviors.
4. Develop routines. Routinely create an environment that feels dependable and safe to a child.
5. As part of the family routine have regular one to one time with a child.

A HEALTHY FAMILY MEANS ALL OF ITS MEMBERS ARE INVOLVED

1. The development of self-esteem is an active process. Empower children by their demonstrated importance in family functioning.
2. The best way to teach values and build skills is by doing things with a child.
3. Identify a child's contributions to family life.
4. Laugh and be playful with a child.
5. Include a child in appropriate family decision making.

ENCOURAGE COMMUNICATION

1. Be interested in a child's life and their experiences. It is through talking about things that happen that children are able to learn valuable lessons and better understand themselves.
2. Encourage a child to talk to you about things that are important to them.
3. When a child shares their experiences, thoughts, and ideas with you actively listen and encourage their problem solving of issue.
4. Avoid criticizing and giving directions. Respect them. Ask them what they think.
5. Give a child the time and attention required to understand their point of view. They are individuals. Expect them to have their own ideas.

6. Use active listening behaviors (face them and use eye contact) and reflect to them what you hear them saying. When you repeat to them what you think they are saying it demonstrates interest, respect, and that they are important.

7. When there is an opportunity to teach values to a child in a meaningful way take advantage of it. It will feel natural instead of contrived.

GUIDING YOUR CHILD TO APPROPRIATELY EXPRESS ANGER

Everyone is familiar with the devastating situations in which children have killed other children as an expression of their extreme anger with being treated badly and being humiliated. While it is imperative that bullies and cruel social behaviors be dealt with, it is also important that children be taught how to appropriately express feelings of anger. Learning how to effectively problem-solve and deal with difficult emotions is a preventive measure for positive mental health and preventing violent behavior. Young people turn to violence when they don't see other ways of managing difficult situations. They may be reacting to the moment without anticipating the consequences of their actions. The following tips can help a child to learn internal management, use of resources, and self-responsibility.

1. *Be a good listener.* Pay attention to what your children are saying about what they feel and how they are thinking about things in their life. Unfortunately, children are confronted at an earlier age about more adult-oriented issues such as relationships, sex, and romanticizing. Failure and rejection are also difficult issues to deal with. Young people are not prepared mentally or physically to effectively manage many of these issues and can find themselves overwhelmed and in trouble.

2. *Be comforting and reassuring.* Tell your children that you care about what they think and feel. Show confidence in them by helping them to explore their choices for managing the issues confronting them.

3. *Normalize the experience of anger.* Everyone gets angry. Share the positive ways that you have found to deal with anger and other difficult feelings.

4. *Encourage children to express their feelings honestly and appropriately and then to move on to fun and interesting activities.* Distracting oneself with other activities helps to refocus on other things and not get stuck and miserable with anger.

5. *Teach problem-solving and conflict resolution skills.* Give your children some ideas about how to deal with difficult situations and encourage them to talk about what they try to do in those situations, what works, what doesn't, and what they may do next time they are confronted with a similar situation.

6. *Catch them being good.* It is always important to reinforce good behavior by acknowledging it. When your children deal with their anger in positive ways, reinforce their positive choices. Use every opportunity to build and reinforce strengths and skills.

If you do not feel that your efforts are successful, talk to a professional about community resources (such as anger management classes) and therapy.

THE FAMILY MEETING

The Family Meeting is a regularly scheduled meeting of all family members. It creates the opportunity to promote healthy family functioning by:

1. Providing time for clarifying rules or establishing new rules as a family goes through new stages of growth and change.
2. Making decisions and problem solving. List any family problems. Choose one to solve. State the result that is desired. List and discuss all possible solutions. Choose one solution and make a plan to carry it out. Set a date to review it.
3. To acknowledge and appreciate good things happening in the family.
4. Identifying strength of individual family members, and of the family as a whole.
5. To list fun activities for the family.
6. To encourage all family members to share their ideas. Try to see and understand each other's point of view.
7. A time to practice assertiveness and democracy. Role model respectful and effective communication. Parents should role model the skills of reflective listening, "I" messages, and problem solving so that children can learn.
8. To promote commitment of all family members to the functioning of the family.
9. To provide an opportunity for all family members to be heard.
10. Expressing feelings, concerns, and complaints.
11. Distributing chores and responsibilities fairly among family members.
12. Expressing positive feelings about one another and giving encouragement.

GUIDELINES

1. Meet at a regularly scheduled time which is convenient for everyone.
2. Share the responsibility of the meeting by taking turns in chairing the meeting.
3. Reserve an hour for the family meeting. If the children are young, try 20 to 30 minutes.
4. Each person has a chance to speak.
5. One person speaks at a time.
6. Listen when others are speaking.
7. No one is forced to speak, but participation is encouraged.
8. No criticism or teasing. Do not allow the meeting to become a regular gripe session.
9. All family members must have an opportunity to bring up what is important to them.
10. Focus on what the family can do as a group rather than on what any one member can do.
11. Share things that are going well. Recognize efforts and accomplishments.

12. The goal of the family meeting is communication and agreement. Be sure to accomplish plans for family fun.

13. End the meeting by summarizing the decisions and clarifying commitments. Thank everyone for respectfully attending and participating.

DEVELOPING POSITIVE SELF-ESTEEM IN CHILDREN AND ADOLESCENTS

1. Demonstrate a positive perspective rather than a negative one. "Catch" your children doing something good. This communicates love, care, acceptance, and appreciation. Be careful not to undo a positive statement. For example, "you did a great job of cleaning your room, too bad you don't do it more often."

2. Keep your promises. This facilitates trust in parents, while they are role modeling being respectful and responsible. Consistency is important.

3. Create opportunities out of your children's mistakes. For example, "what did you learn? What would be helpful next time?"

4. Show appreciation, approval, and acceptance. Listen for the feelings behind the words. Active listening to what a child says shows respect and is a way to reflect their worthiness. Being genuinely interested fosters mutual care and respect.

5. Have reasonable and appropriate consequences. Discipline should be a part of learning and encouraging responsible behavior. If a consequence is too long or severe it creates feelings of hopelessness, and a feeling that they have nothing to lose. As a result, it is likely to lead to more opposition and acting out.

6. Ask your children for their opinions, involve them in family problem solving and decision making whenever possible and appropriate.

7. Help your children develop reasonable age-appropriate goals for themselves and help them recognize their progress toward goals.

8. Avoid making comparisons between siblings or peers. Each person is unique and has something special to offer. Recognizing individual attributes is a good thing because it helps a child or adolescent to become more aware of their strengths or assets.

9. Support your children in activities in which they feel accomplished and successful. Everyone feels good about themselves when they are successful.

10. Spend time doing things with your children. The amount of time as well as the quality of time is important. Remember, your children grow quickly and time that has past can never be recaptured. Be sure to take time to have fun and enjoy your children.

11. Encourage your children's efforts and accomplishments. Genuine encouragement of efforts, progress, and accomplishments promotes positive self-esteem. Children learn to accept themselves, identify their assets and strengths, build self-confidence, and develop a positive self-image.

12. Communicate your love by saying it and demonstrating it. Feeling loved is feeling secure. Love is communicated by mutual respect, which is a cornerstone in the development of independence and responsibility.

13. Accept your children for who they are. This facilitates self-acceptance, self-like, and self-love.

14. Have faith in your children so that they can learn to expect the best in themselves.

15. Focus on contributions, assets, and strengths so that children feel that they are important and have something to offer. Let them know that what they offer counts.

UNDERSTANDING AND DEALING WITH LIFE CRISES OF CHILDHOOD

Everyday family life is full of stressors, crises, and necessary adjustments. An aspect of general growth and development includes the experience of being exposed to difficult/stressful situations and learning to cope with them. Growing up means learning to cope effectively with a full range of life experiences—both good and bad. Your child's ability to effectively cope with any given situation is related to the amount of distress it elicits, if they previously have experienced anything similar in which they were able to resolve, and how supportive parents and other adults are in facilitating the effective management of stressors. As an adult, you probably have had years of experience in dealing with all kinds of crises and have probably learned to cope with them. If this is not the case it is recommended that you consult with a therapist on the issues of problem solving, conflict resolution, and crisis resolution. If you are unable to cope effectively with stressors and crises it will be very difficult for you to help a child to successfully resolve and learn to cope with the stressors in their life.

A central task for all parents is teaching your child how to deal with stressors, pressures, and demands so that as they move into their adult life they are able to cope effectively. How your child responds to difficult circumstances will be influenced by how you help them deal with life crises they experience. While crises are often associated with emotional distress it is also a time of opportunity. It is a time of learning. The very essence of a crisis demands that a person search and explore new methods of coping and developing alternatives for dealing with it. As a result, a crisis presents a person, child or adult, an opportunity for growth and increased effectiveness in coping.

Parents are confronted with two major problems in helping children face and cope with stress:

1. To deal with your own reactions to the stress.
2. Facilitate optimal coping of the child by giving adequate support, encouraging and helping with the development of alternatives to deal with difficult situations, and by giving positive feedback and reinforcement for efforts toward management and resolution of stressors and crises.

WHAT IS A CRISIS?

A crisis can be defined as a person's evaluation of an experience as dangerous, threatening, traumatic, outside of anything they have ever experienced, and with an uncertainty of how they will handle it. A crisis is unique to the individual. What is experienced as a crisis for one person will not necessarily be a crisis for another person. It involves a person's interpretation and feelings about an experience along with speculation and questions about why it happened and what the consequences of it will be.

Losses such as death, divorce, relocation, and job change, and new or frightening experiences such as a physical trauma or hospitalization are frequently thought of in terms of what a crisis means. However, some positive events such as a marriage, birth of a child, job promotion, and acceptance to a desired college can also be experienced as a crisis. With any experience that is new there is some level of stress, expectation of performance, concern of how to deal with it, and questions about what may happen as a result of it. This can be just as overwhelming for a person as an event interpreted as a negative experience. When a person experiences a crisis in relation to a positive experience they may also feel guilty or upset with themselves expressing that they are confused because this should be a happy or pleasing experience.

Recognizing and understanding that the crisis is not the event, but the individual's interpretation of the event allows insight into why two different people may react differently to the same event. One child may begin school confident, secure, and grown up, while another child may feel fearful, rejected, or punished. Other events that may trigger a crisis include loss, loneliness, independence, sexuality, high expectations of performance (by self or others), and feeling overwhelmed by a situation that is interpreted as being out of their control. Therefore, everyone has different areas of vulnerability of sensitivity resulting from their past experiences which will influence their interpretation and response to situations. There is not an issue or event that across the board will be interpreted as a crisis for every person. Each person will interpret and react to life experiences in their own unique manner as a result of personality, disposition, coping ability, support, issues of emotional security, and previous life experiences will all work together as a person responds to a crisis event.

WHAT HAPPENS DURING A CRISIS

When an event precipitates a crisis there is a disruption in equilibrium and stability. Anxiety and tension begin to rise. The person tries to understand what is happening and why it is happening. The less a person is able to understand the situation, the more tension and anxiety they experience. This can lead to feeling overwhelmed, out of control, and helpless. With this psychological and emotional experience there may also be feelings of shame, depression, anger, or guilt. A child may be unable to verbally express their fears or may be afraid to express them. The confusion of fear, anxiety, and other emotions is the crisis.

When preparing yourself to help children deal with life events that they may interpret and experience as a crisis, it is helpful to consider the following:

1. Children tend to be self-centered. This is especially true of young children and adolescents. They seem to interpret things as if the world revolves around them—everything is taken personally. Because of this they may interpret themselves as being the cause of something that they have no power or control of, which can be overwhelming.

2. Children tend to interpret things in a literal or concrete manner. This can cause a crisis via misunderstanding. For example, telling a child that death is like sleep, or having a medical or dental procedure won't hurt because they will be knocked out. What the parent means and what the child interprets such statements as meaning are likely to be different.

3. Fantasy is reality for young children. This could be a situation in which one parent is seeking divorce and the child fears that they will also be abandoned or divorced by this parent. Sometimes a child experiences a form of fantasy called magical thinking, which means that a child has a belief that they had the power to make something happen by thinking it. An example of this is when a

child is angry and thinks or says "I wish you were dead" and someone is harmed in some way. They may believe that harm came to the person because of their thoughts or wish.

4. The effect of childhood loss or separation. Most of the crises experienced by a child involve a loss or separation of some kind. The loss or separation can be fantasy or real. There are direct losses such as divorce or death, or indirect losses such as starting school, a hospitalization, or staying for a brief period with a relative. Losses are a threat to feeling safe and secure. Losses can involve feelings such as sadness, depression, loneliness, rejection, abandonment, anger, guilt, and confusion.

Because life has a normal level of stress and changes, it would be impossible to hide from children the problems that confront a family. Children are very sensitive and can feel when things are not right at home. Therefore, instead of allowing a child to interpret what is going on it is better to give them age-appropriate information in a manner that helps them maintain their feelings of safety and security.

CRISIS RESOLUTION

1. *Promoting objectivity.* Help the child see the situation for what it is. For example, while the child is at school mom/dad won't forget about them, or parents did not divorce because the child was bad, etc.

2. *Validate feelings.* Recognize and accept how the child feels about a given situation. Denying their feelings is a rejection and is also confusing. When feelings are denied it leads to a misinterpretation of feelings later on.

3. *Elicit their thoughts and feelings about what has happened.* Encourage them to vent their thoughts and feelings appropriately instead of keeping them inside.

4. *Facilitate problem solving and taking appropriate action.* This means identifying exactly what the problem is, what the alternatives are for managing it or resolving it, and then taking action. It also includes utilizing resources and self-care behaviors such as getting adequate rest/sleep, nutrition, exercise, and balance in their life—not just being focused on the crisis.

Helping the child to understand what has happened, why it happened, how it is happening, what it means to them, how it affects them are the objectives for facilitating resolution of the crisis for the child. The efforts of understanding and support to the child early in life when faced with crises pays off later because it lays the foundation of coping skills for dealing with crises later in life.

WHAT DO YOU NEED TO DO TO HELP A CHILD

1. As with any relationship interaction you need to be the best you can be before you can offer healthy support, guidance, and facilitate problem solving for effective coping. This means that you need to understand and cope with your own reactions to events before you can help a child learn to cope. When a

child experiences a crisis parents experience their own personal reactions. Additionally, the body language or nonverbal communication your child experiences from you will have a significant impact on how they interpret an event. A child tends to reflect their parents reaction to an event.

2. Attempt to understand the child's experience of the event. Remember the tendency of the child to be self-centered. This will give you insight into how the child might personalize a given experience. Is the child fearing a loss or rejection and abandonment? Is the situation frightening or do they feel that they are to blame for what has occurred? What kind of feelings might the child be trying to express?

3. Validate the child's feelings. Acknowledge and accept the feelings that the child is experiencing. In order for the child to master the situation they must be able to understand and effectively express what it is they are feeling. Reflecting the child's emotional experience ("I understand that you feel sad because we could not keep the kitten") because it offers acceptance and a label to their emotion which allows them to connect their feelings to the event and lets them know that having such a feeling for that experience is okay.

4. Understand the stage of loss that a person experiences, which are a series of feelings which people go through when working through a loss and/or death.
   A. *Denial* that the event is happening.
   B. *Anger* that the event happened, or that they have been abandoned.
   C. *Depression* (and guilt) often experienced as sadness and loneliness associated with the object, or feeling guilty that something has happened to another and harboring a belief that somehow they could have prevented it.
   D. *Bargaining* in an attempt or as a plea to not accept what has happened, or being willing to do anything to take it back.
   E. *Acceptance* of the reality of what has occurred.

People do not necessarily go through these stages in the sequence that they are given, or go through a stage and never return to that stage again. Everyone goes through these stages in their own unique way based on how they grieve and cope. However, everyone seems to go through this sequence of feelings in coping with a loss, and children seem to go through these stages in general when coping with a crisis.

5. Accept the child's efforts to deal with the crisis. Be careful to not put them down or shame them. Instead, offer acceptance and support to facilitate the resolution of the crisis. In other words, meet the child where they are at emotionally and guide them by responding appropriately to what they need in moving toward resolving the crisis.

6. Make an effort to hear what the child is trying to express.

7. Respond verbally to the child at their level of understanding. Be direct and keep it simple.

8. Don't push the child to talk about the event. This can result in distressing the child more and leading to withdrawal.

9. Be empathic. Try to understand what the child's experience is. Often, a child experiences a crisis because they believe that they are somehow responsible for what has happened (divorce, death), that they are being punished for

being bad (a new baby takes their place in the family, they are sent to school), or they are being rejected and abandoned. Be consistent and reassuring by what you say and what you do. Give the child adequate time and support to work it out.

10. Whenever possible, prepare a child for a difficult event such as an impending change, loss or death. It is much easier to cope with something when there is some expectation and understanding for what is happening. This will often reduce the intensity of the crisis or avert it all together. A child can be prepared by talking with them, using age-appropriate books, drawing, dolls, etc. Also, if possible avoid too many changes within a given period of time. This would be overwhelming for an adult with good coping skills, let alone a child who is striving to develop the skills necessary to adequately cope with difficult situations.

YOUR CHILD'S MENTAL HEALTH

When a parent has any health concerns, he/she seeks medical advice. Mental health problems may be more difficult to recognize. According the Center for Mental Health Services, one in five children has a diagnosable mental, emotional, or behavioral problem. Sometimes these problems lead to family conflict, school problems and academic failure, violence, or suicide. Even though help is available, two-thirds of the children with mental health problems do not get the help that they need.

Don't confuse normal responses with an illness. It is common for children to at times feel sad or to behave badly. However, if you are not sure, talk to a therapist about your concerns. Overall, if you see severe and persistent troubling behaviors, immediately seek help. The following questions will help to clarify if there is a problem and help you to effectively communicate your concerns to a therapist.

1. Is the child extremely fearful? Is this worry and fear is excessive in comparison to other children your child's age?
2. Does the child want to be alone all the time?
3. Do he or she avoid family and friends?
4. Does the child seem to have lost interest in things he or she formerly enjoyed?
5. Is the child angry most of the time?
6. Does he or she cry a lot?
7. Does the child overact to things?
8. Is the child easily distracted and does he or she seem to have poor concentration?
9. Does he or she have trouble making decisions?
10. Has the child's school performance gone down?
11. Is the child obsessed about his or her looks?
12. Are there unexplained changes in the child's sleeping or eating habits?
13. Does he or she complain about headaches, stomachaches, or other physical problems?

14. Does the child feel that life is too hard to manage or is he or she easily overwhelmed?

15. Does the child talk about suicide?

*If you answered yes to any of these questions, seek professional help.

WARNING SIGNS OF TEEN MENTAL HEALTH PROBLEMS

The teen years can be tremendously fun and interesting. They can also be tough for both the parent and child. Adolescents experience a lot of stress:

1. To be liked
2. To do well in school
3. To get along with their family (when they are trying to separate)
4. To define who they are
5. To plan their future
6. To manage negative peer pressure (substance use, etc.)
7. To deal with continual physical and emotional changes

Most of these pressures cannot be avoided, and worrying about them is natural. However, if your teen is feeling sad and depressed, hopeless, worthless, or overwhelmed, these could be warning signs of a mental health problem. These problems are real, painful, and can become severe. They can lead to increased difficulty and stress, such as family conflict, school problems, and academic failure. Consider the following review of possible problems:

1. Experiences significant changes
   A. Grades go down
   B. Loses interest in things usually enjoyed
   C. Wants to be alone all the time
   D. Avoids family and friends or doesn't get things done
   E. Daydreams a lot
   F. Feels that life is too hard and is overwhelmed
   G. Talks about suicide
   H. Hears voices
   I. Is not taking care of his/her hygiene
   J. Is giving prize possessions away
   K. Is very moody

2. Emotional changes
   A. Feels extremely sad and hopeless without reason
   B. Is angry a lot of the time
   C. Is often tearful
   D. Overreacts to things
   E. Feels worthless or guilty

F. Worries excessively

G. Has excessive anxiety

H. Cannot get over grief from a death of someone he/she was close to

I. Is extremely fearful

J. Is overly concerned about physical appearance

K. Is overly concerned about physical problems

L. Is fearful of his/her own thinking

M. Feels like he/she is out of control (his/her mind is out of control/someone is controlling him/her)

N. Has poor concentration

O. Has difficulty making decisions

P. Worries excessively

Q. Is constant fidgeting

R. Has difficulty remaining seated

S. Has a fear of harming self or others

T. Displays compulsive, ritualistic behavior

    1. Need to wash/clean things

    2. Hand washing

    3. Need for specific order

    4. Other similar behaviors

U. Has racing thoughts

V. Has persistent nightmares

W. Has a sleep disturbance

X. Has a appetite disturbance

3. Self-defeating behaviors

A. Substance use

B. Truancy

C. Lying/stealing

D. Eating excessive amounts of food

E. Forced vomiting

F. Abusing laxatives

G. Excessive exercise/dieting

H. Obsessiveness about weight (bone-thin)

I. Destroying property

J. Breaking the law

K. Hurting people or animals

L. Fascinated with fire/starts fires

M. Engaging in risky, life-threatening activities

If you identify any of these issues of concern, seek professional help for your teen.

TALKING TO CHILDREN

A parent communicating with their child is an important interaction. It is also complex because of the opportunity that it holds for the child in the way of building self-esteem, encouragement, feeling understood, and feeling accepted.

Accept the child as a unique individual separate from yourself. They have their own ideas and special way of looking at things. When a child experiences your acceptance they are more open to you, your support, and your interventions for problem solving. In other words, they feel respected.

Acceptance can be communicated verbally as well as nonverbally. If your verbal communication is accepting but your nonverbal communication is not it will be confusing to the child.

Ways of demonstrating your acceptance include:

1. Taking an interest in the child's activities, hobbies, and interests.
2. Listening to the child, and encouraging them to give details, to express their thoughts and feelings about it, and reflecting to them what you are hearing.
3. Allow and encourage the child to do thing for themselves. They are capable beings.
4. Be careful to avoid lecturing, repeating, ordering, preaching, criticizing, and shaming.

Always make an effort to hear what the child has to say. This means taking the time to listen. If you are in a hurry or have limited time let the child know and make sure that you follow up later to complete the conversation. For example, the morning can be rushed trying to get everyone ready for work and school. If this is not a good time for discussing things or sharing then clarify and offer other time frames for quality sharing.

Be accepting of the child's feelings. Treating a child as a unique, worthwhile person requires genuine positive regard, respect, and acceptance.

RULES FOR LISTENING

1. When a child is talking to you be facing them physically and use eye contact.
2. Avoid shaming, criticizing, preaching, nagging, threatening, or lecturing.
3. Treat a child in the respectful manner that you would treat a friend.
4. Be accepting and respectful of their feelings.
5. Restate in your own words the child's feelings and beliefs. Reflective listening is a demonstration of interest and understanding in what they are saying.
6. Be open and encouraging.
7. Allow and facilitate the child's learning. Resist jumping in with your own solutions.
8. Encourage a child to identify their own solution to problems. This encourages self-esteem.

RULES FOR PROBLEM SOLVING AND EXPRESSING YOUR THOUGHTS AND FEELINGS TO CHILDREN

1. Communicate your feelings with "I" messages. When you use "I" messages you are making a statement about how their behavior affects you and how you feel about it. "You" messages are blaming and disrespectful.
2. When there is a conflict:
   A. Decide who owns the problem.
   B. Limit your talking to perception of feelings and answering questions.
   C. Initiate problem solving. Invest the child in understanding the conflict and what to do about it.

3. Communicate belief in the child by what you say, how you say it, and with body language.

4. Always be encouraging. People learn from their mistakes. Encourage the child to learn from all of their experiences.

5. Be patient. Allow children the time to think and to express their responses to what it is you are sharing with them.

6. Admit that as an adult you do not have all the answers, but together you can explore alternatives and find solutions to their questions or difficult situations.

7. Engage in purposeful conversation, talking with one another to understand what the other means. They are worthy of your time.

8. Offer a non judgmental attitude which demonstrates respect.

9. Avoid pressure, sarcasm, ridicule, put-downs, and labeling.

DO'S

__ take an interest in what the child is interested in
__ allow the child to do things for himself
__ encourage the child to try new things
__ be accepting of their feelings
__ encourage their expression of thoughts and ideas
__ talk to the child honestly, simply, and at their level
__ ask one question at a time, and listen to their answer

DON'TS

__ do not tell a child that their fears are stupid
__ do not lie or make false promises
__ do not invade their privacy. Don't push them to talk about something that causes them to clam up more.
__ do not re-do tasks that they have completed. Be encouraging.
__ do not deny their feelings, "you shouldn't feel that way"
__ do not be controlling. Clarify rules, boundaries/limits, and safety issues. Children need room to grow.

GUIDELINES FOR DISCIPLINE THAT DEVELOPS RESPONSIBILITY

For discipline to be a learning experience that shapes positive, appropriate, and responsible behavior requires that the consequences be:

1. logically related to the misbehavior.

2. given in a manner that treats a person with dignity. Also separate the behavior from the person.

3. based on the reality of the social order with clarification on its importance for community living.

4. concerned with present and future behavior, not bringing up the past.

5. verbally expressed in a way that communicates respect and goodwill.

6. tied to choices, i.e., all choices have a consequence, some are positive and some are negative. Choosing a certain behavior is acknowledging a willingness to accept the associated consequences.

7. a defining factor for telling the difference between a privilege and a right.

HELPFUL HINTS

1. Don't look at discipline as a win or lose situation. The goals are:
   A. to provide the opportunity to make one's own decisions and to be responsible for their own behavior.
   B. to encourage children to learn the natural order of community life (rules are necessary to promote optimal freedom of choice for all and to maintain safety).
   C. to encourage children to do things for themselves for the development of self-respect, self-esteem, and taking responsibility for their own behavior.

2. Be both firm and kind.

3. Don't lecture. Be brief, clear, and respectful.

4. Don't fight.

5. Don't be worn down or manipulated.

6. Be consistent.

7. Be patient. It takes time for natural and logical consequences to be effective.

8. Don't be reactive. Parents' responses often reinforce children's goals for power, attention, revenge, or displays of inadequacy. Be calm and respectful when you intervene.

STEPS IN APPLYING LOGICAL CONSEQUENCES

1. Provide choices and accept the child's decisions. Allow them the space and time to learn. Use a friendly tone of voice that communicates respect and goodwill.

2. As you follow through with a consequence be assuring that they may be able to try again at a later time. Encourage them to express the purpose of the consequence for demonstrated mutual understanding.

3. If the misbehavior is repeated, extend the time that must elapse before the child is given another opportunity. Be careful not to make the mistake of initially choosing a time frame which is too long. Children do not share your concept of time, and the purpose of the consequence may be lost.

SURVIVING DIVORCE

Divorce is one of the most stressful life experiences to endure. However, as with all times of crisis it can also be a time of opportunity and new beginnings. It is a time to learn, to grow personally, and to develop new relationships and discover community resources. The first step in learning how to deal with divorce to understand how it is affecting you emotionally and physically. Once you have an increased awareness for how you are being affected, you can then acknowledge and accept your feelings, which becomes a springboard of learning new ways to take care of yourself. This is a very stressful time, but you will learn that you can deal with such a big change in your life and even go on to thrive.

PHYSICAL STRESS

Whenever a person goes through a stressful experience, the body is affected. Ongoing stress can even lead to physical illness. Some physical experiences include headaches, stomach upset, sleep disturbance, appetite disturbance, and exacerbation of preexisting illnesses such as asthma or back pain. Pay attention to you body and take care of yourself.

EMOTIONAL STRESS

Many difficult emotions are associated with divorce. You may experience feelings of

1. Failure
2. Anger
3. Resentment
4. Worry
5. Depression
6. Loss
7. Sadness
8. Fear
9. Frustration
10. Loneliness
11. Helpless

In addition to such feelings, there is also the fact that you miss sharing your life with someone. You miss the warmth, friendship, financial security, and intimacy you had or hoped you would have had. If you have children, that job also becomes more difficult. Often, parents who have divorced find that the level of demand in caring for their children significantly increases because they are no longer sharing those responsibilities in the same home. There is less time to spend with children during a time that their needs are greater. If you are not the one who wanted the divorce, you may be struggling with feeling angry and you may be resentful for having such changes and losses forced on you. You have to be careful to not put the children in the middle of your anger and grief. There may also be conflict stressors associated with custody and child support. You may have worries about your children being alienated from you. Divorce is even more painful if is seems like everyone around you seems to be happily married or you get little or no support from family and friends.

SELF-CARE

1. Recognize your feelings and find positive ways to deal with them
2. Reach out to other, use your social resources
3. Find social support in your community with groups dealing with divorce and other activities
4. Take good care of your body (sleep, nutrition, laughter, exercise)
5. Take risks by trying new activities and getting distracted from your problems
6. Nurture yourself, do things that feel good and do not have a harmful side

Doing these things can make you stronger, more confident, and more content.

Differences between Biological Families and Stepfamilies

Biological family	Stepfamily
Marriage is a new beginning	Marriage brings together two families
Traditions and history develop	Different traditions and history—not shared
Couple's relationship comes before relationship with children	Biological parent-child relations come before new marital relationship
Family lives in same home	Children spend time in two parental homes
Couple develops parenting role and skills gradually and together	Couple brings their own individual parenting ideas and skills to marriage

Since approximately 50% of first marriages and approximately 60% of second marriage end in divorce, understanding what happens in marriage is important if you want to improve the outcome of your marriage when it is complicated by stepfamily issues. As with all marriages, the factors necessary for success are the following:

1. Honor
2. Validation
3. Respect
4. Responsibility
5. Communication
6. Discipline
7. Parent-centered structure

HONOR

Honor embodies the meaning of marriage vows. It is the feeling demonstrated to a marital partner that he/she is the most important person in your life.

VALIDATION

Validation means to listen, acknowledge, and accept that everyone is entitled to their own thoughts and feelings. There are few things that feel as bad as when we share our thoughts and feelings and they are denied as real, accurate, or important by someone important.

RESPECT

One never minimizes how their choices and behavior affect the people that they love, especially their life partner. Treat others as you desire to be treated. Respect is the foundation of trust.

RESPONSIBILITY

Responsibility describes how one thinks and behaves in a way that demonstrates doing what is right. It is the recognition that we have obligations and values, which clarifies how to take care of and nurture a couple's relationship.

COMMUNICATION

Open and honest communication is the foundation of a successful stepfamily. Do not avoid talking about difficult issues. Instead problem-solve the issues that confront you as a couple and your family (children) together.

DISCIPLINE

It is imperative that a couple approach parenting issues as a team. The children in a family need the consistency offered by the team approach. Likewise, the couple benefits from being able to depend on an alliance with their team member.

PARENT-CENTERED STRUCTURE

A couple's bond needs to be strong. When there is a healthy couple relationship, there is greater success in dealing with difficult family issues.

HELPING CHILDREN COPE WITH SCHEDULING CHANGES

A schedule change could be a return to work following a long leave of absence, change from a traditional lifestyle (Mom has been at home), or family/parent adjustments of any kind, which present a disruption to a child's schedule or learned expectation of parental contact. The following are some suggestions to consider:

1. Talk with your child in age-appropriate terms. Talk factually about the change and explain in age-appropriate language what that means. Remain focused on the positive aspects and consider that even what you view as a negative may not be experienced in the same manner by your child. Likewise, what you see as positive may be stressful to your child. Explain what you will be doing and how important it is.

2. If possible, take your children to your place of work (or familiarize them with whatever is associated with change) so that they have a picture of where you will be or what is involved. If there is a receptionist, introduce them for added comfort should there be a time they need to call you. If at all possible, call them at predetermined times to check in.

3. Outline changes that will improve your lives and make things easier. This is an opportunity to develop positive family behaviors. Family members should all have a contribution in self-responsibility and home maintenance. Children are likely to feel empowered when they feel that they have positive contributions. Think of age-appropriate ways that children can help around the house and develop a reward system for reinforcing the development of self-responsibility.

4. Make sure that your children know that you are thinking of them without repeatedly reinforcing how much you miss them or how sad you are. They may begin to feel responsible for making you happy or develop other negative feelings about work or change. Instead, do sweet things like leaving them fun notes.

5. Be emotionally available to your children when you are with them. Sitting in front of the television or being busy with chores when you are home is not a demonstration of taking the time to be with them. Talk to and *listen* to your children. Keep the lines of communication open so you will know what is happening in their lives and how they feel about it. This way you will know what are they interested in, what do they like at school, what are they struggling with, who their friends are, and so forth.

6. Each day, allot specific child time where there is no phone, no television, no interruptions of any kind. Even if it is only a short period of time, you are telling your children how important they are, which reinforces positive self-esteem. This is an investment in your child. One thing you can do is it read to your child. Reading with children is a special time; it fosters reading as being enjoyable, a quiet time, and it can be used as a nonstressful means for working on difficult issues. Think of the possibility that reading may facilitate children to be more open to learning life lessons.

7. Demonstrate a focus on the positives and what *is* working. Demonstrating genuine gratitude for what one has improves coping with limitations and encourages letting go or accepting what cannot be changed.

8. If you feel that your child is keeping difficult emotions inside or you just want to stimulate the sharing of thoughts and feelings, play the "finish the sentence" game. Create sentence stems where the child gets to complete the sentence. This game not only creates the opportunity to understand what your child is thinking and feeling, it is also an opportunity for your child to find out that you have similar feelings about some things. Examples include the following
   A. "I Wish..."
   B. "I feel happy when..."
   C. "I feel unhappy when..."
   D. "I don't understand..."
   E. "When I grow up I will never..."
   F. "When I grow up I will..."

9. Even when you find yourself tired and frustrated, don't give into blaming your significant other for hardships created by the changes associated with necessary adjustment. If you talk in terms of feeling punished for taking responsibility for what needs to be done, consider the effect on children and how they may be reinforced to view their own issues of responsibility.

10. Remember, you are the role model for positive self-talk and self-care. Your child is learning from watching you:
   A. How to interact with the world
   B. How to simply do what needs to be done without negativity and procrastination
   C. How to problem-solve and resolve conflicts
   D. How to appropriately get needs met

IS YOUR BEHAVIOR IN THE BEST INTEREST OF YOUR CHILDREN?

Though we often consider a separation or divorce to be a time when parents engage in behaviors that may be emotionally and psychologically damaging to children, the concern of children could be expanded in general to marital distress as well. Therefore, carefully consider the following, and if you do any of the things listed, stop immediately. Try to put yourself in the shoes of your child, who needs a healthy relationship with both parents.

1. Do not put your child in the middle
   A. Children should not be placed between two parents communicating information from one to the other. Parents need to act like adults and communicate directly.

2. Do not put your child in the position of having to choose to be with one parent over the other
   A. Parents are supposed to be in the family leadership role. This means that children are supposed to be able to rely on parents to make the decisions that are best for them.
   B. Allow your children to be children, not to take on adult worries and stress
   C. Parents are supposed to protect, nurture, and encourage children

3. Do not use your child as a confidant
   A. Do not speak to your children about the adult issues that you struggle with
   B. Do not speak to your children about your view of the faults of other parents
   C. Do not try to get children "on your side" against the other parent

4. Do not allow your child to be responsible for you emotionally
   A. When your children are exposed to your emotional displays of sadness, fear, anger, and so on, they may come to believe that they are responsible for protecting you and making you feel better because they
      1. See you as fragile and unable to fulfill all aspects of your parent role
      2. See you as a victim of the other parent

If you are doing any of these behaviors, then something is wrong. As a parent, you need to stop thinking about yourself and your needs and take responsibility for what you are doing to your children. If you need support, understanding, and to problem-solve how to deal with your own difficult feelings, get help so that you can learn to do things differently before you damage your children and their relationship with the other parent.

Your children are entitled to the following:

1. To be a carefree child who does not have to worry about you or adult issues.
2. To have a healthy relationship with both parents.
3. To be able to trust that their parents will protect them and their emotions.
4. To be encouraged and supported in their lives.

THE RULES OF POLITENESS

The Do's	The Don'ts
Give sincere and positive appreciation. If you have an issue to resolve, sit down and discuss it in a constructive manner to manage your differences.	Don't complain or nag.
Be courteous and considerate.	Don't be selfish.
Express interest in the activities of others. Try to listen and ask questions.	Don't hog the conversation.
Give others a chance to finish speaking.	Don't suddenly interrupt.
Speak honestly and in a caring way.	Don't put others down.
Critique your ideas, but don't criticize yourself.	Don't put yourself down.
Focus on the present situation. If you have an issue, sit down and discuss some constructive solutions.	Don't bring up old resentments.
Think of the needs and wants of others. Be empathic. If you have an issue to resolve, sit down and work out a constructive solution.	Don't think only of your own needs and wants.
Be sensitive to others as you choose topics to discuss.	Don't embarrass or humiliate others.

SELF-MONITORING

Self-monitoring is the process of observing and recording your thoughts, feelings, and behaviors. It is used to:

1. Define or redefine the problem or target of change as needed.

2. Increase or decrease desired target behaviors, thoughts or feelings.

3. Evaluate the progress toward your goal(s).

Self-monitoring is important for increasing your awareness for which management skills and behaviors have been most helpful, and in planning the steps you will take to ensure continued progress and success. Initiate self-monitoring by:

1. Identify
   A. Target behaviors, thoughts, and/or feelings to be changed
   B. Desired Behaviors
   C. Goals

2. Identify methods supportive of making desired changes and reaching your goals
   A. Objectives
   B. Strategies

3. What has been most helpful, and how do you plan to maintain positive changes

QUESTIONS TO ASK YOURSELF

1. Suppose someone who used to know you well, but has not seen you for some time sees you when you complete the program. What would be different about you then than now?

2. When you are successful, what will you be doing differently?

3. How would you like to benefit from the program, and how will you make that happen?

4. What do you want to be thinking, feeling, and doing?

5. How much control do you have over making this happen?

6. What changes will these goals require of you?

7. Can these goals be achieved without the help of anyone or anything else?

8. To whom is this goal most important?

9. Who, specifically, is responsible for making this happen?

It is important that goals be feasible and realistic.
Part of self-monitoring includes:

1. Goal Setting

2. Accomplishment

3. Listing Strengths

4. Resources

GOAL SETTING

In order to accomplish the tasks that will make the most difference in the quality of your life experience it is required that you develop appropriate goals. To successfully reach your goals requires that you develop a plan using objectives or steps which will lead to the completion of your selected goal(s).

1. Goal: _____

   Objective: _____

   _____

   _____

2. Goal: _____

   Objective:_____

   _____

   _____

3. Goal: _____

   Objective:_____

   _____

   _____

4. Goal: _____

   Objective:_____

   _____

   _____

5. Goal: _____

Objective:_____

_____

_____

ACCOMPLISHMENTS

From the time that you begin your program of change and personal growth it is important to keep a log of what you accomplish in how you think, how you manage your feelings and the difficulties in your life, and behavioral changes.

_____

_____

_____

_____

_____

_____

_____

_____

_____

_____

STRENGTHS

As you continue to work toward your goals of personal growth you will learn more about yourself, your abilities, and your assets. These are your strengths. As you identify them write them down. Your strengths contribute significantly to how you manage your life. When you combine your strengths with your skills and your resources you will experience yourself as much more effective in how you choose to live your life.

1. _____

2. _____

3. _____

4. _____

5. _____

6. _____

7. _____

8. _____

9. _____

10. _____

RESOURCES

Developing a list of resources can be very helpful. It will have to be updated from time to time. Write down whatever resources you are aware of at this time and continue to add to it as you go through this program. Examples of resources include trusted individuals, community meetings, sponsors, etc.

1. _____

2. _____

3. _____

4. _____

5. _____

6. _____

7. _____

8. _____

9. _____

10. _____

TEN RULES FOR EMOTIONAL HEALTH

1. *Take care of yourself.* Take time to relax, exercise, eat well, spend time with people you enjoy and activities which you find pleasurable. When you are the best you can be the best that you can be in relationships.

2. *Choose to find the positives in life experiences instead of focusing on the negatives.* Most clouds have a silver lining and offer opportunities for personal understanding and growth. When you accept that things are difficult and just do what you need to do then it doesn't seem so hard.

3. *Let go of the past.* If you can't change it and you have no control over it then let it go. Don't waste your energy on things that cannot benefit you. Forgive yourself and others.

4. *Be respectful and responsible.* Don't worry about other people; do what you know is right for you. When you take care of business you feel good. Don't get caught up in blaming others.

5. *Acknowledge and take credit for your successes and accomplishments.* Avoid false modesty.

6. *Take the time to develop one or two close relationships in which you can be honest about your thoughts and feelings.*

7. *Talk positively to yourself.* We talk to ourselves all day long. If we are saying negative and fearful things then that is the way we feel.

8. *Remove yourself from hurtful or damaging situations.* Temporarily walk away from a situation that is getting out of control. Give yourself some space and problem solve a positive approach to dealing with it.

9. *Accept that life is about choices and is always bringing change to you to which requires adjustment.*

10. *Have a plan for the future.* Develop long range goals for yourself, but work on them one day at a time.

Chapter 4

Professional Practice Forms
Clinical Forms
Business Forms

Although there is some similarity to several of the forms in each section, there are minor variations which allow them to be used to meet more specific needs. For example, there are several variations of assessment forms which have been designed to be utilized for different reasons and offer slightly different information.

Overall, the forms offer a basic selection of the breadth of forms used in a general mental health practice. At the same time there are some forms whose use does not necessarily fall under the general practice expectation, but may fulfil needs of expectation as a reviewer of someone else's work or working toward the development of a new specialty or service.

Clinical Forms

CASE FORMULATION

If you are preparing to consult with a treatment team, insurance case reviewer, or referring physician, consider the following informational format:

If the consult is with a case reviewer, the initial information presented should include the following:

1. Identifying information
   A. Provider name and identification (ID) number (Social Security number or tax ID)
   B. Member name, identification, and date of birth (DOB)

2. Treatment modality
   A. Type of session (individual, conjoint/family, or group)
   B. Number of sessions to date and session frequency
   C. Number of additional sessions needed to complete treatment

GENERAL CONSULT INFORMATION

1. Diagnostic information
   A. Multiaxial diagnosis
      1. On Axis IV, be specific. General examples include the following:
         a. Problems with primary support group
         b. Economic problems
         c. Housing problems
         d. Educational problems
         e. Occupational problems
         f. Problems with access to health care
         g. Problems in interaction with legal/criminal system
         h. Problems related to social environment
         i. Problems related to stage of life issues
         j. Other psychosocial and environmental problems

2. Medical presentation
   A. Psychotropic medications
   B. Substance abuse
   C. Elaboration on Axis III issues presenting
      1. Management problems
      2. Medical instability
      3. Factors influencing emotional/psychological functioning

3. Clinical presentation
   A. Crisis issues
      1. Harm to self
      2. Harm to others
      3. Child abuse/neglect
      4. Other related issues
   B. Symptoms/behavior
   C. Stability and compliance
   D. History of abuse/neglect/assault
   E. Treatment history (including hospitalizations) and course of assoc. treatment
   F. Family history and involvement in treatment

4. Relevant history of presenting problem(s)
5. Current status
    A. Descriptive current level of functioning
    B. Situational issues impeding or facilitating improvement

6. Treatment goals and objectives
    A. Integrating empirically supported treatments

GENERAL CLINICAL EVALUATION

The general clinical evaluation systematically reviews all domains associated with understanding an individual and his/her level of functioning. Depending on the presentation of a given area, the assessment will vary in intensity as needed. Areas of evaluation include the following:

1. Presenting problem/reason for evaluation
2. Referral source with associated information
3. History of the presenting problem
4. Psychiatric history
    A. Chronology of episodes of mental illness and associated course of treatment including medication, treatment programs, and treatment providers
    B. Responses to prior treatment (medication, dosage, duration, side effects, benefits, complaints)

5. Medical history
    A. Medical illness (medication(s), treatment, procedures, hospitalizations)
    B. Undiagnosed health problems
    C. Injuries, trauma
    D. Sexual/reproductive history
    E. Headaches/chronic pain
    F. Allergies/drug sensitivities
    G. Disease(s), infection
    H. Health-related behaviors (exercise, nutrition, use of substances, etc.)

6. Substance use history
    A. Specific substances
    B. Frequency/amount
    C. Route of administration
    D. Pattern of use (episodic/continual/single/recreational/mood management)
    E. Association between substance use and mental illness
    F. Perceived benefits

7. Personal history
    A. Developmental milestones/stage-of-life experiences
    B. Response to transitions/adjustments
    C. Genetic influences (inherited/consequences, potential of passing on to children)
    D. Psychosocial issues
        1. Family (experiences and genogram)
        2. Education

    3. Religion/spiritual beliefs

    4. Culture/ethnicity (immigration, political repression, war experience, natural disaster)

    5. Legal issues (past, current)

E. Current level of functioning

    1. Mood management

    2. Family (marriage, parenting)

    3. Personal relationships/resources

    4. Work

    5. School

    6. Social environment

F. Past level of functioning

    1. Mood management

    2. Family (marriage/parenting)

    3. Personal relationships/resources

    4. Work

    5. School

    6. Social environment

8. Mental status examination (MSE)

A. The MSE is a systematic review of observed information collected during the interview

    1. Appearance, grooming, general behavior

    2. Facial expressions

    3. Mood

    4. Affect

    5. Characteristics of speech and language

    6. Movement (rate, repetition, posturing, purposeful, unusual movements)

    7. Thoughts and perception

        a. Spontaneous thoughts (concerns, worries, impulses, perceptual experiences)

        b. Cognitive/perceptual distortions (hallucination, delusions, ideas of reference, obsessions, compulsions)

        c. Issues of risk (danger to self, danger to others, violent, self-injurious) (insight, judgment, impulse control)

    8. Associations (loose or idiosyncratic associations, contradictory statements)

    9. Understanding/insight of the current situation

    10. Cognitive status

        a. Level of consciousness

        b. Orientation

        c. Attention and concentration

        d. Memory (short term, intermediate, long term)

        e. Language function (naming, fluency, comprehension, repetition, reading, writing)

        f. Fund of knowledge

        g. Calculation

        h. Abstract reasoning (explaining similarities, explaining proverbs)

        i. Executive functions (judgment, resisting distraction, inhibition of impulsive answers, recognizing contradictions)

9. Diagnostic tests
    A. There may be the use of paper-and-pencil tests or inventories, which may used later to assess improvement in patient functioning or to monitor other areas of progress

10. Initial diagnostic impression and diagnoses to be ruled out

11. Initial treatment plan

12. Recommendations or requests of the treatment team members are to follow up on in establishing a comprehensive treatment plan

TREATMENT PLAN

_____

Name: Date:

DOB: SS#:

Referral source:

Current medications:
(and purpose of medications)   Prescribing physician: _____

_____   Primary care physician: _____

_____   Current health problems:_____

_____   _____

_____   _____

_____   _____

                                            Date of last physical exam: _____

                                            Approximate date and time frame of treatment

Prior inpatient and/or outpatient treatment (Reason for treatment, Provider, Outcome of treatment) physical and emotional reasons

_____

_____

_____

Is there a family history of the following? (If yes, explain)

Alcoholism: _____

Drug abuse/dependency: _____

Emotional/psychological problems: _____

Health issues (hypertension, diabetes, cardiac, others): _____

_____

_____

Do you use substances (daily basis, binging/party, other patterns, how much)?

_____

_____

Is there a history of sexual abuse or sexual assault?

_____

_____

Is there a history of anger problems or domestic violence?

_____

_____

DIFFICULTIES EXPERIENCED

Thoughts/Feelings/Mood

__ Depression
__ Anxiety
__ Sadness
__ Fear
__ Fatigue
__ Euphoria
__ High energy
__ Financial stress

__ Intrusive thoughts
__ Anger/frustration
__ Not liking self
__ Not liking others
__ Sudden mood changes
__ Obsessive/ruminative thoughts
__ Thought of hurting yourself
__ Legal worries/problems
__ Hear things other people don't

__ Dissociation
__ Depersonaliztion
__ Derealization
__ Thoughts of hurting others
__ Excessive worry/stress
__ Negative thoughts
__ Believing you are better than others
__ Confusion
__ Memory difficulties
__ Difficulty with attention and concentration
__ Suspicious(Distrustful)
__ See things other people don't

Behaviors

__ Compulsive behavior/rituals
__ Difficulty with daily routine
__ Difficulty getting to appt. on time
__ Let others take advantage of you
__ Using alcohol/drug to cope
__ Dependency upon others

__ Angry/hostile
__ Withdrawal from other
__ Isolation
__ Self destructive/sabotaging
__ Abuse of others
__ Hyperactivity
__ Not able to relax

__ Lying
__ Stealing
__ Reactive
__ Avoidant
__ Controlling
__ Argumentative
__ Decrease/lack of sexual interest
__ Preoccupation with sex

Experience in Workplace

__ Pattern of tardiness
__ Absenteeism
__ General performance
__ General satisfaction

__ Negative feelings about work
__ Difficulty with supervision
__ Difficulty with coworkers
__ History of work problems

Physical Functioning

__ Ulcers
__ Bowel problems/changes in habit
__ Abdominal pain/vomiting
__ Changes in urinary patterns
__ Changes in menstrual problems
__ Colitis/irritable bowl
__ Headache
__ Hearing/vision problems
__ Sweating/flushes

__ Hyperventilation
__ Shortness of breath
__ Easily fatigued
__ Back pain
__ Joint pain
__ Swelling legs/ankles/feat
__ Chest pain
__ Shakiness/trembling

__ Hypertension
__ Hypoglycemia
__ Thyroid dysfunction
__ Sleep disturbance
__ Appetite disturbance
__ Hypoglycemia
__ Skin problems

Presenting problem identified by client (why is the person coming to therapy and why now?):
As stated by client

_____

_____

_____

_____

_____

PRESENTING PROBLEMS PERCEIVED BY CLINICIAN

Personal	**Addictions**	**Crisis Issues**
Depression	Alcohol	Suicidal ideation/ death wish
Anxiety	Smoking	• H/o suicide attempts
Stress	Amphetamine	Self destructive behavior
Grief	Cocaine	• Homicidal ideation
Self-esteem	Hallucinogens	• H/o violent behavior
	Huffing	• Potential for violent behavior
Interpersonal	Opeatis	Child abuse
Significant other	Sedatives	Domestic violence
Marital	Tranquilizers	Dependent adult abuse/neglect
Family	Eating	Elder abuse
Child	Gambling	
Divorce	Sex	
Friendships	Stealing	
Work/School	**Health**	
• Career/vocational	Weight	
• Performance	Appetite	
• Interpersonal	Sleep	
• Authority	Pain	
	Other	

DSM IV Diagnosis

Axis I_____

_____

Axis II _____

_____

Axis III _____

_____

Axis IV _____

_____

Axis V _____

_____

	Problem	Goal	Interventions	Time frame to complete goal	How progress monitored
1					
2					
3					
4					
5					
6					

_____   _____

Therapist's signature   Date

_____   _____

Client's signature   Date

MENTAL STATUS EXAM

The mental status exam serves as the basis for diagnosis and understanding of the dynamic elements which contribute to an individual's current level of psychological and emotional functioning.

A satisfactory assessment should include objective behavioral observation as well as information elicited through selected questioning of the individual. Sensitivity, tact, and respect to the individual and their reactions will facilitate cooperation.

The following outline for the mental status exam breaks down the type of information needed for a thorough evaluation. In order to foster feelings of interest and compassion from the therapist it is best to begin the evaluation by discussing the present difficulties or primary complaint and then proceed in a natural manner. This is accomplished by blending specific questions into the general flow of the interview.

CONTENTS OF EXAMINATION

1. Appearance, Behavior, and Attitude
    A. Appearance—apparent age, grooming, hygiene/cleanliness, physical characteristic (build/weight, physical abnormalities, deformities, etc.), appropriate attire. The description of appearance should offer adequate detail for identification. It should take into consideration the individual's age, race, sex, educational background, cultural background, socioeconomic status, etc.
    B. Motor Activity—gait (awkward, staggering, shuffling, rigid), posture (slouched, erect), coordination, speed/activity level, mannerisms, gestures, tremors, picking on body, tics/grimacing, relaxed, restless, pacing, threatening, overactive or underactive, disorganized, purposeful, stereotyped, repetitive.
    C. Interpersonal—rapport with the interviewer. Evaluation process, cooperative, opposition/resistant, submissive, defensive.
    D. Facial Expression—relaxed, tense, happy, sad, alert, day-dreamy, angry, smiling, distrustful/suspicious, tearful.
    E. Behavior—distant, indifferent, evasive, negative, irritable, labile, depressive, anxious, sullen, angry, assaultive, exhibitionistic, seductive, frightened, alert, agitated, lethargic, somnolent.

2. Characteristics of Speech
   A. Descriptors—normal, pressured, slow, articulate, amount, loud, soft, dysarthric, apraxic, accent, enunciation.
   B. Expressive Language—normal, circumstantial, anomia, paraphasia, clanging, echolalia, incoherent, blocking, neologisms, perseveration, flight of ideas, mutism.
   C. Receptive Language—normal, comprehends, abnormal.

3. Mood and Affect
   A. Mood—a symptom as reported by the individual describing how they feel emotionally, such as: normal, euphoric, elevated, depressed, irritable, anxious, angry.
   B. Affect—observed reaction or expressions. Range of affect includes: broad, restricted, blunted, flat, inappropriate, labile, mood congruent, mood incongruent.

4. Orientation and Intellectual Ability
   A. Orientation—time, person, place, and self. The individual should be asked questions such as the day of the week, the date, where he lives, where he is at, and if he knows who he is.
   B. Intellectual Ability—above average, average, below average
      1. General information—the last four presidents, governor of the state, the capital of the state, what direction does the sun set, etc.
      2. Calculation—serially subtracting 7 from 100 until he can go no further. Simple multiplication word problems such as, "if a pencil costs 5 cents, how many pencils can you but with 45 cents?"
      3. Abstract Reasoning—proverbs. This is the ability to make valid generalizations. Responses may be literal, concrete, personalized, or bizarre. Example, "Still waters run deep", "A rolling stone gather no moss".
      4. Opposites—slow/fast, big/small, hard/soft.
      5. Similarities—door/window, telephone/radio, dog/cat, apple/banana.
      6. Attention—digit span, trials to learn four words.
      7. Concentration—months of the year or days of the week backward.
      8. Reasoning and Judgment—is able to connect consequences to choices and behaviors.

5. Memory—immediate (10 to 30 sec)
   short term (up to $1\frac{1}{2}$ hours)
   recent (2 hours to 4 days)
   recent past (past few months)
   remote past (6 months to lifetime)

6. Thought Processes/Content—deals with organization and composition of thought. Examples include: normal, blocking, loose associations, confabulation, flight of ideas, ideas of reference, illogical thinking, grandiosity, magical thinking, obsessions, perseveration, delusions, depersonalization, suicidal ideation, homicidal ideation.

7. Hallucination—none, auditory, visual, olfactory, gustatory.

8. Insight—good, fair, poor. Understanding, thought, feeling, behavior.

9. Impulse Control—good, fair, poor. The ability/tendency to resist or act on impulses.

A Mental Status Exam review form can be a helpful adjunct to the initial assessment report.

MENTAL STATUS EXAM

Appearance: Grooming   __Normal   __Disheveled   __Unusual
            Hygiene   __Normal   __Body Odor   __Bad Breath
                      __Other _____

Motor Activity   __Relaxed   __Restless   __Pacing   __Sedate
                __Threatening   __Catatonic   __Posturing
                __Mannerisms __Psychomotor Retardation
                __Tremors   __Tics   __Other _____

Interpersonal   __Cooperative   __Oppositional/Resistant
               __Defensive   __Other _____

Speech   __Normal   __Pressured   __Slow   __Dysarthric   __Apraxic
   Expressive Language   __Normal   __Circumstantial   __Anomia
                          __Paraphasia   __Clanging   __Echolalia
                          __Incoherent   __Neologisms
   Receptive Language   __Normal   __Abnormal _____

Mood   __Normal   __Euphoric   __Elevated   __Depressed   __Angry
        __Irritable   __Anxious

Affect   __Broad   __Restricted   __Blunted   __Flat
        __Inappropriate   __Labile

Orientation   __Normal   __Abnormal _____

Estimated IQ   __Above Average   __Average   __Below Average

Attention   __Normal   __Distractible   __Hypervigilant

Concentration   __Normal   __Brief

Memory   Recent Memory   __Normal   __Abnormal
          Remote Memory   __Normal   __Abnormal

Thought Processes   __Normal   __Blocking   __Loose Associations
                     __Confabulation   __Flight of Ideas
                     __Ideas of Reference   __Grandiosity
                     __Paranoia   __Magical Thinking   __Obsessions
                     __Perseveration   __Delusions
                     __Depersonalization   __Suicidal Ideation
                     __Homicidal Ideation   __Other _____

Hallucination   __None   __Auditory   __Visual   __Olfactory
               __Gustatory

Judgment   __Good   __Fair   __Poor

Insight   __Good   __Fair   __Poor

Impulse Control   __Good   __Fair   __Poor

MENTAL STATUS EXAM

Date: _____

Name: _____

INITIAL INTERVIEW

Presenting Problem:

Sleep patterns:

Appetite change:

Drug/alcohol use:

Marital status:

Marriage quality:

Children:

APPEARANCE
Clothing
    Clean
    Dirty
    Disheveled
    Atypical
Physical Hygiene
    Good
    Fair
    Poor

BEHAVIOR
Posture
    Normal
    Slumped
    Rigid
    Unsteady
    Atypical
Facial Expression
    Anxious
    Sad
    Hostile
    Cheerful
    Inappropriate
    Other_____

General Body Movements
    Accelerated
    Slowed
    Appropriate
    Inappropriate
Speech (speed and volume)
    Increased/loud
    Decreased/slowed
    Normal
    Mute
    Atypical
Relationships with Others
    Domineering
    Submissive
    Provocative
    Suspicious
    Uncooperative
    Cooperative
    Physically/emotionally abusive

FEELINGS (AFFECT AND MOOD)
    Appropriate
    Inappropriate
Range of Affect
    Broad
    Restricted
Lability of Affect
    Labile
    Stable
Prominent Mood
    Euphoria
    Hostility
    Anxiety
    Sadness
    Fearful
    Other_____

PERCEPTION
Illusions
    Present
    Absent
Hallucinations
    Absent
    Present
    Visual
    Olfactory
    Tactile
    Responding to hallucinations
    Not responding to hallucinations
Thought processes
Orientation
Disoriented
X-4 Person/place/time/situation

Memory
Impaired
Not impaired
Immediate
Recent
Remote
Comments:
Thought content
    Obsessions
    Compulsions
    Phobias
    Dearealization

Depersonalization
Suicidal ideation
Homicidal ideation
Delusions
No thought disorder
Sexually preoccupied
Associational Disturbance
    Present
    Absent
Judgment
    Impaired
    Not impaired

Comments:

_____

_____

_____

_____

_____

_____

_____   _____

Therapist   Date

INITIAL CASE ASSESSMENT

Name: _____ Date of 1st Contact: _____ Date of 1st Session: _____

IDENTIFYING INFORMATION:

_____

_____

_____

PRESENTING PROBLEM:

_____

_____

_____

SITUATION STRESSORS:

_____

_____

_____

MENTAL STATUS EXAM:

_____

_____

_____

SYMPTOMS OF IMPAIRED FUNCTIONING:

_____

_____

_____

PATIENT'S STRENGTHS AND ASSETS:

_____

_____

_____

DIAGNOSIS:

AXIS I: _____   AXIS IV: _____
AXIS II: _____   AXIS V: CURRENT _____
AXIS III: _____ PAST: _____

DIAGNOSTIC COMMENTS:

_____

_____

_____

_____

_____

_____

TREATMENT GOALS:

_____

_____

_____

_____

_____

_____

_____

TREATMENT PLAN:

_____

_____

_____

_____

_____

_____

_____

THERAPIST _____   DATE ___ ___ ___

INITIAL EVALUATION

Person(s) present at interview:

_____

1. Presenting Problem
   A. Presenting problems and precipitating events
   B. History of problems
   C. Medications/Prescribed by whom
   D. Primary Care Physician (PCP)

2. Interpersonal Relationships
   A. Current living arrangement
   B. Present family relationships
   C. Relationships in Family-of-Origin (past emphasis)
   D. Marital/significant other relationships (past and present)
   E. Peers and social relationships

3. Medical and developmental history

_____

_____

_____

4. Vocational and educational information

_____

_____

_____

5. Other mental health and community agency involvement (past and present)

_____

_____

_____

_____

6. Diagnostic impression
   A. Client mental status
   B. Strengths and weaknesses
   C. Diagnosis
      Axis:
         I   _____

         II _____

         III _____

IV _____

V _____

  D. Observations about other family members and relationships

7. Treatment Disposition
   A. Goals (what will be accomplished)
   B. Objectives (what interventions to reach goals)

_____   Date_____

BRIEF MENTAL HEALTH EVALUATION REVIEW

Name: _____   DOB: _____

Date first examined: _____   Type of Service
                                                 __ Outpatient
                                                 __ Case management

Date of most recent visit: _____

Presenting Problem: _____

_____

Diagnosis

Axis I _____

Axis II _____

Axis III _____

Axis IV _____

Axis IV _____Current   _____ Last year

Medications: _____

_____

Current Mental Status Examination (circle and comment on abnormal findings)
Appearance and Behavior

    Grooming: well-groomed   disheveled   eccentric   poor hygiene

    Motor activity: normal tremor,   retarded agitated   hyperactive

    Speech: normal   slow   rapid   pressured   slurred   mute   delayed   soft
        loud   tuttering   aphasia

    Interview behavior: cooperative   guarded evasive

    Behavior disturbance: none   irritable   aggressive   violent/poor   impulse   contol
        manipulative   apathetic

Comment: _____

_____

Sensorium and Cognitive Functioning

    Orientation: oriented x4   disoriented (person, place, time, situation)

    Concentration: intact   slight distracted   impaired (mild, moderate, severe)

    Memory: normal   impaired (immediate, recent, remote) and degree (mild,
        moderate, severe)

    Intelligence: above average   average   below average   borderline   mental
        retardation

Comment: _____

_____

Mood and Affect

Mood: normal anxious depressed fearful elated euphoric angry

Affect: appropriate labile expansive blunted flat

Perception

Hallucinations: none auditory visual olfactory gustatory

Illusions: none misidentified

Thought Processes

Associations: goal directed blocking circumstantial tangential loose
  neologisms

Content-delusions: none persecution somatic broadcasting grandiosity
  religious nihilistic ideas of reference

Judgment: good fair poor

Insight: good fair poor

Impulse control: good fair poor

Comment: _____

_____

Substance Abuse

Current alcohol use: none social abuse (occasional, binge, pattern, daily)
  Specify type, amount, frequency: _____

_____

_____

Current illicit drug use: none abuse (occasional, episodic, daily) cannabis
  cocaine heroin amphetamines sedatives
  hallucinogens hypnotic inhalants
  Specify drug, amount, frequency: _____

_____

_____

History of substance abuse: _____

_____

_____

Detox, treatment program, tox screen (specify date): _____

_____

_____

History of Sexual Abuse or Assault: _____

_____

_____

Suicidal Ideation: __Yes __No

Homicidal Ideation: __Yes __No

Progress in Treatment and Prognosis: _____

_____

_____

_____   _____
Therapist name   Title/license number

_____
Address

_____   _____
Phone   FAX/e-mail

LIFE HISTORY QUESTIONNAIRE

The purpose of this questionnaire is to obtain a comprehensive understanding of your life experience and background. Completing these questions as fully and as accurately as you can will benefit you through the development of a treatment program suited to your specific needs. Please return this questionnaire when completed, or at your scheduled appointment.

PLEASE COMPLETELY FILL OUT THE FOLLOWING PAGES

Date _____

Name _____

Address _____

Telephone numbers (day) _____ (evenings)_____

DOB_____ Age _____ Occupation _____

By whom were you referred?_____

With whom are you now living? (list people)_____

_____

Where do you reside?   __house   __hotel   __room   __apartment   __other

Significant relationship status (check one)
__single
__engaged
__married
__separated
__divorced
__remarried
__committed relationship
__widowed

If married, husband's (or wife's) name, age, occupation?

_____

1. Role of religion and/or spirituality in your life:
   A. In childhood _____
   B. As an adult _____

2. Clinical
   A. State in your own words the nature of your main problems and how long they have been present:

B. Give a brief history and development of your complaints (from onset to present):

C. On the scale below please check the severity of your problem(s):
__mildly upsetting
__moderately severe
__very severe
__extremely severe
__totally incapacitating

D. Whom have you previously consulted about your present problem(s)?_____

E. Are you taking any medication? If "yes", what, how much, and with what results?

3. Personal Data

A. Date of birth_____ Place of birth_____

B. Mother's condition during pregnancy (as far as you know): _____

C. Check any of the following that applied during your childhood:
__Night terrors   __Bedwetting   __Sleepwalking
__Thumb sucking   __Nail biting   __Stammering
__Fears   __Happy childhood   __Unhappy childhood

Any others:

D. Health during childhood?
List illnesses_____

E. Health during adolescence?
List illnesses_____

F. What is your height?_____   Your weight_____

G. Any surgical operations? (Please list them and give age at the time)

H. Any accidents:

I. List your five main fears:

1. _____

2. _____

3. _____

4. _____

5. _____

J. *Underline* any of the following that apply to you:

headaches	dizziness	fainting spells
palpitations	stomach trouble	anxiety
bowel disturbances	fatigue	no appetite
anger	take sedatives	insomnia
nightmares	feel panicky	alcoholism
feel tense	conflict	tremors
depressed	suicidal ideas	take drugs
unable to relax	sexual problems	allergies
don't like weekends and vacations	overambitious	shy with people
can't make friends	inferiority feelings	can't make decisions
can't keep a job	memory problems	home conditions bad
financial problems	lonely	unable to have a good time
excessive sweating	often use aspirin or painkillers	concentration difficulties

Please list additional problems or difficulties here.

_____

_____

_____

_____

K. Circle any of the following words which apply to you:

Worthless, useless, a "nobody," "life is empty"

Inadequate, stupid, incompetent, naive, "can't do anything right"

Guilty, evil, morally wrong, horrible thoughts, hostile, full of hate

Anxious, agitated, cowardly, unassertive, panicky, aggressive

Ugly, deformed, unattractive, repulsive

Depressed, lonely, unloved, misunderstood, bored, restless

Confused, unconfident, in conflict, full of regrets

Worthwhile, sympathetic, intelligent, attractive, confident, considerate

Please list any additional words:

_____

L. Present interests, hobbies, and activities_____

_____

M. How is most of your free time occupied? _____

_____

N. What is the last grade of school that you completed?_____

O. Scholastic abilities: strengths and weaknesses_____

_____

P. Were you ever bullied or severely teased? _____

Q. Do you make friends easily?_____

Do you keep them?_____

4. Occupational Data

A. What sort of work are you doing now?

B. List previous jobs.

C. Does your present work satisfy you? (If not, in what ways are you dissatisfied?)

D. How much do you earn?_____

How much does it cost you to live?_____

E. Ambitions/Goals_____

Past_____

_____

Present_____

_____

5. Sex Information

A. Parental attitudes toward sex (e.g., was their sex instruction or discussion in the home?)

B. When and how did you derive your first knowledge of sex?

C. When did you first become aware of your own sexual impulses?

D. Did you ever experience any anxieties or guilt feelings arising out of sex or masturbation? If "yes," please explain.

E. Please list any relevant details regarding your first or subsequent sexual experience.

F. Is your present sex life satisfactory? (If not, please explain).

G. Provide information about any significant heterosexual (and/or homosexual) reactions.

H. Are you sexually inhibited in any way?_____

6. Menstrual History

Age of first period?_____

Were you informed or did it come as a shock?_____

Are you regular?_____   Duration_____

Do you have pain?_____   Date of last period_____

Do your periods affect your moods?_____

7. Marital History

How long did you know your marriage partner before engagement?_____

How long have you been married?_____

Husband's/Wife's age_____

Occupation of husband or wife_____

A. Describe the personality of your husband or wife (in your own words)

B. In what areas is there compatibility?

C. In what areas is there incompatibility?

D. How do you get along with your in-laws? (This includes brothers and sisters-in-law.)

How many children do you have?_____

Please list their gender and age(s)._____

_____

E. Do any of your children present special problems?

F. Any history of miscarriages or abortions?

G. Comments about any previous marriage(s) and brief details.

8. Family Data
   A. Father
      Living or deceased? _____

      If deceased, your age at the time of his death. _____

      Cause of death. _____

      If alive, father's present age. _____

      Occupation: _____

      Health: _____

   B. Mother
      Living or deceased? _____

      If deceased, your age at the time of her death. _____

      Cause of death. _____

      If alive, mother's present age. _____

      Occupation: _____

      Health: _____

   C. Siblings
      Number of brothers: _____ Brothers' ages: _____

      Number of sisters: _____ Sisters' ages: _____

   D. Relationship with brothers and sisters:

      Past: _____

      _____

      Present: _____

      _____

   E. Give a description of your father's personality and his attitude toward you

      (past and present): _____

      _____

      _____

F. Give a description of your mother's personality and her attitude toward you (past and present): _____

_____

_____

G. In what ways were you punished by your parents as a child?

H. Give an impression of your home atmosphere (i.e., the home in which you grew up, including compatibility between parents and between parents and children).

I. Were you able to confide in your parents? _____

_____

J. Did your parents understand you? _____

K. Basically, did you feel loved and respected by your parents? _____

_____

If you have a step-parent, give your age when parent remarried: _____

_____

L. Describe your religious training:

M. If you were not raised by your parents, who did raise you, and between what years?

N. Has anyone (parents, relatives, friends) ever interfered in your marriage, occupation, etc.?

O. Who are the most important people in your life?

P. Does any member of your family suffer from alcoholism, epilepsy, or anything which can be considered a "mental disorder"?

Q. Are there any other members of the family about whom information regarding illness, etc., is relevant?

R. Recount any fearful or distressing experiences not previously mentioned?

S. What do expect to accomplish from therapy, and how long do you expect therapy to last?

T. List any situations which make you feel calm *or* relaxed.

U. Have you ever lost control (e.g., temper or crying or aggression)? If so, please describe.

V. Please add any information not brought up by this questionnaire that may aid your therapist in understanding and helping you.

9. Self-Description (Please complete the following):

A. I am a person who _____

B. All my life _____

C. Ever since I was a child _____

D. One of the things I feel proud of is _____

E. It's hard for me to admit _____

F. One of the things I can't forgive is _____

G. One of the things I feel guilty about is _____

H. If I didn't have to worry about my image _____

I. One of the ways people hurt me is _____

J. Mother was always _____

K. What I needed from mother and didn't get was _____

L. Father was always _____

M. What I wanted from my father and didn't get was _____

N. If I weren't afraid to be myself, I might _____

O. One of the things I'm angry about is _____

P. What I need and have never received from a woman (man) is _____

Q. The bad thing about growing up is _____

R. One of the ways I could help myself but don't is _____

10. A. What is there about your present *behavior* that you would like to change?

B. What feelings do you wish to alter (e.g., increase or decrease)?

C. What sensations are especially:

    1. pleasant for you?

    2. unpleasant for you?

D. Describe a very pleasant image of fantasy.

E. Describe a very unpleasant image of fantasy.

F. What do you consider your most irrational thought or idea?

G. Describe any interpersonal relationships that give you:

    1. joy

    2. grief

H. In a few words, what do you think therapy is all about?

11. With the remaining space and blank sides of these pages, give a brief description of you by the following people:
A. Yourself
B. Your spouse (if married)
C. Your best friend
D. Someone who dislikes you

This has been adapted from Lazarus (1977).

ADULT PSYCHOSOCIAL

IDENTIFYING INFORMATION (age, gender, ethnicity, marital status):

_____

_____

Presenting Problem:

_____

_____

Current Social Information:

1. Describe the present living arrangements (include with whom you are living with, and a brief description of these relationships):

   _____

   _____

2. How long have you been married/dating/living together? Describe this relationship (include occupation and age of significant other): _____

   _____

   _____

3. How many children do you have? (name, sex, age): _____

   _____

   _____

4. Are there any significant problems with any of these children? (describe):_____

   _____

   _____

   _____

5. Give details of previous relationships/marriages: _____

   _____

   _____

6. Any history of abuse (emotional, physical, sexual) in current or previous relationships:

_____

_____

_____

FAMILY HISTORY

1. Describe your childhood and adolescence (include home atmosphere, relationship with parents): _____

_____

_____

_____

2. Any history of significant life events such as death, abuse (physical, emotional, sexual) divorce, separation, other?: _____

_____

_____

_____

3. List mother and father by age, include occupation: _____

_____

_____

_____

4. List siblings by age and describe how you relate to them (past and present): ___

_____

_____

_____

5. Have any family members been treated for/have emotional problems? Describe:

_____

_____

_____

DRUG AND ALCOHOL ABUSE

1. Any family history of drug and/or alcohol usage? List and describe: _____

_____

_____

_____

2. Any personal history of drug/alcohol usage? List and describe: _____

_____

_____

EDUCATIONAL HISTORY

1. Describe all school experiences, high school, college, vocational school. Were there any problems with truancy, suspensions, special education, vocational training, etc.?: _____

_____

_____

EMPLOYMENT HISTORY

1. Present employment status and where (positive and negative aspects of what is going on at work): _____

_____

_____

2. If on leave of absence or disability, will you return to present job?: _____

_____

_____

SOCIALIZATION SKILLS

1. List clubs and organizations you belong to: _____

_____

_____

2. What do you do for pleasure and relaxation?: _____

_____

_____

SUMMARY

This _____ year old (include sex, marital status, ethnicity) is currently participating in outpatient treatment for_____(summary of reasons for treatment).

1. What/who seems to be placing the most stress on you at this time?: _____

   _____

2. Are there any legal issues pending? _____ Yes _____ No (describe): _____

   _____

3. Are you having financial problems at this time?: _____

   _____

4. Describe your plans regarding any help you would like to have with yourliving arrangements: _____

   _____

   _____

TREATMENT PLANS AND RECOMMENDATIONS

1. _____

2. _____

3. _____

4. _____

_____   _____
Therapist   Date

CHILD/ADOLESCENT PSYCHOSOCIAL

IDENTIFYING INFORMATION

Date of assessment: _____

Name of child _____ Sex: (M) _____ (F) _____

Birth date _____ Place of birth _____ Age _____

Address (number and street) _____

(city) _____ (state) _____ (zip code) _____

Telephone (___) _____ Religion (optional) _____

Education (grade) _____ Present school _____

Referral Source: _____

I give permission for (therapist) to contact (physician/teacher/etc.) regarding treatment issues, symptoms, behaviors or other information necessary for the treatment of (minor patient).

Parent Signature _____ Date _____

CHIEF COMPLAINT:

Presenting Problems: (check all that apply)

__Very unhappy
__Irritable
__Temper outbursts
__Withdrawn
__Daydreaming
__Fearful
__Clumsy
__Overactive
__Slow
__Short attention span
__Distractible
__Lacks initiative
__Undependable
__Peer conflict
__Phobic

__Impulsive
__Stubborn
__Disobedient
__Infantile
__Mean to others
__Destructive
__Trouble with the law
__Running away
__Self-mutilating
__Head banging
__Rocking
__Shy
__Strange behavior
__Strange thoughts

__Fire setting
__Stealing
__Lying
__Sexual trouble
__School performance
__Truancy
__Bed wetting
__Soiled pants
__Eating problems
__Sleeping problems
__Sickly
__Drugs use
__Alcohol use
__Suicide talk

Explain:

How long have these problems occurred? (number of weeks, months, years)

_____

What happened that makes you seek help at this time? _____

_____

Problems perceived to be: __very serious __serious __not serious

What are your expectations of your child? _____

_____

What changes would you like to see in your child? _____

_____

What changes would you like to see in yourself? _____

_____

What changes would you like to see in your family? _____

_____

PSYCHOSOCIAL HISTORY:

CURRENT FAMILY SITUATION:

Mother—Relationship to child   __natural parent   __relative
    __step-parent   __adoptive parent

Occupation _____

Education _____   Religion _____

Birthplace _____   Birth date _____

Age _____

Father—Relationship to child   __natural parent   __relative
    __step-parent   __adoptive parent

Occupation _____

Education _____   Religion _____

Birthplace _____   Birth date _____

Age _____

Marital History of Parents:
    Natural Parents: __married   when _____   age_____ _____
                  __separated   when _____
                  __divorced   when _____
                  __deceased   M or F _____
    Step-parents: __married   when _____

If child is adopted:

Adoption source:

_____

Reason and circumstances:

_____

Age when child first in home:

_____

Date of legal adoption:

_____

What has the child been told?

_____

LIVING ARRANGEMENTS: Places   Dates

Number of moves in child's life _____   _____   _____

                                              _____   _____

Present Home __renting __buying   _____   _____

                 __house __apartment   _____   _____

Does the child share a room with anyone else?   __Yes __No

If yes, with whom?_____

If no, how long has he/she had own room?_____

Was the child ever placed, boarded, or lived away from the family?   __Yes   __No

Explain: _____

What are the major family stresses at the present time, if any? _____

_____

What are the sources of family income? _____

_____

BROTHERS and SISTERS: (indicate if step-brothers or step-sisters)

Name	Age	Sex	School or Occupation	Present Grade	Living at home (yes or no)	Use drugs or alcohol (yes or no)	Treated for drug abuse (yes or no)
1. _____	___	___	_____	_____	_____	_____	_____
2. _____	___	___	_____	_____	_____	_____	_____
3. _____	___	___	_____	_____	_____	_____	_____
4. _____	___	___	_____	_____	_____	_____	_____
5. _____	___	___	_____	_____	_____	_____	_____
6. _____	___	___	_____	_____	_____	_____	_____

List all other extended family members by their relation to the patient who have drug and/or alcohol problems (legal or illegal), history of depression, self-destructive behavior, or legal problems.

1. _____

2. _____

3. _____

4. _____

5. _____

6. _____

Others living in the home (and their relationship):

1. _____

2. _____

HEALTH OF FAMILY MEMBERS: (excluding patient)

Name	Relationship to child	Type of Illness	When Occurred	Length of Illness
1. _____	_____	_____	_____	_____
2. _____	_____	_____	_____	_____
3. _____	_____	_____	_____	_____
4. _____	_____	_____	_____	_____

Does or did any member of the child's family have any problems with:
__reading   __spelling   __math   __speech
(if yes, please explain.)

Is there any history in the child's family of:
__mental retardation   __epilepsy   __birth defects   __schizophrenia
(if yes, please explain.)

CHILD HEALTH INFORMATION:

Note all health problems the child <u>has had</u> or <u>has now</u>.

	AGE		AGE
__High fevers	____	__Dental Problems	____
__Pneumonia	____	__Weight Problems	____
__Flu	____	__Allergies	____
__Encephalitis	____	__Skin Problems	____
__Meningitis	____	__Asthma	____
__Convulsions	____	__Headaches	____
__Unconsciousness	____	__Stomach Problems	____
__Concussions	____	__Accident Prone	____
__Head Injury	____	__Anemia	____
__Fainting	____	__High or Low Blood Pressure	____
__Dizziness	____	__Sinus Problems	____
__Tonsils Out	____	__Heart Problems	____
__Vision Problems	____	__Hyperactivity	____
__Hearing Problems	____	__Other Illnesses, etc.	____
__Earaches	____	(Explain)	____

Has the child ever been hospitalized?   __Yes   __No
If yes, please explain.

Age	How Long	Reason
_____	_____	_____
_____	_____	_____

Has child ever been seen by a medical specialist?   __Yes __No

Age	How Long	Reason
_____	_____	_____
_____	_____	_____

Has child ever taken, or is he/she taking presently any
   prescribed medications?   _Yes   _No

Age	How Long	Reason
_____	_____	_____
_____	_____	_____

Name of Primary Care Physician_____

DEVELOPMENTAL HISTORY:

Prenatal—Child wanted?   __Yes __No   Planned for?   __Yes __No
Normal pregnancy?   __Yes __No
If mother ill or upset during pregnancy, explain:

Length of pregnancy:_____
Paternal support and acceptance: (explain)

BIRTH:

Length of active labor: __hrs.   __Easy   __Difficult
Full term: __Yes   __No
If premature, how early: _____

If overdue, how late: _____

Birth weight: __lbs.   __oz.
Type of delivery: __spontaneous   __cesarean   __with instruments
                    __head first   __breech
Was it necessary to give the infant oxygen?   __Yes   __No   If yes, how long: _____
Did infant require blood transfusions?   __Yes   __No
Did infant require X-ray?   __Yes   __No
Physical condition of infant at birth:
(If yes explain)   anorexia   __Yes   __No
                   trauma   __Yes   __No
                   other complications   __Yes   __No
Did mother abuse alcohol/drugs during pregnancy?   __Yes   __No

NEWBORN PERIOD:

			How Long
irritability	__Yes	__No	_____
vomiting	__Yes	__No	_____
difficulty breathing	__Yes	__No	_____
difficulty sleeping	__Yes	__No	_____
convulsions/twitching	__Yes	__No	_____
colic	__Yes	__No	_____

| normal weight gain | _Yes | _No | _____ |
| was child breast fed | _Yes | _No | _____ |

DEVELOPMENTAL MILESTONES:

Age at which child:

sat up: _____

crawled: _____

walked: _____

spoke single words: _____

sentences: _____

bladder trained: _____

bowel trained: _____

weaned: _____

Describe the manner in which toilet training was accomplished:

EARLY SOCIAL DEVELOPMENT:

Relationship to siblings and peers:

        __individual play __group play
        __competitive   __cooperative
        __leadership role __a follower

Describe special habits, fears, or idiosyncrasies of the child:

EDUCATIONAL HISTORY:

Name of School	City/State	Dates attended: from	to	Grades completed at this school
preschool_____	_____	_____	_____	_____
elementary_____	_____	_____	_____	_____
junior high_____	_____	_____	_____	_____
high school_____	_____	_____	_____	_____

Types of classes: __regular   __learning disability __continuation
       __emotionally handicapped __opportunity   __other
Did child skip a grade? __Yes __No Repeat a grade? __Yes __No
(If yes, when and how many years appropriate grade level at present time?

Did child have any specific learning difficulties?   __Yes __No
Has child ever have a tutor or other special help with school work?   __Yes __No
Does child attend school on a regular basis?   __Yes __No
Does child appear motivated for school?   __Yes __No
Has child ever been suspended or expelled?   __Yes __No

ACADEMIC PERFORMANCE:

Highest grade on last report card? _____

Lowest grade on last report card? _____

Favorite subject? _____

Least favorite subject? _____

Does child participate in extracurricular activities?   __Yes __No (explain)

In school, how many friends does child have: __a lot __a few __none

What are child's educational aspirations?   __quit school
                                              __graduate from high school
                                              __go to college

Has child had special testing in school? (If yes, what were the results?)
Psychological   __Yes __No   Vocational   __Yes __No

List child's special interests, hobbies, skills:

_____

_____

_____

_____

_____

Has the child ever had difficulty with the police?   __Yes __No (if yes, explain)

Has child ever appeared in juvenile court?   __Yes __No (if yes, explain)

Has child ever been on probation?   __Yes __No

From	To	Reason	Probation Officer

Has child ever been employed?   __Yes __No

Job	Employe	How long

ADDITONAL COMMENTS:

_____

_____

_____

_____

_____

_____

_____

_____

_____

_____

_____

Therapist   Date

PARENT'S QUESTIONNAIRE

Name of child: _____   Date: _____

Name of parent (filling out form): _____

Answer all of the questions by indicating the degree of the problem. Write "N" for never, "S" for sometimes, or "O" for often in front of the number for each question.

QUESTION

_____1. Picks at things (nails, fingers, hair clothing)

_____2. Talks back to authority figures (attitude)

_____3. Has problems with making or keeping friends

_____4. Excitable, impulsive

_____5. Wants to run things

_____6. Sucks or chews (thumb, clothing, blankets, etc.)

_____7. Cries easily/often

_____8. Emotionally reactive

_____9. Has a chip on his/her shoulder

___10. Tendency to daydream

___11. Difficulty learning

___12. Always squirming, restless, and moving around

___13. Experiences fear and anxiety in new situations/meeting new people

___14. Breaks things/destructive

___15. Lies, makes up stories

___16. Does not follow rules

___17. Gets into trouble more than peers

___18. Shy and does not assert self

___19. Has problems with speech (stuttering, hard to understand, baby talk)

___20. Denies mistakes and is defensive

___21. Blames other for mistakes

___22. Steals

___23. Argumentative

___24. Disrespectful

___25. Pouts and sulks

___26. Obeys rules but is resentful

___27. When hurt or angered by someone, holds a grudge

___28. Develops stomachache or headache when stressed

___29. Worries unnecessarily

___30. Does not finish tasks

___31. Emotionally sensitive and easily hurt

___32. Bullies others

___33. Cruel and insensitive

_____34. Clingy and in need of constant reassurance

_____35. Easily distracted

_____36. Frequent headaches or stomachaches

_____37. Rapid mood changes

_____38. Fights a lot and creates conflicts

_____39. Power struggles with authority

_____40. Childish or immature (wants help when should be able to do it independently)

_____41. Does not get along well with siblings

_____42. Easily frustrated

_____43. Perfectionism prevents trying new things

_____44. Problems with sleep

_____45. Problems with eating

_____46. Has bowel problems

_____47. Vomiting, nausea, or other complaints of pain or physical distress

_____48. Feels he/she is treated differently in the family than siblings

_____49. Passive and gets pushed around

_____50. Self-centered, brags, little understanding of others

SELF-ASSESSMENT

What is happening in your life which resulted in this appointment? _____

_____

What would you like to see accomplished in therapy? _____

_____

CHIEF COMPLAINT (CHECK ALL THAT APPLY TO YOU):

__ Depression
__ Low energy
__ Low self-esteem
__ Poor concentration
__ Hopelessness
__ Worthlessness
__ Guilt
__ Sleep disturbance (more/less)
__ Appetite disturbance (more/less)
__ Thoughts of hurting yourself
__ Thoughts of hurting someone
__ Isolation/social withdrawal
__ Sadness/loss
__ Stress
__ Anxiety/panic
__ Heart pounding/racing
__ Chest pain
__ Trembling/shaking
__ Sweating
__ Chills/hot flashes
__ Tingling/numbness
__ Fear of dying
__ Fear of going crazy
__ Nausea
__ Phobias
__ Obsessions/compulsive behaviors
__ Thoughts racing
__ Can't hold onto an idea
__ Easily agitate
__ Excessive behaviors (spending, gambling)
__ Delusions/hallucinations
__ Not thinking clearly/confusion

__ Feeling that you are not real
__ Feeling that things around you are not real
__ Lose track of time
__ Unpleasant thoughts won't go away
__ Anger/frustration
__ Easily agitated/annoyed
__ Defies rules
__ Blames others
__ Argues
__ Excessive use of drugs and/or alcohol
__ Excessive use of prescription medications
__ Blackouts
__ Physical abuse issues
__ Sexual abuse issues
__ Spousal abuse issues
__ Other problems/symptoms:

_____

_____

_____

_____

_____

_____

_____

_____

Previous outpatient therapy? _____Yes _____No, with _____

What was accomplished? _____

__medications, list: _____

Previous hospitalization? ___Yes ___No Number of hospitalizations ___ECT? _____

If yes, when _____

BRIEF MEDICAL HISTORY

Name:_____ Age:_____ DOB:_____ Date:_____

Primary Care Physician: _____

Last medial exam: _____

List any medical problems that you are currently experiencing: _____

_____

Name of the physician monitoring this condition(s): _____

List any medications you are currently taking: _____

_____

Who prescribed the medication(s): _____
Have you ever seen a psychiatrist or counselor before?

Yes _____   No _____   When: _____

Please Explain: _____

_____

Check any of the following problems that you experience:

__ lack of appetite	__ sleep disturbance	__ depression
__ excessive drinking	__ headaches	__ bowel problems
__ anger management	__ sexual problems	__ bladder control problem
__ problem drug use	__ appetite disturbance	__ difficulty relaxing
__ nervousness	__ stomach problems	__ fears/phobia
__ fatigue	__ pain (where)	__ obsessive thoughts
__ panic attacks	__ low self-esteem	__ compulsive behaviors
__ anxiety	__ relationship problems	__ marital/family problems
__ loneliness	__ difficulty concentrating	__ poor impulse control
__ nightmares	__ feelings of unreality	__ confusion
__ intrusive thoughts	__ flashbacks	__ difficulty trusting

ILLNESSES AND MEDICAL PROBLEMS

Please mark with an "X" any of the following illnesses and medical problems you have had and indicate the year when each started. If you are not certain when a illness started, write down an approximate year or ago it occurred.

ILLNESS	X	YEAR	N/A	ILLNESS	X	YEAR	N/A
Eye or Eyelid Infection				Venereal Disease			
Glaucoma				Genital Herpes			
Other Eye Problems				Breast Disease			
Ear Condition				Nipple Drainage			
Deafness or Decreased Hearing				Headaches			
Thyroid Problems				Head Injury			
Strep Throat				Stroke			
Bronchitis				Convulsions/Seizures			
Emphysema				Black Outs			
Pneumonia				Dizziness			
Allergies, Asthma, or Hayfever				Mental Problems			
Nose Bleeds				Arthritis			
Tuberculosis				Gout			
Other Lung Problems				Cancer or Tumors			
Difficulty Breathing				Bleeding Tendency			
High Blood Pressure				Diabetes			
High Cholesterol				Measles/Rubeola			
Arteriosclerosis (hardening of arteries) .				German Measles/Rubella			
Heart Attack				Polio			
Chest Pain				Mumps			
Irregular Heart Beat				Scarlet Fever			
Heart Murmur				Chicken Pox			
Other Heart Conditions				Mononucleosis			
Stomach/Duodenal Ulcer				Eczema			
Nausea				Psoriasis			
Vomiting				Skin Rash			
Weight Loss				Open Wounds			
Weight Gain				Infection			
Difficulty Swallowing				Muscle Stiffness			
Diverticulosis				Muscle Weakness			
Colitis				Muscle Pain			
Other Bowel Problems				Bone Fracture			
Blood in Stools				Bone Stiffness			
Diarrhea				Others			
Hemorrhoids				. . . .			
Easily Fatigued				. . . .			
Hepatitis				. . . .			
Liver Problems				. . . .			
Gallbladder Problems				. . . .			
Hernia				. . . .			
Kidney or Bladder Disease				. . . .			
Prostate Problem (male only)				. . . .			
Ovarian Problem (female only)				. . . .			
Last menstrual period				. . . .			
Last Pregnancy				. . . .			
Menstrual Flow Pattern				. . . .			

MEDICAL REVIEW CONSULT REQUEST FOR PRIMARY CARE PHYSICIAN OF AN EATING DISORDER (EDO) PATIENT

Dear Attending Physician:

This patient has presented for psychological treatment for an eating disorder. In order for effective, comprehensive treatment to be rendered, all professionals involved must share information, including the screening and monitoring of medical complications associated with the eating disorder. Before psychological treatment proceeds, a physical examination is required, which includes the following routine lab work. If abnormalities are presented, a list of selected studies may be required. Please forward the results of your examination and lab studies. Your consultation is appreciated.

Laboratory Studies for Evaluation of Eating Disorders
Routine:

>   Complete blood count
>   Electrolytes, glucose, and renal function tests
>   Chemistry panel
> >   Liver function tests
> >   Total protein and albumin
> >   Calcium
> >   Amylase
>   Hormones
> >   Thyroid function tests
> >   A.M. plasma cortisol
> >   Luteining hormone
> >   Follicle stimulating hormone
> >   Estrogen (female)
> >   Testosterone (male)
>   Chest x-ray
>   Electrocardiogram
>   Dual photon absorptiometry

Selected:

>   Magnetic resonance imaging for brain atrophy
>   Abnormal x-ray for severe bloating
>   Lower esophageal sphincter pressure studies for reflux
>   Lactose deficiency tests for dairy intolerance
>   Total bowel transit time for severe constipation

Regards,

_____

Signature

Adapted from E. Anderson (1991). *Medical complications of eating disorders.*

SUBSTANCE USE AND PSYCHOSOCIAL QUESTIONNAIRE

(To be filled out by client)

Client Name: _____

Sex: _____   Date of Birth_____   Age: _____   Marital Status: M/D/S

Living Arrangements: _____

_____

Referral Source: _____

Presenting Problems: _____

_____

1. Use of alcohol and/or drugs

Type	How used	Age started	Amount	Frequency	Last time used

2. Has there been any change in the pattern of alcohol/drug use in the last 6 months to 1 year __Yes __No. If yes, describe: _____

_____

_____

3. Preferred alcohol or drug: _____

_____

_____

4. Preferred setting for alcohol/drug use (home, work, bars, alone, with friends):

_____

_____

5. Longest period of time you have gone without using alcohol or drugs? _____

_____

6. What medication(s) are you currently being prescribed, what are you taking it for, and who is prescribing it? _____

_____

_____

7. Do you use alcohol or drugs to get started in the morning? _____

_____

_____

8. Have you ever felt annoyed when other people criticize your substance use? __

_____

9. Has your physician ever told you to cut down or stop using alcohol/drugs? __

_____

10. Have you ever felt the need to cut down on the use of alcohol/drugs (if yes, explain):

_____

_____

11. Has the use of alcohol/drugs caused you to be late to or miss work? _____

12. Has the use of alcohol/drugs affected your home life or relationships? _____

13. How do you feel about your use of alcohol/drugs? _____

_____

14. Have you ever attended AA/NA meetings? _____

_____

TREATMENT HISTORY

1. Number of attempts to stop alcohol/drug use_____. By what means? _____

_____

2. Length of time you abstained from alcohol/drug use: _____

   Why did you start again? _____

3. Previous experiences with detox: _____

_____

_____

4. Previous treatment experiences (list problems, type of treatment, location, and what you learned and accomplished):_____

_____

_____

FAMILY HISTORY

1. Alcoholism and/or drug dependence of mother, father, siblings or grandparents?

_____

2. High blood pressure? _____

3. Diabetes? _____

4. Liver disease? _____

SOCIAL HISTORY

1. Occupation: _____

2. Level of education completed: _____

_____

SYMPTOMS (If Yes, Please Explain)	Yes/No	Explain
Depression	_____	_____
Fatigue/decreased activity level	_____	_____
Sleep problems	_____	_____
Appetite problems or changes	_____	_____
Memory problems/changes	_____	_____
Suspicious	_____	_____
Anxiety	_____	_____
Fever, sweaty	_____	_____
Shortness of breath	_____	_____
Chest pain/discomfort	_____	_____
Palpitations	_____	_____
Dizziness	_____	_____
Indigestion/nausea	_____	_____
Vomiting (with blood)	_____	_____
Abdominal pain	_____	_____
Diarrhea	_____	_____
Black "tarry" stools	_____	_____
Trouble getting an erection	_____	_____
Tremors	_____	_____
Blackouts	_____	_____

SYMPTOMS (If Yes, Please Explain)	Yes/No	Explain
Periods of confusion	_____	_____
Hallucinations	_____	_____
Staggering/balance problems	_____	_____
Tingling	_____	_____
Headaches/vision changes	_____	_____
Muscle weakness	_____	_____
Suicidal attempts/thoughts	_____	_____

MEDICAL PROBLEMS

Has your physician told you that you have any of the following:

Diabetes	__Yes	__No
Cirrhosis	__Yes	__No
Hepatitis	__Yes	__No
Anemia	__Yes	__No
Gout	__Yes	__No
High blood pressure	__Yes	__No
Delirium tremens	__Yes	__No
Gastritis	__Yes	__No
Pancreatitis	__Yes	__No

Goals of participating in treatment at this time? _____

_____

_____

_____

_____

_____

_____

CHEMICAL DEPENDENCY PSYCHOSOCIAL ASSESSMENT

Date: _____   Age: _____

S.O. Name _____   Phone: _____

Religious/ethnic/cultural background: _____

_____

Marital Status: _____   Children: _____

Living with Whom: _____

Present Support System (family/friends): _____

Chemical History:

Chemical Use	Route	Age Started	Amt.	Freq.	Last Dose? Last Used	Length of Use

Description of Presenting Problems (patient's view): _____

_____

Previous Counseling:

When	Where	Therapist/Title	Response To

Family/S.O. Relationships/History of Chemical Use: _____

_____

_____

_____

S.O. Relationships and History of Chemical Use: _____

_____

_____

_____

Effects of on Family/Support System: _____

_____

_____

Daily Activities that: A. support abstinence: _____

                              B. encourage usage: _____

History of Sexual/Physical Abuse (victim/abuser): _____

_____

Sexual Orientation: _____

Education: _____

Vocational History: _____

Leisure/Social Interests: _____

_____

Current Occupation: _____

Current Employer: _____

Impact of on Job Performance: _____

_____

EAP?   Yes__ No__ Name: _____   Phone: _____

Socioeconomic/Financial Problems: _____

_____

_____

Legal: _____ DWI: Yes__ No__ Court Ordered: Yes__ No__

Patient's Perceptions of Strengths and Weaknesses: _____

_____

_____

Preliminary Treatment Plan: List presenting problems based on initial assessment of the
                          client's physical, emotional, cognitive, and behavioral status.

Detox: Yes__ No__ Explain: _____

Rehab: Yes__ No__ Explain: _____

Problem #1: _____

Problem #2: _____

Problem #3: _____

Immediate treatment recommendations to address identifying problems: _____

_____

_____

_____

_____

_____   _____
Therapist   Date

INITIAL EVALUATION CONSULTATION NOTE TO PRIMARY CARE PHYSICIAN

Date: _____

Name: _____

Primary Care Physician: _____

Reason for Referral: _____
(Presenting Problem)

_____

Medications currently prescribed: _____

Medical problems currently experiencing: _____

Previously seen by therapist or psychiatrist: _____

Symptoms:

__depression   __anxiety   __hopeless/helpless
__tearful   __fears/phobias   __anger/frustration
__sleep disturbance   __shakiness/trembling   __depersonalization
__appetite disturbance   __palpitations   __derealization
__difficulty concentrating __sweating/flushes/chills   __obsessive thoughts
__memory problems   __dizziness/nausea   __compulsive behaviors
__social isolation   __fatigue   __relationship problems
__activity withdrawal   __irritability/on edge   __family problems
__headaches   __hypervigilance   __issues of loss
__abdominal distress   __intrusive thoughts   __stress
__suicidal ideation   __bowel problems   __difficulty relaxing
__homicidal ideation   __asthma/allergies   __work problems
__sexual abuse/assault   __mania   __legal/financial problems
__eating disorder   __school problems/truancy   __hyperactive
__defies rules   __annoys others   __easily annoyed
__spiteful/vindictive   __blames others   __argues
__uses obscene language   __excessive drinking   __drug use
__somatic concerns

History of Current Problem (Relevant History, Reason for Treatment):

_____

_____

_____

_____

_____

Mental Status:

Mood   __Normal __Depressed __Elevated __Euphoric __Angry __Irritable __Anxious

Affect   __Normal __Broad __Restricted __Blunted __Flat __Inappropriate __Labile

Memory   __Intact __Short-term Problems __Long-term Problems

Processes   __Normal __Blocking __Loose Associations __Confabulations __Flight of Ideas __Ideas of Reference __Grandiosity __Paranoia __Obsession __Perseverations __Depersonalization __Suicidal Ideation __Homicidal Ideation

Hallucinations   __None __Auditory __Visual __Olfactory __Gustatory __Somatic __Tactile

Judgment   __Good __Fair __Poor

Insight   __Good __Fair __Poor

Impulse Control   __Good __Fair __Poor

Initial Diagnostic Impression:

Axis I. _____

Axis II. _____

Axis III. _____

Axis IV. _____

Axis V. _____

Initial Treatment Plan:

__Brief psychotherapy

__Supportive psychotherapy

__Decreased symptomatology

__Stabilize

__Cognitive restructuring

__Specialized group

__Child Protective Services

__AA/Alanon

__Chemical dependency treatment

__Self-esteem enhancement

__Parent counseling

__Grief resolution

__Psychological testing

__Medication evaluation with PCP

__Medical referral

__Improve coping

__Utilization of Resources

__Social skills training

__Problem solving/conflict resolution

__Stress management

__Behavior modification

__Pain management

__Suicide alert

__Impatient care/Partial hospitalization

__Legal alert

__Potential violence

Next Appointment _____

_____

Therapist

BRIEF CONSULTATION NOTE TO PHYSICIAN

Dear Dr. _____ ;

_____ was seen on _____ .

Purpose of visit:

Preliminary findings reveal:

I tentative diagnosis:

Return appointment: _____
If you have further questions please feel free to contact me.

Sincerely,

OUTPATIENT TREATMENT PROGRESS REPORT

Name: _____   Date: _____

SS#: _____   DOB: _____

Date of initial interview: _____   Number of sessions: _____

Describe treatment motivation and compliance: _____

_____

_____

Current Risk Factors

- Suicidality: ☐ None   ☐ Ideation   ☐ Plan   ☐ Intent w/o means   ☐ Intent with means
- Homicidality: ☐ None   ☐ Ideation   ☐ Plan   ☐ Intent w/o means   ☐ Intent with means
- If risk exists: Client is able to contract not to harm: ☐ Self   ☐ Others
- Impulse control: ☐ Sufficient   ☐ Moderate   ☐ Minimal   ☐ Inconsistent   ☐ Explosive
- Substance abuse: ☐ None   ☐ Abuse   ☐ Dependence   ☐ Unstable Remission
- Medical risks: ☐ Yes   ☐ No   If "yes," explain:_____

Risk History (Explain significant history of behaviors that may affect the current level of risk.)

Functional Impairments (Explain how symptoms impact current functioning or place client at risk.)

Diagnosis

- Axis I—Primary_____   Secondary_____
- Axis II— _____
- Axis III— _____
- Axis IV— (*Identify Stressors*)_____
- Axis V (*GAF*) Current _____ Highest in past 12 months _____

Current Medication

☐ None   ☐ Psychiatric   ☐ Medical   ☐ No information_____

Specify (*include dosage, frequency, and compliance*):_____

_____

A: Measurable Behavioral Goals with Target Dates for Resolution

1.

2.

3.

B: Planned Interventions

1.

2.

3.

C. Objective Outcome Criteria by Which Goal Achievement Is Measured

1.

2.

3.

D. Progress Since Last Update

E. Referrals

F. Discharge Planning

Comments:

_____

_____

_____

_____

_____

_____

_____

_____

_____

_____

_____

_____

_____

_____

_____

_____

_____

_____

_____

_____

_____

_____

_____

_____   _____
Therapist   Date

_____
Patient

PROGRESS NOTE FOR INDIVIDUAL WITH ANXIETY AND/OR DEPRESSION

_____

Symptoms List: Check off any symptoms that have been most bothersome or have occurred frequently during the past week.

Date: _____

Name: _____

General Symptoms
- ❑ Fever
- ❑ Repetitive, senseless thoughts
- ❑ Repetitive, senseless behaviors
- ❑ Fainting or feeling faint
- ❑ Tremors, trembling, or shakiness
- ❑ Seizures
- ❑ Easy bruising
- ❑ Skin rash
- ❑ Violent behavior

- ❑ Constant worry
- ❑ Irritability
- ❑ Tension
- ❑ Headache
- ❑ Feeling in a dreamlike state
- ❑ Fearful feelings
- ❑ Fear of losing control
- ❑ Jumpiness
- ❑ Restlessness
- ❑ Sweating
- ❑ Dizziness/lightheadedness
- ❑ Keyed up/on edge

Section 1: If constant worry plus three other symptoms in Section 2 are checked, consider a diagnosis of persistent anxiety.

- ❑ Agitation
- ❑ Nervousness
- ❑ Trouble concentrating
- ❑ Insomnia/trouble sleeping
- ❑ Decrease in sex drive
- ❑ Trouble making decisions

Section 2: If any symptoms are checked in this section, plus either of the first two symptoms in Section 3, consider a diagnosis of depression with associated anxiety.

- ❑ Sad/depressed/down in the dumps
- ❑ Lack of/loss of interest in things
- ❑ Helpless feelings
- ❑ Fatigue, lack of energy
- ❑ Weakness
- ❑ Increase or decrease in appetite
- ❑ Increase or decrease in weight
- ❑ Frequent crying or weeping
- ❑ Frequent thoughts of death or suicide
- ❑ Worthless feelings
- ❑ Excessive feelings of guilt
- ❑ Hopeless feelings
- ❑ Feeling life is not worth living
- ❑ Sleeping too much
- ❑ Frequent negative thinking
- ❑ Memory problems

Section 3: If six or more symptoms in this area are checked, consider a diagnosis of depression.

❏ Fear of doing something uncontrollable
❏ Fear of dying
❏ Chills
❏ Seeing or hearing things that are not real
❏ Fear of going crazy

Please list medications and dosages
Do you smoke?   _No   _Yes. How much?
Do you drink or use other substances?   _No   _Yes. How much and how often?
Do you have thoughts of harming yourself? _____
Do you have thoughts of harming another person? _____

*May be used as a progress note. Have patient check off symptoms. Remove the printing on the right side of page and line to write progress note.

Adapted from Bristol Meyer Squibb Well Being Chart.

CLINICAL NOTES

1. Mental Status:
   A. Appearance: WNL__   Unkempt__   Dirty__   Meticulous__   Unusual__
   B. Behavior: WNL__   Guarded__   Withdrawn__   Noncompliant__   Hostile__
   Uncooperative__   Provocative__   Manipulative__   Hypoactive__
   Hyperactive__   Suspicious__   Cooperative__   Pleasant__
   Under-the influence__
   C. Mood/Affect: WNL__   Flat__   Depressed__   Euphoric__   Anxious__
   Fearful__   Irritable__   Angry__   Labile__   Incongruent__
   D. Cognitions: WNL__   Loose__   Scattered__   Blocked__   Illogical__
   Dilusional__   Paranoid__   Hallucinations__   Grandiose__
   Fragmented__   Somatic__
   E. Safety: Danger to self/others?   Yes__   No__
   If yes, describe:_____
   Safe to return home?   Yes__   No__
   If no, state planned intervention below.

2. Intervention and/or Teaching:

_____

_____

_____

3. Patient Response/Participation:

_____

_____

_____

Signature: _____   Date:_____

****

1. Mental Status:
   A. Appearance: WNL__   Unkempt__   Dirty__   Meticulous__   Unusual__
   B. Behavior: WNL__   Guarded__   Withdrawn__   Noncompliant__   Hostile__
   Uncooperative__   Provocative__   Manipulative__   Hypoactive__
   Hyperactive__   Suspicious__   Cooperative__   Pleasant__
   Under-the influence__
   C. Mood/Affect: WNL__   Flat__   Depressed__   Euphoric__   Anxious__
   Fearful__   Irritable__   Angry__   Labile__   Incongruent__
   D. Cognitions: WNL__   Loose__   Scattered__   Blocked__   Illogical__
   Dilusional__   Paranoid__   Hallucinations__   Grandiose__
   Fragmented__   Somatic__
   E. Safety: Danger to self/others?   Yes__   No__
   If yes, describe:_____

Safe to return home?   Yes___   No___
If no, state planned intervention below.

2. Intervention and/or Teaching:

_____

_____

_____

_____

_____

_____

3. Patient Response/Participation:

_____

_____

_____

_____

_____

_____

Signature: _____   Date:_____

Printed by permission from Cosette Taillac-Vento, LCSW

WNL = Within Normal Limits

DISABILITY/WORKER'S COMPENSATION

Patient Name: _____ Sex ____ M _____ F DOB _____

Address: _____

Work Phone: _____ Home Phone: _____

Occupation: _____

SS#: _____ Date Last Worked: _____

Date Disability Commenced On: _____

Approximate date patient may resume work: _____

Has patient previously been treated at this office? _____ Yes _____ No

If yes, give dates/circumstances: _____

_____

Description of patient complaint: _____

_____

_____

Symptoms experienced: _____

_____

Diagnosis (including DSM IV/CPT code): _____

_____

Type of treatment rendered and frequency: _____

_____

Referral to Residential Treatment Facility: _____ Yes _____ No

If yes, where and for what purpose: _____

_____

Profession: _____ Practice in the State of: _____

Name on License: _____ License #: _____

Signature: _____ Date: _____

Address: _____

Phone: _____ Fax: _____

SOCIAL SECURITY EVALUATION MEDICAL SOURCE STATEMENT, PSYCHIATRIC/PSYCHOLOGICAL

_____

Please evaluate, give examples, and provide comments on the patient's ability in the following categories:

1. Ability to relate and interact with supervisors and co-workers.

2. Ability to understand, remember, and carry out an extensive variety of technical and/or complex job instructions.

3. Ability to understand, remember and carry out simple one-or-two step job instructions.

4. Ability to deal with the public.

5. Ability to maintain concentration and attention for at least 2 hour increments.

6. Ability to withstand the stress and pressures associated with an 8 hour workday and day-to-day work activity.

7. Please comment on the patient's ability to handle funds.

8. Please comment on expected duration and prognosis of patient's impairments.

9. Please comment on the onset and history of the patient's impairments, as well as response to treatment.

10. Specify any side effects from medication and restrictions related thereto.

11. Does patient require any additional testing or evaluations? Please specify.

_____   _____
Therapist   Date

WORKER'S COMPENSATION ATTENDING
THERAPIST'S REPORT

_____

Employee: _____   Claim Number: _____

Employer: _____   Date of Injury:_____ Date of Next Appt:____

Date of This Exam: _____   Patient Social Security No: _____

Current Diagnosis: _____

_____

PROGRESS

Since the last exam, this patient's condition has:
__Progressed as expected   __progressed slower than expected
__not progressed significantly   __worsened
__plateaued. No further progress expected   __been determined to be non-work related

Briefly describe any change in objective or subjective complaint: _____

_____

TREATMENT

Treatment Plan: (only list changes from prior status): __No change   __Patient is/was

discharged from care on: _____

Est. Discharge Date: _____   Medications: _____

Therapy Type _____   Duration _____   Times per Week _____

Diagnostic Studies: _____

Hospitalization/Surgery: _____

Consult/Other Services: _____

WORK STATUS

The patient has been instructed to:
__ return to full duty with no limitations or restrictions
__ remain off the rest of the day and return to work tomorrow
__ with no limitations   __with limitations listed below
__ return to work on _____

Work limitations: _____

Remail off work until _____

Estimated date patient can return to full duty: _____

DISABILITY STATUS

__ Patient discharged as cured

Please supply a brief narrative report if any of the following apply:

__ Patient will be permanently precluded from engaging in his/her usual and customary occupation

__ Patient's condition is permanent and stationary

__ Patient will have permanent residuals   __Patient will require future medical care

Therapist Name: _____   Address: _____

Signature: _____   _____

Date: _____   Telephone: (   ) _____

BRIEF PSYCHIATRIC EVALUATION
FOR INDUSTRIAL INJURY

Date: _____

Name: _____

Date of first examination: _____

Date of most recent visit: _____

Frequency of visits:_____

Diagnosis (axis I):_____

_____

_____

Type of service
- Outpatient psychotherapy
- Intensive Outpatient
- Urgent care
- Case Management

Medication

1._____

2._____

3._____

4._____

CURRENT MENTAL STATUS EXAM (circle and comment if abnormal findings)

Appearance and Behavior
Grooming: Well-groomed, disheveled, eccentric, poor hygiene
Motor activity: Normal, tremor, retarded, agitated, hyperactive
Speech: Normal, slow, rapid, pressured, slurred, mute, delayed, soft, loud, stuttering, aphasia
Interview behavior: Cooperative, guarded, evasive
Behavioral disturbance: None, irritable, aggressive, violent, poor impulse control, manipulative, apathetic
Comments: _____

Sensorium and Cognitive Functioning
Orientation: Oriented in all spheres, disoriented (person, place, time, situation)
Concentration: Intact, slightly distracted, impaired (mild, moderate, severe)
Memory: Normal, impaired (immediate, recent, remote) and degree (mild, moderate, severe)
Intelligence: Above average, average, below average, borderline, mental retardation
Comments: _____

Mood and Affect
Mood: Normal, anxious, depressed, fearful, elated, euphoric, angry
Affect: Appropriate, labile, expansive, blunted, flat
Comments: _____

_____

_____

Percepion

Hallucinations: None, auditory, visual, olfactory

Illusions: None, misidentification

Specify: _____

Thought Process

Associations: Goal directed, blocking, circumstantial, tangential, loose, neologisms

Content-Delusions: None, persecution, somatic, broadcasting, grandiosity, religious, nihilistic, ideas of reference

Content-preoccupations: None, obsessions, compulsions, phobias, sexual, suicidal, homicidal, depersonalization

Comments: _____

Judgment: Intact, impaired (mild, moderate, severe)

Comments: _____

PROGRESS IN TREATMENT AND PROGNOSIS: _____

_____

_____

ALCOHOL AND DRUG ABUSE

Current alcohol use: None, social, abuse (occasional, binge pattern, daily)

Current illicit drug use: None, social, abuse (occasional, binge pattern, daily)

Detox, drug program, or tox screen: (Specify dates and results) _____

_____

_____

History of alcohol/drug abuse:_____

CURRENT WORK-RELATED SKILLS

(Comment on reason for limitation and degree of limitation, if there is impaired ability.)

Able to understand, remember and perform simple instructions:_____

_____

Able to understand, remember and perform detailed, complex instructions:_____

_____

Able to maintain concentration for two-hour periods: _____

_____

Able to interact with coworkers and supervisors: _____

_____

Able to sustain an ordinary routine without special supervision: _____

_____

Able to handle the responsibilities common to a basic work environment: _____

_____

Do you believe this patient is capable of managing funds in his/her own best interest?

Yes_____   No_____   Comments:_____

Name of reporting doctor: _____

Address:_____   Signature:_____

City, state:_____   Title:_____

Telephone number:_____   Date:_____

BRIEF LEVEL OF FUNCTIONING REVIEW FOR INDUSTRIAL INJURY

Name: _____ Date _____

DOB: _____ SS#: _____

Mental Status Assessment <u>based on last office visit</u>

<u>Provide assessment based on last office visit.</u> Circle response.

1. Sensorium: Alert   Clear   Clouded   Drowsy   Other_____
2. Orientation: Normal   Disoriented as to: Time   Place   Person   Situation
3. Behavioral attitudes: Cooperative   Hostile   Withdrawn   Guarded/Resistant
   Indifferent/Passive
4. Appearance: Well-groomed   Adequate   Unkempt   Inappropriate
   Other _____
5. Attention and concentration: Good   Fair   Distractible   Other _____
6. Speech: Rate   Normal   Slow   Rapid   Halting   Pressured
   Other _____
   Quality   Clear   Mumbled   Slurred   Other_____
   Tone   Normal   Low   Inaudible   Loud   Other_____
7. Psychomotor activity: Normal   Retarded   Accelerated   Restless   Agitated
8. Mood: Euthymic   Depressed   Elevated   Hypomanic   Manic
   Anxious   Angry   Irritable   Labile
9. Affect: Congruent w/mood & thought   Incongruent w/mood & thought
   Intensity: Full   Bland   Blunted   Flat
   Range: Constricted   Normal
10. Thought Process: Goal Directed/Relevant   Tangential   Circumstantial
    Loose Associations   Flight of ideas
11. Thought Content   Obsessions   Preoccupations   Grandiose   Paranoid
    Somatic religious   Phobia   Fears
    Hallucinations: Auditory (Command Type   Y   N)   Visual
    Tactile   Olfactory
    Delusions: _____
    Suicidal Ideation: No   Yes   Plan/Intent: No   Yes
    Risk: Low   Moderate   High
    Homicidal Ideation: No   Yes   Plan/Intent   No   Yes
    Risk: Low   Moderate   High
12. Insight & psychological mindedness   Excellent   Good   Fair   Poor
13. Evidence of possible organic/neurological pathology   No   Yes   Comments:
14. Vegetative symptoms:

_____

_____

Circle the response that applies to the patient's ability to perform ADL's

	Performance Areas	ADL's	Performance of ADL's			
1	Mathematical skills	Balance checkbook	Yes	No	N/A	?
2	Word processing skills	Operate personal computer at home	Yes	No	N/A	?
		Write letters	Yes	No	N/A	?
3	Problem solving/judgment	Schedule day	Yes	No	N/A	?
		Schedule children's day	Yes	No	N/A	?
		Driving	Yes	No	N/A	?
4	Attention/ concentration	Read newspaper or books	Yes	No	N/A	?
		Follow movie/TV shows	Yes	No	N/A	?
5	Initiate work	Shopping	Yes	No	N/A	?
		Planning/cooking meals	Yes	No	N/A	?
		Initiate and complete domestic chores (washing dishes, laundry, yard work, etc.)	Yes	No	N/A	?
6	Memory	Remember doctor's appointments	Yes	No	N/A	?
		Recalling phone conversations	Yes	No	N/A	?
		Remembering medications/dosages	Yes	No	N/A	?
7	Social interactions	Socialize with family/friends	Yes	No	N/A	?
		Attend social outings/church	Yes	No	N/A	?
		Pariticipate in hobbies	Yes	No	N/A	?
		Participate in exercise /sports	Yes	No	N/A	?
		Take trips/vacations	Yes	No	N/A	?
8	Maintain personal hygiene	Bathe/shower regularly	Yes	No	N/A	?
		Neat grooming	Yes	No	N/A	?
		Dressed appropriately	Yes	No	N/A	?
9	Supervise others	Supervise children/family members	Yes	No	N/A	?
		Organize home activities	Yes	No	N/A	?
10	Understand and carry out instructions	Medication compliant	Yes	No	N/A	?
		Manage physical health needs	Yes	No	N/A	?
		Return phone calls	Yes	No	N/A	?

How are these functions assessed?

_____

_____

_____

_____

What are the treatment plan target dates?

Goal: _____ Target date: _____

Goal: _____ Target date: _____

Goal: _____ Target date: _____

What are the current: Medications   /   Dosage   /   Frequency   /   Response

DSM IV AND ICD 9 code of Diagnostic Categories for which the patient is being treated:

    a. Axis I (ICD or billing codes)

_____

    b. Axis II

_____

    c. Axis II

_____

    d. Axis IV

_____

    e. Axis V

_____

Current symptoms   GAF = ☐   GAF = ☐

                                        current   past year

_____

_____

_____

_____

Released to return to work: _____ or Estimate for return to work:_____

The patient is unable to return to work at this time because he/she is unable to perform the following job-related duties:_____

_____

_____

The reason(s) that he/she is unable to return to work:_____

_____

_____

_____

_____

_____

_____

Circumstances that have contributed to the patient's recovery taking longer include the following: _____

_____

_____

_____

_____

_____

The person could return to work with the following modifications or restrictions:_____

_____

_____

_____

_____

_____

_____

_____   _____
Signature of Therapist   License number

_____   _____
Address   Phone

OUTLINE FOR DIAGNOSTIC SUMMARY

DIAGNOSTIC SUMMARY

Date: _____

Patient Name: _____

Date of Birth: _____

Sources of Information (includes but not limited to, mental status exam, history and physical, psychiatric evaluation, psychosocial and treatment plan).

Identification of the Patient (demographic information, include but not limited to, age, race, marital status, etc.):

_____

_____

_____

_____

_____

Presenting Problems (includes, but not limited to, why was the patient hospitalized, drug of choice, route of admission, frequency of use, pattern of use, medical problems, mood, affect, mental status, legal problems, etc.):

_____

_____

_____

_____

_____

Treatment Plan/Recommendations/Goals (includes problem list, therapeutic interventions and goals):

_____

_____

_____

_____

_____

Discharge Plan (includes, but not limited to, follow-up with therapy, a physician, a sponsor, a 12-step recovery program, vocational guidance, etc.):

_____

_____

_____

_____

_____

_____

_____   _____
Therapist   Date

DISCHARGE SUMMARY

_____

NAME OF PATIENT:_____

IDENTIFICATION OF PATIENT:

_____

_____

PRESENTING PROBLEM:

_____

_____

TREATMENT GOALS: *WERE GOALS MET? (yes/no)*

_____   _____

_____   _____

_____   _____

_____   _____

DISPOSITION/CONSULTS/REFERRALS/PROGNOSIS:

_____

_____

_____

_____

INITIAL DIAGNOSIS: *DISCHARGE DIAGNOSIS:*

Axis I _____   Axis I _____

Axis II _____   Axis II _____

Axis III _____   Axis III _____

Axis IV _____   Axis IV _____

Axis V _____   Axis V _____

Date of 1st session: _____   Date of last session: _____   # of sessions: _____

_____   _____
Date   Therapist

Business Forms

PATIENT REGISTRATION

_____

(PLEASE PRINT)   Today's Date: ___/___/_____

Patient's full name: _____ SS#: _____

Home Address: _____ City: _____ State: _____ Zip: _____

Home Phone: ( )_____ Sex: _____ Age: _____ Date of Birth: ___/___/_____

Patient Employer: _____ Phone Number: ( )_____

If Student: _____ H.S._____ College: _____

Family Physician:_____ Referred By: _____

Person to Contact in Emergency: _____ Phone: ( )_____

INSURED/RESPONSIBLE PARTY INFORMATION

Please complete this section regardless of insurance coverage.

Full Name of Insured: _____ Relationship: _____ Occupation: _____

Home Address: _____ Phone: ( )_____

Employer and Address: _____ Phone: ( )_____

Insured's SS#_____ Driver's License No._____ State_____

Full Name of spouse: _____ SS#:_____

Spouse's Employer: _____ Phone: ( )_____

Insured's Primary Ins. Co.: _____ I.D.No.: _____ Group NO.: _____

Secondary Ins. Co.: __No   __Yes; Company: _____ Policy No.: _____

Job Related Injury-Workmens Comp. Co.:   __No __Yes; Company: _____

OFFICE BILLING AND INSURANCE POLICY

1. I authorize us of this form on all of my insurance submissions.
2. I authorize the release of information to my insurance company(s).
3. I understand that I am responsible for the full amount of my bill for services provided.
4. I authorize direct payment to my service provider.
5. I hereby permit a copy of this to be used in place of an original.

Name: _____ I.D.# _____

Signature: _____ Date: _____

It is your responsibility to pay any deductible amount, co-pay, co-insurance amount or any other balance not paid by your ins. the day and time serviced provided.

There will be a $25.00 service charge on all returned checks.

In event that your account goes to collections, there will be a 20% collection fee added to your balance.

There is a 24-hour cancellation policy which requires that you cancel your appointment 24 hours in advance between the hours of 8am to 4pm Monday through Friday to avoid being charged.

Signature _____ Date _____

CONTRACT FOR SERVICES WITHOUT USING INSURANCE

Financial Agreement

I have agreed to pay privately for my therapy.

The agreed upon charge is $_____ for the first visit and then $_____ per session thereafter. Paperwork or other requests will be a separate cost if not done during the allotted time. Additionally, I acknowledge that my insurance will not reimburse me for my decision to see _____ privately. _____ is not to bill my insurance.

Name: _____ Date: _____

FEE AGREEMENT FOR DEPOSITION AND COURT APPEARANCE

Date:

To:

From:

Re:

When served with a subpoena *duces tecum* for my appearance in person or a deposition subpoena for my appearance, the following fee policies will be in effect. This is the case unless you receive a signed, written amendment from me.

My fee for scheduled appearance is $_____/hour paid in advance. The fee is due with the subpoena. If the fee is not paid at that time, arrangements for payment are the duty of the party requesting the appearance and must be made on receipt of this communication.

The fee is required for my scheduling the day or any fraction of the day. The fee is due whether or not I am actually called on that day. The fee is due even if the appearance is canceled by anyone other than me for any reason and at any time. These are my usual and customary fee arrangements.

Further required attendances will be charged at additional daily rates under the same circumstances. These terms are not negotiable.

Please determine the number of days you need me, specify same, and send me a check for $_____ per day by return mail if you want me to obey your subpoena. Then I will get back to you with my availability.

For payment purposes, my Federal Tax Identification Number or my Social Security Number is _____.

_____

Signature of Therapist

LIMITS ON PATIENT CONFIDENTIALITY

We are required to disclose confidential information if any of the following conditions exist:

1. You are a danger to yourself or others.
2. You seek treatment to avoid detection or apprehension or enable anyone to commit a crime.
3. Your therapist was appointed by the courts to evaluate you.
4. Your contact with your therapist is for the purpose of determining sanity in a criminal proceeding.
5. Your contact is for the purpose of establishing your competence.
6. The contact is one in which your psychotherapist must file a report to a public employer or as to information required to be recorded in a public office, if such report or record is open to public inspection.
7. You are under the age of 16 years and are the victim of a crime.
8. You are a minor and your psychotherapist reasonably suspects you are the victim of child abuse.
9. You are a person over the age of 65 and your psychotherapist believes you are the victim of physical abuse. Your therapist may disclose information if you are the victim of emotional abuse.
10. You die and the communication is important to decide an issue concerning a deed or conveyance, will or other writing executed by you affecting as interest in property.
11. You file suit against your therapist for breach of duty or your therapist files suit against you.
12. You have filed suit against anyone and have claimed mental/emotional damages as part of the suit.
13. You waive your rights to privilege or give consent to limited disclosure by your therapist.
14. Your insurance company paying for services has the right to review all records.

*If you have any questions about these limitations, please discuss them with your therapist.

Signature: _____ Date: _____

I am consenting to my (or my dependent) receiving outpatient treatment.

Signature: _____ Date: _____

RELEASE OF INFORMATION

I authorize _____ to contact my primary care physician (name) _____ regarding an appointment being made for follow-up, as well as information pertaining to psychological and emotional function.

Signature: _____ Date: _____

TREATMENT CONTRACT

The therapist and I have discussed my/my child's case and I was informed of the risks, approximate length of treatment, alternative methods of treatment, and the possible consequences of the decided on treatment which includes the following methods and interventions: For the purpose of

__Stabilization
__Decrease and relieve symptomatology
__Improve coping, problem solving, and use of resources
__Skill development
__Grief resolution
__Stress management
__Behavior modification and cognitive restructuring
__Other _____

While I expect benefits from this treatment I fully understand and accept that because of factors beyond our control, such benefits and desired outcomes cannot be guaranteed.

I understand that the therapist is not providing emergency service and I have been informed of whom/where to call in an emergency or during the evening or weekend hours.

I understand that regular attendance will produce the maximum possible benefits but that I or we am/are free to discontinue treatment at any time in accordance with the policies of the office.

I understand that I am financially responsible for any portion of the fees not covered or reimbursed by my health insurance.

I have been informed and understand the limits of confidentiality, that by law, the therapist must report to appropriate authorities any suspected child abuse or serious threats of harm to myself or another person.

I am not aware of any reason why I/we/he/she should not proceed with therapy and I/we/he/she agree to participate fully and voluntarily.

I have had the opportunity to discuss all of the aspects of treatment fully, have had my questions answered, and understand the treatment planned. Therefore, I agree to comply with treatment and authorize the above named clinician(s) or whomever is designated to administer the treatment(s) to me or my child.

Name of Patient: _____

Signature of Patient/Parent/Guardian: _____

Therapist Signature: _____ Date: _____

CONTRACT FOR GROUP THERAPY

1. As a group member I expect to benefit from participation, I recognize that I have rights and responsibilities as a group member.

2. The goals of this group are:

   A. _____

   B. _____

   C. _____

3. I will attend all group meetings and be on time. If there is an emergency which prevents me from attending I will contact the group facilitator as soon as possible. If for some other reason I am not able to attend a group meeting I will let the group know at least one week in advance.

4. If for some reason I decide to not continue to participate in group or I am unable to, I will let the group know 2 days before the last group meeting that I attend.

5. I agree to not socialize with group members outside of group.

6. I have been informed and understand the limits of confidentiality, that by law, the group facilitator must report to appropriate authorities any suspected child abuse and any serious threats of harm to myself or another person.

7. The cost of group is $ _____, or $ _____ per session, which begins at_____ am/pm and ends at _____ am/pm on _____ days. The first group meeting is scheduled for _____.

8. Respectfully and with full understanding I accept the following rules:

   A. Only first names will be used.

   B. There will be no side conversations or comments, whoever is speaking will be given full attention and respect.

   C. Children or other unauthorized visitors are not allowed in group.

   D. Recording of the group meetings is not allowed.

   E. I agree to not disclose information/problems of any group member outside of group.

   F. I will not disclose the identity of any group member outside of group.

   G. No food or drink will be allowed in group.

   H. I will not abuse any substances on the day of a group meeting.

Name: _____ Date: _____

RELEASE FOR THE EVALUATION AND TREATMENT OF A MINOR

As parent or legal guardian of _____.
I authorize his/her evaluation and treatment. As parent or legal guardian, I have the right to request information concerning the above minor's evaluation and treatment.

Signature _____   Date _____

Witness _____   Date _____

AUTHORIZATION FOR THE RELEASE OR EXCHANGE OF INFORMATION

Patient Name: _____   DOB: _____

Information To Be Released By Or Exchange With:

Name: _____

Address: _____

Information To Be Released By Or Exchanged:

__ History and Physical Exam
__ Discharge Summary
__ Psychiatric Evaluation
__ Psychological Test Results
__ Chemical Recovery History
__ Dates of Hospitalization

__ Court/Agency Documents
__ Mental Status
__ Treatment Plans
__ Progress Notes
__ Therapist Orders
__ Diagnoses
__ Crisis Intervention Reports
__ Medical Records

__ Family Systems Eval
__ Nursing Notes
__ Consultation Reports
__ Educational Records
__ Educational-Tests and Reports
__ Attendance Record
__ Psychosocial Report
__ Lab results

Other (specify) _____

_____   Date: _____
Patient Signature

CLIENT MESSAGES

In-Chart Log

Client's name: _____

Phone calls/messages

Date: _____ Time: _____ am/pm

Content: _____

_____

Response: _____

_____

Date: _____ Time: _____ am/pm

Content: _____

_____

Response: _____

_____

Date: _____ Time: _____ am/pm

Content: _____

_____

Response: _____

_____

Date: _____ Time: _____ am/pm

Content: _____

_____

Response: _____

_____

AFFIDAVIT OF THE CUSTODIAN OF MENTAL HEALTH RECORDS TO ACCOMPANY COPY OF RECORDS

_____

I, _____ declare that:
  (custodian of records)

1. I am the (a) duly authorized custodian of the mental health records of and have the authority to certify said records; and
2. The copy of the mental health records attached to this affidavit is a true copy of all the records described in the subpoena duces tecum; and
3. The records were prepared by _____ in the ordinary course of business; and
4. The documents contained herein are subject to privilege and may be subject to confidentiality provisions. They are to be reviewed by a judge of competent jurisdiction prior to further distribution.

I declare under penalty of perjury that the foregoing is true and correct.

_____
(Signature of custodian)

REFERRAL FOR PSYCHOLOGICAL

Evaluation Testing Therapy (circle one)

Date: _____

Client: _____ Age: _____ Sex: _____

Telephone # (H) (   )_____ (W) (   ) _____

Address: _____

Referral Sources: _____ Agency _____

PSYCHIATRIC HISTORY

1. Nature and length of client involvement with referral source:

   _____

   _____

   _____

2. Background information regarding client and family:
   A. Household members and ages.
   B. Behavioral description of client/family interactional style.

   _____

   _____

3. Is client presently taking medications: _____Yes _____No _____DK

   If yes, specify medication: _____

   Dosage level: _____

   Medical/Psychiatric condition: _____

4. Behavioral description of client:

   _____

   _____

   _____

   _____

5. Questions to be addressed by, and purpose of this referral?

_____

_____

_____

_____

6. What has client been told about this referral?

_____

_____

_____

7. What is the client's attitude toward and expectation of this referral?

_____

_____

_____

_____

_____

8. List other agencies involved:

_____

_____

_____

_____

_____

_____
Therapist

RELEASE TO RETURN TO WORK OR SCHOOL

Date _____

This is to certify that _____ has been under my care and has

been unable to attend work/school since _____. They are released to return

to work/school on _____.

Remarks/Limitations/Restrictions:

_____

_____

_____

_____
Therapist

NOTICE OF DISCHARGE FOR NONCOMPLIANCE OF TREATMENT

Date:

Dear :

This letter is to inform you that I am discharging you from further professional attendance because you have not complied with appropriate recommendations throughout the course of your treatment.

Since you have the need of professional services it is recommended that you promptly seek the care of another mental health professional to meet your needs. If for some reason you are unable to locate another mental health practitioner, please let me know and I will try to assist you.

Effective 14 days from the date, I will no longer be available to attend to your mental health needs. This period will give you ample time to find another mental health professional.

When you have selected another mental health professional, I will, upon your written authorization, provide a summary of your chart to the new provider.

Sincerely,

DUTY TO WARN

Although confidentiality and privileged communication remain rights of all clients of mental health practitioners according to the law, some courts have held that if an individual intends to take harmful acts or dangerous action against another human being, or against themselves, it is the practitioner's duty to warn the person or the family of the person or the family of the person who is likely to suffer the results of harmful behavior, or the family of the client who intends to harm himself of such an intention.

I, as a mental health practitioner, will under no circumstances inform such individuals without first sharing that intention with the client, unless it is not possible to do so. Every effort will be made to resolve the issue before such a breach of confidentiality takes place.

_____
Therapist

I have read the above statement and understand the therapist's social responsibility to make such decisions when necessary.

Name _____ Date _____

MISSED APPOINTMENT

It appears that circumstances have prevented you from meeting with me for an appointment on_____ at _____. Please contact me if you are interested in rescheduling the appointment. If I do not hear from you I will assume that you are not interested in my services at this time. In that event, please feel free to call again in the future if I can be of service to you.

Sincerely,

RECEIPT

—————————————

(letterhead)

RECEIPT

Date of service: _____

Name: _____

DOB: _____ SS#: _____

Service provided: _____

Diagnosis code: _____

Amount paid: _____

RECEIPT

_____

(letterhead)

RECEIPT

Date of service: _____

Name: _____

Service provided: _____

Amount paid: _____

BALANCE STATEMENT

Date _____

Name _____

    Our records show that you have a balance due for _____

in the amount of _____.

    Date of service was _____.
    Please bring your account current.

CLIENT SATISFACTION SURVEY

To be completed by client or parent/guardian if client is a minor.

1. The problems, feelings, or situation that brought me to the therapist are:
   __Much improved
   __Improved
   __About the same
   __Worse
   __Much worse

2. Because of therapy, I understand the problems well enough to manage them in the future:
   __Strongly agree
   __Agree
   __Not certain
   __Disagree
   __Strongly disagree

3. My therapist was:
   __Very helpful
   __Somewhat helpful
   __Neither helpful nor unhelpful
   __Somewhat unhelpful
   __Very unhelpful

4. If I needed help in the future, I would feel comfortable calling this therapist:
   __Definitely yes
   __Probably yes
   __Maybe
   __Probably not
   __Definitely not

5. I would recommend this therapist to others that need help:
   __Definitely yes
   __Probably yes
   __Maybe
   __Probably not
   __Definitely not

6. The interest shown by my therapist in helping me to solve my problems was:
   __Very satisfactory
   __Satisfactory
   __Neither satisfactory nor unsatisfactory
   __Unsatisfactory
   __Very unsatisfactory

7. How long has it been since your last visit?
   __Less than 1 month
   __1 or 2 months
   __3 to 5 months
   __6 months or more (how many) _____

8. Treatment ended with this therapist because:
   __The concerns which brought me to the therapist were worked out to my satisfaction.
   __Most of the significant concerns which brought me to seek therapy were worked out satisfactorily. There are some minor problems which we can now handle.
   __We reached the number sessions set by the therapist at the beginning of treatment. Significant problems remained that were not dealt with adequately.
   __I felt that more treatment would not be helpful at this time, even though significant problems remained.
   __The therapist felt that more treatment would not be helpful at this time, even though significant problems remained.
   __There was a change in a work or school schedule that made it impossible to arrange further appointments.

9. After you received counseling with this therapist, have you or any members of your family received any counseling elsewhere for the same problems you came here for?
   _____YES _____NO

10. Additional Comments:

   _____

   _____

   _____

   _____

   _____

   _____

   _____

THANK YOU FOR YOUR TIME.

_____   _____
SIGNATURE (OPTIONAL)   DATE

FORM FOR CHECKING OUT AUDIOTAPES, VIDEOTAPES AND BOOKS

_____

Date: _____

_____ has borrowed the following:

_____

_____

_____

_____

The tape(s) will be returned by _____. It is understood that for each tape or book not returned during this period of time I will be charged $10.00.

Signature _____

QUALITY ASSURANCE REVIEW

Patient Number: _____

Therapist Number: _____

Initial Assessment Date: _____

Termination Date: _____

INITIAL ASSESSMENT

1. Presenting problem	__Yes	__No
2. Relevant history	__Yes	__No
3. Reason for treatment	__Yes	__No
4. Mental status	__Yes	__No
5. Current medications	__Yes	__No
6. DSM IV diagnosis	__Yes	__No
7. Treatment plan	__Yes	__No

PROGRESS NOTES

1. Do progress notes relate logically to assessment, diagnosis, and treatment plan	__Yes	__No
2. Does each progress note express:		
Client concern/problem	__Yes	__No
Therapist Intervention	__Yes	__No
Client response to intervention	__Yes	__No
3. Treatment plan	__Yes	__No
Other Issues		
1. Signed release of information	__Yes	__No
2. Something relating to limits of confidentiality	__Yes	__No
3. Client agreement with therapist (fee, office policy)	__Yes	__No
4. Discharge summary	__Yes	__No

BIBLIOGRAPHY

Ackerman, R., & Michaels, J. (1990). Recovery source guide, 4th ed., Health Communication, Deerfield Beach, FL.

Agras, W. S. (1965). An investigation in the decrements of anxiety responses during systematic desensitization therapy. *Behav. Res. Ther., 2,* 267–270.

Agras, W. S., Barlow, T. H., Chapin, H. N., Abel, G. G., & Leitenberg, H. (1974). Behavioral modification of anorexia nervosa. *Archives of General Psychiatry, 30,* 279–286.

Aguilera, D., & Messick, J. (1982). Crisis intervention: Therapy for psychological emergencies. New York: New American Library/Mosby.

Alban, L. S., & Nay, W. R. (1976). Reduction of ritual checking by a relaxation-delay treatment. *Journal of Behavior Therapy and Experimental Psychiatry, 44,* 656–664.

Alberti, R., & Emmons, M. (1975). Stand up speak up talk back: The key to self-assertive behavior. New York: Pocket Books.

Alexander, J. F., Barton, C., Schiavo, R. S., & Parsons, B. V. (1976). Systems-behavioral intervention with families of delinquents: Therapist characteristics, family behavior, and outcome. Monterey, CA: Brooks/Cole.

Alexander, J. F., & Parsons, B. V. (1982). *Functional family therapy.* Monterey, CA: Brooks/Cole.

Allport, G. (1961). *Pattern and growth in personality.* New York: Holt, Rinehart & Winston.

Altmaier, E. M., Ross, S. L., Leary, M. R., & Thornbrough, M. (1982). Matching stress inoculation's treatment components to client's' anxiety mode. *Journal of Counseling Psychology, 29,* 331–334.

American Psychiatric Association (2000). *Practice guidelines for the treatment of psychiatric disorders.* Washington D. C.: American Psychiatric Association.

American Psychiatric Association DSM-III-R (1987). Diagnostic and statistical manual of mental disorders. 3rd ed. Washington, D.C.: American Psychiatric Association.

American Psychiatric Association (1994). Diagnostic and statistical manual of mental disorders, 4th ed. (DSMIV) Washington D. C.: American Psychiatric Association.

Anastopolous, A. D., & Shelton, T. L. (2001). *Assessing attention deficit/hyperactivity disorder.* New York: Kluwer Academic Plenum.

Anderson, P. K. (1988). *Adult children of alcoholics: Coming home*. Glen Abbey Books, Seattle.

Anthony, J., & Edelstein, B. (1975). Thought-stopping treatment of anxiety attacks due to seizure-related obsessive ruminations. *Journal of Behavioral Therapy and Experimental Psychiatry, 6,* 343–344.

Aranoff, G. M., Wagner, J. M., & Spangler, A. S. (1986). Chemical interventions for pain. *Journal of Consulting and Clinical Psychology.*

Arrick, M., Voss, J. R., & Rimm, D. C. (1981). The relative efficacy of the thought-stopping covert assertion. *Behaviour Research and Therapy, 19,* 17–24.

Ascher, L. M., & Phillips, D. (1975). Guided behavior rehearsal. *Journal of Behavior Therapy and Experimental Psychiatry, 6,* 215–218.

Atwood, J., & Chester, R. (1987). Treatment techniques for common mental disorders. New Jersey: Jason Aronson, Inc.

Auerswald, M. C. (1974). Differential reinforcing power of restatement and interpretation on client production of affect. *Journal of Counseling Psychology, 21,* 9–14.

Austad, C. S., & Berman, W. H. (1991). *Psychotherapy in managed health care: The optimal use of time and resources*. Washington, D.C.: American Psychological Association.

Azrin, N. H., Gottlieb, L., Hugart, L., Wesolowiski, M. D., & Rahn, T. (1975). Eliminating self-injurous behavior by educative procedures. *Behaviour Research and Therapy, 13,* 101–111.

Baker, S. B., & Butler, J. N. (1984). Effects of preventative cognitive self-instruction training on adolescent attitudes, experiences and state anxiety. *Journal of Primary Prevention, 5,* 10–14.

Baker, S. B., Thomas, R. N., & Munson, W. W. (1983). Effects on cognitive restructuring and structured group discussion as primary prevention strategies. *School Counselor, 31,* 26–33.

Baldwin, C. (1977). *One on one: Self-understanding through journal writing*. New York: M. Evans.

Bandura, A. (1969). Principles of behavior modification. New York: Holt, Rinehart & Winston.

Bandura, A., Jeffrey, R. W., & Gajdos, E. (1975). Generalizing change through participant modeling with self-directed mastery. *Behaviour Research and Therapy, 13,* 141–152.

Barlow, D. H. (Ed). (1981). Behavioral assessment of adult disorders. New York: Guilford Press.

Barlow, D. H. (1992). Cognitive-behavioral approaches to panic disorder and social phobia. *Bulletin of the Menninger Clinic, 56* (Suppl. 2), A29–A41.

Barsky, A. J., & Klerman, G. L. (1983). Overview: Hypochondriasis, bodily complaints, and somatic styles. *American Journal of Psychiatry.*

Bauer, G., & Kobos, J. (1984). Short-term psychodynamic psychotherapy: reflections on the past and current practice. *Psychotherapy, 21,* 153–170.

Bauer, G., & Kobos, J. (1987). Brief Therapy: Short-term psychodynamic intervention. New Jersey: Jason Aronson, Inc.

Beattie, M. C. (1987). *Codependant no more*. Center City, MN: Hazelden.

Beck, A., Rush, J., & Emery, G. (1979). *Cognitive therapy of depression*. New York: Guilford Press.

Beck, A. T. (1976). *Cognitive therapy and emotional disorders*. New York: International Universities Press.

Bell, J. (1977, June). Rescuing the battered wife. *Human Behavior,* 16–23.

Bellak, L., & Small, L. (1965). *Emergency psychotherapy and brief psychotherapy*. New York: Grune & Stratton.

Bellak, A. S., Hersen, M., & Himmelhoch, J. (1981). Social skills training, pharmacotherapy, and psychotherapy for unipolar depression. *American Journal of Psychiatry, 138,* 1562.

Bemis, K. (1980). Personal communication. In P. C. Kendall & S. D. Hollon (Eds.), *Assessment Strategies for Cognitive-Behavioral Interventions*. New York: Academic Press.

Bepko, C., & Krestan, J. A. (1985). *The responsibility trap*: A *blueprint for training the alcoholic family*. The Free Press: New York.

Berman, A. (1991). *Adolescent suicide*: *Assessment and intervention*. Washington, DC: American Psychological Association.

Bernstein, N. (1979). Chronic illness and impairment. *Psychiatric Clinics of North America, 2*, 331–346.

Biere, J. (1996). Trauma symptom checklist for children (TSCC). Odessa, FL: PAR.

Bishop, G. D. (1987). Lay conceptions of physical symptoms. *Journal of Applied Social Psychology*.

Bodin, A. M. (1996). Relationship conflict–verbal and physical: Conceptualizing an inventory for assessing process and content. In F. W. Kaslow (Ed.), Handbook of rotational diagram and dysfunctional family patterns (pp. 371–393) N. Y.: Wiley.

Bolby, J. (1973). *Attachment and loss*: *Separation, anxiety, and anger*. Basic Books: New York.

Bolstad, O. D., & Johnson, S. M. (1972). Self-regulation in the modification of disruptive classroom behavior. *Journal of Applied Behavior Analysis, 5*, 443–445.

Bonger, B. (1991). *The suicidal patient*: *Clinical and legal standards of care*. Washington, DC: American Psychological Association.

Booth, G. K. (1984). Disorders of Impulse control. In H. H. Goldman (Ed.), *Review of general psychiatry*. Los Altos, CA: Lange Medical Publications.

Borck, L. E., & Fawcett, S. B. (1982). *Learning counseling and problem solving skills*. Haworth Press: New York.

Borman, L. D., Borck, L. E., Hess, R., & Pasquale, E. L. (Eds.) (1982). *Helping people to help themselves*. Self-Help and Prevention: New York.

Bowen, M. (1978). *Family therapy in clinical practice*. New York: Jason Aronson.

Brammer, L. M., & Shostrom, E. L. (1982). *Therapeutic psychology*: *Fundamentals of counseling and psychotherapy*. Englewood Cliffs NJ: Prentice-Hall.

Brown, J. (1991). *The quality management professional's study guide*. Pasadena, CA: Managed Care Consultants.

Brown, S. (1985). Treating the alcoholic: A developmental model of recovery. N.Y.: John Wiley & Sons.

Brown, S. (1988). *Treating adult children of alcoholics*: *A developmental perspective*. Wiley: New York.

Brownell, K., Colleti, G., Ersner-Hershfield, R., Hershfield, S., & Wilson, G. (1977). Self-control in school children: Stringency and leniency in self-determined and externally imposed performance standards. *Behavior Therapy, 8*, 442–455.

Bruch, H. Psychotherapy of anorexia nervosa and developmental obesity. In R. K. Goldstein (Ed.), *Eating and weight disorders*. New York: Springer.

Budman, S. H. (Ed.). (1981). *Forms of brief therapy*. New York: Guilford Press.

Budman, S. H., & Gurman, A. S. (1988). Theory and practice of brief therapy. New York: Guilford Press.

Budman, S. H., Hoyt, M. F., & Friedman, S. (1992). The first session of brief therapy: A book of cases. New York: Guilford Press.

Buggs, D. C. (1975). *Your child's self-esteem*. New York: Doubleday.

Campbell, O. C. (Ed.) (1995). Assessing dangerousness: Violence by sex offenders, batteries and child abuseness Newbury Park, CA: Sage Publications.

Canino, I. A., & Spurlock, J. (2000). *Culturally diverse children and adolescents*. New York: Guilford Press.

Cantwell, D. P., et al. (1978). In M. Rutter & E. Schopler (Eds.), *Autism: A reappraisal of concept and treatment*. New York: Plenum Press.

Carkhuff, R. R., & Pierce, R. M. (1975). *Trainer's guide: The art of helping.* Amherst, MA: Human Resources Development Press.

Carrington, P. (1978). *Learning to mediate: Clinically standardized mediation (CSM) course workbook.* Kendall Park, NJ: Pace Educational Systems.

Carter, L., & Minirth, F. (1995). *The freedom from depression workbook.* Nashville: Thomas Nelson Publishers.

Cautela, J. R. (1969). *Behavior therapy and self-control: Techniques and implications.* New York: McGraw Hill.

Cautela, J. R., & Groden, J. (1978). *Relaxation: A comprehensive manual for adults, children, and children with special needs.* Champaign IL: Research Press.

Cermak, T. L. (1986). *Diagnosing and treating codependence.* Minneapolis, MN: Johnson Institute Books, 61.

Chiauzzi, E. (1991). *Preventing relapse in the addictions: A biopsychosocial approach.* New York: Pergamon Press.

Claiborn, C. D. (1982). Interpretation and change in counseling. *Journal of Counseling Psychology, 29,* 439–453.

Cohen, D. J., & Volkmar, F. R. (Eds.). (1997). *Handbook of autism and pervasive developmental disorders* (Rev. ed.). New York: Wiley.

Cormier, W. H., & Cormier, L. S. (1975, 1985). Interviewing strategies for helpers: Fundamental skills and cognitive behavioral interventions (2nd ed.). Monterey, CA: Brooks/Cole.

Craske, M. (1988). Cognitive-behavioral treatment of panic. In A. J. France & R. E. Hales (Eds.), American Psychiatric Press Review of Psychiatry (Vol. 7, pp. 121–137). Washington, DC: American Psychiatric Press.

Daley, D. (1989). A Psycho-educational approach to relapse prevention. *Journal of Chemical Dependency Treatment, 2*(2),105–124.

Daley, D., & Sproule, C. (1991). *Adolescent relapse prevention workbook.* Holmes Beach, FL: Learner Publications.

Daley, D. (1993). *Preventing relapse.* Minnesota: Hazelden.

Davanloo, H. (1978). *Basic principles and techniques in short-term dynamic psychotherapy.* New York: Spectrum Publications.

Davis, M., Eshelman, E. R., & McKay, M. (1988). *The relaxation and stress reduction workbook.* Oakland, CA: New Harbinger Publications.

Davis, A., Rosenthal, T. L., & Kelley, J. E. (1981). Actual fear cues, prompt therapy, and rationale enhance participant modeling with adolescence. *Behavior Therapy, 12,* 536–542.

Day, R. W., & Sparacio, R. T. (1980). Structuring the counseling process. *Personnel and Guidance Journal, 59,* 246–250.

Deffenbacher, J. L., & Suinn, R. M. (1982). The self-control of anxiety. In P. Karoly & F. H. Kanfer (Eds.), *Self-management and behavior change.* New York: Pergamon Press.

DeShazer, S. (1985). *Keys to solutions in brief therapy.* New York: Norton.

DeWitt, K. N. (1984). Adjustment disorder. In H. H. Goldman (Ed.), *Review of general psychiatry.* Los Altos, CA: Lange Medical Publications.

Docherty, N. M., DeRose, M., & Andreasen, N. C. (1996). Communication disturbances in schizophrenia and mania. *Archives of General Psychiatry, 53,* 358–364(E).

Doenges, M., Townsend, M., & Moorhouse, M. (1989). *Psychiatric care plans: Guidelines for client care.* Philadelphia: F. A. Davis.

Drabman, R. S., Spitalnick, R., & O'Leary, K. D. (1973). Teaching self-control in disruptive children. *Journal of Abnormal Psychology, 82*, 10–16.

DuPaul, G. J., Power, T. J., Anastopolous, A. D., & Reid, R. (1998). *ADHD Rating Scale IV checklists, norms and clinical interpretation.* New York: Guilford Press.

Dutton D. G. (1993). A scale for measuring propensity for abusiveness. *Journal of Family Violence, 10* (2), 203–2.

Dyer, W. W., & Friend, J. (1975). *Counseling techniques that work.* Washington DC: American Personnel and Guidance Association.

Eberle, T., Rehm, L., & McBurrey, D. (1975). Fear decrement to anxiety hierarchy items: Effects of stimulus intensity. *Behavioral Research Therapy, 13*, 225–261.

Edelstein, M. G. (1990). *Symptom analysis: A method of brief therapy.* New York: Norton.

Egan, G. (1976). *Interpersonal living: A skills contract approach to human-relations training in groups.* Monterey, CA: Brooks/Cole.

Eisenstein, S. (1980). The contributions of Franz Alexander. In H. Davanloo (Ed.), *Short-term dynamic psychotherapy.* New York: Jason Aronson.

Eisler, R. M., Hersen, M., & Miller, P. M. (1973). Effects of modeling on components of assertive behavior. *Journal of Behavior Therapy and Experimental Psychiatry, 4*, 1–6.

Eisler, R. M., Hersen, M., Miller, P. M., & Blanchard, E. F. (1975). Situational determinants of assertive behavior. *Journal of Consulting and Clinical Psychology, 43*, 330–340.

Emery, G., & Campbell, J. (1986). *Rapid relief from emotional distress.* New York: Rawson Associates.

Erickson, L., Bjornstad, S., & Gotestam, K. G. (1986). Social skills training in groups for alcoholics: One-year treatment outcome for groups and individuals. *Addictive Behaviors, 11*, 309–329.

Evans, I. M. (1974). A Handy record-card for systematic desensitization hierarchy items. *Journal of Behavior Therapy and Experimental Psychology, 5*, 43–46.

Everstine, D. S., & Everstine, L. (1983). *People in crisis: Strategic therapeutic interventions.* New York: Brunner/Mazel.

Falloon, I. R. H. (1985). *Family management of schizophrenia: A study of the clinical, social, family and economic benefits.* Baltimore, MD: Johns Hopkins University Press.

Fawcell, J. M. D. (Ed.). (1993). Predicting and preventing suicide. *Psychiatric Anals, 23*, 5.

Ferster, C. B. (1961). Positive reinforcement and behavior deficits of autistic children. *Child Development, 32*, 437–456.

Filsinger, E. (1983). *Marriage and family assessment: A sourcebook for family therapy.* Beverly Hills, CA: Sage.

Fisch, R., Weakland, J., & Segal, L. (1982). *The tactics of change: Doing therapy briefly.* San Francisco: Jossey-Bass.

Fishman, S. T., & Lubetkin, B. S. (1983). *Office practice of behavior therapy.* New York: Grune & Stratton.

Flegenheimer, W. (1985). History of brief psychotherapy. In A. Horner (Ed.), *Treating the oedipal patient in brief psychotherapy.* New York: Jason Aronson.

Flor, H., Kerns, R. D., & Turk, D. C. (1987). The role of spousal reinforcement, perceived pain, and activity levels of chronic pain patients. *Journal of Psychosomatic Research, 31*(2), 251–259.

Foccaro, E. F., Kramer, F., Zemishlanz, Z., Thorne, A., Rice, C. M., II, Giordano, B., Patel, B. M., Torres, J., Nora Neufeld, R., Mohs, R. C., & Davis, K. L. (1990). Pharmacological treatment of noncognitive behavioral disturbances in elderly demented patients. *American Journal of Psychiatry, 147*, 1640–1645.

Fordyce, W. E. (1976). Behavioral concepts in chronic pain and illness. In P. O. Davison (Ed.), *Behavioral management of anxiety, depression and pain.* New York: Brunner/Mazel.

Fredricksen, L. W. (1975). Treatment of ruminative thinking by self-monitoring. *Journal of Behavior Therapy and Experimental Psychiatry, 6,* 258–259.

Fremouw, W. J., & Brown, J. P., Jr. (1980). The reactivity of addictive behaviors to self-monitoring: A functional analysis. *Addictive Behavior, 5,* 209–217.

Fremouw, W. J., & Heyneman, N. (1983). Obesity. In M. Hersen (Ed.), *Outpatient behavior therapy.* New York: Grune & Stratton.

Friedman, S., & Fanger, M. T. (1991). *Expanding therapeutic possibilities: Getting results in brief psychotherapy.* New York: Lexington Books.

Galassi, M. D., & Galassi, J. P. (1977). *Assert yourself: How to be your own person.* New York: Human Sciences.

Gambrill, E. (1981). *Behavior Modification: Handbook of assessment, intervention, and evaluation.* San Francisco: Jossey-Bass.

Gardner, R. A. (1989). *Family evaluation in child custody, mediation, arbitration and litigation.* Creskill, NJ: Creative Therapeutics.

Garvey, W., & Hegrenes, J. (1966). Desensitization techniques in the treatment of school phobia. *American Journal of Orthopsychiatry, 36,*147–152.

Geffner, R., & Mantooth, C. (2000). *Ending spouse/partner abuse: A psychoeducational approach for individuals and couples.* New York: Springer.

Geller, B., Craney, J. L., Bolhofner, K., *et al.* (2002). Two year prospective follow-up on children with a prepubertal and early adolescent bipolar disorder phenotype. *American Journal of Psychiatry, 159,* 927–933.

Giles-Sims, J. (1983). *Wife battering: A systems theory approach.* New York: The Guilford Press.

Giovacchini, P. (1986). *Developmental disorders: The transitional space in mental breakdown and creative integration.* New Jersey: Jason Aronson.

Glaister, B. (1982). Muscle relaxation training for fear reduction of patients with psychological problems: A review of controlled studies. *Behavior Research Therapy, 20,* 493–504.

Goldfried, M. R. (1982). *Behavioral assessment: An overview.* New York: Plenum Press.

Goodman, M., Brown, J., & Deitz, P. (1992). *Managing managed care: A mental health practioner's survival guide.* Washington DC: American Psychiatric Press.

Goodman, F., & Jamisin, K. (1990). *Manic-depressive illness.* New York: Oxford University Press.

Goodwin, S. E., & Mahoney, M. J. (1975). Modification in aggression through modeling. *Journal of Applied Behavior Analysis, 9,* 114.

Gorski, T., & Miller, M. (1988). *Staying sober workbook.* Independence, MO: Independence Press.

Goulding, M. M., & Goulding, R. L. (1979). *Changing lives through redecision therapy.* New York: Brunner/Mazel.

Gresham, F. M., & Nagle, R. J. (1980). Social skills training with children: responsiveness to modeling and coaching as a function of peer orientation. *Journal of Consulting and Clinical Psychology, 48,* 718–729.

Grisso, T. (1988). *Competency to stand trial evaluations: A manual for practice.* Sarasota, FL: Professional Resource Exchange, Inc.

Grotstein, J. S., Solomon, M. F., & Lang, J. (Eds.). (1987). *The borderline patient.* Hillsdale, NJ: Analytic Press.

Gustafson, J. P. (1986). *The complex secret of brief psychotherapy.* New York: Norton.

Hackett, G., & Horan, J. J. (1980). Stress inoculation for pain: What's really going on? *Journal of Counseling Psychology, 27*,107–116.

Haley, J. (1961). *Control in brief psychotherapy.* New York: Grune & Stratton.

Haley, J., & Hoffman, L. (1967). *Techniques of family therapy.* New York: Grune & Stratton.

Haley, J. (1977). *Problem-solving therapy.* San Francisco: Josey-Bass.

Hamby, S. (1995). Dominance scale: Durham NH: University of New Hamphire Press.

Hay, W. M., Hay, L. R., & Nelson, P. O. (1977). The adaptation of covert modeling procedures to the treatment of chronic alcoholism and obsessive-compulsive behavior. *Behavior Therapy, 8*, 70–76.

Hays, V., & Waddell, K. J. (1976). A self-reinforcing procedure for thought stopping. *Behavior Therapy, 7*, 559.

Helfer, R., & Kempe, R. (1987). *The battered child.* Chicago: The University of Chicago Press.

Hersen, M., & Bellack, A. S. (1976). A multiple baseline analysis of social-skills training in chronic schizophrenia. *Journal of Applied Behavior Analysis, 9*, 239–246.

Hersen, M., Eisler, R. M., Miller, P. M., Johnson, M. D., & Pinkston, J. G. (1973). Effects of practice, instructions, and modeling on components of assertive behavior. *Behavior Research and Therapy, 11*, 443–451.

Horner, A. (1985). Treating the oedipal patient in brief psychotherapy. In A. Horner (Ed.), New York: Jason Aronson.

Horowitz, M. J. (1976). *Stress response syndromes.* New York: Aronson.

Horowitz, M. J., et al. (1984). Personality styles and brief psychotherapy. New York: Basic Books.

Housekamp, B. M., & Foy, D. W. (1991). The assessment of post-traumater stress disorder in battered women. *Journal of Interpersonal Violence, 6*, 367–375.

Housekamp, B. M., & Foy, D. W. (1991). The assessment of post-traumatic stress disorder.

Hoyt, M. F. (1979). Aspects of termination in a brief time-limited psychotherapy. *Psychiatry, 42*, 208–219.

Hoyt, M. F. (1985). Therapist resistance to short-term dynamic psychotherapy. *Journal of the American Academy of Psychoanalysis, 13*, 93–112.

Hoyt, M. F. (1986). Mental-imagery methods in short-term dynamic psychotherapy. In M. Wolpin et al. (Eds.), *Imagery 4.* New York: Plenum.

Hoyt, M. F. (1987). Notes on psychotherapy with obsessed patients. *The Psychotherapy Patient, 3*(2), 13–22.

Hoyt, M. F. (1989). Psychodiagnosis of personality disorders. *Transactional Analysis Journal, 19*, 101–113.

Hoyt, M. F. (1990). On time in brief therapy. In R. A. Wells & V. J. Gianetti (Eds.), *Handbook of brief psychotherapies.* New York: Plenum Press.

Hoyt, M. F. (1991). Teaching and learning in short-term psychotherapy within an HMO: with special attention to resistance and phase-specific parallel process. In C. S. Austad & W. Berman (Eds.), *The Handbook of HMO Psychotherapy in Prepaid Health Care Setting.* Washington DC: American Psychological Association.

Hoyt, M. F. (1995). *Brief therapy and managed care: Readings for contemporary practice.* San Francisco: Jossey-Bass.

Institute for the Advancement of Human Behavior. Child abuse and the mental health professional (manual). P.O. Box 7226, Stanford, CA 94309.

Jacobs, D., & Brown, H. (Eds.). (1989). *Suicide understanding and responding.* Madison, CT: International University Press.

Jacobson, G., Strickler, M., & Morley, W. E. (1968). Generic and individual approaches to crisis intervention. *American Journal of Public Health, 58,* 339.

Jacobson, J. W. (1982a). Problem behavior and psychiatric impairment within a developmentally disabled population: I. Behavior frequency. *Applied Research in Mental Retardation, 3,* 121–139.

Jacobson, J. W. (1982b). Problem behavior and psychiatric impairment within a developmentally disabled population. II Behavior severity. *Applied Research in Mental Retardation, 3,* 369–381.

James, J., & Cherry, F. (1988). *The grief recovery handbook.* New York: Harper and Row.

Jarvinen, P. J., & Gold, S. R. (1981): Imagery as an aid in reducing depression. *Journal of Clinical Psychology, 37,* 523–529.

Johnson, S. L. (1997). Therapist's Guide to Clinical Intervention: The 1,2,3's of Treatment Planning. San Diego: Academic Press.

Jones, M. C. (1924). The elimination of childrens fears. *Journal of Experimental Psychology, 7,* 383–390.

Kandal, D., & Faust, R. (1975). Sequence and stages in patterns of adolescent drug use. *Archives of General Psychiatry, 32,* 923–932.

Kanfer, F. H. (1980). *Self-management methods.* New York: Pergamon Press.

Kaplan, H. (1979). *Disorders of sexual desire and other new concepts and techniques in sex therapy.* New York: Brunner/Mazel.

Kaplan, H. (1985). *Comprehensive evaluation of disorders of sexual desire.* Washington, DC: American Psychiatric Press.

Kaplan, H. I., & Sadock, B. J. (1981). *Modern synopsis of comprehensive textbook of psychiatry III.* (3rd ed.), Baltimore: Williams & Wilkins.

Kazdin, A. E. (1974). *Self-monitoring and behavior change.* Monterey, CA: Brooks/Cole.

Keefe, F. J., & Williams, D. A. (1989). New direction in pain assessment and treatment. *Clinical Psychology Review,* 549–568.

Kellner, R. (1987). Hypochodriasis and somatization. *Journal of the American Medical Association.*

King, S. H. (1962). *Perceptions of illness and medical practice.* New York: Russell Sage Foundation.

Kleiman, K. R., & Ranskin, V. D. (1994). *This isn't what I expected.* New York: Bantam Books.

Kolodny, R., Masters, W., & Johnson, V. (1979). *Textbook of sexual medicine.* Boston: Little, Brown and Company.

Kozloff, M. A. (1973). *Reaching the autistic child: A parent training program.* Champaign IL: Research Press.

Kroop, P. R., & Hart, S. D. (1997). Assessing risk for violence in wife assaulters: The spousal assault risk guide. In C. D. Webster & M. A. Jackson (Eds.), Impulsivity, theory, assessment and treatment (pp. 302–325) N.Y.: Guilford Press.

Krumboltz, J. D., & Krumboltz, H. B. (1972). *Changing childrens behavior.* Englewood Cliffs, NJ: Prentice-Hall.

Kubler-Ross, E. (1969). *On death and dying.* New York: MacMillan.

Lacy, J. I. (1967). Somatic response patterning and stress: Some revisions of activation theory. In M. H. Appley & R. Trumbull (Eds.), *Psychological stress: Issues in research.* New York: Appleton-Century-Crofts.

Lange, A., & Jakubowski, P. (1976). *Responsible assertive behavior: Cognitive/behavioral procedures for trainers.* Champaign, IL: Research Press.

Lazarus, A. A., Davidson, C. G., & Polefka, D. A. (1965): Classical and operant factors in the treatment of a school phobia. *Journal of Abnormal Psychiatry, 70,* 225–229.

Lazarus, R. (1966). *Psychological stress and the coping process.* New York: McGraw Hill.

Lazarus, A. A. (1976). *Multi-modal behavior therapy.* New York: McGraw-Hill.

Lazarus, A. A. (1981). Multi-modal behavior therapy. Part 3. New York: Springer.

Lehrer, P. M., & Woolfolk, R. L. (1982). Self-report assessment of anxiety: Somatic, cognitive, and behavioral modalities. *Behavior Assessment, 4,* 167–177.

Lewinsohn, P. M. (1974). A behavioral approach to depression. In R. J. Friedman & M. M. Katz, (Eds.), *The psychology of depression.* Washington DC: V. H. Winston and Sons.

Lewis, J. A., Dana, R. Q., & Blevins, G. A. (1994). *Substance abuse counseling: An individual approach* (2nd ed.), Pacific Grove, CA: Brooks/Cole Publishing.

Liberman, R. P., King, L. W., DeRisi, W. J., & McCann, M. (1975). *Personal effectiveness: Guiding people to assert themselves and improve their social skills.* Champaign, IL: Research Press.

Linehan, M. (1987). Dialectical behavior therapy for borderline personality disorder. *Bulletin of the Menniger Clinic, 51*(3), 261–276.

Linehan, M. (1995). *Treating borderline personality disorder: Dialectical approach program manual.* New York, Guilford Press.

Linton, S. (1994). Chronic back pain: Integrating psychological and physical therapy—an overview. *Behavioral Medicine, 20,* 101–104.

Lion, J. (1972). *Evaluation and management of the violent patient.* Springfield, IL: Charles C. Thomas.

Lovaas, O. I., & Newsom, C. D. (1976). *Behavior modification with psychotic children.* Englewood Cliffs, NJ: Prentice Hall.

Maxmen, J. S., & Ward, N. G. (1995). Essential psychopathology and its treatment: N.Y.: WW Norton & Co.

Mace, N., & Rabins, P. (1981). *The 36 hour day.* Baltimore: John Hopkins University.

Malan, D. (1979). *Individual psychotherapy and the science of psychodynamics.* Boston: Butterworths.

Mann, J. (1973). *Time-limited psychotherapy.* New York: McGraw-Hill.

Maltsberger, J. (1986). *Suicide risk: The formulation of clinical judgment.* New York: New York University Press.

Marlatt, G. A., & Gordon, J. R. (Eds.). (1985). *Relapse prevention: Maintenance strategies in the treatment of addictive behaviors.* New York: Guilford Press.

Mash, E., & Barkley, R. (1989). *Treatment of childhood disorders.* New York: Guilford Press.

Maxmen, J. S., & Ward, N. G. (1995). *Essential psychopathology and its treatment.* New York: W. W. Norton.

Marsh, E. J., & Barkley, R. A. (1989). *Treatment of childhood disorders.* New York: Guilford.

McKay, M., & Fanning, P. (1992). *Self-esteem.* Oakland, CA: New Harbinger Publications.

McKay, M., Fanning, P., & Paleg, K. (1994). *Couple skills.* Oakland, CA: New Harbinger Publications.

McKay, M., Rogers, P., & McKay, J. (1989). *When anger hurts: Quieting the storm within.* Oakland, CA: New Harbinger Publications.

McCracken, J. (1985). Somatoform disorders. In J. Walker (Ed.), *Essentials of clinical psychiatry.* Philadelphia: Lippincott.

McGlashen, T. H., & Fenton, W. S. (1997). The positive/negative distinction in schizophrenia: Review of natural history validators. *Archives of General Psychiatry, 49,* 63–72(F).

McFall, R. M., & Dodge, K. A. (1982). Self-management and interpersonal skills learning. New York: Pergamon Press.

Meichenbaum, D. H., & Goodman, J. (1971). Training impulsive children to talk to themselves: A means of developing self-control. *Journal of Abnormal Psychology, 77*, 115–126.

Meichenbaum, D. H., & Turk, D. (1976). The cognitive-behavioral management of anxiety, anger, and pain. In P. O. Davidson (Ed.), *The behavioral management of anxiety, depression, and pain.* New York: Brunner/Mazel.

Meichenbaum, D. H. (1976). A cognitive-behavior modification approach to assessment. In M. Hersen & A. S. Bellack (Eds.), *Behavioral assessment: A practical handbook.* New York: Pergamon Press.

Meichenbaum, D. H. (1985). *Stress-inoculation training.* New York: Pergamon Press.

Melton, G., Petrila, J., Poythress, N., & Slobogin, C. (1987). *Psychological evaluations for the courts: A handbook for mental health professionals and lawyers.* New York: Guilford Press.

Meyer, R. G. (1983). *The clinician's handbook: The psychopathology of adulthood and late adolescence.* Boston: Allyn & Bacon.

Miller, A. (1988). *The enabler: When helping harms the one you love.* Claremont, CA/Ballantine, NY: Hunter House.

Miller, W. (1989). *Matching individuals with interventions: Handbook of alcoholism treatment approaches.* New York: Pergamon Press.

Mirin, S., & Weiss, R. (1983). Substance abuse. In E. Bassuk, S. Schoonover, & A. Gelenberg (Eds.), *The Practioner's guide to psychoactive drugs* (pp. 221–290) New York: Plenum Press.

Mitchell, J. T., & Everly, G. S. (2000). Critical incident stress management and critical incident stress debriefings: Evolutions, effects, and outcomes. In B. Raphael & J. P. Wilson (Eds.), *Psychological debriefings: Theory, practice and evidence* (pp. 71–90). New York: Cambridge University Press.

Monti, P. M., Abrams, D. B., Kadden, R. M., & Cooney, N. L. (1989). *Treating alcohol dependence: A coping skills training guide.* New York: Guilford Press.

Morrison, J., & Anders, T. F. (1999). *Interviewing children and adolescents: Skills and strategies for effective DSM IV diagnoses.* New York: Guilford.

Murphy, L. B. (1974). Coping, vulnerability, and resilience in childhood. In G. V. Coehlo, et al. (Eds.), *Coping and adaption.* New York: Basic Books.

Murphy, L., & Moriarty, A. (1976). *Vulnerability, coping, and growth from infancy to adolescence.* New Haven, CT: Yale University Press.

National Mental Health Association (NMHA). 1021 Prince Street. Alexandria, VA. 22314–22971.

Nay, W. R. (1979). *Multi method clinical assessment.* New York: Gardner Press.

Nelson, R. O. (1983). Behavioral assessment: Past, present, and future. *Behavioral Assessment, 5,* 195–206.

Neimeyer, R., & Feixas, E. (1990). The role of homework and skills acquisition in the outcome of cognitive therapy for depression. *Behavior Therapy, 21,* 281–292.

Neimiah, J., & Sifneos, P. (1970). Affect and fantasy in patients with psychosomatic disorders. In O. W. Hill (Ed.), *Modern trends in psychosomatic medicine,* (Vol. 2, pp. 26–34). New York: Appleton-Century-Crofts.

N. H. Consensus Development Panel on Depression in Late Life. (1992). *JAMA 268,* 1018–1024 (G).

O'Hanlon, W. H., & Weiner-Davis, M. (1988). *In search of solutions: A new direction in psychotherapy.* New York: Norton.

O'Leary, K. D., Vivian, D., & Malone, J. (1992). Assessment of physical aggression against women in marriage: The need for multimodal assessment. *Behavioral Assessment, 14*(1), 5–14.

O'Leary, K. D., Heyman, R. E., & Neidig, P. H. (1999). Treatment of wife abuse: A comparison of gender specific and conjoint approaches. *Behavior Therapy, 30,* 475–506.

Othmer, E., & DeSouza C. (1985). A screening test for somatization disorder (hysteria). *American Journal of Psychiatry, 142*, 1146–1199.

Patsiokas, A. J., et al. (1979). Cognitive characteristics of suicidal attempts. *Journal of Consulting and Clinical Psychology, 47*, 478-484.

Perry, S., Frances, A., & Clarkin, J. (1985). *A DSM-III casebook of differential therapeutics*. New York: Brunner/Mazel.

Peterson, L., & Brownlee-Duffeck, M. (1984). Prevention of anxiety and pain due to medical and dental procedures. In M. C. Roberts & L. Peterson (Eds.), *Prevention of problems in childhood: Psychological research and application* (pp. 195–308). New York: Wiley.

Pollin, I., & Golant, S. K. (1994). Taking charge: Overcoming the challenges of long term illness. N.Y.: Times Books.

Pollin, I., & Kanaan, S. (1995). *Medical crisis counseling: Short-term therapy for long-term illness*. New York: Norton.

Pope, S. J. (2002). Nonadherence with mood stabilizers: Prevalence and predictors. *Journal of Clinical Psychiatry, 63*, 384–390.

Pruder, R. S. (1988). Age analysis of cognitive-behavioral group therapy for chronic pain patients. *Psychology and Aging, 3*(2), 204–207.

Rada, R. (1981). The violent patient: Rapid assessment and management. *Psychosomatics, 22*, 101–109.

Rasgon, N., Bauer, M., Glenn, T., & Whybrow, P. (2002). Gender differences in mood patterns in bipolar disorder. Research presented at 155th Annual Meeting of the American Psychiatric Association, Philadelphia, May 2002.

Root, M. P. P. (1992). Reconstructing the impact of trauma on personality. In L. S. Brown & M. Ballon (Eds.). Personality and psychopathology: Feminist reappraisals (pp. 229–265) NY: Guilford Press

Rosenbaum, R. (1990): Strategic psychotherapy. In R. A. Wells & V. J. Giannetti (Eds.), *Handbook of the brief psychotherapies*. New York: Plenum Press.

Rosenbaum, R., Hoyt, M. F., & Talmon, M. (1990). *The challenge of single-sessions therapies: Creating pivotal moments*. New York: Plenum Press.

Rosenberg, K. (1993). *Talk to me: A therapist's guide to breaking through male silence*. New York: Plenum Press.

Rosenberg, L. (1983). The technique of psychological assessment as applied to children in foster care and their families. In M. Hardin (Ed.), *Foster children in the courts* (pp. 550–574). Boston: Butter-worth.

Russell, M. L., & Thoresen, C. E. (1976). Teaching decision-making skills to children. In J. D. Krumboltz & C. E. Thoresen (Eds.), *Counseling methods*. New York: Holt, Rinehart, and Winston.

Samaan, M. (1975): Thought-stopping and flooding in case of hallucinations, obsession, and homicidal-suicidal behavior. *Journal of Behavior Therapy and Experimental Psychiatry, 6*, 65–67.

Schetky, D. H., & Slader, D. L. (1980). Termination of parental rights. In D. H. Schetky & E. P. Benedek (Eds.), *Child Psychiatry and the Law*.

Seligman, M. E. P. (1991). *Learned optimism*. New York: Knopf.

Seligman, M. (1990). *Learned optimism: How to change your mind and life*. New York: Pocket Books.

Sifneos, P. (1972). *Short-term psychotherapy and emotional crisis*. Cambridge, MA: Harvard University Press.

Sifneos, P. E. (1987). *Short-term dynamic psychotherapy*. New York: Plenum.

Simos, B. G. (1979). *A time to grieve: Loss as a universal human experience*. New York: Family Services Association of America.

Small, L. (1979). *The briefer psychotherapies*. New York: Brunner/Mazel.

Smith, R. E., & Sarason, I. G. (1975). Social anxiety and the evaluation of negative interpersonal feedback. *Journal of Consulting and Clinical Psychology, 43*, 429.

Sonkin, D., Martin, D., & Auerbach Walker, L. (1985). *The male batterer: A treatment approach.* New York: Springer Publishing Company.

Sonkin, D. J. (2000). Count-mandated perpetuator assessment and treatment handbook. :CA: Author.

Spates, C. R., & Knafer, F. H. (1977). Self-monitoring, self-education, and self-reinforcement in childrens learning: A test of a multistage self-regulation model. *Behavior Therapy, 8*, 9–16.

Spitzer, R., Williams, J., & Gibbon, M. (1987). Structured clinical interview for DSM III-R, personality disorders module. New York: Guilford (BMA Audio Casettes a Division of Guilford Publications, Inc.).

Stahl, P. (1999, March). Alienation and alignment of children. *California Psychologist, pp. 23–29.*

Stoudemire, G. (1988). Somatoform disorders, factitious disorders, and malingering. In J. Talbott, R. Hales, & S. Yudofsky (Eds.), *Textbook of psychiatry.* Washington DC: American Psychiatric Press.

Strupp, H. H., & Binder, J. (1984). *Psychotherapy in a new key: A guide to time limited dynamic psychotherapy.* New York: Basic Books.

Tatarsky, A., & Washton, A. (1992). *Intensive outpatient treatment: A psychological perspective.* New York: Brunner/Mazel.

Taylor, C. B. (1983). DSM-III and behavioral assessment. *Behavioral Assessment, 5*, 5–14.

Terman, M., Williams, J., & Terman, J. (1991). Light therapy for winter depression: clinician's guide. In P. Keller (Ed.), Innovation in clinical practice: A source book (pp. 179–221). Sarasota, FL: Pro-Resources.

The National Alliance for the Mentally Ill (NAMI). 200 North Glebe Road, Suite 1015, Arlington, VA 22203–3754.

Turk, D., & Genest, M. (1979). Regulation of pain: The application of cognitive and behavioral techniques for prevention of remediation. In P. Kendall & S. Hollon (Eds.), *Cognitive-behavioral interventions: Theory, Research, and Procedures.* New York: Academic Press.

Turner, R. M. (1983). Cognitive-behavior therapy with borderline personality disorder. *Carrier Foundation Letter, 88*, 1–4.

Turner, R. M. (1988). The cognitive-behavioral approach to the treatment of borderline personality disorder. *International Journal of Partial Hospitalization, 5*, 279–289.

Turpin, J. (1975). Management of violent patients. In R. Shader (Ed.), *Manual of Psychiatric Therapeutics.* Boston: Little Brown.

Vaillant, G., & Perry, J. (1985). Personality disorders. In H. Kaplan & B. Sadock (Eds.), *Comprehensive textbook of psychiatry* (4th ed.). Baltimore: Williams & Wilkins.

Veinot, T. (2001). Who is the abuser? A screening challenge. Website http://www.womenabuseprevention.com/ht.screening.html.

Wachtel, P. L. (Ed.). (1982). *Resistance: Psychodynamic and behavioral approach.* New York: Plenum Press.

Waldinger, R. (1986). *Fundamentals of psychiatry.* New York: American Psychiatric Press.

Walls, R. T., Werner, T. J., Bacon, A., & Zanc, T. (1977). Behavioral checklists. In J. D. Cone & R. P. Hawkins (Eds.), *Behavioral assessment: New directions in clinical psychology.* New York: Brunner/Mazel.

Walker, L.(1979). *The battered woman.* New York: Harper and Row.

Washton, A. M. (1989). *Cocaine abuse: Treatment, recovery, and relapse prevention.* New York: Norton.

Washton, A. M. (1995). *Psychotherapy and substance abuse*: A practitioners handbook. New York: Guilford Press.

Watson, D., & Tharpe, R. (1981). *Self-directed behavior: Self-modification for personal adjustment.* Monterey, CA: Brooks/Cole.

Watzlawick, P., Weakland, J., & Fisch, R. (1974): *Change: Principles of problem formation and problem resolution.* New York: Norton.

Weiner, H. (1977). *Psychobiology and human disease.* New York: Elsevier.

Weiner, I., & Hess, A. (1987). *Handbook of forensic psychology.* New York: Wiley.

Weissman, H. N. (1991): The child custody evaluation: Methodology and assessment. *Family Law News, 14,* 2.

Weissman, M. M., Klerman, G. I., Markowitz, J. S., & Ouellette, R. (1989). Suicidal ideation and attempts in panic disorders and attacks. *New England Journal of Medicine, 321,* 1209–1214 (C).

Wells, R. A., & Giannetti, V. J. (1990). *Handbook of brief psychotherapies.* New York: Plenum Press.

Wells, R. A., & Phelps, P. A. (1990). *The brief psychotherapies: A selective overview.* New York: Plenum Press.

Wernick, R. L. (1983). *Stress inoculation in the management of clinical pain: Application to burn pain.* New York: Plenum Press.

West, D. (1979). The response to violence. *Journal of Medical Ethics, 5,* 128–131.

Wetzel, R. D. (1976). Hopelessness, depression, and suicidal intent.

Wexler, D. (1991). *The adolescent self: Strategies for self-management, self-soothing, and self-esteem in adolescents.* New York: Norton.

Whitfield, C. L. (1992). *Boundaries and relationships in recovery.* Deerfield Beach, FL: Health Communications.

Williams, R., & Williams, V. (1993). *Anger kills.* New York: Harper Perennial.

Wills-Brandon, C. (1990). *Learning to say no: Establishing healthy boundaries.* Deerfield Beach, FL: Health Communications.

Wilson, C. P., & Mintz, I. L. (1988). *Psychosomatic symptoms: Psychodynamic treatment of underlying personality disorder.* Northvale, NJ Jason Aronson.

Winokur, M., & Dasberg, H. (1983). Teaching and learning short-term dynamic psychotherapy. *Bulletin of the Menninger Clinic, 47,* 36–52.

Woititz, J., & Garner, L. (1991). *Lifeskills for adult children.* Deerfield Beech, FL: Health Communications.

Wolberg, L. R. (1980). Crisis intervention. In L. R. Wolberg (Ed.), *Handbook of short-term psychotherapy.* New York: Grune & Stratton.

Wolberg, L. R. (1980). *Handbook of short-term dynamic psychotherapy.* New York: Grune & Stratton.

Wolff, P. (1972). Ethnic differences in alcohol sensitivity. *Science, 125,* 449–451.

Wolpe, J., & Lazarus, A. A. (1966). *Behavior therapy techniques.* New York: Pergamon.

Wolpe, J. (1982). *The practice of behavior therapy* (3rd ed.), New York: Pergamon.

Woolfolk, R. L., & Lehrer, P. M. (Eds.). (1984). *Principles and practice of stress management.* New York: Guilford Press.

Wooten, V. (1994). Medical causes of insomnia. In M. H. Kryger, T. Roth, & W. C. Dement (eds.), *Principles and practice for sleep medicine* (2nd Ed.) (pp. 509–522). Philadelphia: Saunders.

Yamagami, T. (1971). The treatment of an obsession by thought-stopping. *Journal of Behavior Therapy and Experimental Psychiatry, 2,* 133–135.

Yapko, M. (1990). *When living hurts: Directives for treating depression.* New York: Brunner/Mazel.

Zorick, F. (1994). Overview of insomnia. In M. H. Kryger, T. Roth, & W. C. Dement (Eds.), *Principles and practice of sleep medicine* (2nd ed.) (p.483–485). Philadelphia: Saunders.

Zweben, J. E. (1992). Issues in the treatment of the dual diagnosis patient. In B. C. Wallace (Ed.), *The chemically dependent: Phases of treatment and recovery.* New York: Brunner/Mazel.

INDEX

A

Abuse
   neglect and child abuse 195
      indicators 196
      prevention 195
      treatment 197
   psychoactive substances
      abstinence 38
      addiction 37
      assessment, chemical dependency
         psychosocial 185
         somatic 185
      categories of pharmacological
         intervention 41
      checklist, withdrawal symptoms 185
      chemical use history 186
      common drugs of abuse 43–44
      denial 38
      developmental model 37
      obsessive-compulsive 37
      pathways of use 37
      self-control 39
      symptoms leading to relapse 42
      treatment settings 41
   spousal/partner (Domestic Violence: DV)
      assessing 187, 192
      assessing lethality 188
      counseling victims 194–195
      cycle of domestic violence 190
      domestic violence, safety planning 399
         create a file of important documents 400
         create a safe room 399
         documentation 399
         evaluate the problem 402
         important to remember 398
         know when/how to leave 401
         money and keys 400
         pack a suitcase 400
         problem resolution 403
         safe place to go 399
         struggle with leaving 401
      intervention 193–194

   predicting a potentially violent
      relationship 397
   stage model 191
   systems model 191
Accomplishments 428
Activities of daily living (ADL's) 128
   care of environment and chore
      responsibilities 129
   child care 129
   financial 129
   level of required assistance 129
   living situation 129
   meals 129
   self-care skills 128
   shopping 129
   transportation 130
ADHD/ADD 174, 177
Adjustment disorder, see also Disorders 81
   adjusting and adapting 298
   treatment 82
Adult children of alcoholics 393
Adult psychosocial 403–465
Affidavit for custodial records 524
Alzheimer's disease, ten warning signs 632
   eating history 169
   mood eating scale 169
   medical review consult request for primary
      care physician for eating disorder
      patient 480
Anxiety disorder 65
   anxiety assessment 111
   cycle of anxiety provoking emotional
      disturbance 69
   cycle of phobic anxiety 124
   how your body reacts to stress and
      anxiety 351
   managing anxiety 242
   obsessional disorders 125
      assessment of 125
   overanxious disorder 16
      treatment, 66–69
   progress note for anxiety 494

Anxiety disorder *(continued)*
  PTSD 346
    separation anxiety 13
    trauma response 70
    treatment 66–69, 345
    what is panic anxiety 344
Anger 283–289, 408
Antidepressant medication and other
    treatment 63
Assertive communication, *see also* Skills 257
  development 261
    practice assertive responses 263
    saying no 264–265
    steps of positive assertiveness 263
Assessing lifestyle and health 371
Assessing special circumstances 109–222
  activities of daily living 128–130
  ADHD behavioral review 177
  adult ADD screening 174
  assessment of phobic behavior 139
  chemical dependency assessment 179
  chemical dependency psychological
    assessment 182
  child abuse and neglect 195
  child custody evaluation 198
  chronic mental illness 130
  chronic pain, assessment and intervention 182
  counseling the individual in a medical
    crisis 147
  crisis evaluation 132
  crisis intervention 133
  cycle of depression 113
  cycle of phobic anxiety 124
  dangerousness 119
  dealing with the challenges of long term
    illness 151
  dispositional review: foster/temporary
    placement 211
  eating disorder evaluation
    anorexia 170
    bulimia 172
  eating disorder screening questionnaire 167
  eating history 167
  evaluation and disposition considerations
    for families where parental alienation
    occurs 207
  forensic evaluation 219
  gravely disabled 127
  identifying traumatic stress 135
  obsessional disorders, overview 125
  pain identification 160–162
  parental alienation syndrome 202–206
    treatment 209
  postpartum depression and anxiety
    141–144
  professional guidelines for crisis
    intervention 145
  psychiatric work related disability
    evaluation 213
  psychological pre-employment
    evaluation 217
  report outline 220
  self-care behaviors 142
  somatic problem 164
  spousal/partner abuse 187

  stage model of domestic violence 191
  structured interview for depression 112
  suicide 115
  the patient with psychosomatic illness
    who has an underlying personality
    disorder 165
  visitation rights report 211
  withdrawal symptoms checklist 185
Assuming the patient role, benefits 372
Authorization for release or exchange of
    information 522
Avoidant personality disorder 89

B

Behavior
  affect, of inappropriate 99, 101
  appropriate boundaries, lack of 101
  autonomy difficulties 18, 92
  avoidant 14, 88
  bipolar disorder, hypersexuality 101
  body image, 20, 24, 73
  bonding 199, 201
  bulimia nervosa, *see also* Disorders, eating
    physical symptoms 22
    psychological symptoms 22
  defensive 10
  dependent 92
  isolative 14, 97
  manipulative 101
  oversensitive 89, 92
  responses, negative 94, 101
  self-destructive, *see also* Harm 101
  social interaction, dramatized 99
Borderline personality disorder 101

C

Caregiver of elderly patients 363–366
Caregiver stress 34
Case conceptualization xxvi
Characteristics of adult children of
    alcoholics 393
Chemical dependency, *see* Evaluation, skills
Child Abuse and neglect 195
Child custody evaluation
  ability of the child to bond 199
  ability of the parents to bond 199
    other pertinent information 199
  bonding study versus custody evaluation 201
  dispositional review
    foster/temporary placement 211
    report outline 212
  guidelines for psychological evaluation 198
  interaction between parent-child(ren) 201
  parental alienation 202–209
  visitation rights report 211
Chronic mental illness (CMI), *see also*
    Disorders, schizophrenia 130
  general guidelines for assessment 131
Chronic Pain
  assessing and measuring pain 157
  assessment and intervention 157
  clinical interview 158
  factors affecting experience of pain 157
  identification chart 160
  interventions 162

management scale 161
six stages of treatment 162
Codependency *see also* Skills 383, 387, 388,
389, 390
Common axis I and axis II diagnosis xxvii
Communication, *see also* Skills
of difficult feelings 266
Competency evaluation, *see also*
Evaluation 220
Compulsive overeating, *see also* Disorders,
eating
physical symptoms 23
psychological symptoms 23
Compulsive personality disorder 90
Counseling the individual in a medical
crisis 147
central crisis issues 149
dealing with the challenges of long-term
illness 151
treatment framework and
conceptualization 147
working through the challenges of long-term
illness 154
Couples 396–397, 402–403, 406, 422
Criminal evaluation, *see also* Evaluation 220
Crisis
what happens during 412
what is a crisis 411
Crisis intervention 133
assessment of phobic behavior 139
childhood, life crises 411
critical incident stress debriefing (CISD) 134
effects of time 137
how does treatment affect someone 136
identifying traumatic stress 135
professional guidelines 145
recovery from traumatic stress 135
screening for survivors 135
trauma and vehicular accidents 137
Crisis resolution 413
Critical problem solving 247–249
Cross-cultural issues 61–62

D
Daily activity schedule 322
Daily living skills, *see also* Skills
activities of daily living (ADL) 128
Dangerousness, *see also* Violence,
potential for
assessment 119
assessment outline 120
objectives and treatment focus 122
Decision making, *see also* Skills 272
Decision tree xxi
Defense mechanisms, *see also* Skills 282
Delirium 35–36
Delusional 45
Dementia 31, 32–35
conditions
causing dementia that are not
reversible 359
causing reversible symptoms 358
diagnosis 359
symptoms 358
what is dementia 358

Dependent behaviors, *see* Behavior
Dependent personality disorder 92
Depression, *see also* Disorders
51–52, 324
additional considerations 64
causes 314
children 61
co-occurring with other illnesses
56–57
decreasing the intensity of 313
elderly 64
management of 314
mood 314
recognizing stages of 313
risk of relapse 118
suicide risk 52
surviving the holiday blues 317
symptoms checklist 315
treatment of 52–56, 63
Desensitization 357
Differences xxiii
Differentiation
emotional states, internal sensations 21
Disorders
adjustment 81
anxiety 65
attention deficit hyperactivity 7
avoidant 14
disruptive behavior 7
dissociative 78
eating 18
first evident in infancy, childhood or
adolescence 1
identity 26
impulse control 84
mood 51
organic mental syndrome 31
overanxious 16
personality
avoidant 89
borderline 101
compulsive 90
dependent 92
histrionic 99
narcissistic 100
passive-aggressive 94
paranoid 95
schizotypal 97
schizoid 98
physical factors affecting psychological
functioning 104
psychoactive substance abuse 37–41
schizophrenia, delusions and related
psychotics 45–49
disorders 45–49
separation anxiety 13
sexual 80
sleep, *see also* Skills 367
somatoform 72
Disabled, gravely 127
daily living, activities 128
indicators, behavioral 129
Dispositional review 212
Disruptive behavior disorder 7
Dissociative disorder 78

Domestic violence 398
    create a file with important documents 400
    create a safe room in your home 400
    document the abuse 399
    find a safe place to go 399
    have money and keys 400
    know when and how to leave 401
    most important to remember 399
    pack a suitcase 401
    struggle with leaving 401
Duty to warn 529

E

Elderly, caregiver of parents 363
    advise for those close to the situation 366
    common problems of 365
    coping strategies 365
    tips for the caretaker 366
Education
    family 2–3, 6, 8, 13, 16, 17, 21, 25–26, 41,
        47, 55, 68
    teacher 9, 14, 17
Effective management of stress 229
Emotional IQ 237
Enabler, the companion to the dysfunctional/
        substance abusing person 383
Ethics
    educational guidelines xx, xxi, xxv
    professional practice xx, xxi, xxv
Evaluation
    ADHD behavioral review 177
    adult ADD screening 174
    adult psychosocial 463
    anorexia 170
    bulimia 172
    brief consultation note to physician 490
        industrial 505
    brief medical history 478
    brief mental health evaluation review 451
    chemical dependency psychosocial 485
    chemical dependency psychosocial
        assessment 182
    child custody
        bond ability, child 199
        bond ability, parent 199
        custody versus bonding study 201
        dispositional review 211
        parent-child interaction 201
        psychological guidelines 198
        report outlines 200
        visitation rights 211
    chronic pain 157
    client satisfaction survey 534
    clinical notes 496
    competency 220
    compulsory psychosocial evaluation 218
    criminal evaluation 220
    disability, workers compensation 498
    discharge summary 51
    domestic violence 182, 192
    duty to warn 529
    forensic evaluation 219
    general clinical evaluation 436
    illness and medical problems 479
    initial case assessment 447

    initial evaluation 449
    initial evaluation consultation note to
        primary care physician 488
    worker's compensation attending therapist
        report 500

F

Factitious disorder 77
Family meeting, *see also* Skills 409
Fatigue or sleep deprivation 344
Forensic evaluation 219
Fear
    bad memories 341
    dealing with 380
Forms
    affidavit of the custodian of mental health
        records to accompany copy of
        records 524
    authorization for release/exchange of
        information 522
    balance statement 533
    client messages 523
    client satisfaction survey 534
    clinical
        adult psychosocial 463
        brief consultation note to physician 490
        brief level of functioning review for
            industrial injury 505
        brief medical history 478
        brief mental health evaluation review 451
        brief psychiatric evaluation for industrial
            injury 502
        case formulation 435
        chemical dependency psychosocial
            assessment 485
        child/adolescent psychosexual 467
        clinical note 496
        disability/worker's compensation 498
        discharge summary 511
        duty to warn 529
        general clinical evaluation 435
        illness and medical problems 475
        life history questionnaire 454
        medical review consult request for primary
            care physician of an eating disorder
            (EOO) patient 480
        mental status at time of offense 220
        mental status exam 442, 444, 445
        notice of discharge for noncompliance of
            treatment 528
        outpatient treatment progress report 491
        outline for diagnostic summary 509
        parent's questionnaire 475
        progress note for individual with anxiety
            or depression 494
        self assessment 477
        social security evaluation, medical source
            statement, psychiatric/psychosocial 499
        substance use and psychosocial
            questionnaire 481
            family history 483
            medical history 484
            social history 483
            treatment history 482
    treatment plan

contract for group therapy 521
contract for services without using
    insurance 515
fee agreement for disposition and court
    appearance 517
form for checking out audiotapes
    and books 536
limits on patient confidentiality 519
missed appointments 530
notice of discharge for noncompliance of
    treatment 528
receipt 531, 532
referral for psychological evaluation 525
treatment contract 520
quality assurance preview 537

G
Geriatric (elderly) xxi, 31, 66
Goal development 273
Goals 427
Gravely disabled xxi, 127
    activities of daily living 128
    chronic mental illness 130
    guidelines for discipline that develops
        responsibility 419
Grief
    cycle of 303
    grief 304
    history of losses graph 307
    life changes 298
    losses/opportunities 301
Guidelines
    professional practice xxi
Guilt 327

H
Harm xxi, xxii, xxix, 18
    Tarasoff, *see also* Duty to warn 529
Health inventory 370
Healthy adult relationship 396
Heart disease and depression 375
Helping children cope with scheduling
    changes 423
History of loss graph 307
Histrionic personality disorder 99
How does codependency work 390
How to build a support system 312
How to handle angry people 295
How to predict the potentially violent
    relationship 397
How to stop using food as a coping
    mechanism 377

I
Identify feeling states 20, 21
Identity 26, 80
Imaging, mental/visual 239
Impulse control 7, 84
Interventions
    crisis
        common responses 133
        critical incident stress debriefing (CISD) 134
        early intervention 133–134
        effects of time 137
        guidelines, professional 145

how does traumatic stress affect
        someone 136
identifying traumatic stress 135
medical crisis 147
recovery from traumatic stress 135
response pattern 133
screening for survivors 135
self-care behavior 146, 235
vehicular accidents 137
critical issues xxi
level of functioning xix, xxii

J
Journal
    writing 22, 267, 308
        steps 1–4 308
        steps 5–15 309

L
Loss, *see* Grief

M
Malingering 77
Management
    anxiety, *see also* Skills, managing anxiety
        65, 144, 238, 274, 278–279, 281,
        319, 334–345, 347, 351–353,
        355–357, 367, 368
    depression, *see also* Skills, depression
        52, 274, 278–279, 281, 301, 303–304,
        310, 312–315, 318, 319, 322–327,
        329–330, 334, 342, 344, 357,
        367–368
    stress, *see also* Skills, stress management
        226, 229–231, 235, 238, 249, 274,
        278–279, 281, 298, 301, 308, 319,
        334, 351, 366–368, 370–371, 373
    time, *see also* Skills, time management 92,
        270, 271
Mania, *see also* Disorders 58, 62
Medical causes of psychiatric illness 106
Medical crisis counseling 147
    central crisis issues 149
    challenges of long-term illness 151
    treatment framework and
        conceptualization 148
    working through long-term illness issues 154
Medication
    compliance with 45, 48, 55, 59
    evaluation of 8, 41, 53, 63, 66, 84
    side effects of 32, 36, 48, 55, 60, 66, 69
Meditation 245
Mental retardation 1
Mental states 442, 444, 445
    contents of exam 442
Modalities, treatment xxiii, xxix
Mood disorders 51–64
    additional treatment considerations 64
    antidepressant medication 63
    bipolar hypersexuality 62
    depression 52
    depression co-occurring with other illness 56
    mania 58
Mood eating scale 169

N

Narcissistic personality disorder 100
Nonverbal communication 260
    checklist 255
Nurturing, self 334

O

Obesity and self esteem 379
Obsession with weight 378
Obsessional disorder 125
    assessment 125
Occupational history 214
Organic mental syndromes 31
Outline for diagnostic summary 509
Outpatient treatment progress report 491
Overanxious disorder 16

P

Pain, chronic assessment and intervention 157
Pain identification chart 160
Pain management 233
    interventions 161
    pain management scale 161
Panic anxiety, what is it 344–345
Parent questionnaire 475
Parental alienation syndrome
    behaviors
        children 205
        parents 204
    child's own scenarios 203
    criteria for establishing primary custody 203
    evaluation and disposition considerations 207
    family dynamics and environmental/
        situational issues 203
    parental programming 202
    subtle and unconscious influencing 202
    three categories of parental alienation 206
    treatment 209
Parenting a healthy family 406
    a healthy family means all of its members
        are involved 407
    be an active parent 407
    creating effective family rules 406
    effective co-parenting 406
    encourage communication 407
    maintain effective family rules 406
Patient registration 515
Patient with psychosomatic illness who has an
        underlying personality disorder 165
Personal bill of rights 262
Personality disorders
    avoidant 89
    borderline 107
    compulsive 90
    dependent 92
    histrionic 99
    narcissistic 100
    paranoid 95
    passive-aggressive 94
    schizoid 98
    schizotypal 97
Pervasive development disorder 5
Physical factors affecting psychological
        functioning 104
    stages of adjustment 105

Placement, foster/temporary 211
Plan of action for dealing with anxiety 353
Positive attitude 318
Postpartum depression and anxiety 141
    definitions of 141
    how to break the postpartum cycle 144
    psychosis 143
Post traumatic stress disorder (PTSD) 346
Power of positive thinking 318
Practice reframing how you interpret
        situations 281
Preventing
    body weight and body image problems in
        children 378
    violence in the workplace 289
        bully in the workplace 291
        dangerous employee 290
        how to handle angry people 295
        negative work environment 290
        what management can do to minimize
            employee stress 296
        workplace violence 291
Problem solving diagram 249
Professional care guidelines for crisis
        intervention 145
Progress note for individual with anxiety
        and/or depression 496
Psychiatric work-related disability evaluation 213
    description of client
        at time of interview 213
        current complaints 213
    developmental history 215
    family history 214
    findings from psychological assessment 215
    history of present illness 213
    identifying information 213
    interviews with collateral sources 216
    occupational history 214
    past psychiatric history and relevant medical
        history 214
    review
        of medical records 215
        employment or personnel records 216
    social history 215
    summary and conclusions 216
Psychoactive substance abuse disorders 37
    categories of pharmacological
        interventions 41
    substance abuse and/or dependence 38
    treatment settings 41
Psychological factors affecting physical
        condition 86
Psychological pre-employment
        evaluation 217
Psychosomatic illness with underlying
        personality disorder 165

Q

Questionnaire
    parent's 475
    relationship 396
    substance use and psychosocial 481
Questions to ask yourself 426
Quotient
    emotional IQ 237

R

Rational thinking
  realistic self-talk 279
  reframing 277
  reframing your interpretation 281
  self-talk 274
  thinking distortions 278
  thought stopping 276
Recognizing the stages of depression 313
Recommendations for family members of
      anorexic individuals 25
Registration, patient 515
Relationship
  graph 307
  questionnaire 396
Relaxation exercises 238
  brief progressive relaxation 241
  confronting the provocation 245
  deep breathing 238
  guide to meditation 245
  it's time to talk to yourself 245
  mental imagery 239
  mental relaxation 239
  preparing for the provocation 244
  progressive muscle relaxation 242
  tensing the muscles 239
Resources 429
Risk, situations in practice xxiii
Rules
  for emotional health 429
  of politeness 426

S

Saying no 264
Schizophrenia *see also* Disorders
  phases of treatment 49
  summary of treatment recommendations 49
  thought disorder 45
  treatment setting 49
  understanding 359–360
Seasonal anniversary of losses 342
Self assessment 477
Self-care
  behaviors 146
  plan 235
Self-esteem
  affirmations 334
  boosters 333
  characteristics
    of high self-esteem 338
    of low self-esteem 336
  low 330
  review 332
  self-nurturing 334
Self monitoring 318, 426
Separation anxiety 13
Setting priorities 274
Sexual disorders *see also* Disorders 80
Shyness 339
Skills
  adjusting/adapting 298
    developmental perspective 299
    life changes 298
  accepting no for an answer 265
  accomplishments 428

affirmations for building self-esteem 334
anger
  barriers to expressing anger 288
  decreasing the intensity of 287
  handling, general principles regarding
      anger 286
  how to handle angry people 295
  inappropriate expression 288
  management of 283
  penalties for not expressing 288
  recognizing the stages of 287
  steps for letting go of 289
  taking responsibility 284
  understanding your experience of 285–286
  ways to deal with
areas of potential conflict 268
  list of potential conflicts 268
assertive communication 257, 262
  assertive inventory 258
  consequences of saying yes 265
  developing assertiveness 261
  non-verbal assertive behavior 261
  overcoming guilt of saying no 264
  personal bill of rights 262
  practicing assertive responses 263
  saying no 264
  the steps of positive assertiveness 263
  verbal assertive behavior
assessing lifestyle and health 371
assuming the patient role, benefits of
    being sick 372
bad memories and fear 341
caregiver of elderly parents 363
  advice for others close to the situation 366
  common problems experienced by
      caregivers 365
  tips for the caretaker 366
  warning signs of caregiver stress 366
characteristics
  of adult children of alcoholics 393
  of high self-esteem 338
  of low self-esteem 336
chemical imbalance 329
codependency
  characteristics 388
  classic situation 388
  enablers 383
  how does it work 390
    effects on children of codependents 392
    how it affects one's life 391
    rules 391
    stages of recovery
    what can you do 392
  suggested diagnostic criteria 389
  what is codependency 387
communication
  components of effective communication 253
    active listening 253
    effective listening 257
    how to present yourself 256
    how to say it 256
    improving communication skills 256
    I statements 253
    non-verbal communication checklist 255
    reflection 254

Skills (continued)
  confronting and understanding suicide 323
  couple's conflict, rules for fighting fair 403
  crisis resolution 413
    what do you need to do to help
      a child 413
  critical problem solving
    developing good problem solving
      skills 248
    managing intervention during problem
      solving 248
    preparing to learn problem-solving
      skills 248
    stages of problem solving 248
    steps for problem solving 249
  daily activity schedule 322
  dealing with fear 380
  decision making
    steps for 272
  defense mechanisms 282
    definitions of 283
  definition, the natural emotional response to
      the loss of a cherished idea, person or
      thing 303
  dementia
    conditions causing dementia that is not
      reversible 359
    conditions causing reversible
      symptoms 358
    diagnosis 359
    symptoms 358
    what is dementia 358
  depression 324
    symptom checklist 315
  detaching with love versus controlling 382
  developing and utilizing social supports 310
    characteristics of a supportive
      relationship 310
  domestic violence (DV)
    create a file with your important
      documents 400
    create a safe room in your home 400
    document the abuse 399
    find a safe place to go 399
    have money and keys 400
    most important to remember 399
    pack a suitcase 401
    predicting potentially violent
      relationships 397
    safety planning 399
    struggle with leaving 401
  eating history 376
  effective management of stress 229
    assertiveness 230
    conflict resolution 230
    critical problem solving 229
    self-care 230
    time management 230
    tips 230
  emotional IQ 237
  family meeting 409
    developing positive self-esteem in
      children and adolescents 410
    guidelines 409
  fatigue or sleep deprivation 344

feeling
  like your life is out of control 326
  overwhelmed and desperate 325
goals
  steps for developing 273
goal setting 427
grief
  acceptance 306
  bargaining 305
  depression 305
  never happened 304
grief cycle 273
guiding your child to appropriately express
    anger 408
guidelines
  for completing your first step toward
    emotional health 399
  for discipline that develops
    responsibility 419
  helpful hints 420
  steps in applying logical consequences 420
  for family members/significant others of
    alcoholic/chemically dependent
    individuals 381
  to follow if someone you know has an
    eating disorder 379
guilt 327
health inventory 370
healthy adult relationships 396
heart disease and depression 375
helping children cope with scheduling
    changes 423
how does codependency work 390
how to
  get the most out of your day 236
  build and keep a support system 312
  predict the potentially violent
    relationship 396
  stop using food as a coping
    mechanism 377
how your body reacts to stress and
    anxiety 351
improved coping skills for happier
    couples 402
improving communication skills 256
  body language, how to present
    yourself 256
  effective listening 257
  quality of voice, how to say it 256
improving your health 373
is life what you make it 308
is your behavior in the best interest of your
    children 425
journal writing 308–309
learning history 300
list of feeling words
  difficult/unpleasant 269
  pleasant 269
list of symptoms leading to relapse 386
loneliness 329
losses/opportunities
  finding the solution, the five stages of
    recovery loss 302
  how do you know you are ready 302
  how you deal with loss 302

other ways 302
what are the myths of dealing with loss 302
what is meant by resolving grief/loss 301
why are people not prepared to deal with loss 301
low self esteem 330
managing anxiety 347
what do you do 349
pain management 233
panic anxiety
symptoms 345
treatment 345
what is panic anxiety 344
parenting a healthy family 406
a healthy family means all of its members are involved 407
be an active parent 407
creating effective family rules 406
effective co-parenting 406
encourage communication 407
maintain the parent role 407
personal bill of rights 262
plan of action for dealing with anxiety 353
post traumatic stress disorder (PTSD) 346
power of positive attitude 315
practice reframing how you interpret situations 281
preventing body weight and body image problems in children 378
preventing violence in the workplace 289
bully in the workplace 291
negative work environment 290
the dangerous employee 290
workplace violence 291
problem solving diagram 249
rational thinking 274
reframing 277
self-talk 274
thought stopping 276
realistic self-talk 279
recognizing the stages of depression 313
relationship graph 307
relaxation exercises 238
brief progressive relaxation 241
brief relaxation 241
confronting the provocation 245
deep breathing 238
guide to meditation 245
it's time to talk to yourself 245
mental imagery 239
mental relaxation 239
preparing for the provocation 244
progressive muscle relaxation 242
tensing the muscles 239
resources 429
risks 252
saying no 264
overcoming guilt of 264
consequences of saying yes 265
seasonal anniversary of losses 342
self-care plan 235
self-esteem review 332
self-monitoring
checklist 319
questions to ask yourself 426

self-nurturing, a component of self-esteem 334
setting priorities 274
sleep disorders 367
treatment focus and objectives 367
some examples of individual time management options 234
standing up to shyness 339
socializing 340
stress
what is stress 223
review 225
stress management 226
busting stress 229
early warning signs 228
signals of 228
substance abuse/dependence personal evaluation 385
successful stepfamilies
communication 423
discipline 423
humor 422
parent-centered structure 423
respect 422
responsibility 422
validation 422
survey of stress symptoms 350
estimate your stress level 350
physical symptoms 350
psychological symptoms 350
surviving divorce 420
systematic desensitization 357
talking to children 417
do's 419
don'ts 429
rules
for listening 418
for problem solving and expressing your thoughts and feelings to children 418
ten
rules for emotional health
self-esteem boosters 333
steps for giving feedback 264
steps for letting go of anger 289
tips for better sleep 368
warning signs of Alzheimer's disease 362
warning signs of caregiver stress 366
ways of responding to aggression 265
the classic situation 388
thinking distortions 278
time management
four central steps to effective time management 270
how to start your own time management program 270
tips
for stress management 230
to simplify your life 231
how to improve planning 233
ten signs that you need to simplify your life 232
understanding
and dealing with life crises of childhood 411
anger 285
schizophrenia 359

utilizing your support system 315
warning signs of relapse 356
warning signs of teen mental health
  problems 416
what happens during a crisis 412
what is a crisis 412
what management can do to minimize
  employee stress 295
what motivates me 339
why victims of domestic violence struggle
  with leaving 401
writing 267
Sleep disorders
  fatigue or sleep deprivation 344
  tips for better sleep 368
  treatment and objectives 367
Social security evaluation, *see also*
  Forms 499
Solution focused approach to treatment xxv
Solving problems 247, 249
Somatic problems 164–165
Somatoform disorder, *see also* Disorders 72
Spousal/partner abuse 187
  assessing abuse 187
Stage model of domestic violence 191
Standing up to shyness, *see also* Skills 339
Steps for letting go of anger 289
Strengths 428
Stress 223
  management 229–230
  what is stress 223
Structural interview for depression 112
Substance abuse/dependence personal
  evaluation 385
Substance use and psychosocial questionnaire 481
  family history 483
  medical problems 484
  social history 483
  treatment history 482
Successful stepfamilies, *see also* Skills 422
  communication 423
  discipline 423
  humor 422
  parent-centered structure 423
  respect 422
  responsibilities 422
  validation 422
Suggested diagnostic criteria for
  codependence 389
Suicide 115, 360
  adolescent 116
  assessment outline 115
  depression and suicide risk relapse 118
  treatment focus and objectives 117
Summary, treatment plans and
  recommendations 466
Survey of stress symptoms, *see also*
  Skills 350
Surviving divorce, *see also* Skills 420
Surviving the holiday blues 317

Systematic desensitization
  the ten steps of 357

T
Talking to children, *see also* Skills 417
Ten
  rules for emotional health 429
  self-esteem boosters 333
  steps for giving feedback 264
  steps for letting go of anger 289
  tips for better sleep 365
  warning signs of Alzheimer's disease 362
  ways of responding to aggression 265
The classic situation 388
Thinking distortions 278
Time management, *see also* Skills 270
Tips
  for stress management 230
  to simplify your life *see also* Skills 231
Traumatic stress and vehicular accidents 137
Treatment contracts 520
Treatment plan xxiv, 439

U
Understanding
  and dealing with life crises of children 411
  anger 285
  schizophrenia 359
    potential for violence 360
    suicide 360
    symptoms and perceptual disturbance 360
    what causes schizophrenia 360
Utilizing your support system 318

V
Violence, potential for 119–121
Visitation rights report 211

W
Warning signs
  of relapse 356
  of teen mental health problems 416
What management can do to minimize
  employee stress 298
What motivates me 339
Why victims of domestic violence struggle with
  leaving 401
Withdrawal symptoms
  checklist 185
  psychological 185
  somatic 185
Worker's compensation
  attending therapist's report 500
  disability status 500
  progress 500
  treatment 500
  work status 500
Writing 267